ıp to this line

£18.00

MONEY, BAN
AND
ECONOMIC AC

by

GAIL E. MA

Georgetown Uni
United States General Ac

ACADEMIC P

New York/London/Toronto/Syd
A Subsidiary of Harcourt Brace J

MONEY, BANKING, AND ECONOMIC ACTIVITY

Cover photo by Dan Lenore

Academic Press, Inc.
111 Fifth Avenue, New York, New York 10003

United Kingdom Edition published by
Academic Press, Inc. (London) Ltd.
24/28 Oval Road, London NW1 7DX

ISBN: 0-12-468950-7

Library of Congress Catalog Card Number: 80-70228

Printed in the United States of America

To the memory
of my grandparents

CONTENTS

4

5

6

PREFACE

This text is an outgrowth of a series of lectures in a course on money and banking given by me over the past decade. My decision to write it and its differentiating characteristics arise from a basic dissatisfaction with numerous other texts in the field. They universally incorporate macroeconomic theory and analyze the role of money in that frame of reference. However, in the main, they neglect to apply microeconomic analysis, forgetting that commercial banks and other depository financial institutions can be treated as firms which manufacture a product called money. Thus, most other texts discuss the demand for money as a part of their macroeconomic model, but neglect to provide a theoretical rationale for a supply schedule of money. This text attempts to correct this oversight. Once commercial banks and other financial intermediaries are treated as firms which manufacture money, the theoretical foundations for the money supply schedule are readily forthcoming. One can then discuss the determinants of the position and slope (elasticity) of that schedule and the factors which account for its shift over time. Having isolated the determinants, their historical values can then be examined. These values, then, provide a proximate explanation for the movement of the stock of money over time.

Moreover, this micro-theoretic framework also enables one to give a careful description of the functions of other deposit-type financial institutions, to contrast and compare them with those which create money, and to understand how their activities influence the supply of money, credit, and economic activity.

The students taking my course in money and banking, for whom this text is written, were drawn from diverse academic interests. Some were economics majors, but the majority were from fields associated with business administration and business education (one student over this period was a major in a mortuary science program). The proportion of each group of majors was by no means constant. Accordingly, the emphasis given various topics, as well as the depth of the material covered, was subject to change. This text, therefore, is designed to accommodate both a diverse and shifting population of student majors. This is accomplished by including after various key chapters, a series of appendices whose purpose is to add depth and sophistication to various topics. They can be used to supplement basic material as the need arises.

The macro- and microeconomic theory used in this text is at a level a little above that taught in most principles courses. The macroeconomic theory is rather Keynesian in its outlines, but can be and is easily adapted to explaining such alternatives as Monetarism.

The material covered in the text neglects one topic generally found in similar books: monetary history. This omission is due to a belief that: "It is not enough to know the past. It is necessary to understand it" (from the French poet-diplomat, Paul Claudel). To understand what history teaches is, unfortunately, often involved, time consuming, and controversial. The magnitude of this task can be appreciated when it is realized that Professors Milton Friedman and Anna Schwartz devote almost 1000 pages to an interpretation of U.S. monetary history from 1867 to 1960. In addition, several hundred pages of additional material would have to be included if their critics were given an equal hearing. Thus, monetary history is best left to specialized study.

This textbook could not have been completed without the valued assistance of a number of very special people. Professors Jay Levin of Wayne State University and Roger Trenary of Kansas State University read the entire manuscript and made many useful suggestions for improvement. My mentor, Professor H. Peter Gray of Rutgers University, read and made many useful comments on the chapters on international finance. I also discussed many topics in the text with Professor William Bomberger of the University of Florida, with whom I have written a number of academic papers, and Mr. John Haltiwanger, a Ph.D. candidate at the Johns Hopkins University. Such a selfless use of their time on my behalf is gratefully appreciated. They are truly valued friends and colleagues. Dr. Theresa Vaughan provided her able editorial assistance to make my prose readable. She did this with a graciousness and understanding that a teacher usually reserves for a pupil. Typing and stylistic support were entrusted to the very capable and conscientious hands of Ms. Cheri Miller and her assistants, Kathy Taylor and Dawn Zoppa. They remained good natured through endless drafts and changes. A debt of gratitude is owed to the several hundred students who sat through my lectures as the approach developed in this text took its form, and to the individuals and institutions who graciously consented to my requests to quote from their work. Finally, I would like to acknowledge the great debt I owe to two editors of Academic Press: Susan Anderson who, for the second time, saw merit in one of my manuscripts, and Susan Loring, in whose capable hands the manuscript was transformed into this book.

1 THE IMPORTANCE OF MONEY

Throughout human history money has played many opposing roles. Its possession has been seen both as a major factor promoting happiness and as a sign of avarice and greed. Literature presents nefarious characters for whom the mere possession of money is an end in itself and the source of untold pleasure. The wisdom of Benjamin Franklin contains references to the productivity of money, for it supposedly begets money and its offspring begets more. Yet, in medieval times Church scholars held that money was barren or unproductive. To charge interest on a loan was regarded as usury and imperiled the immortal soul.

Among the debates waged by economists, those concerning the role of money have undoubtedly been the most intense, controversial, and long lasting.

The amount of money in existence has been linked to a number of very important economic variables that in one way or another influence our daily lives. These variables include the amount of employment (or unemployment), the interest rates that prevail in the marketplace, the rate of flow of gross national product, the spending on new capital goods (investment), the general level of commodity prices (inflation or deflation), the state of a nation's international balance of payments, and the distribution of national income among wages, salaries, interest, rents, and profits.

Recessions, depressions, or times of great prosperity; commodity price inflation or deflation; high or low market interest rates; and balance-of-payments deficits or surpluses, have all been connected in some way to the supply of money. This is merely to say that what is commonly called the business cycle has been linked to the supply of money.

Figure 1:1 is designed to show this relationship for several key variables for the United States during the past 100 years. The data plotted in the figure represent indices of the level of these variables, with the shaded areas designating years of recession or economic downturn.

One cannot help but be struck by the close long-run relationship between the stock of money,[1] real and nominal gross national product, and the level of commodity prices. Since real GNP and employment are closely related in the short run, the money stock is also closely related to employment.

[1] In Figure 1:1 the money stock is measured as the sum of currency, coin, and total bank deposits—both saving and demand.

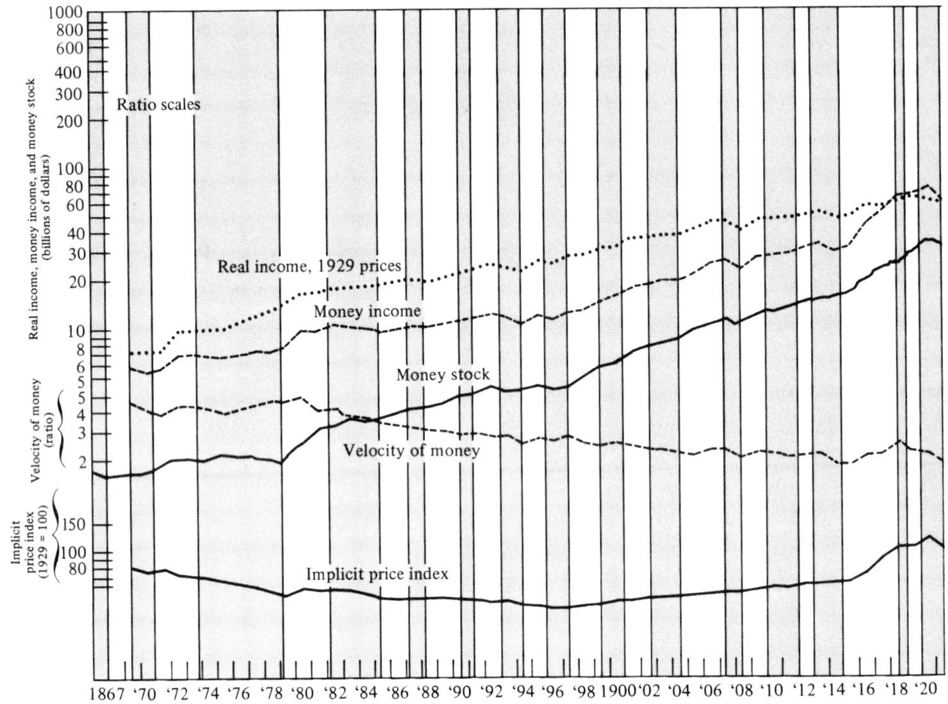

FIGURE 1:1

Money stock, income, prices, and velocity in reference cycle expansions and contractions, 1867–1975.

Shaded areas represent business contractions, unshaded areas business expansions.

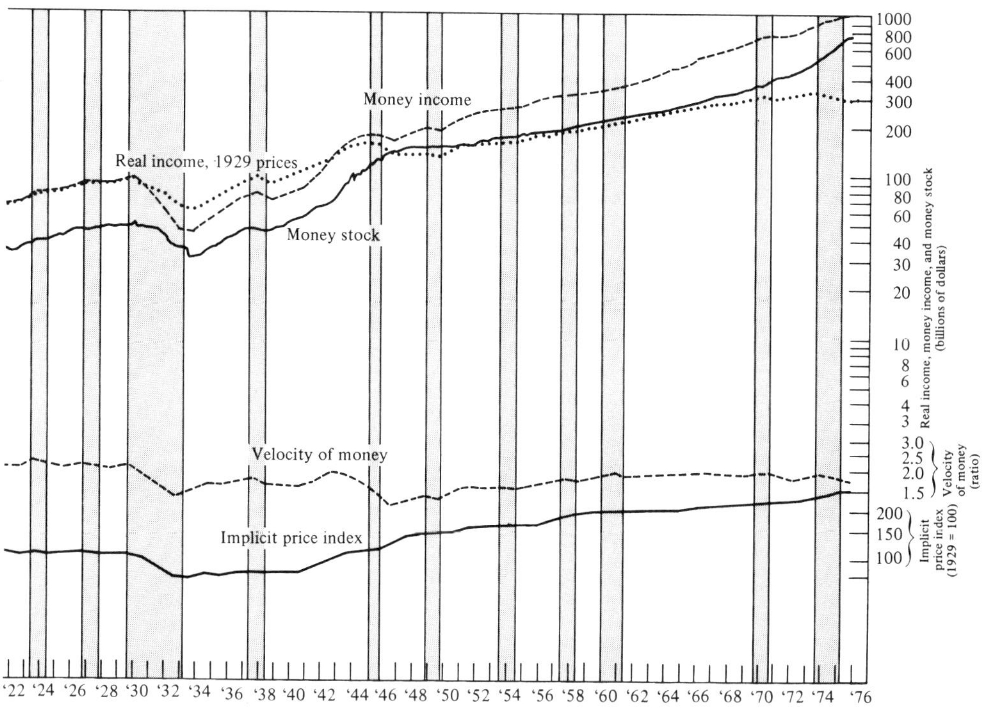

(Courtesy of Milton Friedman and Anna Schwartz, A Monetary History of the United States, 1867–1960 *(Princeton, N.J.: Princeton University Press, 1963) Chart 62. Update to 1975 uses Kuznets's Net National Product data, furnished by the National Bureau of Economic Research.)*

Understanding the relationship of money to the economic variables reproduced, in part, in Figure 1:1, is not a simple task, and it is compounded by a serious difficulty: those who have investigated this relationship are by no means unanimous in their judgment on exactly how money and these other variables are related. Rather, as noted, this relationship has been the subject of a long, intense, and continuing controversy which arose soon after money was invented and which has flared anew with great vigor in the United States in the post-1965 era.

One group[2] sees in the supply of money the cause of the *majority* of business cycles. In an earlier era this group saw variations in the money supply itself as the cause of the business cycle. More recently, it has identified variations in the growth rate of the money supply as the major cause of changes in the rate of growth of real gross national product, employment, the market rate of interest, and the general level of commodity prices. For this group, the *majority* of all business cycles have their origin in an unsteady growth rate of the money supply and the business cycle could be minimized if the rate of growth of the money supply were held steady.

Examining Figure 1:1, members of this group would hold that the shaded areas indicating recessions and the light areas indicating years of expansion were preceded by variations in the growth rate of the money supply. Without such variations, the line depicting the growth of real gross national product would have been fairly straight, with an upward slope depending upon the growth of the labor force, the accumulation of capital, and the rate of technological change. In addition, the level of prices (or the rate of inflation) would have shown little variation over time.

A second group holds that the majority of business cycles are due to nonmonetary causes ranging from sun spots to Arab oil sheiks, with the most emphasis being placed on the degree of optimism or pessimism with which the purchasers of producer (capital) and consumer durable goods view the future. For this group, historical variations in the money supply such as can be computed from Figure 1:1 are not the cause of the majority of business cycles, but rather the result of other forces that govern the course of the cycle. In fact, a majority of this group would go so far as to say that the business cycle would occur even if the money stock grew at a constant rate over time. However, this is not to suggest that money does not matter for this group. Quite the contrary. Money supply variations can be used to offset to one degree or another the forces that cause the business cycle. What is important for this group is not the money supply or its variations per se, but rather what money does to the market interest rate. It is variations in the interest rate that are to be used to offset these other nonmonetary forces in any program to stabilize the level of economic

[2] Since at this point we are merely outlining various views of the cause of the business cycle, we will not identify the persons holding these views.

activity. Thus, for this group, the importance of the money supply derives from its effect on the market interest rate.

This controversy over the relationship of the money stock to economic activity might be cast aside as some unimportant discussion that has only slight relevance to the real world were it not for one salient factor. How one views the cause of the business cycle determines the conduct of monetary policy and the management of the money supply.

For the people in the first group, proper monetary management, or one designed to stabilize the economy, calls for a constant rate of growth of the money supply over time. Exactly what the rate should be depends upon the growth rate of real gross national product.

For the other group, since the interest rate is the important variable, proper monetary management would probably center on a variable growth rate of the money supply designed to produce the "right" interest rate. To either group, the policy of the other is likely to destabilize the economy.

Given these two assessments of the relationship of the money supply to economic activity, there should be no mystery why economists fiercely disagree as to policy. Having fundamentally different views of the cause of the business cycle, they have fundamentally different views on the proper management of the money supply.

This book will not deal exclusively with the controversy over the role of money. While some parts of this text will be devoted to this subject, a great deal of time and effort will be spent on other topics designed to impart more basic information. Among them are what is money, the role of financial institutions and financial markets, the ability of financial institutions to create money, the role of the central bank as a controller of the money supply, and finally, the role of money in economic activity.

2 WHAT IS MONEY? 2

The discussion in Chapter 1 indicated that money has long played an important role both as a cause of business cycles and, in a policy context, as a means of achieving economic stability. It should come as no surprise then that a definition of money is of some importance if one proposes to use the supply of money in a program aimed both at stabilizing economic activity at high levels of employment and at avoiding the excesses of inflation or deflation of commodity price levels. It may, however, come as a surprise that several different and often competing definitions of money have emerged that imply that, for a given country at a given time, different collections of assets should be called money. On the other hand, in some countries, or at different periods in the history of a given country, the range of assets may be so limited that all the different definitions of money apply to the same collection of assets.

In order to convey some measure of the variability of definition, this chapter will examine three definitions of money that have been used: the traditional, the empirical, and the liquidity. The greatest amount of space and detail of examination will be given to the traditional definition, for the recent analysis of Brunner and Meltzer[1] has restored this definition to the prominence it historically enjoyed. These authors have explained in a highly satisfactory way the origin, use, and holding of money. The two other definitions either merely accept the existence of money (i.e., they cannot explain its origin) or define money in such a way that one cannot readily distinguish it from all other assets.

THE TRADITIONAL DEFINITION

The Brunner-Meltzer revitalization of the traditional definition of money has as its purpose an explanation of the origin, use, and holding of money. As a part of this explanation, the important economic functions performed by money become evident. For this reason, this definition is often called the functional definition.

There are several ways to explain how a monetary economy arises. The method used here will be to consider an individual living in isolation who suddenly discovers other people.

Robinson Crusoe, as long as he lives alone, clearly has no need for money. But if Robinson Crusoe should discover a group of people living on

[1] Karl Brunner and Allen Meltzer, "The Use of Money: Money in the Theory of an Exchange Economy," *The American Economic Review*, Vol. 61, No. 5 (Dec. 1971): 784–805.

his island who are producing goods and services some of which are like his, some qualitatively superior to his, and some different from his, then it would probably occur to him that an exchange of some sort might be beneficial to him. That is, he would realize that through exchange, he could obtain more of the goods he especially likes or are qualitatively superior to those he produces or are different from any he could produce. These he could obtain in exchange for the goods he produces, which to others have the same desirable characteristics he sees in theirs.

Since the goods or services that Crusoe produces are his income, the purpose of exchange is to convert this income into a more desirable combination of goods and services.

Entering into this newly discovered society with a desire to exchange, Crusoe would probably be confronted with several immediate problems. Who is offering for sale what goods and services? Where are they located? What are the differences in quality among similar goods? Who desires what he brings to the market? At what price ratios are the exchanges offered? (That is, how many of good X are being exchanged for good Y?) To answer these questions will require the expenditure of time and effort to acquire information about what can be called the conditions of the market. In other words, Crusoe will have to do some "shopping." Obviously, it will be easier to find out information about the characteristics of some goods and services than others. What the following analysis demonstrates is that the use of money can reduce the time, effort, and other costs of acquiring information about market conditions, and therein is to be found a large part of its social usefulness.

The Unit-of-account role

One of the greatest problems our hypothetical Crusoe will encounter is the number of exchange ratios between goods. If only four commodities, A, B, C, and D, are offered for sale, the number of exchange ratios or relative prices will be six in number:

A–B
A–C
A–D
B–C
B–D
C–D

The first involves the number of units of good A that can be exchanged for good B. If this should be one for three, then the relative price of B in terms of A is 1/3. That is, each unit of B will exchange for 1/3 unit of A. Similar determinations for the other goods will produce six relative prices. In a more formal sense, the number of relative price ratios can be expressed as $N(N\text{-}1)/2$, where N refers to the number of goods and services exchanged. It can be seen that as N becomes large, the number of relative prices becomes astronomical and trade becomes increasingly complex. If Crusoe wants to be a sharp trader, he will need to acquire, process, and store a lot of information on relative prices.

Suppose now that one of the goods brought to market, say A, is used as the good in terms of which all other goods are expressed. Then the number of exchange ratios declines from $N(N\text{-}1)/2$ to $N\text{-}1$. In our case using four goods, only the first three price ratios will be required (A–B, A–C, A–D). With this development, the cost of acquiring, processing, and storing information declines. Hence, one of thc significant functions of money is to serve as a *unit of account* or *standard of value*, which means that money is the common denominator in terms of which the market value of all goods is expressed and their relative importance measured. In our society the unit of account is the dollar, and if one object sells for \$5 and another for \$100, then the latter is 20 times more valuable than the former in our market.

The unit-of-account function of money should not be underemphasized. The gains that accrue to society are analogous to the social gain derived from the use of other common units of measurement for distance, weight, temperature, and so on. One can easily imagine the confusion that might emerge if in place of the two units of temperature we now have, 200 or 2000 were used.

Medium-of-exchange function

A second problem for Crusoe, potentially greater than the vast array of possible exchange ratios, will be to find someone who wants what he is willing to give in exchange and who will give him what he wants. Thus, a double coincidence of wants must prevail if any kind of *direct* exchange is to take place. It is possible that in the newly discovered society Crusoe can find no one, even after an exhaustive, time-consuming search, with whom he can trade directly. Does this mean that Crusoe will have to return home unsatisfied? No, for another option is open to him—*indirect* exchange. He might be able to convert his goods and services into others, and these into still others, and finally, after a number of successive transactions, wind up with the bundle of goods and services he most prefers. There are, however, certain drawbacks to this process. At each step in this series of transactions or transactions chain, Crusoe may incur further costs. First, he must acquire information about the qualities of the goods and services exhanged, including whether the seller has legal entitlement to those offered for sale. While he is acquiring this information, time passes and he may be forced to consume some of the goods brought to market (thus, information acquisition reduces his income and can be an important cost in making transactions). Second, the transactions themselves may be spaced in time so that the goods acquired at each step in the transactions chain must be held or stored. In storage they may deteriorate or lose value as relative supplies or market prices fluctuate. Finally, the act of exchange itself may involve a cost or brokerage fee. The sum of all of these costs can be called the *transactions cost of indirect exchange*.

Certain social institutions may develop to reduce the costs of acquiring information and making transactions. Among them would be a central marketplace or fair to which all might bring their wares for exchange. Since in most societies supplies of and demand for goods and services are far from invariant, relative exchange ratios are likely to be constantly changing. Thus, even with a central marketplace, Crusoe will have a continuous problem acquiring, processing, and storing information as well as arranging indirect exchanges.

Without a central market, the cost of information acquisition and transactions will be much higher. The higher these costs, the smaller will be the surplus from his income (the goods and services he produces) that Crusoe will have available to consume. Since this will also be true for other people on the island, they will not find most exchanges advantageous, and thus the volume of transactions will be lower.

Money and transaction costs

If in place of barter exchange monetary exchange is allowed, it will aid Crusoe primarily by reducing the cost of acquiring information and making exchanges. Monetary exchange does this by reducing the number of exchanges or the length of the transactions chain by which the initial bundle of goods and services brought to the market is exchanged or converted into the bundle of most desired goods and services.

Suppose a commodity exists whose quality is well known to many others and which has certain desirable technical properties: it can be finely subdivided (divisibility), is easily transferred from place to place (portability), and does not deteriorate or depreciate markedly with the passage of time (durability). Crusoe could exchange his initial market basket of goods and services for this commodity, hold an inventory in this commodity, and then exchange it directly for the most desired goods and services as the need arises.

Obviously, the use of such a commodity could save Crusoe a considerable amount of transaction costs, depending upon the degree to which the transactions chain is shortened. If the use of this commodity reduces the number of transactions or the length of the transactions chain, it reduces the amount of information that must be acquired as well as the direct cost (brokerage fees, etc.) of exchange itself.

How much of this commodity will be held as an inventory depends upon its marginal productivity in the sense of saving transaction costs versus the marginal cost of holding it. In the case of a commodity held as money, the marginal cost of holding it can be measured by its rate of deterioration over time, which, given its technical characteristics, means its rate of exchange relative to other goods and services. In other words, the marginal cost of holding money can be measured by the rate of commodity price inflation or loss of relative exchange value.

Since the use of an exchange route or transactions chain involving money is advantageous for Crusoe, it must also be advantageous for the majority of the other members of society. In general, the transactions patterns of society will tend to converge on one or a few assets as the dominant means used to make exchanges. It follows that the foremost function of anything used as money is that it serve as the principal medium or means of making exchanges. Unless it is feasible as a medium of exchange, no asset can hope to serve as money.

The emergence of a dominant transactions medium

Thus far the analysis of the medium-of-exchange function has shown how desirable it would be if some asset existed that was widely known and had certain desirable characteristics. The time is now at hand to explain why some assets fulfill these purposes and others do not. The explanation has two parts.

First, an asset is more likely to be adopted as a medium of exchange if it has the desirable technical properties enumerated above: divisibility, portability, and durability. Second, the public at large must be able to identify the quality of the asset at very little cost without having to spend much time and effort. This probably explains the adoption of metals such as gold, silver, and copper of a given weight and fineness as early money. These two factors explain the evolution of the monetary form over time. Paper currency came to replace metal coins as the dominant means of making transactions because it had greater portability, thus saving time in making transactions. Checks then came to replace both currency and coin in many transactions because they have various cost-saving advantages in terms of ease of transportation in any amount and between individuals, involve much less loss due to theft, and provide a convenient form of receipt. Today various electronic means of making transactions are superseding checks, again because they save time and costs, and thereby increase the efficiency of exchange.

When the various economies of the world are examined, two aspects of their monetary systems are of immediate interest. First, as a rule, the same unit serves as both the unit of account and the medium of exchange.[2]

[2] A curious exception to this rule is the case of Great Britain. There the medium of exchange is the pound sterling, whereas a common unit of account is the guinea, which measures one pound one shilling (1 1/10 pounds). This anomaly no doubt arose because when the gold guinea was first issued in 1663, it was valued at one pound. Subsequently, in 1917, a gold revaluation caused its value to rise to one pound one shilling.

Second, in very different places in the world a narrow and similar range of assets is used to make or receive payments. That is, coins, paper currency, and checks are used in societies whose state of development and institutional structures are markedly different.

Other functions of money

The traditional definition of money notes two other functions that money performs that are derived from its primary functions as a unit of account and medium of exchange: the store-of-value and standard-of-deferred-payments functions.

Store of value

Money is a *store of value* insofar as it is a generalized form in which wealth can be held. This function follows from the medium-of-exchange function. Whenever one sells goods for money and holds the money before exchanging it for other goods and services, a portion of one's wealth is being held as an inventory of money.

Standard of deferred payments

To say that money is a standard of deferred payments is simply to say that in contracts calling for future payments the payments agreed on will be in terms of money. This function is derived from the role of money as a unit of account and medium of exchange, for whenever a standardized asset with well-known properties becomes widely used as a medium of exchange and unit of account, it so reduces the cost of information and exchange that it induces individuals to enter into contracts calling for future payments in this unit.

The money assets

The traditional definition of money would define as money any asset or collection of assets that simultaneously fulfills the four functions of unit of account, medium of exchange, store of value, and standard of deferred payments.

Until the early 1970s, only two assets fulfilled these functions in the United States: currency, including coins issued by the Federal Reserve System (our central bank) and the U.S. Treasury; and the demand deposits (checking accounts) issued by commercial banks. A series of changes in the rules and regulations governing financial institutions now makes it possible for a broader collection of assets to perform these functions. These changes started in 1972 when the mutual savings banks in New Hampshire and Massachusetts acquired the right to offer interest-bearing accounts against which a check or draft can be drawn to transfer ownership. These are known as Negotiable Order of Withdrawal (NOW) accounts. Similar privileges were extended to savings and loan associations and commercial banks in 1974. Subsequently, NOW accounts were made available throughout New England.[3]

In March 1980 Congress passed a landmark piece of legislation entitled "The Depository Institutions Deregulation and Monetary Control Act of 1980." Under its provisions, NOW accounts were legalized throughout the United States for all depository institutions. This law also removed legal challenges to two other practices that had broadened the range of assets used for making transactions: credit union share drafts and automatic transfers from savings.

The former practice was instituted in 1976 when federally chartered credit unions throughout the United States were authorized to offer share drafts that allow their owners to transfer their deposits to others by instruments that resemble checks. Thus far approximatley 1,000 of the 23,000 eligible credit unions offer this service to their owners.

Automatic transfers from savings commenced on November 1, 1978, when all federally insured commercial banks (which constitute 98% of all banks) were authorized to automatically transfer funds from savings accounts to demand deposit accounts to cover any deficiencies in the latter, for individuals (natural persons only, not corporations) and business firms organized as sole proprietorships. Should eligible customers elect this service, a portion of savings accounts can be regarded as a means of payment. Thus, today a wider range of assets offered by a number of different financial institutions can be used as the means of payment. Even though they have different names, they all represent deposits that are subject to checking. That is, their owner can transfer ownership to a third party by means of a check. These accounts, then, are the equivalent of commercial bank demand deposits and will be treated as such for analytical purposes.

Money and monetary policy

Regardless whether the purpose of monetary policy is control of the money supply or interest rates, the traditional definition implies that control must extend to those financial institutions that issue the means of exchange:

[3] These recent changes are discussed more fully in Chapters 5 and 15. On the basis of this early experience in the New England states, commercial banks are likely to emerge as the dominant holders of NOW accounts: they hold 73% in Connecticut, 78% in Maine, 84% in Rhode Island, 93% in Vermont, 57% in Massachusetts, and 64% in New Hampshire.

For a discussion of the NOW account phenomenon, see the following articles in the *New England Economic Review* published by the Federal Reserve Bank of Boston: Katharine Gibson, "The Early History and Initial Impact of NOW Accounts" (Jan.–Feb. 1975): 17–26; Ralph C. Kimball, "Recent Developments in NOW Account Experiment in New England" (Nov.–Dec. 1976): 3–19; and "The Maturing of the NOW Account in New England" (July–Aug. 1978): 27–42; and Donald Basch, "The Diffusion of NOW Accounts in Massachusetts" (Nov.–Dec. 1976): 20–30.

commercial banks, savings and loan associations, mutual savings banks, and perhaps credit unions. (The nature and importance of each of these institutions is explained in Chapter 3.) The U.S. Treasury escapes control because in issuing coins it only responds to the preferences of the public as to the desired composition of its money holdings. That is, the public decides how much money it wishes to hold as currency, coin, and deposits, and the Treasury and the central bank respond by issuing the requisite notes and coins.

Other stores of value

While it is true that currency and the deposits of certain financial institutions are the dominant means of exchange in the United States, it is also obvious that many other assets are substitutes for these two: e.g., bonds, common and preferred shares of stock, insurance annuities, commodities, real estate, deposits at some financial institutions. The existence of these alternative stores of value raises the possibility that they may be able to exert an independent influence on the supply of money or on the amount of spending that occurs in the economy. If this is possible, what problems does it pose for those who see control of the money supply as the key to economic stability? The question will be discussed in detail in Chapter 5, for it has been raised many times.

Social productivity of monetary exchange

Before we consider the alternative definitions of money, we will examine the social productivity of monetary over barter exchange.

If it is true that a common unit of account reduces the total cost of acquiring, processing, and storing information, then such an account should serve to expand the number and range of transactions. In other words, the adoption of a unit of account broadens or increases the size of the market because by reducing the cost of exchange, it increases the return to resources devoted to exchange. As Adam Smith observed over 200 years ago, the degree of individual specialization in production is dependent upon the size of the market—the larger the market, the greater the degree of specialization, and the greater the specialization, the larger the volume of goods and services available to the public, or the more time people will have available for leisure. It is this increase in real per capita income or leisure that constitutes the social advantage of monetary over barter exchange.

When money is used in exchange it also serves to reduce the amount of income that must be allocated to the acquisition of information and to the storage of goods used in making transactions as an initial bundle of goods and services is converted into an ultimate bundle. In this fashion monetary exchange serves to increase either the real income available to the individual for consumption or the amount of time available for leisure. Since monetary exchange also serves to reduce the costs of transactions, it leads to an expansion of the market, which encourages a greater degree of specialization, and thus a rise in real per capita income.

Moreover, any developments that improve the efficiency of monetary exchange contribute to these same ends. Thus, simplification of the number and types of money should reduce information and transactions costs. In the United States the slow reduction in the number and types of currency issues over the past 100 years has been a step in raising per capita real income.

The social productivity of money is not constant, but depends in part on changes in market conditions. The number of new products introduced into the market, technical changes and innovations that alter the number and quality of goods and services, and changes in relative prices induced through fluctuations in economic activity are all conditions that enhance the attractiveness of monetary exchange, for these factors contain the potential of increasing the costs of information acquisition. In the absence of monetary exchange such changes would increase the time required to find out about market conditions and perhaps alter or lengthen the transactions chain by which an initial endowment of goods and services or labor time is converted into an ultimate market basket of goods and services. Monetary exchange, on the other hand, minimizes these costs.

It is an interesting fact that even in countries with astronomical inflation rates monetary exchange continues to prevail. This indicates that the gain to the individual from using money in a transactions chain exceeds the cost imposed by inflation on money holding.

The social productivity of money depends only on monetary exchange. It does not depend upon what definition of money is used. The group of assets that emerges from the two alternative definitions to be discussed next can also be called money, and thus they have a social productivity.

THE EMPIRICAL DEFINITION OF MONEY

One of the foremost proponents of the empirical approach to the definition of money is Professor Milton Friedman, long associated with the University of Chicago. With his collaborator Anna Schwartz, Friedman concludes:

> *. . . the definition of money is to be sought for not on grounds of principle but on grounds of usefulness in organizing our knowledge of economic relationships. "Money" is that to which we choose to assign a number by specific operations; it is not something in existence to be discovered . . . ; it is a scientific construct to be invented, like "length" or "temperature" or "force" in physics.*[4]

[4] Milton Friedman and Anna J. Schwartz, *Monetary Statistics of the United States* (New York: National Bureau of Economic Research, 1970), p. 137.

In another context Friedman and Schwartz have argued that money is anything that serves as a temporary abode of purchasing power which permits the individual to separate the act of purchase from the act of sale. Such a definition of money has no ready counterpart in a definable group of assets—almost anything can serve as a temporary abode of purchasing power.

In attempting to discover what this group of assets is, individuals who advance the empirical approach generally hold that variations in the money supply cause the business cycle. Thus, one way of discovering what money is is to see which group of assets is most closely associated with economic activity, and one method for measuring closeness is correlation analysis. Various collections of assets are formed and their variations are measured relative to variations in some definition of economic activity, namely, gross national product. Then the components of whichever collection shows the closest movement relative to the selected measure of economic activity are designated as money.[5] In performing their calculations for the United States, Friedman and his followers are most apt to use the various measures of the money supply constructed by the Federal Reserve. While the components of these measures have changed from time to time, the Federal Reserve's most recent revisions, made in January 1980, are[6]

M-1*A* = Currency plus demand deposits at commercial banks less demand deposits held by foreign banks and official institutions. (This measure corresponds closely to what was previously designated as M_1.)

M-1*B* = *M*-1*A* plus other checkable deposits at all depository institutions including NOW accounts, Automatic Transfer from Savings Accounts (ATS), credit union share drafts, and deposits at mutual savings banks.

M_2 = *M*-1*B* plus savings and small-denomination time deposits (under $100,000) at all depository institutions, overnight repurchase agreements (RP's) at commercial banks, money market mutual fund shares, and certain Eurodollar deposits. (A description of each of these assets is contained in the pages to follow.)

M_3 = M_2 plus large-denomination time deposits at all depository institutions and term RP's at commercial banks and savings and loan associations.

[5] Correlation analysis only measures whether two series move together or inverse to each other or have no relation to each other. It does not in any way imply cause and effect. Thus, a high correlation of money with GNP doesn't necessarily imply that money makes GNP change or vice versa.

[6] Since these definitions are so new, the older definitions are given below. In several instances in the pages to follow, reference is made to these older definitions.
M_1 = Currency plus demand deposits at commercial banks.
M_2 = M_1 plus savings deposits at commercial banks and small denomination (under $100,000) time deposits at commercial banks.
M_3 = M_2 plus all deposits of savings and loans, mutual savings banks, and credit unions.

In addition, the Federal Reserve has adopted a broad measure of liquid assets. This is equal to M_3 plus other liquid assets such as term Eurodollars, bankers acceptances, commercial paper, Treasury bills, and other Treasury securities and U.S. savings bonds.

These collections are called money series and still others have been constructed. To discover which of these alternatives is *the* money supply, those who use the empirical definition look at the relationship between money supply alternatives and GNP. In some studies the *level* of each series (e.g., the dollar value of M per unit of time) is correlated with levels of gross national product, while in others *changes* in each measure of money are correlated with levels of gross national product. In terms of Figure 1:1, the time series listed as money could be the M-1s, M_2, M_3, or any other M series. The movements in the series that most nearly parallel movements in the level of GNP would be the one designated "money."

Unfortunately, the "best" choice of a money series has not been consistent over time. As Figure 2:1 shows, the growth rate of the M-1s, M_2, and M_3 has not been uniform. Since the three stocks of money have not grown evenly over time, for some historic periods the M-1s correlate better with gross national product, while for other time periods the best correlation is obtained using M_2 or M_3. Had each series moved together

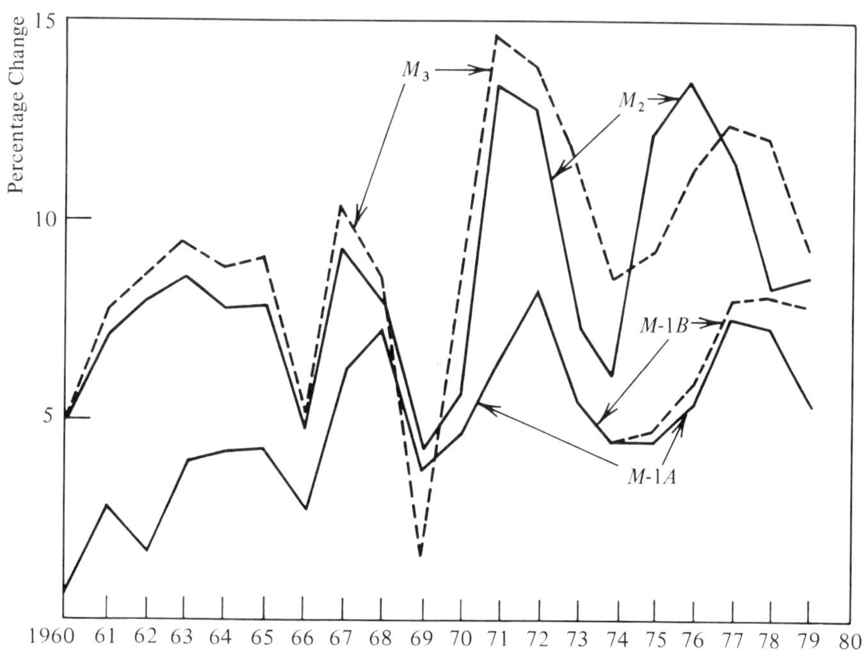

FIGURE 2:1
Percentage change of **M-1s**, $\mathbf{M_2}$, *and* $\mathbf{M_3}$ *over time (Courtesy of the Federal Reserve.)*

uniformly, each would have provided the same correlation, making it irrelevant which measure was selected.[7]

Analyzing and explaining history is one thing, making projections into the future is quite another. Policymakers who rely on the empirical approach to the definition of the money supply could be handicapped by an inability always to determine which group of assets should be controlled to impart stability to future economic activity. Is it to be the M-1's, M_2, or M_3 whose growth rate is to be regulated? This question is of critical importance to those who believe in the superiority of the empirical approach to the definition of money and its implications for the conduct of monetary policy.

A COMPARISON OF THE TRADITIONAL AND EMPIRICAL DEFINITIONS

If one looks to the past, the traditional and empirical definitions do not single out the same collection of assets as money. The traditional definition, concentrating on the means of payment, would indicate that M-1A or M-1B contains the proper set of assets. On the other hand, the empirical definition, using correlation analysis, would imply M_2 or M_3 as the appropriate set. Because M-1A, M-1B, and M_2 are widely used monetary aggregates and are reported in the financial press, the analysis in this text will concentrate on explaining their determinants.

THE LIQUIDITY DEFINITION

The liquidity definition of money is superficially related to the empirical definition in that it attempts to determine by mathematical estimation what

[7] The literature using some variation of the empirical approach is extensive. For a sample see Milton Friedman and David Meiselman, "The Relative Stability of Monetary Velocity and the Investment Multiplier in the United States, 1897–1958," in *Commission on Money and Credit, Stabilization Policies* (Englewood Cliffs, N. J.: Prentice-Hall, 1963). In this early study M_2 was selected as the best definition. In Friedman's later study with Anna Schwartz (see footnote 4) a broader definition of money close to M_3 was selected as best. However, in Richard H. Timberlake, Jr., and James Fortson's "Time Deposits in the Definition of Money," *American Economic Review,* Vol. 57, No. 1 (March 1967): 190–3, it was concluded that nothing was gained by using M_2 over M_1. Other studies providing conflicting evidence on the best definition of money are George G. Kaufman, "More on an Empirical Definition of Money," *American Economic Review,* Vol. 59, No. 1 (March 1969): 78–87; David T. Hulett, "More on an Empirical Definition of Money: Note," *American Economic Review,* Vol. 61, No. 3, Pt. I (June 1971): 462–8; and Frederick C. Schadrack, "An Empirical Approach to the Definition of Money," in *Monetary Aggregates and Monetary Policy* (Federal Reserve Bank of New York 1974), pp. 28–34. This welter of confusing evidence implies that the findings on the best definition of money are sensitive to whether the money stock is measured quarterly or annually, whether a long or short time span is used, whether certain lags are used in the estimation procedure, and which of various measures of economic activity money is linked with. It should also be noted that M_1 and M_2 measures of money used in these studies are not the same as those defined by the Federal Reserve in January 1980 and used in this text. The newer definitions reflect changes in the range of assets that can be used to make transactions.

should be called money. It differs primarily in not including the total value of financial assets other than currency and demand deposits.

In this approach currency and demand deposits are regarded as the basic means of payment. Given any asset, one may measure its liquidity by the ease with which it can be converted into the means of payment. Ease is determined by two factors: how quickly the asset can be converted and whether the conversion takes place at or about the price paid for the asset. The problem now posed is to measure the liquidity of other assets that are possible substitutes for the two means of payment—substitute stores of value according to the traditional definition.

An early test to measure liquidity was proposed by John Gurley.[8] Suppose that the amount of the two means of payment is reduced by $100. By how much will, say, time and saving deposits at commercial banks have to be increased in order to keep the structure of interest rates (i.e., the relationship of short-term to long-term interest rates) constant? If this would require an equivalent $100 increase, then time and savings deposits are as liquid as the two means of payment. If it would require a $200 increase, then they are only half as liquid. The degree of liquidity of any asset could be calculated similarly. The degree of liquidity, then, becomes the weight that is attached to the dollar value of these assets in arriving at a definition of money. For example, a weight of 1 is given the dollar value of currency and demand deposits, whereas only one-half the dollar value of time and savings deposits might be assigned to the total of these assets if it were discovered that they are only half as liquid.[9] Needless to add, the liquidity definition yields a much larger measure of the money supply than the other two definitions and implies that to control the money supply, a large number of financial institutions will have to be controlled by the monetary authority.

A variation on this approach is to see how sensitive the demand for the means of payment is to the rate of return on alternative financial assets (e.g., savings and time deposits). The method used to make these estimates is theoretically equivalent to calculating what is called the *cross elasticity of demand*.

It will be recalled from microeconomic theory that the cross-elasticity calculation seeks to measure how sensitive the demand for one good is to a change in the price of another good. As the calculated coefficient approaches infinity, the two goods approach being perfect substitutes. As the coefficient approaches zero, the two goods are completely independent of each other. When the price of the other good is a yield or rate of return, a reinterpretation of the usual approach is required. Thus, if the rate of return on an asset alternative to the means of payment declines and this

[8] John G. Gurley, "Liquidity and Financial Institutions in the Postwar Economy," Study Paper 14, Joint Economic Committee, 86th Congress, 2nd Session (Washington, D.C.: U.S. Government Printing Office, 1960).

[9] In actual fact, Gurley grouped all other financial assets together and assigned them a weight of .5, although he believed that other values would work almost as well.

leads to an increase in the demand for money, the calculated coefficient will be negative. A negative number, therefore, means substitutability.[10]

There have been a number of econometric attempts to calculate the cross elasticities of the various assets to the means of payment. An examination of the work of Feige, Lee, Chetty, Edwards, and Steinhaur and Chang reveals many problems.[11] Whether the alternative financial assets are substitutes for the means of payment, and the degree to which they are substitutes, appear to depend on whether aggregated or disaggregated data are used (national as opposed to state or regional data), the time period of the data used in the calculations, whether interest rate levels or differentials are used, whether the data are of a cross-sectional or time-series nature, whether linear or multiplicative demand equations are estimated, whether certain variables are included in the estimation, whether only current or lagged values of these variables are used, and so on.

Some of these investigations yield the conclusion that there are financial assets that have either the same degree or a higher degree of "moneyness" than the means of payment themselves![12] Obviously, something is amiss in several of these estimates. Nevertheless, they are an interesting, though not very compelling, approach to an estimation of the stock of money. In addition, these studies generally support Gurley's objection to including the total sum of each of these assets, such as time and savings deposits, in such measures as M_2 and M_3.

A fundamental objection to the liquidity approach is that it assumes the existence of money. It cannot explain the origin, use, or holding of a money asset.

While this textbook will use the traditional definition of money or that which emerges from a consideration of the functions of money, all can readily agree with Friedman and Schwartz that "after centuries of consideration in the literature, the best way to define money remains a live issue today."

[10] As will be explained, the rate of return on certain types of assets is negatively related to their market prices. Thus, if the rate of return falls, market price will rise. Inserting a rising market price into an equation used to estimate cross elasticity will produce a positive coefficient, indicating, in accordance with theory, a substitute relationship.

[11] E. L. Feige, *The Demand for Liquid Assets: A Temporal Cross-Section Analysis* (Englewood Cliffs, N.J: Prentice-Hall, 1964); T. H. Lee, "Substitutability of Non-bank Intermediary Liabilities for Money," *Journal of Finance* 21 (Sept. 1966):441–57, and "Alternative Interest Rates and the Demand for Money: The Empirical Evidence,"*American Economic Review* 57 (Dec. 1967): 1168–81; V. K. Chetty, "On Measuring the Nearness of Near Moneys," *American Economic Review* 59 (June 1969): 270–81; F. R. Edwards, "More on Substitutability Between Money and Near-Monies," *Journal of Money, Credit and Banking*, Vol. 4, No. 3 (Aug. 1972): 551–71; L. Steinhauer and J. Chang, "On Measuring the Nearness of Near-Moneys: Comment," *American Economic Review*, Vol. 64, No. 1 (March, 1972): 221–5.

[12] It should be noted that the individuals who seek to measure cross elasticities are rather unclear about their definition of "moneyness." In general, the term supposedly indicates the services from money. But since these other financial assets cannot be used as a means of payment, "moneyness" must mean some other lesser services usually described as liquidity, safety, convenience, etc. If this is the case, it seems incredible that an inferior substitute turns out to have an equal or greater degree of moneyness than the means of payment.

MONETARY SYSTEMS

We will now consider the type of monetary system or the type of money used by a society. The importance of such a consideration springs from the fact that the supply of some types of money is more easily managed than that of others. That is, some types of money allow monetary authorities greater flexibility in consciously manipulating the supply of money.

Monetary systems can be classified according to various criteria. If the money supply is distinguished by the nature of the issuer, bank money is separable from government money. One might also distinguish money by whether or not it is convertible into commodities or into other money. Finally, money might be distinguished by the commodity out of which it is made. While each classification can be useful in a specific context or in dealing with a specific problem, the commodity classification is the one of interest here, for it determines in part if the money supply can be managed.

Differentiating monetary systems on the basis of the commodity out of which money is made produces a twofold classification: *full-bodied* and *credit* monies.

Full-bodied monies

A monetary system using full-bodied monies is one in which the exchange value of money in the market is equal to the exchange value of the commodity out of which money is made.

In many primitive societies, including our own in its early history, full-bodied monies are commonly used. When cows, rice, tobacco, wool, or other commodities are employed as a means of exchange, their exchange value or purchasing power or their command over other goods depends on their purchasing power as a commodity. Thus, if 100 pounds of tobacco is the standard means of exchange, its purchasing power as money will depend upon the commodity value of 100 pounds of tobacco. This will, in turn, depend upon the relative supply of tobacco in terms of others goods and services. As it would be unlikely that the exchange value would remain invariant over time, individuals could speak either of an inflation or deflation of prices in terms of the standard unit of account. What they would mean is simply that 100 pounds of tobacco on the average buys either less or more of all other goods.

As societies become more organized and sophisticated, they usually specify a unit of account and define it in terms of a certain weight of metal, with gold, silver, and copper being common choices.

Thus, in the United States the dollar was originally defined in 1781 as 23.22 grains of fine gold.[13] Once the step of defining the unit of account as a certain weight of metal is taken, the monetary authority must face the problem of ensuring that this weight of metal always has an exchange value

[13] Since there are 480 grains of gold per ounce, equating 23.22 grains to the dollar establishes $20.67 as the price per ounce of gold.

as money equal to its exchange value as a commodity. To the extent that it is successful in doing so, it has no control over the supply of money. Suppose, for example, someone finds a new gold field or invents a new mining process that significantly reduces mining costs. These developments should expand the supply of gold, causing its price as a commodity to fall relative to all other prices. To prevent the commodity price of gold from falling, the monetary authorities must buy up all the metal not otherwise used as a commodity at the established price of 23.22 grains per dollar or $20.67 per ounce. It does this by receiving for free coinage all of the metal not demanded for nonmonetary purposes at the established price of $20.67 per ounce. Interestingly, since this will expand the supply of money relative to the quantity of goods and services available for sale, it should push up on average all prices, thereby causing the relative purchasing power of gold as money to decline.

Conversely, if the nonmonetary demand for gold should rise and threaten to increase the commodity value of the metal above its money value (i.e., 23.22 grains of gold would exchange for more than a dollar's worth of commodities), the monetary authority must either sell gold from whatever stocks it has accumulated or allow the public to melt coins and sell the bullion as a commodity.

The difficulty of maintaining equality between the commodity and money values of a metal is compounded if two metals (such as gold and silver) are used as money. In this case, the monetary authority has the added burden of maintaining the fixed price between the two metals themselves, i.e., it must keep the relative price ratio constant.

A full-bodied monetary system does not preclude the use of paper money or checking deposit money. The former is merely a warehouse receipt for its commodity equivalent (a paper dollar becomes the warehouse receipt for 23.22 grains of gold held in some vault), whereas checking deposit money can, at most, be only some multiple of the amount of full-bodied money entrusted to financial institutions for safekeeping.[14]

Credit monies

A credit monetary system is one that uses money whose exchange value as money is much greater than the exchange value of the commodity from which it is made.

Most advanced societies use credit monies and such monetary systems often are a part of an evolution that started with commodity monies. Sometime during the history of the nation its monetary authorities broke the link between the paper money in circulation and the commodity for which it serves as a warehouse receipt. In the United States this occurred in 1933 when President Roosevelt and Congress abolished the right of domestic citizens to exchange paper notes for gold.

[14] Explaining why checking deposit money can at maximum be some multiple of full-bodied money would involve explaining money creation, a subject reserved for Chapter 4.

A basic question is how such credit monies, which are worth very little as a commodity, remain in general circulation. For some, the answer centers around the fact that our coins and paper notes bear the legend "In God We Trust," and thus to repudiate or refuse to accept the notes in exchange for goods and services would reveal an absence of faith.[15] More seriously, the ability of credit monies to remain in circulation rests mainly upon a comparison of the benefits from monetary exchange with the costs of holding a portion of one's wealth in the form of an inventory of money. As the benefits of monetary exchange have already been fully explored, it remains only to emphasize that the cost of holding wealth in a money form can be measured by the loss in purchasing power that money may sustain if commodity prices in general rise.

To maintain credit monies in circulation, the cost of holding money must be kept low, which means that inflation must be kept low. This can be accomplished by maintaining the growth of the money supply in some reasonable relationship to the growth in real goods and services. Such a policy will ensure the reasonable stability of purchasing power that is essential if credit monies are to be used as means of exchange.

CREDIT MONEY AND MONETARY MANAGEMENT

Once money no longer depends on a commodity such as gold and silver, the ability to vary its supply becomes much greater, and hence monetary authorities have more discretion in regulating its supply. This flexibility is not absolute, however; it depends on the type of financial arrangement among the nations of the world. If these international financial arrangements have as their central feature a system of fixed exchange rates and any imbalances in purchases and sales between nations are settled in some commodity such as gold, then the use of credit monies domestically does not imply full freedom for monetary authorities. The requirement of maintaining fixed exchange rates between national currencies will impose a constraint on the domestic issue of money. In particular, the price levels in the various countries will need to move in similar directions and by similar amounts. If they do not, trade imbalances will develop and to restore equality will, among other things, require some variation in the issue of money.

If, however, the exchange rate is free to fluctuate, the balance of

[15] Dean Acheson, onetime Secretary of State, related that on the eve of the Allied invasion of Europe in 1944 a discussion arose over the nature of the currency to be issued in the areas liberated by the Allies. The discussion centered heavily on who should issue the currency. To divert the participants to matters bearing on the acceptability of the new notes, the British delegate, Sir Edward Playfair, suggested that the new currency could benefit from the U.S. practice of using a motto on its coins. In place of "In God We Trust" he suggested one from the book of Job: "I know that my Redeemer liveth." See Acheson, *Present at the Creation* (New York: Norton, 1969), p. 284.

international commerce need not constrain domestic monetary authorities in their efforts to regulate the supply of money.[16]

CREDIT MONIES AND INFLATION

It has been claimed that credit monetary systems result in an inflationary bias in monetary management—that is, the use of credit monies tends to raise the average rate of world inflation. In response to this charge it must be noted that there is nothing inherent in such a system that would make it more inflation-prone than a full-bodied monetary system.

For instance, the gold and silver brought back by Spain from the New World in the early sixteenth century set off in Europe a century of price inflation so severe that it prompted a number of investigations as to its origins. Among these were several rather comprehensive statements linking the supply of money to the price level. Thus, even with the hardest of hard money, significant inflations are possible.

The phenomenon known rather arbitrarily as *hyperinflation* has occurred only in nations using credit monies. After World War I Germany, Austria, Hungary, Poland, and Russia fell victim to this disease when their governments sought to pay their bills by money creation. Later, in the World War II period, Greece, China, and once again Hungary were similarly afflicted. The hyperinflation in Hungary after World War II was by far the most intense in recorded history. From July 1, 1945, to August 1, 1946, the Hungarian price level rose from an index number of 8000 to 24×10^{28}. In the final two months of this period alone the index rose from 75×10^{10} to 24×10^{28}. Amazing stories emerged from this experience. We are told, for example, that during a two-hour wait in the bread queue the price of a loaf rose from 10,000 to 50,000 pengö (the Hungarian unit of account). Such stories should not obscure one interesting fact. Despite the extraordinary rise in prices, monetary exchange continued throughout these episodes of hyperinflation. Such is the advantage of monetary exchange that it will persist until an extremely high cost is imposed on money holding. Only when this cost is extremely high do individuals seek out other transaction chains involving barter or the use of more stable valued foreign currencies. Only then do we observe what is called the collapse of the monetary system.

A considerable historical experience shows that credit monetary systems are not inherently inflationary.

THE EFFECT OF INFLATION ON CREDIT MONIES

Severe inflation in the short run or a sustained period of mild inflation can cause credit monies to become full-bodied monies. Throughout much of this century the U.S. Treasury minted subsidiary coins that contained silver

[16] In Chapter 16 the ability to alter the money supply in economies engaged in international trade is explored in greater detail.

PAYING CASH FOR:

SILVER COINS

(1964 and Before)

DIMES, QUARTERS AND HALVES PRICES ARE SUBJECT TO SILVER MARKET FLUCTUATIONS, BUT THE LEAST WE HAVE RECENTLY PAID IS
$16.00 per $1.00 face value

DIMES	**$1.70 each**
QUARTERS	**$4.25**
HALVES	**$8.50**

FIGURE 2:2
(Courtesy of The Washington Post, *February 19, 1980.)*

and issued silver certificates the $1 denomination of which were warehouse receipts for .7734 troy ounce of silver. The secular (long-term) inflation since the mid-1930s and the increased industrial demand for silver slowly increased the metal's price as a commodity. When its commodity price rose above $1.293 per troy ounce, the silver bullion behind the silver certificate and the silver in minor coins made them worth more as a commodity than as money. As Figure 2:2 shows, market incentives were created to remove these coins from circulation. In 1968 the Treasury revoked the right to redeem silver certificates for silver bullion.[17] If copper prices continue to rise, a similar fate may await the penny.

SOCIAL BENEFITS OF PAPER MONEY

The use of paper money either as a warehouse receipt for a commodity (gold or silver) or as a pure credit money confers a benefit upon society.

Insofar as the paper is a substitute for the gold or silver, its social usefulness lies in its potential for saving resources. To maintain a given volume of money requires either the maintenance of a given amount of metal money or its equivalent in paper. Using paper generally involves a smaller resource cost than using metal.

[17] One of the earliest laws incorporated into monetary economics was that proposed by Sir Thomas Gresham, which is commonly stated as: Bad money drives out of circulation good money. What Gresham meant was that the overvalued money circulates and the undervalued money is hoarded. In the case at point, so long as the minor coins made with silver exchanged for those made from cheaper metals on a one-for-one basis, the overvalued coins (those made from the less valued metals) were used in exchange, while the undervalued coins (those made with silver) were hoarded or, in some cases, melted down in violation of law. History is replete with similar examples, most of which arose when full-bodied coins were used.

In the case of pure credit money, the resource saving is more substantial, for metal does not have to be dug up, refined, and then buried again in vaults. All the metal is available for nonmonetary uses.

Finally, the use of paper money encourages the development of a fractional reserve banking system. With this development, a given money supply can be produced and maintained at a lower resource cost than one composed of metal. Moreover, the use of fractional reserve banking develops and expands the number of exchanges made with money, thereby increasing the efficiency and productivity of the economy.

SUMMARY

This chapter explored several of the alternative definitions of money and accepted the so-called traditional or functional definition, which ultimately recognizes the principal services of money to an economy. By reducing the cost of acquiring, processing, and storing information about the market, and the costs of making transactions, money performs a socially useful function. In general, its social productivity raises the real income of each individual either by permitting a larger volume of goods and services to be consumed or by allowing the individual to spend more time in leisure.

Finally, monetary systems were examined according to the degree of flexibility they give monetary management in varying the supply of money.

STUDY QUESTIONS

1. What benefits accrue to a society from using a single unit of account?
2. What benefits accrue to a society from using only a single medium of exchange?
3. Given the benefits listed in response to the above two questions, why isn't there one unit of account and medium of exchange for the entire world?
4. Explain the origin of money. That is, why do you think money came into being and use?
5. Does the ability of credit money to remain generally acceptable depend upon its being designated by governments as "legal tender," i.e., legally acceptable in the discharge of obligations?
6. Why do you think individuals hold a part of their wealth in the form of money, which yields no explicit interest income (e.g., currency and certain forms of demand deposits)?
7. Suppose the government minted two half dollars, one composed of silver and the other of copper. Suppose further that both are worth more as money than as commodities, but that the silver half dollar more nearly approximates its value as a commodity than the copper half dollar.

Would both half dollars circulate side by side? Would your answer be the same if the silver half dollar were worth more as a commodity than as money?

8. Suppose that there is no unit of account, but very high speed, efficient, low-cost computers exist that can print out at a moment's notice the entire array of relative prices in a given market. Would there then be any reason to introduce a unit of account and medium of exchange into the society?
9. It has become increasingly common to use credit cards to make transactions. Why aren't they included in the four most common measures of the money supply? (If they were, what would be added to the money supply?)

SELECTED REFERENCES AND READINGS

Brunner, Karl, and Meltzer, Allan. "The Use of Money: Money in the Theory of an Exchange Economy." *American Economic Review,* Vol. 61, No. 5 (December 1971).

Feige, Edgar, and Pearce, Douglas. "The Substitutability of Money and Near-Monies: A Survey of the Time-Series Evidence." *Journal of Economic Literature,* Vol. 15, No. 2 (June 1977).

Friedman, Milton, and Schwartz, Anna. *Monetary Statistics of the United States.* New York: National Bureau of Economic Research, 1970.

Galbraith, John Kenneth. *Money, Whence it Came, Where it Went.* Boston: Houghton Mifflin Co., 1975.

Gambs, Carl M. "Money—A Changing Concept in a Changing World." *Monthly Review,* Federal Reserve Bank of Kansas City (January 1977).

Johnson, Harry G. "Monetary Theory and Policy," reprinted as Chapter 1 in *Essays in Monetary Economics.* London: Allen & Unwin, 1967.

Laidler, David E. W. "The Definition of Money, Theoretical and Empirical Problems." *Journal of Money, Credit and Banking* (August 1969).

Melitz, Jacques. *Primitive and Modern Money.* Reading, Mass.: Addison-Wesley, 1974.

Renshaw, Edward F. "A Note on Economic Activity and Alternative Definitions of the Money Supply." *Journal of Money, Credit and Banking* (August 1975).

3 FINANCIAL INTERMEDIARIES

One characteristic differentiating developed from underdeveloped countries is the number, range, and diversity of specialized financial institutions. These institutions (commercial banks, credit unions, savings and loan associations, mutual savings banks, insurance companies, pension funds, etc.) are known collectively as financial intermediaries. The name *intermediary* refers to the fact that these institutions stand between the ultimate borrower and the ultimate lender; their function is to expedite the flow of funds from the latter to the former. Since it is often observed that credit is the lifeblood of the economy, these financial intermediaries can be viewed as credit merchants whose role is to keep an economy healthy.

It is no accident that a highly developed system of financial intermediaries is generally found only in highly developed economies. Financial institutions and economic development interact to a high degree. Most economically advanced societies achieved that status in large part because their financial institutions grew in size, diversity, and sophistication. Also, while financial institutions contribute to economic development, economic development in itself, by expanding the size of markets, makes possible the further evolution of financial institutions.[1]

The fundamental way in which financial intermediaries contribute to economic development is by reducing the costs involved in the lending process. Cost reductions are achieved through three different means. First, financial institutions can increase the overall supply of loanable funds. Second, they can reduce the risks involved in the lending process. Third, many financial institutions are highly specialized lenders, they only make certain types of loans. Through specialization they acquire lending expertise, which enables them to lower the direct cost of negotiating, evaluating, accounting, appraising, and collecting loans.

Through these three means the overall cost of lending is reduced, which is reflected in a lower interest rate structure. A lower interest rate structure stimulates a higher rate of capital formation, which increases the sophisti-

[1] John Gurley and Edward Shaw are pioneers in examining the interaction of real and financial development. See their "Financial Aspects of Economic Development," *American Economic Review*, Vol. 45, No. 4 (Sept. 1953): 515–38; "Financial Intermediaries and the Saving-Investment Process," *Journal of Finance*, Vol. 11, No. 2 (May 1956): 257–76, and "The Growth of Money and Debt in the United States, 1800–1950: A Suggested Interpretation," *Review of Economics and Statistics*, Vol. 39, No. 3 (Aug. 1957): 250–62.

cation of the production process, the expansion of markets, and the rate of economic growth and development.

In order to justify all these conclusions it will be necessary to analyze the lending process itself, to examine the growth of American financial intermediaries over time, and finally, to discuss the degree to which each intermediary is specialized.

THE LENDING PROCESS

An examination of the lending process reveals both the risks involved and the methods financial intermediaries use to reduce those risks and to increase the overall supply of loanable funds.

At any moment in time, society will be composed of two groups of individuals: those whose income exceeds their expenditures and those whose expenditures exceed their income. The first group can be called ultimate savers or ultimate lenders. By spending less of their income than they receive, they are in effect saving a portion of their income. Since their income is earned through the production of goods and services, their financial savings has as its counterpart a quantity of real goods and services that they produced but did not wish to consume. For the economy to run smoothly, these real goods and services must be transferred to those persons or institutions (including business and government) that desire to spend more than they receive as income (i.e., buy more goods and services than their income during this period will permit). This second group of net spenders can be called ultimate borrowers. In order to buy more goods and services than they produce through earning an income, they must command financial resources in addition to those they earned as income (or in the case of the government, received in the form of tax revenue). This requires them to borrow the additional purchasing power of the net savers.

This borrowing can either be done *directly,* that is, the ultimate borrower can obtain the additional purchasing power directly from the ultimate saver-lender by issuing some evidence of debt; or *indirectly,* by borrowing from a financial intermediary. The intermediary has obtained the surplus funds from the ultimate lender by issuing some evidence of debt or providing a service such as insurance or rights to a future pension. Figure 3:1 sets out the nature of the lending process.

Before we consider the nature of the risks involved in lending, it should be noted that these two types of lending are not mutually exclusive in one society. It is true that in primitive societies most lending is probably direct, while in advanced societies a large amount of lending is indirect. However, the government in advanced societies is a large borrower and its borrowing is often done directly. On a lower level, a student often borrows money from parents to meet the expenses of an education. Such lending is direct.

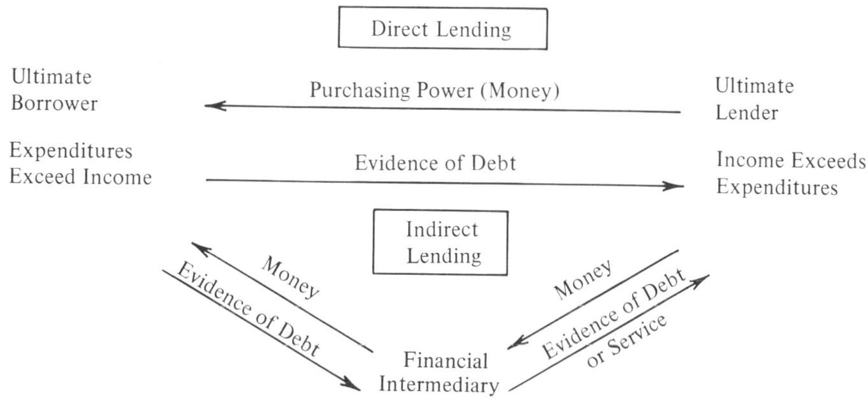

FIGURE 3:1
The lending process

There is no guarantee that the surplus funds of the ultimate saver will be lent to the ultimate borrower, with or without a system of financial intermediaries. However, the presence of financial intermediaries makes it more likely that such funds will not lie idle, for a basic function of an intermediary is to bring together borrower and lender. In doing so, financial intermediaries increase the potential supply of loanable funds to the market.

The risks of lending

In any lending arrangement two types of risks usually arise. The first is the well-known *default risk,* which means simply that the borrower may not be able to repay the loan in whole or in part at the time repayment is scheduled. The ultimate lender then suffers a monetary loss equal in whole or part to the defaulted loan. To the extent that the borrower pledged specific assets to secure the loan, the degree of the loss suffered by the lender is reduced.

The second type of risk is concerned with the *liquidity* of the asset acquired in relation to that given up by the ultimate lender. The property of liquidity pertains to the ability of the ultimate lender to dispose of the asset quickly and at a price reasonably close to that given for it. Liquidity is related to several characteristics of the asset. First, is the asset issued by a well-known firm, individual, or government unit whose financial position is above suspicion? If so, the asset is potentially highly marketable. Second, what is the length of time before the asset matures, that is, before the ultimate borrower can redeem the asset? Generally, the longer the term to maturity, the less liquid an asset is. Third, does the asset bear interest? If the asset bears interest and is in the nature of a bond, the longer the term to maturity, the greater will its market price fluctuate for a given change in market interest rates.[2] For this reason also, longer-term assets are generally less liquid than those with maturity dates close at hand.

Finally, how well developed is the market for this type of asset? For example, are prices quoted daily, are the assets sold on a nationwide exchange, do financial institutions deal in them? The more highly developed the market for a type of asset, the more liquid it is.

FINANCIAL INTERMEDIARIES AND RISK REDUCTION

The market interest rate functions to induce potential lenders to bear the two risks of default and illiquidity. If these risks can be reduced, ultimate lenders ought to be willing to supply their surplus funds at lower rates of interest to borrowers. Can financial intermediaries lower these risks? If the primary ultimate borrower is the federal government, which borrows by issuing short-term securities, then intermediaries will probably not decrease the risks of lending. The reason is that since the federal government has the power to levy and collect taxes, it need never default on its obligations. Hence, these loans are virtually free of the default risk. Second, short-maturity obligations have a high degree of liquidity. They are highly marketable and their market price does not fluctuate greatly even for sizable movements in market interest rates.

On the other hand, though assets representing personal loans acquired by the ultimate lender may have a low default risk, they are probably highly illiquid and therefore are made at market rates of interest in excess of those paid by the government. The potential rate asked by the lender may be so high as to discourage a great deal of borrowing, thus reducing the number of borrowers.

For nongovernment lending, financial intermediaries can reduce for the ultimate lender the two risks involved. To see this, consider first the default risk.

The default risk

Intermediaries can reduce the default risk in either of two ways, which theoretically are available to the ultimate lender, but at a cost. Since the mid-1930s a large number of financial institutions—commercial banks, credit unions, mutual savings banks, savings and loan associations—have

[2] See pp. 159–60 for a rigorous proof of this position. This applies only to negotiable securities such as bonds. It does not apply to non-negotiable securities such as the familiar Series E savings bond issued by the federal government.

been able to acquire at low rates federal insurance on their deposits.[3] Thus the ultimate saver who entrusts his excess funds to most financial institutions acquires an insured deposit (to a maximum of $100,000 per person), which reduces the default risk to zero.[4]

Even in the absence of deposit insurance, financial intermediaries can reduce the default risk for the ultimate lender by diversifying the loans they make. It is well known that loan defaults can move together over time. That is, defaults rise during economic downturns and fall during economic upturns. However, since different types of loans have different default risks, i.e., their risk of default is not positively and perfectly correlated, diversification of loans (making them to different individuals whose activities are not related to the business cycle in the same way) serves to reduce the overall risk of default. (Similarly, diversification can be used to stabilize earnings.) If, however, defaults among all loans were perfectly correlated, diversification could not achieve overall lowering of the diversification risk. While diversification of loans is possible for any lender, it is less likely to be achieved by the small lender whose surplus funds are small and for whom diversification may require extra costs—each loan involves the cost of acquiring information about the ability of the borrower to discharge his obligations in a timely fashion.

Either through the use of federal deposit insurance or through diversification, financial intermediaries reduce the default risk. Because this is so, ultimate lenders ought to be willing to entrust to these intermediaries their surplus funds at a lower interest rate than they would require if they were making the loans directly.

It should also be noted that individuals can serve as their own life insurance companies or pension funds, i.e., act as their own intermediary. This can be accomplished by holding surplus funds in a money or security form to provide a reserve for survivors in case of death or to supplement their own earning power when it diminishes because of accident or old age.

When an individual serves as his own life insurance company or pension fund, the same questions arise as when a loan is made to others. In deciding

[3] Economists of such diverse opinion as Milton Friedman and John Kenneth Galbraith are unanimous in holding that the creation of the Federal Deposit Insurance Corporation in 1934 was one of the most significant institutional developments in American banking. By finally creating a lender of last resort to the financial community, a role traditionally reserved for a central bank, this Act of Congress freed the American banking system from periodic currency runs that either brought on or exacerbated financial crises. It is significant that since the creation of federal deposit insurance, the United States has *never* had a run on its banking system. It is ironic that powerful opposition to this reform was led by the American Bankers Association, which held it to be unsound, unscientific, unjust, dangerous, and otherwise unsatisfactory!

[4] There is no reason why the ultimate saver could not acquire asset insurance. The premium would undoubtedly be substantially higher than that paid by a financial institution, because, among other things, the institution's default risk is likely to be smaller than an individual's because of diversification.

what form in which to hold these retained earnings, the individual will have to contend with default risk and the possible illiquidity of some assets. An additional problem is that the accumulated assets may be insufficient to provide an adequate reserve if death or disabling accidents occur early in life. For these reasons, entrusting surplus funds to life insurance companies and pension funds appears to many to be a wiser alternative than serving as one's own insurance company and pension fund.

Liquidity risk

As already noted, one factor determining the rate of interest is the liquidity of the asset acquired by the ultimate lenders relative to the liquidity of their surplus funds.

In general, the deposit claims against financial intermediaries given to ultimate lenders in return for their surplus funds are highly liquid. In the case of checking deposit claims on financial institutions, they are money itself. In most other instances these claims are represented by a deposit that, although non-negotiable (i.e., title cannot be transferred by giving the deposit to someone else), can either by custom or law be converted into the means of payment on demand. That is, the deposit can be withdrawn in currency or a draft (check) drawn against a financial institution. Certain classes of time deposits have fixed maturities and can only be converted into the means of payment when they fall due. The popular time certificates of deposit (CD's) issued by commercial banks are negotiable and can be sold in an organized market, which enhances their liquidity.

The availability of depository claims issued by financial intermediaries as a form for holding the surplus funds of ultimate lenders ought to reduce the liquidity risk inherent in the lending process.

THE ABILITY OF INTERMEDIARIES TO DECREASE THEIR OWN RISKS

Thus far the discussion has shown how the liquidity and default risks can be reduced for the ultimate lenders. While they have been reduced for these individuals, they have been shifted to the intermediary. In order for interest rates to be reduced for the ultimate borrower, the intermediaries must be able to reduce the default and liquidity risks for themselves.

As to the default risk, the possibility of diversification of loans should serve to lower this category of risk for the financial intermediary. In addition, after operating for some time, most intermediaries build up precautionary reserves so that any losses they might sustain do not automatically lead to financial failure.

Several means of reducing the liquidity risk are available to financial intermediaries either by their very existence or because of positive things they can do to achieve risk reduction. First, the various diversified financial institutions are a basic part of the infrastructure known as the financial market. By their existence they help to create "the market," and the existence of a financial market where securities are actively traded tends to enhance the liquidity of all securities. Second, operation over time permits financial intermediaries to hold a volume of similar securities of varying maturities. For example, a savings and loan association that customarily makes loans on home mortgages will have some mortgages currently coming due, while others will come due in 1, 2, 5, 10, 15, 20, 25, or 30 years, depending on when they were purchased. Similarly, other financial institutions acquire assets of differing maturity dates to add to their overall liquidity.

Finally, some financial institutions avail themselves of "lenders of last resort." In the United States the central bank or Federal Reserve is such a lender and can, by timely purchase of U.S. government securities or other means, add liquid funds to the financial system when necessary.

These three means should serve to reduce the liquidity risk of financial intermediaries below that for the individual ultimate lender.

Since both lending risks are lower for the intermediary than for the ultimate lender, the intermediary should be willing to pass on the funds entrusted to it to most ultimate borrowers at lower interest rates than those for which the funds could be obtained directly. So long as there is competition among financial intermediaries, the market will work to ensure that the funds are transferred at lower interest costs.

SPECIALIZATION AND COST REDUCTION

The process of making loans can be involved and complicated. The lender must first evaluate the credit worthiness of the potential borrower, especially the ability to repay the sums advanced according to schedule. This involves evaluating the future earning capacity of the borrower, which may be no easy task. In addition, once the loan is approved, if it is sizable in amount, the lender may have to sell other assets in order to raise the requisite sum. Rearrangement of asset holdings or the portfolio is never costless. Finally, the loan must be administered and collected to ensure it is repaid in a timely fashion. Moreover, the intermediary often must maintain offices to solicit funds and provide services to the ultimate lender. In most economic endeavors specialization serves to reduce the cost of production, and so it is with financial intermediaries. As will be explained, intermediaries tend to specialize in making one type of loan, and with this specialization comes expertise in evaluating the ability of the ultimate borrower to discharge his obligations. Of course, sometimes the intermediary's experts are too optimistic and the institution acquires some bad or doubtful assets as a result. Nevertheless, specialization tends to reduce the costs associated with the evaluation of loans, the placement of funds, and the administration and collection of loans. The market then works to ensure that these cost reductions are passed on to the ultimate borrower in terms of lower interest rates.

It should also be noted that the existence of large financial intermediaries reduces the cost of soliciting funds for the ultimate borrower as well. It should not be forgotten that the ultimate borrower has two options available for raising funds—the direct and indirect—and these two may not be equally costly. To the extent that the required funds can be obtained from one or a few intermediaries as opposed to thousands of people, solicitation costs are reduced, as well as the costs of meeting a repayment schedule, i.e., sending out checks for interest and repayment of the principal sum borrowed.

A MIXED BLESSING?

Thus far this chapter has concentrated on explaining the considerable social gains that come from the indirect lending process. However, the indirect lending process may contribute to economic instability from time to time. These periodic episodes, when serious, are called financial panics or runs, and when less intense, it has become fashionable to refer to them as credit crunches.

The cause of some of these periods of financial distress is *disintermediation,* which is simply the opposite of intermediation. That is, rather than entrust their surplus funds to intermediaries, ultimate lenders decide that it is more profitable to lend them directly to ultimate borrowers. Not only do they commit their current surplus funds in this direction, but they also withdraw past surplus funds from intermediaries and lend these directly. When the funds are withdrawn from intermediaries, these institutions are forced to draw down their holdings of money or else sell in the market some of their assets in order to raise immediate money balances. If a great number of intermediaries must do this simultaneously, distressed selling will occur, the supply of financial securities offered for sale will rise, prices will fall, and some financial institutions will incur losses and perhaps even be forced into bankruptcy. In addition, some institutions will be compelled to call in loans, or not renew others for established customers, thereby putting them in financial distress. Under these conditions, the financial or credit market tightens and loans are difficult to come by.

To see why disintermediation can cause such problems, the functioning of financial intermediaries must be understood. They perform their role as middlemen by borrowing from ultimate savers at a lower interest rate than that at which they lend to ultimate borrowers. The difference between the two rates constitutes their profit. One reason why these two rates are different and profit emerges is that these institutions *lend long* and *borrow short*. That is, they customarily lend at long term to ultimate borrowers, and because the assets they give to the ultimate lenders from whom they obtain their funds are usually payable on demand, they are borrowing at short term. Whenever short-term rates rise in general or advance toward equality with the long-term rate, the intermediaries have problems retaining their deposits. To retain these deposits, they must meet the rate paid on other competitive short-term securities, and to do this, they must increase the interest rate they pay all depositors. At the same time the earnings from their assets remain relatively constant, or if the long-term rate is also moving in a general upward direction, their earnings are increasing only in relation to the new loans they are making at the higher rate (and the rate of new to existing loans may be rather low—10% to 20% per year). As their profits are squeezed, the intermediaries cannot effectively compete to retain their deposits, and severe disintermediation may lead to severe financial and economic distress. The profit squeeze can become very marked whenever short-term rates rise above the long-term rate.

DISINTERMEDIATION AND REGULATION Q

In the United States this tendency to disintermediation whenever there is a general rise in short-term interest rates is exacerbated by the legalized price-fixing made possible by Regulation Q (which governs the practices of the Federal Reserve System). Regulation Q authorizes various federal monetary agencies to set legal ceilings on the interest rates that federally insured financial institutions can pay on their time and savings deposits.[5]

Regulation Q ceilings either cause or aggravate disintermediation when they prevent financial institutions from effectively competing to retain the funds they have on deposit. In the post-1965 period, during which market interest rates reached 100-year highs, financial intermediaries were hit, on several occasions, by massive disintermediations (1966 and 1969) that the financial press called "credit crunches."

In an effort to ease the financial pressure on the intermediaries, the Regulation Q ceilings have been raised on a number of occasions and even

[5] The Banking Act of 1933 authorized the Federal Reserve to set interest rate ceilings on all banks that were members of the system. The rate was set by statute at zero for demand deposits. The Banking Act of 1935 extended this power to the Federal Deposit Insurance Corporation (FDIC), authorizing it to set similar ceilings on the interest rates paid on deposits by all insured banks that are not members of the Federal Reserve System. In September 1966 legislation further authorized the FDIC to set ceilings on deposit rates paid by insured mutual savings banks, and gave the Federal Home Loan Bank Board the same power over the rates paid by savings and loan associations. For a comprehensive discussion of Regulation Q, see Charlotte E. Ruebling, "The Administration of Regulation Q," *Monthly Review*, Federal Reserve Bank of St. Louis (Feb. 1970): 29–40; and Clifton B. Luttrell, "Interest Rate Controls—Perspective, Purpose and Problems," *Monthly Review*, Federal Reserve Bank of St. Louis (Sept. 1968): 6–14.

abolished for large ($100,000 or more) negotiable certificates of deposit.[6] In 1980, Congress established the Depository Institution Deregulation Committee whose function is to phase out Regulation Q over a six-year period. Figure 3:2 shows these ceiling rates compared to other short-term interest rates against which the financial intermediaries must compete.

Even though Congress is now intent on phasing out Regulation Q, it would be a useful exercise to examine why it was instituted, whether it was ever effective in accomplishing its goals, and whether it imposed an economic cost on society. This exercise is useful because it will point out what occurs when those unschooled in the logic of a market's operation unknowingly pass laws which are irrational to market participants. We will see that markets evolve ways to function in spite of such laws. As a footnote to history, it should be noted that the undesirable consequences of Regulation Q were known for at least twenty years. Either the lethargy of Congress or the power of vested interests prevented this law for a long time from being repealed.

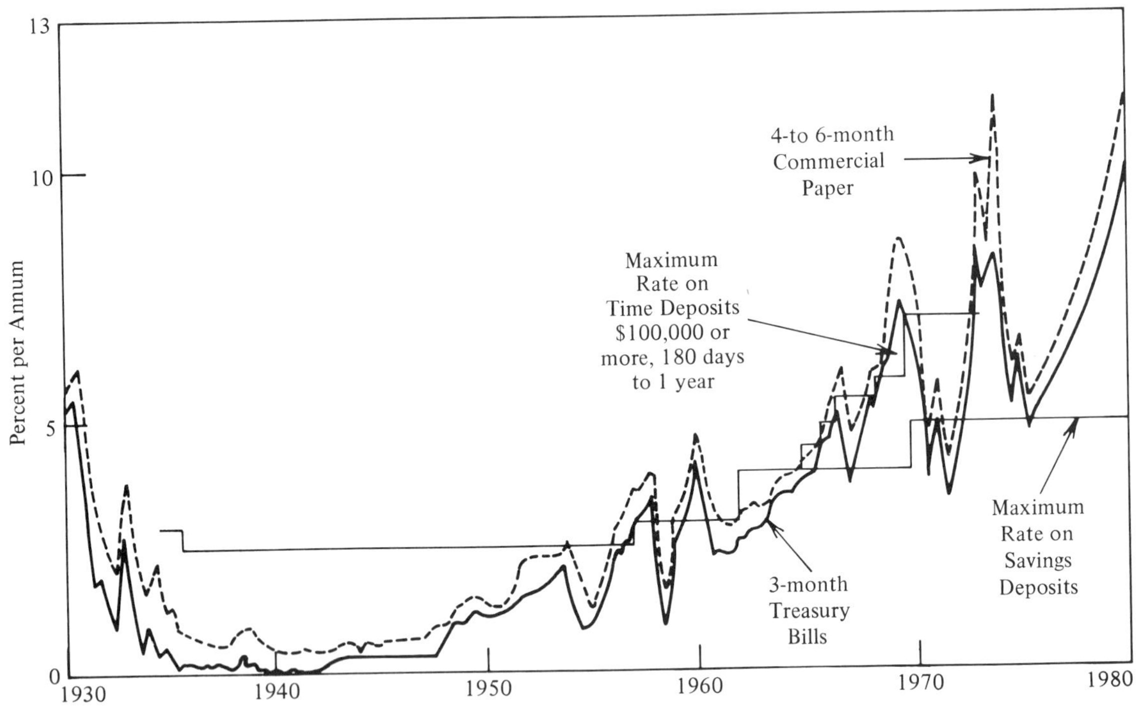

FIGURE 3:2
Regulation Q ceilings and other short-term rates (Courtesy of the Federal Reserve Bulletin.*)*

[6] It should be noted that in the 20-year period from 1936 until 1957 the ceiling rates remained unchanged and were usually above the prevailing short-term market rates. It was only the general rise in market rates starting in the 1950s that again focused concern on the disintermediary effects of Regulation Q.

HISTORICAL RATIONALIZATIONS FOR REGULATION Q

Originally, Regulation Q was intended to prevent another depression like that of the 1930s. It was believed that unregulated competition among financial institutions, especially commercial banks, which could pay interest on all classes of deposits, so increased the costs of bankings that to recover normal profits banks were led to make highly risky loans. These loans then became uncollectible with the onset of the Great Depression in 1929, and this contributed substantially to the great number of bank failures. The obvious solution, or so it appeared, was to regulate the amount of (explicit) interest that could be paid by banks on their deposits. The rationale behind this law is interesting.[7]

Until the early 1930s the dominant type of financial intermediary was the commercial bank. Because industrial firms and merchants in areas remote from financial and commercial centers ordered goods from these places, banks in the remote areas frequently kept deposits in the banks at these larger centers to finance the activities of their commercial and industrial customers. Since the recipient banks could lend out these funds at a profit, they began to compete for them by paying interest on these balances. This practice of paying interest on interbank deposits arose, then, in response to market competition.

Since these interbank deposits were subject to withdrawal on demand, the depository banks tended to lend them out at short term—in an increasing proportion as callable loans to stock brokers, i.e., as loans collateralized by shares sold on the stock exchanges. Whenever the demand by the rural banks for their deposits coincided with a slump in the financial markets, a degree of panic would develop, since the larger banks would find it difficult to honor these withdrawal requests. Thus, the payment of interest on interbank deposits, which was seen as a cornerstone of the system, came to be viewed as one of the causes of the recurrent financial panics in the United States and a symptom of unsound banking practices. In the last half of the nineteenth century commercial banks began the practice of issuing demand deposits to their customers rather than paper bank notes (currency). Individual banks then saw in these deposits a source of funds for expanding their own lending power. They naturally sought to compete for them by offering interest payments. Thus the practice of paying explicit interest on all deposits developed.

The onset of the Great Depression in 1929 set in motion a large number of bank failures, which revived the belief that the payment of interest on deposits led to risky loans and increased the vulnerability of banks to adverse economic developments. In order to restore soundness to the

[7] For an extensive discussion of the history of Regulation Q, see Charles M. Linke, "The Evolution of Interest Rate Regulation on Commercial Bank Deposits in the United States," *National Banking Review*, Vol. 3, No. 4 (June 1966): 449–69.

banking system, it was believed, such unregulated competition must be stopped—and it was in 1933, despite the fact that there was very little substantive evidence to support the contention that bank failures were caused by the payment of interest on deposits.[8] The notion that this practice led to unsound loans was also unsubstantiated. The evidence seems to be that those loans made during the 1920s that became uncollectable in the 1930s, were in themselves evidence of unsound banking practices. The obvious solution was government-imposed price fixing.

RECENT RATIONALIZATIONS FOR REGULATION Q

In more recent years the rationalization for Regulation Q shifted. It was put forth as a major tool of monetary stabilization since it has an impact on the availability of credit, i.e., on the ability of financial institutions to make loans.[9] If the ceiling rates were set low enough, financial institutions would find it difficult to attract and retain deposits, and therefore the volume of credit they could make available to the market is reduced. The conclusion then drawn was that the total volume of credit was reduced, which caused total demand to fall.

This conclusion is questionable. What generally occurred was not a decrease in the *total volume* of credit, but rather a change in the *allocation* of credit. That is, lenders who would ordinarily lend through intermediaries lent directly. Therefore, those who customarily borrowed directly had better access to credit whereas those who borrowed indirectly found credit harder to come by.

In addition, in the administration of Regulation Q, and until it is phased out, mutual savings banks and savings and loan associations are permitted to quote a 0.25 higher interest rate on regular savings deposits than that paid by commercial banks. This added amount is intended to shelter these intermediaries from the competition of commercial banks, and thus ensure a flow of funds to the housing industry, which is largely financed by these two nonbank intermediaries.

[8] For recent investigations into this contention, see George J. Benston, "Interest Payments on Demand Deposits and Bank Investment Behavior," *Journal of Political Economy,* Vol. 72, No. 5 (Oct. 1964): 431–49; and Albert M. Cox, Jr., "Regulation of Interest on Bank Deposits," *Michigan Business Studies,* Vol. 17, No. 4, Bureau of Business Research, Graduate School of Business Administration (Ann Arbor: University of Michigan, 1966).

[9] Two other reasons of lesser importance were also advanced to justify Regulation Q. First, the regulation supposedly reduced the interest rate paid by borrowers from financial institutions, for the latter are in a position to acquire funds more cheaply from ultimate lenders. Second, the regulation reduced the geographic flow of deposits from small banks that do not issue time certificates of deposit to the large banks that do. This argument is an interesting variation of an older argument that by paying interest on interbank deposits, rural areas of the country were deprived of needed productive funds. It would be difficult to produce evidence to substantiate either of these contentions.

THE EFFECTIVENESS OF REGULATION Q

Of crucial importance to the discussion of Regulation Q is the question of its effectiveness. Did the regulation prevent banks from paying interest on demand deposits and did it limit the interest rate that banks and other intermediaries paid on their time and savings deposits? Most assuredly the answer was no! While banks are forbidden to pay an explicit interest rate on demand deposits, they did pay an implicit rate. This was commonly accomplished by subsidizing the cost of maintaining a checking account at a bank. That is, the banks do not charge their customers the full cost of maintaining their checking accounts, and the remission of these service charges was an implicit rate of interest. Other common methods used by banks to pay an implicit interest are granting favorable loan treatment (including reduced interest rates) to their large customers,[10] providing a host of services to their customers (including preparation of their payroll), and, ultimately, allowing customers to transfer funds from savings deposits to demand deposits to make up deficiencies in the latter. With this last method banks devised a way to pay explicit interest on demand accounts.

In an effort to evade the ceilings on time and savings deposits financial intermediaries provided extra services of the types noted, or offered premiums to induce new deposits or retention of those funds already on deposit. The premiums can range from clocks and dishes to television sets and automobilies, depending on the size and duration of the deposit.

These innovative practices devised to avoid Regulation Q were so widespread that there should be no doubt that financial institutions were getting around a law that was at variance with the logic of the marketplace. However, these efforts to evade the law were not without cost to the economy, for they represented an inferior and less efficient way to accomplish a given objective.

THE COST OF REGULATION Q

Since the resources available to society are limited relative to the demands made upon them, these resources ought to be used as efficiently as possible. Regulation Q forced financial intermediaries to pay implicit interest in a form that customers may value less highly than an equivalent amount of generalized purchasing power (money). This can lead to the inefficient use of resources. For example, if the banks provide free checking in lieu of charging customers the cost of writing checks and paying explicit interest on their deposit, customers will tend to write more checks than they would

[10] The prohibition of interest payments on demand deposits extends to interbank deposits as well. Nevertheless, banks still compete for these valuable accounts and have devised a number of ways to court those bankers who control these deposits—as the public discovered when the affairs of a Georgia banker, one Thomas Bertrum Lance, were aired in public.

have written were they paying the actual cost. A higher volume of checks leads banks (society) to commit resources to check clearing and processing that could be used elsewhere. To take another example, banks and other intermediaries may build extra branches or keep longer hours, for these are other services made available to customers in an effort to evade the legal ceilings on the payment of explicit interest.

In addition, to the extent that the law leads to a diversion of funds from an indirect to a direct lending route, ultimate borrowers who are discriminated against (i.e., borrowers who traditionally borrow indirectly) must devote more time and effort to secure the means of finance.

Regulation Q also served to alter the institutional structure of the U.S. financial system in a number of ways. First, the interest rate advantage given savings and loan associations and mutual savings banks permitted them to attract and retain a larger volume of funds than would otherwise be the case. The result was that commercial banks diminish in relative size and importance over time. Second, the interest rate advantage promoted expansion of nonregulated financial institutions relative to those in the regulated sector. The spectacular growth of credit unions in recent years (see Table 3:1) can be attributed to their immunity from such regulations. This growth by the nonregulated sector is inefficient in the sense that it would not have occurred except for the imposition of the ceilings on deposit interest rates. Thus, when more efficient firms are prevented by law from competing, less efficient firms enter the market. This invasion by the nonregulated sector led the regulated sector to adopt various innovations to retain the funds that had traditionally gone to them. On the part of savings and loans and mutual savings banks, this meant providing customer services that resembled those provided by commercial banks through checking accounts—these institutions originated NOW accounts and have recently rushed into electronic means of permitting their customers to make payments to third parties (for a more extensive discussion of these innovations, see Chapters 5 and 15).

As a final indictment of this effort to thwart the logic of the marketplace, it should be noted that Regulation Q discriminates against savers of modest means who cannot, largely because of high transactions costs, shift to higher-yielding assets whenever interest rates rise above the ceilings. Moreover, because Regulation Q exacerbates any tendency to disintermediation and reintermediation, it generally forced regulated financial intermediaries to adopt more cautious lending policies, i.e., to maintain more liquid portfolios.

Few regulations on financial institutions were so unanimously condemned by economists as this one. Its basic fault was that it regulated only a few financial institutions. It did not regulate with any logic the so-called money or financial market. As a result, it led to manifold waste of economic resources and forced an unnatural development upon the institutional structure of the U.S. financial market.

TABLE 3:1
Total assets of selected financial intermediaries 1900–1978 (billions of dollars)

Year	Commercial Banks	Savings and Loan Associations	Mutual Savings Banks	Credit Unions	Life Insurance Companies	Total	% Commercial Banks
1900	10.0	.5	2.4	—	1.7	14.6	68
1912	21.8	.9	4.0	—	4.4	31.1	70
1922	47.3	2.8	6.6	.01	8.7	65.1	72
1929	65.6	7.4	9.9	.04	17.5	100.4	65
1939	65.0	5.4	11.9	.19	29.2	111.7	58
1949	157.7	14.5	21.5	.83	59.6	254.1	62
1959	242.8	63.5	40.6	4.8	119.6	471.4	52
1965	374.1	129.6	58.2	10.6	158.7	731.2	51
1970	576.2	176.6	79.0	18.0	207.3	1057.1	55
1972	739.0	243.6	100.6	22.0	239.4	1344.6	55
1974	919.6	295.5	109.6	31.9	263.3	1619.9	57
1976	1030.8	392.0	134.7	45.2	321.6	1923.0	54
1978	1303.9	523.6	158.2	62.6	389.0	2437.3	53

Data through 1949 from Raymond W. Goldsmith, *Financial Intermediaries in the American Economy Since 1900* (Princeton, N.J.: Princeton University Press, 1958). Subsequent data obtained from various issues of the *Federal Reserve Bulletin*.

THE STRUCTURE AND GROWTH OF FINANCIAL INTERMEDIARIES

The data shown in Table 3:1 reveal two main facts. First, the dominant position of commercial banks among all financial intermediaries is at once apparent. Second, the relative importance of commercial banks has by no means been constant. Rather, they have lost ground during certain periods, but their position appears to have been relatively stable during the past 20 years. Their current stability may be due to the development of the negotiable time certificate of deposit (the so-called CD), which provided them with a very effective means of competing for highly liquid business funds (another example of an innovation in response to Regulation Q).

FINANCIAL INTERMEDIARIES AND THE VOLUME OF CREDIT

From our discussion so far it might appear that all financial intermediaries are merely brokers for the loanable funds represented by the prior saving of ultimate lenders and that these savings limit the total amount of loanable funds available to borrowers. To a large degree this is not the case, as we shall see in the following two chapters. To be sure, a large source of loanable funds is the saving of ultimate lenders. However, financial intermediaries in general do have the ability to alter the volume of credit or loanable funds over and above those provided from current saving. Their ability to alter the flow of such funds depends in part on the decision of individual wealth owners on the form in which they will hold their wealth. This is often called the *portfolio decision* because it concerns the composition of the individual's portfolio of assets. Financial intermediaries can influence this choice primarily through the type of deposit instrument they issue and the rate of interest or other service attached to it.

Among all the financial intermediaries, commercial banks have traditionally been singled out for special attention and analysis, for until recently they alone created the principal means of payment, or money, in our society. This was their differentiating characteristic. Because they alone created demand deposits, they had the power to alter the flow of credit or loanable funds, a power not even remotely approximated by other financial intermediaries singly or as a group. However, today the commercial banks share this power with three other deposit-issuing financial institutions listed in Table 3:1. As a group, these institutions have the power to increase the flow of loanable funds independent of the flow of savings from ultimate savers.

FINANCIAL INTERMEDIARIES AND LENDING SPECIALIZATION

Financial intermediaries fall into two distinct categories. The first contains a number of institutions that issue deposits that either are the means of payment themselves or are generally convertible into the means of payment and are subject to government-imposed reserve requirements against their deposit liabilities. Customarily, their deposit liabilities are grouped under the general heading of those subject to checking and those of a saving or time nature. Also, most share the feature of lending at long term while borrowing at short term.

The second category of financial intermediaries is distinguished from the first in that its members do not issue deposits. Typical of this group are life insurance companies and pension funds, whose basic function is to sell protection against the hazards of death, disability, and old age.

Each of these financial intermediaries tends to specialize in certain types of loans. In the remainder of this chapter we shall examine briefly the main types of financial intermediaries.

Commercial Banks

The historic function of commercial banks, indeed, the origin of their name, comes from their early specialization in making commercial loans to business. These loans are designed to provide business firms with working capital. They are short term in nature, and enable firms to buy and carry inventories of raw materials and finished goods as well as to pay salaries.

TABLE 3:2
*Consolidated commercial bank balance sheet**
(billions of dollars, Sept. 30, 1978)

		Assets		Liabilities and Capital
Cash		$ 158.4	Demand deposits	$ 369.0
Securities		262.2	Time deposits	368.6
Loans			Savings deposits	223.3
Real estate	$203.4		Other liabilities	146.3
Commercial	213.1		Capital and retained earnings	91.3
Installment	131.6			
Other	146.3	694.4		
Other assets		83.5		
TOTAL ASSETS		$1198.5	TOTAL LIABILITIES AND CAPITAL	$1198.5

Courtesy of the *Federal Reserve Bulletin*, July 1979.
*All insured banks.

The completion and sale of the product puts business in possession of funds with which to repay the loan. Over time, commercial banks have expanded the range of their lending activities, but the commercial loan is still prominent, as Table 3:2 shows.

Since commercial banks generally have a more diversified asset structure than other deposit-type intermediaries, they are in a relatively better position to meet disintermediation withdrawals. In fact, a substantial portion (13%) of their assets is in the form of currency or currency claims on the central bank.

Savings and Loan Associations

Next among financial intermediaries in terms of asset size are the over 6000 savings and loan associations found in the United States. Savings and loan associations are an outgrowth of the old building and loan associations, which represented an attempt to organize the savings of individuals of modest means as a source of funds for home construction. As shown in Table 3:3, their early specialization in home mortgages continues to this day, partly because of legislation that restricts their lending. Here is the most dramatic example of lending long and borrowing short. Over 83% of their assets is in home mortgages, which customarily are issued for a 20–40-year period. Since the savings and loan institutions have been making such loans for a considerable period of time, it is clear that the due dates of

TABLE 3:3
Consolidated savings and loan balance sheet
(billions of dollars, Dec. 31, 1978)

	Assets		Liabilities and Capital
Mortgages	$432.9	Share capital (deposits)	$431.0
Securities and cash	44.9	Undistributed profits	29.0
Other assets	45.9	Advances from the FHLBB	32.0
		Other liabilities	31.7
TOTAL ASSETS	$523.7	TOTAL LIABILITIES AND CAPITAL	$523.7

Courtesy of the *Federal Reserve Bulletin*, July 1979.

these mortgages will be distributed over time, with some having 40 years to run until they mature.

As a source of additional liquidity, the federally chartered savings and loans (some 75% have federal charters and these have 98% of all assets of such institutions) can borrow from a lender of last resort (the regional Federal Home Loan Banks—FHLBB), which acts as the governing institution for the savings and loans. Reference to Table 3:3 shows that some 6% of their funds are obtained from such borrowings.

As of March 31, 1980, in the landmark bill to deregulate financial institutions, Congress now allows savings and loans, mutual saving banks, and credit unions to borrow from the Federal Reserve. It is too early to see how these institutions will avail themselves of this new facility.

Mutual savings banks

Mutual savings banks originated in the concern of public-spirited citizens for the savings of the relatively poor working classes. To protect these savings, they organized banks to receive deposits and use the funds for relatively safe investments. As witness to their conservative investment strategy, only a minute percentage of these banks failed during the Great Depression.

As Table 3:4 reveals, their growth as measured by asset size over time has been very slow, mainly because they are almost totally confined to the northeastern part of the United States, a section whose economic growth rate has been generally below the national average.

While Table 3:4 shows that almost two-thirds of their assets are confined to mortgages, mutual savings banks, unlike the other deposit-type intermediaries, have invested a relatively high percentage of their assets in corporate securities—both bonds and common stock.

TABLE 3:4
Consolidated balance sheet of mutual savings banks (billions of dollars, Dec. 31, 1978)

		Assets		Liabilities and Capital
Loans			Deposits	$142.7
Mortgages	$95.2		Other liabilities	4.6
Other	7.2	$102.4	Capital and reserves	10.9
Securities				
U.S. government	5.0			
State and local	3.3			
Corporate	39.7	48.0		
Other				
Cash	3.7			
Other	4.1	7.8		
TOTAL ASSETS		$158.2	TOTAL LIABILITIES AND CAPITAL	$158.2

Courtesy of the *Federal Reserve Bulletin*, July 1979.

Like the savings and loan institutions, they have also lent long and borrowed short to a greater degree than commercial banks, and hence are more vulnerable to disintermediation than the latter.

Credit unions

In recent years, as measured by asset size, the credit unions have been the most rapidly growing of the deposit-type financial intermediaries. They are a twentieth-century development and represent the attempt by individuals belonging to some common organization (labor union, fraternal or religious association, vocational affiliation, etc.) to pool small amounts of savings to make low-cost loans for the purchase of consumer durable goods such as automobiles, home appliances, boats, and leisure vehicles. Loans for these purposes are relatively small and have short maturity dates (12 to 36 months). In recent years some credit unions have been making mortgage loans, but these are a minute fraction of total loans. At the end of 1978 total credit union assets stood at $62.6 billion.

Life insurance companies

Life insurance companies are differentiated from the classes of financial intermediaries discussed above in that they do not issue deposit accounts. Rather, their principal liability (over 80%) represents reserves against claims by their policyholders in the case of death, accident, and so forth.

TABLE 3:5
Consolidated asset position of life insurance companies (billions of dollars, Dec. 31, 1978)

Government securities		
Federal	$ 4.8	
State and local	6.3	
Foreign	8.5	$ 19.6
Business securities		
Bonds	161.9	
Stocks	35.4	197.3
Mortgages		105.9
Real estate		11.8
Policy loans		30.2
Other assets		24.2
TOTAL ASSETS		$389.0

Courtesy of the *Federal Reserve Bulletin*, July 1979.

Because of the massive accumulation of statistics on life expectancy over many years, life insurance companies are in the highly favorable position of being able to calculate with reasonable accuracy the claims against their assets to be expected in any given year. The major item of uncertainty among the managers of assets of life insurance companies is the number of policyholders who will exercise the option to borrow against the equity built up in their policy (that is, borrow against the so-called cash-surrender value of their policies).

Because of the general reluctance of policyholders to borrow against their policies, the general ability to predict death benefits, and the highly stable or predictable flow of premium income, insurance companies have greater flexibility than other financial intermediaries in making investments. That is, they don't have to hold a large volume of highly liquid assets with which to meet unforeseen contingencies. As shown in Table 3:5, they have committed almost half their assets to business and government securities—especially corporate bonds. In addition, they are a major source of funds for commercial mortgages.

Money market mutual funds

The spectacular rise in market interest rates in the early 1970s gave rise to a new type of financial institution—the money market mutual fund. These funds, rather than holding common stock and bonds as other mutual funds do, maintain in their portfolios high-yielding short-term securities such as

U.S. Treasury bills, commercial paper, and large-denomination negotiable certificates of deposit.

Individuals can purchase shares in these funds at a lower minimum outlay than they would need to purchase the securities held by the fund directly. In addition, most money market mutual funds give shareholders the option of writing checks against their share holdings. The minimum amount of a single check is, however, usually $500. Also, some funds will transfer on a same-day notice deposits into a prearranged bank account against which checks can be drawn. Money market mutual funds thus are a sort of hybrid containing some of the characteristics of deposit-type financial intermediaries. Assets in these funds have recently grown rapidly, from $10.3 billion in December 1978 to $43.6 in December 1979.[11]

In addition to these major financial intermediaries, there are a number of institutions of secondary importance such as private pension funds, investment companies (mutual funds), finance companies, and mortgage companies. These intermediaries will not be discussed in detail here, although they do perform important services.

THE FLOW OF LOANABLE FUNDS THROUGH PRIVATE INTERMEDIARIES

As the final step in this survey of financial intermediaries and their relative importance, Table 3:6 sets out their individual contribution to the annual flow of loanable funds for 1978. Table 3:6 reveals that a total of $288.5 billion was advanced by financial intermediaries in the credit market in 1978. This contrasts with $90.3 billion of direct credit market lending in the same year. Thus, in the United States the majority of lending is through intermediaries, even though direct lending is far from insignificant.

TABLE 3:6
Credit market funds advanced by private financial institutions (billions of dollars)

Commercial banks	$121.9
Savings institutions	78.2
Insurance and pension funds	70.1
All other	18.4
TOTAL	$288.5

Courtesy of the *Federal Reserve Bulletin*, July 1979 (Table A45).

[11] Data are from reports of the Federal Reserve System.

SUMMARY

This chapter examined the indirect lending process and the risks that are involved. Two risks were identified: default and liquidity. It was then explained how financial intermediaries could reduce these risks both to ultimate lenders and to themselves. In so doing, they work to reduce interest rates prevailing in the economy.

However, financial intermediation also exposes a society to the potential instability caused by disintermediation, which can be exacerbated by such constraints as those imposed by Regulation Q.

The last part of the chapter discussed the purpose and magnitude of the principal financial intermediaries and the degree to which each specializes in the expediting of the flow of loanable funds or credit to borrowers, drawing attention to deposit-type financial institutions. In the next chapter we shall consider the special role played by these intermediaries in varying the total supply of loanable funds in excess of the amount entrusted to them by ultimate lenders.

STUDY QUESTIONS

1. Explain how financial intermediaries lower the default and liquidity risks such that they can decrease the costs of borrowing and lending.
2. Explain what is so dangerous about borrowing short and lending long that financial intermediaries can be called a "mixed blessing."
3. How do rising market interest rates lead to disintermediation?
4. Under what circumstance can the setting of a maximum price such as under Regulation Q be ineffective, i.e., cause no problem for the market?
5. How can a price remain below its legal ceiling?
6. Why is forbidding banks to pay interest on certain classes of deposits likely to be futile? How is such legislation circumvented? Is the method used to circumvent the legislation likely to be efficient?
7. If indirect lending is so beneficial, why does direct lending continue to exist?
8. It has been said both that "credit is the lifeblood of the economy" and "debt is the burden of the economy." Evaluate these gems of wisdom.

SELECTED REFERENCES AND READINGS

Black, Robert P., and Harless, Doris E. *Nonbank Financial Intermediaries*. Richmond, Va.: Federal Reserve Bank of Richmond, 1969.

Brockschmidt, Peggy. "Credit Union Growth in Perspective." *Monthly Review*, Federal Reserve Bank of Kansas City (Feb. 1977).

Fand, David. "Intermediary Claims and the Adequacy of Our Monetary Controls." *Banking and Monetary Studies,* edited by Deane Carson. Homewood, Ill.: Richard D. Irwin, 1963.

Goldsmith, Raymond W. *Financial Institutions*. New York: Random House, 1968.

Gurley, John G., and Shaw, Edward S. "Financial Aspects of Economic Development." *American Economic Review,* Vol. 45, No. 4 (Sept. 1955).

Higgins, Bryon. "Interest Payments on Demand Deposits: Historical Evolution and the Current Controversy." *Monthly Review,* Federal Reserve Bank of Kansas City (July–Aug. 1977).

Krooss, Herman E., and Blyn, Martin R. *A History of Financial Intermediaries*. New York: Random House, 1971.

Polakoff, Murray E., et al. *Financial Institutions and Markets*. Boston: Houghton Mifflin, 1970.

Ruebling, Charlotte E. "The Administration of Regulation Q." *Monthly Review,* Federal Reserve Bank of St. Louis (Feb. 1970).

4 THE SUPPLY OF MONEY 4

In the preceding chapter deposit-type financial institutions together with other financial intermediaries were seen to play a major role in facilitating the transfer of funds from ultimate lenders to ultimate borrowers. In this chapter it will be shown that the deposit-type intermediaries can alter the total volume of loanable funds independently of the total amount provided by ultimate lenders. They do this through their ability to create the means of payment. Because a number of deposit-type intermediaries have this ability, the explanation may become cumbersome. To simplify the language of the discussion, the word *depository institution* (or DI) will be used to describe all money-creating intermediaries.[1] When these intermediaries are referred to as a group, the term *financial system* will be used. When the discussion is applicable to only one intermediary, it will be identified by its appropriate name, for example, commercial bank (or, more commonly, bank).

In order to explain the creation of money, we will start the analysis with a very simple and unrealistic example. Then, through successive stages, the unrealistic assumptions will be relaxed, until finally, we shall examine a financial system that closely approximates the one currently prevailing in the United States.

Since it is possible to get lost in the explanation, it should be stated at the outset that we shall be addressing the following questions:

1. What does it mean to say "DIs create money"? Can DIs create money in some reasonable sense? If so, how do they do it?
2. What limitations (if any) are, or can be, imposed on the creation of money by DIs? What are the sources of these limitations?
3. Can the supply of money be deliberately controlled? If so, how and by what agencies? In particular, how does a central bank (the Federal Reserve) act to control the money supply, and how effective is it?

[1] It should be remembered that the deposit-type intermediaries to which this discussion is applicable are commercial banks, savings and loan associations, mutual savings banks, and credit unions.

THE BALANCE SHEET

Because an accounting aid known as a balance sheet plays a prominent role in the explanation, its basic form must be understood. The purpose of the balance sheet is to display the total amount of a firm's assets (what it owns), its total liabilities (what it owes to others), and, after subtracting the second from the first, the residual amount, which represents the net claim on the assets by the owners of the firm (or the firm's capital).

The familiar *T*-account is the balance sheet commonly used. Assets are listed on the left, while liabilities and capital are listed on the right. If no errors are made, the balance sheet balances after every transaction, for what is obtained as an asset must be related either to a new liability claim or to an increase in the net worth of the owners.

MONEY CREATION

Case I: Demand deposits

Case I is intended to demonstrate the way in which DIs create money.[2] In order to focus attention exclusively on this process, it will be assumed that deposits subject to checking (hereafter called demand deposits) are the only type of money (i.e., currency does not exist), that no other financial assets exist, that the financial system consists of many DIs, and that each DI's ability to manufacture or create demand deposits is subject to two constraints. First, the DIs must have reserves, which are supplied by the central bank.[3] The sum of these reserves—and ultimately, as our cases expand, any currency that comes to be held by the non-DI public—will be called the *monetary base* or *high-powered money.* Second, for every dollar of demand deposits the DIs have outstanding, they must have on hand a certain amount of reserves or high-powered money. These *reserve requirements* are set by the monetary authorities; for the examples in this chapter, they will be assumed to be 20%. That is, for every dollar of demand deposits, the DIs must have 20 cents in reserves.

In order to analyze Case I graphically, four DI balance sheets are displayed below in Table 4:1, representing a small portion of the total number of depository institutions in the United States. In exchange for capital stock, the monetary authorities give to DI No. 1 $100 in reserves or high-powered money. This addition of reserves appears as an asset in DI No. 1's balance sheet and is offset by $100 in capital stock (this assumes that DI No. 1 is owned by the monetary authorities).

[2] Those interested in the historic evolution of deposit creation should see Appendix A at the end of this chapter.

[3] The main method used by the central bank in the United States to supply reserves to the financial system is through its purchase of U.S. government securities. However, as these securities do not exist in this example, assume that reserves are slips of green paper denominated in dollars which the central bank gives to DIs in exchange for their capital stock.

TABLE 4:1
Balance sheets of representative DIs

DI No.1				DI No.2	DI No.3	DI No.4
Assets		Liabilities				
Reserves	$100	Capital	$100			
TOTAL	$100	TOTAL	$100			

If the financial system operates under the constraint of a 20% legal reserve requirement, what is the maximum loan that DI No. 1 can make? Surely, it could loan out a sum equal to its initial endowment of reserves. If this were done, its balance sheet would appear as Table 4:2. In making the loan, the DI merely gives the borrower a checkbook with a $100 balance. In such a situation, $100 of money was "created" in the sense that the non-DI public now has $100 more in money than it had before the loan was made. Since demand deposits have risen, the money supply must also have increased by the same sum.

This example of money creation is so simple that many either refuse to believe it or have great difficulty accepting it. They seem to think that where high finance is involved, the process of money creation must be more subtle or much more involved. However, it is not. The simple fountain pen and some printed paper have provided these lenders with the alchemy for turning base metal into coin of the realm, which so eluded Merlin in Arthurian times.

Consider now the question of whether it is possible for the DI to make such a loan. In this example, the only constraint on the DI was that it must have 20 cents in high-powered money or reserves for each dollar of demand deposits it carries on its books, and indeed, the loan made by DI No. 1 meets these requirements.

Notice that DI No. 1 really only needs $20 of reserves to cover its $100 in demand deposits, so that it has $80 of excess reserves to serve as cover for further deposit liabilities. To comply with the law, DI No. 1 then separates its reserves into those *required* by law and those that are *excess*. When this separation is carried out, its balance sheet appears as Table 4:3.

TABLE 4:2
Balance sheet of DI No. 1 after loan

Assets		Liabilities and Capital	
Reserves	$100	Demand deposits	$100
Loans	$100	Capital	$100
TOTAL	$200	TOTAL	$200

TABLE 4:3
Balance sheet of DI No. 1 after reserve allocation

Reserves:		Demand	
Legal (LR_D)	$ 20	deposits (D)	$100
Excess (ER)	80		
Loans	100	Capital (K)	100
TOTAL	$200	TOTAL	$200

As DI No. 1 still has excess reserves of $80, might it not make additional loans in order to expand its asset holdings and, on the basis of the interest earned from these loans, its total profits? This depends upon what the owner of the demand deposit is likely to do with that deposit. If he intends to leave the deposit untouched at the DI, and the DI knows this, the DI can continue to make additional loans. However, this is highly unlikely, for the individual obtained the deposit by selling an IOU to the DI, and is probably going to spend this money quickly. Suppose that checks are drawn against that deposit for the entire $100 and given to various individuals who all, for convenience of exposition, deposit them to their accounts in DI No. 2.[4] The owners of DI No. 2 will then present them to DI No. 1 for payment. DI No. 1 will pay these checks by transferring to DI No. 2 $100 in reserves or high-powered money. Since DI No. 2 is only required to hold $20 in high-powered money as reserves against its demand deposit liabilities of $100, the other $80 in reserves obtained from DI No. 1 is shown as excess reserves. The balance sheets of the two DIs would appear as Table 4:4.

DI No. 2 is now faced with the same decision that DI No. 1 faced before. What is the maximum sum that can safely be lent out? Learning from the experience of DI No. 1, DI No. 2 can expect to lose all or a substantial portion of its reserves for every dollar it lends. Thus, DI No. 2 formulates the rule of lending only a sum equal to the amount of its excess reserves:

TABLE 4:4
Balance sheets after deposits of check in DI No. 2

DI No. 1				DI No. 2			
Loans	$100	Capital	$100	Reserves:			
				LR_D	$ 20	D	$100
				ER	80		
TOTAL	$100	TOTAL	$100	TOTAL	$100	TOTAL	$100

[4] In a financial system such as that in the United States with many thousand depository institutions, it is highly improbable that checks drawn against deposits in a given DI would be returned to that DI as deposits.

in the case at hand, \$80. If it is assumed that DI No. 2 makes loans equal to this amount and individuals who receive these loans in the form of demand deposits draw drafts against these deposits, the experience recounted above is merely repeated. If the individuals who receive these checks deposit them for convenience in DI No. 3, the balance sheets of the financial system will appear as in Table 4:5.

If DI No. 3 follows the experience of DIs No. 1 and No. 2, it will also confine its new loans to the sum of its excess reserves, in this case, \$64. Such a sum may be lent and drafts drawn against the deposit created and redeposited in DI No. 4. This process may continue for a long time, but notice that at every new step the amount of a possible new loan is reduced. For DI No. 2, it is \$80; for DI No. 3, it is \$64; and so on. Since our ultimate interest is in the total amount of demand deposits (money) that the financial system can create for a given amount of new high-powered money and legal reserve requirements, there must be an easier way to obtain the answer than to work it through a large number of balance sheets. In fact, such a route is readily available, and a clue to obtaining it can be found in these three balance sheets. By examining the successive balance sheets, it will be seen that the amount of deposits created becomes successively smaller (\$100, \$80, \$64, etc.). Why does this occur? Because high-powered money is successively being transferred from excess reserves to legal reserves as each DI expands the volume of demand deposits. Ultimately, when the initial increase in high-powered money is all committed to legal reserves, the financial system will be unable to create any more demand deposits (money).

If the increase in the monetary base or high-powered money given originally to DI No. 1 is symbolized as ΔB and the increase in legal reserves

TABLE 4:5
Balance sheets of the financial system after loans by DI No. 2

DI No. 1				DI No. 2			
Loans	\$100	Capital	\$100	Reserves:		*D*	\$100
				LR_D	\$ 20		
				Loans	80		
TOTAL	\$100	TOTAL	\$100	TOTAL	\$100	TOTAL	\$100
DI No. 3				DI No. 4			
Reserves:		*D*	\$ 80				
LR_D	\$ 16						
ER	64						
TOTAL	\$ 80	TOTAL	\$ 80				

for demand deposits is symbolized as ΔLR_D, then demand deposit or money creation will end when

$$\Delta B = \Delta LR_D \tag{4:1}$$

Since the change in legal reserves for demand deposits (ΔLR_D) is equal to the product of the legal reserve requirement (symbolized as r) and the change in demand deposits, ΔD, they can be expressed as

$$\Delta LR_D = r\Delta D \tag{4:2}$$

which can be substituted into Equation (4:1) to yield

$$\Delta B = r\Delta D \tag{4:3}$$

Since our interest centers on the amount of demand deposits that can be created for a given ΔB and r, Equation (4:3) can be rearranged as

$$\Delta B\left(\frac{1}{r}\right) = \Delta D \tag{4:4}$$

If the initial values for ΔB and r used above are substituted into Equation (4:4), it yields a direct answer to the question concerning the amount of demand deposits (money) that can be created:

$$\$100\left(\frac{1}{.2}\right) = \$500$$

Thus, if the monetary base is increased by \$100 and the reserve requirement against demand deposits is 20%, the financial system can ultimately create \$500 in demand deposits (money).[5] This conclusion depends in large

[5] The money-creation formula can be derived in a more rigorous mathematical manner. Reference to Figure 4:5 shows that the demand deposits created behave according to the sequence \$100 + \$80 + \$64 + \$52 + . . . + 0. Using ΔB as the change in the monetary base and r as the legal reserve ratio, this sequence can be expressed as:

Total Demand Deposits Created

$$(D) = \Delta B + \Delta B(1-r) + \Delta B(1-r)^2 + \Delta B(1-r)^3 + \ldots + \Delta B(1-r)^N \tag{4:1'}$$

or

$$\Delta D = \Delta B[1 + (1-r) + (1-r)^2 + (1-r)^3 + \ldots + (1-r)^N] \tag{4:2'}$$

which mathematically is the sum of an infinite series when $N = \infty$. This formulation can be simplified if each side of the equation is multiplied by $(1 - r)$. This yields

$$\Delta D(1-r) = \Delta B[(1-r) + (1-r)^2 + (1-r)^3 + (1-r)^4 + \ldots + (1-r)^{N+1}] \tag{4:3'}$$

If Equation (4:3′) is subtracted from (4:2′), it yields

$$\Delta D - \Delta D(1-r) = \Delta B[1 - (1-r)^{N+1}] \tag{4:4'}$$

Since $(1 - r)^{N+1}$ goes to zero as N approaches infinity, ∞, Equation (4:4′) simplifies to

$$\Delta D(r) = \Delta B$$

or

$$\Delta D = \Delta B\left(\frac{1}{r}\right) \tag{4:5'}$$

measure on the highly restrictive set of assumptions used to construct Case I.

In a more rigorous fashion, the analysis of Case I states that the amount of demand deposits (money) that can be created by the financial system is the product of the change in the *monetary base,* ΔB, and the *deposit (money) multiplier,* $1/r$. In this example, the amount of demand deposits created and the amount of money created are identical, so the terms *deposit multiplier* and *money multiplier* can be used interchangeably. In several of the cases to follow, this will not be true and a distinction between the two will be required.

A reconsideration of a neglected aspect of the analysis

Before continuing, it may be wise to reconsider the set of DI balance sheets depicted by Table 4:5. It can be seen that DIs No. 2 and No. 3 hold reserves that are only a fraction (20%) of their demand deposit liabilities. What in this situation is to prevent these two DIs from having a reserve deficiency if the individuals who own these deposits suddenly transfer them to DIs No. 1 or No. 4 or any of a host of other DIs not shown? The answer is nothing. However, in the world we live in, the total volume of demand deposits in a given DI are, under usual circumstances, reasonably stable, i.e., while the total may fluctuate, it does not change much, for deposits gained and lost by the DIs tend to cancel out.

Summary—Case I

We now summarize the main aspects of and conclusions to be drawn from Case I.

First, the amount of demand deposits (money) that the financial system could create was seen to depend upon the increase in the monetary base (ΔB) and the reserve requirement set against demand deposits (r). Later it will be shown that these two factors are the principal tools used by the central bank to manage the money supply.

Second, who controls the amount of demand deposits (money) that the financial system *can* create? In this elementary case, it was an unnamed monetary authority; only this authority could produce changes in the monetary base, and it set the reserve requirement applicable to demand deposits.

Third, what is the role of the financial system in creating money? In order to get the maximum expansion of deposits, each DI would lend out a sum equal to the amount of its excess reserves. Of course, the DIs may well decide not to make maximum possible loans. It should also be noted that money creation does not depend exclusively on DIs making loans. It can occur when they purchase financial securities or real assets from individuals.

Finally, how long does it take to get the maximum $500 expansion? Theoretically, the maximum expansion will never occur, for it would require an infinite number of loans to reach this maximum sum. However, as the simple illustration shows, loans by the first four DIs will have created $296 worth of deposits ($100 + $80 + $64 + $52) or approximately 60% of the maximum.

Case II: Case I plus excess reserve holdings by DIs

In Case I our DIs held no excess reserves above those imposed by the monetary authorities. This is not a realistic situation. Figure 4:1 shows the historical experience for the past 50 years of commercial banks only, because until recently only commercial banks could issue deposits subject to checking. The excess reserve holdings by other depository institutions either is insignificant or the data are not readily available. However, even though they can now issue demand deposits, it is not certain that their excess reserve holdings will mirror those of commercial banks. This is

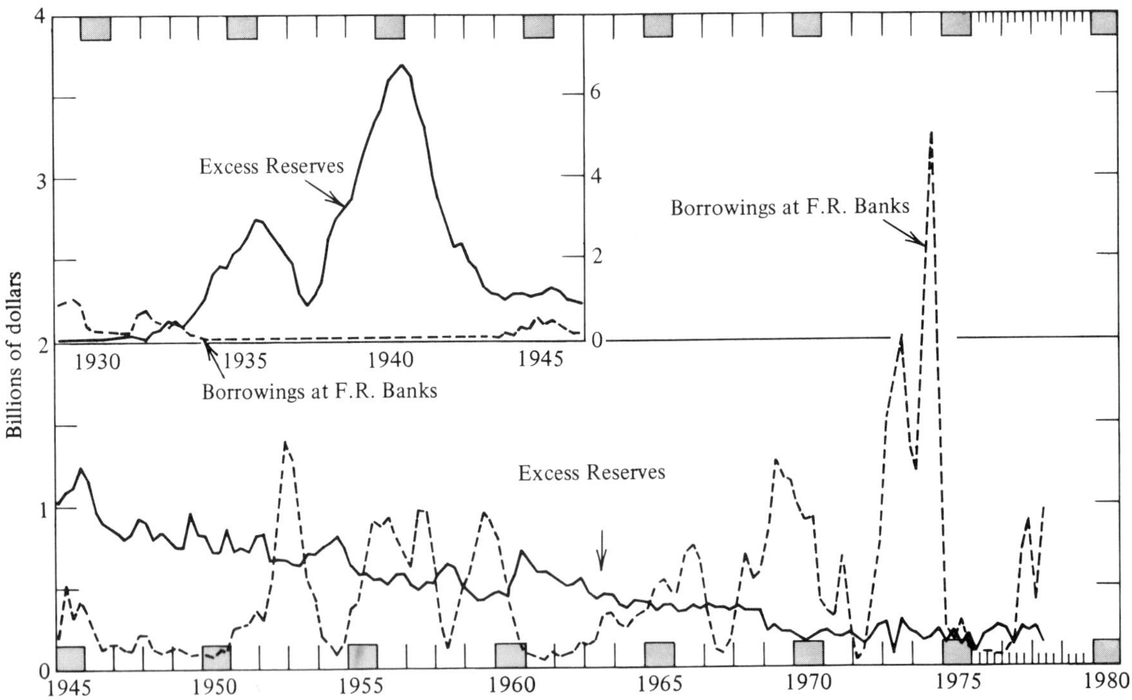

FIGURE 4:1
Excess reserves and borrowings of member banks (averages of daily figures, quarterly) (Courtesy of the Federal Reserve.)

because the types of assets they hold are different from those held by commercial banks. Nevertheless, we will assume their behavior to be the same as that of the commercial banks.

As a first approximation to explain this behavior on the part of the DIs, it will be assumed that their desired holdings of excess reserves is some constant fraction of their demand deposit liabilities. Thus, their demand for excess reserves, ER_D, is some constant fraction, e, of demand deposits, D, or

$$ER_D = eD \tag{4:5}$$

and for any change in their demand deposits, ΔD, the same relationship holds, or

$$\Delta ER_D = e\Delta D \tag{4:6}$$

How does the holding of reserves above those the DIs are legally obligated to hold affect the amount of demand deposits (money) that can be created for a given addition to the monetary base? Intuitively, it would appear to reduce the possible amount of new demand deposits created, since if the DIs voluntarily hold reserves rather than lend them out, fewer deposits will be supplied by them for a given change in the monetary base. To verify this, the example used in Case I will be retained. The initial transaction by which the monetary base is increased is, therefore, the same.

When DI No. 1 creates the first \$100 demand deposit that, through spending, winds up in DI No. 2, however, the balance sheet of that DI will be different from that in Case I. If the value of $e(= ER_D/D)$ is assumed to be 5% (that is, for every dollar in demand deposits, the DIs desire to hold 5 cents in excess reserves), the new situation will be as shown in Table 4:6.

If DI No. 2 follows the rule of always lending out a sum equal to the excess reserves it does not desire to hold as an asset, it will make a loan for and create demand deposits of \$75 in contrast with the \$80 created in Case

TABLE 4:6
Balance sheet allocation after receiving initial new deposit

DI No. 1				DI No. 2			
Loans	\$100	Capital	\$100	Reserves:		D	\$100
				LR_D	\$ 20		
				ER_D	5		
				ER	75		
TOTAL	\$100	TOTAL	\$100	TOTAL	\$100	TOTAL	\$100

I. If these deposits are, in turn, spent and deposited in DI No. 3, which loans on the basis of the same rule, the situation will appear as in Table 4:7.[6] If DI No. 3 continues the same lending practice, it will offer for loan $56 as opposed to the $64 noted in Case I.

Again, observing the balance sheets of all the DIs will permit a direct computation of the maximum amount of demand deposits (money) that can be created for given values of ΔB, r, and e. The ability of the financial system to expand demand deposits will cease when the initial increase in the monetary base becomes absorbed as required reserves for demand deposits and as desired holdings of excess reserves, or

$$\Delta B = \Delta LR_D + \Delta ER_D \tag{4:7}$$

and since $\Delta LR_D = r\Delta D$ and $\Delta ER_D = e\Delta D$, Equation (4:7) becomes

$$\Delta B = r\Delta D + e\Delta D \tag{4:8}$$

which when factored yields

$$\Delta B = \Delta D(r + e) \tag{4:9}$$

Appropriate division reduces this to

$$\Delta B\left(\frac{1}{r + e}\right) = \Delta D \tag{4:10}$$

Substituting $\Delta B = \$100$, $r = .20$, and $e = .05$ gives

$$\$100\left(\frac{1}{.2 + .05}\right) = \$400$$

TABLE 4:7
*Bank balance sheets after loans by DI No. 2**

DI No. 2				DI No. 3			
Reserves:		D	$100	Reserves:		D	$75
LR_D	$ 20			LR_D	$15		
ER_D	5			ER_D	4		
Loans	75			ER	56		
TOTAL	$100	TOTAL	$100	TOTAL	$75	TOTAL	$75

*Sums are rounded to the nearest dollar.

[6] To avoid showing cents, the sums are rounded to the nearest dollar.

This confirms our initial belief that when DIs are allowed to hold reserves above the legal limit, the maximum amount of demand deposits that can be created is reduced. The reason for the reduction is that the value of the denominator of the deposit (money) multiplier rose from .2 to .25, reducing thereby the value of the multiplier from 5 to 4.

Excess reserve holdings—some additional considerations

Thus far the demand for excess reserves by DIs was assumed to be a constant proportion of their demand deposit liabilities. However, reference to Figure 4:6 shows that since 1940 the excess reserve holding by commercial banks has exhibited a general secular decline. During this same historic period the amount of demand deposits has risen substantially. Therefore, the average value of e has, over the longer run, been declining. If one confines attention to a short-run period of a few years, it can be seen that the average value of e both rises and falls relative to its longer-run trend.

The essential point of this discussion is that the demand for excess reserve by DIs is *not* a constant proportion of demand deposits. Rather, the average value of e is a variable. On what factors does its value depend? To this discussion we now turn.

Every dollar of excess reserves held by a DI reduces its lending power, and hence its profits. If some measure of the market interest rate is used to indicate the earnings of DIs per dollar lent, as this rate rises, the loss of potential profits will be greater for each dollar held as excess reserves. Other things being equal, as the market interest rate rises, DIs should be more eager to make loans, and in the process create a larger amount of demand deposits or money.

While the market interest rate measures the opportunity cost to DIs of holding excess reserves, one other factor must be considered before conclusions can be drawn about the behavior of these lenders. This other factor concerns the *benefit* from holding excess reserves. The nature and measure of this benefit is made clear when the consequences of a reserve deficiency are examined. Suppose a DI has a reserve deficiency, which means that the amount of reserves that it is legally required to hold, (rD), is greater than its actual holding of reserves. How does it solve the deficiency? In the American financial system a reserve deficiency can be temporarily met in one of two ways. The first involves borrowing from the central bank by selling to it or, in financial terminology, *discounting* certain eligible assets. In the second, deficient DIs can borrow from other DIs with surplus reserves. Such borrowings are called "federal funds" and the interest rate charged on these borrowings is known as the *federal funds rate*.

Holding excess reserves, therefore, enables a bank to avoid a reserve deficiency and, as a result, to avoid incurring the payment of the discount or federal funds rate. Thus, a measure per dollar of the benefit of holding excess reserves is provided by either the discount or the federal funds rate.

It is the difference between the cost and the benefit of holding excess reserves that is the key variable influencing the behavior of these lenders. As the difference between the market interest rate and the discount rate becomes larger, the greater is the net opportunity cost of holding excess reserves and the smaller should be the volume of such reserves held by DIs. The smaller the difference in rates, the smaller the net opportunity cost; consequently, there should be more holdings of excess reserves by DIs.

If the net difference between rates becomes large enough, nothing prevents the financial system as a whole from having a net reserve deficiency, i.e., the financial system may be in debt to the central bank. Figure 4:1 shows that this was true for commercial banks during the late 1960s and the first half of the 1970s when market interest rates were at 100-year highs.

A demand schedule for excess reserves

The preceding discussion makes it possible to derive a demand schedule on the part of the financial system for excess reserves. Analogous to the demand schedule for a commodity, the vertical or price axis of the demand schedule becomes the net opportunity cost measured in percent of holding or demanding excess reserves, whereas the horizontal or quantity axis measures the quantity of excess reserves (in dollars) the financial system demands or desires to hold. Figure 4:2 shows such a demand schedule. Unlike the demand schedules for commodities, this one extends into the negative quantity range, indicating negative excess reserves (i.e., reserves borrowed from the central bank by some DIs exceed positive excess reserves held by other DIs).

The slope and position of this demand schedule require some explanation. Given the net opportunity cost, the amount of excess reserves DIs desire to hold may depend on expectations of general economic conditions. For example, if these lenders expect a serious recession to develop or worsen, they might wish to hold or demand larger excess reserves at each net opportunity cost. This means that the demand schedule would shift to the right. Conversely, if they expect highly stable conditions, they might wish to hold or demand smaller excess reserves at each net opportunity cost; i.e., the schedule would shift leftward.

Alternatively, the variability of the total amount of demand deposits at individual DIs might influence their demand for excess reserve. For example, the more variable or unpredictable these totals, the greater the likelihood that larger excess reserve balances will be demanded at each net opportunity cost.

Further considerations influencing this demand schedule for excess re-

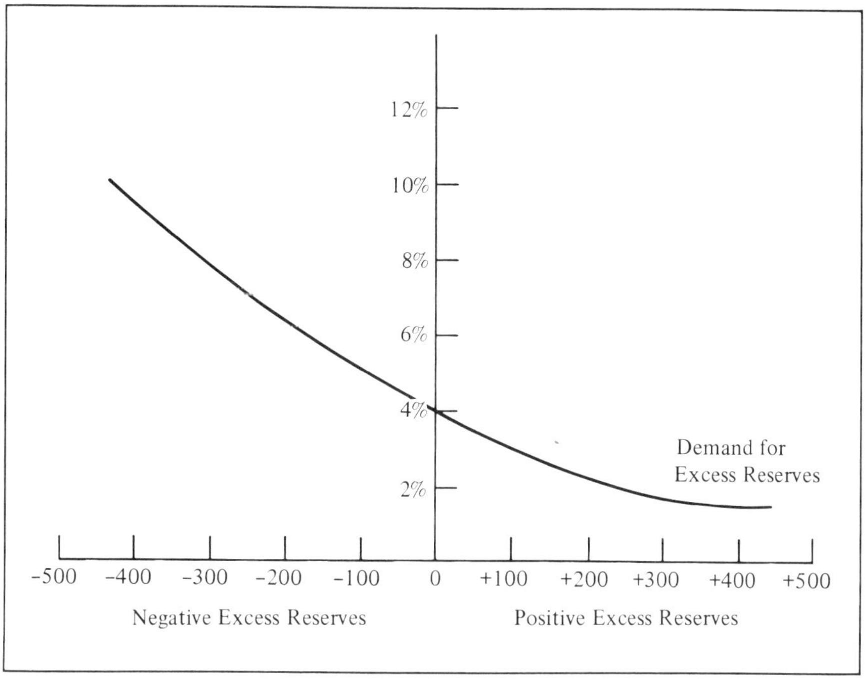

FIGURE 4:2
Demand schedule for excess reserves

serves over time include the type of support the central bank lends to smooth out business cycles, the difficulties of obtaining funds at the central bank's discount window, and institutional changes such as the advent of deposit insurance. All these factors can account for the shifts that take place in the schedule over time.

The demand schedule for excess reserves and the supply schedule of money

The essential feature of this demand schedule for excess reserves is that it makes the average numerical value of the desired excess reserve ratio, e, depend upon the relationship of the market interest rate to the discount rate. For example, assume that, given some initial values of B, r, and e, DIs are now unwilling to make more loans and create more deposits. Further, suppose that at the prevailing market interest rate and discount rate, the net opportunity cost of holding excess reserves is 2%, so that from Figure 4:2 it can be seen that DIs' desired holdings or demand for excess reserves is approximately $250 million. Now, for unspecified reasons, allow the market interest rate to rise relative to the discount rate so that the net opportunity cost rises to 6%. DIs as a group will then wish to have a reserve deficiency of some \$200 million. The process of moving from an excess reserve surplus of \$250 million to an excess reserve deficiency of \$200 million is the process of making loans and creating demand deposits or increasing the money supply. Thus, as the interest rate rises, the financial system as a whole is willing to supply a larger amount of money.

In terms of the formula given in Equation (4:10), the average value of e or ER_D/D moves from a positive value of $\$250/D$ to a negative value of $-\$200/D$. This movement increases the value of the deposit or money multiplier for $\left(\frac{1}{r-e}\right) > \left(\frac{1}{r+e}\right)$.[7]

This positive relationship of the supply of demand deposits (money) to the market interest rate is of great importance. Among other things, it permits the derivation of a supply schedule for money. Such a supply schedule is set forth in Figure 4:3. As the market rate of interest rises while the discount rate is held constant, DIs are willing to supply a larger quantity of money. (For convenience, the supply schedule is drawn as a straight line.)

The elasticity of the money supply schedule Now that the derivation of the money supply schedule has been explained, it is important to specify what

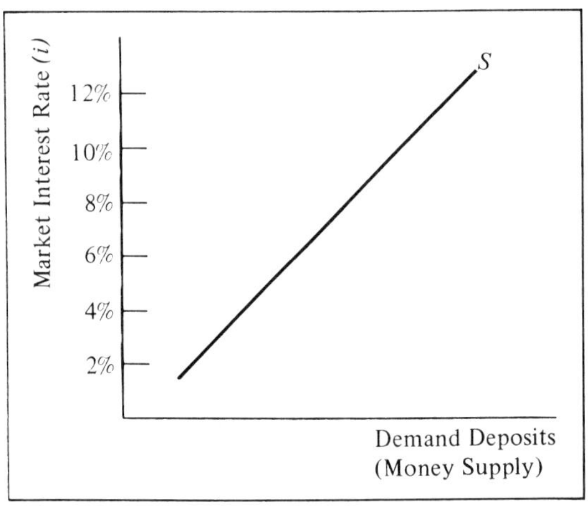

FIGURE 4:3
Supply schedule of money

[7] Technically, when operating on the negative side of the demand schedule, the monetary base as well as the multiplier changes (for borrowing reserves from the central bank through discounting to cover a reserve deficiency) augments high-powered money. So long as the change in excess reserves is confined to the positive side of the demand schedule, only the multiplier changes. Appendix D presents alternative multiplier and monetary base schemes that seek to alter the kind of problem posed here when operating on the negative side of the demand schedule.

the value of its slope depends upon. That is, how responsive is the financial system in increasing the supply of demand deposits (money) to a given change in the market interest rate or decrease in the discount rate? The answer to this question depends upon the sensitivity of the DI's demand for excess reserves to the net opportunity cost of holding them. Which is to say that the interest elasticity or slope of the money supply schedule is directly related to the interest rate (or net opportunity cost) elasticity of the DI's demand schedule for excess reserves. If slight increases in the interest rate relative to the discount rate cause DIs substantially to decrease their holdings of excess reserves (the demand schedule is in this case highly elastic), then the supply schedule of demand deposits (money) will be highly elastic.

Whether the supply schedule of money is elastic or inelastic is a question that can only be resolved by statistical estimation. The estimates thus far have indicated that it is quite inelastic, i.e., large changes in the net-opportunity cost produce only small changes in the supply of money.[8]

Summary—Case II

The purpose of Case II has been to move the example of demand deposit (money) creation one step closer to reality by allowing depository institutions to hold excess reserves. Initially, it was assumed that these desired holdings were a constant proportion of their demand deposit liabilities, i.e., the average value of e was a constant. Given this assumption, a formula was developed to allow a direct computation of the maximum amount of demand deposits (money) the financial system could create.

When this formula was compared with that developed in Case I, it was seen that the value of the denominator of the money multiplier was larger, which reduced its magnitude. In addition, this more complex multiplier introduced the financial system as a factor in determining the supply of money. That is, the reserve-holding behavior of commercial banks, mutual savings banks, savings and loan associations, and credit unions helps to determine the amount of money the financial system can create.

Finally, in an effort to make this example more realistic, the desired holding or demand for excess reserve by DIs was related to behavioral variables: the market rate of interest and the discount rate of the central bank. Given the expectations of these lenders about economic conditions and the variability of total demand deposit liabilities, the behavioral rela-

[8] See Ronald Teigen, "Demand and Supply Functions for Money in the United States: Some Structural Estimates," *Econometrica*, Vol. 32, No. 4 (Oct. 1964):476–509. Subsequently, Teigen reestimated his equations on the basis of improved data in "Demand and Supply Functions for Money: Another Look at Theory and Measurement," *Econometrica*, Vol. 44, No. 2 (Mar. 1976):377–85. See also William Gibson, "Demand and Supply Functions for Money in the United States: Theory and Measurement," *Econometrica*, Vol. 40, No. 2 (Mar. 1972):361–9. (It should be noted that in these studies, money was measured as M_1.)

tionship between the price or net-opportunity cost of holding excess reserves and the quantity demand was a negative one.

Since holding smaller excess reserves means more desired lending on the part of DIs, and hence more deposit creation, a supply schedule for money was derived, and its slope was positively related to the market rate of interest.[9] It is the construction of the supply schedule of money and relating the slope of that supply schedule to the profit-maximizing behavior of these lenders that is the major contribution of Case II.

Case III: Case II plus currency holding by the public

Thus far the public has used only demand deposit money. Case III shows the effects of currency holdings or a demand for currency by the public.

Before the effect of currency holding is analyzed, the source of the currency issue ought to be explained. Recall that in the first two examples the ability of DIs to create demand deposits has depended on their possession of what has been called high-powered money (the monetary base). In fact, high-powered money can be thought of as currency issued by the monetary authorities, for in the American financial system currency is the ultimate means of payment into which deposits are convertible.

The legal reserve obligations of the financial system are held mainly as currency in their own vaults, or as currency claims on the central bank, represented by their deposits at the central bank.[10]

In order to concentrate on demand deposit creation, it was assumed in the first two examples that currency did not circulate. When currency is allowed to circulate, what will its effect be on the amount of demand deposits DIs can create for any given increase in the monetary base? Certainly less than in Case II, for now DIs do not have at their disposal that portion of high-powered money that the public retains in currency. When DIs retain high-powered money, it can serve to support multiple

[9] Some students are apt to make an elementary error after reading Case II. They should now believe that deposits are created when individuals borrow from DIs. They may, however, find it hard to believe that individuals are willing to borrow more, and hence allow more demand deposits to be created, as interest rates *rise*. This is not the message of Case II. Case II is limited to a consideration of the *desired* behavior of DIs, and DIs wish to lend more and create more demand deposits as market interest rates rise. Whether the public is willing to borrow is irrelevant to the example. Our interest is in the desired behavior of DIs. Similarly, in asking the farmer how much wheat he desires to produce or supply to the market, we would find him willing to supply a larger quantity as the market price rises. What quantity the public would demand at market prices is not important for the derivation of the supply schedule of wheat. DIs can be considered as firms that have as their products the principal form of money used in our economy. They stand willing to supply a larger quantity as profitability measured by market interest rates rise (assuming a constant discount rate).

[10] Presently, for many financial institutions, state laws govern the form in which reserves may be held. Some laws permit interbank deposits to count as reserves in meeting the legal obligations. However, in The Depository Institutions Deregulation and Monetary Control Act of 1980, Congress subjected all commercial banks, savings and loans, mutual savings banks, and credit unions to a uniform set of reserve requirements. Because this change is so drastic, it will be phased in over a period of four to eight years.

dollars of demand deposit money. When high-powered money circulates as hand-to-hand currency, it supports only an equal dollars' worth of money.

As in Case II, the analysis of the effect of currency holding by the public will proceed in two steps. The first will be highly simplified by the assumption that the desired currency holdings by the public are a constant proportion of their demand deposit balances. Second, we shall take into account the fact that the desired currency holdings—in other words, the public's demand for currency—are influenced by many factors.

If it is assumed that the public's desired currency holdings, C, is a constant proportion, c', of its demand deposit balances, D, the relationship can be expressed as

$$C = c'D$$

and

$$\Delta C = c'\Delta D \tag{4:11}$$

For simplicity, and without loss of generality, we may assume that the average value of $c' = .25$. That is, for every dollar held as a demand deposit, the public desires to hold or demands on the average 25 cents as currency.

In terms of a balance-sheet presentation like that of Cases I and II, and given the same values for B, r, and e, the first transaction by which high-powered money is added to the system is the same. DI No. 1 now makes the same \$100 loan. However, the borrower will not return the entire loan to DI No. 2 as a deposit. Some portion, \$20, will be withheld as currency (shown in Table 4:8 by ΔC).[11]

TABLE 4:8
Bank balance sheets after first loan by DI No. 1

DI No. 1				DI No. 2			
Loans	\$100	Capital	\$100	Reserves:		D	\$80
				LR_D	\$16		
				ER_D	4		
				ER	60		
TOTAL	\$100	TOTAL	\$100	TOTAL	\$80	TOTAL	\$80
			$\Delta C = \$20$				

[11] The amount of currency retained by the public is computed as follows:

The \$100 loan $= C + D$ where $C = c'D$ or

$= c'D + D$

$= (c' + 1)D$, and since $c' = .25$,

$= 1.25D$

$= 5/4D$

so $D = 4/5 \times \$100 = \$80$

$C = \$100 - D = \$20$

TABLE 4:9
Bank balance sheets after second round of lending

DI No. 2				DI No. 3			
Reserves:		*D*	\$80	Reserves:		*D*	\$48
LR_D	\$16			LR_D	\$10		
ER_D	4			ER_D	2		
Loans	60			*ER*	36		
TOTAL	\$80	TOTAL	\$80	TOTAL	\$48	TOTAL	\$48

$\Delta C = \$12$

On the basis of the excess reserves it does not desire to hold, DI No. 2 can feel secure in lending out \$60. This is to be compared with \$80 in Case I and \$75 in Case II. If the \$60 is lent out, only \$48 will be redeposited in DI No. 3, with \$12 being added to currency holdings by the public. The balance sheets are shown in Table 4:9.

If DI No. 3 follows suit in an effort to increase its profits, it will lend out \$36 by creating an equivalent amount of demand deposits that will, in due course, be spent, with some portion added to currency in circulation and some portion redeposited in the banking system.

Again, by examining the balance sheet presentation, it will be noted that the ability of the financial system to manufacture demand deposits will end when the initial increase in the monetary base (ΔB) is fully absorbed as legal reserves, desired excess reserves, and net additions to currency in circulation outside the financial system, or

$$\Delta B = \Delta LR_D + \Delta ER_D + \Delta C \tag{4:12}$$

Substituting for each right-hand element its equivalent (for ΔLR_D and ΔER_D, see Case II) we have

$$\Delta B = r\Delta D + e\Delta D + c'\Delta D \tag{4:13}$$

By manipulations like those of Case II, this becomes

$$\Delta B \left(\frac{1}{r + e + c'}\right) = \Delta D \tag{4:14}$$

Since the addition of a demand for currency increases the denominator of the demand deposit multiplier, it reduces the amount of demand deposits the financial system can create for any given change in the monetary base. By substituting our assumed values into Equation (4:14), we find that

$$\$100\left(\frac{1}{.20 + .05 + .25}\right) = \Delta D$$

$$\$100(2) = \$200$$

an amount that indeed is less than the corresponding amount for Case II.

Introducing a demand for currency, then, reduces the amount of demand deposits that DIs can create from \$500 in Case I to \$400 in Case II, and to \$200 in Case III. Thus, the value of the demand deposit multiplier has fallen from 5 to 4 to 2.

The money supply

Case III differs from the two previous cases in that the supply of money is not the same as the supply of demand deposits. The disparity arises because the public is allowed to hold currency, which is a component of the money supply and therefore different from the supply of demand deposits.

Fortunately, a formula can be derived that will enable us to compute directly the amount by which the money supply increases for a given change in the monetary base. This measure of the money supply, which coincides historically with the traditional definition of money, can also be designated as the *M*-1*B* measure as set forth by the Federal Reserve. Such a designation will be used here.

To make this calculation, the change in the money supply, $\Delta M\text{-}1B$, is defined to consist of the change in demand deposits, ΔD, and the change in currency in circulation outside the financial system, ΔC, or

$$\Delta M\text{-}1B = \Delta D + \Delta C \qquad (4{:}15)$$

Since $\Delta C = c'\Delta D$ (Equation (4:11)), we have

$$\Delta M\text{-}1B = \Delta D + c'\Delta D \qquad (4{:}16)$$

or

$$\Delta M\text{-}1B = \Delta D(1 + c') \qquad (4{:}17)$$

Substituting for ΔD (from Equation (4:14)) gives

$$\Delta M\text{-}1B = \Delta B\left(\frac{1 + c'}{r + e + c'}\right) \qquad (4{:}18)$$

The quantity $\left(\frac{1 + c'}{r + e + c'}\right)$ is known as the *M*-1*B money multiplier.* It differs from the demand deposit multiplier only in terms of its numerator, which is larger by the addition of c'. Thus, as expected, the M-1B money multiplier is larger than the demand deposit multiplier. As a check, the assumed values of the variables are substituted into Equation (4:18), yielding

$$\Delta M\text{-}1B = \$100\left(\frac{1.25}{.2 + .05 + .25}\right)$$

$$\Delta M\text{-}1B = \$100\,(2.5)$$

$$\Delta M\text{-}1B = \$250$$

The currency-to-demand-deposit ratio: its appearance in the data

Thus far the average currency-to-demand-deposit ratio, c', has been assumed to be constant. An examination of some actual data shows that this assumption is generally false over most periods of time. To facilitate analysis of the actual behavior of the ratio, we shall give three different real examples. Since our evidence is historical in nature, it uses only the demand deposits issued by commercial banks, for similar deposits did not exist for other depository institutions until recently.

The first example consists of a single-year period. Reference to Figure 4:4 shows that the ratio c' fluctuates considerably. We shall call such

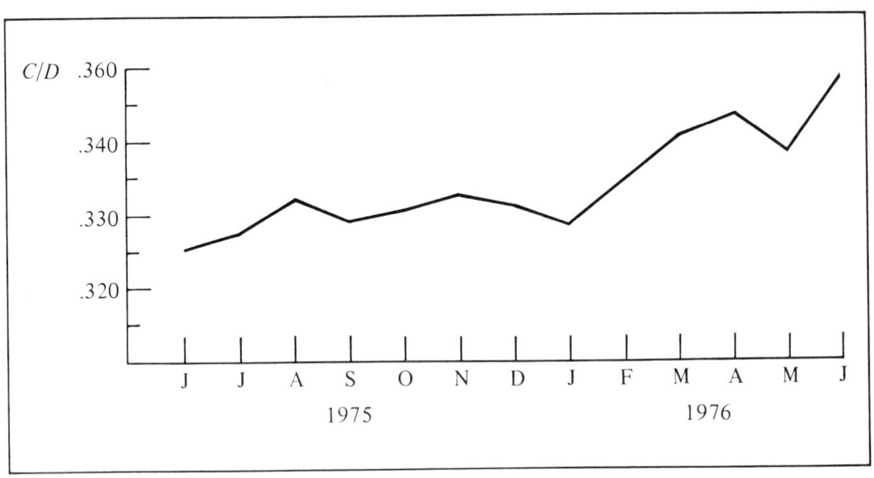

FIGURE 4:4
Seasonal movements in the C/D *ratio (Courtesy of the* Federal Reserve Bulletin.)

changes within a single year the *seasonal movement* in the currency/demand deposit ratio.

A second example would be the behavior of c' through the business cycle. Not all business cycles are of the same length or intensity. Each consists of a downswing, a bottom or trough, an upswing, and a peak. The number of months in the downswing is generally different from the number in the upswing. Thus, business cycle phases are not symmetrical in time.

In the United States the National Bureau of Economic Research (NBER), a nonprofit research organization located in New York City, performs the task of designating the dates for business cycles in the United States. Using various criteria, the NBER designates the month each cycle reaches its respective troughs and peaks. From 1867 through 1980 it has officially designated 29 complete cycles.

In a rough sort of way the movement of the currency/demand deposit ratio is similar in each cycle. The ratio starts to rise in the latter part of the expansion phase of each cycle and ends its rise midway through the contraction phase. Thereafter, the ratio falls, reaching a low point in the latter part of the expansion phase.[12] That is, in the upswing of the cycle the currency/demand deposit ratio tends to rise, whereas midway through the contraction phase the ratio starts to decline.

There are several exceptions to this general observation. First, if the downswing of the business cycle was associated wtih a widespread failure of financial institutions, individuals were often led to convert assets, especially bank deposits, to currency. In this case, the ratio or demand for currency relative to demand deposits rose in the depth of the cycle. Reference to Figure 4:5 will show this to be the case for the Great Depression of 1929–1933.

Second, during hyperinflations of the type experienced in Europe and China in this century (when prices are advancing at rapid rates on a daily basis), it sometimes takes so long for a check to clear through a bank (for the title to the deposit to be transferred) that individuals increasingly insist on currency payment to avoid the loss in purchasing power. Table 4:10 sets out the currency/deposit ratios for the European countries for which data are available to make such computations. Except for Germany, the ratio or demand for currency relative to demand deposits tends to rise during each hyperinflation period and to return to a value close to its preinflation level.

As a third and final example, in Figure 4:5 we show the behavior of the currency/deposit ratio over a long period of time—the so-called secular evidence. This evidence shows that for the United States, the long-run

[12] See Phillip Cagan, *Determinants and Effects of Changes in the Stock of Money, 1875–1960* (New York: NBER, 1965), pp. 135–7.

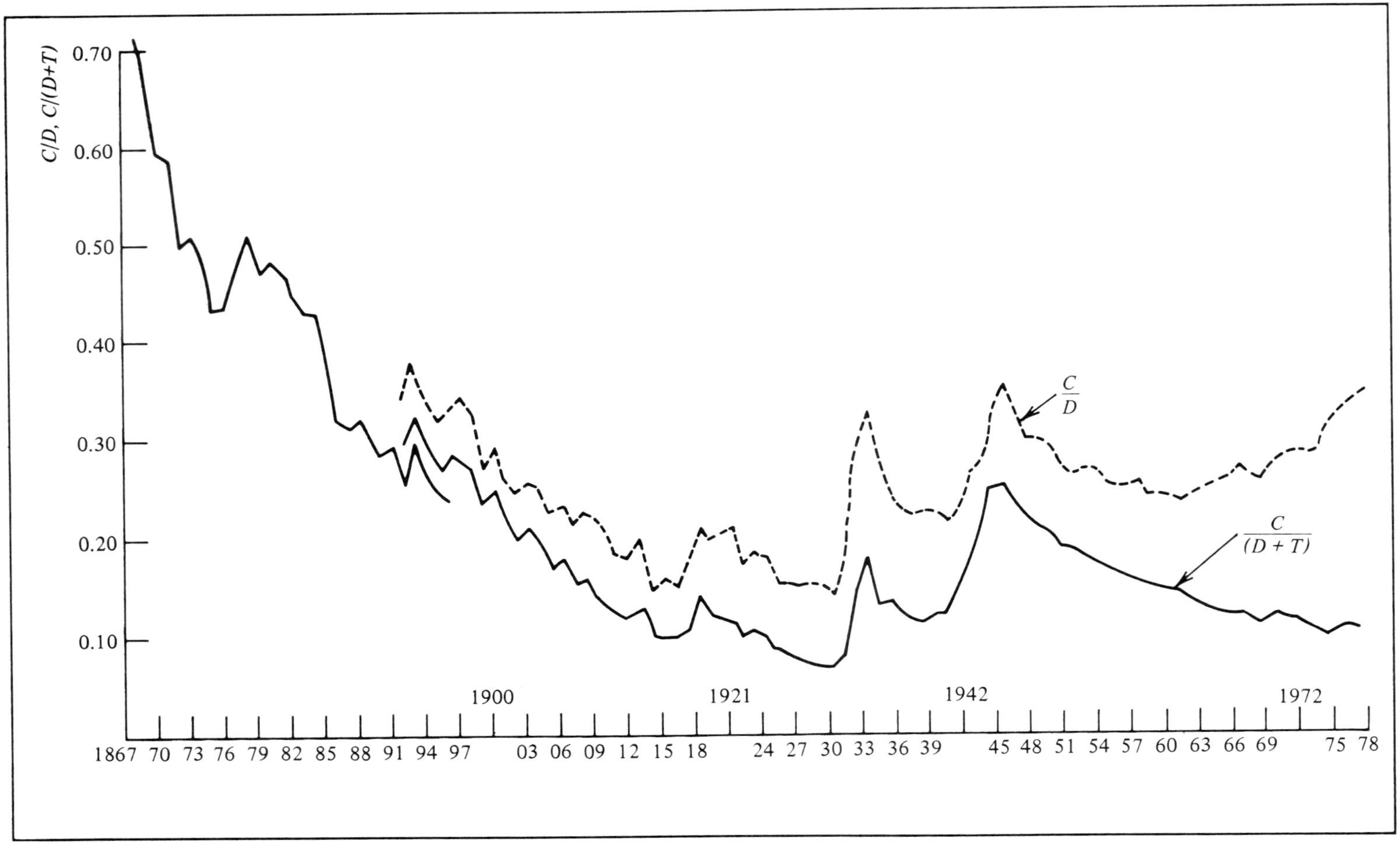

FIGURE 4:5
Secular movement of the C/D *and* C/(D + T) *ratios. The* C/D *ratio runs from 1892 to 1976, while the* C/(D + T) *ratio is from 1867 to 1976.* C/D *represents the ratio of currency to the demand deposits of commercial banks, while* C/(D + T) *represents the ratio of currency to the sum of the demand, time, and savings deposits of commercial banks. (Courtesy of* Historical Statistics of the United States *and Council of Economic Advisors* Annual Report for 1976. *Data for 1867 to 1947 reported as of June 30, while that from 1947 to 1976 are reported as of December 31.)*

TABLE 4:10

*Currency/Deposit ratios for selected European hyperinflations**

	1919	1920				1921				1922				1923				1924			
Country	4	1	2	3	4	1	2	3	4	1	2	3	4	1	2	3	4	1	2	3	4
Austria	.28	.28	.24	.27	.32	.27	.20	.18	.30	.25	.21	.43	.36	.34	.35	.35	.34	.30	.29	.26	.24
Hungary					.65	.61	.75	.75	.82	.84	.80	1.18	1.31	1.20	1.95	3.36	3.81	2.39	1.15	.94	.62
Poland	1.76				3.00	2.73	2.60	2.74	3.33	2.99	2.92	3.34	2.35	3.56	2.73	3.55	1.77	—	1.70	1.76	1.84
Germany	.31	.38	.41	.47	.48	.45	.45	.47	.55	.36	.25	.24	.59	.36	.25	.37	.22				

Note: The dates in brackets signify the hyperinflation periods.

*Deposits represent both demand and savings deposits.

Courtesy of W. A. Bomberger and G. E. Makinen, "Indexation, Inflationary Finance and Hyperinflation: The 1945–46 Hungarian Experience," *Journal of Political Economy,* Vol. 88, No. 3 (June 1980): 550–60.

trend of the ratio has been in a downward direction, although the post-World War II period appears to show a reversal of that trend.[13]

The currency/demand deposit ratio and the supply of money

At the conclusion of the discussion of Case II a supply schedule for money was derived (Figure 4:3) and shown to have a slope upward to the right (a positive slope). What are the implications of the currency/deposit ratio for this schedule?

Reference to Equation (4:18) will provide an answer. For a given value for c' of .25, an interest rate, i, equal to i_0, and assumed values for ΔB, r, and e, the change in the money supply was \$250. If the values of ΔB, r, and c' are kept constant, but e is allowed to vary in response to a rise in market interest rates, the money supply will again slope upward and its elasticity will depend on the net-opportunity cost and elasticity of the DI's demand for excess reserves, just as in Case II. Thus, the addition of the c' ratio only changes the position of the supply schedule, it does not change its slope. This is shown in Figure 4:6.

If the value of c' or the desired currency ratio were reduced from .25 to .10, the money supply for $i = 0$ (and a fixed discount rate) and the assumed values of ΔB, r, and e would be \$287.50. Thus, whenever the desired currency ratio, c', falls, the supply schedule for money would shift to the right from S to S'. This is exactly what one should expect, for if the public desires to hold or demands less currency, it deposits the redundant issue with the financial system, where each dollar serves as reserves for multiple dollars of deposit money. Conversely, if the public desires to hold or demands more currency relative to demand deposits (the value of c' rises), the supply schedule will shift to the left.

If the total demand for money is ignored for the moment, any time the public demands more currency relative to demand deposits, the actual money stock will shrink! Again, a moment's reflection will confirm this. If the public desires to hold or demands more currency, it will convert demand deposits into currency. Every time the banks lose currency, they lose

[13] In an intriguing recent contribution Garcia and Pak question the post-World War II rise in the c′ ratio. They argue that banking statistics on demand deposits are understated because commercial banks have been persuading their large customers to use their demand deposits to purchase securities on an overnight basis (this is explained extensively in Chapter 5). This practice enables banks to pay interest on demand deposit accounts. These accounts are used by their owners during the day, but are converted to securities before closing time. Because of this, they do not appear on the books of the commercial banks as demand deposits. Hence, the "true" value of demand deposits is understated. If one adds these converted accounts to the recorded statistics on demand deposits, the c′ ratio shows little upward trend. See Gillian Garcia and Simon Pak, "The Ratio of Currency to Demand Deposits in the United States," *Journal of Finance*, Vol. 34, No. 3 (June 1979):703–15.

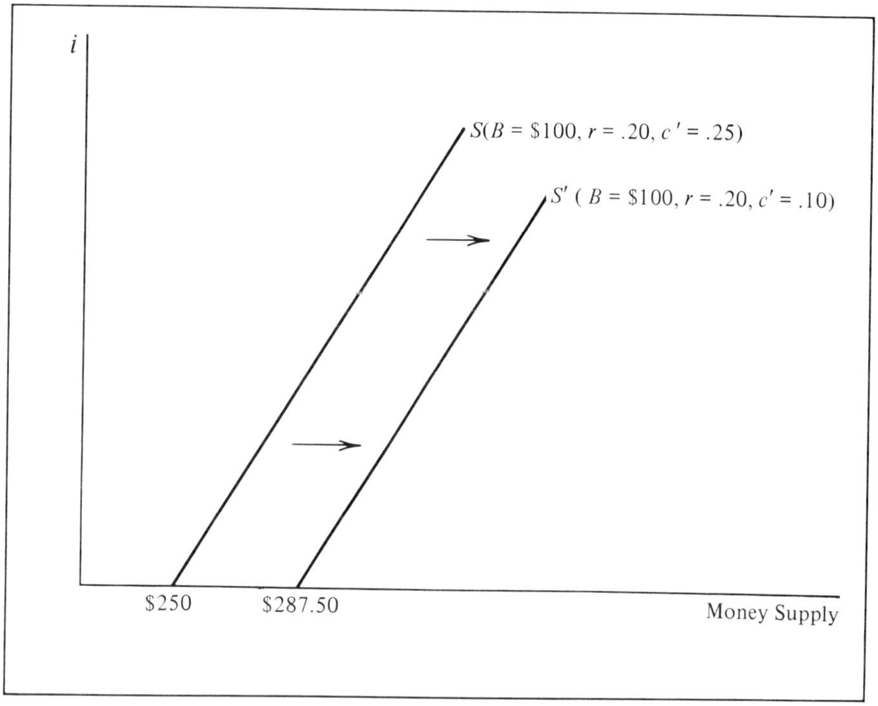

FIGURE 4:6
Money supply schedule with the c′ *ratio*

reserves. Our analysis shows that a dollar of reserves lost will cause the banks to contract their demand deposit liabilities by some multiple number of dollars.

The important thing to remember is that a change in the currency/deposit ratio, c', or the demand for currency is one factor that causes the money supply schedule to shift. The extent of the shift depends upon the magnitude of the change.

The *C/D* ratio data and the supply of money The three types of time periods used in studying the behavior of the currency/demand deposit ratio can now be linked to movements in the supply of money.

If the monetary authorities held both the monetary base and reserve requirements constant, the supply of money would, nevertheless, fluctuate over the course of a given year. From Figure 4:14 it can be seen that since the ratio or demand for currency, in general, rises from June of 1975 to December of 1975, the money supply would, in general, fall in the absence of central bank action. (A similar rise in demand can be seen for the January–June period of 1976.) From long years of experience, the monetary authorities are aware that c' has a seasonal pattern and they attempt to compensate for it when compensation contributes to their overall money supply or interest rate goals.

The behavior of the ratio over a business cycle is more important. Since the ratio or demand for currency tends to move with the cycle, it means that as the economy moves into a recession (downswing), an active force is at work to expand the money supply (a falling c' ratio). Since the ratio or demand for currency starts to rise in the expansion phase of the cycle, the money supply tends to decrease as economic recovery sets in (which may help to explain the ensuing cyclical downswing). The sharp rise in the ratio in the United States during the onset of the Great Depression in 1929–1933 was an important influence leading to the largest contraction of the U.S. money supply in the twentieth century (it fell 34% measured on an M_2 basis and 29% measured as M_1, as these aggregates were measured prior to 1980).

Interestingly, the data in Table 4:10 for the European hyperinflations indicate that the movements in the currency/deposit ratio were, on the whole, a restraining influence on the amount of money created, and thus on the subsequent course of the inflation. The general decline of the c' ratio over the past century would seem to have contributed to the long-run growth of the money supply.

At any given moment in time every individual stands at a certain point in the year, in the business cycle, and in history. Thus, at any given moment factors related to the season, the business cycle, and the long sweep of history are working to change the demand for currency. A variable ratio, as we shall see, presents problems for those who wish to control the supply of money.

Behavioral factors affecting the currency/demand deposit ratio[14]

A number of empirical attempts have been made to explain the seasonal, cyclical, and secular movements of the c' ratio. Prominent as explanatory variables have been per capita real income (or wealth), the rate of interest, the relative importance of various types of transactions, the spread of

[14] Considerable analysis on this ratio has been completed. See the seminal work by Phillip Cagan, op. cit.; James Tobin, "Monetary Interpretation of History: A Review," *American Economic Review*, Vol. 60, No. 3 (June 1965):464–85; A. C. Hess, "An Explanation of Short-Run Fluctuations in the Ratio of Currency to Demand Deposits," *Journal of Money, Credit and Banking* (Aug. 1971):666–79; and W. E. Becker, Jr., "A Theoretical and Statistical Analysis of the Currency-Demand Deposit Ratio for the U.S., 1952–1971," *Journal of Finance* (Mar. 1975):57–74. See also Peter M. Gutmann, "The Subterranean Economy," *Financial Analysts Journal* (Nov./Dec. 1977):26–34; Edgar Feige, "How Big Is The Irregular Economy?," *Challenge* (Nov./Dec. 1979):5–13; and Peter M. Gutmann, "Statistical Illusion, Mistaken Policies," *Challenge* (Nov./Dec. 1979):14–7.

various institutional practices such as commercial banking, the state of confidence in the future course of the economy, and the rate of income taxation.

Seasonal movements The types of expenditures made in the United States for final goods and services, for financial transactions, and for factor payments (wages, salaries, interest, rents, and profits) do not use equally currency and demand deposits per dollar of expenditures. Some types of transactions (e.g., those for consumer nondurable goods) are more "currency intensive" (involve the use of currency more heavily) than others per dollar of payment, while other transactions (financial, or the purchase of durable goods) are more demand-deposit intensive. Over the course of a year the mix of transactions changes. For example, around the Christmas holidays retail sales, which are relatively currency intensive, rise. Similarly, during the summer months currency-intensive transactions associated with out-of-doors sports events, movies, a higher volume of travel, and the like tend to rise relative to demand-deposit–intensive transactions. The seasonal variation in the currency/demand deposit ratio reflects the variability of different types of transactions over the year.

Cyclical movements The general procyclical movement of the c' ratio (its increase in the upswing of the cycle and its fall in the downswing) has been associated with several factors.

First, the composition of currency- and demand-deposit–intensive transactions does not remain constant over the course of a business cycle. In the downswing of the cycle retail sales and wage payments fall relative to total transactions and all factor payments. Since these are relatively currency intensive, the demand for currency relative to demand deposits falls, causing the c' ratio to decline. In the upswing these currency-intensive transactions rise relative to those intensive in demand deposits, causing the ratio to rise.

Second, the market rate of interest has been observed to exhibit a general procyclical pattern—falling in the downswing and rising in the upswing of the business cycle. If demand deposits are better substitutes for interest-bearing assets than is currency, as the interest rate falls, demand deposits will rise relative to currency and the C/D ratio will fall. In the upswing of the business cycle, as the interest rate rises, individuals will be led to substitute interest-bearing assets for demand deposits, causing the volume of demand deposits to decline and, as a consequence, the C/D ratio to rise.[15]

Thus, movements in the mix of transactions and the market interest rate over the cycle can help to explain the cyclical movements in the c' ratio.

[15] Using data for 1947 through 1969, Hess is able to explain part of the movement in the C/D ratio using a short-term interest rate.

Secular movements Although many attempts have been made to explain the secular movements in the demand for currency or c' ratio, most of them cannot be verified empirically.

We list here some of the most important attempts. First, consider the effect of the rise in per capita real income over time. It is held that demand deposits offer certain advantages over currency: they are more secure, they offer a more convenient method for making most exchanges, and a canceled check provides a convenient receipt of payment. Because of these advantages, as real per capita income rises, a greater proportion of money balances should be held in the form of this superior means of payment. Hence, one should observe a declining c' ratio over time. Since per capita real income has risen over time, it may serve to explain in Figure 4:5 the movement of the C/D ratio to the late 1920s, but the subsequent movement in the ratio has been in the opposite direction. A rising per capita income may hold the explanation for the general movement in the $C/(D + T)$ ratio, which includes time deposits.

Second, long-period movements in the market interest rate may explain movements in the ratio because demand deposits and currency are not equally good substitutes for assets that pay these interest rates. Thus, long-run declines in the market interest rate may well lead to a rise in demand deposit holdings relative to currency if the former are better substitutes for interest-paying assets than the latter, causing the c' ratio to decline. The c' ratio should rise for secular rises in interest rates.

Third, the invention of money substitutes can influence this ratio. The rapid growth in the use of demand deposits and the spread of commercial banks in the post-Civil War period undoubtedly contributed to the decline in the $C/(D + T)$ and the C/D ratio up to the late 1920s. The introduction of credit cards must also be viewed in this light. They generally serve as a better substitute for currency than for demand deposits, exercising downward pressure on the ratio.

Fourth, as with the explanation for the seasonal and cyclical variations in the ratio, as the mix of transactions making up total expenditures changes over time, the ratio c' changes also. In particular, the increasing importance of expenditures for consumer services as opposed to durable goods, and the widespread increase in travel over the past several decades, are believed to have contributed to the relative rise in demand for currency.

Finally, a number of conjectures are made for specific short-run movements in the demand for currency. The sharp rise in demand during 1930–1933 is associated with the inordinate number of banking failures of the period. The rises in wartime periods are associated with either of two factors. First, the desire to avoid high rates of wartime income taxation is thought to encourage the use of (raise the demand for) currency to conceal evidence of income. Second, the numerous black-market activities during World War II also contributed to the use of currency to minimize evidence of illegal exchanges.[16] Obviously, none of these explanations alone suffices to rationalize the entire secular movement in the c' ratio. Some combination is required.

Summary—Case III

In Case III we considered the effect of a demand for currency on the part of the public. Initially, it was assumed that the ratio of desired currency holdings to demand deposits was a constant, i.e., the demand for currency was a constant fraction of demand deposits. Currency demand was seen to have the effect of reducing the potential supply of money that DIs could create. Every dollar of currency held by the public reduces correspondingly the DIs' potential reserves that could be used to support multiple dollars of demand deposit liabilities. It is little wonder that currency is called high-powered money!

The introduction of a demand for currency into the money supply formula also introduces the behavior of the public as a force determining the supply of money alongside that of the central bank and deposit-type financial institutions.

Finally, it was observed that the currency/demand deposit ratio is not constant but varies on a seasonal, cyclical, and secular basis. Factors accounting for this behavior are generally thought to be the growth in real per capita income, the market rate of interest, the rate of income taxation, the composition or mix of transactions, the development and availability of money substitutes, and a host of other largely once-and-for-all influences.

Case IV: Case III plus savings deposits

The M-1B money supply

This final effort to construct an example of money creation is more in line with actual experiences than the preceding three examples. In Case IV the public will be allowed to hold or demand savings deposits.

As in the previous cases, the desired savings deposit holdings by the public will be assumed to bear a constant relationship to its demand deposit holdings. Using T as the symbol for dollars of savings deposits and t as the

[16] An interesting explanation has been offered for the continued rise in the ratio during the 1960's and 1970's. Professor Peter Gutmann claims that currency is used to finance a vast subterranean economy in which illegal transactions and those made to avoid income taxation flourish. This so-called irregular economy has been growing rapidly, he asserts, and he seeks to measure its size by using the C/D ratio. More recently, Professor Edgar Feige has advanced a similar argument and obtains a measure of the irregular economy which is about one-third of the official economy as recorded in the official GNP statistics. See footnote 14 for the appropriate references.

ratio of the amount of desired savings deposits to the amount of demand deposits ($t = T/D$), we have the relationship

$$T = tD$$

and

$$\Delta T = t\Delta D \qquad (4:19)$$

Unlike currency holding by the public, the addition of savings deposits as a third alternative asset does not lead to a drain of high-powered money from DIs into the hands of the public.

Once DIs are allowed to supply deposits other than those of a demand nature, however, a complication is introduced into the analysis because of a peculiarity of American law: the reserve requirements applicable to savings deposits are lower than those applicable to demand deposits.[17] Therefore, when the DI's legal reserves are calculated, it will be necessary to specify whether they apply to demand or to savings deposits. In terms of the equation used to determine the money supply, r' will represent the requirements applicable to savings deposits:

$$\begin{aligned} LR_T &= r'T = r'tD \\ \Delta LR_T &= r'\Delta T = r't\Delta D \end{aligned} \qquad (4:20)$$

Once savings deposits are introduced into the analysis of the money supply, the amount of money (measured as M-1B) the financial system can create for any given amount of monetary base should be less than if such deposits did not exist. To make this clear, the balance-sheet presentation will be given first, followed by an exposition in terms of the money supply formula.

As an example of the necessary calculations, the value of r' is assumed to be .10 and that of t to be 1.00.

As in the three previous cases, the initial transaction by which DI No. 1 obtains its reserves and its initial loan equal in value to its excess reserves

[17] An interesting history surrounds these different reserve requirements. During the Civil War the federal government made an attempt to force all commercial banks to acquire federal charters. By this act, reserve requirements were made uniform for all types of deposits, and hence banks did not distinguish between the two types of deposits in their records.

With the passage of the Federal Reserve Act in 1913, the required reserves ratios were for the first time differentiated by type of deposit. The rationalization was that while savings deposits arose from a saving motive, demand deposits represented the holding of money for current transactions, and therefore had a higher turnover rate. This higher turnover rate supposedly made the total demand deposit balance more volatile, which justified, in the eyes of the monetary experts, higher reserve requirements on such deposits in order to protect the banks from insolvency. As in other parts of American banking law, there was not a great deal of empirical support for this distinction.

TABLE 4:11
Balance sheets after DI No. 1 makes initial loan

DI No. 1				DI No. 2			
Loans	\$100	Capital	\$100	Reserves:		Deposits:	
				LR_D	\$ 8.9	D	\$44.4
				LR_T	4.5	T	44.4
				ER_D	2.2		
				ER	73.2		
TOTAL	\$100	TOTAL	\$100	TOTAL	\$88.8	TOTAL	\$88.8

$\Delta C = \$11.2$

is the same. However, when DI No. 2 obtains the deposits from the checks drawn against DI No. 1, the result is different (Table 4:11), for now it grants savings deposits.[18]

When DI No. 2 follows the rule of lending out its undesired excess reserves of \$73.2, the proceeds of the loan will be added either to currency in circulation, desired excess reserve holdings, or demand and savings deposits at DI No. 3 (Table 4:12).

When Tables 4:11 and 4:12 are compared to similar stages in the money creation process in Cases II and III, it will be seen that while the amount of excess reserves and loans is greater, the quantity of money measured as *M-1B* is less. At first sight this may seem paradoxical. It isn't, however. The amount of loans can be larger because the reserve requirements

TABLE 4:12
Balance sheets after DI No. 2 lends out its excess reserves

DI No. 2				DI No. 3			
Reserves:		Deposits:		Reserves:		Deposits:	
LR_D	\$ 8.9	D	\$44.4	LR_D	\$ 6.5	D	\$32.5
LR_T	4.5	T	44.4	LR_T	3.3	T	32.5
ER_D	2.2			ER_D	1.6		
Loans	73.2			ER	53.6		
TOTAL	\$88.8	TOTAL	\$88.8	TOTAL	\$65.0	TOTAL	\$65.0

$\Delta C = \$8.2$

[18] To compute the allocations on both the liability and asset sides of the balance sheet, remember that loans made by DI No. 1 will be held in even proportions as demand and savings deposits and that 25% of the demand deposits will be held as currency. Thus, the loan of \$100 is allocated 1.00/2.25 for each class of deposits and 25/2.25 as currency. In the example the numbers are rounded.

applicable to savings deposits are only one-half as large as those applicable to demand deposits. Thus, it should come as no surprise that a larger volume of loans can be made for the same amount of high-powered money. The same result could be achieved if the reserve requirement on demand deposits were reduced by one-half.

Without carrying Case IV to its conclusion, it can be seen from the balance-sheet presentation that money creation will end when the initial increase in the monetary base, ΔB, is absorbed into required reserves against demand deposits (ΔLR_D) and savings deposits (ΔLR_T), as desired excess reserves (ΔER_D) and public currency holdings (ΔC). That is, when

$$\Delta B = \Delta LR_D + \Delta LR_T + \Delta ER_D + \Delta C \tag{4:21}$$

Substituting for each element its equivalent yields

$$\Delta B = r\Delta D + r't\Delta D + e\Delta D + c'\Delta D \tag{4:22}$$

Factoring the common term ΔD and dividing both sides of the equation by the sum of r, $r't$, e, and c' gives

$$\Delta B \left(\frac{1}{r + r't + e + c'}\right) = \Delta D \tag{4:23}$$

Given that $\Delta M\text{-}1B = \Delta D + \Delta C$ and that $\Delta C = c'\Delta D$, the change in the $M\text{-}1B$ measure of the money supply is

$$\Delta M\text{-}1B = \Delta D(1 + c') \tag{4:24}$$

From Equation (4:23) we have

$$\Delta M\text{-}1B = \Delta B \left(\frac{1 + c'}{r + r't + e + c'}\right) \tag{4:25}$$

where the fraction in parenthesis is the $M\text{-}1B$ money multiplier. Note that it differs from the demand deposit multiplier of Equation (4:23) by having a larger numerator. Its denominator is identical.

Using the values assumed for the variables in Equation (4:25), the increase in the $M\text{-}1B$ measure of the supply of money can be calculated:

$$\Delta M\text{-}1B = \$100 \left(\frac{1.0 + .25}{.20 + .10(1.0) + .05 + .25}\right)$$

$$\Delta M\text{-}1B = \$100 \left(\frac{1.25}{.60}\right)$$

$$\Delta M\text{-}1B = \$208.30$$

which is almost 20% less than the sum created in Case III.

The M_2 money supply

For analytical purposes and simplicity, let us assume that the M_2 definition of the money supply includes only savings deposits. If this concession is granted, we can easily compute the amount of M_2 money that DIs can create. Defining the change in the M_2 measure of money as

$$\Delta M_2 = \Delta D + \Delta C + \Delta T \tag{4:26}$$

and substituting for the last two elements their equivalents yields

$$\Delta M_2 = \Delta D + c'\Delta D + t\Delta D$$

or

$$\Delta M_2 = \Delta D(1 + c' + t)$$

Then, substituting for ΔD from Equation (4:23), we have the desired result:

$$\Delta M_2 = \Delta B \left(\frac{1 + c' + t}{r + r't + e + c'}\right) \tag{4:27}$$

It should be noted that the M_2 multiplier differs from that for the M-$1B$ measure of money only by having a larger numerator.[19]

When the values assumed above are substituted for each variable in Equation (4:27), the change in the M_2 money supply can be computed:

$$\Delta M_2 = \$100 \left(\frac{1.0 + .25 + 1.0}{.20 + .10(1.0) + .05 + .25}\right)$$

$$\Delta M_2 = \$100 \left(\frac{2.25}{.60}\right)$$

$$\Delta M_2 = \$375$$

This is substantially larger than the amount of M-$1B$ money created for the same change in high-powered money.

Factors determining the desired savings deposit/demand deposit ratio

Inspection of Figure 4:7 will show that the assumption of a constant value of t is unrealistic, for the actual ratio has fluctuated markedly over time. Since the t ratio has changed so markedly over time, what variables are

[19] Each of the multipliers developed in Cases I through IV are presented below in comparative form.

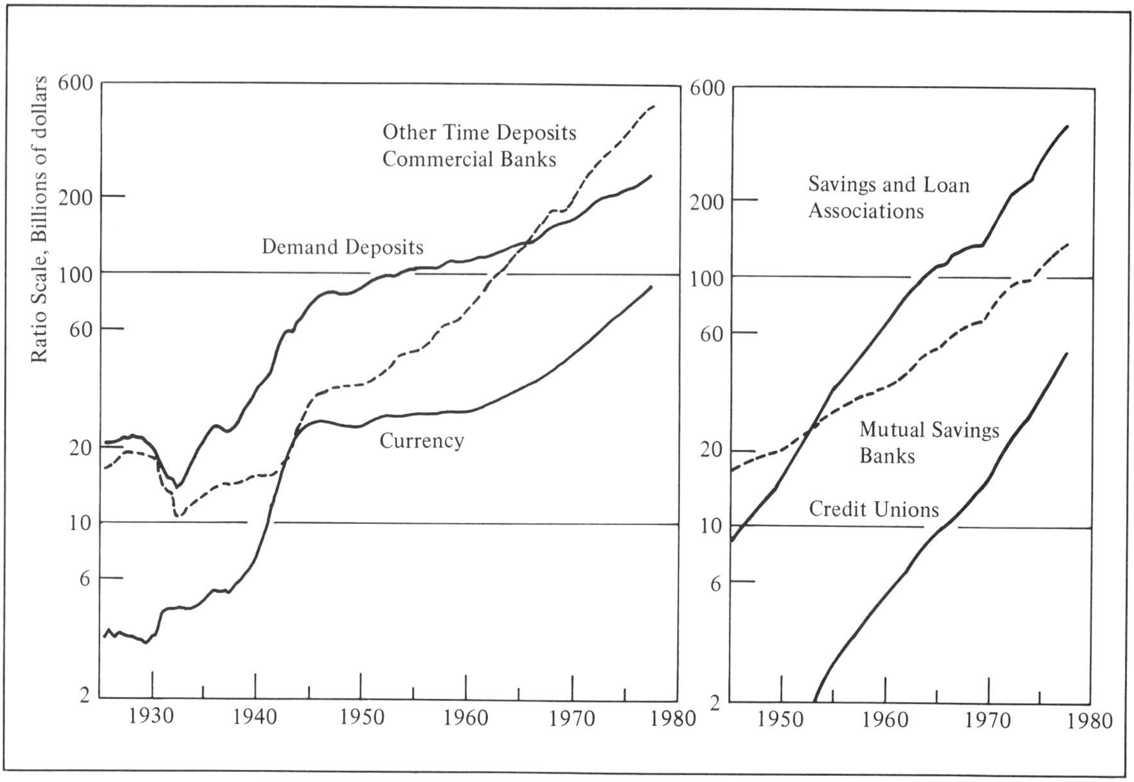

FIGURE 4:7
Historic movements in the major components of $\mathbf{M}_2$. *Data are semiannual (all dates, 1926–1946; seasonally adjusted, quarterly averages, 1947-). (Courtesy of the Federal Reserve.)*

responsible for its changes? In economic theory two variables have been singled out to explain most of the movement in this ratio.

The first is changes in per capita real income. It is believed by economists that, for most people, savings deposits are a sort of luxury good, whereas demand deposits are necessities. Therefore, as real per capita income grows over time, the holding of, or demand for, savings deposits will increase relative to demand deposits and the ratio will rise.

Whether the data will show such a trend depends, in part, on the strength of the second factor, which is the rate of interest paid on these deposits relative to the rate paid on substitute assets (deposits in other intermediaries, Treasury bills, commercial paper, etc.) and the service charges levied less any interest (explicit or implicit) paid on demand deposits.

If the yield on savings deposits rises either because their explicit interest rate rises or because the service charges less interest paid on demand deposits are increased, people should be expected to shift some of their funds from demand to savings deposits, holding a relatively larger proportion of their wealth in the latter. Such changes will increase the value of t and decrease the M-1B money supply.

The influence of either factor on the t ratio should be measurable through econometric means.

The t ratio and the supplies of money (M-1B and M_2)

If the value of all the other variables contributing to the money supply is held constant ($\Delta B, r, r', e, c'$, and $i=0$), and the initial value of the savings deposit interest rate and real per capita income are also held constant, the supply schedule of M-1B, shown in Figure 4:8, can be calculated according to Equation (4:25).

If the interest rate paid on savings deposits is now allowed to increase, it will cause the desired t ratio to rise. Suppose for the sake of argument that the t ratio increases from 1.0 to 1.25. This rise will increase the denominator of the M-1B money multiplier, and hence the M-1B money supply will be reduced. The reduction is seen as a leftward shift in the supply schedule.

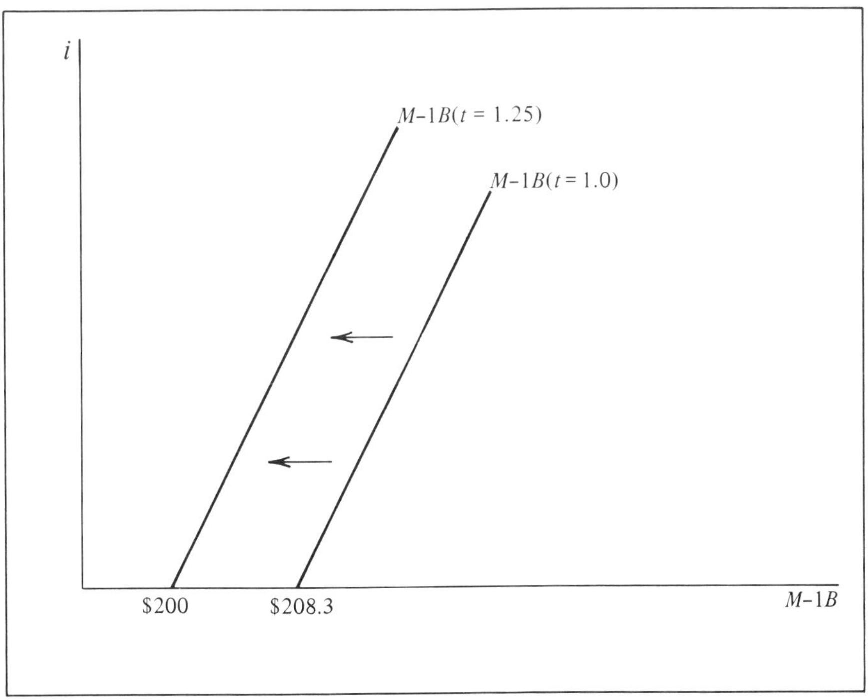

FIGURE 4:8
The supply of **M-1B** *money with time deposits*

Because the rise in the interest rate payable on savings deposits causes the desired t ratio to rise, it increases the numerator of the M_2 multiplier by more than it increases the denominator (the former is increased by Δt, whereas the latter rises only by $r'\Delta t$). Hence, the M_2 money supply will increase, i.e., the schedule will shift to the right, as shown in Figure 4:9.

Summary—Case IV

When the public was allowed to hold both demand and savings deposits, the amount of M-1B money that the financial system could create for a given amount of high-powered money was reduced.

However, the introduction of the ratio of savings to demand deposits into the denominator of the M-1B money multiplier opened an alternative route through which the asset choices by the public could influence the M-1B supply of money.

Finally, once savings deposits are introduced explicitly into the analysis, it is but a short step to consider an M_2 measure of the money supply and

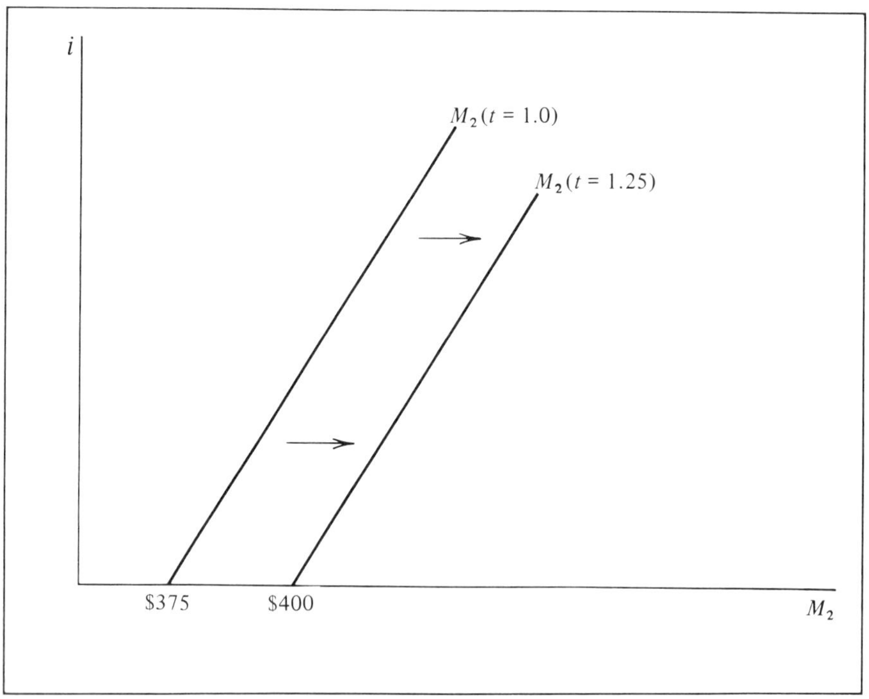

FIGURE 4:9
The supply of M_2 *money and changes in the* t *ratio.*

to examine the interaction between these two measures when the variables determining the volume of savings deposits relative to demand deposits are allowed to change.

A comparison of demand deposit and money multipliers

Our development of demand deposit and money multipliers has proceeded by viewing four cases of increasing complexity. In order to facilitate comparison, they are reproduced below.

Case I—demand deposits

Change in Demand Deposits	Change in the *M*-1*B* Money Supply
$\Delta B = \Delta LR_D$	$\Delta M\text{-}1B = \Delta D$
$\Delta LR_D = r\Delta D$	$\Delta M\text{-}1B = \Delta B(1/r)$
$\Delta B = r\Delta D$	
$\Delta D = \Delta B(1/r)$	
$(1/r)$ = Demand Deposit Multiplier	$(1/r)$ = *M*-1*B* Money Multiplier

Case II—Case I plus excess reserve holdings by banks

Change in Demand Deposits	Change in the *M*-1*B* Money Supply
$\Delta B = \Delta LR_D + \Delta ER_D$	$\Delta M\text{-}1B = \Delta D$
$\Delta LR = r\Delta D$	$\Delta M\text{-}1B = \Delta B\left(\frac{1}{r+e}\right)$
$\Delta ER = e\Delta D$	
$\Delta B = r\Delta D + e\Delta D$	
$\Delta B = \Delta D(r+e)$	
$\Delta D = \Delta B\left(\frac{1}{r+e}\right)$	
$\left(\frac{1}{r+e}\right)$ = Demand Deposit Multiplier	$\left(\frac{1}{r+e}\right)$ = *M*-1*B* Money Multiplier

Case III—Case II plus currency holding by the public

Change in Demand Deposits	Change in the M-$1B$ Money Supply
$\Delta B = \Delta LR_D + \Delta ER_D + \Delta C$	$\Delta M\text{-}1B = \Delta D + \Delta C$
$\Delta LR_D = r\Delta D$	$\Delta C = c'\Delta D$
$\Delta ER_D = e\Delta D$	$\Delta M\text{-}1B = \Delta D + c'\Delta D$
$\Delta C = c'\Delta D$	$\Delta M\text{-}1B = \Delta D(1 + c')$
$\Delta B = r\Delta D + e\Delta D + c'\Delta D$	$\Delta M\text{-}1B = \Delta B\left(\frac{1 + c'}{r + e + c'}\right)$
$\Delta B = \Delta D(r + e + c')$	
$\Delta D = \Delta B\left(\frac{1}{r + e + c'}\right)$	
$\left(\frac{1}{r + e + c'}\right) =$ Demand Deposit Multiplier	$\left(\frac{1 + c'}{r + e + c'}\right) =$ M-$1B$ Money Multiplier

Case IV—Case III plus savings deposit holding by the public

Change in Demand Deposits	Change in the M-$1B$ Money Supply	Change in the M_2 Money Supply
$\Delta B = \Delta LR_D + \Delta ER_D + \Delta C + \Delta LR_T$	$\Delta M\text{-}1B = \Delta D + \Delta C$	$\Delta M_2 = \Delta D + \Delta C + \Delta T$
$\Delta LR_D = r\Delta D$	$\Delta C = c'\Delta D$	$\Delta C = c'\Delta D$
$\Delta ER_D = e\Delta D$	$\Delta M\text{-}1B = \Delta D + c'\Delta D$	$\Delta T = t\Delta D$
$\Delta C = c'\Delta D$	$\Delta M\text{-}1B = \Delta D(1 + c')$	$\Delta M_2 = \Delta D + c'\Delta D + t\Delta D$
$\Delta LR_T = r't\Delta D$	$\Delta M\text{-}1B = \Delta B\left(\frac{1 + c'}{r + e + c' + r't}\right)$	$\Delta M_2 = \Delta D(1 + c' + t)$
$\Delta B = r\Delta D + e\Delta D + c'\Delta D + r't\Delta D$		$\Delta M_2 = \Delta B\left(\frac{1 + c' + t}{r + e + c' + r't}\right)$
$\Delta B = \Delta D\,(r + e + c' + r't)$		
$\Delta D = \Delta B\left(\frac{1}{r + e + c' + r't}\right)$		
$\left(\frac{1}{r + e + c' + r't}\right) =$ Demand Deposit Multiplier	$\left(\frac{1 + c'}{r + e + c' + r't}\right) =$ M-$1B$ Money Multiplier	$\left(\frac{1 + c' + t}{r + e + c' + r't}\right) =$ M_2 Money Multiplier

SOME FINAL THOUGHTS ON THE *M-1B* SUPPLY OF MONEY

In an effort to focus on the creation of money by the financial system, four cases or examples were constructed, ranging from the highly abstract (Case I) to a reasonable approximation of the world around us (Case IV). Each example introduced a new variable into the money creation process and, by holding the other variables constant, the impact of the new variable on the money supply was isolated. From this analysis it emerged that the money supply was positively related to an increase in the monetary base, B, and negatively related to each of the four ratios: excess reserves, e; currency, c'; legal reserves, r; and savings deposits, t. Since each ratio was, in turn, related to behavioral variables, the money supply also could be related to these same variables. Thus, the money supply is positively related to the market rate of interest and negatively related to the discount rate, the interest rate on savings deposits, the service charges on demand deposits, and the ratio of consumption to income and to rises in per capita real income, among other factors.

Our analysis so far has neglected various points that are important in the real world, primarily the substantial interaction among the variables in their ultimate determination of the money supply. To examine this interaction and provide further insight into the actual money supply process, assume that the monetary authorities have increased the monetary base held by DIs, i.e., they have given DIs additional excess reserves. This increase in reserves relative to their demand deposit liabilities will make the actual value of e (ER/D) greater than its desired value for the prevailing market interest and discount rates. It is important to note that since the actual value of e exceeds its desired value, the actual money multiplier is smaller than that which will prevail when e is again at its desired value.

In an attempt to again restore equality between the actual and desired values of e, the financial system will seek to lend out undesired excess reserves, creating demand deposits and expanding credit in the process. As the money supply expands, market interest rates will fall, which, in turn, will increase the desired value of e.

The increase in the money supply should have a positive impact on economic activity and the course of the business cycle. As economic conditions change, the desired amount of currency, c', held by the public is likely to diverge from the actual amount, which, in turn, makes the actual money multiplier different from the desired multiplier. As the public attempts to restore equilibrium between the actual and desired values of c', the financial system will either gain or lose reserves, depending upon which ratio is larger, and the money multiplier will either fall or rise.

If the change in economic activity has a further impact on market interest rates, the desired values of e and t (the savings deposit ratio) may change, causing a disparity to emerge again between actual and desired magnitudes. Attempts to restore equality will induce further movements in the money multiplier and the money supply.

The process by which the system moves from one equilibrium to another following a change in the monetary base is complicated and centers around attempts by the financial system and the public to adjust the actual values of e, t, and c' to their desired values. It is this adjustment process that explains how the money supply grows over time.

WHAT DETERMINES THE SUPPLY OF MONEY?

At the beginning of this analysis of money creation the student was told that several important questions were to be addressed. In a condensed form, the two following questions remain to be answered explicitly:

1. What determines the money supply?
2. Who determines the money supply?

The time is now at hand to explore both of these questions.

The *M*-1*B* money supply equation developed at the end of Case IV exhibits all the determining factors (developed so far) of the money supply:

$$M\text{-}1B = B\left(\frac{1 + c'}{r + r't + e + c'}\right)$$

where

M-$1B$ = narrow measure of the money supply (dollars held by the nonbank public consisting of various deposits subject to checking and currency);[20]

B = monetary base, consisting of the reserves of the financial system and the currency holdings by the non-DI public;

c' = the average desired ratio of currency to demand deposits held by the non-DI public;

r = reserve requirement per dollar applicable to demand deposits (reserve/demand deposit ratio);

r' = reserve requirement per dollar applicable to savings deposits (reserve/savings deposit ratio);

e = the average desired ratio of excess reserves held by DIs to their demand deposit liabilities;

t = the average desired ratio of savings deposits held by the public to their holdings of demand deposits.

It is important to measure the relative magnitude of each of these factors as a force affecting the money supply. In Figure 4:10, the relationship between the money supply (*M*-1*B* measure) and the monetary base is graphed. To the extent that parallel movements between the money supply and the monetary base do not exist, the divergence is caused by changes in the multiplier. Over much of the period 1952–1976 the two series moved together, which implies that the monetary base exercises a dominant influence over the money supply.

[20] In the United States it has long been common practice to exclude federal government holdings of both demand deposits and currency from the definition of money. *M*-1*B* excludes foreign holdings of money as well.

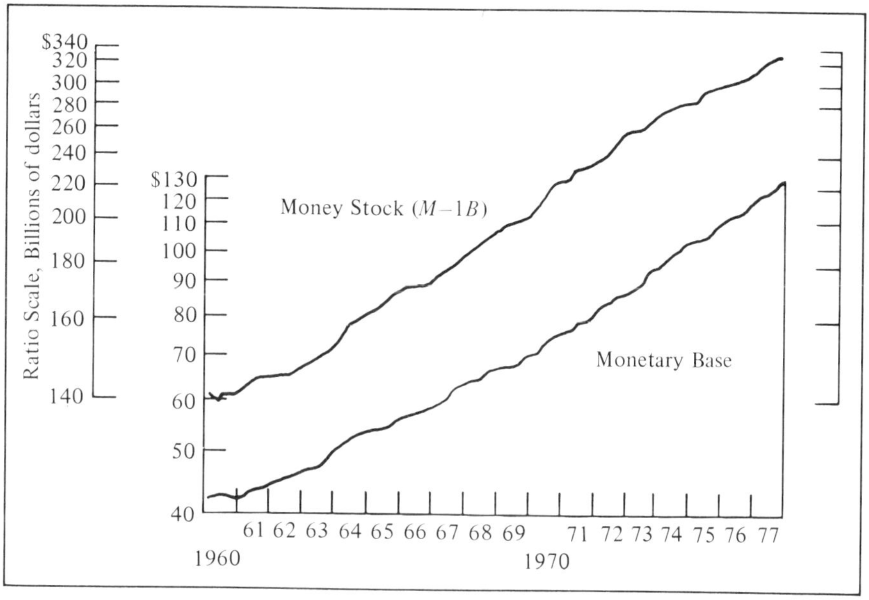

FIGURE 4:10
Movements in the **M-1B** *supply of money and the monetary base (Monetary base computed from* Monthly Review, *Federal Reserve Bank of St. Louis (July 1977). Money stock taken from* Federal Reserve Bulletin. *All data seasonally adjusted.)*

The relatively weak contribution of the money multiplier to changes in the money supply over the longer run is confirmed by reference to Figure 4:11, which shows that over a 25-year period the *M-1B* multiplier varied from a low of 2.5 to a high of approximately 2.8. Such a slight variation over the longer run does not imply that the multiplier is an unimportant source of movement for the money supply over a business cycle or shorter-run period. Quite the contrary. In his classic study of money and the business cycle Phillip Cagan found that while increases in high-powered money accounted for 91% of the secular growth in the money supply from 1875 to 1955, 46% of the cyclical fluctuations in the rate of growth of the money supply could be accounted for by movements in the currency/deposit ratio, 26% by movements in the reserve ratio, and 27% by the movements in high-powered money.[21] Thus, on a cyclical basis the money multiplier exercises a dominant influence on the money supply. Recent work by Peter Frost,[22] updating Cagan's work to 1974, confirms his finding

[21] Cagan, op. cit.

[22] Peter A. Frost, "Short-Run Fluctuations in the Money Multiplier and Monetary Control," *Journal of Money, Credit, and Banking,* Pt. 1 (Feb. 1977): 165–81. It should be noted that in the work of both Cagan and Frost money is measured differently from the methods reported in this text. This evidence should, therefore, be regarded as suggestive in nature.

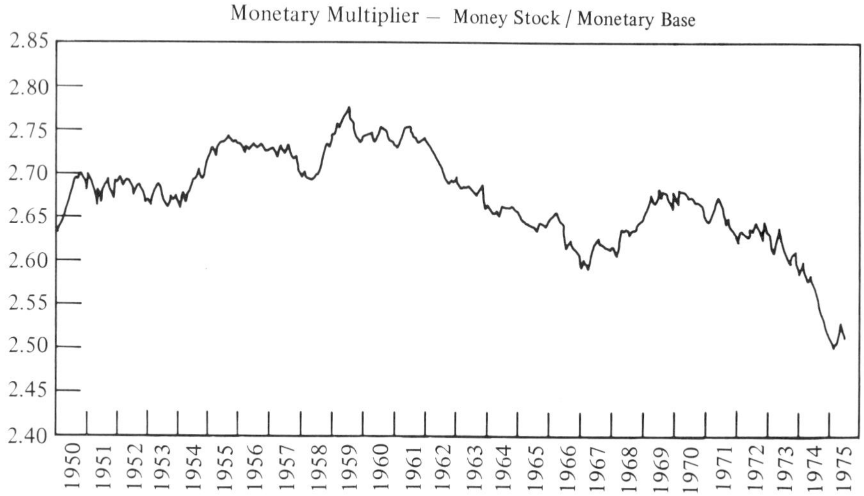

FIGURE 4:11
Historic movements in the **M-1B** *money multiplier (Courtesy of the Federal Reserve Bank of St. Louis.)*

on the short-run importance of the money multiplier and, in particular, the importance of the currency/deposit ratio in the short-run movements of the supply of money.

Even though the money multiplier appears fairly constant over the longer run, it certainly does not follow that the variables making up the multiplier are themselves constant. Figure 4:12 shows that over a 25-year period considerable variation is to be found, especially in the currency/demand deposit (c') and savings deposit/demand deposit (t) ratios. For convenience, all of the reserve holding by commercial banks ($r + r' + e$) are summarized in one variable labeled r.

WHO CONTROLS THE MONEY SUPPLY?

Once the "what controls" question is disposed of, the "who controls" question is easier to address. All that must be done is to discover who controls the variables that affect the supply of money.

Among the variables contributing to the supply of money, the monetary base is a prime candidate for most significant. In each example in this chapter an unspecified monetary authority was the source of high-powered money. In the American institutional structure "the monetary authority" is principally the central bank (Federal Reserve System), together with (to a much lesser degree) the United States Treasury. However, since all depository institutions can borrow reserves from the Federal Reserve, they also

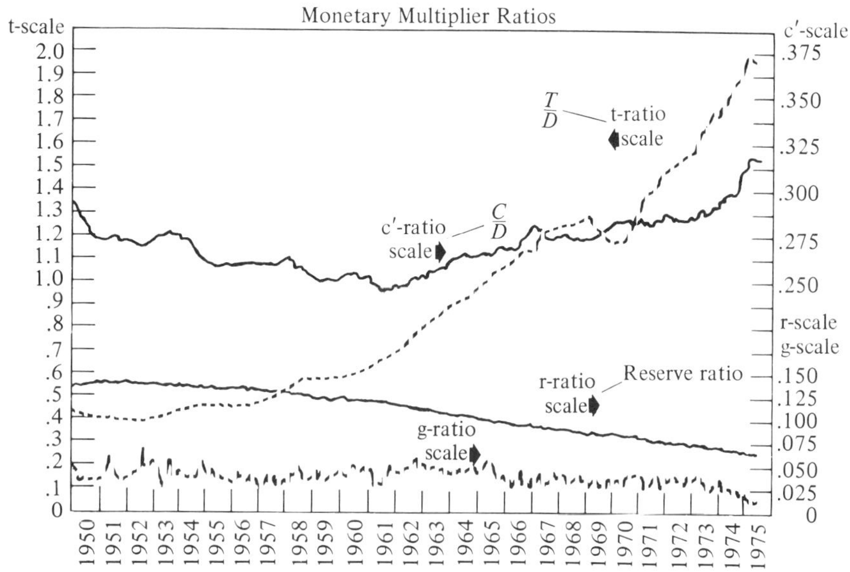

FIGURE 4:12
Historic movements in the components of the **M-*1*B** *multiplier (Courtesy of the Federal Reserve Bank of St. Louis.)*

have some control over the monetary base. Their decision to borrow can be influenced by variations in the discount rate and in the administration of what has been called "the discount window" by the Federal Reserve. The latter phrase refers to the ease with which the central bank grants the discount. Since DIs can influence the amount of the monetary base, a distinction is often made between the borrowed and unborrowed base, the latter being supplied by the central bank.

Both the currency and savings deposit ratios (c' and t) are determined by the behavior of the general public as to the form in which it wishes to hold its wealth. If the interest rate can be manipulated by the central bank, it can exercise some influence over these two ratios and the behavior of the public. However, one would not be justified in concluding that the central bank consciously attempts to control the money supply by manipulating these two ratios.

The excess reserve holdings are determined by the financial institutions themselves. In the previous analysis their behavior was linked to the net-opportunity cost of holding these reserves, given their views of the variability of total deposits and the future stability of the economy.

Since every change in the discount rate by the central bank tends to alter the net cost of holding excess reserves, the central bank has a tool for influencing the future course of the supply of money. Here again, it would be a mistake to conclude that the central bank considers the discount rate a major tool of monetary policy to be used to alter the volume of excess reserves held by the banks.

Presently, the values of r and r' are determined jointly by several agencies in the American financial system. For those commercial banks that belong to the Federal Reserve System (less than 50% of all commercial banks, but they hold 70% of all commercial bank deposits), r and r' are set by the Federal Reserve. For those banks that do not belong to the system, reserve requirements are set by banking commissions in the respective 50 states.[23] Reserve requirements of federally chartered savings and loan associations (representing 98% of all assets) are set by the Federal Home Loan Bank Board, while the reserve requirements of mutual savings banks are determined by the state banking commissions where such banks are legal. However, in 1980 Congress granted the Federal Reserve power to set reserve requirements on all depository institutions. This power is to be phased in over a period of four to eight years. Since reserve requirements are not presently uniform across all jurisdictions, r and r' must be regarded as suitably weighted averages, where the weights are the deposits of the various financial institutions.

CAN THE CENTRAL BANK CONTROL THE MONEY SUPPLY?

The answer to this question depends upon a consideration of several factors, especially time. If the central bank had available to it accurate data on all the variables that affect the money supply on a minute-by-minute basis, or if it could predict with perfect accuracy what those variables would be on the same time basis, it would have a very close control over the supply of money, insofar as it chose to use the monetary tools described above. However, even in this era of high-speed computers that so greatly facilitate both the collection of data and the prediction of the future, the state of technology is not advanced enough to give the central bank this information.

In its attempts to control the money supply the central bank tries to alter the monetary base, giving due consideration to the probable value of the multiplier (which the central bank attempts to predict from historical data). Frequently, actual events diverge from those predicted and the central bank may either over- or undershoot its target, which then necessitates remedial action to correct for the error.

Only a few skeptics would doubt that the central bank could hit an annual money supply target confined to a fairly narrow range. As the time span is

[23] See Appendix C for a complete discussion of the reserve requirements applicable in each of the 50 states and their enforcement. These requirements will prevail during the phase-in period.

reduced to half a year, a quarter, a month, a week, a day, or an hour, the ability of the central bank to remain on target diminishes largely because of the impossibility of getting accurate data on a timely basis.[24]

SUMMARY

In this chapter we constructed a supply schedule for money and identified in a relatively simple fashion the variables determining the slope of the schedule and the cause of its shift over time.

The supply schedule was constructed through four separate cases that moved the analysis from an elementary to a more sophisticated level. As a byproduct, it was shown how DIs manufacture or create money.

Central to the money-creation process is the monetary base or high-powered money that can serve either as DI reserves or as circulating currency in the hands of the public, and the reserve requirements that specify how much of the base DIs must hold for each dollar of deposit liabilities outstanding. It is through the control of these two elements that the central bank attempts to exercise its control over the money supply. However, at any moment in time this control is shared with the financial system, the public, and the U.S. Treasury.

STUDY QUESTIONS

1. Individual bankers have long disclaimed any ability to create money. They rightly claim that they only take in currency or deposits and pass them along to people who want to borrow. Under the circumstances, they don't create anything, much less money. Are they correct? If not, explain to them how their actions increase the supply of money.
2. If in a world with both currency and demand deposits there were no legally imposed reserve requirements, would an unlimited expansion of demand deposits take place for a given primary deposit?
3. Suppose that the only form of money was demand deposits. Would financial institutions manufacture an unlimited volume of money if there were no legal reserve requirements?
4. Should an individual banker who wishes both to maximize profits and to remain in business make loans and increase demand deposits by some multiple of his bank's reserves?
5. In the examples constructed in this chapter the willingness of financial institutions to lend has been based upon the interest rates they re-

[24] In Chapter 17 it will be shown that for an open economy, this conclusion may be subject to modification.

ceive—the higher the rate, the greater their willingness to lend, and in the process create deposits and money. However, individuals are likely to display a greater willingness to borrow only if interest rates are lowered. Hence more deposits and money will result only when interest rates are lowered. Which is it to be? Will the quantity of money supplied be greater or less as interest rates rise?

6. Why would any rational financial institution willingly hold reserves when they could be lent out at a profit?
7. Suppose that the financial system was not supplied with extra reserves at Christmas. What would likely happen to the aggregate money supply?
8. When the price level is rising very rapidly, why might the public prefer to hold its money as currency rather than as a demand deposit? Under what circumstances could the reverse be true?
9. How would the typical movement of the currency/demand deposit ratio over the business cycle influence the movement of the money supply over the same cycle?
10. Increase the monetary base by X dollars and trace the movement of the actual and desired money multiplier until a new equilibrium is obtained. Which component of the money multiplier is likely to do most of the adjusting?
11. Relate the process in question 10 to the rightward shift of the money supply schedule. Under what circumstance would the supply schedule not shift?
12. How might each of the following circumstances affect the money multiplier?
    a. an increase in the effective rate of income taxation.
    b. a rise in market interest rates.
    c. an increase in the rate of inflation.
    d. widespread failures of financial institutions.
    e. wartime controls in prices.
    f. a growth in the illegal drug traffic.

SELECTED REFERENCES AND READINGS

Anderson, Leonall C. "Three Approaches to Money Stock Determination." *Monthly Review,* Federal Reserve Bank of St. Louis (Oct. 1967).

Becker, William E., Jr. "A Theroetical and Statistical Analysis of the Currency–Demand Deposit Ratio for the U.S., 1952–1971." *Journal of Finance,* Vol. 30, No. 1 (Mar. 1975).

Black, Robert. "The Impact of Member Banks Reserves on the Money Supply." *Southern Economic Journal,* Vol. 29, No. 1 (Jan. 1963).

Burger, Albert E. *The Money Supply Process.* Belmont, Cal.: Wadsworth, 1971.

Cagan, Phillip. *Determinants and Effects of Changes in the Stock of Money, 1875–1960.* Princeton, N.J.: Princeton University Press, 1965.

Fand, David I. "Can the Central Bank Control the Nominal Money Stock?" In "Some Issues in Monetary Economics." *Monthly Review,* Federal Reserve Bank of St. Louis (Jan. 1970).

Frost, Peter A. "Short-Run Fluctuations in the Money Multiplier and Monetary Control." *Journal of Money, Credit and Banking,* Vol. 9, No. 1, Part 2 (Feb. 1977).

Hess, Allan C. "An Explanation of Short-Run Fluctuations in the Ratio of Currency to Demand Deposits." *Journal of Money, Credit and Banking* (Aug. 1971).

Kohn, Donald L. "Currency Movements in the United States." *Monthly Review,* Federal Reserve Bank of Kansas City (Apr. 1976).

Nichols, Dorothy M. *Modern Money Mechanics.* Chicago: Federal Reserve Bank of Chicago, 1961.

Poindexter, Carl J. "The Currency-Holding Behavior of the Public and the Strength of Monetary Controls." *The Bulletin,* New York University Graduate School of Business Administration, No. 67 (Nov. 1970).

Tolley, George. "Providing for Growth in the Money Supply." In *Monetary Theory and Policy,* edited by Richard Thorn. New York: Random House, 1966.

4 4

APPENDIX A– THE ORIGIN OF COMMERCIAL BANKING[1]

We started the examination of the money-creation process presented in this chapter by assuming that a financial system existed, and that monetary authorities imposed upon lenders reserve requirements and provided them with reserves for their deposit liabilities. Admittedly, this was highly unrealistic. However, once the origins of commercial banking are examined, it will be seen that little was lost in starting off on such an abstract level. The essentials of the process were preserved.

In the Anglo-Saxon world commercial banking as we know it might never have happened when it did were it not for the lack of respect for private property by an English king. It evolved from the goldsmith business and can be traced to the middle decades of the seventeenth century, although there is evidence that commercial banking developed several centuries earlier in the great Renaissance cities of Italy.[2]

Crude money lending and money changing were present during the reign of Elizabeth I (1533–1603), and the practice developed whereby merchants would deposit money (coins) in the Tower of London, which served as the British mint. In 1640 Charles I expropriated the sum then on deposit (approximately £200,000). Having learned from this loss, the merchants decided to seek a depository free from the danger of royal confiscation. A natural place was the strongboxes owned by goldsmiths, and these businesses soon commenced the practice of accepting deposits for which they gave a receipt payable to the specific order of the depositor or to the bearer. As these receipts were negotiable, they passed from hand to hand in exchange for goods and services. From time to time they would be presented for conversion into coin. This first innovation was the forerunner of the bank note or banker's currency.

[1] The historic dates and other references are taken from an article by an anonymous author entitled "The Goldsmith Banker," *The Three Bank Review,* No. 21 (Sept. 1955): 42–52.

[2] See Raymond de Roover, *The Rise and Decline of the Medici Bank, 1397–1494* (New York: W.W. Norton & Co., 1966); Abbot Payson Usher, "The Origins of Banking: The Primitive Bank of Deposit, 1200–1600," *The Economic History Review,* Vol. IV, No. 4 (Apr. 1934): 399–428; Charles F. Dunbar, "The Bank of Venice," *Quarterly Journal of Economics,* Vol. 6, No. 3 (Apr. 1892): 308–35; and Frederic C. Lane, "Venetian Bankers, 1496–1533: A Study in the Early Stages of Deposit Banking," *Journal of Political Economy,* Vol. 45, No. 2 (Apr. 1937): 187–206.

Shortly thereafter, as early as 1680, the practice developed whereby the depositor could write a note requesting that a sum of money be paid to a third party or to the bearer. This innovation was the forerunner of the modern check, which is merely an order to a bank requesting that a deposit be transferred to a third person or bearer.

Thus far the description of early banking would imply that each goldsmith maintained 100% reserves against deposit liabilities. That is, that he held in coin an amount equal to their deposits. Yet the historic record shows that this is not true. It must have occurred to the goldsmith early on that it was unlikely all depositors would ask for their deposits in gold on the same day. Thus he found it feasible to lend out some of the coin held as reserves (issue deposit receipts against loans), even though an equivalent amount of coin was not on deposit.

The books of the goldsmith might appear as Table 4A:1. Transaction No. 1 marks the receipt of coin from the merchants of the city.

Believing that not all depositors would request coin redemption on the same day, the goldsmith decides to lend out £100 by issuing a negotiable deposit against which drafts can be drawn. Transaction No. 2 designates the loan.

Total deposits are now £ 200, while reserves stand at £100 (50% of deposit liabilities), and earning assets amount to £100. With the advent of this type of lending, fractional reserve banking was born. The total amount of loanable funds is now £100 greater than that provided through the past saving necessary to add £100 of coin to the money supply.

Fractional reserve banking must have developed shortly after the goldsmiths entered the banking business, because periodically they computed balance sheets, or as they called it "casting up ye shop." Some of these early balance sheets indicate that coin reserves varied from 35% to 50% of deposit liabilities.

From this brief explanation of the origins of commercial banking in England it can be seen that the examples developed in Chapter 4 to explain money creation contained the essentials—the ability to increase the money supply (deposits of the goldsmiths) depended upon the presence of the ultimate means of payment (coin or high-powered money) and a reserve requirement either legally or voluntarily imposed.

TABLE 4A:1
Balance sheet of Goldsmith

No. 1	Gold coin	£100	Deposits	£100	No. 1
No. 2	Loan	£100	Deposits	£100	No. 2

APPENDIX B–
BANK CREDIT RATHER THAN MONEY

The annals of central banking are replete with references that focus on the volume and composition of bank credit, rather than the supply of money, as the chief determining factors of the behavior of the economy.[1] Thus, prosperity, inflation, recession, depression, and so on are related not to the supply of money or its growth rate, but rather to the volume of credit and its allocation among competing users. In the credit view, the supply of money is important only insofar as it influences the overall flow of credit or loanable funds.

Whereas conventional money supply analysis focuses attention on the liability side of a bank's balance sheet, the "credit volume view" theorists look on the asset side, giving particular attention to the amount and type of loans and the rate of interest at which they are made, the latter reflecting the terms or availability of credit.

One explanation for the popularity of the "credit volume" viewpoint among central bankers is that bankers were wed to the real bills doctrine, one of whose precepts was that as long as banks accepted for discount only "sound" commercial bills, the economy would avoid the excesses of inflation and deflation. The notion of a "sound" commercial bill was one where the proceeds were used for productive purposes—to enable a firm to complete the production of its goods and services or to carry a reasonable inventory. An "unsound" bill was one whose proceeds were used for speculative purposes. Acumen gained through years in the business apparently enabled bankers to discern the sound from the unsound.

An additional aspect of the credit view seems to be that the type of asset acquired by a bank has an important influence on total spending. Thus, if a bank acquires a commercial bill, this is seen as having a more significant impact on the gross national product than if it should buy a Treasury bill held by the public. The former supposedly increases the demand for productive factors, whereas the latter merely alters the composition in which liquid assets are held.

It is unlikely that there is a dollar-for-dollar relationship between bank credit and the money supply. While bank loans and investments (whose

[1] To update this view, one need only substitute DI for commercial bank. Indeed, people who are favorably disposed toward this view would likely advocate using the current Federal Reserve liquidity aggregate in place of any measure of the money supply.

sum most closely approximates bank credit) constitute a major fraction of bank assets, demand deposit liabilities are a minority of total bank liabilities. The amount of bank credit is, therefore, likely to be much larger than the value of the demand deposit liabilities of banks. Moreover, the growth rate of the two need not coincide over time. If time deposits grow at a faster rate than demand deposits, bank credit can expand at a faster rate than the latter.

When a broader measure of the money supply such as M_2 is used, the growth of bank credit and of money more nearly approximate each other.[2] Divergence arises principally because banks have some nondeposit sources of funds and can loan out their liquid assets in order to expand the volume of loans and investments. Such means of expanding credit may be significant in the short run.

Whether the flow of credit is a better target than the money supply for the central bank to concentrate on in its endeavor to stabilize economic activity is, in part, an econometric problem. For those who judge the significance of relationships from correlation analysis, either measure of the money supply (M_1 or M_2) has a stronger correlation with economic activity than does a measure of the flow of bank credit.[3]

The importance of the bank credit view versus the money supply view is in large part related to the implications of each for monetary policy. One of the great economic tragedies of this century was the Great Depression of 1929–1933. From the available evidence, it would appear that the majority of the Board of Governors of the Federal Reserve System embraced the credit view. As market interest rates declined in this period, the majority believed that credit conditions were easy and that the Depression must, therefore, have its origins in causes outside the banking system. Since credit conditions were assumed to be easy, the Federal Reserve was thought to be powerless to combat the Depression.

On the other hand, the money supply in the four years 1929–1933 as measured on an M_1 basis contracted by 29%, and as measured on an M_2 basis by over 33%. For those who believe that the money supply and economic activity are related, the depth of the Depression was substantially influenced by the massive reduction in the supply of money. According to this view, the Federal Reserve is responsible for allowing the contraction to occur and, by implication, for the depth of the Depression.

[2] Using trend-free data from the first quarter of 1950 through the second quarter of 1976, the Federal Reserve Bank of Kansas City reports a correlation of .54 for M_1 and the sum of loans and investments by banks, and .67 for M_2 and the sum of loans and investments. See J. A. Cacy, "Commercial Bank Loans and the Money Supply," *Monthly Review*, Federal Reserve Bank of Kansas City (Nov. 1976): 3–10, especially Table 2. In this study, both M_1 and M_2 were measured as they were prior to 1980.

[3] Ibid.

APPENDIX C–
BANK RESERVE REQUIREMENTS AND THEIR ENFORCEMENT: A COMPARISON ACROSS STATES[1]

NATURE OF STATE RESERVE REQUIREMENTS

Specification of required reserves and reserve assets

Information on reserve requirements of individual states for various classes of deposit liabilities and on the types of assets that are counted as reserves is presented in Table 4C:1. This information was obtained from the bank supervisors of each state.[2]

Reserve requirements differ greatly among states, with Illinois being the only state with no statutory requirements. Most states have higher reserve requirements on demand deposits than on time and savings deposits, and in three states the reserve requirement ratios apply to total deposits. Two states, Massachusetts and Rhode Island, do not require any reserves on time and savings deposits. In 19 states various types of deposit liabilities, primarily government deposits, are not subject to reserve requirements.

All states with reserve requirements count vault cash and demand deposits at corresponding banks as reserves.[3] In 27 states the banking authorities must approve correspondent banks as depositories if demand balances due from those banks are to be counted as reserves by nonmember banks. In 18 states cash items in the process of collection (CIPC) are also

[1] Reproduced from an article in the *Monthly Review* of the Federal Reserve Bank of St. Louis (Mar. 1978) by R. Alton Gilbert and Jean M. Louat.

[2] Most of the state bank supervisors provided this information in October or November of 1977.

[3] Correspondent banks hold deposit balances of other banks and provide services to those banks.

TABLE 4C:1
State reserve requirements

State	Deposits Subject to Reserve Requirements	Current Reserve Requirement Ratios	Reserve Assets Eligible to Meet Requirements: Vault Cash	Demand Balances Due from Banks	Securities	Other
Alabama	T Dem	10%	X	X		
	TS	3%	X	X		
Alaska[1]	T Dem-US_d-SL_d	20%	X	X		
	TS-US_t-SL_t	8%	X	X		
Arizona[1]	T Dem-US_d-SL_d-R_d	10%	X	X^2	X^3	{CIPC}
	TS-US_t-SL_t-R_t	4%	X	X^2	X^3	
Arkansas	T Dem	FR	X	X^2		{CIPC[4]}
	S	3%	X	X^2		
	T	{3% first $5 million, plus 5% over $5 million}	X	X^2		
California[1]	T Dem-US_d-SL_d-R_d -CIPC- Due From[5]	FR	X	X^2		
	TS-US_t-SL_t	5%	(at least 20%)		(up to 80%)[6]	
Colorado[1]	T Dep-US_d-SL_d-US_t-SL_t	15%	X	X^2	X^6	
Connecticut	T Dem-Due From-CIPC	{12% first $5 million, plus 12.5% over $5 million}	{at least one-sixth}	{X^2}	{up to one-sixth[7]}	
	T	3%				
Delaware[1]	T Dem-US_d-SL_d	{7% first $100 million, plus 9% over $100 million}	{at least 50%[2, 8]}		{up to 50%[9]}	
	TS-$US_t$$SL_t$	3%				
Florida[1]	T Dep-US_d-SL_d-US_t-SL_t	20%	X	X	X^6	
Georgia[1]	T Dem-US_d-SL_d-R_d	15%	(at least 50%)[2, 10, 11]		(up to 50%)[12]	
	TS-US_t-SL_t-R_t	5%	X	X	X^{13}	CDs[14]

Hawaii	T Dem-US_d-SL_d	12%	at least 25%	up to 75%[2]		
	TS-US_t-SL_t	5%				
Idaho	T Dem	15%	X	X[2]		
	TS	5%	X	X[2]		
Illinois	(No statutory reserve requirements)					
Indiana	T Dem	10%	X	X		CIPC
	TS	3%	X	X		CIPC
Iowa	T Dem	7%	X	X[2]		
	TS	3%	X	X[2]		
Kansas[1]	T Dem-US_d-SL_d	FR	X	X		
	TS-US_t-SL_t	FR	X	X		
Kentucky	T Dem	7%	(at least 75%)[15]		(up to 25%)[16]	
	TS	3%	X	X	X	CDs[17]
Louisiana	T Dem-CIPC	7.5% first $2 million, plus 10% $2-$10 million, plus 12% $10-$100 million, plus 13% $100-$400 million, plus 14% over $400 million	at least 50%		up to 50%[18]	
	TS	3%				
Maine	T Dem-TTL	10%	X	X[2] [11]	X[19]	Fed funds sold
	S	2%	X			
	T	4%	X			
	NOW	8%	X			
Maryland	T Dem-US_d-SL_d	15%	(at least two-thirds)		(up to one-third)[20]	
	TS-US_t-SL_t	3%	X	X	X[21]	
Massachusetts	T Dem plus time deposits subject to withdrawal within 30 days	Boston - 20% Others - 15%	at least 15%	up to 80%	up to 80%[9]	
Michigan	T Dem	11%	X	X[2]		
	TS	6%	(at least 10%)[2]		(up to 90%)[13]	

TABLE 4C:1
Continued

State	Deposits Subject to Reserve Requirements	Current Reserve Requirement Ratios	Reserve Assets Eligible to Meet Requirements: Vault Cash	Demand Balances Due from Banks	Securities	Other
Minnesota	T Dem	The following percentages are not marginal requirements but apply to total demand deposits: 7% \$0-\$2 million; 9.5% \$2-\$10 million; 11.75% \$10-\$100 million; 12.75% \$100-\$400 million; 16.25% over \$400 million	at least 70%[15] (Vault Cash and Demand Balances combined)		up to 30%[19]	
	S	3%				
	T	3% maturing in 30–179 days; 2.5% maturing in 180 days to 4 years; 2% maturing in 4 or more years				
Mississippi	T Dem	FR	at least 70% (Vault Cash and Demand Balances combined)		up to 30%[22]	
	TS	FR				
Missouri	T Dem	FR	at least 50%, including CIPC[2] (Vault Cash and Demand Balances combined)		up to 50%[23]	
	TS	3%				
Montana	T Dem	7.5% first 2 million, plus 10% over \$2 million	X	X[2]		
	TS	3%	X	X[2]		
	Due to Banks[24]	10%	X	X[2]		
Nebraska	T Dem	15%	at least 50% (Vault Cash and Demand Balances combined)		up to 50%[25]	
	TS	5%				
Nevada[1]	T Dem-US_d-SL_d	FR	X	X[2]		
	TS-US_t-SL_t	FR	X	X[2]		
New Hampshire	T Dem	12%	at least 60% (Vault Cash and Demand Balances combined)		up to 40%[26]	
	TS	5%				
New Jersey	T Dem	FR	X	X[2]		CIPC
	TS	FR	X	X[2]		CIPC

New Mexico	T Dem	12%	at least 50%, including local CIPC[2]		up to 50%[27]	
	TS	4%				
New York	T Dem-CIPC-Due From[5]	Same as FR except one percentage point lower on all deposit size categories	X	X[2]		
	TS	FR	X	X[2]		
North Carolina[1]	T Dem-US_d-SL_d	8% first $2 million, plus 10% $2-$10 million, plus 12% $10-$100 million, plus 13% $100-$400 million, plus 15% over $400 million	X	X[2]		CIPC
	S	3%	X	X[2]		CIPC
	T-US_t-SL_t	Maturing within 180 days: 3% first $5 million 6% over $5 million Maturing in 180 days or more: 3%	X	X[2]		CIPC
North Dakota	T Dem	8%	X	X[2]		
	TS	2%	X	X[2]		
Ohio	T Dem	7%	X	X		
	S	3%	at least 40%[28]		up to 60%[29]	
	T	Time deposits of $100,000 and over maturing in less than 6 months: 3% first $5 million 6% over $5 million Other time deposits: 3%				
Oklahoma	T Dem	FR	X	X[2]		CIPC
	TS	FR	X	X[2]		CIPC
Oregon	T Dem-US_d	12%	X	X[2]		CIPC
	TS-US_t	4%	X	X[2]	X[21]	CIPC
Pennsylvania	T Dem	12%	at least 50%[2]		up to 50%[30]	
	S	3%				
	T	3% first $5 million, plus 5% over $5 million				
Rhode Island[1]	T Dem-US_d	15%	X	(up to 60%)[2]	X[31]	
	(no reserve requirements on time and savings deposits)					

TABLE 4C:1
Continued

State	Deposits Subject to Reserve Requirements	Current Reserve Requirement Ratios	Reserve Assets Eligible to Meet Requirements: Vault Cash	Demand Balances Due from Banks	Securities	Other
South Carolina	T Dem	7%	X	X		CIPC[32]
	TS	3%	X	X		CIPC[32]
South Dakota[1]	T Dep-US_d-SL_d-US_t-SL_t	17.5%	(at least 40%)[2] [15]		(up to 60%)[13]	
Tennessee	T Dem	10%	X	X		Local CIPC
	TS	3%	X	X		
Texas	T Dem	15%	X	X[2]		CIPC
	TS	5%	X	X[2]		Time Deposits and CIPC[33]
Utah	T Dem	FR	X	X		
	TS	FR	X	X		
Vermont[1]	T Dem-US_d-SL_d	27%	X	X	X[34]	
	TS-US_t-SL_t	6.5%	X	X		
Virginia	T Dem-R_d	10%	X	X[11]		CIPC
	TS-R_t	3%	(at least 75%)[11] [15]		(up to 25%)[35]	
Washington	T Dem	7% first \$2 million, plus 9.5% \$2-\$10 million, plus 11.75% \$10-\$100 million, plus 12.75% \$100-\$400 million, plus 15% over \$400 million	X	X		CIPC
	TS	Maturing in 30-179 days: first \$5 million - 3% over \$5 million - 6% Maturing in over 4 years: 1% Other maturities: 3%	X	X		CIPC
West Virginia	T Dem	7%	at least 20%	X		CIPC
	TS	3%		X		CIPC

Wisconsin	T Dem			
	Reserve Banks[36]	20%	at least two-thirds	up to one-third[37]
	Other	12%		
	TS			
	Reserve Banks[36]	20%	at least five-twelfths	up to seven-twelfths[37]
	Other	12%		
Wyoming[1]	T Dem-US_d-SL_d	20%	at least 50%[2] [15]	up to 50%[38]
	TS-US_t-SL_t	10%		

[1]Exemption applies only to public deposits which are secured by pledged securities.
[2]Demand balances at approved depository banks.
[3]Unpledged U.S. Government securities maturing within six months.
[4]Cash items in the process of collection on insured local banks, where local banks are those domiciled in the same or immediately adjoining municipalities.
[5]Demand balances at banks other than approved depository banks.
[6]Unpledged negotiable direct U.S. Government obligations.
[7]U.S. Government bonds.
[8]Unsecured trust funds held as demand deposits due from other banks may not be counted as part of reserves.
[9]Unpledged debt obligations of the State, its political subdivisions, or the United States.
[10]If amount of deposit is in excess of 10 percent of depositing bank's capital and surplus, state must approve depository.
[11]Net of reciprocal deposits.
[12]Unpledged U.S. Government or agency obligations maturing within one year, or certificates of deposit maturing within one year. The maximum amount deposited with any one bank shall not exceed $100,000 or 10 percent of the depositing bank's reserve requirement, whichever is greater.
[13]Unpledged U.S. Government or agency obligations.
[14]Unpledged certificates of deposit not used to meet reserve requirements against demand deposits.
[15]Includes CIPC.
[16]Up to 25 percent of reserve requirements against demand deposits may be met with U.S. Government or agency obligations maturing within one year or certificates of deposit of any Kentucky bank.
[17]Certificates of deposit of any Kentucky bank.
[18]Up to one-half of required reserves may be met with unpledged direct U.S. Government obligations maturing within one year or obligations of the State of Louisiana maturing within two years, except that state obligations may account for no more than one-fourth of total required reserves.
[19]Unpledged U.S. Government or agency obligations maturing within one year.
[20]Debt obligations of the State, its political subdivisions, or the United States.
[21]Debt obligations of the State or the United States.
[22]Up to 30 percent of required reserves may be invested in direct obligations of the U.S. Treasury or other obligations fully guaranteed by the U.S. Government which mature within one year; a portion of the 30 percent maximum, not to exceed one-half, may be met with negotiable certificates of deposit issued by Mississippi banks which mature within one year.
[23]Up to 50 percent of required reserves may be invested in unpledged U.S. Government obligations maturing within five years and unpledged Federal funds sold to approved depositories.
[24]Nonmember banks designated as reserve depositories must maintain, in addition to the reserve requirements on all demand deposits, reserves of 10 percent on demand deposits due to other banks.
[25]Up to one-half of required reserves many be met with unpledged U.S. Government securities, at market value, or obligations of the Commodity Credit Corporation, at face value.
[26]U.S. Government obligations maturing within two years.

(Continued from previous page)

[27]Direct unpledged U.S. Government obligations maturing within 100 days.
[28]Of required reserves on time and savings deposits, 5 percent may consist of unassigned values of life insurance policies owned by the bank, covering the lives of directors, officers, or employees of the bank, under which the bank is sole beneficiary of the cash surrender value of the policy.
[29]Debt obligations issued, insured, or guaranteed by the United States.
[30]Debt obligations of the Commonwealth, its policy subdivisions, the United States, or other marketable obligations approved by the state banking authorities.
[31]U.S. Government or agency obligations maturing not more than 91 days from computation of reserves.
[32]Cash items collectible within 10 days.
[33]The reserve requirement on time and savings deposits may be met with time deposits at approved depositories.
[34]Of total required reserves, 40 percent must be in the form of vault cash, demand balances due from other commercial banks, and direct U.S. Government obligations maturing within one year. The remaining 60 percent may be held in U.S. Government or agency obligations of any maturity, and one-third of this 60 percent may be obligations of the State of Vermont.
[35]Unpledged U.S. Treasury obligations maturing within one year.
[36]Approved by state banking authorities as reserve bank.
[37]U.S. Government securities and general obligation bonds and notes of the State of Wisconsin maturing within 18 months.
[38]Unpledged U.S. Treasury bills.

Key to Coding

FR	Same as reserve requirements of Federal Reserve	SL_t	State and local government time deposits
T Dep	Total deposits	Due From	Demand deposits due from domestic commercial banks
T Dem	Total demand deposits	R_d	Reciprocal demand deposits
T	Time deposits	R_t	Reciprocal time deposits
S	Savings deposits	CIPC	Cash items in process of collection
US_d	U.S. Government demand deposits	TTL	Treasury tax and loan accounts
US_t	U.S. Government time deposits	NOW	Negotiable Orders of Withdrawal
SL_d	State and local government demand deposits	CD	Certificate of Deposit

counted as reserves. Nonmember banks may meet various proportions of their required reserves with earning assets in 22 states, with remaining shares of required reserves to be met with cash assets. In six states nonmember banks may meet all of their reserve requirements with interest-earning assets, generally unpledged U.S. Treasury securities or state and local government securities; therefore, they have no *cash* reserve requirement.

COMPARISON OF FEDERAL RESERVE AND STATE RESERVE REQUIREMENTS

Reserve requirement ratios are higher in some states than those for Federal Reserve member banks. However, reserve burdens of member banks relative to those of nonmembers cannot be determined just by comparing reserve requirements of the Federal Reserve to those of the various states because of several differences in the types of assets that are counted as reserves for members and nonmembers.

Nonmember banks may hold their cash reserves in the form of vault cash and demand balances at correspondents. Eighteen states allow nonmember banks to count cash items in the process of collection as reserves, and in other states many nonmember banks effectively count CIPC as reserves by classifying their uncollected funds as demand balances due from correspondents. Member banks, on the other hand, may hold their cash reserves only as vault cash and reserve balances at their Reserve Banks. Member bank reserve balances are only *collected* reserves since members receive credit to their reserve accounts for checks deposited with their Reserve Banks on a time schedule approximating the time required for collection of the checks.

Most member banks with total deposits up to about $50 million hold demand balances at correspondents almost as large as the demand balances held by nonmember banks of similar size. An important explanation of this behavior by member banks is that most of them in that size range make little use of Reserve Bank services, using those of correspondent banks instead.[4] As a result, member banks tend to hold substantially higher ratios of cash to total deposits than nonmembers of comparable size.

MONITORING AND ENFORCING RESERVE REQUIREMENTS

State reserve requirements have little relevance for banks unless states establish methods of monitoring the reserve positions of nonmember banks and forcing them to keep their reserves up to required levels. In the survey, state bank supervisors were asked to describe their methods of monitoring

[4] R. Alton Gilbert, "Utilization of Federal Reserve Bank Services by Member Banks: Implications for the Costs and Benefits of Membership," *Monthly Review*, Federal Reserve Bank of St. Louis (Aug. 1977): 2–15.

TABLE 4C:2

Enforcement of state reserve requirements

State	(1) Reserve Settlement Period	(2) Periodic Reports	(3) Penalty for Deficiencies	(4) Comments
Alabama	Weekly	None[1,2]	Federal Reserve discount rate plus 2 percent per annum on each $1,000 of average deficiency.	Penalties on reserve deficiencies became effective in December 1975. From then to April 1977, $6,000 in penalties were collected. The high deficiency rate was due to elimination of local clearings as reserve assets in December 1975.
Alaska	Reserves not averaged	None[1]	No dollar penalty.[5] Possible penalty for failure to keep records of reserve positions—$5,000.	
Arizona	Biweekly	Biweekly	No dollar penalty	
Arkansas	15 days	None[1]	8 percent per annum	Numerous reserve deficiencies were discovered during examinations prior to 8 percent penalty, but such occurrences have decreased since instituting the penalty.
California	Biweekly	Biweekly	Penalty rate ranges from 6 percent to 12 percent per annum depending upon size of deficiency relative to total deposits.[7]	
Colorado	Weekly	None[1]	No dollar penalty	
Connecticut	Semimonthly	None[3]	No dollar penalty[4,5,7]	
Delaware	Semimonthly	Semimonthly	No dollar penalty[7]	

Florida	30 days	None	No dollar penalty[5,7]	Reserve assets are compared to required reserves as of the examination date. If reserves are deficient that day, a 30 day average is calculated.
Georgia	Biweekly	None[1,2]	$50 per day for failure to notify state of deficiency.[4,5,7]	Violations of reserve requirements occur rarely.
Hawaii	Weekly	None[1]	No dollar penalty[4,7]	
Idaho	Biweekly	Biweekly	No dollar penalty[4,5]	A bank may not make additional loans while its reserves are deficient. This penalty would be imposed only after two warnings.
Indiana	Biweekly	None[1]	No dollar penalty[4,7]	
Iowa	5 days	None	$100 per day of reserve deficiencies.	Compliance with reserve requirements is checked as of examination period. Reserve deficiencies are infrequent and penalties are applied only as a last resort.
Kansas	None	None[1]	No dollar penalty[6,7]	
Kentucky	Biweekly	None[1]	No dollar penalty	
Louisiana	Semimonthly	None[1,2]	If reported deficiency in reserves is not restored within period satisfactory to state, or if state banking authorities discover unreported deficiency, penalty of 6 percent per annum may be imposed.	Reserve deficiencies do not occur frequently.

TABLE 4C:2
Continued

State	(1) Reserve Settlement Period	(2) Periodic Reports	(3) Penalty for Deficiencies	(4) Comments
Maine	Weekly	Weekly	Penalty at variable rate not to exceed 10 percent per annum; imposed when deficiency is greater than 2 percent of required reserves.[4]	
Maryland	Reserves not averaged	None. Reserve requirements are calculated on a day-to-day basis at the time of examination.	No dollar penalty. Continued violations can lead to removal of directors and officers of a bank.	
Massachusetts	Weekly	Weekly	No dollar penalty assessed for reserve deficiency. Penalty for not reporting deficiency is $1,000 per week or imprisonment for not more than one year.	
Michigan	Biweekly	Biweekly	No dollar penalty	Repeated reserve deficiencies could bring about a cease and desist order from the state. A penalty of $50 is assessed for not filing reports on reserve positions.
Minnesota	Biweekly	None[1]	For each biweekly period of reserve deficiency, penalty of $50 or 12 percent per annum on reserve deficiency, whichever is greater.	Penalties for reserve deficiencies assessed on 54 out of 547 nonmember banks in 1976.

Mississippi	Biweekly	None[1]	$50 tor each day a bank's reserves are deficient, unless covered by excess reserves in the previous or following biweekly period.	In recent history all reserve deficiencies have been covered by excess reserves in the previc .s or following biweekly periods.
Missouri	Weekly	None[1]	No dollar penalty[4,6]	
Montana	Weekly	None[1]	No dollar penalty[4]	Examinations disclose few reserve deficiencies, and most of those are of one week duration.
Nebraska	Weekly	None[1]	8 percent per annum on reserve deficiencies plus $5 per day of reserve deficiencies.[4,5,7]	
Nevada	15 days	None[1]	No dollar penalty	Excessive or continued deficiencies discovered during examinations are reported to bank management and Board of Directors. Banks have 60 days after examination to rectify reserve deficiencies.
New Hampshire	Reserves not averaged	None	No dollar penalty[4,5]	
New Jersey	Semimonthly	None[1]	No dollar penalty[6]	Violations of reserve requirements are infrequent.
New Mexico	Reserves not averaged	None.[2] Reserves are checked as of examination date.	If reserve deficiency is discovered as of examination date, the penalty is $100 per day while deficiency continues.	
New York	Weekly, with lagged reserve requirements and carry-over provision identical to that of the Federal Reserve	Weekly	Penalties range from 6 percent to 12 percent per annum, depending upon size of deficiency relative to deposit size of bank.	Penalties are not mandatory, but imposed only if a bank is deficient for two consecutive weeks.

TABLE 4C:2
Continued

State	(1) Reserve Settlement Period	(2) Periodic Reports	(3) Penalty for Deficiencies	(4) Comments
North Carolina	Biweekly	None[2]	No dollar penalty[4,5]	Penalties are not imposed with significant frequency.
North Dakota	Weekly	None[1]	If a bank is deficient in reserves as of examination date, it has 30 days to rectify, or the state may impose a penalty of $100 or 7 percent per annum on deficiency, whichever is greater.	
Ohio	Biweekly	None[2]	No dollar penalty[6,7]	
Oklahoma	Semimonthly	Semimonthly	After two consecutive periods of deficiency, penalty at rate of 2 percentage points per annum above the Federal Reserve discount rate is assessed.	In 1976, 13 penalties were assessed on 7 banks. Penalties may be waived, but this is rarely done, except for penalties under $25.
Oregon	Reserves not averaged	None[1]	If bank has a reserve deficiency on any day, it has three days to eliminate the deficiency, or a penalty is assessed. The penalty rate is 2 percentage points per annum above the Federal Reserve discount rate.	

Pennsylvania	Biweekly	None[1,2]	No penalty for reserve deficiency, but a $50 fine assessed per day for not reporting a deficiency within three days.	
Rhode Island	Weekly	Semiannually	No dollar penalty[4,5,7]	
South Carolina	Reserves not averaged	None[1]	No dollar penalty	Very few reserve deficiencies found by examiners.
South Dakota	Weekly	None[1]	$50 per day of reserve deficiency	Very few penalties each year.
Tennessee	Weekly	None[1]	No dollar penalty[4,5,7]	
Texas	Weekly	None[1]	Three grace periods per year, fine of $50 for fourth weekly period of reserve deficiency, with fines increasing up to $500 per period for 10 or more periods of reserve deficiency.	
Utah	Biweekly	None[1,3]	No dollar penalty[4,7]	No record for penalties for reserve deficiencies ever having been imposed.
Vermont	Reserves not averaged	None[3]	No dollar penalty	Only occasionally are banks found to have reserve deficiencies.
Virginia	Biweekly	None[1]	No dollar penalty	Violations of reserve requirements could be punishable as a misdemeanor. State banking authority is not aware of the penalty ever having been imposed.

TABLE 4C:2
Continued

State	(1) Reserve Settlement Period	(2) Periodic Reports	(3) Penalty for Deficiencies	(4) Comments
Washington	Semimonthly	None[1,2]	Penalty is $100 per reserve settlement period of deficiency or prime rate plus 2 percentage points times average deficiency, whichever is smaller.	In 1976, 11 fines were imposed.
West Virginia	Biweekly	Biweekly	Penalty rate is 2 percentage points per annum above Federal Reserve discount rate.[4]	In 1975, 19 penalties imposed for reserve deficiencies, in 1976, 38 penalties imposed.
Wisconsin	Biweekly	None[1]	If bank does not make up deficiency within 30 days after notice from state, a fine of $100 for each biweekly period of reserve deficiency may be imposed.[4,7]	Violations occur infrequently, and no penalties have been imposed during the past 15 years.
Wyoming	Biweekly	Biweekly	No dollar penalty[4,5,7]	

[1]Records of reserve positions must be kept by banks for inspection by examiners.
[2]Banks must report reserve deficiencies to state shortly after deficiencies occur.
[3]Reserve are checked at time of examination. Spot checks are made for periods between examinations.
[4]Making loans is restricted during periods of reserve deficiency.
[5]Declaring dividends is restricted during periods of reserve deficiency.
[6]Banks with reserve deficiencies may be forced to comply with reserve requirements through cease and desist orders.
[7]Continued failure to comply with reserve requirements can lead to liquidation of the bank by the state.

and enforcing reserve requirements. Their responses are presented in Table 4C:2. This information does not indicate whether state reserve requirements actually influence behavior of nonmember banks, but is presented to fill a void in information available on state reserve requirements.

One aspect of reserve requirements presented in Column (1) is reserve settlement periods, that is, the periods over which reserves and deposit liabilities are averaged in determining whether banks are meeting their reserve requirements. Half of the states have either two-week or semimonthly reserve settlement periods, while 15 states have weekly reserve settlement periods. Eight supervisors indicated that either reserves of nonmember banks in their states are not averaged or no reserve settlement period is specified. In such states examiners determine a bank's reserve assets and required reserves as of the examination date. If a bank's reserves are not adequate as of that day, some states then average reserves held and required reserves over longer periods of time. Other states give the bank a specified period of time to bring their reserves up to required levels.

Monitoring procedures are described in Column (2) of Table 4C:2. In 11 states nonmember banks are required to file reports with their supervisors on daily reserves and deposit liabilities at the end of each reserve settlement period. In 28 other states banks are required to keep such records for inspection by state bank examiners, but do not send reports on reserve positions to their supervisors. Eight states require banks to send notice of reserve deficiencies to their supervisors within a few days after reserve settlement periods in which such deficiencies occur. States generally impose fines on banks which do not send such notices.

One of the ways states enforce reserve requirements is to impose dollar penalties for reserve deficiencies; 19 states now do this. Information on those penalties is presented in Column (3) of Table 4C:2. Some supervisors indicated that in their states dollar penalties are seldom imposed, either because their banks seldom have reserve deficiencies or because penalties are often waived. However, other supervisors indicated that penalties are imposed often in their states, giving specific frequencies and total dollar amounts.

States that do not have dollar penalties for reserve deficiencies generally have other enforcement powers. The most common non-dollar penalties are prohibitions on making loans or paying dividends while banks have reserve deficiencies. Also, in 14 states bank supervisors have authority to declare banks with reserve deficiencies unsound and to close them. The supervisors indicated that these nondollar penalties are seldom imposed.

SUMMARY

The reasons most commonly given for declining Federal Reserve membership deal with the level and form of reserve requirements on Federal Reserve member banks relative to those imposed by states on nonmember banks. Upon examination, however, comparisons of reserve requirements of member and nonmember banks are difficult. Deposits subject to reserve requirements differ between the Federal Reserve and state banking agencies, and among states. The periods over which reserve accounts must be settled also vary among states, from weekly (as with the Federal Reserve) to monthly periods (as in one state).

APPENDIX D–VARIATIONS ON A THEME

A number of ways exist to combine a money multiplier and a monetary base in order to produce a given money supply. The choice of any particular combination depends upon the uses that will be made of it. In this appendix three formulations, alternative to the one derived in this chapter, are set forth, and each is briefly discussed in terms of its possible use.

I. THE RESERVE ADJUSTMENT FORMULATION

To derive the reserve adjustment multiplier, it will be assumed that all deposits are subject to one reserve requirement, r, set by the Federal Reserve and made applicable to all depository institutions.

Whenever the Federal Reserve changes the reserve requirement, it changes the value of the money multiplier, computed as in this chapter. However, when it adds reserves directly to DIs, it alters the monetary base. Among others, two economists, Karl Brunner and Allan Meltzer, have thought it desirable to confine to the monetary base all actions taken by the central bank, and to confine to the multiplier all actions affecting the money supply that do not have their origin in central bank activity. In order to make this separation, they propose that when reserve requirements are changed, the equivalent of the increase or decrease in reserves be added to or subtracted from the monetary base and an appropriate neutralizing adjustment be made to the multiplier.

In terms of the formulas developed in this chapter, the separation can be accomplished by adding to the monetary base B a sum designated as RA to indicate the reserve adjustment, that is, the addition to the base that would have the same effect on the money supply as would the reduction in the reserve requirement. To incorporate the adjustment into the formula, it will be assumed that RA is some constant proportion of demand deposits, or $RA = aD$.

Now the money supply formulas can be derived as in the four cases set forth in this chapter:

$$B + RA = LR_D + C + RA \qquad (4D{:}1)$$

$$
\begin{aligned}
RA &= aD \\
LR_D &= rD \\
C &= c'D \\
B + RA &= rD + c'D + aD \\
&= D(r + c' + a)
\end{aligned}
$$

$$(B + RA)\left(\frac{1}{r + c' + a}\right) = D \tag{4D:2}$$

Defining the money supply as *M-1B* yields

$$
\begin{aligned}
M\text{-}1B &= D + C \\
&= D + c'D \\
&= D(1 + c')
\end{aligned}
$$

Substituting from Equation (4D:2) the equivalents for D gives

$$M\text{-}1B = (B + RA)\left(\frac{1 + c'}{r + c' + a}\right) \tag{4D:3}$$

As an example, suppose that initially we have the following values for the variables in Equation (4D:3): $B = \$100$, $r = .25$, $c' = .25$, $RA = 0$, and hence, $a = 0$. The money supply is then \$250. Now, let the reserve requirements be reduced from .25 to .15. As a result, the money supply will rise to \$312.50. The same effect could have been produced by keeping r at .25 and increasing the base from \$100 to \$125.

According to Brunner and Meltzer, the reduction in reserve requirements would be handled by allowing RA to rise from 0 to \$25. The money supply would remain at \$312.50, of which \$250 would be demand deposits (\$312.50 $= D + c'D$ or $1.25D$). Since RA is \$25 and D is \$250, the value of $a = .10$. Thus, in Equation (4D:3) we have

$$
\begin{aligned}
M\text{-}1B &= (\$100 + \$25)\left(\frac{1 + .25}{.15 + .25 + .10}\right) \\
&= \$125\left(\frac{1.25}{.50}\right) \\
M\text{-}1B &= \$312.50
\end{aligned}
$$

The value of a is allowed to rise to offset the decline in the value of r. The multiplier remains unchanged and the change in the reserve requirement shows up as a change in RA, or what Brunner and Meltzer call the extended monetary base.[1]

II. THE UNBORROWED RESERVE FORMULATION

Since depository institutions have the privilege of borrowing reserves from the Federal Reserve, a number of economists believe that to measure the contribution of the base and the multiplier to the money supply accurately, the base should not contain borrowed reserves. If BR stands for borrowed reserves, the money supply can be derived in the usual fashion:

$$B - BR = LR_D + C - BR \tag{4D:4}$$

If BR is assumed to be a constant fraction, b, of demand deposits, D, Equation (4D:4) can be expressed as

$$\begin{aligned} B - BR &= rD + c'D - bD \\ &= D(r + c' - b) \\ (B - BR)\left(\frac{1}{r + c' - b}\right) &= D \end{aligned}$$

Given the M-$1B$ definition of money as

$$M\text{-}1B = D + C$$

appropriate substitutions and factoring yield

$$M\text{-}1B = (B - BR)\left(\frac{1 + c'}{r + c' - b}\right) \tag{4D:5}$$

In this situation, if DIs borrow reserves, the effect on the money supply is confined exclusively to the multiplier. This is because reserve borrowing causes both B and BR to rise by the same amount, so that $\Delta B - \Delta BR$ is zero. However, the ratio $b = BR/D$ rises. Since b enters the denominator of the multiplier negatively, it increases the value of the multiplier and the

[1] For recent work on the U.S. money stock and money multiplier that makes use of this approach, see A. E. Burger and R. H. Rasche, "Revisions of the Monetary Base," *Monthly Review*, Federal Reserve Bank of St. Louis (July 1977): 13–28.

money supply, exactly as would have been the case had BR and b not been in the formulation.

III. UNBORROWED RESERVES AND RESERVE ADJUSTMENT

The third and final formulation of the money supply combines the two given above. Thus, to derive the money supply, the initial formulation is given as

$$(B - BR + RA) = rD + c'D + aD - bD$$
$$= D(r + c' + a - b) \qquad (4D{:}6)$$
$$(B - BR + RA)\left(\frac{1}{r + c' + a - b}\right) = D$$

and hence, $M\text{-}1B = D + C$,

$$M\text{-}1B = (B - BR + RA)\left(\frac{1 + c'}{r + c' + a - b}\right) \qquad (4D{:}7)$$

In this formulation changes in borrowed reserves are confined to the multiplier, whereas changes in the reserve requirements are confined to the adjusted or extended monetary base.

Which method is used to partition the increase in the money supply among the variables contributing to it depends in large part on the problem at hand and the preferences of the investigator.

5 THE ECONOMIC ROLE OF NONMONEY-CREATING FINANCIAL INTERMEDIARIES

In Chapter 3 the principal financial intermediaries in the United States were described and their most recent balance sheets presented in order to examine the process of financial intermediation and to note the degree to which institutions indulge in specialized forms of lending.

Until the late 1970s an analytical distinction was made between commercial banks and other similar deposit-type financial intermediaries, such as savings and loan associations and mutual savings banks. The basis of this distinction was that only commercial banks could supply demand deposits, the principal means of payment. With the recent major changes in the legal and regulatory structure governing financial institutions, this distinction is no longer warranted. Other depository institutions are now virtually indistinguishable from commercial banks in the type of services they offer and the deposits they supply to the public. For that reason, the *M*-1*B* measure of the money supply was selected for use in this text. However, suppose that *M*-1*A* measure had been chosen instead. How, then, would one account for the activities of savings and loans, mutual savings banks, and credit unions? That is, once the deposits of these institutions are excluded from the definition of money, what variable or variables measure the effect of their lending activities? The discussion to follow will be concerned with this issue. It will also provide a useful frame of reference with which to understand new innovations in domestic and international monetary systems. It will also enable us to comprehend the significance of a long controversy in monetary economics over the uniqueness of commercial banks.

It has been customary to refer to the deposit-type financial intermediaries other than commercial banks as thrift institutions or thrifts. We will use this distinction in our discussion. Before we examine the implications of using the *M*-1*A* definition, let us examine the nature, significance, and reasons for the legal and regulatory changes and how they tend to blur the once sharp distinction between commercial banks and thrifts.

RECENT DEVELOPMENTS ALTERING THE FUNCTIONS OF FINANCIAL INTERMEDIARIES

We have noted in several places that the structure and function of financial intermediaries in the United States are undergoing a rapid transition both in response to technological change and in order to avoid the disruptive effects of the disintermediation brought on by the interest rate ceilings embodied in Regulation Q. A more comprehensive discussion of these changes is given below; let us for the present note the nature of these changes. They involve an effort on the part of thrift institutions to participate fully in the system of making payments for goods and services, hitherto monopolized by the commercial banks. Table 5:1 sets out chronologically these major institutional changes.

The changes listed in Table 5:1 accomplished four major alterations in the character of the public's monetary assets:

1. They expanded the number of instruments that can be used for making payments, and in the process they broadened the range of financial intermediaries that can participate in the payments process.
2. They increased the liquidity of savings accounts by making it possible in some instances to make transactions using savings account balances.
3. They *tended* to decrease the liquidity of time deposits by allowing institutions to offer longer-term deposits and to impose a higher penalty for early withdrawal. On the other hand, they allowed institutions to offer six-month money market certificates at rates of interest competitive with those paid by the U.S. government when it borrows for a similar term.
4. They expanded the range of liquid assets available to certain customers.

In order to highlight these changes, the information on Table 5:1 is rearranged and shown in Table 5:2.

Why have these developments occurred?

There is but one basic reason to account for these developments: they are an innovational response to the disruptive effects of disintermediation. Since disintermediation occurs, basically, because of the restrictions of Regulation Q, these new practices represent the market's response to government regulations.

The regulated thrift institutions (mutual savings banks and savings and loan associations) have attempted to gain access to funds hitherto available only to commercial banks in an effort to stabilize their overall flow of funds. Since this action involves attracting demand deposit funds, commercial banks have been forced to offer similar services in order to avoid a

TABLE 5:1
Selected regulatory and institutional changes

Date	Commercial Banks	Other Financial Institutions
Sept. 1970		Savings and loan associations (S&Ls) are permitted to make preauthorized non-negotiable transfers from savings accounts for household-related expenses.
June 1972		Massachusetts mutual savings banks (MSBs) begin to offer Negotiable Order of Withdrawal (NOW) accounts.
Sept. 1972		New Hampshire MSBs begin to offer NOW accounts.
Jan. 1974	All depository institutions in Massachusetts and New Hampshire (except credit unions) are authorized by congressional actions to offer NOW accounts. This action limited interest-bearing negotiable deposits to these two states. Thus, interest-bearing negotiable transfer accounts at banks begin on an experimental basis.	
Jan. 1974		Nebraska S&L begins Point-of-Sale (POS) electronic funds transfer system. First Federal S&L of Lincoln, Nebr., places an electronic terminal in a "Hinky Dinky Supermarket." The terminal allows customers of the S&L to pay for groceries, make deposits to, or withdrawals from, their savings accounts.
Apr. 1974	State of Washington enacts legislation that allows state-chartered commercial banks, MSBs, S&Ls to establish any number of automated facilities throughout the state, provided that those operating these facilities share the cost and operations of the terminals when asked to do so by the state authorities. Commercial banks are required to share facilities with other commercial banks and have the option of sharing them with thrift institutions. Thrifts are permitted, but not required, to share facilities.	
May 1974		Experimental 24-hour electronic facility opens on a shared basis by 15 Washington MSBs and S&Ls.
June 1974		New York State bank regulation permits MSB to offer non-interest-bearing NOW accounts (NINOWs).

TABLE 5:1
Continued

Date	Commercial Banks	Other Financial Institutions
Aug. 1974		Administrator of the National Credit Union Administration grants 3 federal credit unions temporary authority to begin offering share drafts. These 3 credit unions were joined by 2 state credit unions in a 6-month pilot program (launched Oct. 1974).
Sept. 1974		Pennsylvania attorney general rules MSB may legally offer a form of negotiable order of withdrawal account.
Dec. 1974	Comptroller of the Currency's interpretive ruling permits national banks to operate Customer-Bank Communication Terminals (CBCTs).	Federal Home Loan Bank Board (FHLBB) adopts a regulation that gives depositors traveling more than 50 miles from their homes access to their savings account balances through any other federally insured S&L by means of a Travelers Convenience Withdrawal (wire or telephone access).
Jan. 1975		California state-chartered S&L offers Variable Rate Mortgages (VRMs). Minnesota MSB introduces Pay-by-Phone service.
Apr. 1975	Commercial banks are authorized to make transfers from a customer's savings account to a demand deposit account upon telephone order from the customer.	FHLBB adopts two regulations: 1. Authorizes Federal S&Ls to offer their customers bill-paying service from interest-bearing savings accounts. 2. Allows Federal S&L service corporations and companies to make consumer loans (limited to states that allow such activity and subject to state restrictions).
May 1975	CBCT operated exclusively by a national bank is subjected to a 50-mile geographical restriction unless CBCT is available to be shared with one or more deposit institutions. A national bank may use a CBCT established and operated by some other institution and may participate in a statewide EFTS system.	

June 1975		Oregon governor signs into law legislation that allows the state's only MSB to offer checking accounts.
June 31, 1975	U.S. District Court Judge Robinson rules CBCTs authorized for national banks by the Comptroller of the Currency are illegal and must be shut down. (About 72 CBCTs, owned by national banks, have been installed in various parts of the country under the interpretive ruling issued by Comptroller Dec. 12, 1974.) Robinson's decision directly attacks the Dec. 12, 1974 interpretation, calling the terminals branches, both as defined by the U.S. Supreme Court in its 1969 Plant City case and as construed by Congress when it passed the McFadden Act in 1928.	
Sept. 1975	Commercial banks are authorized to make preauthorized non-negotiable transfers from a customer's saving account for any purpose. Previously (since 1962), such transfers were limited to mortgage-related payments.	Massachusetts MSB introduces VRM program.
Oct. 1975		State legislation permits state-chartered thrift institutions in Maine to offer personal checking accounts.
Nov. 1975	Federal Reserve amends definition of savings deposits in Regulations D and Q to permit business savings accounts, up to $150,000, at member banks.	
Dec. 1975		State legislation permits thrift institutions in Connecticut to offer personal checking accounts. While the authority to offer share drafts was still officially temporary, additional credit unions begin to offer share draft accounts following the end of the 6-month pilot program initiated in fall 1974. As of years end, 222 credit unions (roughly 1%) in 44 states approved to offer share drafts to their shareholders.

TABLE 5:1
Continued

Date	Commercial Banks	Other Financial Institutions
Jan. 1976		Federal Reserve System adopts a policy for automated check clearing systems (ACHs) to offer their services on a nondiscriminatory basis to all types of financial institutions. Illinois S&Ls begin offering non-interest-bearing NOW accounts.
Feb. 1976		Congress authorizes all depository institutions in New England to offer interest-paying NOW accounts (effective Mar. 1, 1976). New York governor signs legislation permitting checking accounts, including overdraft privileges, at state-chartered MSBs and S&Ls.
May 1976	U.S. Court of Appeals for the District of Columbia upholds earlier ruling by the U.S. District Court for the District of Columbia that national banks' CBCTs are branches under the McFadden Act.	
Oct. 4, 1976	U.S. Supreme Court lets stand ruling that CBCTs are bank branches.	
Feb. 14, 1977	Iowa statewide electronic banking system begins operating and represents the nation's first shared statewide network, encompassing a broad range of large and small banks in Iowa. (At last count, the system had 33 participating banks; 92 merchant terminals operate through a switch or central computer).	
Apr. 1977		All but 15 of the nation's 470 MSBs have either NOW accounts, traditional checking accounts, or a combination of the two. Legislation enacted to expand credit union lending authority, including authority to make 30-year mortgage loans.
Nov. 1978	All federally insured banks are authorized to make automatic transfers from saving to demand deposit accounts to cover deficiences. All depository institutions in New York State authorized to offer NOW accounts.	

Mar. 31, 1980	U.S. Congress provides that all depository institutions may offer interest earning NOW accounts to individuals and non-profit organizations, after Dec. 31, 1980.	All S&Ls may use remote service units. All federally insured credit unions may offer immediately share drafts. All federal credit unions are authorized to make real estate loans. All federally chartered S&Ls are given permission to hold a broader portfolio of assets, issue credit cards and engage in trust activities.

TABLE 5:2
Chronology of developments in the 1970s affecting the character of the public's monetary assets

I. Developments leading to new transactions instruments

June 1972: State-chartered MSBs began offering negotiable orders of withdrawal (NOWs) accounts in Massachusetts.

Sept. 1972: State-chartered MSBs began offering NOWs in New Hampshire.

Jan. 1974: Depository institutions in Massachusetts and New Hampshire authorized to offer NOWs.

Oct. 1974: Temporary experimental share draft programs first approved for federal CUs.

Mar. 1976: Depository institutions in Connecticut, Maine, Rhode Island, and Vermont authorized to offer NOWs.

May 1976: State-chartered MSBs and S&Ls in New York State authorized to offer consumer demand deposits. (Prior to this time they could offer payment orders of withdrawal (POW) deposits. In addition, thrift institutions in some states have been permitted to offer non-interest-earning transactions balances to households. State-chartered S&Ls in Illinois, for example, have been able to offer non-interest-bearing negotiable orders of withdrawal (NINOWs) accounts since Oct. 1975.)

Mar. 1978: Final regulations for permanent share draft programs at federal CUs became effective.

Nov. 1978: Depository institutions in New York State authorized to offer NOWs.

Nov. 1978: Federal Home Loan Bank Board proposed authorizing federally chartered S&Ls to offer payment order accounts (POAs). (See also Nov. 1978 in **II.** below.)

Mar. 1980: Congress grants all depository institutions (CBs, S&L, MSBs, CUs) the right to offer interest earning NOW accounts after Dec. 31, 1980. S&Ls also may use remote service units and federally chartered CUs may issue share drafts immediately.

II. Developments increasing liquidity of savings accounts

Sept. 1970: S&Ls permitted to make preauthorized non-negotiable transfers from savings accounts for household-related expenditures.

Jan. 1974: Point-of-sale (POS) terminals permitting remote withdrawal of deposits from savings balances at S&Ls allowed.

Apr. 1975: Telephone transfers from savings balances at CBs permitted. (Telephone transfers from savings balances at thrift institutions have been allowed since the 1960s.)

Apr. 1975: S&Ls permitted to make preauthorized third-party non-negotiable transfers from savings accounts for any purpose.

Sept. 1975: CBs permitted to make preauthorized third-party non-negotiable transfers from savings accounts for any purpose.

Nov. 1978: Prearranged automatic transfer services (ATS) from savings balances at CBs and thrifts having transactions balances authorized.

III. Developments expanding liquid investment alternatives available

Early 1974: Money market mutual funds came into existence on a large-scale basis. (These funds, which invest in money market instruments, allow their shareholders to redeem shares by checks drawn on accounts established at designated banks, by wire transfer, or by mail.)

TABLE 5:2 *Continued*

Nov. 1974: Savings accounts at CBs for domestic government units permitted.
Nov. 1975: Savings accounts at CBs for businesses, up to $150,000 per account per customer, permitted.

IV. Developments affecting nature of time deposits

Jan. 1970: Increase in interest rate ceilings on 2½-year deposit approved.
June 1970: Interest rate ceilings on time deposits of $100,000 or more maturing in less than 90 days suspended.
May 1973: Interest rate ceilings on time deposits of $100,000 or more maturing in 90 days or more suspended.
July 1973: Increase in interest rate ceilings on 4-year deposit approved.
July 1973: Substantial penalty on early withdrawal of time deposits imposed.
July 1973: Interest rate ceilings on multiple maturity time deposits of $100,000 or more suspended.
Dec. 1974: Increase in interest rate ceilings on 6-year deposit approved.
June 1978: Increase in interest rate ceilings on 8-year deposit approved.
June 1978: 6-month money market certificates with ceiling rate tied to 6-month Treasury bill rate authorized.

CBs: commercial banks; CUs: credit unions; MSBs: mutual savings banks; S&Ls: savings and loan associations.

reduction in relative size and importance. Thus, banks have contrived ways to pay explicit interest on demand deposits.

Additionally, the form in which the thrifts are able to make these transfers of funds from one account to another has been aided by technology. Increasingly, the use of paper instruments to transfer funds is giving way to the use of computers (see Chapter 15 for a comprehensive discussion of this innovation).

As we noted in Chapter 3, federal regulators are slowly dismantling Regulation Q. Large-denomination ($100,000 and above) negotiable certificates of deposit are no longer (since 1973) subject to interest rate ceilings; depository institutions can now offer six-month saving certificates (in minimum deonominations of $10,000) that match the rate paid by the Treasury on the short-term funds it borrows; and commercial banks, by using automatic transfer from savings, can now pay what is in essence explicit interest on demand deposits, for certain classes of customers.

The effect of the institutional changes

These changes to the structure of money-creating institutions have been significant. However, domestic monetary systems underwent similar changes in the past, though not quite so rapidly. The principal change in days gone by came with the growth of commercial banks. Their liabilities, either in the form of their own notes or deposits, came to supersede gold and silver as the dominant means for making transactions. Then, as now, the question arose as to the proper definition of money. Ultimately, it was settled by broadening the definition to include the means of payment supplied by commercial banks. The same issue arose when various thrifts were granted the power to supply deposits that could be used to make transactions. The Federal Reserve responded by redefining M_1, M_2, and M_3 to recognize the broadened group of assets that are transactions media and the growing difference between savings and time deposits. No doubt the future will bring further changes.

THE HISTORICAL CONCERN WITH THRIFT INSTITUTIONS

For many years the Federal Reserve defined one measure of the money supply as consisting of the demand deposits liabilities of commercial banks and currency in the hands of the public. This measure was designated M_1 and corresponds very closely to what is now designated M-1A.

Both definitions exclude the deposits of thrift institutions from the money stock. Nevertheless, economists using these definitions have long been mindful that the thrifts may have significant effects on overall economic activity and therefore important implications for monetary policy.

Interest in the thrifts arose primarily because economists believed that they were capable of influencing the aggregate flow of money spending. Obviously, it would be a waste of time and effort to concentrate monetary policy on control of the commercial banks' ability to create money if nonbank intermediaries could exert an independent influence on total spending. Under such circumstances, the amount of money spending would be independent of the money supply and control of money spending would necessitate control over the credit-creating powers of the thrift institutions.

Thus, our first task will be to see how the thrifts can influence the flow of credit and money spending. To accomplish this, we will assume that the money stock is measured on an M-1A basis. Indeed, this is how one would analyze the economic effect of thrifts using the old M_1 definition. Our analysis will provide us with a frame of reference with which to evaluate the economic effects of financial intermediaries whose liabilities are presently excluded from M-1B (for example, see the discussion of Eurodollar banks in Chapter 17).

Credit creation by thrift institutions

A demand deposit transfer

The ability of the thrift institutions to influence the flow of money spending depends upon their ability to attract a *primary deposit*. This is a deposit that comes from outside the thrift system, that is, from a commercial bank or from currency held by the public. The primary deposit is emphasized quite simply because if one thrift institution attracts a deposit from another thrift institution, the ability of the thrift institutions as a group to expand credit remains unchanged. This ability to expand credit only on the basis of a primary deposit holds true for commercial banks as well. In order to expand credit and the money supply, they must have a net addition to their reserves as a group.[1] This can only come about through the deposit of currency or an asset swap with the central bank, whereby the commercial banks sell an asset or discount one at the Federal Reserve and obtain in exchange an increase in their reserves.

In order to demonstrate the potential power of the thrift institutions to increase the flow of credit, the commercial banking system will be assumed to be all loaned up (which means the banks have no reserves to lend out).

If all the balance sheets of the commercial banks are added together, the result would be what is known as a *consolidated balance sheet*. If these banks were fully loaned up, the hypothetical consolidated balance sheet might appear as Table 5:3.

Suppose now that the owner of a demand deposit transfers it from a commercial bank to a savings deposit at a thrift institution. Before the thrift balance sheet is examined, the disposition of the check by the thrift institution must be explained. Since the thrift institution exists to make loans, it must hold its lending power in the means of exchange—either demand deposits in commercial banks or currency. Similarly, it must hold reserves in the means of payment in order to honor withdrawals of deposits made by its depositors. Since holding large quantities of currency for this purpose would require expensive vaults (not to mention increasing the risks of robbery), thrift institutions are inclined to hold the vast majority of their reserves as simple demand deposits in commercial banks. Thus, the commercial banking system literally serves as the depository for the reserves of the nonbank intermediaries. When the thrift institutions come into possession of a check from someone making a deposit, they will probably return a substantial portion, if not all, of the check as a net addition to their reserves, held as a commercial bank demand deposit.

TABLE 5:3
Consolidated balance sheet of the commercial banking system

Reserves:		Deposits:	
Demand (20%)	$ 200	Demand	$1000
Time (10%)	100	Savings	1000
Loans	1700		
TOTAL ASSETS	$2000	TOTAL LIABILITIES	$2000

[1] Here the different reserve requirements for different thrift institutions and different classes of commercial banks are ignored.

While this purchase of a savings deposit in the thrifts only changes the ownership of the demand deposits at commercial banks without altering their total, it serves to increase the lending capacity of the thrift institutions—it is a primary deposit for them. Their consolidated balance sheet would appear as Table 5:4. The balance sheet of the banks would be unchanged from Table 5:3.

Since the thrift institutions are in business to make profits, they will not wish to hold the entire $100 as reserves. Rather, they will prefer to lend the money out by purchasing an asset—perhaps a home mortgage. The individual from whom the mortgage is purchased will receive a check drawn against the thrift institutions' account at some commercial bank. The purchase of the home mortgage expands credit without expanding the supply of money and it allows total money spending to rise as well.

The disposition made of the check by its recipient (who sold the mortgage to the bank) is of crucial importance for the continuation of the credit-creation process. If the check is redeposited in a thrift institution, the credit-creation process will continue, just as the money-creation process examined in Chapter 4 continued in Case I for depository institutions when their reserves were augmented by the monetary authority. As in that case, credit creation by the thrift institutions will end when the initial primary deposit is totally absorbed into their required reserves. However, historical experience showed that the thrift institutions were not so fortunate as commercial banks, for individuals and business seemed to have marginal preferences for placing deposits in these institutions. That is, they were more likely to deposit their receipts in commercial banks than in thrift institutions. Thus, the recipient of the check would probably deposit it in the commercial banking system. This loss by the thrift institutions of a deposit back to the banking system is analogous to the loss of a deposit by the commercial banks to currency in circulation. In each case, the ability to further expand deposits and the flow of credit comes to an end.

Nevertheless, to the extent that thrift institutions could attract demand deposits from commercial banks, they could expand the flow of credit without, at the same time, having any effect on commercial bank credit and the money supply.

One should be careful to note an additional aspect of this example. The activities of the thrift institutions in attracting away from commercial banks a deposit that is then lent to others represents an additional level of intermediation. The original act of intermediation occurred when the com-

TABLE 5:4
Consolidated balance sheet of thrift institutions

Reserves:			
Bank deposits	$100	Savings deposits	$100

mercial banks created the demand deposit. When the thrifts attracted this deposit and increased their loans, an additional or higher level of intermediation took place. Hence, a basic economic effect of thrift institutions is to enable an economy to increase the aggregate flow of credit through higher levels of intermediation.

A savings deposit transfer

A savings deposit held at a commercial bank was thought more likely to be transferred to a thrift institution than a demand deposit, for a savings deposit appeared to be a closer substitute for the saving-type deposits long offered by these institutions, i.e., both types of deposits have similar characteristics and, unlike demand deposits, have not been a means of payment.

In the case of a savings deposit transfer from the banks to the thrift institutions, the analysis becomes more complicated, for the thrift institutions will certainly transfer the savings deposit back to the commercial banks as a demand deposit. Since the reserve requirements for these two classes of deposits are unequal, the commercial banks will probably develop a reserve deficiency, forcing them to contract the money supply and the flow of bank credit.

A deposit of currency

As a third and final example, individuals will be assumed to withdraw currency from circulation and deposit it with the thrift institutions.

As with the two previous cases, this primary deposit increases the lending capacity of these institutions and the potential flow of credit. However, depending upon the disposition of the currency, this case is likely to be markedly more expansionary. Its expansionary potential becomes obvious when the thrift institutions transfer a considerable portion of the currency deposit to the banking system to add to their reserves. The commercial banks will now be the recipient of a primary deposit, which will augment their lending and deposit-creating capability.[2] Since both sets of institutions have, in effect, been recipients of primary deposits, the total flow of credit or loanable funds should be greater than for the two cases analyzed previously.

Left unanswered thus far is the question of what determines the ability of the thrift institutions to attract primary deposits. This ability is obviously related to the rate of interest they pay on their deposits relative to the rate

[2] In terms of a money multiplier, the effect would be seen as a fall in the currency/demand deposit ratio that, by reducing the denominator of the multiplier, increases its magnitude and the money supply.

paid by commercial banks and the rates available on various types of securities that individuals can hold as substitutes. Since thrift deposits are by convention payable on demand, the thrifts must in general compete with other short-term borrowers to attract funds. Thus, the short-term interest rates are an important measure of the competitive price that the thrift institutions must meet or exceed to increase their flow of primary deposits. Their ability to meet these rates is, in turn, governed by the earnings on their assets, and these earnings are related to the long-term interest rates prevailing when the assets were acquired. A notable exception occurs in the case of money market mutual funds. As the difference between the long- and short-term interest rates closes, institutions such as the thrifts that lend at long term and borrow at short term have a decreased ability to attract deposits. Also, it must be remembered that commercial banks do not remain passive as they see their deposits lost to the thrift institutions. In an attempt to retain the funds deposited with them, they raise their savings deposit rate as much as possible. In the administration of Regulation Q, the monetary authorities allow the thrift institutions a 0.25% advantage over banks on most savings and time deposits. Thus, the banks may be at a slight disadvantage in competing for funds.

Certain characteristics of their balance sheets are also relevant in examining the ability of the thrift institutions to attract deposits. As explained in Chapter 3, commercial bank assets are, on the whole, more liquid than those of the thrift institutions. While this means that commercial banks may earn less overall, a more liquid asset structure gives them greater flexibility in managing their investments, which can improve their profit positions in the shorter run and thereby give them greater power to attract and retain funds.

Considerations such as these must be taken into account when one examines the ability of the thrift institutions to attract deposits from the banking system or from individuals holding idle currency.

The above three examples have been constructed on the basis of the historic relationship of thrifts to commercial banks. The first two examples demonstrated that the activities of the thrifts can be viewed as representing advanced stages of intermediation, which serve to augment the aggregate flow of credit made available to the economy.

These examples are relevant in a world such as ours today in which the distinction between commercial banks and thrifts has become blurred. As will be seen in Chapter 17, the relationship of Eurodollar banks to U.S financial institutions is identical to the historic relationship of thrifts to commercial banks. That is, Eurodollar banks represent advanced stages of intermediation that serve to increase the flow of credit throughout the world economy. This anaylsis is also relevant to the relationship of money market mutual funds to depository institutions. These funds represent advanced stages of intermediation. To increase lending they must attract deposits from depository institutions.

MONETARY ANALYSIS AND THE PLACE OF THRIFT INSTITUTIONS

Economists have formulated two different ways to view money spending on newly produced goods and services. One, developed in the work of the British economist Lord Keynes, is now a central feature of all macroeconomics textbooks. According to this viewpoint, spending is the sum of spending for consumer nondurable goods, C, investment in durable goods, I, and spending by various levels of government, G. Thus, $C + I + G$ is regarded as total spending for newly produced goods and services.

Before the Keynesian analysis, economists expressed the amount of money spending as the product of the average stock of money, M, and the number of times this stock was turned over or spent per year. They called this turnover rate the velocity of circulation, V. The product $M \cdot V$ was regarded as equal to total money spending. It is more helpful to consider the effects of thrift institutions in terms of this older, pre-Keynesian approach.

If the thrift institutions attract only savings deposits from commercial banks, the above example (pp. 139–40) suggests that their impact will be both on the M-1A money supply (they will reduce it) and on the turnover rate of money (they will raise it). Their net impact on MV is therefore uncertain.

If, however, the thrift institutions attract away only demand deposits from the commercial banks, their impact will be more or less exclusively confined to the turnover rate, V, of the given supply of money. The degree to which MV rises depends upon the ability of the thrift institutions to retain reserves after they lend them out.

It may not be obvious in the second case how the thrift institutions raise the turnover rate of money. A moment's reflection will make it clear. In persuading someone to give up a demand deposit for a thrift deposit, these institutions are, in effect, activating an idle balance. That is, the individual originally holding the demand deposit was not planning to spend it. By influencing him to swap it for a substitute, the thrift institutions can then activate the demand deposit by lending it to someone who wishes to increase spending. If, however, the thrift institutions receive currency in return for a deposit, then both the money supply and its turnover rate or velocity will rise.

In this analysis the activities of the thrifts are seen to influence the velocity or turnover rate of money. Whenever the deposits of a thrift come to be counted as a part of the money stock, then, of course, its activities cease to influence velocity directly and are confined to the money stock. Thus, the more inclusive is the range of assets called money, the smaller becomes its turnover rate. By broadening this range of assets, recent changes allowing savings and loans, mutual savings banks, and credit unions to offer deposits subject to transfer by check, have decreased the velocity of money.

THE DISTINGUISHING CHARACTERISTICS OF COMMERCIAL BANKS

Off and on for almost 200 years some economists in the English-speaking world have argued that commercial banks are really no different from other depository institutions or, indeed, from any commercial firm that allows its customers to buy from it on credit. In this view all three types of firms merely provide credit to the market.

The arguments of the British over this question for the first half of the nineteenth century formed a part of the famous controversy between two groups of monetary theorists known as the Currency and Banking schools. The uniqueness of commercial banks again became a controversial issue in the 1950s when a Royal monetary commission known as the Radcliffe Committee[3] concluded that while commercial banks were important, they were only one source of total "liquidity" (or credit) and it was "liquidity," or liquidity individuals thought they could obtain, that was the most important determining factor of total spending.[4] In the view of the Radcliffe Committee, commercial banks were much like any institution that creates credit—including business firms—and since all were sources of liquidity, monetary policy need not single out one or the other for special controls. Interestingly, when it came to banks, the Committee recommended that controls be placed not on the deposit liabilities of banks, which are part of the money supply, but on the assets that banks buy—in effect, the monetary authorities were to be given the power to ration the flow of credit by deciding what type of assets banks could buy.

Coincidentally, on this side of the Atlantic similar views were being advanced by John Gurley and Edward Shaw. Their work was inspired by a massive study on the amount of savings in the United States over time and its flow through financial intermediaries published by Raymond Goldsmith in successive installments during the late 1950s.[5] Goldsmith's work showed that while all financial intermediaries grew rapidly during the first half of the twentieth century, the thrift institutions grew relative to commercial banks, causing the latter to diminish in importance (see Table 3:1, which uses Goldsmith's data for confirmation).

Gurley and Shaw concluded that the decline in the relative importance of

[3] For a discussion of the English monetary debates, see Gail E. Makinen, *Money, The Price Level, and Interest Rates* (Englewood Cliffs, N. J.: Prentice-Hall, 1977), Ch. 3 and 10.

[4] It is interesting that the Radcliffe Committee never defined liquidity. Since it was potential liquidity that supposedly influenced spending rather than actual liquidity, it became impossible to test their theory empirically.

[5] R. W. Goldsmith, *The Share of Financial Intermediaries in National Wealth and National Assets, 1900–1949* (New York: NBER, Occasional Paper 42, 1954); *A Study of Saving in the United States* (Princeton, N.J.: Princeton University Press, 1955); and *Financial Intermediaries in the American Economy Since 1900* (Princeton, N.J.: Princeton University Press, 1958).

commercial banks weakened the ability of the central bank to control economic activity, so long as such control extended only to the money-creating ability of commercial banks. Thus, direct control of the credit-creating ability of deposit-type thrift institutions was called for through an enlarged monetary authority. They further argued that in the future the theoretical distinction drawn in textbooks between commercial banks and thrift institutions should be discontinued as invalid. (This, it should be noted, was before the thrifts acquired the right to issue demand deposits.)

In 1960 a major economist, James Tobin[6] of Yale University, advanced similar doubts about the validity of the theoretical distinction made in the literature between commercial banks and the thrift institutions. Rather, he believed, all financial institutions offer the public assets that, while they may be differentiated one from another (each has its unique attributes), all share certain attributes that make them to one degree or another interchangeable substitutes in the portfolios of individuals and businesses. To the extent that these assets are substitutes, the thrift institutions have the power to alter the flow of money spending.

Many economists in both England and the United States have adhered to the views of the Radcliffe Committee, Gurley and Shaw, and Tobin. In an attempt to distill the merits of this long monetary controversy, an analysis of the similarities and differences among deposit-type financial intermediaries would seem worthwhile.

We first note that commercial banks and thrift institutions are identical in that each serves the function of transmitting funds from ultimate lenders to ultimate borrowers. That is, they make indirect lending possible. In this process both serve to decrease risks, and to the extent that they also secure cost reductions through achieving scale economies in the lending process, they reduce market interest rates.

Second, both types of financial intermediaries have the ability to create loanable funds over and above those made available through saving. One purpose of this chapter was to demonstrate this fact. Examples were constructed to show that the mere choice by the individual of the form in which to hold his wealth can influence the supply of loanable funds. The decision by an individual to shift from a commercial bank deposit to one in a thrift institution was seen to influence the overall supply of loanable funds from all intermediaries independent of the supply of new savings.

For any given primary deposit, the same two factors influence the amount of credit that each type of financial intermediary can create:

1. The legally or conventionally imposed reserve requirement;
2. The extent to which newly lent funds are redeposited within the system.

[6] J. Tobin, "Commercial Banks as Creators of Money," in Deane Carson, ed., *Banking and Monetary Studies* (Homewood, Ill.: Richard D. Irwin, 1963).

While the reserve requirements faced by each type of institution are different, it is primarily with regard to the redeposit feature that the two types of intermediaries were distinguishable.

When commercial banks expanded deposits and credit on the basis of a given addition to their reserves, they could count on a substantial redeposit of newly created funds, even if in the process of money expansion some of the funds were deposited in thrift institutions. Because thrift institutions held their reserves in commercial banks, these deposits would return to the banks, and thus not reduce the amount of ultimate expansion (which is calculated by multiplying the addition to the banks' reserves by the money multiplier). The principal factor that reduced the amount of money that commercial banks could create was the drain of currency into circulation. This drain, together with the reserves that the banks need to hold, served to bring the money-expansion process to an eventual halt.

Thrift institutions, on the other hand, could not count on a high redeposit rate. When they lent out funds, they expected to lose a substantial amount of reserves per dollar lent. These "lost funds" would probably find their way to commercial banks as deposits. The reason for this large reserve loss on the part of the thrift institutions was that commercial banks provided the means of payment used in the society; that is, they administered the payments system that served to make their deposits very attractive to both individuals and businesses.

Even if thrift institutions were to hold their reserves in their own vaults, or at a central depository such as the Federal Reserve, as commercial banks do, it would have done little to alter the large reserve loss they suffered per dollar lent, although it would have reduced the lending capability of the banking system.

In many essential respects thrift institutions were similar to commercial banks, but the latter were singled out for control by the monetary authorities because their ability to expand credit on the basis of a primary deposit was substantially larger. The reason for this was that they were able to retain reserves to a much greater extent than the thrift institutions for each dollar lent. The commercial banks' reserve-retention ability was directly related to the fact that they have in the past created the principal means of payment used in the economy. This was their historic uniqueness and the main reason for their special treatment by monetary authorities.

THRIFT INSTITUTIONS AND MONETARY POLICY

Both the work of the Radcliffe Committee in England and that of Gurley and Shaw, and Tobin in the United States suggested that the rapid growth of thrift institutions posed special problems for the secular and cyclical conduct of monetary policy. Similar views are heard today concerning the effect of Eurodollar banks and such domestic innovations as money market mutual funds.

These two groups believed that since thrift institutions had been growing more rapidly than commercial banks on a secular (long-run) basis, their deposit liabilities must be regarded as better substitutes in the portfolios of ultimate savers than similar types of deposits offered by commercial banks. Thus, the thrift institutions were thought to be inducing people to convert from time deposits at banks to similar deposits at thrift institutions. If this were true, one ought to observe a secular rise in the turnover rate (velocity) of conventionally defined money that could not be explained by other factors.

On a theoretical basis, a secular trend either upward or downward in velocity should pose no difficulty for the smooth functioning of monetary policy. It merely requires that the growth in the supply of money be adjusted for this trend so that the required growth in money spending can be achieved.

When the data on the velocity on money are examined for the period running from the end of the Civil War to World War II, one does *not* find a secularly rising velocity. Quite the contrary, velocity falls. After World War II the turnover rate of money appears to be rising, and this is consistent with the Gurley-Shaw view. However, empirical work to explain the secular behavior of velocity has been able to achieve satisfactory results without having to consider the activities of thrift institutions.

It was on the cyclical or short-run level that the main argument against traditional monetary policy was waged. It was asserted that the thrift institutions and other intermediaries had the power to offset partially or totally variations in the supply of conventional money. Thus, when the monetary authorities reduced the M-1A supply of money, the thrift institutions supposedly raised their turnover rate to offset the deflationary impact of the money supply reduction, thereby allowing money spending, MV, to remain more or less constant. As a consequence, it was argued, monetary policy ought to have concentrated on regulating the credit-creating ability of all types of financial intermediaries.

As we noted, the ability of the thrift institutions to raise the velocity of money follows from their ability to attract deposits from banks, and this ability, in turn, depends on the spread between long- and short-term interest rates. In addition, to the extent that the thrift institutions attract time deposits from banks, their activities curtail the flow of bank credit, leaving their impact on total spending, MV, uncertain.

Whether the thrift institutions had the power to change V to counter movements in M is a purely empirical question, and the evidence does not support the view that they can cause compensatory changes in V.

Nevertheless, suppose the thrift institutions did have such power, but it was not unlimited. Need it hamper monetary policy, which centers on control over the conventional money supply? The answer is no so long as the monetary authorities can estimate with precision the movements in the short-run or cyclical turnover rate of money. If they have this ability, they can compensate for velocity movements when they change the supply of money.

It should be borne in mind that if the power of the thrift institutions to vary the velocity of money had been unlimited, then money spending, or MV, would be independent of the conventionally defined money supply, and any monetary policy that centers on control of M would be totally useless. This fact, more than any other, served to weaken the argument of those who asserted that the thrift institutions had such power. The available evidence from a wide variety of studies did not support the conclusion that the volume of money spending is independent of the supply of money.

THRIFT INSTITUTIONS AND THE MONEY MULTIPLIER

The impact of thrift institutions on the money supply can be incorporated into the money multiplier, under the simplifying assumption that the public holds a certain proportion, k, of their (commercial bank) demand deposits, D, as deposits, S, in thrift institutions, or

$$S = kD \tag{5:1}$$

$$k = S/D \tag{5:2}$$

The mere holding of thrift deposits would not reduce the ability of commercial banks to create money for a given change in the monetary base, so long as the thrift institutions held *all* of their reserves as deposits in commercial banks. However, the thrift institutions could curtail the money-creating ability of commercial banks if they held some of their reserves in currency or cash in their own vaults, as evidence indicates they did. Thus, when deposits were transferred to them from commercial banks, they would return only a portion of the deposit and request currency for the remainder, in order to bolster their currency reserves. For convenience, let it be assumed that their currency reserves, P, are some constant fraction, p, of their deposit liabilities.

Thus, pS represents the total currency holdings of the thrift institutions. Since $S = kD$ from Equation (5:1), their currency reserves are equal to

$$pkD \tag{5:3}$$

When an increase in the monetary base, ΔB, is given to the system, the ability of commercial banks to create money will end when this addition is absorbed into any or all of the following: reserves required against demand deposits, ΔLR_D, and savings deposits, ΔLR_T; voluntary holdings of reserves by banks, ΔER_D; holdings by the public as currency, ΔC; or currency reserves by the thrift institutions, ΔP.

Substituting for each its equivalent,

$$\begin{aligned} \Delta LR_D &= r\Delta D \\ \Delta LR_T &= r'\Delta T = r't\Delta D \\ \Delta ER_D &= e\Delta D \\ \Delta C &= c'\Delta D \\ \Delta P &= p\Delta S = pk\Delta D \end{aligned}$$

yields

$$\begin{aligned} \Delta B &= r\Delta D + r't\Delta D + e\Delta D + c'\Delta D + pk\Delta D \\ &= \Delta D(r + r't + e + c' + pk) \end{aligned}$$

$$\Delta B\left(\frac{1}{r + r' + e + c' + pk}\right) = \Delta D \qquad (5{:}4)$$

If the change in the money supply is defined as[7]

$$\Delta M\text{-}1A = \Delta D + \Delta C$$

then since $\Delta C = c'\Delta D$, we have

$$\begin{aligned} \Delta M\text{-}1A &= \Delta D + c'\Delta D \\ &= \Delta D(1 + c') \end{aligned}$$

Substitution from Equation (5:4) yields

$$\Delta M\text{-}1A = \Delta B\left(\frac{1 + c'}{r + r't + e + c' + pk}\right) \qquad (5{:}5)$$

Comparing the money multiplier in Equation (5:5) with the money multipliers developed for the M-1B money supply in Chapter 4 reveals several differences. First, the additional variable pk is added to the denominator of the multiplier. Second, the values of c', r, r', t, and e may be different in magnitude. Basically, however, the effect of the holding of currency reserves by the thrifts is identical to the effect produced by public holdings of larger currency balances (allowing c' to rise).

[7] Remember that ΔD consists only of the demand deposits supplied by commercial banks.

FEDERAL FUNDS AND REPURCHASE AGREEMENTS

The M_2 and M_3 definitions of money include repurchase agreements (or RPs), both overnight and term, and supplied by both commercial banks and savings and loan associations. In this concluding section RPs, which represent a rather major money market innovation, are discussed. Since they share many of the attributes of federal funds, with which they are often confused, both markets will be described and analyzed.[8] Because the market for federal funds is the older of the two, it will receive our attention first.

In Chapter 4, federal funds were described as transactions between depository institutions that have excess reserves for sale and those that desire to borrow to make up a reserve deficiency. Today such lending is a very important part of that market, but the market is more extensive than this. Federal funds lending is generally in minimum sums of $1 million and on an overnight basis.[9] The loans are generally unsecured and for that reason are frequently made only between parties who enjoy a very high degree of mutual confidence.

The federal funds market had its origin in the early 1920s among a few large banks in New York City. At the time, some were faced with reserve deficiencies while others enjoyed reserve surpluses. It grew to a daily borrowing of about $250 million by 1929, but the Great Depression considerably reduced both its size and growth.

The market revived and grew substantially after the end of World War II. Its growth is highly correlated with the ups and down of market interest rates. This growth has also been aided by legal interpretations that have broadened participation in the market and increased its profitability.

In 1963 the restriction on the amount that one federally chartered bank could lend to another on an unsecured basis was removed when federal funds transactions were declared to be purchases and sales rather than borrowing and lending. This lending restriction had previously prevented smaller banks from participating in the market.

In 1964 the Federal Reserve permitted member banks to purchase (borrow) the deposits held in those banks by nonmember banks (these are called correspondent balances). This change permitted many other smaller banks to ask their correspondents to engage in federal funds transactions on their behalf under the threat that otherwise they would move their

[8] Much of the information in this section is drawn from Charles M. Lucas, Marcos T. Jones, and Thom B. Thurston, "Federal Funds and Repurchase Agreements," *Quarterly Review*, Federal Reserve Bank of New York (Summer 1977): 33–48.

[9] These transactions (as well as those for RPs) involve what is known as "immediately available funds." These are transactions in which the borrower acquires immediate and unconditional title to the funds. They are unlike the typical check transaction, wherein a depositor acquires unconditional title to the funds only after the check has cleared, a process which often takes a number of days.

balances elsewhere. Note carefully that this enabled the small banks to earn interest on their correspondent balances. Before 1964 Regulation Q had forbidden the payment of explicit interest on correspondent balances. They were treated as though they were ordinary demand deposits.

It should also be noted that presently federal funds borrowing from commercial banks that are members of the Federal Reserve System is not subject to reserve requirements. How a transaction might emerge is shown in Table 5:5, in which a correspondent balance (CB) is purchased as federal funds (FFP). Since federal funds are not subject to reserve requirements, the excess reserves of commercial banks rise. Because the bank in question has positive excess reserves, these can be sold in the federal funds market. (Such a transaction is shown in the bottom portion of the table.) Thus, the same bank can both purchase and sell federal funds. The net result is that both the depository bank and the depositor bank earn interest on funds that would otherwise lie idle.

Another significant change that expanded the market occurred in 1970, when federal funds borrowing from certain other customers was permitted and exempted from reserve requirements. These favored customers included agencies of the United States government, savings and loan associations, mutual savings banks, and agencies and branches of foreign banks operating in the United States.

Thus, today the supply of funds comes mainly from smaller commercial banks, thrifts, agencies of the federal government, and a few other sources. The demand for these funds is chiefly from the very large banks in this country and arises from what is described in Chapter 6 as the practice of liability management. This practice is also important for repurchase agreements.

The market for repurchase agreements shares several characteristics with the federal funds market: both involve mainly transactions for one business day, although some are for a longer term, both involve immediately available funds; and in both the liabilities created are not subject to the reserve requirements imposed by the Federal Reserve. Repurchase agreements are secured loans and they may be executed with a broader range of individuals than would be eligible to participate in the federal funds market. Because of the size of the typical transaction ($1 million or more), the principal

TABLE 5:5
Federal funds transactions

Bank Balance Sheet	
ER +	CB − FFP +
ER − FFS +	

additional participants are nonfinancial corporations and state and local governments. Again, note that repurchase agreements are a way of paying explicit interest on what are essentially demand deposits.

Table 5:6 shows a typical repurchase agreement. A large corporation sells its demand deposit account to the commercial bank. The purchase by the bank is typically secured by a U.S. Treasury security. (For the repurchase agreement to be exempt from reserve requirements, it must be secured by a security of the federal government or one of its agencies). The repurchase agreement obligates the corporation to buy back its deposit the next day. The difference between the selling price and purchase price represents the interest earned by the corporation.[10] Since the repurchase liability on the bank's books is not subject to reserve requirements, the excess reserves of the banking system rise. These, in turn, can be lent to regular customers or sold as federal funds.

On November 30, 1979, overnight RPs issued by commercial banks were \$20.3 billion, while term RPs issued by commercial banks and savings and loan associations were \$29.7 billion (\$21.5 and \$8.2 billion, respectively). The overnight repurchase agreements raise an interesting question concerning the accuracy of the measure of the old M_1 and the current M-1A and M-1B stock of money. Overnight repurchase agreements are executed before the close of bank business. As a result, the daily total of demand deposits will be less than they would be without the repurchase agreements. Some economists hold that the dollar value of overnight repurchase agreements constitutes "missing money" and should be watched closely in judging the growth rate of monetary aggregates. For that reason, they may prefer the M_2 or M_3 measure of the money supply for policy purposes.

TABLE 5:6
Repurchase agreement

Bank Balance Sheet	
ER +	DD −
	RP +

[10] For those who find the description of an RP transaction a trifle confusing, it may be clearer to think of this as a case in which the corporation uses its demand deposit to purchase a security from a bank with the promise that the bank will repurchase it on the following day. The difference between the price paid for the security by the corporation and that at which it sells it back to the bank represents its profit. The form of the transaction given above conforms to what legally occurs.

SUMMARY

This chapter has drawn a sharp distinction between money- and non-money-creating financial institutions. This was largely accomplished by using the historic distinction between commercial banks and so-called thrifts. As a result, we acquired a frame of reference for understanding such recent innovations as Eurodollar banks and money market mutual funds. We also were able to evaluate the merits of a long argument about the uniqueness of commercial banks.

The ability of thrift institutions to create credit and expand the volume of loanable funds was seen to depend on the same set of factors that govern the ability of banks to create money:

1. The availability of a primary deposit;
2. The reserve-holding behavior of the institution;
3. The ability to retain deposits once credit or money creation starts.

It should be emphasized that the credit-creating power of the thrifts holds regardless of what financial institutions are called banks. Thus, even though much of the analysis of this chapter was carried out as if only commercial banks created money, its conclusions are not altered when the definition is broadened to include other depository institutions. Those institutions not included in the definition are seen largely to influence the velocity or turnover rate of conventional money.

Indeed, one can define money any way one wishes. The narrower the definition, the greater will be the variability of the velocity or turnover rate. The broader the definition, the less variable money's velocity.

The chapter concluded with a discussion of the markets for federal funds and repurchase agreements, both of which have grown significantly in the past decade.

STUDY QUESTIONS

1. Why should we be concerned about the ability of non-money-creating institutions to alter the flow of credit?
2. Suppose new instruments were evolved for making transactions. Under what circumstances should they be included as a part of the money supply? In thinking about your answer, remember that demand deposits were once excluded from the definition of money.
3. Historically, why have commercial banks been distinguished from other deposit-type financial institutions?
4. If the deposits of financial institutions are not included in the definition of money, where will they show up when one examines money spending? Explain how these institutions can raise or lower money spending. Is this ability unlimited?

5. Given the information in question 4, does the existence of such institutions render the central bank helpless in its attempt to control money spending?
6. If total money spending is defined to be equal to $M \cdot V$, what should one expect to happen to the movement of V over time as the deposits of an increasingly large number of financial institutions are counted as money?

SELECTED REFERENCES AND READINGS

Bloch, Ernest. "Two Decades of Evolution of Financial Institutions and Public Policy." *Journal of Money, Credit and Banking,* Vol. 3, No. 2 (May 1971).

Gurley, John. "The Radcliffe Report and Evidence." *American Economic Review* Vol. 50, No. 4 (Sept. 1960).

———and Shaw, Edward S. *Money in a Theory of Finance.* Washington, D.C.: Brookings Institution, 1960.

Guttentag, Jack, and Lindsey, Robert. "The Uniqueness of Commercial Banks." *Journal of Political Economy,* Vol. 76, No. 5 (Sept.–Oct. 1968).

Shelby, Donald. "Some Implications of the Growth of Financial Intermediaries." *Journal of Finance,* Vol. 13, No. 5 (Dec. 1958).

Smith, Warren L. "Financial Intermediaries and Monetary Controls." *Quarterly Journal of Economics,* Vol. 73, No. 4 (Nov. 1959).

Thorn, Richard. "Non-Bank Financial Intermediaries, Credit Expansion and Monetary Policy." *Staff Papers* 6 (International Monetary Fund, 1958).

Tobin, James. "Commercial Banks as Creators of Money." in *Banking and Monetary Studies,* edited by Deane Carson. Homewood, Ill.: Richard D. Irwin, 1963.

———and Brainard, William. "Financial Intermediaries and the Effectiveness of Monetary Controls." *Papers and Proceedings of the American Economic Association,* Vol. 53, No. 2 (May 1963).

Wood, John H. "Two Notes on the Uniqueness of Commercial Banks." *Journal of Finance,* Vol. 25, No. 1 (Mar. 1970).

6 THE THEORY AND PRACTICE OF COMMERCIAL BANKING

Among all intermediaries, commercial banks have historically occupied and presently occupy a dominant and vital place in the U.S. financial system. Because of this, and because they were not as legally circumscribed in the range of assets they could acquire as, for example, savings and loan associations, theories were developed to guide bankers in their asset selections. These theories will be discussed in this chapter. As an incidental part of the discussion, we will discover the types of loans depository institutions make. We start the discussion by examining the characteristics of the balance sheet of a commercial bank.

The theories discussed in this chapter have applicability for other depository institutions that also create means of payment, to the extent that the laws governing their asset choice are liberalized. In addition, some aspects of these other depository institutions' balance sheets are the same as those of banks.

THE BANK BALANCE SHEET

An example of the types of assets that banks select, and some special characteristics of the balance sheet that influence their asset choices or *portfolio behavior,* are given in Table 6:1, which reproduces the actual balance sheet of a large midwestern bank.

This balance sheet (and bank balance sheets in general) has many attributes found in the balance sheets of industrial and commercial enterprises. However, it also has some notable differences, and these differences exercise a constraint on bank asset selection. They mainly concern liabilities.

Definite and certain liabilities

First, all commercial bank liabilities have a definite and certain value at any moment in time. That is, the bank knows with certainty the amount of its outstanding liabilities. Their value is not affected by market interest rates, or by the bank's decision to pay off a customer. It is a common practice in

TABLE 6:1
Consolidated balance sheets of Manufacturers National Corporation and subsidiaries

	December 31	
	1979	1978
Assets		
Cash and due from banks	$ 412,377,000	$ 490,686,000
Interest-bearing deposits with banks	175,800,000	133,040,000
Investment securities (market value of $833,000,000 in 1979 and $732,000,000 in 1978)	896,331,000	772,821,000
Trading account securities	21,779,000	10,536,000
Federal funds sold	26,721,000	164,433,000
Commercial loans	941,300,000	885,967,000
International loans	198,055,000	178,463,000
Real Estate Construction Loans	109,176,000	105,268,000
Real Estate Mortgage Loans	1,101,973,000	1,031,175,000
Installment loans	418,496,000	327,257,000
Total loans (net of unearned installment income of $38,951,000 in 1979 and $44,995,000 in 1978)	2,769,000,000	2,528,130,000
Less allowance for loan losses	(24,233,000)	(24,568,000)
Net loans	2,744,777,000	2,503,562,000
Lease financing	48,229,000	25,610,000
Properties and equipment	73,646,000	64,227,000
Customers' liability on acceptances outstanding	17,895,000	48,993,000
Accrued income and other assets	108,203,000	77,607,000
Total assets	$4,525,758,000	$4,291,515,000
Liabilities and Shareholders' Equity		
Demand deposits	$1,091,648,000	$1,093,795,000
Savings deposits	790,316,000	901,188,000
Time deposits	1,564,568,000	1,363,274,000
Deposits in foreign office	161,110,000	103,277,000
Total deposits	3,607,642,000	3,461,534,000
Federal funds purchased and securities sold under agreements to repurchase	440,511,000	345,654,000
Other borrowed funds	73,370,000	89,355,000
Acceptances outstanding	17,895,000	48,993,000
Accrued expenses and other liabilities	93,658,000	76,983,000
Subordinated and other notes	51,509,000	50,823,000
Total liabilities	4,284,585,000	4,073,342,000
Shareholders' equity:		
Preferred stock—no par value:		
Authorized and unissued—250,000 shares		

TABLE 6:1 *Continued*

	December 31	
	1979	1978
Common stock—$10 par value:		
Authorized—8,000,000 shares		
Issued—5,058,749 shares in 1979		
and 5,015,340 shares in 1978	50,587,000	50,153,000
Capital surplus	40,424,000	39,777,000
Retained earnings	150,327,000	128,408,000
Less cost of 7,020 shares of common stock in treasury	(165,000)	(165,000)
Total shareholders' equity	241,173,000	218,173,000
Total liabilities and shareholders' equity	$4,525,758,000	$4,291,515,000

Assets carried at approximately $212,000,000 were pledged at December 31, 1979, to secure public deposits (including State of Michigan deposits of $54,731,000) and for other purposes as required by law.
Courtesy Manufacturers National Corporation, Detroit, Michigan.

business for creditors to grant a deduction from the face value of the sum due if they are paid within a certain time period.

Because outstanding liabilities are fixed in value, banks will try to acquire assets whose values are similarly stable.

Demand nature of liabilities

Second, unlike most businesses, banks have creditors who are entitled to payment on demand either legally (those who hold demand deposits can request currency conversion on demand) or by convention. The latter category of creditors includes all who hold ordinary time and saving deposits, even though most banking laws permit banks to request advance notice (often 30 days) of withdrawal. Since such notice is rarely requested, for all practical purposes this distinction may be ignored.

An increasingly common type of bank liability, the negotiable certificate of deposit (the CD), is an exception. These certificates have a stated maturity date and the banks are not required to redeem them until they come due. So the portion of total liabilities they represent is not payable on demand either by law or custom. Banks have other nondeposit sources of funds that are similar to corporate bonds. These are sometimes called capital notes and they have a fixed maturity date. Despite these exceptions, the vast majority of bank liabilities, consisting of demand and ordinary time and savings deposits, are payable on demand.

The influence of this liability structure upon asset selection is rather straightforward. Banks will acquire as assets either currency itself or other highly liquid assets—those that can be converted quickly and at little cost into the means of payment. These highly liquid assets will typically be the debt obligations of a widely known institution whose solvency is not subject to doubt (e.g., the federal government) and whose maturity date, or time to maturity, is close at hand.

Although the balance sheet shown in Table 6:1 is not very detailed, one can estimate that over 9% of all assets are held as currency, and almost 21% of all assets are commercial loans, which typically have short maturities. Another common short-term asset, although not shown explicitly in Table 6:1, consists of Treasury securities, which are often bills.[1] Thus, bank assets are typically much more liquid than those of other depository institutions.

Small capital accounts

A third characteristic of the bank balance sheet, which it shares with other financial institutions and which serves to distinguish it from nonfinancial enterprises, is the very small value of its capital account (shareholders' equity) relative to its assets. This means that the owners of the bank supply only a small portion of the funds that the bank lends. Over much of the past century the capital accounts of banks have averaged somewhat less than 10% of the value of their assets. For example, in the 1979 balance sheet of the Manufacturers National Corporation total shareholder equity is about 5 1/2% of the value of the bank's assets.

Such small capital accounts will dictate an unusually conservative lending strategy on behalf of individual banks, manifested in a preference for a safe, secure type of loan, such as those made to governments or to private business or individuals that are supported by ample collateral. Banks are unlikely to be the source of risk capital for business: they cannot sustain large and continuous losses, for every dollar of loss is written off against their capital accounts. If they were to make high-risk loans and lose, then in a short time their thin capital accounts would be reduced to zero. Once liabilities exceed assets, a bank is reduced to insolvency and a receiver is appointed to make a distribution of the assets or to merge the bank with another in an effort to preserve the value of assets that might otherwise have to be sold at distressed prices.

Thus, small capital accounts impose upon banks the constraint of holding assets whose values are relatively stable and do not fluctuate greatly with the phases of the business cycle or with the public's state of confidence in the future.

[1] The U.S. government issues four types of securities differentiated by their time to maturity. The shortest-term securities are called Treasury bills and they mature in less than a year—commonly 90 days. Certificates of Indebtedness generally mature in from one to five years. Notes run about five years, and bonds usually mature at a minimum of ten years. Some run for twenty years.

Liabilities form the money supply

The fourth and final characteristic of the bank balance sheet, deriving from the special place occupied by banks in our financial system, which exercises a constraint on asset selection, concerns the fact that the demand deposit portion of bank liabilities forms the principal component of the U.S. money supply. Because the money supply is an important determinant of economic activity, public authority has imposed regulations on banks to prevent large fluctuations in the money supply arising from bank insolvencies.

Public regulation of banking varies from state to state, and from state to federal jurisdiction, depending upon the authority chartering the bank. Nevertheless, there are some common characteristics in the regulations on the quantity and quality of the assets that banks purchase. In general, laws seek to enforce asset diversification on banks, as well as the maintenance of a reasonable degree of liquidity (the latter was, after all, the primary purpose of legal reserve requirements). Most of these regulations also involve such things as prohibiting or limiting the amount of loans to the officers and directors of banks and to any one customer, specifying that banks cannot buy common stock or risky bonds (those with a low rating according to Moodys or Standard and Poors, etc.). These various laws constraining the asset selection of banks arose over a long period in response to banking abuses.

In summary, the asset selection of banks is influenced by the fixed value of their liabilities. Because over three-quarters of their liabilities are by law or convention payable on demand, because they have in general very small capital accounts relative to their assets, and because their liabilities are the principal component of the money supply, various laws have been enacted restricting the bank's portfolio choices.

THE ASSET AND LIABILITY STRUCTURE OF A TYPICAL LARGE BANK

We could use the balance sheet in Table 6:1 as a typical example of all banks, in order to learn what type of assets such a bank holds. Alternatively, we could use the consolidated bank balance sheet shown in Table 3:2. For this exercise we will use the former.

As noted, over 9% of the assets are held as "cash and due from banks." This asset category consists of currency held in the bank's own vaults and its deposits at the central bank, which together can serve to meet its legal reserve obligations. The account may also include correspondent balances at other banks and checks in the process of collection.

Almost 20% of the bank's assets are held in investment securities, probably those issued by various levels of government. An advantage of some of these securities (the state and municipal bonds) is that the income from them is tax exempt. Depending upon the tax rate applied to bank profits, the tax-free income from state and municipal securities may be equal to a considerable interest premium, which undoubtedly accounts for the rapid increase in the amount of these securities held by banks in the past few years. For example, if state and municipal securities yield 6%and the bank pays 50% of its profits in taxes, the yield is equivalent to one subject to taxation of 12%. In fact, it would be in the interest of a bank to pay more than 6% to obtain savings deposits, which could then be invested in state and municipal securities yielding less than that amount, so long as the bank has other operating income against which its interest costs could be offset. This explains the seeming paradox that a bank may pay more than 6% to attract funds which it then invests in securities earning only 6%.[2]

Over 20% of the assets of this bank are invested in commercial loans, which are short term in duration and designed to provide business with working capital. The name *commercial bank* comes from this type of loan and commercial banking originated with this type of lending.

Only a small portion (about 9%) of the assets is tied up in consumer installment loans of the type that enable individuals to buy durable goods (such as automobiles), on time. As noted earlier, other lending institutions, such as credit unions and finance companies, specialize in this type of lending.

Last among the loans are those for real estate, in which this bank holds almost 27% of its assets. Such loans could be to individuals to enable them to buy a home, but are more likely to be to business.

Finally, under 2% of the bank's assets are in its own equipment and premises, consisting of the main office and its branches throughout the Detroit area. Since this balance sheet is a consolidated one for a bank holding company, it may contain the assets of other smaller banks, as well as those for any trust activities of the bank.

Of the total deposits, less than one-third are of a demand nature. Slightly over two-thirds are time and savings deposits, which tells us that the major source of bank funds is not demand deposits. In fact, insofar as their deposit structure is concerned, banks look a great deal like other depository institutions.

It appears from the balance sheet that this bank both bought and sold

[2] To see this, suppose it costs a bank 8% to borrow funds that it then invests in tax-free securities yielding 6%. The bank's interest costs per $100 borrowed is $8, while its earnings are $6 per $100 invested. However, its interest costs can be offset against taxable income in order to calculate its overall tax liability. If the tax rate is 50%, then its net interest cost to obtain the funds is not $8 per $100, but $4. Thus, the bank's profit by investing in tax-free securities is $6 minus $4, or $2 per $100. This conclusion holds only to the extent the bank has other operating income subject to taxation.

federal funds. This market has already been discussed in detail[3] and it was shown that it is possible for a bank to both buy and sell federal funds. This is not an anomaly. This bank is also active in the market for repurchase agreements, which should come as no surprise, for it is the large banks that make this market operate.

Total shareholders' equity, consisting of capital stock, retained earnings, and capital surplus (which probably arose because the original shares were sold at prices above those stated on the securities' par or face value), is slightly in excess of 5 1/2% of the value of the bank's assets.

The size of the capital accounts reveals that almost 95% of the funds by which assets were acquired were obtained from the bank's creditors. Only 5 1/2% were supplied directly or indirectly by the owners of the bank.

THE RELATIONSHIP BETWEEN MARKET INTEREST RATES AND BOND PRICES

Before examining the various theories put forth to explain the type of assets that banks should purchase, we shall consider a fundamental relationship that every student of money and banking must understand. This is the relationship between market interest rates and the market price of negotiable debt instruments.[4] The relationship is an inverse one, that is, as market interest rates rise (fall), the market price of negotiable debt securities falls (rises). Moreover, the longer the time to maturity of the debt security, the greater will be the change in its market price for a corresponding change in the interest rate. This means that if the market interest rate rises from 3% to 4%, the market price of a security that has 20 years to run will fall in price by substantially more than will the price of a security with a maturity date of but one year.

Consider a rise in market interest rates from 3% to 4% and two securities, one with a time to maturity of one year and one with a maturity date that never comes. (The latter is typified by a British security called a *consol,* which pays interest every year but is not redeemable at face value.)

Assume each security has a face value of $100 and bears interest at 3% (its coupon rate). Thus, if each security were issued today at its face value, a prospective buyer would pay $100. In the case of the one-year security, the owner would receive $103 when the security was redeemed one year

[3] See Chapter 5.

[4] For want of a better word, such securities are often called *bonds,* but this term may be misleading. We do not mean the common Government Series E bonds, which individuals purchase as part of a payroll savings plan. Such securities are not negotiable. The individual in whose name the security is issued can only sell them back to the government. Negotiable debt securities are not issued in the name of a specific individual and they can be sold to anyone. Usually, an active market for them exists, in which prices are actively quoted. This is the type of security where the price moves inversely to market interest rates.

later. The owner of the consol would receive \$3 per year for as long as it was owned.

Now assume that the market interest rate rises from 3% to 4% and that all newly issued securities bear a coupon equal to the new higher market rate. How is it possible for those who own the old securities bearing the 3% coupon to dispose of them when newly issued securities of the same class bear a 4% coupon? The only way is to make them as attractive as the new securities. Since the owner of the 3% coupon securities cannot change the coupon, the only option available to him is to offer the security at a discount, i.e., to sell it for a sum less than its face value. Suppose the short maturity security were offered for sale for \$99. A purchaser would buy it for \$99 and one year hence the government would redeem it for \$100 and also pay him \$3 interest. His total profit, therefore, is \$4, and since his investment was \$99, his yield would be \$4/\$99 or slightly in excess of 4%. Thus, to yield exactly 4%, the security would be offered for sale at a sum less than \$100, but greater than \$99 (at \$99.03, to be precise).

From this example involving a short-maturity security, it can be seen that if market interest rates rise (from 3% to 4%, or a percentage increase of one-third), the market price will fall (in this case from \$100 to \$99.03, or a percentage change of less than 1%).

On the other hand, consider our consol (whose face value, recall, is also \$100). To calculate its market price or present value, the money value of the coupon is divided by the market interest rate.[5] If the money value of the coupon is \$3 or 3% and the market interest rate is also 3%, the consol will have a market price of \$100 (\$3/.03), and in Britain consols will be said to be at par. If the market interest rate rises to 4%, the market price of the consol will fall to \$75 (\$3/.04). Thus, a rise in interest rates from 3% to 4% (or 33 1/3%) will cause the price of consols to decline from \$100 to \$75 (or 25%). It follows that the longer the term to maturity, the greater will be the decline in market prices for a *given* change in market interest rates.

THE THEORIES OF COMMERCIAL BANKING

The constraints enumerated previously on the type of assets that banks may acquire are not very specific, except, of course, in those cases where the law specifically forbids banks from acquiring certain classes of assets.

[5] In general, the formula for computing the market or present value for a debt security is simply the sum of the discounted value of the coupon interest payments plus the principal or face value, or

$$\text{Market value} = \frac{\text{Coupon}}{(1+i)^1} + \frac{\text{Coupon}}{(1+i)^2} + \ldots + \frac{\text{Coupon}}{(1+i)^N} + \frac{\text{Face Value}}{(1+i)^N} \qquad (6{:}1)$$

where i is the market rate of interest per year or its equivalent on a fractional year basis and 1,2, . . . , N refer to the number of years or fractions thereof to maturity.

In the special case of the consol where $N = \infty$, the final term in Equation (6:1) is equal to zero and the remainder of the equation collapses to Coupon/i.

Within these general constraints, banks have great leeway in selecting assets. One of the primary considerations in the selection process is the profit motive: banks are in business to make a profit, and they attempt to maximize this quantum. Profit maximization, however, cannot serve as the only guide for asset selection. If it did, banks might, legal restraints aside, be led to lend against the security of highly risky long-term mortgages. Therefore, considerations of risk must enter their calculations, and the risk is related to both the default potential of the borrower and the potential liquidity of the asset to be acquired.

As we noted earlier, banks must pay more attention to the liquidity of their asset structure because most of their liabilities are legally or conventionally payable on demand. Thus, the liquidity of assets is an important consideration for banks. As one would expect, the more liquid the asset, the lower its yield. In the case of money itself, its explicit yield is zero.

A persistent problem in bank portfolio management is the selection of assets so as to ensure liquidity without reducing profits to zero. The ability to keep a desirable balance between profits and liquidity can only be tested over the longer run, the test being whether the bank survives as a growing enterprise. Unfortunately, the American experience with commercial banking is indeed a sad one. We have probably had more bank failures than any other developed country. During the period 1929–1934 almost half of all the banks in this country failed (to be sure, these were mainly small banks). Illiquidity of asset structure in the face of massive deposit withdrawals was a major cause of these catastrophes in American economic history.

Several theories have been proposed to help banks select assets that yield reasonable profits while keeping the liquidity risk acceptably low. In the main, these theories seem more concerned with liquidity than profitability. Older theories take the liability structure of the banks as a given, and then seek to rationalize the type of asset a bank should purchase. In contrast, the most recent approach to asset management holds that the liability structure of banks can also be managed, and that through such management banks can achieve greater flexibility in asset selection. In particular, they will be able to acquire a larger proportion of the higher-yielding, longer-term assets.

The real bills doctrine

One of the earliest attempts to provide banks with a theory of asset selection was the real bills doctrine. This doctrine recognizes that bank liabilities are by law or convention payable on demand (during the eighteenth, nineteenth, and early twentieth centuries, when this theory was popular, almost all bank liabilities were payable on demand). Consequently, bank assets must also be of a highly liquid nature. That is, bank assets must be in a form that can be quickly converted into currency or other means of payment to meet any sudden withdrawals of deposits or requests that notes be converted into gold (disintermediation).

Since one attribute of liquidity is linked to the time to maturity of an asset, a short-term asset will, other things being equal, be more liquid than a long-term asset. Thus, the real bills doctrine held that banks should confine their lending to short-term, self-liquidating commercial loans. The purpose of these loans was to supply business with working capital, i.e., with funds to hire workers and acquire inventories in order to complete the production of goods. When the goods were sold, the proceeds would be used to retire the loan—hence, the loans were said to be self-liquidating.

If the borrower could not repay the loan, the bank could always claim the goods that were the collateral for the loan, sell them, and hold the proceeds (because of the collateral, these commercial loans were called real bills).

From the viewpoint of the *individual* bank, such commercial loans were an ideal type of liquidity reserve to be used to meet any disintermediation crisis that might arise. They were often called an ideal secondary reserve that supplemented the basic or primary reserves of coin and notes held by the banks to ensure adequate liquidity in time of need.

From the viewpoint of *all* banks as a group, however, the value of this type of loan was not so clear. Suppose, for example, that all banks were simultaneously exposed to disintermediation, i.e., a desire on the part of the public to convert deposits to currency. Could the banks as a group sell off their commercial loans to raise currency? Probably not, for the principal market for commercial loans was made by bankers on behalf of themselves. If all must simultaneously raise currency, a substantial segment of the market no longer exists—not everyone can be a seller!

Moreover, if the borrowers defaulted on their loans, which would be likely in times of economic distress, and the banks came to possess the collateral or goods, their mass sale to raise currency would decrease the price of the goods, and therefore the proceeds the banks would realize. If the decrease in proceeds was at all substantial, the banks could suffer losses that would impair their small capital accounts, reducing some to a state of insolvency.

Thus, the principal deficiency of the real bills doctrine was that while it was valid for an individual bank, it had serious shortcomings when applied to the banking system as a whole. However, with the advent of a central bank in the United States, that would grant discounts on the basis of commercial paper, the holding of such assets remained attractive to banks, as the balance sheet in Table 6:1 shows.

An additional deficiency of the real bills doctrine was that it required banks to forego loans to business for the acquisition of fixed capital (plant and equipment). During the period when this doctrine was in vogue banks were the principal financial intermediary. Under such conditions, if business could not acquire funds for fixed capital acquisition from banks, it might not be able to acquire them at all.

The real bills doctrine and the supply of money

An interesting implication of the real bills doctrine concerns the determinants of the stock of money. The doctrine implies that the actual stock of money in existence is determined exclusively by the demand for it. Thus, the money supply analysis developed in Chapter 4 centering on the monetary base and money multiplier is incorrect according to the real bills doctrine.

A basic premise of the real bills doctrine is quite similar to the traditional approach to the definition of money developed in this text, which is that money is useful because it eliminates the hazards involved in barter. From this premise, the real bills doctrine concluded that the demand for money was governed by the "needs of trade." Should the "needs of trade" expand, the demand for money would rise and individuals and businesses would obtain the necessary funds from banks by offering commercial bills at discount. The banks would then purchase or discount the bills, supplying in return the necessary demand deposits or money. Should the banks fail to accept all the discounts, it is not at all clear what the consequences were supposed to be. Some who expounded the real bills doctrine implied that if the funds could not be secured from banks, they might be obtained from other financial intermediaries or from expanded credit terms given by tradesmen. On the other hand, if commercial banks came to possess additional reserves, the real bills doctrine held that they could not expand the money supply in excess of that required to meet the needs of trade. The reason for this was that no one would borrow money at interest unless it could be used productively in business. Thus, expanding the monetary base would not lead to a rise in the money stock in active circulation unless it was coincident with a rise dictated by an increase in the needs of trade.

Of crucial importance to the validity of the real bills doctrine was some explanation of the forces determining the "needs of trade." Unfortunately, no explanation was given. So long as it was assumed that the "needs of trade" were given, and that no one would borrow money at interest unless it could be used productively in business, the conclusion of the real bills doctrine concerning the nature of the money stock seemed valid.

As early as 1797, however, a remarkable English banker, Henry Thornton,[6] exposed the fallacy of this doctrine. He reasoned that the "needs of trade" was a variable depending upon the relative profitability of using money in business. The relative profitability was, in turn, related to the difference between the yield on capital and the interest rate charged by banks on loans. Thus, if banks acquired additional reserves and lowered the lending rate in an effort to induce more loans, the relative profitability of borrowing would increase and the needs of trade would expand. In terms of the analysis in Chapter 4, Thornton was merely saying that an increase

[6] See Henry Thornton, *The Paper Credit of Great Britain* (New York: Augustus Kelly, 1965).

in bank reserves would shift the supply schedule of money along a fixed money demand schedule and the money stock would, therefore, rise.

Though long known to be incorrect, the real bills doctrine still has its adherents, especially among bankers. One suspects that its popularity in banking quarters is due to the fact that the doctrine holds banks blameless for most aspects of the business cycle—after all, the doctrine holds that it is the demand for money, not the supply, that governs the money stock.

Shiftability thesis

A concerted attack on the real bills doctrine was undertaken in the early twentieth century by H. G. Moulton.[7] Among other things, Moulton argued that the liquidity of a bank's assets came not from the type of loans it made, but from the shiftability (or salability) of the securities it held. In Moulton's words, "liquidity is tantamount to shiftability."[8] In theory, Moulton's argument could be taken to mean that it is the marketability, not the time of maturity of a security, that makes it an ideal secondary reserve. Thus, long-term securities that are highly salable could serve as the liquidity reserves of a bank.

The popularity of this theory among bankers spread with the growth and development of the market for short-term debt. Before the 1920s the volume of short-dated securities was rather small, consisting mainly of commercial paper. This was, in part, a consequence of a very small public debt. In the late 1920s the short-term sector of the securities market underwent a marked change. In 1929 the Treasury introduced the Treasury bill as a means for drawing on short-term funds. It was a highly desirable (shiftable) asset for banks. Moreover, the increase in the public debt subsequent to 1930 increased the supply of these securities to the market.

Unfortunately, the shiftability thesis suffers from the same shortcoming as the real bills doctrine: it is inapplicable to the banking system at large in the absence of a central bank as a lender of last resort. If all banks were faced with the need for liquidity and were forced to sell their securities, distressed selling would take place, security prices would fall sharply, and banks would face the same situation as they did under similar conditions with the real bills doctrine. It should be noted that, like the real bills doctrine, the shiftability thesis accepts as a given the liability structure of banks and offers suggestions on asset selection designed to achieve liquidity.

Just before the shiftability thesis was developed, a major change occurred in American banking. In 1913 the United States for the first time in almost 80 years again had a central bank—the Federal Reserve. One of the powers

[7] H.G. Moulton, "Commercial Banking and Capital Formation," *Journal of Political Economy* 26 (July–Aug. 1918): 705–31.

[8] Ibid., p. 723.

given this central bank was to purchase at discount certain classes of assets from member commercial banks—basically commercial paper and some agricultural loans. Being eligible to be sold at discount certainly improved the liquidity of these assets in those instances when the banks as a group were subject to massive disintermediation.

The anticipated income doctrine

In the late 1940s Herbert Prochnow,[9] a Chicago banker, advocated the theory that the liquidity of assets did not reside in any special type of loan, but could arise through establishing a structure of term loans whose periodic amortization would provide the bank with a continuous flow of funds. The amortizability of these loans depended upon the reliability of the borrower, which in turn depended upon whether his "anticipated income" was sufficiently large to meet the installment schedule of the loan. From this viewpoint, all loans of whatever maturity are quite similar.

The major purpose of this theory was to show how banks could derive liquidity from their portfolio of loans and securities. Its secondary purpose was not so much to provide a theory of liquidity as to set a standard by which banks could evaluate the credit worthiness of potential borrowers: was their expected income sufficient to enable them to meet the repayment schedule?

Prochnow was realistic enough to admit that if all banks (or a single bank) were subject to massive deposit withdrawals, they would have to have recourse to the discount window of the Federal Reserve, and perhaps would require additional forms of aid designed to ease restraint in the credit market.

Asset allocation theory

The last in this line of theories designed to improve liquidity for banks argued that the maturity structure of bank assets ought to be determined by the maturity structure of bank liabilities. Since under normal circumstances the turnover rates of different bank liabilities may be different, the maturity structure of assets need not be uniform. In particular, the higher the proportion of demand deposits to total deposits, the larger should be the proportion of liquid short-term assets to total assets. This is because demand deposits have a higher turnover rate than savings deposits, rendering their total amount over any short period less predictable. Greater possible fluctuations in their total sum would necessitate a higher proportion of liquid assets.

[9] Herbert Prochnow, *Term Loans and Theories of Bank Liquidity* (New York: Prentice-Hall, 1949).

Liability management

In the early 1960s the theoretical literature regarding asset selection changed significantly. This change was based upon the view that bank liquidity could be achieved by management of the liability side of the balance sheet as well as the asset side.

The principal means for achieving this management was the development of the negotiable certificate of deposit (the CD). This debt instrument was introduced to the financial world by the First National Bank of New York in 1961 in an attempt to attract the increasingly interest-sensitive corporate funds.[10] Shortly after the First National Bank announcement other large banks in New York announced the formation of a market to buy and sell CDs. The formation of this market served to enhance the liquidity and general acceptability of the CD. It is now an established part of American banking.

The principal advantage of the CD, from the viewpoint of the bank, is that it has a fixed maturity date. That is, the banks do not have to pay these certificates on demand, but only when they mature. Thus, the banks know with certainty when a portion of their liabilities will fall due, and this knowledge gives them additional flexibility in managing the maturity structure of their assets. In particular, it enables them to acquire a higher proportion of longer-maturity assets.

The major impediment to the liability management approach came when market interest rates hit and exceeded those set by Regulation Q. First in 1966, then in 1969, banks found it very difficult to attract and retain funds through the use of CDs. The Regulation Q ceilings prevented them from effectively competing for funds. The abolition of these ceilings for CDs over $100,000 provided greater flexibility for banks. However, at times market interest rates have risen so sharply and to such heights that even in the absence of ceilings banks could not pay the necessary rates to attract and retain funds. The ceilings, and later the very high market rates, have dampened the enthusiasm bankers once felt for the liability management approach to liquidity.

In essence, the CD represents a nondeposit source of funds similar to corporate bonds. However, the CDs usually have short-term maturities compared to bonds.

This chronological review of the various theories of liquidity management and their shortcomings should not be taken to mean that all have been discredited. Quite the contrary. The theories should be viewed as complementary in nature and various elements of each can be found in generally accepted banking practices today. For example, a substantial portion of

[10] The American banking system emerged from World War II with a high proportion of highly liquid funds. In the 1950s this liquidity was worked off and the rate of interest moved upward. With rising interest rates, corporate treasurers became increasingly concerned with the investment of their short-term funds.

bank assets is held in the form of commercial loans, which are highly regarded as secondary reserves. Banks hold a large number of short-term highly marketable securities from which they derive considerable liquidity. For any given type of loan or security and for loans and securities in general, establishing a maturity structure is a sound principle of portfolio management, as is a thorough investigation of the ability of the borrower to discharge his obligations over a given period. Finally, the CD has become an important instrument by which banks raise loanable funds. Thus, current bank portfolio management seems to retain the portions of each theory that under changed institutional circumstances (the establishment of the Federal Reserve) remain valid.

SUMMARY

Being more precise about the assertion that banks make loans was the purpose of this chapter. Several characteristics of the balance sheets of banks that influence or constrain the selection of those assets were discussed.

Finally, a fundamental problem facing bankers was analyzed: that of earning adequate profits while maintaining that liquidity of assets which is necessary because of the demand nature of the bank's liabilities. Several theories attempting to resolve this problem were presented, with main attention focused on the current theory of liability management.

STUDY QUESTIONS

1. Why do banks as profit-oriented institutions hold currency, which yields no income?
2. What is it that makes commercial loans so desirable that they constitute a high proportion of bank loans?
3. Under what circumstances would a bank pay more to attract funds from depositors than it could earn by lending these funds to others?
4. What characteristic of bank balance sheets would lead bankers to be cautious lenders?
5. Explain why as market interest rates rise, the market prices of existing debt securities typically decline.
6. Explain the implications of the commercial loan theory of banking for the supply schedule of money.
7. How would the asset allocation theory of bank portfolio management prove to be deficient during a period when depositors stage a run on the banking system?

8. How do you think the advent of deposit insurance influenced the balance sheet of banks?
9. If banks should be given permission to pay explicit interest on all their deposits, how do you think this would influence their balance sheets?

SELECTED REFERENCES AND READINGS

Carson, Deane, and Scott, Ira O. "Commercial Bank Attributes and Aversion to Risk." In *Banking and Monetary Studies*, edited by Deane Carson. Homewood, Ill.: Richard D. Irwin, 1963.

Markowitz, Harry. "Portfolio Selection." *Journal of Finance*, Vol. 7, No. 1 (Mar. 1952).

———. *Portfolio Selection: Efficient Diversification of Investments*. New York: John Wiley, 1959.

Moulton, H.G. "Commercial Banking and Capital Formation." *Journal of Political Economy*, Vol. 26, No. 4 (July–Aug. 1918).

Prochnow, Herbert. *Term Loans and Theories of Bank Liquidity*. New York: Prentice-Hall, 1949.

Roll, Richard. "Investment Diversification and Bond Maturity." *Journal of Finance*, Vol. 26, No. 1 (Mar. 1971).

Schweitzer, Stuart A. "Bank Liability Management for Better or Worse." *Business Review*, Federal Reserve Bank of Philadelphia (Dec. 1974).

7

CENTRAL BANKING

It has been observed that a people who do not remember their history are forced to relive it, and there is ample evidence to support this observation. However, to remember historical facts is one thing; to interpret them or to understand what they have to teach us is quite another. Interpretation requires a frame of reference, and as noted several times, economists are blessed with at least two alternative frameworks. One attributes to the money supply the causal role in the business cycle; the other subordinates the influence of money to other so-called real factors.

When discussing the American experience with central banking, two avenues of exposition are available. One could merely recite factual detail, or one could attempt to interpret these acts of the central bank in one or the other frame of reference. In this chapter we shall take a factual approach. We shall consider the American experience with central banking without attempting more than a superficial interpretation of the economic history of this institution. To a degree, this approach is forced upon one because for much of the historical period surveyed, insufficient data are available for interpretative purposes.

The presentation of the American experience with central banking will devote special attention to the evolution and development of the three tools used by central bankers to affect the supply of money, and hence the level of economic activity. These three tools are the discount rate, the legal reserve ratio, and open-market operations.

THE HISTORY OF AMERICAN CENTRAL BANKING[1]

The First Bank of the United States

Shortly after the United States became a federal republic the first Secretary of the Treasury, Alexander Hamilton, persuaded the Congress to charter a central bank appropriately called the First Bank of the United States in 1791. The bank was chartered over the vigorous opposition of the political faction led by Thomas Jefferson. Its enabling legislation provided a 20-year

[1] For a detailed history, the reader is referred to the excellent work of Paul Studenski and Herman E. Krooss, *Financial History of the United States* (New York: McGraw-Hill, 1952); and Bray Hammond, *Banking and Politics in America* (Princeton, N.J.: Princeton University Press, 1957).

charter. Being a corporation, the bank was, for its time, an ambitious undertaking. It was then the largest corporation in the United States, with a capital stock of $10 million, of which $2 million was subscribed by the federal government.

The ability of the bank to issue paper notes was limited by its charter to the amount of its capital stock. Had all the capital been subscribed in specie (gold and silver coin), the money stock would have remained unchanged—notes issued in the course of buying assests would have ultimately replaced the specie held as reserves. However, in the case of the government, its capital shares were paid for in bonds.

It should be noted that the bank was a largely private corporation that in addition to serving as a central bank, engaged in the practice of commercial banking for a profit. Its headquarters were in Philadelphia and, in the course of time, it established some ten branches throughout the territory of the United States—mostly at the major seaports, where it collected the tax on imported merchandise. This revenue was the principal source of income for the federal government.

From what records exist, the following conclusions seem warranted with regard to the functioning of the First Bank:

1. It served as an adequate fiscal agent for the federal government by collecting taxes, selling public lands and government bonds, and serving both as a depository and disbursing agent for public funds.
2. It promoted the geographic mobility of liquid capital through its branch banking network. Since such transfers aided internal economic development, the bank's activities in this area must be deemed successful.
3. By establishing correspondent relations with various European banks, especially those in London and Paris, the First Bank served as a means for channeling foreign capital to the United States. Since the United States was then an underdeveloped country, foreign capital was an important source of development funds.
4. Finally, the First Bank prevented the relatively few private state-chartered banks from overissuing their notes by regularly presenting these notes for specie conversion.[2]

[2] Demand deposit banking was virtually nonexistent at the time. Rather, banks gave out their own paper notes or currency when they acquired assets. These notes were redeemable in specie, which necessitated the maintenance of reserves on the part of banks. However, unlike checks, these notes were usually not returned to the issuing banks immediately upon receipt by individuals or other banks. Being negotiable, they often circulated for a long time. Thus, the typical bank could get along on very small reserves. Because the First Bank insisted on conversion, it forced the small banks to hold larger reserves than they otherwise would have, thereby reducing their lending capability and profits and the flow of credit or loanable funds to the private sector.

It should be noted that issuing paper currency instead of demand deposits does not alter the money supply process described in Chapter 4. Only the words describing bank liabilities are changed—notes outstanding replace demand deposits. Because reserve holdings by banks are lower for a system using paper notes rather than demand deposits, the money multiplier is likely to be higher.

It would be an error to conclude that the First Bank engaged in any type of sophisticated monetary management. Its primary role in monetary management was confined to keeping private banks from overissuing their notes. The money supply itself was determined largely by the international flows of specie associated with movements in the balance of our international accounts. The more we sold abroad and foreigners invested here relative to our purchases abroad, the larger was the inflow of gold and silver coin (and the growth of our money supply) and vice versa.

Despite the fact that the First Bank appeared to function adequately, its charter was not renewed and our first brief experience with central banking ended in 1811.[3] Many factors influenced the decision not to renew the charter. Foremost among them was the longstanding opposition of the Jeffersonian Democrats, who had argued from its inception that Congress did not have the constitutional power to charter a central bank.

Certainly among the First Bank's opponents were the farmers, manufacturers, and merchants, who found credit more difficult to obtain because the bank held down the note issue, and consequently, the flow of loanable funds emanating from the state-chartered banks.

Almost immediately after the demise of the First Bank the United States entered into a second war with Great Britain, the War of 1812. Because they are financed in ways that create much money, wars cause inflation, and inflation generally brings with it temporary prosperity. Banking then becomes a very profitable business and the number of banks, as well as the volume of their note issue, rises. Loans that in more sober times would appear of dubious quality may, under the false prosperity of war conditions, appear sound and be the source of an advance of notes. The War of 1812 was no exception and the number and amount of notes in circulation expanded. During most of the war the banks were freed from the obligation to redeem their notes in specie, which greatly served to expand their rate of production.

In 1814 the end of the war precipitated a partial collapse of the banking system and a contraction in the issue of notes. The small, often undercapitalized, banks, which loaned excessively to one or a few customers and kept inadequate reserves, were the principal victims in this financial crash. Because news in general, and news of bank failures in particular, did not travel rapidly in that time, the notes issued by unknown banks often were accepted at a discount. The farther from the eastern seaboard the bank, the larger the discount applied to its notes. In some cases, the discounts were in excess of 50% of the face value of the note.

In the midst of this monetary chaos the voices of reform were raised, and the Jeffersonian Democrats responded in 1816 by chartering the Second Bank of the United States, once again for a period of 20 years.

[3] In 1810, when the bank's charter was presented for renewal, the House of Representatives passed the Act 73–35. The Congress then adjourned, and when it reconvened, the Senate voted 17–17 for renewal. Vice President Henry Clinton, in his role as president of the Senate, broke the tie in favor of the opposition and the bank died.

The Second Bank of the United States

The new bank was larger than the First Bank, but in all other respects it was similar. Its capital was the then formidable sum of $35 million, which was again equal to the dollar amount of notes it could issue. Five million dollars of this capital was subscribed by the federal government. The bank ultimately opened 27 branches throughout the territory of the United States.

Its initial start was uncertain, occurring as it did in the midst of an economic depression; one of its branches even passed into bankruptcy. Nevertheless, the Second Bank survived and, in time, prospered under its third president, the remarkable Nicholas Biddle.

Biddle graduated from the University of Pennsylvania at the age of 15 and served as an aide to James Monroe while the latter was minister to Russia and Secretary of State. Precocious, talented, and aristocratic in manner, this man was to guide the Second Bank to its apex and, ultimately, see it in ruins and himself indicted in connection with its bankruptcy.

The story of the Second Bank closely involves the political activity of the era. Before discussing this, however, the economic effects of the Second Bank should be noted.

The historical record again indicates that this bank performed its tasks in a satisfactory fashion:

1. It aided domestic commerce, production of goods and services, and exchange by providing the public with a currency known to be secure and bills that were immediately recognizable.
2. It regulated the ability of state-chartered banks to issue notes by presenting these notes regularly to the state-chartered banks for specie redemption (it should be noted that the state banks reciprocated in kind). This was the only type of monetary management that it engaged in. The overall supply of money was still governed by the state of the international balance of payments. It should also be noted that such regulation undoubtedly contributed to the stability of the banking system by diminishing the number of bankruptcies.
3. Through its system of branches, it encouraged the geographic mobility of capital in the United States.
4. Through correspondent relations with foreign banks, it provided the means for transmitting foreign capital to the United States, which, in dollars terms, was an important source of the wherewithal for social overhead structures (canals, turnpikes, and railroads).
5. It facilitated foreign trade and commerce by attempting to stabilize the exchange rate of the dollar and other foreign currencies.
6. It served as a fiscal agent for the federal government: it collected taxes, sold public lands, purchased and sold government bonds, acted as a depository for and disperser of public funds, etc.

The destruction of the Second Bank is a shameful episode in American history. Both Andrew Jackson and Biddle were strong personalities with fundamentally different views on the desirability of paper money, and it was perhaps inevitable that they would clash. The clash came in 1832, when the rechartering of the Second Bank became a leading political issue in the presidential election. When Jackson won an impressive victory despite Biddle's use of bank funds on behalf of the opposition, the fate of the bank was sealed. In their final effort to humilate each other, Jackson withdrew federal deposits from the bank and made its notes ineligible for important transactions with the government, while Biddle attempted to precipitate a recession by contracting the bank's loans and its notes.

In 1836 the bank was chartered by the state of Pennsylvania and continued to operate until it went bankrupt in 1839. Biddle was indicted for fraud in connection with the bankruptcy, acquitted, and died soon thereafter. The United States was not again to have a central bank until 1913.

Our historical survey so far suggests at least two conclusions. First, without a central bank or an equivalent authority acting as a restraining influence on commercial banks, many practices that weaken the banking system arise: undercapitalization, excessive loans to one or a few customers (lack of asset diversification), excessive issue of notes relative to reserves, little or no examination to see that existing laws are enforced, etc.

Second, central banks, whose duty it is to regulate other banks, should not be allowed to operate for private profit. Both the First and Second Banks were giant corporations compared to their rivals. They attained this size both through a public grant of the right to organize as a corporation and through the subscription of public funds to their capital stock. Granting such large institutions the power to regulate their business rivals gives them an unfair advantage, which naturally raises the strong opposition of the regulated, on the grounds of conflict of interest. When banks are regulated by a "nonprofit" central bank, they may still feel oppressed, but their objections are likely to be less frequent and intense since the regulator is not also a competitor.

1836–1863

For the 27 years following the end of the Second Bank, the American banking system expanded within the confines of the laws of the individual states. In some jurisdictions banking laws were fairly strict; in other places self-regulating schemes such as the Suffolk System in the northeast states gave rise to a relatively safe banking system. However, in most of the country the banking industry was in a state of anarchy. Every abuse known to banking was to be found. A great variety of notes were in circulation (it is estimated that there were upward of 20,000, of which between 25% to 50% were either issued by defunct banks or were counterfeit). Surely such a plethora of notes must have constituted a handicap to exchange, production, and distribution. Many of the notes were circulated at a substantial discount and it was not uncommon for individuals to keep books that listed the issues with ratings of good and bad—and to consult them before accepting the notes.

The National Banking Act

To reform the banking system and at the same time finance the Union side of the Civil War, the federal government in 1863 made a major effort to involve itself in commercial banking. This effort did not involve a central bank. Rather, the government sought to nationalize the note issue of the country by forcing all banks to take out federal charters. This was accomplished by placing a 10% tax on the notes of all banks that did not join the new system. However, at that time demand deposits were superseding notes as the medium of exchange, and as the tax did not apply to deposits, many banks refused to join the new system.

To strengthen the banking system, the new National Banking Act contained provisions designed to correct those abuses thought responsible for repeated bank failures. Undercapitalization was to be corrected by specifying the size of each bank's capital stock. The larger the city where the bank was located, the larger was to be its capital stock.

Inadequate reserves were to be corrected by specifying obligatory reserve holdings by banks. In applying these requirements, the country was divided into three categories: Central Reserve cities (New York and Chicago), Reserve cities, and the rest of the country. Thus, three categories of banks were created. Banks in the first category were required to hold in their own vaults reserves in specie equal to 25% of their note and deposit liabilities. Reserve city banks faced identical requirements, but could hold up to one-half of their reserves as deposits in Central Reserve city banks (which they often did since these deposits earned interest). The reserve requirement for country banks was 15%, two-fifths of which had to be held in their own vaults, with three-fifths eligible for interbank deposit. Later, it will be shown that this system of reserve holding was a major shortcoming of the National Banking Act, for it permitted three banks to expand notes or deposits on the basis of the same dollar of reserves.

The Office of the Controller of the Currency was created to provide continuous supervision of the banks. It was hoped that its audit staff and unannounced visits to the banks would ensure compliance with the law.

Finally, to provide notes that would be safe beyond doubt, the act provided that they must be secured by the bonds of the federal government (this was the means used to finance the Civil War). Thus, the notes were backed both by government bonds and a reserve requirement. To prevent the excessive issue of national bank notes, Congress limited the issue of eligible bonds against which notes could be issued to a total of $300 million.

Despite these safeguards, the financial system endured recurrent financial panics. These happened in 1873, 1884, 1893, 1903, and 1907. Their basic cause was the reserve requirement provisions of the National Banking Act, which enabled one class of bank to hold deposits in other banks as reserves.

For example, when $100 was deposited in a country bank, $15 had to be held as reserves. However, 60% of this sum, or $9, could be deposited in a Reserve city bank. Twenty-five percent of this $9 deposit, or $2.20, had to be held as legal reserves by the Reserve city bank. This gave the Reserve city bank $6.80 in excess reserves, on the basis of which notes or deposits could be created. In this way two banks counted the same dollar as reserves.

This was not the end, though, for the Reserve city banks could then take one-half of the $2.20 in legal reserves or $1.10 and deposit it in Central Reserve city banks. Against this deposit of $1.10, the Central Reserve city banks needed to hold only 25%, or about 28 cents. They then acquired 82 cents in excess reserves or new lending power. When notes or deposits were created against these reserves, three banks counted the same dollar as reserves.

What happened when the country banks withdrew their deposits from the Reserve city banks? If they did not have sufficient excess reserves, the latter were forced to contract credit and to withdraw their deposits from Central Reserve city banks. These, in turn, were forced to contract credit to come up with sufficient reserves to pay off their deposit withdrawals.

Often, of course, the Reserve city and Central Reserve city banks could anticipate withdrawals by country banks, which might coincide with such events as harvests. Periodically, however, these withdrawals would coincide with a slump on the financial markets. As country bank deposits were frequently lent as call money to stock brokers, the simultaneous occurrence of a withdrawal and depressed stock market prices spelled panic. The brokers could not sell securities to repay bank loans and the city banks, in turn, found it difficult to honor withdrawal requests by country banks. A full-scale financial panic then ensued, often confined to New York City banks. The panic of 1907 gave rise once again to a loud cry for banking reform—especially for the creation of some form of central bank.

These financial panics would probably not have developed if either of two reforms had been instituted. First, the interbank holding of reserves could have been forbidden; second, some system whereby banks with reserve deficiencies could have borrowed reserves from some central agency or other banks could have been set up. Either reform, especially the second, would have eased any financial panic considerably.

In 1908 the Congress passed the Aldrich–Vreeland Act, which allowed banks to form regional associations that, under certain circumstances, could make emergency issues of currency on discount of certain classes of assets. This act was a major step in the direction of reform.[4]

One other shortcoming of the National Banking Act will be considered.

[4] The act expired on June 30, 1915, and was tested but once. At the outbreak of World War I the New York Stock Exchange closed and depositors started a run on New York banks. To stem the run, emergency issues of currency were authorized by a regional Association of National Banks and the potential financial panic subsided as soon as individuals knew they could obtain currency for their deposits.

It was alleged that the currency supply was inelastic, or unresponsive to a demand for it. It will be recalled that National Bank notes could be issued only on security of government bonds and that the total value of bonds issued during the Civil War was fixed at $300 million. This sum diminished in the post–Civil War era as the government ran heavy budget surpluses. If a national bank was faced by a demand for notes and did not have or could not acquire the bonds that notes could be issued against, it simply could not issue additional notes. Other expedients to meet the demand might be resorted to by the banks, such as issuing greenbacks, silver certificates, or specie. Still, the inflexibility of these notes was a handicap to the smooth functioning of the financial system. The early enactment of a law modelled along the lines of the Aldrich–Vreeland Act would have served admirably to grant needed flexibility to the system.

Finally, before we examine the Federal Reserve System, one significant aspect of the National Banking Act should be noted. This was the imposition of legal reserve requirements upon banks. The purpose of these requirements was not to control the money supply, although, given the monetary base, they did set an upper limit on that total. Rather, their purpose was to make the banks hold a considerable portion of their assets in a highly liquid, non-interest-yielding form. Thus, the initial effect of the reserve requirements was to force some combination of portfolio diversification and liquidity upon banks.

The Federal Reserve System

A provision of the Aldrich–Vreeland Act authorized the formation of a National Monetary Commission, one of its purposes being to formulate plans for a central bank. The commission was dominated by the Republican members of Congress and its principal consultant was a Wall Street banker, Paul M. Warburg.

The details of the plan drawn up by Warburg need not concern us, for the proposal was defeated by a coalition of Democrats and Progressive Republicans when it was presented to the Congress in 1912. In the general election of that year the three major political parties (Democratic, Regular Republican, and Bull-Moose) all included planks in their platforms calling for some form of central bank.

With the victory of Woodrow Wilson, the task of developing a central bank fell to the Democrats. However, the party was by no means unified in its approach. Its eastern or gold wing, led by Carter Glass of Virginia, favored a privately owned central bank, regional in character, having notes that would not be the liability of the federal government. Its midwestern agrarian wing was led by William Jennings Bryan, who may have seen in the central bank and its paper currency issue the means for raising farm prices, which his long campaign for the free coinage of silver had failed to achieve. Whether this is true or not, a fear of such proposals as those associated with Bryan was persistent among eastern Democrats.

FIGURE 7:1

Boundaries of Federal Reserve districts and their branch territories. — *Boundaries of Federal Reserve districts.* — *Boundaries of Federal Reserve branch territories.* • *Board of Governors of the Federal Reserve System.* ◉ *Federal Reserve Bank cities.* • *Federal Reserve branch cities. (Courtesy of the Federal Reserve.)*

President Wilson, with the advice of the noted lawyer Louis Brandeis, worked out a bill that would be acceptable to the two wings of his own party as well as to the banking community.[5] This was completed in a fairly short time and President Wilson signed the bill creating the Federal Reserve System just before the end of 1913.

Our central bank is certainly a curious one, perhaps because of the political influences under which it developed. The United States was divided into 12 regions and each region was given its own central bank. This division, which cuts across states, is shown in Figure 7:1.

Ostensibly, the reasons for this arrangement were twofold. At that time the U.S. economy was far more regional in character than it is now. Thus, it was thought that regional central banks could best deal with the peculiarities of each locale. Second, it was believed that the regional approach was the most effective way to prevent the central bank from being dominated by "Wall Street," or the New York financial interests.

The act provided for the creation of a Board of Governors, located in Washington, D.C., which was charged with the supervision and coordination of the system. Its seven members are appointed for 14-year terms by the President. The lengthy term was supposed to make the monetary authorities largely independent of the government. One of the seven is designated as chairman, and while he is equal to the others in terms of voting power, he does have certain prerogatives that increase his power and prestige relative to the other governors. Fortunately, during most of the bank's history the chairmen have been reasonably competent. A brief biographical sketch of the 12 men who have held the position of chairman since the inception of the Federal Reserve is given on page 179.

In its early days the authority in the system was uncertain, and conflicts developed between the New York bank and the Washington board. By various rulings of the Attorney General, power over the system came ultimately to reside in the Washington board. This power consists of control over the tools of central banking. Thus the board came to control the discount rate and the setting of reserve requirements, and its members form a majority of those charged with formulating open-market operations.

The Wilson compromise provided that the Federal Reserve would be privately owned by the commercial banks in the country that desired to buy its capital stock (i.e., join the system), that its note or currency issue would be the liability of the federal government (in order to prevent any overissue, a gold reserve requirement was imposed. It has since been suspended), and that it would serve as the sole depository of bank reserves (subsequently, banks have been given the option of counting vault cash as

[5] A number of individuals have claimed to have originated the Federal Reserve System; among them are Aldrich, Warburg, Glass, and H. Parker Willis, adviser to the House Banking Committeee.

The 12 Chairmen of the Federal Reserve Since 1914

Since its creation in 1914 the office of chairman of the Board of Governors of the Federal Reserve System had been held by these 12 men:

Charles S. Hamlin, Massachusetts attorney; former Assistant Secretary of the Treasury; later, special counsel to the Fed's Board of Governors. He served as Fed chairman from 1914 to 1916.

W. P. G. Harding, former president of the First National Bank of Birmingham, Alabama. Fed chairman from 1916 to 1922.

Daniel R. Crissinger, attorney. He was president of the City National Bank of Marion, Ohio, and served as Comptroller of the Currency under President Warren G. Harding. He later was Fed chairman from 1923 to 1927.

Roy A. Young, ex-governor of the Minneapolis Federal Reserve Bank, who was Fed chairman from 1927 to 1930.

Eugene Meyer, attorney, president of Eugene Meyer and Company. He was a governmental adviser on nonferrous metals and a director of the War Finance Corporation before his term as Fed chairman from 1930 to 1933. Later he was editor and publisher of the *Washington Post* and chairman of the Washington Post Company.

Eugene H. Black, attorney; governor of the Federal Reserve Bank of Atlanta; served as Fed chairman from 1933 to 1934.

Marriner S. Eccles, former banker and corporate executive at the First Securities Corporation, Utah International, the Amalgamated Sugar Company, and others. He was the driving force behind the Banking Act of 1935, leading to the restructuring of the Federal Reserve System. He remained a member of the board until 1951, after serving as Fed chairman from 1934 to 1948.

Thomas B. McCabe, former president of the Scott Paper Company; ex-chairman of the Federal Reserve Bank of Philadelphia. He served as Fed chairman from 1948 to 1951, and later was a public governor of the New York Stock Exchange.

William McChesney Martin, Jr., president of the New York Stock Exchange at age 31, ex-director and president of the Export-Import Bank under President Harry S. Truman. He served as chairman of the Fed from 1951 to 1970.

Arthur F. Burns, former professor of economics at Columbia University and Rutgers; ex-chairman of the President's Council of Economic Advisers, the Advisory Board on Economic Growth and Stability, and the Cabinet Committee on Small Business; a member of the President's Advisory Committee on Labor-Management Policy. He was appointed Fed chairman by President Richard M. Nixon in 1970. He resigned from the Board in 1978.

G. William Miller, Massachusetts attorney, former chairman of Textron Inc., a conglomerate business firm, and former member of the Board of Directors of the Boston Federal Reserve. He served as chairman approximately 18 months, resigning to become Secretary of the Treasury.

Paul Volcker, New York economist; former Under Secretary of the Treasury and former president of the New York Federal Reserve Bank. In moving from the New York Fed to the Board of Governors, Mr. Volcker was forced to take a 50% pay cut. This was because the New York Fed is privately owned and its salary structure is not related to federal government pay scales, which govern the salaries of the members of the Board of Governors.

reserves). In addition, means were devised that would allow the central bank to deal with financial panics, particularly the ability to issue the new currency, Federal Reserve notes, to banks on the discount of certain classes of assets—particularly short-term commercial paper. Finally, the act continued the three-fold reserve requirement classification of the National Banking Act. To induce banks to join the new system, the reserve requirements were reduced substantially: 13% for the demand deposits held by Central Reserve city banks (those located in the 12 cities with a Federal Reserve bank), 10% for those demand deposits held by Reserve city banks (in the 24 cities with a branch of the Federal Reserve), and 7% for demand deposits in country banks. Time and savings deposits in all classes of banks were subject to a 5% reserve requirement.

In response to economic problems over the past 65 years, Congress has from time to time amended the act, altering the structure of the Federal Reserve System, or broadening it powers, or curtailing its activities. A major part of this evolution is concerned with the three tools of central banking often called the instruments of *general credit control* because they supposedly do not influence the allocation of credit, only its overall flow. To that discussion we now turn.

THE TOOLS OF CENTRAL BANKING

Of the three tools of central banking, the discount rate was originally thought to be the most important. This was because the reserve requirements were fixed by law and could not be altered at the discretion of the board and open-market operations had not yet been discovered.

The discount rate

The discount rate is the interest rate the Federal Reserve charges depository institutions who avail themselves of the *privilege* of borrowing from it either by discounting[6] (selling) assets to it, or by seeking an *advance* on their own promise to pay secured by government bonds. Until March 31, 1980, only member commercial banks could exercise this privilege. Subsequently, in enacting the "Depository Institutions Deregulation and Monetary Control Act of 1980," Congress extended this privilege to virtually all depository institutions.

[6] Technically, the central bank *rediscounts* the assets, for in buying them in the first place depository institutions discounted them, i.e., made the loan less the interest due them.

The operation of the discount rate is straightforward. When it is raised relative to prevailing market interest rates, it supposedly discourages depository institutions from borrowing and encourages those who have borrowed not to renew their discounts. This, in turn, is supposed to make it more difficult for customers to obtain loans, thereby slowing the money supply's rate of growth and putting upward pressure on market interest rates.[7] The opposite occurs when the discount rate is lowered relative to prevailing market rates.

In fact, however, the discount rate has never played an important role in U.S. monetary policy for a number of reasons. Foremost among them is that open-market operations, once discovered, proved to be the most flexible and powerful tool of central banking. The second reason is that frequent changes in the discount rate are thought to have disruptive effects on bond prices, and one provision of the Federal Reserve Act pledges it to maintain orderly conditions in those markets. The third reason is that the precise effect of a change in the discount rate on the supply of money and monetary conditions in general is uncertain. That is, its effect on either the borrowed portion of the monetary base or the money multiplier is not clear.

From time to time, however, the discount rate is changed, often as a means of signifying a major change in Federal Reserve policy. Thus, a concerted effort to ease credit may be signaled by a reduction in the discount rate, or a hike in the rate may signal a major effort to tighten monetary conditions. Often such changes are accompanied by other signs, including statements by the chairman of the Board of Governors.

At the very least, changes in the discount rate give Wall Street brokers a handy reason for explaining that day's movement in the Dow Jones average.

Before we conclude this discussion of the discount rate, its relation to a fundamental purpose of central banking and, indeed, to the Federal Reserve System should be noted. A principal purpose of a central bank is to serve as a *lender of last resort* to the financial system. We have recounted the periodic financial panics that gripped the United States from time to time. Each was associated with runs on banks and the subsequent suspension of the convertibility of deposits and notes for specie. One rationale for the Federal Reserve was that it should prevent such crises. To accomplish this, it was given the power to discount or purchase various eligible assets originally only from member banks. Thus, member banks confronted with massive requests for deposit withdrawals could obtain Federal Reserve notes through the discount process in sufficient quantities to restore

[7] The analysis in Chapter 4 suggests that a change in the discount rate relative to the market interest rate will alter the ratio of excess reserves to demand deposits, which changes the values of the money multiplier and the money supply.

depositor confidence. The original Federal Reserve Act envisioned such a lender-of-last-resort role for the U.S. central bank.

As a footnote to history, it is generally agreed that the Federal Reserve failed when its first major test as a lender of last resort came during the early months of the Great Depression. A convincing case can be made that the United States would have been better served had the Aldrich–Vreeland Act remained in force.

The advent of federal deposit insurance in 1934 has diminished the significance of the lender-of-last-resort role for the Federal Reserve. Nevertheless, additional liquidity and reserves can be obtained through the discount window should the U.S. financial system be subjected to a crisis of confidence. The possibility of recourse to the discount window may be responsible for the absence of such crises during the past 50 years.

Reserve requirements

The original purpose of the legal reserve requirements of the Federal Reserve Act was similar to their purpose in the National Banking Act: to force member commercial banks to hold a certain portion of their assets in a liquid form as a safeguard against the disruptive effects of disintermediation.

The requirements in the 1913 act were set at a fixed ratio, which gave the Board no discretion in varying them. For the first time, lower requirements were applied to time and savings deposits than to demand deposits.

In 1935 the Congress amended the Federal Reserve Act to make the manipulation of reserve requirements a new instrument of central banking. The amendment provided that each class of reserve requirement would be doubled and the Board of Governors would be empowered to move the actual reserve ratio within the range. Thus, under the 1935 provisions, the reserve ratios became:

Demand deposits	
Central Reserve city banks	13–26%
Reserve city banks	10–20%
Country banks	7–14%
Saving deposits (all banks)	3– 6%

In 1962 the reserve requirement range for the upper two classes of banks was made a uniform 10–22%.

The classification of commercial banks by geographic area for purposes of assessing reserve requirements raised several important problems. Foremost among them was that the system was inequitable. Banks in Reserve cities had higher reserve requirements than country banks. Yet they could be physically very close, separated by a line that distinguishes the corporate limits of a city from a suburb, and they may be the same size.

Of course, each dollar impounded as reserves reduces the profit of the bank. It is as though the profits that could be earned from those funds is taxed at 100%.

In addition, the classification system weakened control over the money supply. Shifts in deposits from one class of bank to another would cause the weighted reserve ratio in the money multiplier to change, and with this the money supply as well.[8]

In an effort to redress the equity problem Congress amended the Federal Reserve Act in 1972 to assess reserve requirements by the deposit size of the commercial bank. If a bank was located in a city containing either a Federal Reserve bank or a branch (36 cities in all) or had a demand deposit size of over $400 million, it is a Reserve city bank; otherwise it is classified as a country bank. The reserve requirement for each classification could then be applied to each of the demand deposit intervals. The actual reserve requirements in force on June 30, 1979 are shown in Table 7:1.

If a bank has demand deposits of $40 million, its reserve requirements would be 7% of the first $2 million, 9 1/2% of the next $8 million, and 11 3/4% of the final $30 million—or $4,425,000, which is an average of 11.063%. This is less than the 11 3/4% it would have had to hold in the absence of this scheme. The revision was also designed to encourage smaller commercial banks to join the system, and those that were members to stay in it.

While the 1972 Act sought to redress the equity issue by making banks of similar size hold similar volumes of reserves, it had the disadvantage of

TABLE 7:1
Reserve requirements, June 30, 1979

Demand Deposits (millions of dollars)	Marginal Reserve Requirements June 1979
0–2	7%
2–10	9 1/2%
10–100	11 3/4%
100–400	12 3/4%
over 400	16 1/4%
Time deposits to $5 million	1–3%*
Time deposits over $5 million	1–6%*

*The actual reserve requirement depends upon the maturity of the time deposit. The longer the term, the lower the requirement.

[8] In Chapter 4 our model used only one demand deposit ratio for all depository institutions. This ratio should, in a more complete framework, be interpreted as a weighted reserve ratio.

reducing the Federal Reserve's control over the money supply. The reason was that shifts of deposits from one-size bank to another could alter the value of the weighted reserve ratio, and hence the value of the money multiplier. Thus, even if the monetary base were held constant, a mere shifting of deposits from a bank of one-size to another could change the money supply.[9]

Finally, in the sweeping Monetary Control Act of 1980, Congress changed once again the method of assessing reserve requirements. The Federal Reserve was given the power to set reserve requirements for all depository institutions—all commercial banks, savings and loans, mutual savings banks and credit unions.

Under the provisions of the 1980 Act, the first $25 million of all *transactions* accounts will be subject to a uniform reserve requirement of 3 percent. On all balances above this amount, the Federal Reserve will be able to vary the ratio between 8 and 14 percent. Moreover, in "extraordinary circumstances," to be determined by the Board of Governors, it is empowered to impose an additional reserve requirement of up to 4 percent. For purposes of this legislation, transactions accounts include demand deposits, NOW accounts, telephone transfer, automatic transfer from savings, and credit union share drafts.

Because this legislation is so sweeping in its dimensions, it is to be implemented over time. In particular, the Act provides for an eight-year phase-in for depository institutions which are not Federal Reserve members and a four-year phase down of reserve requirements for member banks (the reserve requirements of member banks have been uniformly higher than for non-member institutions).

Thus, with a single monumental piece of legislation, Congress addressed the equity issue and gave the Federal Reserve more control over the money supply. The latter arises because some uncertainty over the value of the money multiplier is reduced now that uniform legal reserve requirements are to prevail.

Functioning of reserve requirements

A decrease in reserve requirements can be analyzed in two ways: by using either the consolidated balance sheet of the financial system or the money

[9] The rules by which an individual bank must calculate its reserve requirement obligation have been changed several times. Each Wednesday since 1968 a bank computes the averages of its daily deposits and vault cash holding for the week ending that day. This determines the amount of reserves it must have on deposit at the Federal Reserve two weeks hence. For example, if its computed reserve requirements were $10 million and it had held $2 million in vault cash, then during the week ending two weeks hence its deposits at the Federal Reserve would have to be $8 million. On June 4, 1980, the Federal Reserve announced that it would invite public comment on its proposal to change the current system of lagged reserve accounting, instituting instead a system of contemporary reserve accounting, i.e., this week's deposits will determine this week's reserve liability.

multiplier. Let Table 7:2 represent the consolidated balance sheet of the financial system and, to simplify the analyses to follow, let us assume that the system is all loaned up, i.e., depository institutions hold no excess reserves. Moreover, the reserve requirement is assumed to be 20%.

Suppose that the reserve ratio is reduced from 20% to 10%. In terms of Table 7:2, while total reserves do not change, only $100 must now be held against deposit liabilities, leaving $100 in excess reserves. If this is lent out, the money supply will expand by $1,000, as demand deposit liabilities rise from $1,000 to $2,000. At that point, the required reserves will again be $200. (This is simply an application of Case I in Chapter 4.)

If, instead, the reserve ratio is increased from 20% to 40%, the available reserves of $200 can support only $500 in demand deposits. In order to reduce their deposit liabilities by one-half, depository institutions will either call in loans or attempt to sell their marketable assets. In either case, when demand deposits are used to buy assets or retire loans, depository institutions will simultaneously lose an asset and a liability. This mutual canceling of assets and debts will continue until each side of the balance sheet totals $500.

In terms of the simple money multiplier developed as Case I in Chapter 4, a reduction in the reserve ratio, r, reduces the denominator of $1/r$ and consequently increases the quotient or value of the multiplier. An increase in r will decrease the value of the multiplier.

Among a number of economists who doubt whether monetary policy has much effect on economic activity, increases in reserve requirements are considered more effective than decreases, for one can *force* depository institutions to contract deposits by raising the ratio, but one cannot *force* them to lend and create deposits by lowering the ratio. In this view monetary policy is asymmetrical—more effective on the contractionary than on the expansionary side. These doubters often quote the old adage that one can bring a horse to the water, but one cannot make him drink. However, as long as the reserve holding of depository insititutions is linked to various behavioral variables such as the interest and discount rates, monetary policy should be equally effective in restraining and expanding the money supply unless the demand schedule for excess reserves on the part of depository institutions becomes infinitely elastic as the difference between the two rates becomes small.

Despite the fact that the Board of Governors has had the power to alter

TABLE 7:2
Consolidated balance sheet of depository institutions

Legal reserves	$ 200	Demand deposits	$1000
Loans	800		
	$1000		$1000

the reserve ratio since 1935, it has not used it extensively. In the main, control of the money supply has not been affected by variations in the reserve ratio. There are several reasons for this.

Changes in the ratio cannot be made frequently, for member banks must be given advance notice (14 days) so that they can make the necessary alterations in their asset structure to accommodate the change. Such alterations are especially important in those cases where the ratio is to be increased. Moreover, since changes in the ratio were long applicable only to the approximately 6,000 banks that are members of the Federal Reserve System, an increase in the ratio, it was feared, would encourage them to leave.

Finally, changes in the ratio are a relatively clumsy means for achieving a given change in the money supply. The reason for this is that small changes in the ratio can have a large impact on the money supply, and there are limits on the size of the change (i.e., the change in the ratio is seldom less than one-quarter percent).

In actual experience the reserve ratios have been gradually reduced over the past 35 years (since the end of World War II).

Open-market operations

Open-market operations involve primarily the purchase and sale by the Federal Reserve of the various classes of negotiable securities issued by the federal government. In recent years the Federal Reserve has also been empowered to purchase securities issued by various government lending institutions, and foreign currencies (in an effort to regulate the dollar's foreign exchange rate) as well as a form of short-term security known as a banker's acceptance. Federal Reserve dealings in the second and third categories of debt instrument, however, are minor.

This most widely used and flexible tool of central banking was discovered by accident. For some six or seven years after its founding, the Federal Reserve had been engaging in open-market operations, largely to provide itself with operating income, without realizing what its purchases of securities were doing to bank reserves.

Before we analyze open-market operations, we will list some of the basic facts about them. First, the purchase or sale of government securities is made pursuant to instructions issued by the Federal Open Market Committee, which is composed of 12 members (the 7 members of the Board of Governors and 5 of the 12 regional bank presidents). This ensures the participation of the regional banks in the formulation and execution of monetary policy.

Second, the actual decision on how many dollars' worth of securities to buy or sell in order to implement the instructions of the Open Market Committee is made by the New York Federal Reserve Bank acting as agent for the system. The transactions themselves are carried out through private security dealers. Once the New York Federal Reserve decides on the amount of securities to be purchased or sold, the regional banks supply the necessary resources, money or securities as the case may be.

Third, as will be demonstrated, it makes an *initial* difference whether the Federal Reserve deals with depository institutions or with private persons when it conducts open-market operations. Dealings with depository institutions affect only reserves, whereas dealings with private persons affect both reserves and the money supply. Ultimately, the end results on the money supply are likely to be quite similar.

Fourth, the Federal Reserve has distinguished between *defensive* and *dynamic* operations. The former are designated to offset other factors changing the monetary base that, if left alone, would alter the money supply in an undesirable fashion. The latter are designed to alter the reserve position of depository institutions in order to achieve a desired change in the money supply.

Fifth, unlike reserve requirement changes, the effects of open-market operations were not historically limited to member banks. When, for example, the Federal Reserve sells government securities, it does not know on what depository institution the check for purchase will be drawn.

Functioning of open-market operations

To illustrate the operation of this most flexible and often used tool of general credit control, we will assume that the Federal Reserve buys securities worth $100 from the financial system. In Table 7:3 this purchase is shown on the books of the Federal Reserve System as a $100 increase in its assets (bonds) and a $100 increase in its liabilities. The increase in liabilities arises because the Federal Reserve writes a check drawn on itself for $100 and gives it to depository institutions in exchange for the bonds. They then forward the check to the Federal Reserve for payment, which is made either by increasing their reserves by $100 or by issuing $100 in Federal Reserve notes. Either way the monetary base is increased by the amount of the purchase. In theory, the ability of the Federal Reserve to

TABLE 7:3
Open-market purchase from depository institutions

Federal Reserve Balance Sheet				Consolidated Balance Sheet of the Financial System				
Bonds	+$100	Reserves or Federal Reserve notes	+$100	Reserves			*D*	$1000
				Legal		$ 200		
				Excess		+100		
				Loans		500		
				Bonds 300				
					−100	200		
						$1000		$1000

increase the monetary base is unlimited under current legislation. In days gone by, a gold reserve requirement was imposed on the reserve and note liabilities of the Federal Reserve, and it operated, just as conventional reserve requirements do on depository institutions, to limit the Federal Reserve's ability to create high-powered money.

On the books of depository institutions, bond holdings are reduced by \$100 and excess reserves are increased from zero to \$100. Since actual excess reserves (\$100) are greater than desired excess reserves (\$0), they are in a state of disequilibrium. In an effort to restore equality between actual and desired excess reserves, they will make loans and create deposits. In other words, the movement to equilibrium results in the creation of money.

If, instead, these securities had been purchased from the public, then the money supply would have been expanded directly.[10] This increase occurs when the public deposits their Federal Reserve checks. The deposit serves to increase both the money supply and the excess reserves of depository institutions. If the legal reserve ratio is 20%, the \$100 deposit will raise excess reserves by \$80, as opposed to the \$100 increase when the securities are purchased directly from depository institutions. However, if they lend out all of their excess reserves and we add the \$100 of money created directly when the securities are purchased from the public, the total increase in the money supply will be the same in both cases.

The great flexibility of this tool of central banking should be obvious. It gives the Federal Reserve the power to add to (or subtract from) the total of the reserves of depository institutions a sum with its amount limited only by the market value of the smallest denomination of government security.

A contrast and comparison of reserve requirements and open-market operations

Since open-market operations and changes in reserve requirements are alternative ways to accomplish a given change in the money supply, it should be instructive to contrast and compare them.

If a given increase in the money supply is desired, it can be accomplished either by increasing the monetary base (by increasing the reserves of depository institutions through open-market operations) or by increasing the value of the money multiplier through reductions in the reserve ratio. These acts may differ in the way they influence the behavior of depository institutions.

When reserve requirements are lowered, the proportion of earning assets

[10] This is the more likely situation, for the Federal Reserve conducts open-market operations through government security dealers. These dealers sell securities from their inventories and deposit their checks. When their inventories are replenished by purchases, the demand deposits are transferred to the sellers of securities.

to total assets is increased and, as a consequence, the profitability of depository institutions is increased. However, if excess reserves are increased through open-market operations, the proportion of liquid to total assets is increased. Having more liquid assets, they are thought to be inclined to make longer-term loans than would be the case if their reserve requirements were reduced. If less liquid loans are higher yielding, they should prefer to have their excess reserves increased through open-market operations.

The effects of each of these two tools are discriminatory to some degree. Historically, changes in reserve requirements applied only to banks that belong to the Federal Reserve System, while the initial impact of open-market operations is more likely to be felt by the larger than by the smaller financial institutions, even though the effect will ultimately work its way through the entire financial system.

It should be apparent now that open-market operations are more flexible as to *amount* and *timing* than are changes in reserve requirements. Changes in the latter are limited both in size (only certain fractions of a percentage change are allowed) and in frequency (since advance notice is required, the number of changes that can be made is limited). Open-market operations can be carried out at any time, subject to the directives of the Open Market Committee.

A final and major difference is that open-market operations can be used directly to affect the market rate of interest, whereas changes in reserve requirements do so only indirectly. This ability to directly alter interest rates arises because in the execution of open-market operations government securities are either bought or sold. In buying or selling, the market prices of these securities are altered, which, given their coupon interest rate, affects their yield in the market. Since for many security holders privately issued securities are substitutes for government securities, when the yields on the latter are altered, individuals will attempt to realign their asset holdings, either buying government securities and selling private securities, or vice versa. In the process the change in percentage yield begun in the government sector is generalized to the private sector. For example, assume the Federal Reserve buys government securities, which raises their prices and reduces their market yields. Some individuals or institutions will now seek to sell their high-priced, lower-yielding government securities and buy the lower-priced, higher-yielding private securities. The demand for private securities will rise, causing their market prices to rise and their yields to decline. Thus, through substitutions by individuals and institutions of private securities for government securities, open-market operations can have an effect on the yield of the former.

It should also be noted that decreases in reserve requirements, by giving depository institutions excess reserves, can induce them to buy securities, raising the securities' prices in general and decreasing their yields. However, experience shows that open-market operations are able to accomplish this goal faster and more directly.

Selective credit controls

These three tools of central banking—the discount rate, reserve requirements, and open-market operations—are frequently called *general credit control devices,* in recognition of the fact that their main impact is on the overall flow of credit rather than on its allocation to one sector or another. *Selective credit controls* supposedly influence the allocation of credit. Whether this power is more apparent than real is a point of contention.

Today the Federal Reserve has several selective credit control powers. One is its power to set the *margin* requirement for negotiable securities. The Securities Act of 1934 allows the Federal Reserve to specify the margin (the amount of the down payment as a percentage of the purchase price) that the purchaser of stocks and convertible bonds must obtain from his own resources. The remainder can be borrowed from a broker or financial institution. The margin ranges from 25% to 100% of the purchase price of the securities. For example, if the margin is set at 40%, a buyer must provide at least that percentage of the purchase price from his own resources; the remainder, 60% at most, can be borrowed.

The imposition of this legal restriction resulted from the pervasive opinion that the stock market crash of 1929 gave rise to the Great Depression, and that the crash itself was due in large part to extensive reckless speculation by people buying on very small margins.

In March 1980, Congress gave the Federal Reserve the power to specify reserve requirements for money market mutual funds and for the accounts receivable of business that arise when individuals use credit cards. Thus, for example, if Sears allows a customer to charge $10 worth of merchandise using a credit card, it would have to forward to the Federal Reserve upwards of $1.50, on which it would earn no interest. Since this increases the cost of doing business, Sears would, in turn, pass these costs on to their customers. Rising costs would then serve to discourage purchases.

The reserve requirement on money market mutual funds was imposed because of a belief that they were attracting funds away from savings and loans and mutual savings banks, thereby exerting a depressing effect on new home construction.

Thus, these special reserve requirements were designed to discourage personal consumption expenditures and to divert the flow of funds away from new housing construction. Shortly after they were introduced, the U.S. economy moved into a sharp recession and they were relaxed somewhat.

Previously, the Federal Reserve also had the power to specify the minimum down payment and the maximum time over which the balance was to be paid for a variety of consumer durable goods (e.g., houses and automobiles). If a decrease in the purchase of durables was thought desirable, the minimum down payment could be raised and the months over which the balance was to be paid could be shortened. The law authorizing the Federal Reserve to set such conditions on loans for durable goods lapsed at the end of the Korean War in 1953.

The extent to which these controls affect the allocation of credit is debatable, for there are ways to evade them. For example, the imposition of higher margin requirements supposedly forces an individual to come up with more of his own resources to make the purchase and he buys less. However, nothing prevents him from substituting borrowed funds for those of his own he was going to use for nonsecurity purchases and using his own funds to purchase securities. In this case, the higher margin requirements have merely induced the buyer to borrow funds for other than security purchases—funds he would have borrowed to buy securities had it not been for the higher margin requirements.

Considerations such as these have led a number of economists to question the usefulness of selective credit controls.

THE FEDERAL RESERVE AS A FISCAL AGENT

Like our earlier central banks, the Federal Reserve functions as a fiscal agent for the federal government. Foremost among its fiscal functions is the management of government deposits so that the financing of government activities does not have disruptive effects on the money supply. Second in importance is its management of the check-clearing process in the United States. These functions are of interest because they lead to changes in the monetary base.

Management of government deposits

After the demise of the Second Bank of the United States in 1836, the Treasury came ultimately to establish its own system of banks across the country whose purpose was to serve as a depository for government funds. This Independent Treasury System continued until 1913 when the Federal Reserve was formed. Its potential to disrupt the money supply was great. Every time the government received revenue from taxes or bond sales, it would place these funds in its own vaults. Thus, the monetary base would decline, which, given the multiplier, would decrease the money supply. Subsequently, when these funds were expended, the base and the money supply would be restored. The reason the Independent Treasury System was not too disruptive was that the federal government was very small in size compared to gross national product. A federal government on today's scale could have profound effects on the money supply if such a system still prevailed. Interestingly enough, this sytem was used to dampen financial panics. When a panic developed, the Treasury would loan funds from its own vaults to selected commercial banks hit by a run. The banks would then acquire reserves to pay off nervous depositors, thereby restoring confidence. Once the panic abated, the depositors would return currency to the banks, and the Treasury would then reclaim its deposits and transfer them back to its own vaults.

Today the Federal Reserve manages what are called *tax and loan accounts* in some 10,000 commercial banks across the nation. The purpose of these accounts is to prevent the receipts and expenditures of the federal government from disrupting the nation's monetary base. Contrary to earlier practices, the commercial banks of the nation today serve as a depository for the funds of the federal government.

The operation of the tax and loan accounts is rather simple. When the federal government comes into possession of checks issued by individuals who pay taxes or buy new issues of government bonds, the Federal Reserve deposits them on behalf of the government in the commercial banks. Since only deposit ownership is changed, the monetary base remains unaltered.[11] When these deposits are expended by the government, deposit ownership is transferred back to private persons, and again, the monetary base remains unaltered.

The management of tax and loan accounts is the responsiblity of the Federal Reserve. It notifies the commercial banks in advance when the Treasury will make a withdrawal from its account, so that the banks can make any adjustment in their asset structure that such a withdrawal might necessitate.[12]

Thus, the routine operations of the federal government involving the collection of billions of dollars in taxes and additional billions from the sales of securities to finance budget deficits have very little impact on the monetary base, even though they might have an impact on the supply of money.

For a commercial bank to be eligible for a tax and loan account, it must stand ready to hold government securities against the value of the government's deposit. Thus, in case of bankruptcy the funds of the government are not lost or subject to any delay in withdrawal.

Check clearing

An essential service performed by the Federal Reserve is its operation of a complex network for the clearing of the billions of checks written each year. We are interested in this activity of the Federal Reserve because check clearing gives rise to something called *float,* which can cause the monetary base to change over time.[13]

[11] In Chapters 8 and 9, which contain a more comprehensive explanation of the implications of the tax and loan accounts, it will be seen that Treasury operations can influence both the monetary base and the money multiplier. Suffice it to note here that since demand deposits and currency held by the federal government are excluded from the recorded statistics on the money stock, any increase in balances held in tax and loan accounts will reduce the recorded money stock.

[12] The actual mechanics of the Treasury's operations are a bit more complicated than suggested by this paragraph. The Treasury does not actually draw checks against its accounts at the commercial banks. Rather, the funds are first transferred from the commercial banks to the Federal Reserve banks. Only then does the Treasury draw its checks against these funds.

[13] Other depository institutions can use these check-clearing facilities so long as they pay checks drawn on them at their face value (clear at par). If, rather, they accept them at a discount, they cannot use the facilities.

Before the advent of the Federal Reserve, checks could be cleared in large cities by the use of clearing houses, or central locations where banks would bring their checks drawn on one another, separate them, and pay one another any net differences. For checks drawn on banks outside the cities, correspondent balances (i.e., accounts one bank keeps in others) were the method used for clearing. It was not uncommon for a check to take considerable time to clear. An anecdote is told about two banks some 15 miles apart that had to use 20 correspondent banks to clear a check drawn on the one and deposited in the other because they did not themselves have a mutual correspondent balance.

In order to see how modern check clearing works and explain how float arises, consider the following case. Individual A in Detroit draws a check for $100 on a local bank in favor of individual B in Chicago, who deposits it to his account in a local bank. The Chicago bank then sends the check to the Federal Reserve in Chicago for clearing. When the Chicago Federal Reserve gets the check, it does not immediately increase the reserves of the Chicago bank and decrease those of the Detroit bank because it does not know if the check is good. Rather, the Chicago Federal Reserve will increase an asset account it maintains called *Uncollected Cash Items* and a liability account called *Deferred Availability Items,* as shown in Table 7:4.

The Chicago Federal Reserve will then consult the *Deferred Availability Schedule,* which tells it how long it will take for the check to clear. As an illustration, assume this period to be three days. At the end of this time the Chicago Federal Reserve will assume the check to be good and will automatically increase the reserves of the Chicago bank. This is done by reducing Deferred Availability Items and increasing the reserves of the Chicago bank. This entry by itself will increase the reserves of the Chicago bank *without decreasing* the reserves of the Detroit bank. If everything goes according to schedule, the Detroit bank will report the check to be good and, on the same day, an entry will be made decreasing Uncollected Cash Items and the reserves of the Detroit bank. Thus, at the end of three days the balance sheet of the Chicago Federal Reserve will appear as Table 7:5.

From time to time check clearing does not go according to schedule. At holidays and tax collection time the volume of checks rises and they cannot be cleared fast enough. Since it takes longer to clear these checks than is allotted by the Deferred Availability Schedule, the reserves of some banks will be increased without the reserves of others being decreased. Float will be said to rise and the monetary base of the country will increase. Similarly,

TABLE 7:4
Balance sheet of the Chicago Federal Reserve Bank

Uncollected Cash Items	$100	Deferred Availability Items	$100

TABLE 7:5
Balance sheet of the Chicago Federal Reserve Bank

	Reserves:	
	Chicago Bank	+100
	Detroit Bank	−100

snowstorms, floods, strikes, and other disasters may impede the flow of the mail and cause float to rise.

In order to calculate the actual amount of float, the amount of Deferred Availability Items is subtracted from Uncollected Cash Items. This quantity (which varies over time) will have a predictable seasonal pattern because the volume of expenditures in this country has a predictable seasonal pattern. Therefore, the Federal Reserve can undertake defensive open-market operations to counteract unwanted movements in the float.

PROPOSALS FOR REFORM

Because the Federal Reserve was created through a political compromise, it has, in the eyes of many, imperfections that they seek to correct. Proposals for reform have aimed at both the structure of the central bank itself and banking in general.

Reform of the central bank

First, the necessity for maintaining 12 regional banks is questioned. The original purpose of this curious arrangement was dictated by the political climate of the day, which saw in Wall Street an unmitigated evil to be combated. Since this view is hopelessly superficial, the regional arrangement no longer has any rationalization. However, it should be noted in defense of this arrangement that the regional banks do not always agree with the Board of Governors on the proper conduct of monetary policy. The St. Louis bank has long been a sort of rebel in the system, and as one instance of its influence, it has (through a long series of articles in its *Monthly Review,* supported by statistical evidence) persuaded the Washington board to pay closer attention to the rate of growth of the money supply as an indicator of the tightness of monetary policy. Without the regional set-up, it is quite possible that studies of the type supported by the St. Louis bank would have been largely ignored by the Washington board.

Second, many have questioned the high degree of independence of the central bank in this country. The members of the Board of Governors are appointed for very long terms (14 years) and are responsible to no higher authority unless Congress forces upon them some changes. However, this independence is more apparent than real and the Board of Governors is frequently mindful of the intent and will of Congress and the Executive Branch of government.

In 1975 Congress passed House Concurrent Resolution 133 which requested that the Board of Governors consult with congressional committees on a quarterly basis about the system's objectives and plans for the ranges of growth of monetary and credit aggregates over the next 12 months. Such consultations became mandatory with the passage of the Federal Reserve Reform Act of 1977. For the first time since its inception the Federal Reserve must now set forth its objectives and in a limited way provide a standard against which its performance can be evaulated. While it is too early to evaluate the impact of this simple requirement, it may have profound significance, for it furnishes crucial information to the financial market which was not hitherto available.

The United States is one of the very few industrial countries where monetary and fiscal policies are formulated and executed by two separate groups—the Federal Reserve and the federal government. At times it has been difficult to coordinate the two to achieve a common objective because the central bank may have different goals than does the federal government, or a different interpretation of events, or different priorities, or operate within a different theoretical framework. Whether one common authority over both monetary and fiscal policy is desirable is debatable. Those who believe that on balance it is, are prepared to circumscribe the independence of the Federal Reserve and subordinate it more directly to the elected representatives of the people (the President and the Congress).

Reform of commercial banks

The commercial banking system in this country has not escaped criticism. One of its alleged shortcomings, applicable now to all depository institutions, is its ability to expand the supply of money by some multiple of its reserves. Economists who view variations in the growth rate of the money supply as the major cause of the business cycle believe that this ability is the source of much trouble. They have proposed that this power on the part of banks be abolished by the imposition of a 100% reserve ratio. That is, for every dollar of demand deposit liabilities, the banks would have to have one dollar in currency. The effect of this proposal would be to enable banks to alter the composition of the money supply without altering its total. The basic way by which banks could acquire currency to make loans would be by selling capital shares. Otherwise, every dollar of currency they held would serve as reserves for an equal dollar of deposit liabilities.

Under 100% reserve banking, the long-run growth of the money supply would depend on the growth of the monetary base (i.e., currency). This, in turn, would depend upon the deficits of the federal government that would be financed by printing currency or by open-market operations, whereby the Federal Reserve would buy government securities with Federal Reserve notes.

How seriously such proposals are currently viewed by economists is debatable. They would reduce the effect of variations in the money multiplier on the money supply. However, as long as the Federal Reserve has control of the monetary base and can estimate the money multiplier with reasonable accuracy, reforms such as 100% reserve requirements for all banks and other depository institutions are unnecessary.

SUMMARY

The American experience with central banking reflects our national distrust of centralized power. Our first two central banks in the early nineteenth century were chartered for only limited periods, even though they appeared to function satisfactorily. In the periods during which the country functioned without a central bank, a number of serious banking abuses arose that reached such proportions that one wonders how the U.S. economy managed to achieve such a notable rate of economic growth. Perhaps the true costs of that growth have been incorrectly calculated.

The United States again had a central bank with the founding of the Federal Reserve in 1913. Using the three tools of central banking, the Federal Reserve gradually acquired a high degree of control over the U.S. money supply. It is this control that is the principal distinguishing characteristic of the Federal Reserve.

STUDY QUESTIONS

1. In terms of the social productivity of money, explain the usefulness of a widely recognized, uniform, and financially sound currency.
2. Why should state-chartered banks have opposed the First and Second Banks of the United States?
3. Explain the problem of reserve pyramiding which emerged during the national banking period. How might it have been dealt with?
4. Suppose banks had been forbidden to pay explicit interest on interbank deposits. Do you think such a law would have ended the practice during the national banking period?
5. What is the likely effect on the supply of money when the discount rate is increased relative to market interest rates?
6. It has been said that reserve requirements act as a 100% tax on bank profits. Explain what this means.
7. Using the demand schedule for excess reserves developed in Chapter 4, analyze both an increase and a decrease in reserve requirements. Is there any reason to believe that the effectiveness of the change is greater on the contractionary than on the expansionary side?
8. Why are open-market operations regarded as the most flexible tool of central banking?

9. Why does float emerge?
10. Suppose that financial institutions stand willing to hold all reserves made available to them by the central bank. Is there any way to increase the money supply?

SELECTED REFERENCES AND READINGS

Board of Governors of the Federal Reserve System. *The Federal Reserve System, Purposes and Functions*. Washington, D.C., 1975.

Cagan, Phillip. "The First Fifty Years of the National Banking System—An Appraisal." In *Banking and Monetary Studies*, edited by Deane Carson. Homewood, Ill.: Richard D. Irwin, 1963.

Friedman, Milton, and Schwartz, Anna J. *A Monetary History of the United States, 1867–1960*. Princeton, N.J.: Princeton University Press, 1963.

Galbraith, John Kenneth. *Money, Whence It Came, Where It Went*. Boston: Houghton Mifflin, 1975.

Kane, Edward J. "Good Intentions and Unintended Evil: The Case Against Selective Credit Allocations." *Journal of Money, Credit, and Banking*, Vol. 9, No. 1 (Feb. 1977).

Krooss, Herman E., ed. *Documentary History of Banking and Currency in the United States*. New York: McGraw-Hill, 1969.

Martin, David A. "Bimetallism in the United States Before 1850." *Journal of Political Economy*, Vol. 76, No. 3 (May–June 1968).

8 THE DERIVATION OF THE MONETARY BASE 8

SOURCES OF THE BASE

In Chapter 4 the money supply was shown to be the product of the monetary base and the money multiplier. The source of the monetary base was left rather vaguely specified in order to concentrate attention on the process of money creation and the derivation of the money supply schedule.

Initially, the monetary base was assumed to consist of green pieces of paper denominated in dollars that were supplied by the central bank to the financial system. Later, these green pieces of paper were seen to be either Federal Reserve notes or bank reserves held at the Federal Reserve, and to result from open-market operations. It was also shown that discounting and float could affect the size of the monetary base. While that discussion was factually correct, it was piecemeal and sketchy. We will now undertake a systematic discussion of the sources of the monetary base or high-powered money.

At present in the United States there are two institutions, the Federal Reserve and the U.S. Treasury. Each has some liabilities that can be used as either actual or potential reserves of the financial system. That is, these liabilities can either be held as reserves of depository institutions, or as currency in the hands of the public.

In order to isolate the sources of supply of the monetary base, the balance sheets of these two institutions must first be consolidated. Then those liabilities that either are reserves of depository institutions or currency held by the public (i.e., the monetary base) must be singled out. If this is done, the consolidated assets less the remaining liabilities and capital accounts must be equal to the monetary base. This conclusion follows from the construction of a balance sheet. If assets equal liabilities plus capital accounts, then subtracting some subgroup of liabilities plus capital from total assets must yield the remaining liabilities—in this case, the monetary base.

A complete U.S. Treasury balance sheet is unavailable. However, the monetary liabilities of the Treasury are known and these are simply added to both sides of the Federal Reserve balance sheet, which is reproduced here as Table 8:1.[1]

[1] On the left side Treasury currency outstanding is listed. This consists of the paper notes and coins issued by the Treasury. This currency can be held by depository institutions, the public, the Federal Reserve, and the Treasury itself. All such holdings are, therefore, listed on the right-hand side.

TABLE 8:1
Federal Reserve balance sheet and the monetary liabilities of the Treasury

Assets	Liabilities and Capital
1. Gold stock and SDR account	1. Member bank reserve deposits
2. Federal Reserve credit	2. Currency held by all depository institutions
A. Government securities held	3. Currency held by the public
B. Discount and advances	4. Treasury cash holdings
C. Acceptances	5. Deposits at the Federal Reserve
D. Float	A. Treasury
3. Other Federal Reserve asset accounts	B. Foreign
	C. Other
4. Treasury currency outstanding	6. Other Federal Reserve liabilities and capital accounts

This balance sheet can be rearranged to isolate the monetary base. This is accomplished by moving to the left side all the liability and capital accounts that are not themselves a part of the monetary base. The remaining liability items can then be used either as reserves of depository institutions or held as currency by the public. Table 8:2 shows such a division; the positive and negative signs indicate the direction of influence on the monetary base of an increase in the specific item.

In order to substantiate the direction of the influence of the seven items making up the source of the monetary base, a transaction involving each will be analyzed.

TABLE 8:2
Sources and uses of the monetary base

Sources of the base		Uses of the base
1. Gold stock and SDR account	+	1. Member bank deposits at the Federal Reserve
2. Federal Reserve credit	+	2. Currency held by all depository institutions
A. Government security held		3. Currency held by the public
B. Discounts and advances		
C. Acceptances		
D. Float		
3. Other Federal Reserve asset accounts	+	
4. Treasury currency outstanding	+	
5. Treasury cash holdings	−	
6. Deposits at the Federal Reserve	−	
A. Treasury		
B. Foreign		
C. Other		
7. Other Federal Reserve liabilities and capital accounts	−	

Gold Stock and the SDR Account

The gold stock of the United States is subject to change from two sources: domestic mining and, prior to 1973, the state of our international balance of payments. The SDR account stands for Special Drawing Rights and represents an attempt at the international level to create paper gold to supplement what was believed to be an inadequate growth in the output of physical gold to finance international trade and commerce. For the purpose of this analysis, the SDR account will be neglected. (See Chapter 17 for a discussion of SDRs).

For some 40 years prior to 1975, the Federal Reserve, serving as a purchasing agent for the Treasury, bought all the gold domestically mined in the United States. To purchase gold, the Federal Reserve would issue its own check to the gold miner. The miner would deposit the check in his depository institution, which would then forward it to the Federal Reserve for payment. It would be paid by increasing member bank reserves if the miner's depository institution was a member, or by issuing Federal Reserve notes to the depository institution if it was not a member. Either way the monetary base would increase, for either member bank deposits or currency held by depository institutions and the public would rise. Table 8:3 shows the result of a gold purchase on the books of the Federal Reserve and the banking system.

Until it was decided in 1973 to let market forces determine the dollar's foreign exchange rate, the United States was on a sort of international gold standard by which foreign central banks could convert their dollar holdings into gold and we could do the same for our accumulations of their currencies. (Actually, the right of foreign central banks to request gold conversion was suspended in August 1971.)

Consider the case in which U.S. citizens sell more abroad than they buy. This will be represented by a net increase in the deposits in domestic depository institutions balanced by an asset representing the claims of the U.S. financial system on foreign banks. When the U.S. depository institutions withdraw those foreign deposits, they are paid in gold, and the American depository institutions then sell it to the Federal Reserve. Once

TABLE 8:3
Gold purchase

Federal Reserve		Member Banks		Other Depository Institutions	
Gold +	Member bank reserves or Federal Reserve notes +	Reserves +	Deposits +	Currency +	Deposits +

this stage is reached, this case then becomes the exact equivalent of the gold miner selling his output to the Treasury through the Federal Reserve. Either the dollar value of the reserves of depository institutions or Federal Reserve notes outstanding will rise. Thus, all increases in Treasury holdings of gold will lead to a dollar rise in the monetary base.

Federal reserve credit outstanding

Federal Reserve credit consists of four different items. Increases in any of these will serve to increase the monetary base.

Security holdings

The Federal Reserve holdings of government securities arise from open-market operations. When the Federal Reserve buys these securities with a check drawn on itself, it pays the check either by increasing bank reserves, if the bank is a member of the system, or by paying out Federal Reserve notes, which increases currency in circulation.

Table 8:4 illustrates these transactions; the two right-hand balance sheets represent the options.

Discounts and advances

The Federal Reserve rediscount of an asset represents a purchase of that asset from a depository institution. On the other hand, if the Federal Reserve makes an advance, it lends to depository institutions on the basis of the latters' own IOU (secured by government securities). Either of these actions by the Federal Reserve will serve to increase the reserves of depository institutions and the monetary base. This is shown in Table 8:5.

From the viewpoint of the depository institution, the accounting for the two ways to obtain reserves is slightly different. Discounts are shown as a decrease in assets, and advances are shown as a liability. (The Federal Reserve, of course, treats both as a single asset.)

The advance is convenient for those depository institutions that do not have suitable assets (assets that meet the tests) for discount. Reference to Table 8:10 shows that discounts and advances are a very small component of the monetary base.

Float

The origin and impact of float on the monetary base has already been discussed in detail. It will be remembered that float arises when the actual time required to clear a check is greater than that expected under the usual

TABLE 8:4
Open-market operations

A. Purchase from Depository Institutions

Federal Reserve

Assets		Liabilities	
Government securities	+	Member bank reserves or Federal Reserve notes	+

Member Banks

Assets		Liabilities	
Reserves	+		
Bonds	−		

Other Depository Institutions

Assets		Liabilities	
Currency	+		
Bonds	−		

B. Purchase from the Public

Depository Institutions

Assets		Liabilities	
Reserves	+	Demand deposits	+

Public

Assets		Liabilities	
+	Currency or Demand deposits		
−	Bonds		

TABLE 8:5
Federal Reserve grant of a discount or advance

Federal Reserve				Depository Institutions			
Discounts and advances	+	Member bank reserves or Federal Reserve notes	+	Reserves	+		
				Assets discounted	−	←or→	Advances +

conditions. Whenever the actual time is greater than expected, the reserves of some depository institutions are increased without those of others being decreased. Thus, the monetary base varies directly with float.

Acceptances

A substantial amount of trade is financed on terms not requiring immediate payment. The payment is to be made at some date in the future. Suppose, for example, that A sells to B $10,000 in merchandise, and requires payment 60 days in the future. A will draw up a note requiring future payment to him or the holder of the note at some interest rate. If A requires B's bank to endorse the note, then the bank is liable for its payment when it becomes due (in essence the bank substitutes its credit for B's). This negotiable instrument is called a *banker's acceptance.* A can either hold it until it is paid or he can sell it. A market exists for these debt instruments, and the Federal Reserve Act authorizes the central bank to buy or sell banker's acceptances as it sees fit. Therefore, their purchase or sale has exactly the same effect on the monetary base as would an open-market purchase of government securities. The buying and selling of these instruments amounts to open-market operations in private debt securities. A balance sheet presentation is identical to that given in Table 8:4 for the purchase of government securities.

Treasury currency outstanding

"Treasury currency outstanding" consists primarily of coins. A small amount of currency notes is also included, represented in the main by United States notes, the so-called greenbacks issued to finance the Civil War.

To see how a rise in Treasury currency outstanding will increase the monetary base, suppose that the Treasury pays all civil servants in coins. Then the quantity of, "currency held by the public" rises by the amount paid out. If some of the coins are deposited in depository institutions, their reserves rise by this amount and "currency held by the public" decreases by the same amount. Overall, the monetary base is increased by the total amount paid out in coins.

Other Federal Reserve asset accounts

This account is frequently combined in the official statistics with other Federal Reserve liabilities and capital accounts and shown merely as a total sum. For illustrative purposes, it will be shown here separately.

Substantially, "other Federal Reserve asset accounts" represent the plant, buildings, and equipment of the entire Federal Reserve System. From time to time, the Federal Reserve expands its facilities. When it does, it pays for these extensions with checks drawn on itself. The suppliers of these facilities, in turn, deposit these checks in *their* depository institutions which forward them to the Federal Reserve for payment. They are paid either by increasing the reserves of member banks or by paying out Federal Reserve notes, which increases currency in circulation. This transaction is set forth in Table 8:6.

An increase in any one of the four items making up the source of the monetary base discussed thus far will increase the monetary base. By the same token, a decrease in any one item will reduce the monetary base. To see this, merely reverse the example trasactions.

In each of the three items to be discussed, an increase will serve to *reduce* the monetary base, for these items represent the other liabilities and capital accounts of the Federal Reserve and, in part, the Treasury. If the assets in the consolidated balance sheet are held constant, an increase in the other liabilities and capital accounts *must* reduce those liabilities we have designated as the monetary base. For that reason, these accounts are frequently regarded as negative source items.

Treasury cash holdings

Treasury cash holdings represent what may be thought of as petty cash or currency holding to make relatively small payments. To see the negative impact of this item on the monetary base, assume that to accumulate petty cash, the Treasury collects more in taxes than it pays out. Thus, Treasury tax and loan accounts grow in size. From our earlier analysis, we know that these accounts do not give rise to a change in the monetary base, only

TABLE 8:6
Federal Reserve purchase of plant and equipment

Federal Reserve		Member Banks		Other Depository Institutions	
Other Federal Reserve asset accounts +	Member bank reserves or Federal Reserve notes +	Reserves +	Demand deposits +	Currency +	Demand deposits +

TABLE 8:7
Treasury accumulation of currency

Banks	
Reserves −	Treasury deposits −

to a change in the ownership of demand deposits. However, when these deposits are transferred from the banks to the Treasury's own vaults, the monetary base declines. This is because the banks pay off these deposits with their vault cash or from their reserves held at the central bank. Either way, as Table 8:7 shows, bank reserves and the monetary base decline.

Deposits at the Federal Reserve

Treasury deposits

When Treasury deposits are transferred from the tax and loan accounts at banks to the Federal Reserve, as they are just prior to the Treasury's payments for the expenditures of the government, the banks lose reserves equal to the amount transferred. This is because when the Treasury withdraws its balances from a bank, it is given a check by the bank for the sums withdrawn. The Treasury then deposits this check with the Federal Reserve, which cashes the check by decreasing member bank reserves on deposit with it, or by requesting nonmember banks to pay in currency—the latter forming their reserves. As shown in Table 8:8, the reserves of the banks decline.

Foreign deposits

If in the immediately preceding analysis the word "foreign" had been used in place of "the Treasury," the results would be the same. Whenever deposits owned by foreigners are transferred from depository institutions to the Federal Reserve, the reserves of depository institutions, whether held as central bank deposits or as vault cash, will decline as they cover the withdrawals.

TABLE 8:8
Transfer of Treasury deposits to the Federal Reserve

Federal Reserve		Banks	
	Treasury deposits +	Reserves −	Treasury deposits −
	Member bank reserves, or Federal Reserve notes −		

Other deposits

Other deposits at the Federal Reserve are primarily those of nonmember depository institutions. They exist in order to facilitate the check-clearing process.

When nonmembers make deposits at the Federal Reserve, they decrease their holdings of vault cash. Since their cash holdings are a part of the monetary base, the base declines when such deposits are made at the Federal Reserve.

Other Federal Reserve liabilities and capital accounts

This entry on the balance sheet comprises primarily the capital accounts of the central bank. As noted in a previous chapter, the Federal Reserve System is privately owned by the commercial banks that choose to become members (although, as stockholders in modern corporations have long known, ownership and control are two different things).

Each bank that elects to become a member of the system must subscribe to an amount of the share capital of the Federal Reserve equal to 6% of its own capital and retained earnings. One-half of this sum must be paid into the Federal Reserve and one-half is on standby and can be called at the option of the Federal Reserve.

When a member bank subscribes to capital shares, it pays for them with a check drawn on itself. The Federal Reserve "cashes" the check by decreasing those reserves of the bank that are on deposit with it. This transaction is shown in Table 8:9. Since its inception in 1913, the Federal Reserve has paid an annual interest of 6% on these shares.

This completes our analysis of the sources of the monetary base. The importance of this detailed discussion should not be lost. It may be vitally important to know what is causing the monetary base to change over time, for depending on the cause, the action of the central bank may be different. For example, a change in the base due to a decrease in the gold stock may require a different Federal Reserve policy than a change initiated by a rise in the currency holdings by the Treasury or by a change in float.

TABLE 8:9
Subscription to the capital stock of the Federal Reserve

Federal Reserve		Member Banks	
	Reserves − Capital stock +	Reserves − Capital shares of the Federal Reserve +	

MOVEMENTS IN THE SOURCE ACCOUNTS OVER TIME

Since the monetary base grows over time, its growth must be accounted for by movements in the items constituting the sources of the base.

If the accounts that enter the sources of the base with a positive sign increase over time, the monetary base will rise. The same will hold true if those accounts that enter with a negative sign decline over time. For example, if Treasury cash holdings decline, the monetary base will rise, other things being equal. Conversely, if the positive source accounts decline, the monetary base will decrease; the same thing will happen if those accounts entering with a negative sign increase.

Table 8:10 is drawn up to explain the changes in the monetary base over time. The magnitude of each of these accounts should be noted in order to appreciate which ones are most important in explaining the amount of the base and its change over time. The purpose of Table 8:10 is to derive the monetary base as of two separate dates, and then to explain the movement of the base over this six-year period. The net increase was a little over $39 billion. The dominant source item being Federal Reserve purchases of U.S. government and federal agency securities. This alone amounts to over $38.6 billion.

THE COMPONENTS OF THE MONETARY BASE AND CONTROL OF THE MONEY SUPPLY

Once the sources of the monetary base are listed, it becomes obvious that the Federal Reserve does not control all of them. In fact, its control is confined to Federal Reserve credit, although reference to Table 8:10 shows this sum to dwarf all others by a considerable margin.

Because the Federal Reserve does not control all the items in the base, it shares *influence* over the monetary base with the Treasury, depository institutions, and foreigners. This fact has important implications for the *control* of money supply. Among other things, it implies that control will be more difficult, for in deciding how much high-powered money it will supply to the system, the Federal Reserve will have to estimate the most probable value of these other contributions. In carrying out open-market operations, the Federal Reserve will have the added problem of estimating the impact on the monetary base of agents over which it has no control. The art of central banking is not easy. The ability to hit a money supply target on a quarterly basis depends on how well or poorly these estimates are fulfilled.

SUMMARY

The task laid out for this chapter was to explain the factors accounting for the monetary base. This was accomplished through a consolidation of the balance sheets of the Federal Reserve and the federal Treasury. The items

TABLE 8:10

An analysis of the change in the monetary base (in millions of dollars)

	Sources of the Base	Monetary Base as of December 1970	Monetary Base as of December 1976	Factors Changing the Base: Increasing	Factors Changing the Base: Decreasing
1.	Gold Stock	$11,105	$11,598	$ 493	
2.	SDR account	400	1,200	800	
3.	Federal Reserve credit				
	A. U.S. government securities held	61,688	93,412		
	Federal agency securities held		6,916	38,640	
	B. Discounts and advances	321	—		321
	C. Float	3,570	3,536		34
	D. Acceptances	97	519	422	
4.	Other Federal Reserve assets	1,032	3,249	2,217	
5.	Treasury currency outstanding	7,145	10,865	3,720	
6.	Treasury cash holdings	−427	−464		37
7.	Federal Reserve deposits				
	A. Treasury	−849	−6,138		5,289
	B. Foreign	−145	−306		161
	C. Other	−735	−974		239
8.	Other Federal Reserve liabilities and capital	−2,265	−3,253		988
	TOTAL MONETARY BASE	$80,938	$120,160	46,292	7,069
	Holding of the Base				
	Member bank reserve deposits at the Federal Reserve	$23,925	$26,430		
	Currency held by all commercial banks*	7,013	11,530		
	Currency held by the public	50,000	82,200		
		$80,938	$120,160		

Total Change in the Base		*Explanation of Change*	
Base on Dec. 31, 1976	$120,160	Factors increasing the base	$46,292
Base on Dec. 31, 1970	80,938	Factors decreasing the base	7,069
	$ 39,223	Net factors increasing the base	$39,223

Courtesy of the *Federal Reserve Bulletin*.

* During this period only commercial banks issued demand deposits on a nationwide basis. Holdings of currency by other depository institutions was included in currency held by the public.

composing the monetary base were isolated on the liability side of this balance sheet, and the remaining liabilities and capital accounts were then moved to the left-hand side as negative offsets to the assets. From this arrangement it follows that all movements in the monetary base can be explained by movements of the items on the left side of the balance sheet. As an aid to understanding the derivation and movements in the base, a number of accounting transactions were described and explained. Finally, the monetary base itself was computed and its movement between two dates explained.

It was also observed that since others besides the Federal Reserve can influence the movement of the monetary base, control over the money supply is a complex matter. The Federal Reserve, in preparing its own plans, must estimate the most probable impact of others on the monetary base as well as the value of the money multiplier.

STUDY QUESTIONS

1. Why is it important to understand the factors that cause the monetary base to change?
2. Suppose a domestic gold mine sold gold to the public. Would the monetary base rise?
3. Suppose the Treasury bought the gold of domestic mines and minted them into gold coins, which were held in bank vaults. Would the monetary base rise?
4. Which is the easiest way to increase the monetary base?
5. Suppose deposits owned by the Bank of England are moved from commercial banks to the Federal Reserve. What would happen to the monetary base?
6. The Federal Reserve does not control all the components of the monetary base. What additional problems does this introduce for the control of the money supply?

SELECTED REFERENCES AND READINGS

Anderson, Leonall, and Jordan, Jerry L. "The Monetary Base—Explanation and Analytical Use." *Monthly Review*, Federal Reserve Bank of St. Louis (Aug. 1968).

Federal Reserve Bank of Cleveland. "Sources of Commercial Bank Funds: An Example of 'Creative Response.' " *Economic Review* (Nov. 1965).

9

THE FEDERAL TREASURY, THE NATIONAL DEBT, AND THE MONEY SUPPLY

The potential monetary powers of the federal Treasury are formidable. In our earlier discussion of the monetary base it was shown that when the Treasury transfers its balances from the tax and loan accounts it maintains at commercial banks to the Federal Reserve, the monetary base contracts and, given the money multiplier, reduces the money supply. This action on the part of the Treasury is analogous to open-market operations by the central bank in its impact on the monetary base and the money supply.

In the past the Treasury has occasionally exercised powers that resemble those a central bank would exercise. In particular, during the period of the Subtreasury System from 1846 to 1913, the Treasury would periodically transfer funds from its own vaults to commercial banks in an effort to ease a financial panic. In some cases such action was successful (the panic subsided); in others it was not.

Treasury intervention of a central bank variety reached its peak during the tenure of Leslie M. Shaw (1902–1906) as Secretary of the Treasury. Shaw was of the opinion that if the Treasury were given \$100 million in discretionary funds to be deposited or withdrawn from banks as the situation dictated, together with several other powers,[1] all financial panics could be averted.[2]

Current interest in the activities of the Treasury centers on their implications for the money supply. Our discussion will be twofold. First, we will consider the Treasury's financing of the fiscal activities of the federal government, including its management of the national debt. Second, we

[1] Among the other powers Shaw requested was the authorization to vary the reserve requirements of commercial banks. This power and the \$100 million discretionary fund would have given to the Treasury the principal powers now used by the Federal Reserve for stabilization purposes.

[2] For a more extensive discussion of this era, see Milton Friedman and Anna J. Schwartz, *A Monetary History of the United States* (Princeton, N.J.: Princeton University Press, 1963).

will analyze the implications of the tax and loan accounts within the framework of the money supply analysis developed in Chapter 4.

THE FEDERAL GOVERNMENT'S FISCAL ACTIVITIES

As Table 9:1 shows, for most years since 1929, the federal government's combined fiscal activities have shown a deficit. This means that its total expenditures for goods, services, and income transfers have exceeded its revenues from all forms of taxation and contributions to pension funds (such as social security).

Associated with the deficit are two separate but related problems: first, each annual deficit must be financed; and second, the cumulative deficits add to the national debt, and this debt must be refinanced as portions of it mature. Thus, the Treasury must sell debt obligations both to finance new deficits and to refund old ones.

The sale of government securities to finance a deficit

It is the sale of government securities that has the greatest potential for altering the monetary base and the nation's money supply. Assume, for example, that the federal government has a deficit of $100 which the Treasury must finance. That is, in the year in question the total revenue of the government is $100 less than its total expenditures.

The debt obligations the Treasury will put up for sale can be sold in the United States to three parties: (1) the Federal Reserve, (2) depository institutions, and (3) the public. The effect of a sale to each party on the monetary base and the money supply will not be identical. A sale to the Federal Reserve will be most expansionary, while a sale to the public will have the least impact on the monetary base and the money supply.

A sale to the Federal Reserve

To see this, consider first a sale to the Federal Reserve. The Federal Reserve will buy these securities by creating a Treasury deposit, as shown in Table 9:2 and designated by (1). The Treasury then draws checks against these deposits and pays the bills of the government. These checks are then deposited in depository institutions, which forward them to the Federal Reserve for payment. They are paid either by increasing bank reserves or by issuing Federal Reserve notes. This is shown by (2). When depository institutions lend out their excess reserves, the money supply will expand further.

The result of this purchase of securities by the central bank is an expansion of the monetary base and the supply of money. It may be of

TABLE 9:1

Revenue and expenditures of the Federal Government 1929–1980 (millions of dollars)

Fiscal Year	Receipts	Outlays	Surplus or Deficit (−)
1929	3,862	3,127	734
1933	1,997	4,598	−2,602
1939	4,979	8,841	−3,862
1940	6,361	9,456	−3,095
1941	8,621	13,634	−5,013
1942	14,350	35,114	−20,764
1943	23,649	78,533	−54,884
1944	44,276	91,280	−47,004
1945	45,216	92,690	−47,474
1946	39,327	55,183	−15,856
1947	38,394	34,532	3,862
1948	41,774	29,773	12,001
1949	39,437	38,834	603
1950	39,485	42,597	−3,112
1951	51,646	45,546	6,100
1952	66,204	67,721	−1,517
1953	69,574	76,107	−6,533
1954	69,719	70,890	−1,170
1955	65,469	68,509	−3,041
1956	74,547	70,460	4,087
1957	79,990	76,741	3,249
1958	79,636	82,575	−2,939
1959	79,249	92,104	−12,855
1960	92,492	92,223	269
1961	94,389	97,795	−3,406
1962	99,676	106,813	−7,137
1963	106,560	111,311	−4,751
1964	112,662	118,584	−5,922
1965	116,833	118,430	−1,596
1966	130,856	134,652	−3,796
1967	149,552	158,254	−8,702
1968	153,671	178,833	−25,161
1969	187,784	184,548	3,236
1970	193,743	196,588	−2,845
1971	188,392	211,425	−23,033
1972	208,649	232,021	−23,373
1973	232,225	247,074	−14,849
1974	264,932	269,620	−4,688
1975	280,997	326,185	−45,188
1976	300,005	366,439	−66,434
Transition quarter	81,773	94,729	−12,956
1977	357,762	402,725	−44,963
1978	401,997	450,836	−48,839
1979*	455,989	493,368	−37,379
1980*	502,553	531,566	−29,013

*Estimates.
Courtesy of the Department of the Treasury and Office of Management and Budget.

TABLE 9:2
A Federal Reserve purchase of Treasury securities

Federal Reserve				Depository Institutions			
(1) Government securities	+100	(1) Treasury deposit	+100	(2) Reserves	+100	(2) Demand deposits	+100
		(2) Treasury deposit	−100				
		(2) Depository institution reserves or Federal Reserve notes	+100				

interest that a major part of the origin and development of the hyperinflations in Germany, Hungary, Poland, Russia, and Austria at the end of World War I, and in Hungary, Greece, and China at the end of World War II, was due to central bank financing of the activities of the central government. As a part of the stabilization program in most of these countries (except for those that became communist states) such financing was henceforth forbidden. The governments were then forced to raise taxes and cut expenditures until budgets were balanced and the need to create money to finance the deficits ceased.

A sale to the public

If, on the other hand, the public buys the government issues, nothing happens to either the base or the money supply. The public's purchase of the securities is shown on the books of depository institutions as portrayed in Table 9:3 by a deposit transfer to the Treasury (designated as (1)). When the Treasury subsequently draws checks against these deposits to pay the government's bills, the entries will be reversed as the deposits of the Treasury are drawn down and those of the public increased. This reversal is shown as (2). The net result is, of course, no change to either the monetary base or the supply of money. The public merely holds more government bonds than it held previously.[3]

[3] This is a good place to introduce briefly the "crowding-out" effect of government expenditures. It is argued by some that government expenditures replace dollar-for-dollar private expenditures, and thus, on balance, have no expansionary impact on economic activity. In the case at hand, when a private citizen buys government bonds, he must have given up the purchase of a substitute. If the substitute was a private security to finance new private capital goods, the crowd-out is both obvious and total. If a direct purchase of goods or services was the substitute, the effect is the same. Other cases are not so obvious. This will be considered in a later chapter.

TABLE 9:3
A purchase of government securities by the public

Depository Institutions			
	(1)	Demand deposits	−$100
		Treasury deposits	+ 100
	(2)	Demand deposits	+ 100
		Treasury deposits	− 100

A sale to depository institutions

Selling the government issues to the financial system represents an intermediate case. If depository institutions wish to buy Treasury securities and have no excess reserves, they will have to contract private credit and deposits in order to raise sufficient excess reserves to purchase the Treasury issues and create a deposit for the Treasury. When the Treasury spends these funds, the money stock will be restored to its previous level. This case, then, resembles a sale to the private sector in that neither the monetary base nor the supply of money changes.

If, however, depository institutions have excess reserves that they were not otherwise willing to lend, then buying the Treasury issue will lead to an expansion of the money supply. Table 9:4 shows how a purchase of government securities by depository institutions increases the Treasury's deposits (shown as (1)), which, when subsequently spent, will increase private deposits (2).

Since the money supply rose while the monetary base remained constant, this purchase of government securities by depository institutions must have affected only the money multiplier. Indeed, this is the case. The value of the ratio of desired excess reserves to demand deposits in the denominator of the money multiplier declined. This increased the value of the multiplier, and hence the amount of the money supply.

When the federal government runs a surplus, the funds are used to reduce

TABLE 9:4
A purchase of government securities by depository institutions

(1)	Reserves:		(1)	Treasury deposits	+$100
	Legal	+$20			
	Excess	− 20			
	Government securities	+$100	(2)	Treasury deposits	−$100
				Demand deposits	+100

the national debt and effects occur opposite to those just described. Reducing the debt held by the Federal Reserve is the most restrictive way to use the surplus. It will cause both the monetary base and the supply of money to decline. Retirement of the debt held by private individuals will, on the other hand, change neither the monetary base nor the money supply. Reducing the debt held by depository institutions represents an intermediate case.

Debt financing

A refinancing of the existing debts of the government can have similar monetary implications. So long as the holders of the debt continue to replace maturing obligations with new issues, no changes will occur to either the base or the money supply.

Suppose, however, that private holders of the debt do not totally renew their issues when they mature. The securities issued to replace some of these maturing obligations must then be purchased by the Federal Reserve. The Treasury will sell the refinancing issue to the central bank, which makes the purchase by giving the Treasury a deposit, as in Table 9:2. The funds are then used by the Treasury to buy back the maturing issue from the public. The public deposits Treasury checks in depository institutions, and they forward the checks to the Federal Reserve for payment. They are paid by increasing their reserves or Federal Reserve notes. Thus, both the monetary base and the money supply are increased. This refinancing is exactly the equivalent of a Treasury sale to the central bank with the funds used to finance government expenditures (shown in Table 9:2). Thus, Treasury refinancing of the national debt can have monetary implications.

WHEN IS FISCAL POLICY FISCAL POLICY?

Three examples were constructed to demonstrate the options available to the federal government for the financing of a given deficit. Each was discussed in terms of its effects on the monetary base and the supply of money. A sale to the Federal Reserve was seen to have the largest impact on both the monetary base and the supply of money, whereas a sale to the public was seen to have no impact on either. Yet each of these cases was involved with a given fiscal deficit. Here we have the ingredients for controversy.

Fiscal policy is traditionally defined to include all matters related to tax rates and expenditures by the federal government. The impact of fiscal policy is quite frequently measured by some definition of the budget deficit.[4] However, when the financing implications of the deficit are considered, the total expansionary impact of a given level of government expenditures is markedly different from what it would be were these implications not considered. Which of the three examples above should be used when measuring the impact of fiscal policy? For some years after the Keynesian approach to macroeconomic theory became the standard treatment of the subject, no one was concerned with how the deficit was financed. In 1964 a significant reduction in federal taxes was undertaken to accelerate the economic growth rate in the United States. Following that reduction, several attempts were made to calculate its impact on the increase in gross national product. Then, for the first time, serious questions were raised about the method used to finance government deficits.[5] A definition for measuring fiscal policy was distilled from this controversy. Fiscal policy is now defined to involve changes in government spending or tax rates while the monetary base is kept constant. Thus, the pure impact of a fiscal deficit on gross national product is measured when the resulting bonds are sold to the private sector (the second case above). Any sale that gives rise to an increase in the monetary base, then, represents some combination of monetary and fiscal policy. The effects of each must be disentangled before the impact of either can be measured. Needless to add, a great deal of effort has gone into such endeavors.

THE MATURITY STRUCTURE OF THE PUBLIC DEBT

When financing a budget deficit or refinancing the existing national debt as it matures, the Treasury by no means always uses securities with the same time to mature. It has a choice of short-term bills or longer-term bonds (which of the two it uses is generally governed by market conditions). Thus, the maturity structure and the average maturity of the federal debt should be expected to change from time to time. As shown in Table 9:5, this has been the case.

[4] A common measure is the full-employment deficit. Full-employment gross national product is calculated and, given the tax rates, the potential revenue is computed. This "full-employment" revenue is then compared to the actual level of government expenditures. The resulting deficit (or surplus) is the full-employment deficit (or surplus). The definition of full-employment output changes over time to reflect, among other things, changing demographic trends. In 1977 the Council of Economic Advisers defined it to be the level of output that the economy would produce if the Department of Commerce manufacturing capacity utilization rate were 86% and the unemployment rate 4.9%. This definition will likely change in the future.

[5] See, for example, the debate between Walter Heller, the former chairman of the Council of Economic Advisers who engineered the tax cut, and Milton Friedman in *Monetary vs. Fiscal Policy* (New York: Norton, 1969).

TABLE 9:5
The maturity structure of the Federal Debt: December 31, 1970–1976 (millions of dollars)

	All Maturities	Within 1 Year	1–5 Years	5–10 Years	10–20 Years	Over 20 Years
1976	$421,276	$211,035	$141,132	$43,045	$11,865	$14,200
% of total		50.1	33.5	10.2	2.8	3.4
1970	247,713	123,425	82,318	22,554	8,556	10,863
% of total		49.8	33.2	9.1	3.5	4.4

Courtesy of the *Federal Reserve Bulletin*.

The practice of altering the maturity structure of the federal debt is related to a long-held belief that the average maturity of this debt is an important determinant of total spending. This belief follows directly from the liquidity approach to the definition of money explored in Chapter 2. There, it will be remembered, the distinguishing characteristic of demand deposits and currency was that they were perfectly liquid. Other assets had varying degrees of liquidity, depending upon the ease and cost with which they could be converted into the means of payment. Among these other assets are, of course, government securities. During World War II and for some six years thereafter the Federal Reserve supported the prices of all government securities so that their market prices were virtually constant. Under these circumstances, the securities had the attributes of the means of payment[6] and could exercise a direct influence on total spending. In 1951 the support policy was discontinued. Nevertheless, the liquidity of the public debt is still believed to have an effect on total spending, and the average maturity of the public debt rather than the ability of each security to be quickly disposed of at or about the price at which it was purchased is still used as a measure of its liquidity. From this it can be seen that altering the maturity structure has been thought to be a useful tool for countercyclical fiscal policy. In addition, economists have fashioned various theories of public finance to explain the proper method of financing and refinancing the national debt. These theories are interesting in that they may conflict with proposals that advocate the use of the average maturity of the national debt as a countercyclical tool for economic stabilization.

We now turn to an explanation of these public finance theories, together with examination of their implications for using the average maturity of the debt as a countercyclical tool.

[6] That is, their nominal value or purchasing power was fixed and they were negotiable. Under these circumstances, the interest-bearing debt of the government was exactly the same as the non-interest-bearing debt, except that it was in larger denominations, which limited its role as money.

The interest minimization approach

An early approach to Treasury financing of the operations of government stressed the minimization of the total interest cost of the debt over a given time period. Thus, government securities ought to be sold either to finance a current deficit or to refund maturing obligations in those maturities where the market interest rate is such that it minimizes the total interest cost of the debt over a given time period. Such a strategy calls for issuing long-dated securities when interest rates are low and relatively short-dated securities when interest rates are high. This policy is supposed to lead to what is called *procyclical debt issues*. That is, the average maturity of the national debt will lengthen in the downswing of the cycle and shorten in the upswing of the cycle. This result follows from the general pattern of interest rates over the cycle: they are low in the downswing and high in the upswing (especially as the cycle approaches its peak). If this cyclical pattern of interest rates holds true, the Treasury will issue long-dated securities in the downswing of the cycle when rates are low and short-dated maturities in the upswing when interest rates are at cyclical highs.

It was, of course, pointed out that if the average maturity of the public debt is an important determinant of total spending, a debt issue policy designed to minimize interest costs would tend to aggravate the business cycle. In the upswing the average maturity of the debt will fall, thereby stimulating spending, thus booming the boom; and in the downswing the average maturity will rise, exerting a depressing effect on spending. In either case, the effect is opposite to that desired. Hence, any policy of debt management that centers on minimizing the interest cost to the federal Treasury is likely to aggravate the business cycle rather than dampen cyclical swings.

Countercyclical approach

The opposite approach is suggested by our analysis. That is, regardless of total interest cost, the Treasury should seek to reduce the average maturity of the debt in the downswing of the cycle by financing government deficits and refunding the maturing issues with short-term securities. In the upswing the average maturity of the public debt should be lengthened by selling long-term securities.

Whether debt management has any role to play in a countercyclical context is a subject of debate among economists. Those who believe that the cycle is primarily due to an irregular monetary growth rate downgrade the role of managing the average maturity of the public debt for countercyclical purposes. They say this kind of management is not needed if the money supply is properly managed, and when it is used in a countercyclical role, it tends to disrupt securities markets as the government finances its operations first in one sector of the market, then in another. Such shifting, they believe, creates uncertainty about security prices and the structure of interest rates. This uncertainty reduces the efficiency with which the financial market transfers the savings of surplus economic units to the borrowing deficit units—i.e., to compensate for the additional uncertainty, lenders demand higher interest rates.

For those who believe that nonmonetary forces cause the cycle, the average maturity of the national debt is a tool for economic stabilization. They argue that the Treasury should be mindful of its impact when it sells securities to finance deficits and refund maturing obligations.

Since such a large proportion of the national debt is held by the Federal Reserve, insurance companies, and all types of financial intermediaries, it is doubtful that its average maturity has much of an impact on total spending. Very little work has been done on this subject over the past decade or so.

THE TREASURY, THE *g* RATIO, AND THE MONEY SUPPLY

In introducing this chapter reference was made to a previous discussion in Chapter 8, where it was shown that a transfer of Treasury deposits from its tax and loan accounts at commercial banks to the Federal Reserve reduced the monetary base and the money supply. Such a transfer can also affect the money multiplier whenever the multiplier is extended to include demand deposit holdings by the federal government. Such an extension is often made because the holdings of demand deposits and currency by the federal government are excluded from the recorded statistics on the money stock. In this section we will incorporate Treasury demand deposit holdings into a money multiplier along lines analogous to the multipliers developed in Chapter 4. First, however, it would be useful to discuss in greater detail the Treasury tax and loan accounts, for their use by the Treasury has undergone several changes since they were introduced and these changes have raised problems for the Federal Reserve in its efforts to manage the nation's money supply or stabilize interest rates.

Tax and loan accounts

Treasury tax and loan accounts were created by Congress in 1917 as a part of the Liberty Loan Act to finance World War I. Called, appropriately, Liberty Loan Accounts, they were used to deposit the proceeds from the sale of Liberty bonds. Their purpose was to minimize fluctuations in the aggregate level of bank reserves and deposits that would have arisen had these bond proceeds been deposited at the Federal Reserve. For the same reason, in 1918 the Treasury began to use these accounts to deposit the proceeds from federal income and excess profits taxes. Given their expanded use, their name was changed to War Loan Deposits and depository banks were obliged to pay interest to the Treasury at an annual rate of 2%.

The use of these accounts continued after the war. With the passage of the Banking Act of 1933, and its provision against the payment of interest on demand deposits, banks could no longer pay interest to the Treasury on its deposits. Moreover, in 1935 these deposits were made subject to reserve requirement obligations as though they were private demand deposits.

The Treasury increasingly used these accounts as depositories for a wider and wider range of revenues from taxes and bond sales. Even though these deposits earned no interest for the Treasury, the recipient banks provided various services for the government free of charge: sales and redemption of savings bonds, collection of various taxes, handling Treasury checks and other securities, and so forth. In effect, the banks were paying the Treasury an implicit rate of interest.

In 1974, after completing a study of the profitability of these accounts for recipient banks, the Treasury decided that through appropriate cash management procedures, it could raise income from these deposits. It proposed that Congress allow banks to pay explicit interest on them. While the Congress debated this proposal, the Treasury discovered a way to "earn" interest on its deposits—it transferred the bulk of them to the Federal Reserve. By the transfer it reduced the monetary base and forced the Federal Reserve to engage in defensive open-market purchases of government securities. The interest earned by the Federal Reserve on these newly acquired securities was then remitted to the U.S. Treasury. Hence, the Treasury "earned" interest by reducing its interest expense on the national debt.

The 1974 change was quite significant. It meant that the Treasury was substituting a cash-management interest-expense-minimization operation for its former emphasis on minimizing the effects of its operations on the monetary base and the money supply. As a consequence, an increased burden was placed on the Federal Reserve. It was forced to rely more heavily on defensive open-market operations to stabilize fluctuations in the monetary base and the money supply due to Treasury activities.

Congress finally acted on the Treasury request made in 1974. In October 1977 and November 1978 legislation was passed to allow banks to pay interest on Treasury deposits and to permit the Treasury to make an explicit payment for services rendered by banks. Under the provisions of the legislation, banks can treat Treasury deposits in either of two ways. First, under the "remittance option," banks transfer Treasury deposits to the Federal Reserve after one business day.[7] Banks selecting this option pay no interest on these funds, and banks belonging to the Federal Reserve must meet reserve obligations as though these were private demand deposit accounts. Second, under the "note option," funds deposited in tax and loan accounts are transferred to interest-bearing note accounts at the same

[7] It should be noted that qualified taxpayers pay taxes due directly to these accounts. They do not first send checks to the Treasury.

bank after one business day. Once transferred, the banks pay interest based on the federal funds rate (these deposits are exempt from Regulation Q ceilings), and member banks are exempt from a reserve requirement obligation.

With this action by Congress, the Treasury transferred the bulk of its deposits back to the banking system, much as they were maintained before 1974. The new legislation reduced the burden on the Federal Reserve System to minimize the effect of Treasury operations on the monetary base and the money supply.

The *g* ratio and the money supply

To examine the effect of the tax and loan accounts on the monetary base and the money supply,[8] assume initially that federal government deposit holdings, G, bear a constant proportion, g, to public demand deposits, D, or

$$G = gD \text{ and } \Delta G = g\Delta D \tag{9:1}$$

Reserve requirements against Treasury deposits will be designated as r^*. How these differ from reserve requirements against private demand deposits depends on various circumstances. For Treasury deposits in financial institutions that are members of the Federal Reserve, reserve requirements are applied only on those held under the "remittance option." The rate is that prevailing on private demand deposits. In other cases, state reserve requirement regulations apply. Thus, r^* must be interpreted as a weighted average reserve ratio.[9]

To see the implications of the expanded multiplier, we will consider a relatively simple case. All Treasury deposits will be assumed to be held under the "remittance option."

Given some increase in the monetary base, ΔB, money creation will come to an end when this increase is allocated among required reserves for demand, $r\Delta D$, saving, $r'\text{t}\Delta D$, and government deposits, $r^*g\Delta D$, net additions to currency in circulation, $c'\Delta D$, and as excess reserves depository institutions desire to hold, $e\Delta D$, or

$$\Delta B = r\Delta D + r't\Delta D + r^*g\Delta D + c'\Delta D + e\Delta D \tag{9:2}$$

or

$$\Delta B = \Delta D(r + r't + r^*g + c' + e) \tag{9:3}$$

[8] For a more elaborate discussion of this topic, see Richard W. Lang," TTL Note Accounts and the Money Supply Process," *Monthly Review,* Federal Reserve Bank of St. Louis, Vol. 61, No. 10. (Oct. 1979): 3–14.

[9] This will be true only until the transition to uniform reserve requirements is completed in 1988.

Therefore,

$$\Delta D = \Delta B \left(\frac{1}{r + r't + r^*g + c' + e} \right) \tag{9:4}$$

and given the definition of *M-1B* as

$$\begin{aligned} \Delta M\text{-}1B &= \Delta D + \Delta C \\ &= \Delta D(1 + c') \end{aligned} \tag{9:5}$$

we have

$$\Delta M\text{-}1B = \Delta B \left(\frac{1 + c'}{r + r't + r^*g + c' + e} \right) \tag{9:6}$$

When the federal government receives the proceeds of its tax collections and security sales and deposits these in its tax and loan accounts, the value of g rises; consequently, the multiplier declines, as does the *M-1B* measure of the money supply. Subsequently, when the balances held in the tax and loan accounts are transferred to the Federal Reserve so that the Treasury can pay its bills, the monetary base will decline. This decline will be offset in part by a rise in the money multiplier, which occurs because the value of g declines when the transfer takes place. Finally, when the Treasury pays its bills, the monetary base will be restored to its previous level and the money supply will once again return to the level it attained prior to the Treasury operations outlined.

Given the expanded multiplier of Equation (9:6), the problem of monetary management is more complicated, for now the Federal Reserve must attempt to forecast the value of g in its efforts to achieve a given growth rate of the money supply. Reference to Figure 4:12 shows the value of the g ratio over the past 25 years. It appears to be quite stable over time and to have no sharp trend to characterize it as several other ratios in the money multiplier are characterized. Neverthless, the mere fact that the g ratio occurs in the money multiplier gives the Treasury power to alter the money supply. It thus makes more compelling the argument for close Treasury–Federal Reserve cooperation to achieve economic stability.

SUMMARY

The monetary implications of the activities of the federal Treasury are seldom discussed. Yet, in many respects they resemble the powers of the central bank in that they can change the monetary base, the money multiplier, and the money supply. For that reason, it is important that the Treasury and the Federal Reserve know each other's policies and coordinate them.

If the central bank ignores the requirements of the Treasury, additional uncertainty is introduced into forecasting the movements of the monetary base, the money multiplier, and the money supply.

In its broadest role the Federal Reserve must assume a share of responsibility for the stabilization of economic activity in the United States. The Treasury also has an impact and a role to play through its policy of financing the operations of the government and managing the public debt. In this capacity it can either reinforce or run counter to Federal Reserve objectives, depending on the degree of cooperation and coordination between these two agencies.

STUDY QUESTIONS

1. Explain how a Federal Reserve purchase of new securities from the Treasury is identical to an open-market operation in its effect on the monetary base.
2. What is the nature of the controversy over the appropriate measure of fiscal policy?
3. Under what circumstances would interest-bearing Treasury securities acquire liquidity closely approximating that of demand deposits and currency?
4. Why might the interest-minimization approach to debt management be opposed by someone who believes that total liquidity is an important determinant of spending?
5. What facts must individuals know when they advocate a countercyclical approach to debt management?
6. Explain how the receipt of taxes by the federal government and their subsequent deposit in commercial banks reduces the measure of the money supply.
7. Why is it important for the Federal Reserve to be informed about the management of Treasury deposits, i.e., where the Treasury keeps its deposits and when they are to be spent?
8. Suppose the Treasury follows a policy of transferring all its operating balances to the Federal Reserve. What might the response of the Federal Reserve be to such a policy?
9. What do you expect would happen to the monetary base if the Treasury followed the practice of maintaining its tax and loan account balances at a constant amount, for example, $3 million? (All other funds would be held at the Federal Reserve.) On the other hand, what would be the consequences for the monetary base if the Treasury held its Federal Reserve balance at a constant $3 billion?

SELECTED REFERENCES AND READINGS

Cagan, Phillip. "A Partial Reconciliation of Two Views of Debt Management." *Journal of Political Economy,* Vol. 74, No. 6 (Dec. 1966).

Friedman, Milton, and Schwartz, Anna J. *A Monetary History of the United States, 1867–1960.* Princeton, N.J.: Princeton University Press, 1963.

Hamburger, Michael, and Silber, William. "Debt Management and Interest Rates: A Re-examination of the Evidence." *The Manchester School of Economics and Social Studies* (Dec. 1971).

Tobin, James. "An Essay in Debt Management." In *Commission on Money and Credit, Fiscal and Debt Management Policies.* Englewood Cliffs, N.J.: Prentice-Hall, 1963.

10

MONEY AND ECONOMIC ACTIVITY

10

A fundamental purpose of monetary theory is to explain how changes in the supply of money affect the level of real output, the volume of employment, the rate of interest, and the general level of commodity prices. As a part of this explanation, monetary theory should describe in detail the linkages by which the monetary sector is connected with the real sector of the economy. To accomplish this, one must have some basic idea of how an economy functions and the nature of the fundamental relationships between economic variables—in abstract form, an economic model. However, economists disagree on how best to describe the functioning of an economy and how to model its significant relationships. This disagreement naturally presents a dilemma, for if one is to discuss monetary theory, a model should be specified for analytical purposes. Since "orthodoxy" centers on the Keynesian approach, the model to be developed in this chapter will be Keynesian in spirit. Later in the text an opposite view will be carefully described so that the major points of contention between the two schools will become apparent.

Keynesian models are of varying degrees of complexity. Some are fairly detailed and involve a system of several hundred equations that attempt to capture the major behavioral relationships. Simpler models use only a few equations. One's choice of a model should be dictated by the questions one wishes to ask. If the questions are fairly elementary, a relatively simple model is quite adequate.

The model to be developed in this chapter is of the elementary variety, and if one understands the concepts of supply and demand, its construction and functioning should present no difficulties. The model contains three sectors or markets: one for commodities, one for money, and one for labor. Each market will be described separately, and then the entire model will be integrated.

Our first task will be to construct the commodity market. This can be done by first examining the definition of gross national product.

THE COMMODITY MARKET

Gross national product is a measure of the total value of new goods and services produced during a given time period. To say that GNP in 1976 was \$1.7 trillion means that that dollar value of new goods and services was produced during that year. (It should be remembered from an elementary principles course that there are certain difficulties with valuation that, in some cases, lend themselves to amusing examples. However, these difficulties need not concern us here.)

There are at least two different methods of computing the market value of GNP. The first seeks to value GNP according to how it is purchased. Some portion was purchased as nondurable goods for consumption, C; some portion was added to the stock of producer and consumer durable goods (commonly called investment), I; some portion was used collectively or by all units of government, G; and some portion was sold to foreigners as exports, X, less that portion of their GNP that we used or imported, Z. Using these symbols, GNP can be expressed as

$$C + I + G + (X - Z) \equiv GNP \tag{10:1}$$

Initially, our economy will be assumed to have no government spending and no foreign trade. Then GNP can be set equal to

$$C + I \equiv GNP \tag{10:2}$$

A second method for computing GNP recognizes that in producing goods and services, the factors of production must be used, and hence factor income is generated in the form of wages, salaries, interest, rents, and profits.

What do the income recipients do with their factor income? They use some portion for the purchase of nondurable goods or consumption, C. The rest is used for many things. Regardless of what use is made of this portion of income, it will be designated as saving, S. Saving, therefore, represents that portion of income that is *not* used for consumption or the purchase of nondurable goods. This approach yields the equation

$$C + S \equiv GNP \tag{10:3}$$

It is quite important to understand exactly what saving consists of. Since income is earned in the production of goods and services and some portion of this income is consumed, some portion of goods and services is used for consumption. Since some portion of income is saved, some portion of goods and services is not consumed but available for nonconsumption uses (e.g., investment). Therefore, saving can be defined as the supply of goods and services available or potentially available for nonconsumption purposes.

When the activities of the government are considered, this analysis becomes only slightly more complex. The individual can now do three things with his income. Some portion is used for consumption, C; some portion is saved, S; and some portion is paid over to the government in the form of taxes, T. Since taxes also represent income earned but not used for consumption, they can be viewed as the equivalent of saving. In fact, one can think of taxes as a form of social saving in contrast to private saving (it may not make the tax bite any easier). Hence, the combination of private saving, S, and taxes, T, represents the supply of goods and services available for nonconsumption purposes. Later, when taxes are considered in greater detail, it will be shown that there is an interrelationship between S and T so that an increase in T may not increase total saving, $S + T$, by an equal amount.

To move from a definition of GNP to a theory that explains its movement over time, consumption, saving, and investment must be related to various behavioral variables. It is to this discussion we now turn. In order to organize the discussion, saving, or the supply of goods and services available for nonconsumption purposes, will be examined first. Then investment, or the nonconsumption demand for goods and services, will be explained. Finally, the interrelation of supply and demand which involves the concept of commodity-market equilibrium will be explained.

Saving (or the supply of goods and services for nonconsumption purposes)

Why don't income recipients in the aggregate use their income in its entirety for consumption purposes? Once this question is answered, the determinants of saving will be clear.

One can divide the needs or wants of individuals into two classes: those that require immediate gratification (such as freedom from hunger and pain, or shelter from the elements) and those that can be gratified in the future (income for old age and possible disability, for education of children). Further, these needs can be ranked from most urgent to least urgent. Given such a ranking expressing the preferences of individuals, how many of these needs can be satisfied? A fundamental determinant is *real* income. The higher the real income, the greater will be the number of wants that can be gratified. While other factors, specifically the real interest rate, may also affect saving, the model to be developed in this chapter will use real income as the only determinant of saving. Disregarding the real interest rate will not alter any of the fundamental conclusions.

The relationship between real income and real saving is a direct one. That is, the higher the level of real income, the greater will be the absolute amount of real saving. In other words, the larger real income becomes, the larger will be the aggregate supply of goods and services available for nonconsumption purposes. For convenience, the relationship between income and saving will be assumed to be proportional, yielding the saving schedule shown in Figure 10:1.

In terms of this analytical framework with no government, the only factor that could explain a shift in the saving schedule would be a change in the collective view of the merits of current consumption versus future con-

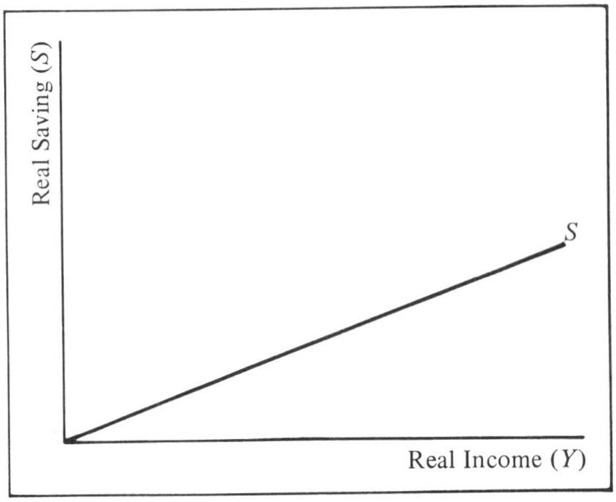

FIGURE 10:1
Real saving and real income

sumption. This change of "preferences" would alter the ranking of wants requiring current rather than future consumption, and conceivably the origin and slope of the saving function.

Since the saving schedule represents in essence the aggregate supply of goods and services available for nonconsumption purposes, a demand for these goods and services will have to be specified before the concept of commodity-market equilibrium can be discussed.

Investment (or the demand for goods and services for nonconsumption purposes)

It should be remembered that for an economist, investment represents durable goods. For business enterprises, these are machinery, buildings, equipment, and inventories; for private individuals, investment consists of a home, furniture, appliances, automobiles, and the like. Given this definition of investment, our task is to specify what determines the amount of real investment desired at some given time by individuals and businesses. Our analysis will show that the market interest rate plays a fundamental role in this determination.

Business investment

In actuality, the decision to invest on the part of business depends on complex circumstances, including the elaborate tax incentive program put in place over the years by the federal government. The approach to investment decision making developed here will be relatively simple compared to some of the elaborate econometric approaches formulated in recent years. Basically, it will be supposed that business will decide to make an addition to its stock of capital goods when the expected *profit* generated by the project is greater than the cost of the project. Consider the case of a business contemplating an addition to its existing plant. Its first task will be to calculate the cost of the addition. This can be done in various ways, which do not concern us here (e.g., by applying costs to the engineering specifications). Suppose this exercise is completed and yields a current cost of $100,000. Let us further suppose that this addition will last for three years and then be scrapped.

The next task will be to calculate how much this extra capacity will add to the annual profits of the firm. This will involve an estimate of how many additional sales will be possible at what price or prices, and how much the additional output will add to the annual costs of production. Suppose these calculations are made and management finds that expected annual profits will rise by $35,000 per year for a total of three years (the estimated life of the new addition).

At first glance it might appear that this project is profitable, for 3 × $35,000 = $105,000, a total greater than the current cost of the capital project, $100,000. However, this would be an unwarranted conclusion, for the costs of the contemplated project must be incurred *today,* whereas the profits accrue mainly in the *future*. The only valid comparison for decision-making purposes involves comparing current magnitudes. How, then, is the future to be translated into the present? By finding the *present value* of the future profits, which can be accomplished by *discounting* them to the present. Discounting involves using an interest rate; hence, the interest rate becomes the means for translating the future into the present.

In accordance with the general formula expressed as Equation 6:1, present value can be reduced to

$$\text{Present value} = \frac{\$35{,}000}{(1+i)^1} + \frac{\$35{,}000}{(1+i)^2} + \frac{\$35{,}000}{(1+i)^3} \qquad (10{:}4)$$

Expressed as Equation (10:4), the crucial role of the interest rate in calculating present value is obvious: present value moves inversely with the interest rate. To see this more clearly, two different interest rates are used.

2%:

$$\$100{,}937 = \frac{\$35{,}000}{(1.02)} + \frac{\$35{,}000}{(1.0404)} + \frac{\$35{,}000}{(1.0612)}$$

10%:

$$\$87{,}040 = \frac{\$35{,}000}{(1.10)} + \frac{\$35{,}000}{(1.21)} + \frac{\$35{,}000}{(1.331)}$$

The use of these two different interest rates exhibits the inverse relationship between their magnitude and present value. From this, it can be concluded that the lower the market rate, the more likely it is that the investment project will be undertaken, for the present value of expected profits will be large relative to current construction costs. The relation is represented graphically in Figure 10:2. The graph shows that as market interest rates fall, the quantity of investment desired by business rises, i.e., that the investment demand schedule is downward sloping.

The slope and position of the investment schedule The slope and position of the investment demand schedule depend upon the number of potential projects and the sensitivity of the present value of expected profits to different interest rates. The more plentiful the number of investment projects, the farther to the right of the vertical axis the investment schedule will lie; whereas the more sensitive the present value of expected future profits to the interest rate, the more elastic (flatter) will be its slope.

The number of investment projects in any given society will depend upon such factors as its state of economic development, the present capital intensity of its methods of production, and the rate of technological change. The sensitivity of the present value of expected profits to interest rates, on the other hand, is likely to depend upon the economic life of the project. The longer this life, the greater the uncertainty of the future profitability of the project. This uncertainty can become so great that changes in the rate of interest used to transform the future into present may have little impact on the decision to invest. If projects of this nature (i.e., whose economic life is long) dominate the investment picture, the investment demand schedule is likely to be highly inelastic (approach the vertical).

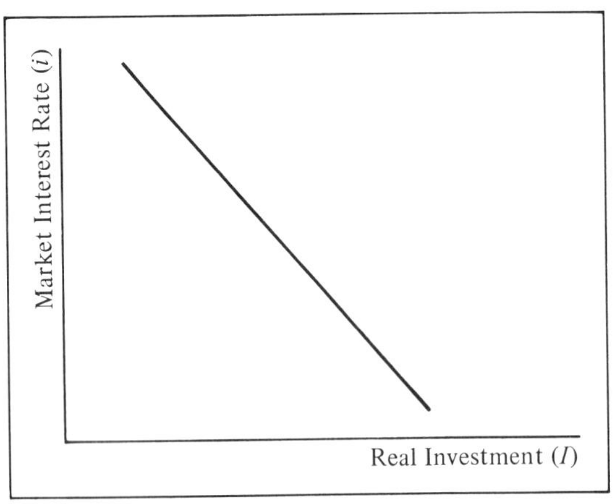

FIGURE 10:2
Investment demand and the market rate of interest

Shifts in the investment demand schedule As with the demand schedules for individual commodities, the investment demand schedule may be subject to shifts from time to time. What causes these shifts to take place? Basically, they are due to changes in the expected profitability of the investment projects. Suppose, for example, that in the problem outlined above expected profitability declined because businessmen became less optimistic about the future. Being less optimistic, they tend to downgrade projected sales or the prices at which the additional goods can be sold. In our example, if this decline in expected profits is from $35,000 per year to $34,000, the project will not be undertaken at an interest rate of 2%. In terms of Figure 10:2, the investment demand schedule will be seen to have shifted to the left, with less investment being desired at each market interest rate.

Conversely, if business becomes more optimistic about the future, expected future profitability will rise and a larger volume of investment will be forthcoming at each interest rate. For example, given a larger expected profit, projects that management was indifferent to undertaking at a 2% rate (i.e., those with a present value of exactly $100,000) will now be undertaken at that rate. The investment demand schedule will be seen as shifting to the right.

Consumer durable goods purchases

The private individual must also come to a decision whether or not to purchase a durable good. In our relatively simple conceptual framework this decision depends on exactly the same type of calculations as those made by business. The reason this is possible is that consumer durable goods yield services over their expected lifetimes, and they can be valued at market prices. For example, a house yields such services as shelter from the elements, an automobile yields transportation services, a television yields entertainment services, and so on for the list of consumer durable goods.

The present value of these services can be computed as in Equation (10:4) and compared with the present market price of the durable good in question. Should the present value exceed the market price, the durable would be purchased. Should it not, the durable would not be purchased. As in the investment decision by business, the present value of the services yielded by the consumer durable should be sensitive to market interest rates. The lower the rate used for discounting, the higher will be the present value of the durable's services and the more likely the consumer will be to buy the durable, i.e., to invest. Thus, the investment demand schedule for consumer durables will have the same configuration as that for producer durable goods. The slope, position, and reason for shifts of this schedule will also be determined by factors similar to those influencing the demand schedule for producer durable goods.

The investment demand schedule and the Keynesian theory of business cycles

Insofar as the Keynesian interpretation of economic history is concerned, a shifting investment demand schedule is the fundamental cause of the business cycle. Recessions and depressions are, then, due to a partial or total collapse of the investment demand schedule caused by pessimism in the business community. Conversely, prosperity is brought about because business becomes optimistic about the future. Shifts in mood, then, are responsible for the cyclical course of the economy through time. This view of the business cycle serves as the rationalization for a countercyclical policy aimed at varying the level of government expenditures or rates of taxation and the rate at which the money supply is increased over time.

Supply–demand and the concept of equilibrium

In the elementary case of a single commodity the price and quantity relationship indicated by the intersection of the demand and supply schedules represents equilibrium in the respective market. If the price of the commodity depicted by Figure 10:3 is P_0, then the quantity demanded is exactly equal to the quantity others are willing to supply. The market is said to be in *equilibrium*. At any other price such as P_1 or P_2, the quantities demanded and supplied would be different and the market would be said to have either excess supply or excess demand. Either situation would be the cause of a change in market price, and thus at prices P_1 or P_2, the market would be in *disequilibrium*.

Similarly, in the context of a macroeconomic model commodity-market equilibrium can be said to prevail when desired or intended saving is equal

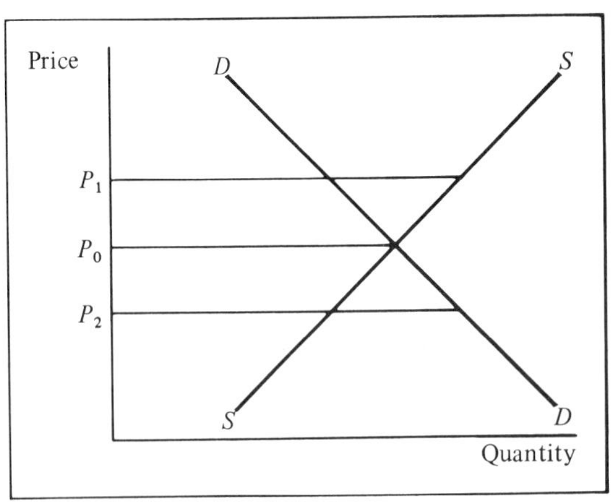

FIGURE 10:3
Single-market equilibrium

to desired or intended investment. Since saving represents the supply of goods and services for nonconsumption purposes, while investment represents the demand for these goods, the equality of saving and investment is simply another way of expressing the equality of supply and demand or commodity-market equilibrium.

This macroeconomic commodity-market equilibrium can also be shown diagramatically. However, since saving and investment are explained by two different variables (real income and the interest rate), it will first be necessary to fix the level of investment. This will be possible once the rate of interest is set. If this rate is assumed to be i_0, then (in the upper portion of Figure 10:4) the level of investment is I_0. Once the level of investment is fixed, it can be plotted (in the lower portion) as a horizontal line, since

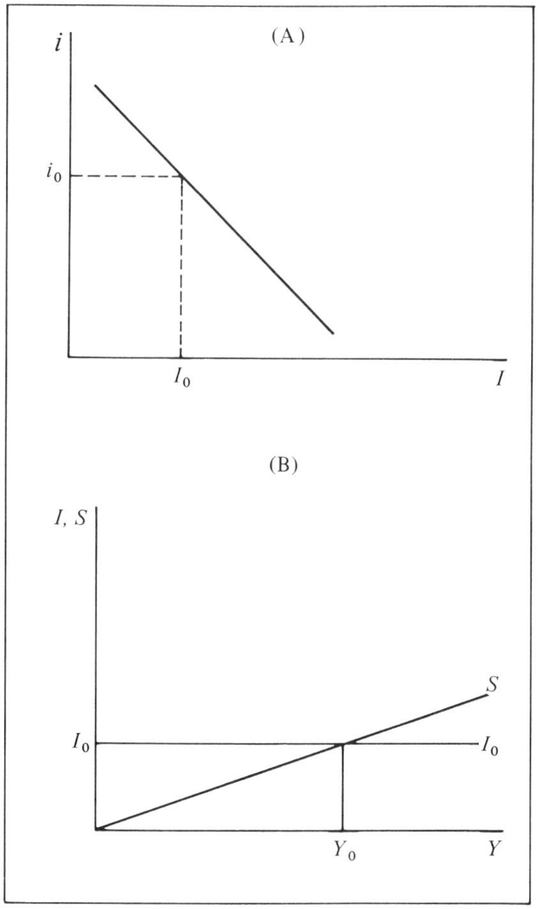

FIGURE 10:4
Commodity-market equilibrium

it does not respond to the level of income. The intersection of investment and saving, S, then yields the equilibrium level of real income, Y_0. Therefore, at interest rate i_0 and real income Y_0, the supply of goods and services for nonconsumption purposes, S_0, is equal to the demand for them, I_0. At any other level of real income either excess supply or excess demand will prevail, i.e., disequilibrium.

The government sector and the commodity market

In order to make our macroeconomic model more realistic, the acitvities of the government must be considered, for they will affect both the supply of and the demand for nonconsumption goods and services.

Consider first the government activities on the demand side of the equation. The various levels of government (local, state, and national) purchase a variety of goods and services. In the United States the public sector has grown considerably since the 1930s and now accounts for some 25% of gross national product. The purchases by the public sector are in many cases, identical to purchases by the private sector for capital formation (military aircraft versus civilian passenger aircraft). In discussing the capital goods purchases of the private sector, we related investment decisions to behavioral variables: the state of expectations and the market rate of interest. Do similar considerations guide the expenditures of the public sector? Generally no, although the urgency of public investment projects may indicate their social yield. Public investment decisions can be somewhat vaguely described as being determined by the democratic process. That is, these decisions, both as to prospective projects and the total amount to be spent, depend upon the interaction among the elected representatives of the people. For this reason the level of government expenditures will be treated as a constant that is not related to any behavioral variable (e.g., the interest rate or the level of real income).

These public sector expenditures will be symbolized by G and the total demand for nonconsumption goods and services, $I + G$, will be symbolized by $\bar{I}$. G can be added to I by drawing a new schedule parallel to I, producing the $\bar{I}$ schedule shown as Figure 10:5.

Taxes

It has been explained that government taxes, T, can be regarded as the social saving of society, for they, like private saving, represent income not used for consumption. However, private saving must be adjusted before being added to taxes to obtain total saving. To see why, consider the problem that arises when a government is imposed upon the model. Assume that this government imposes a tax at a flat rate of 10% upon total income. How do individuals pay that tax? Do they reduce their consumption by the full amount of the levy, or do they reduce their private saving by the full amount, or do they use some combination of the two? To answer that

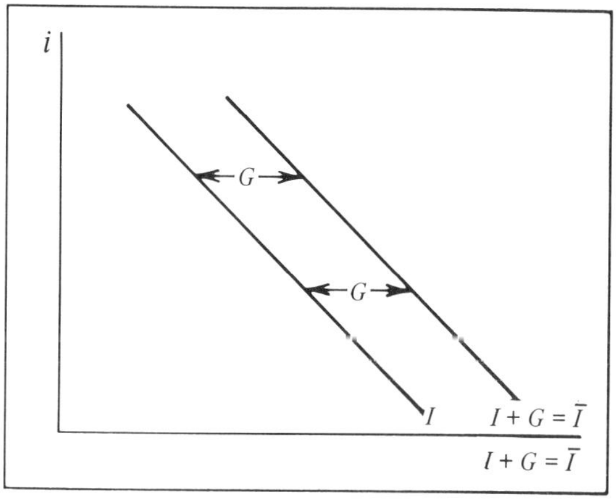

FIGURE 10:5
Aggregate demand for nonconsumption goods and services

question, we must return to the discussion of the determinants of the division of the individual's income between consumption and saving. This, it will be recalled, was seen to be based upon the relative intensity of present needs versus future needs. How, then, do taxes affect the relative intensity of future versus present needs? It is hard to say. One could conceive of a tax related to a specific program, such as social security or unemployment insurance, that might diminish the desire to save. In such a case the tax would be paid primarily by forgoing saving. Otherwise, taxes will be regarded as falling upon both consumption and saving. Thus, a 10% tax will be paid by decreasing both consumption and private saving. If the division of income before taxation was 70% consumption and 30% saving, a 10% tax will be paid by reducing consumption by \$7 and saving by \$3 per \$10 of real income.

So long as a flat rate tax is assumed, it can be graphed as a straight line, as shown in Figure 10:6. The slope of the tax schedule is $\Delta T/\Delta Y$, which is equal to the tax rate of 10%.

The burden of taxation is important to our discussion because if taxes are increased, total saving, $S + T$, will rise, but not by as much as the rise in taxes. In the example above, for an income of \$100, total saving, $S + T$, would rise by \$7 for a \$10 or 10% tax. This result follows from the fact that while taxes will increase by \$10 per every \$100 in income, private saving will decline by \$3. Nevertheless, total saving or the supply of goods and services available for nonconsumption uses will rise.[1]

[1] One school of thought, associated primarily with Milton Friedman, which has acquired a wide following in recent years, holds that temporary changes in taxes will have essentially no effect on economic activity because individuals base their consumption decisions on the income they expect to receive over a long period of time (called their permanent income). Since temporary tax changes do not affect permanent income very much, they are unlikely to have much effect upon economic activity.

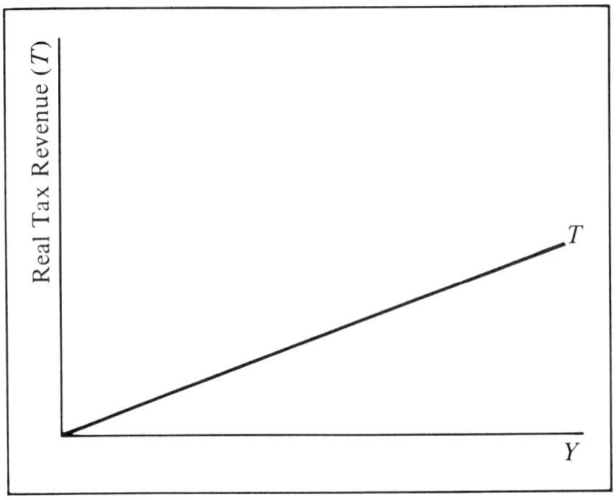

FIGURE 10:6
A flat rate tax

In Figure 10:7 public saving, T, is added to private saving, S, to form the total saving schedule $\bar{S}$. This new schedule shows the total supply of goods and services available for nonconsumption purposes at each real income level.

The slope of the $\bar{S}$ schedule

The slope of the $\bar{S}$ schedule is important, for it contains the essence of the multiplier principle that, although not developed by Keynes, was to play an important role in his *General Theory.*

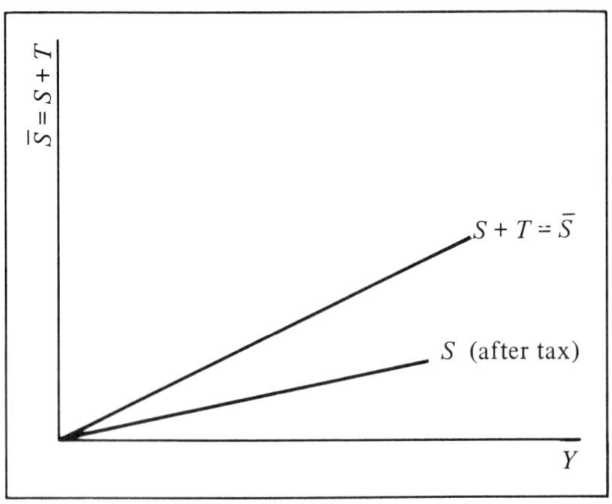

FIGURE 10:7
Total saving

To see the multiplier in action, consider the situation depicted in Figure 10:8. There two separate $\bar{S}$ schedules are shown; one, $\bar{S}_0$, has a relatively flat slope, whereas the other, $\bar{S}_1$, has a relatively steep slope. A given change from $\bar{I}$ to $\bar{I}'$ produces different effects on real income. For the steeper $\bar{S}$ schedule, real income increases from Y_1 to Y_1', while for the flatter schedule, the respective increase is from Y_0 to Y_0'. The latter change is much greater than the former. Why is it larger? The answer can be made on two levels. First, from Figure 10:8 it can be seen that the slope of the $\bar{S}_0$ schedule is flatter or has a smaller value. The slope of the schedule is equal to $\Delta\bar{S}/\Delta Y$, which, in the Keynesian framework, could be called the "marginal propensity of social saving" (or $MP\bar{S}$); its reciprocal, or $1/MP\bar{S}$, is known as the Keynesian multiplier.[2] A flat $\bar{S}$ schedule will produce a relatively small value for the $MP\bar{S}$ and, as a result, a large multiplier. Thus, with a relatively flat $\bar{S}$ schedule such as $\bar{S}_0$, a given change in $\bar{I}$ will produce a relatively large change in real income.

Second, it is possible to describe the multiplier process in such a way that it becomes evident why a smaller marginal propensity to save (or a smaller tax rate) will cause a larger increase in income. Consider a situation where the marginal propensity to save is alternatively 50 cents and 25 cents of each dollar received as income. Now, let government expenditures or private investment increase by $1. Thus, an additional $1 of goods is purchased, that, if it comes from inventory, it is replaced by new output.

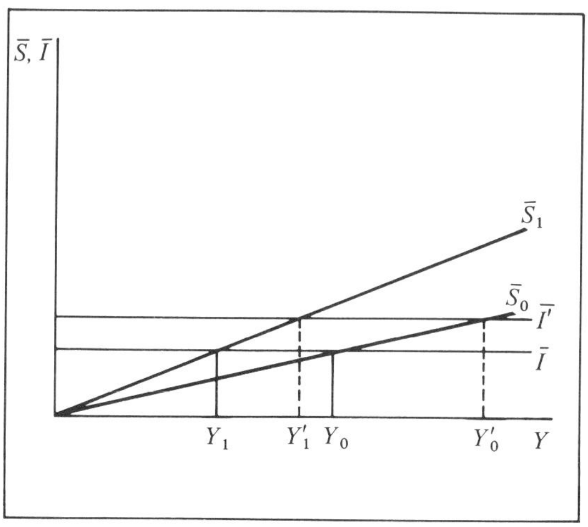

FIGURE 10:8
The Keynesian multiplier

[2] In the Keynesian literature the marginal propensity to save includes only private saving. The marginal propensity derived from the $\bar{S}$ schedule is the sum of the marginal propensity of private saving and the rate of taxation.

In producing the new output, the income of the factors of production increase by exactly \$1. These income recipients, in turn, spend either 50 cents or 75 cents on new output (depending on whether the *MPS* is 50% or 25%). This, in turn, accrues as income to other factors of production, which spend 50% or 75% of *their* new income, and so on. It should be obvious that the new spending over time will be larger the smaller the fraction of income that is saved, i.e., the smaller is the marginal propensity to save. The amount of total spending can be calculated as follows:

Total spending:

Case I: $MPS = .5$ (no taxes):

$$\$1 + \$1(.5) + \$1(.5)(.5) + \$1(.5)^3 + \ldots + \$1(.5)^N.$$

Case II: $MPS = .25$ (no taxes):

$$\$1 + \$1(.75) + \$1(.75)(.75) + \$1(.75)^3 + \ldots + \$1(.75)^N.$$

From this analysis it can be seen that the model for monetary theory developed in this chapter contains the Keynesian multiplier.

Equilibrium in the commodity market

Within the confines of our expanded model the concept of commodity-market equilibrium can be shown and discussed. As with the simple model, equilibrium occurs whenever the nonconsumption demand $(I + G)$ is equal to the available supply $(S + T)$ of such goods and services. In Figure 10:9 equilibrium prevails when the market interest rate is equal to i_0 and the level of real income is Y_0.[3] At those values, nonconsumption demand, $\bar{I}_0$, is equal to the available supply of such goods and services, $\bar{S}_0$.

If the interest rate were lower than i_0 while the level of real income remained at Y_0, disequilibrium would prevail. Such a situation would be characterized as one of excess demand. That is, the demand for goods and services for nonconsumption purposes, $\bar{I}$, would exceed the available supply, $\bar{S}$. To restore equilibrium, one or more variables must change. (When the complete model is developed, a more comprehensive discussion about disequilibrium situations will be possible.)

Similarly, if the interest rate were to lie above i_0 while real income remained fixed at Y_0, disequilibrium would also prevail, for the supply of nonconsumption goods and services, $\bar{S}_0$, would then exceed the demand for them. The extent of the excess supply would serve as a measure of the disequilibrium.

[3] If Figure 10:9 looks a little curious, it is because the axes of the $\bar{S}$ schedule have been reversed to facilitate its integration into a more comprehensive model. Increases in $\bar{S}$ due either to an increase in taxes or to a rise in the private desire to save will be shown by a clockwise rotation of the schedule.

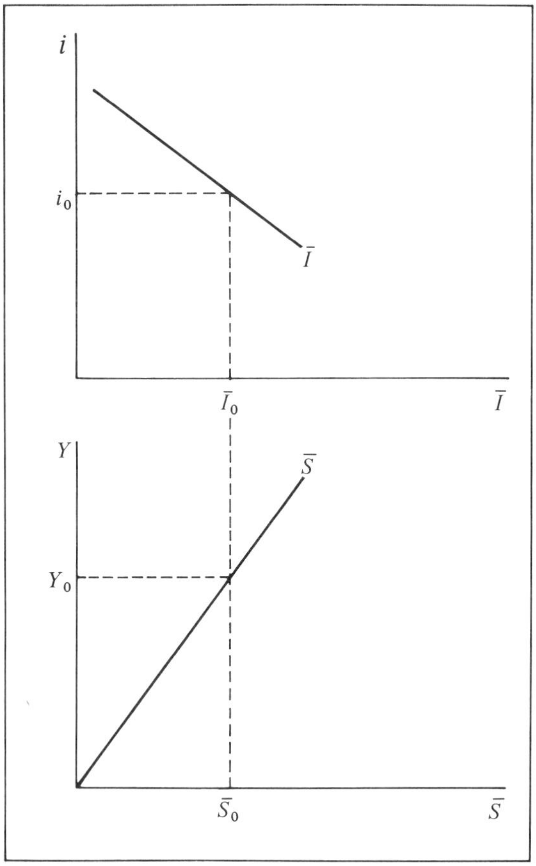

FIGURE 10:9
Commodity-market equilibrium

Thus far our discussion of the commodity market has made no mention of money. It has centered exclusively on the supply and demand for nonconsumption goods and services. This oversight will now be corrected.

THE MONEY MARKET

To parallel the preceding discussion of the commodity market, the money market will be discussed in terms of the supply of and demand for money.

The supply of money

The discussion of the determinants of the supply of money occupied fully the first half of this text. It was designed to explain the factors determining the money supply and to see whether the central bank could control the movement of the supply over time. To this end the various powers of the central bank over the monetary base and the reserves of the financial system were examined in detail. For purposes of this discussion, a relatively sophisticated money multiplier was developed. However, since our interest will now center on broader policy-oriented questions and the role of money as a determinant of economic activity, a relatively simple supply schedule of money will suffice. Essentially, it will be identical with that developed as Case I in Chapter 4. In Case I the supply of money consists only of deposits subject to checking and depends only on the monetary base (possessed solely by depository institutions) and the obligatory reserve requirement imposed by the central bank. Under these circumstances, the money supply schedule is a vertical line when graphed in a diagram such as Figure 10:10. The supply schedule will shift to the right if either the monetary base is increased or the reserve requirement is reduced; it will move to the left for opposite movements in the two determinants.

The demand for money

In developing the definition of money used in this text, the advantages of monetary exchange over barter were noted and discussed in some detail. The advantages of monetary exchange gave rise to the holding of inventories of money. This total could fluctuate according to the volume of monetary transactions to be made, and the cost of holding money, as measured by the rate of depreciation of its purchasing power (or the rate of inflation).

To reconcile this analysis with the Keynesian approach to the demand for money, it must be rephrased. We shall postulate that the demand for money depends upon the volume of monetary exchange, as measured by

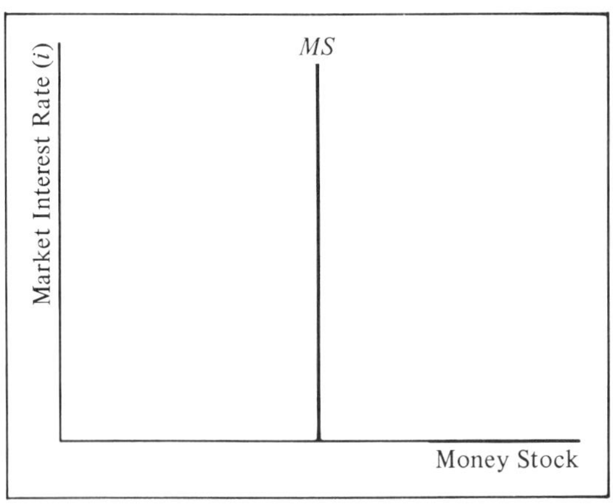

FIGURE 10:10
The supply of money

money income, and the opportunity cost of holding money, as measured by the market rate of interest.[4]

In order to see the parallel between the treatment of money in this text and the approach to money demand formulated by Keynes, the latter's analysis will have to be examined in greater detail.

According to Keynes, the demand for money arises because of three motives: transactionary, precautionary, and speculative. From a consideration of these three motives, it will be seen that the demand for money depends upon money income and the market rate of interest.

Transactions motive

The "transactions motive" may be simply described as follows: Whenever an individual's income and expenditures are not perfectly synchronized, inventories of money are desired in order to bridge the gap between the two.

To see this, consider a society composed of two people. The first receives his income of \$6 in a lump sum on Monday and spends it uniformly over the week. The other individual is just the opposite. His income, also \$6, accrues uniformly over the week and is spent in a lump sum on Monday. The combined income of the two is \$12. How much money is needed to accommodate the two in this type of income/expenditure pattern?

First, examine the money holdings of the first individual. His average daily money holdings can be deduced by subtracting his daily expenditures from his income, or

$$\$6, \$5, \$4, \$3, \$2, \$1, \$0$$

that, when added together and divided by the number of days of the week, will yield an average money holding of \$3 per day.

For the second individual, the pattern of money holding is exactly the opposite, or

$$\$0, \$1, \$2, \$3, \$4, \$5, \$6$$

that, when added together and divided by the number of days of the week, will yield an average money holding of \$3 per day.

Thus, even though their combined income is \$12, only \$6 in money is required to facilitate their joint income/expenditure pattern. Furthermore,

[4] In most Keynesian-type models the rate of inflation does not influence the choice between money and the other financial asset known as a bond. Thus, the opportunity cost of holding money can be measured by the market rate of interest rather than by the rate of inflation. If, however, the individual can hold commodities as an alternative, then the opportunity cost should be measured by the rate of inflation. This latter option is foreclosed in most Keynesian models.

the only reason each holds money is that their respective income and expenditures are not perfectly synchronized. That is, their income is not received in the same amount in which it is spent day by day. The particular pattern that emerges will govern how much money is held as an inventory.

Given the uniform pattern of the above example, the transactions demand for money, M_T, can be set forth in graphical terms, as in Figure 10:11. So long as the income/expenditure pattern remains the same, a doubling of income will simply double money holdings, and so on.[5]

Should, however, one of the individuals be paid more frequently than once per week, the average money holdings per day of the two would necessarily decline. Under these circumstances, income can remain at $12 for the two, but the amount of money demanded will decline. The amount of the decline will depend on the frequency with which they are paid. In terms of Figure 10:11, the transactions demand schedule will be seen to move counterclockwise.

The precautionary motive

A precautionary demand for money arises because the future is thought to be uncertain in many respects and one way of insuring oneself against these uncertainties is to hold a portion of wealth in a highly liquid form. The more uncertain the future and the fewer the liquid assets alternative to money available, the greater ought to be the demand for money for precautionary purposes. That said, most Keynesian analysis conveniently

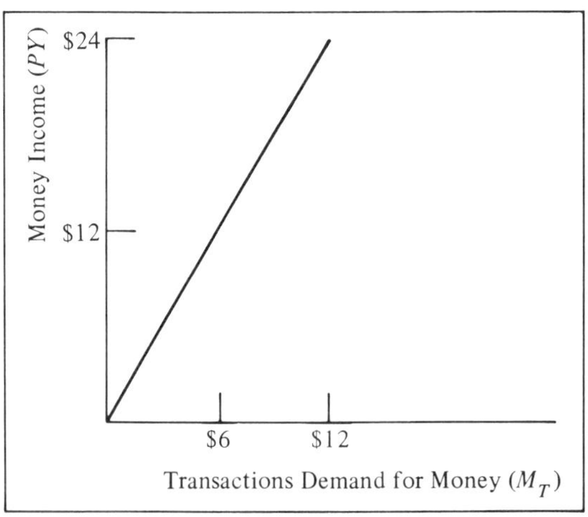

FIGURE 10:11
The transactions demand for money

[5] For a suggested alternative to this general conclusion, see Appendix 10C.

disposes of the precautionary motive for holding money.[6] This is usually accomplished in one of two ways. First, uncertainty is linked to the growth of money income. Therefore, as money income grows, so do the precautionary holdings of money balances. If the precautionary demand is assumed to be linearly related to money income, it can be added to the transactions demand. Alternatively, it is assumed that liquid assets other than money can better meet the uncertainties of economic life (e.g., Treasury bills). Either route disposes of the precautionary demand for money.

Speculative motive

Rather than present here the formal Keynesian approach to the speculative demand for money (given in Appendix 10A), a more generalized asset demand for money will be described. Under this approach, an individual can choose to hold his wealth in two types of assets: a generalized financial security called a bond, or money. Money has no explicit yield, whereas the bond yields interest. The interest yield, then, represents the opportunity cost of holding money. The higher the opportunity cost (the market rate of interest), the smaller will be the quantity of money individuals will desire to hold as an asset, and vice versa for a lower market rate. This relationship can be graphed as in Figure 10:12.

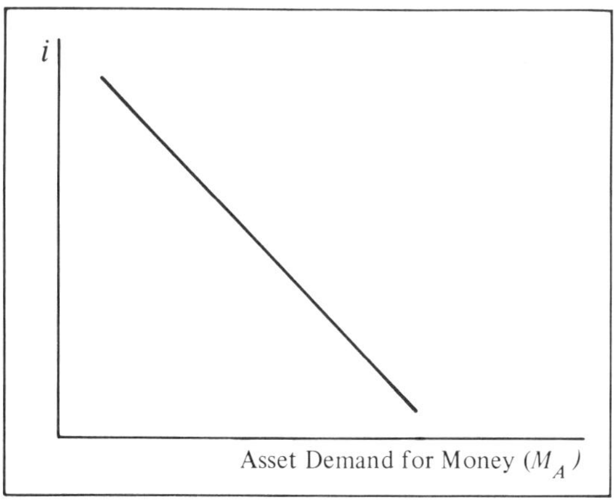

FIGURE 10:12
The asset demand for money

[6] Even Keynes's own presentation of the precautionary demand is curious. When it is introduced in Chapter 13 of the *General Theory,* it is the senior partner in explaining the interest rate, while in Chapter 15 it is reduced to a poor relation eking out an existence as a subsidary to the transactions demand. This seeming switch in importance goes unexplained by Keynes.

Before continuing, let us digress a moment to consider why any rational person would wish to hold money that yields no explicit rate of return, for without such an explanation, the asset demand for money appears to be without much of a foundation. On a fundamental level it can be argued that money has a social productivity. After all, a good deal of effort was devoted in Chapter 2 to explaining the productivity of money. At a minimum, it saves time and income by making indirect exchange possible, and this reduction in the cost of making exchange can be translated into an implicit rate of return. Thus, when the explicit yield on the bond alternative rises relative to the implicit yield on money, there is a decrease in the quantity of money individuals desire to hold.

The combination of the transactions demand, M_T, and the asset demand, M_A, equals the total demand for money. The total demand for money can be depicted in several ways. The method selected depends, in part, on what one wishes to show. In Figure 10:13 two alternatives are graphed. In panel A the total demand for money is confined to one diagram. To do this, the level of money income must first be fixed at, say, PY_0. This, then, determines the amount of money required for transactions, as explained above. The asset demand can then be added, showing that as interest rates fall, the quantity of money demanded rises. The demand schedule is then designated as PY_0 to indicate the level of income to which it is applicable.

Alternatively, the demand for money can be divided between two diagrams. This is shown in panel B of Figure 10:13 and will be the method used in this text. The division can be accomplished in two steps. First, as above, the level of money income must first be fixed. If this is designated as PY_0, then the corresponding amount demand for transactions will be M_{T_0}. The upper diagram in panel B shows the quantity of money demand as an asset.

Money-market equilibrium

Equilibrium in the money market refers to the situation where the total demand for money is equal to the money supply. Because the demand for money is divided between two diagrams, showing equilibrium in the money market will be a little more complicated than if we had chosen to confine demand to one diagram. In effect, the supply of money will have to be distributed between two diagrams. This is easily accomplished once the level of money income is fixed. Should this be PY_0, then the quantity of money required for transactions will be M_{T_0}. The sum M_{T_0} is then subtracted from the total money supply given by the central bank. The residual money supply, *MS*, is then available to satisfy the asset demand and is put into the upper portion of Figure 10:14. The interaction of the asset demand and the residual supply yields the equilibrium interest rate, i_0. Thus, with income level PY_0 and interest rate i_0, the total demand for money (the sum of the

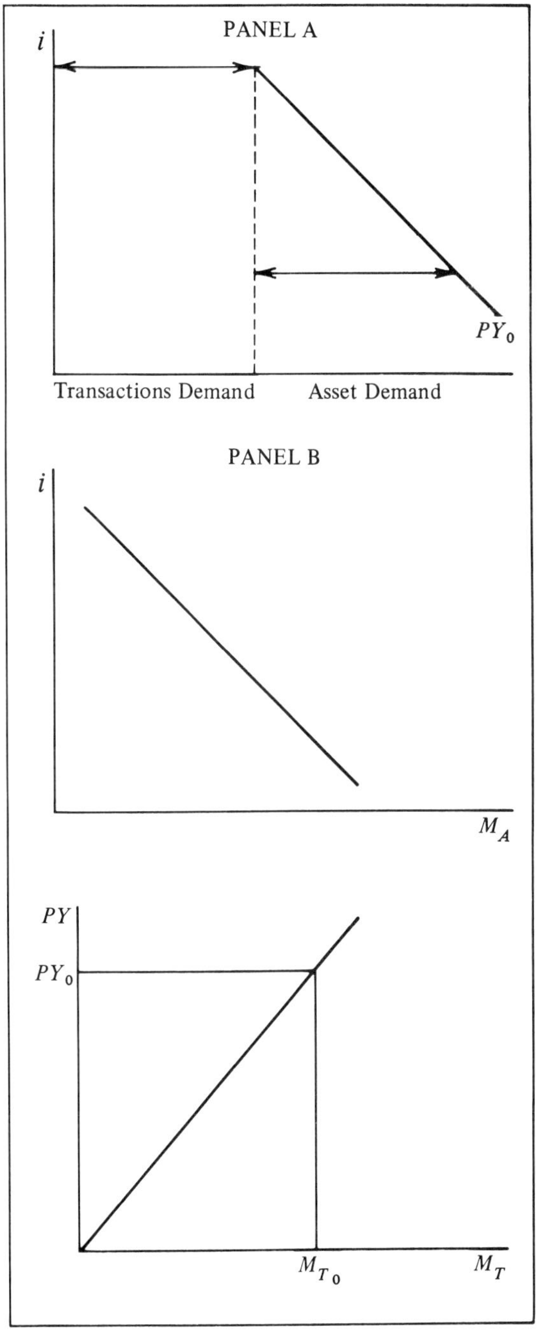

FIGURE 10:13
The total demand for money

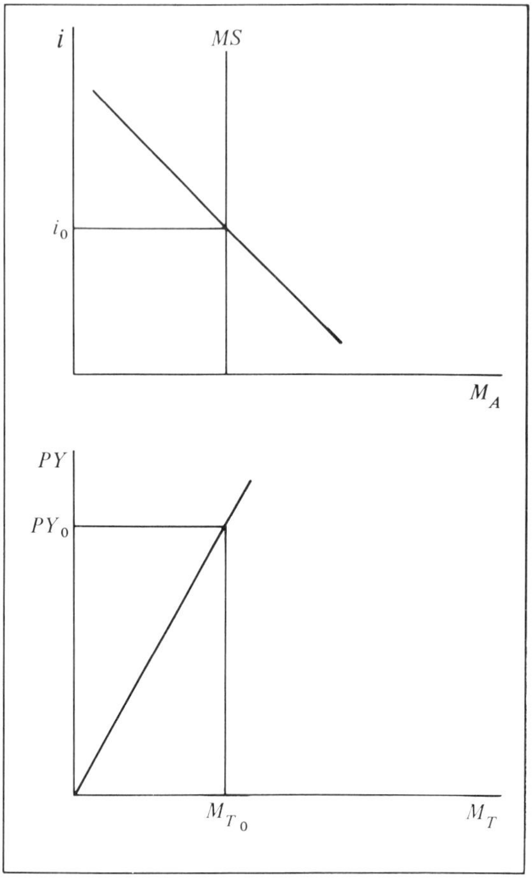

FIGURE 10:14
Money-market equilibrium

transactions and asset demand) is equal to the total supply and money-market equilibrium prevails.

For a more complete understanding of the nature of money-market equilibrium, consider two cases: an increase in the supply of money and a growth in money income. An expansion in the money supply is shown in Figure 10:14 by a rightward shift in the residual money supply schedule *MS* and a fall in the market interest rate. The decline in the rate is necessary to induce the public to hold the larger supply of money.

Should money income, *PY*, rise, a larger quantity of money would be demanded for transactions purposes. This is shown in the lower portion of Figure 10:14 as a movement along the transactions demand schedule. Since a larger quantity of money is required for transactions, the residual money supply available to be held as an asset decreases. This is shown by a leftward shift of the *MS* schedule in the upper portion of the diagram. Thus, as money income rises, a higher interest rate is required to equate demand and supply.

JOINT EQUILIBRIUM IN THE COMMODITY AND MONEY MARKETS

Thus far we have discussed the components and determinants of the commodity and money markets and the conditions for equilibrium in each. Before proceeding to the final market, the joint equilibrium of these two markets (shown in Figure 10:15) must be explained.

In order for the joint equilibrium to prevail, two variables will have to be

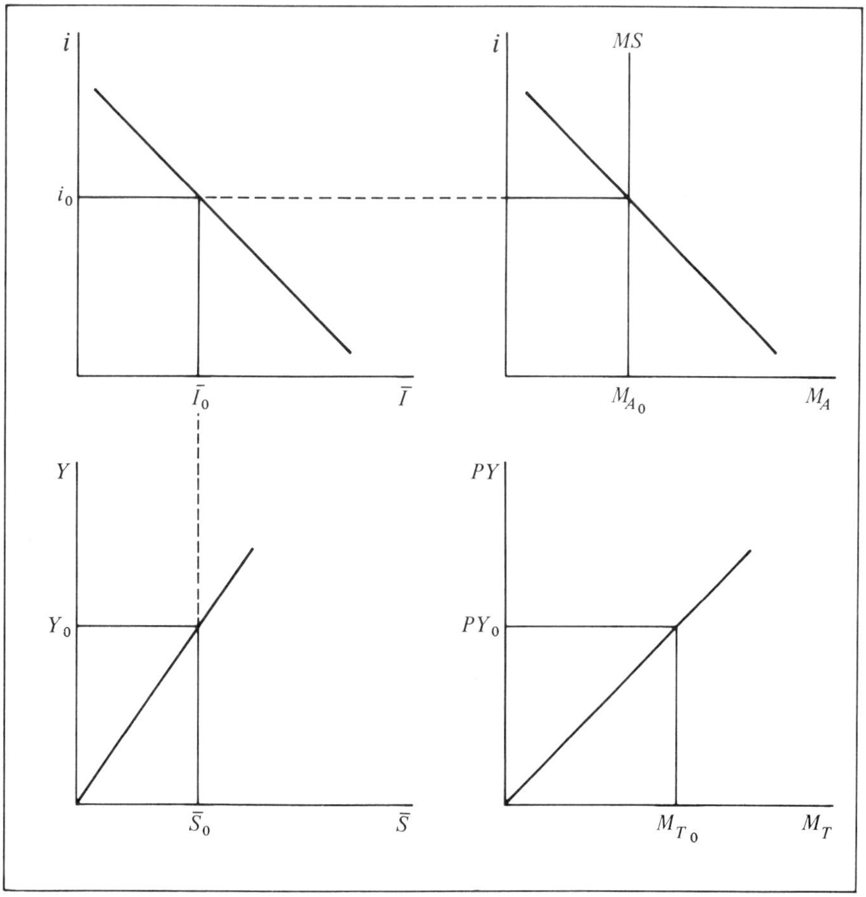

FIGURE 10:15
Equilibrium of the commodity and money markets

specified: the money supply and the price level. (The derivation of the price level is explained below.) Once these are given, the two sets of diagrams can be connected and their joint equilibrium shown.

Two aspects of the model's equilibrium should be noted. First, unless the price level (the P component of money income, PY) is set equal to 1, it is not possible to draw a straight line from the real-income diagram to that depicting money income. Second, the money market is linked to the real or commodity market by the market rate of interest. The market interest rate is said to be the means for transmitting money's influence to the real sector.

THE LABOR (AND OUTPUT) MARKET

The third and final sector of the model consists of the labor market. It is here that the amount of employment is determined. Once this is done, the level of real output is also determined.

This market has in common with the other two the proposition that demand and supply play the most important or main role in explaining its functioning.

The demand schedule for labor

The demand schedule for labor is derivable from the schedule for the marginal physical product of labor, and the assumption that business has as its goal the maximization of profit. Thus, our first step in deriving the demand schedule for labor is to derive its marginal physical product schedule. To do so, one must first examine the relationship between the input of labor into the production process and the output of final product. To measure this relationship, it will be necessary to hold constant the capital stock and the state of technology. If these are allowed to vary, it will be impossible to measure the true contribution of labor to the output of final product without resorting to more complex estimation procedures.

As labor is added to the capital stock, the level of output should rise. This relationship between input and output should prevail over a substantial range of labor time. However, the relation need not be linear. In fact, economists are fond of pointing out that the continual addition of labor to the capital stock is likely, after a while, to produce a diminishing rate of increase in final output, and possibly, after some time, an absolute decline in output. The relationship between the input of labor and real output (which is identical to real income) is depicted in Figure 10:16.

By examining changes in total real income, ΔY, and the changes in labor, ΔN, one can compute the marginal physical product of labor. From Figure 10:16, this can be seen to diminish as more and more units of labor are added to a fixed capital stock.

If the marginal units of output are plotted against incremental units of

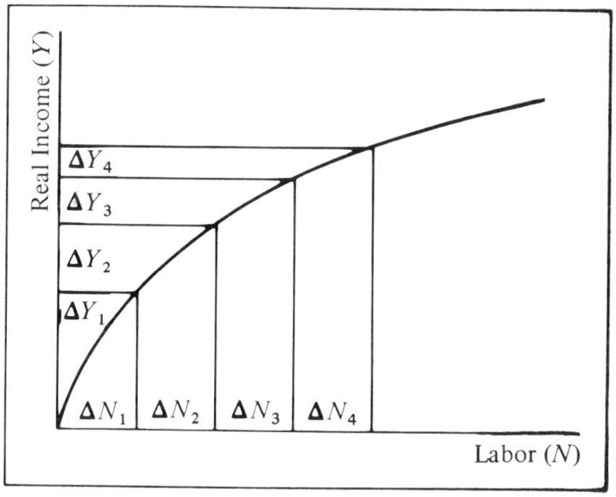

FIGURE 10:16
Real income and labor time

labor, they appear as in Figure 10:17. The slope of this schedule, and hence the marginal physical product of labor, is $\Delta Y/\Delta N$.

To convert Figure 10:17 to a demand schedule for labor, the assumption that business has as its goal the maximization of profit must be made. In the context of a competitive market for final product and labor, this means that production will be carried to the point where marginal cost, MC, is equal to the price received for the final product, P, or

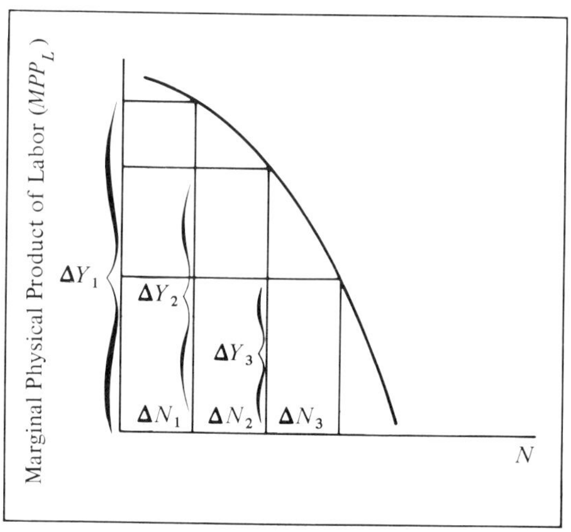

FIGURE 10:17
Marginal physical product of labor

$$MC = P$$

Marginal cost, it will be remembered from microeconomic principles, is the variable cost to produce the last unit of output. This, in turn, is equal to the wage paid the last worker hired, W, divided by the output of his or her labor, MPP_L, or

$$MC = \frac{W}{MPP_L}$$

By substitution into the profit maximization equation, we have

$$\frac{W}{MPP_L} = P$$

which becomes

$$\frac{1}{MPP_L} = \frac{P}{W}$$

and

$$MPP_L = \frac{W}{P}$$

This final equation says that profits are maximized when labor is employed to the point where its marginal physical product is equal to the *real* wage business must pay labor (the real wage is equal to the money wage divided by the price of final output produced by the firm). In moving from an example applicable to an individual firm to one applicable to the entire economy, the real wage is replaced by a suitable index of money wages, divided by a similarly suitable index of the price of final output.

Once the profit maximization condition is expressed, Figure 10:17 can be altered in one of two ways, as shown in Figure 10:18. That is, the vertical axis can show either the real wage or the money wage. The left portion of the figure graphs the relationship shown by the profit maximization equation above, while the right portion graphs the alternative profit maximization equation

$$W = MPP_L \cdot P$$

Both labor demand schedules indicate that to increase employment in the short run, the real wage must decline, i.e., prices must rise relative to money wages.

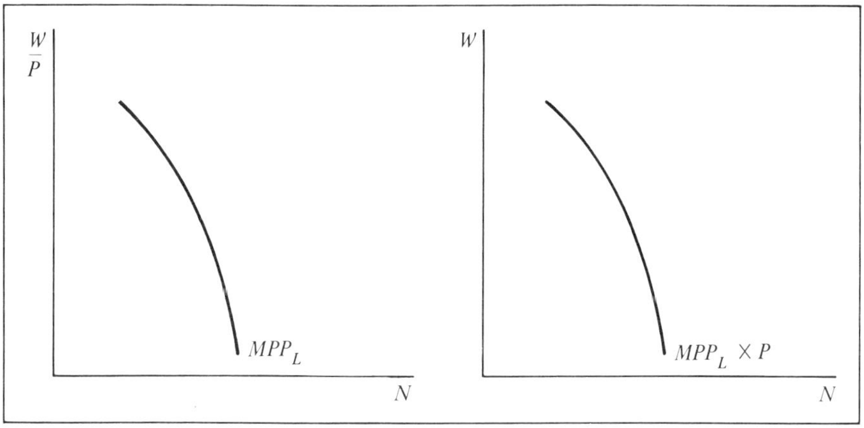

FIGURE 10:18
The demand for labor schedule

The difference between these two demand schedules for labor occurs when the price level changes while money wages are held constant, i.e., when the real wage falls. In the left portion of Figure 10:18 this reduction is shown as a movement along the demand schedule (the quantity of labor demanded is said to increase), while in the right-hand portion the demand schedule for labor shifts to the right.

In this and subsequent chapters the type of diagram shown on the right of Figure 10:18 will be used to depict the demand for labor. Thus, a fall in the real wage will be shown as a rightward shift of the demand schedule.

The supply schedule of labor

It is with the derivation of the supply schedule for labor that one encounters a major controversy in economic theory. The predecessors of Lord Keynes had developed an economic approach to the labor supply schedule under which labor would offer more time to the market only upon payment of a higher *real* wage. That is, the offer of labor time or the supply of labor depended upon the *real* wage. Keynes objected to this in his *General Theory,* stating that

> *. . . ordinary experience tells us, beyond doubt, that a situation where labor stipulates (within limits) for a money-wage rather than a real wage, so far from being a mere possibility, is the normal case. Whilst workers will normally resist a reduction of money-wages, it is not their practice to withdraw their labor whenever there is a rise in the price of wage-goods. It is sometimes said that it would be illogical for labor to resist a reduction of money wages but not to resist*

a reduction of real wages. . . . But, whether logical or illogical, experience shows that this is how labor in fact behaves.[7]

Thus, for Keynes and for many of his followers, the supply of labor depends upon the money wage prevailing in the market, not on the real wage. Later, the consequences of this assumption will be analyzed in great detail, for it has interesting implications in a world of inflation and forms part of the controversy between Keynesian economists and those who follow the dictates of Keynes's predecessors.

Given the Keynesian specification of the labor supply schedule, it can be graphed as in Figure 10:19. One interesting facet of this supply schedule should be observed—that relating to the definition of full employment. Full employment is determined by observing the amount of labor time forthcoming at the prevailing money wage, W_0. Once that is recorded, all others who offer their labor time are assumed to do so only at a higher money wage. These individuals are, then, not the concern of social policy (e.g., unemployment insurance) should they claim to be unemployed.

The combination of the supply and demand schedules determines both the level of employment and real income, as shown in Figure 10:20. The labor market depicted in this figure shows, in Keynesian terms, an "unemployment equilibrium." That is, at the prevailing money wage, W_0, the demand for labor is insufficient to employ all those willing to work, N_{FE}. The distance between N_{FE} and N_0 measures the amount of "involuntary unemployment," or the number of individuals who would be willing to work at W_0 but who cannot find employment.

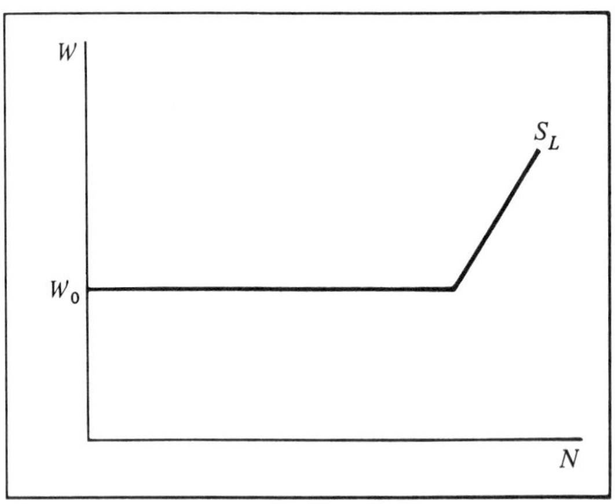

FIGURE 10:19
Labor supply schedule

[7] J. M. Keynes, *The General Theory of Employment, Interest and Money* (New York: Harcourt and Brace, 1936), p. 9.

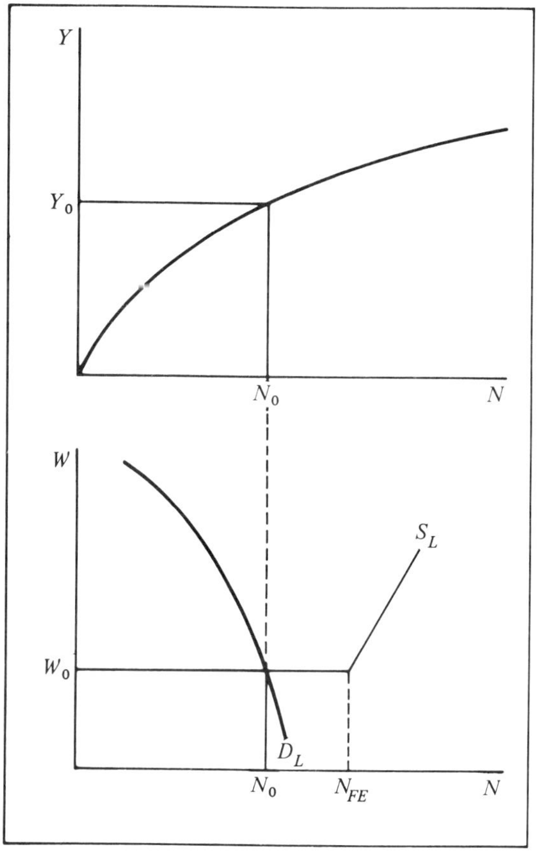

FIGURE 10:20
The level of real income and employment

An unemployment equilibrium

Because the unemployment equilibrium is so crucial to the conclusions that emerge from the Keynesian model, some discussion should be devoted to the validity of this assumption.

From the perspective of *microeconomic* theory, whenever excess supply emerges in the market for an individual commodity, its price is supposed to fall until the quantity supplied is equal to that demanded. If this is true for labor, how can an excess supply of labor or unemployment continue over a long period of time? The explanation of this phenomenon has perplexed a good number of economists.

Among Keynesian economists, Professor James Tobin[8] provides an

[8] James Tobin, "Inflation and Unemployment," *American Economic Review*, Vol. 62, No. 1 (Mar. 1972): 1–18.

explanation for what Keynes had in mind when he described an unemployment situation as an equilibrium. In Tobin's view, the use of "equilibrium" to describe a labor market in which unemployment is present was a most unfortunate choice of words. Unemployment *is* a disequilibrium phenomenon and should not be identified with a state of equilibrium. Tobin argues that the error is the result of Keynes's awkward attempt to deal with dynamic analysis within a static framework. The proper way to view "the" labor market, Tobin believes, is not as one large market but as many separate markets. There is a market for accountants, a market for engineers, a market for teachers, a market for football coaches, and so on. Although people can and do move between markets (e.g., teachers become football coaches), they generally identify themselves as members of one labor market and stay there. Wages are determined in each individual labor market by the supply and demand for labor curves within that market. Although workers usually stay within one labor market, however, they do not ignore the other labor markets. Accountants care about their real wage relative to the real wage of engineers and will not accept a decline in their money wage unless engineers do too, because to do so would mean that the accountants' real wage has fallen relative to the engineers'.

With this picture of "the" labor market in mind, one can see how unemployment emerges. Assume there is a decline in the demand for all labor. To keep full employment would require that all workers—accountants, engineers, teachers, football coaches, and so on—accept a lower real wage. But none want to be the first to drop their money wage. Accountants will not accept a decline in their money wage until engineers do, and engineers will not accept a decline in their money wage until accountants do. Thus, unemployment occurs. If there were some central, economy-wide mechanism that would drop all money and real wages simultaneously so that relative real wages would be maintained, full employment could be restored. But no such mechanism exists in the decentralized, free-labor markets characteristic of the United States and other Western capitalist economies. The result is that excess supply of labor (unemployment) continues for significant periods of time. Because the unemployment can last for such a long period of time, it leaves the impression that an equilibrium exists. In fact, each labor market is in disequilibrium (labor supply is greater than labor demand). The solution to this situation, Tobin and others who hold this view argue, is policies that manipulate aggregate demand along the lines suggested by Lord Keynes.

The Keynesian theory of the price level

Before the three sectors or markets composing the model are put together, the Keynesian theory of the price level must be explained. As formulated by Keynes, the price level depends upon per unit labor costs plus a markup to cover the remuneration for all the other factors that enter the production process. However, since labor payments quite clearly constitute the majority (close to 70%) of all factor payments, changes in this cost item are likely to be the major reason for price level changes.

Two alternative reasons are offered to explain the changes in per unit labor cost that occur over time. First, money wages may increase, that, given constant labor productivity, will increase per unit costs of production. Second, money wages may remain constant but the marginal productivity of labor may decline. This is especially likely to occur in the short run as employment is increased. Under circumstances of diminishing marginal productivity, the extent of the rise in per unit costs depends upon how fast labor's productivity declines at the margin. With substantial unemployment, the marginal decline is likely to be small. As the rate of unemployment diminishes (as full employment is approached), the decline in marginal productivity will accelerate.

Now that we know that the price level depends upon per unit labor cost, which depends, in turn, upon the wage rate, to complete the discussion we must inquire where the wage rate (W_0 in Figure 10:19) comes from. According to Keynes, the wage rate depends upon historical and institutional circumstances, e.g., the extent and militancy of trade unions, the participation of women and children in the labor force, and past inflation. In other words, the wage rate is given, which means that the price level is initially given to the model. This is alleged to be a major shortcoming of the model. It is, in the words of some economists, one equation short, i.e., it does not have an economic or behavioral explanation for the price level. This, of course, makes it difficult to explain changes in the price level or the rate of inflation.

THE COMPLETE KEYNESIAN MODEL

Having completed our discussion of the labor market, we may combine the three sectors or markets that compose the Keynesian model. This model is illustrated in Figure 10:21. Now we are ready to analyze problems in order to understand its functioning.[9]

AN INCREASE IN THE SUPPLY OF MONEY

As an introduction to both the functioning of the model and a more complex discussion to follow, we will analyze the effect of an increase in the supply of money. In order to make the presentation as logical as possible, we will employ a step-by-step process of explanation.

[9] See Appendix 10D for additional problems.

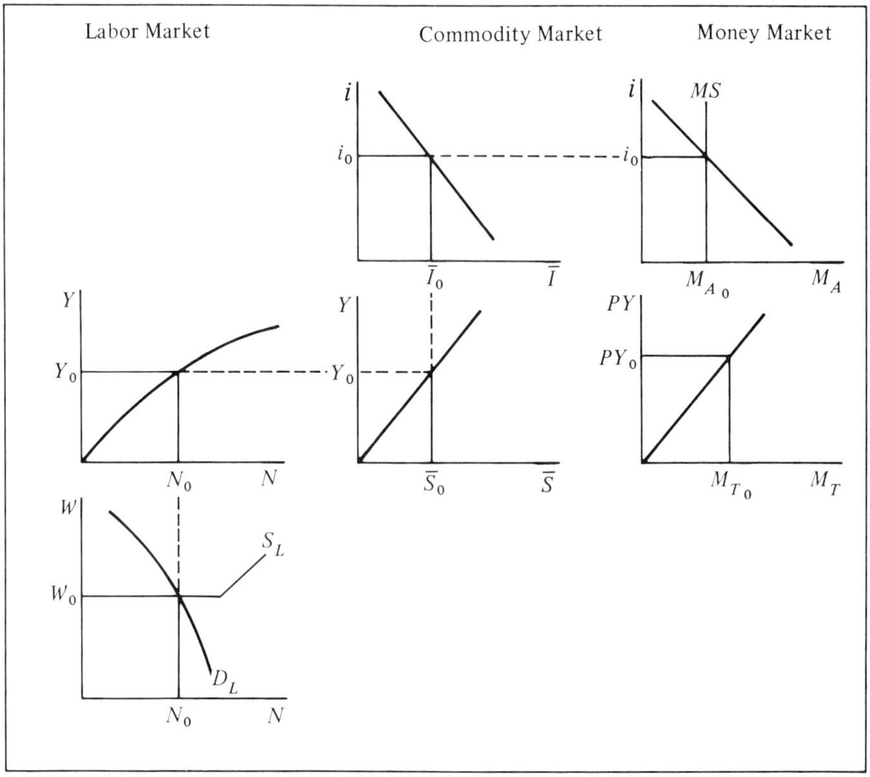

FIGURE 10:21
The complete Keynesian model

1. The central bank, through open-market operations, increases the monetary base (reserves held by depository institutions). The actual reserve holdings of depository institutions will now exceed those they desire to hold. To restore equilibrium between the two, they will make loans and increase the supply of money. This is shown by a shift to the right in the money market by the schedule representing the residual money supply from MS_0 to MS_1 (Figure 10:22). This is sometimes referred to as the "liquidity effect" of a change in the money supply.
2. The decline in the market interest rate from i_0 to i_1 will make it profitable for business and consumers to add to their stock of capital goods, with investment increasing from I_0 to I_1. Note carefully that the influence of an increase in the money supply is being transmitted to the commodity market by a decline in market interest rates (Figure 10:23).
3. As the quantity of investment rises, the manufacturers of these goods find that they must increase their rate of output by hiring more workers or by working the existing staff longer hours. The increase in labor time

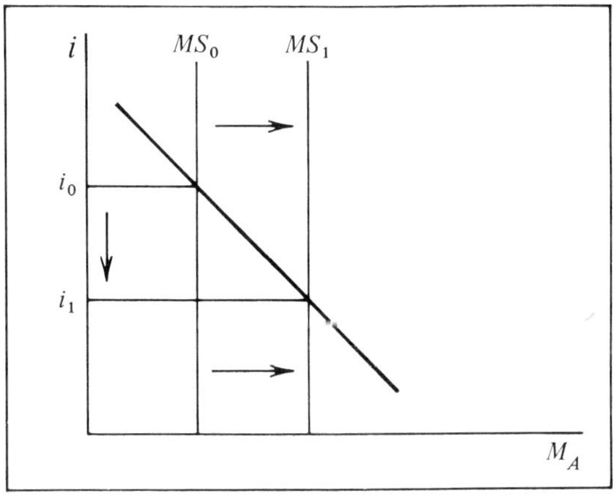

FIGURE 10:22
An increase in the supply of money

employed gives rise to larger incomes, some portion of which is spent on consumer goods. This, in turn, increases the demand for nondurable goods. Increased demand induces the nondurable goods industries to expand output, hire more workers, and generate rising income. This process becomes repetitive and is merely a description of the working out of the multiplier principle. When does the multiplier process come to an end? When a sufficient increase in $\bar{S}$ takes place to offset the rise in $\bar{I}$. When this occurs, $\bar{S}$ is again equal to $\bar{I}$ and the commodity market is again in equilibrium (Figure 10:24).

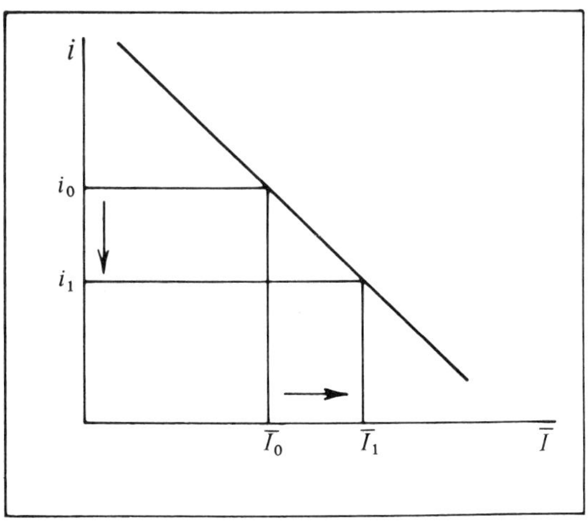

FIGURE 10:23
The decline in market interest rates

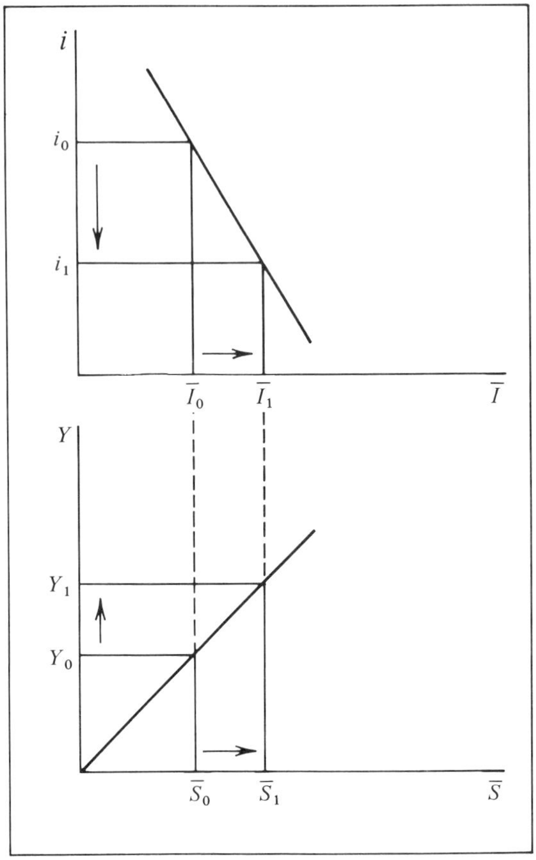

FIGURE 10:24
A rise in real income

4. The increase in real output or income is reflected in a diminished marginal product of labor. This leads to an increase in per unit labor costs and a rise in the price level. As the price level rises, the value of labor's marginal product ($P \times MPP_L$) rises and the demand schedule for labor shifts to the right from D_L to D'_L. Given that an unemployment equilibrium exists, the volume of employment will rise and the unemployment rate will diminish (Figure 10:25). (While this presentation is sequential, it should be noted that steps 3 and 4 are likely to occur simultaneously, for producers, in deciding to expand output, must see prices rise relative to production costs. If prices and costs rise proportionately, real profit will remain unchanged and no incentive will exist to increase production. Thus, prices must rise relative to costs—wages.)
5. As steps 3 and 4 operate, expanding nominal income (both Y and P will rise, causing PY to rise), they set in motion a reversal effect. That is, as

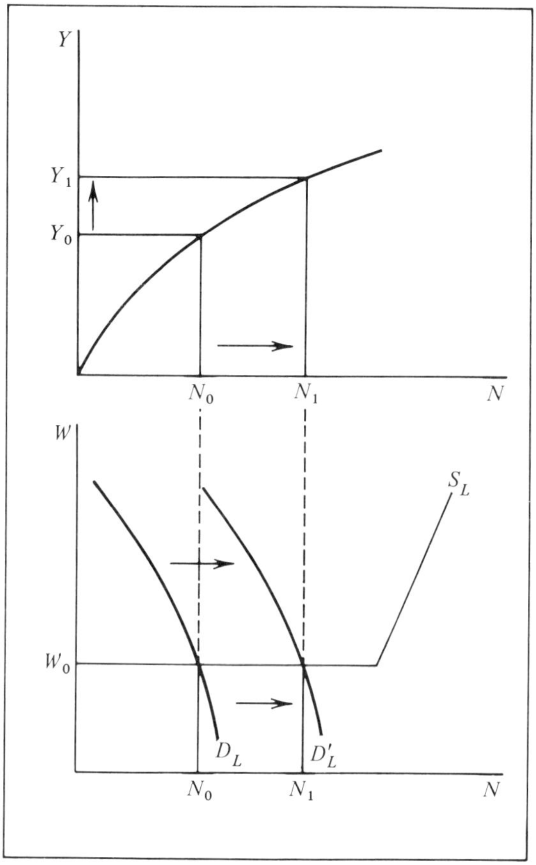

FIGURE 10:25
A rising volume of employment with diminishing unemployment rate

nominal income rises, a larger quantity of money will be required for transactions purposes (because income and expenditures are not perfectly synchronized). Since the supply of money has not increased beyond its initial change in step 1, upward pressure will be put on the market interest rate, causing a switch from holding money balances as an asset to using them to make transactions (the residual supply schedule shifts to the left from MS_1 to MS_2).

As the market interest rate rises, a reversal of step 1 occurs. So long as there is an unemployment equilibrium to start with, the reversal, sometimes called the *income effect* of an increase in the money supply, will be partial rather than total. That is, the income effect will only offset or reverse a portion of the initial liquidity effect of an increase in the money supply (Figure 10:26). On balance, then, the net effect of an increase in the supply of money will be expansionary on real income, employment, and the price level.

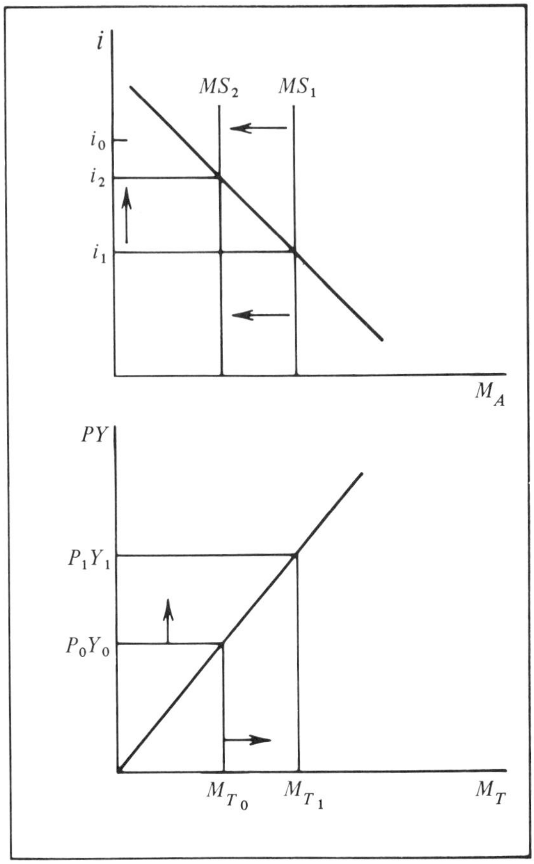

FIGURE 10:26
The income effect on interest rates

6. The net result of this discretionary increase in the money supply will be:
   a. lower market interest rates
   b. a higher level of investment
   c. a higher level of real income
   d. a higher level of employment
   e. a *lower* real wage since money wages, W_0, remained constant while the price level rose from P_0 to P_1
   f. a higher level of commodity prices.

The disquieting and controversial aspect of this analysis (which will be more extensively discussed in the chapters to follow) is the combination of lower market interest rates, a higher price level, and the decrease in the real wage that is necessary to increase the volume of employment.

The modern-day followers of Irving Fisher contend that these two decreases in market interest rates and real wages are unlikely if a longer-run perspective is the focus of analysis. Thus, these conclusions follow from the Keynesian analysis only because the focus of that analysis is on the short run. The Fisherian would ask, for example, what would happen when workers realize that they now work for a *lower* real wage? Will they not demand some sort of compensatory wage adjustment? If and when they do, what will this do to the conclusions enumerated in step 6? Clearly, it will serve to reverse them. The interested student can work them through starting with an upward shift in the labor supply schedule.[10]

Nevertheless, the six steps constitute the typical Keynesian analysis of a discretionary change in the supply of money or, in other words, the role of money in Keynesian monetary theory. Above all else, the analysis emphasizes the crucial role played by market interest rates in transmitting the influence of the money supply to the commodity markets or the real sector of the economy.

FACTORS GOVERNING THE SUCCESS OF MONETARY POLICY

Within the confines of the model developed above, the potency of monetary policy depends upon two elasticities: the interest elasticity of the demand for money, and the interest elasticity or sensitivity of investment. To verify this conclusion, consider first the demand schedule for money as an asset.

Since the influence of a change in the money supply is transmitted to the commodity market through a change in the interest rate, for monetary policy to be successful, a large interest rate change must be forthcoming for a given change in the money supply. In Figure 10:27 three different demand-for-money schedules are plotted. If the money supply is increased from MS_0 to MS_1, the largest change in the interest rate occurs with a demand schedule such as *AA*. In relative terms, demand schedule *AA* is the most inelastic and *CC* is the most elastic.[11]

[10] The Fisherian criticism is considered in great detail in Chapter 12.

[11] Elasticity seeks to measure the relationship between the change in the price of a good and the quantity demanded of that good, or

$$\frac{\Delta Q/Q}{\Delta P/P}.$$

If the price of money is taken to be the interest rate, the resulting formula becomes

$$\frac{\Delta M_a/M_a}{\Delta i/i}.$$

For each demand schedule—*AA, BB, CC*—the numerator will be the same. Clearly, *AA* has the largest denominator, and hence the smallest quotient. It follows that *AA* is the most elastic schedule of the three.

One should be careful to interpret what has been said above. From elementary microeconomic analysis, it will be remembered that elasticity calculations are made for a point on a demand schedule. With the exception of several special cases, all demand schedules have elasticities ranging from elastic to inelastic. The discussion centers on the relative slopes of three schedules. The question asked concerns which slope, relatively speaking, is the most or least elastic.

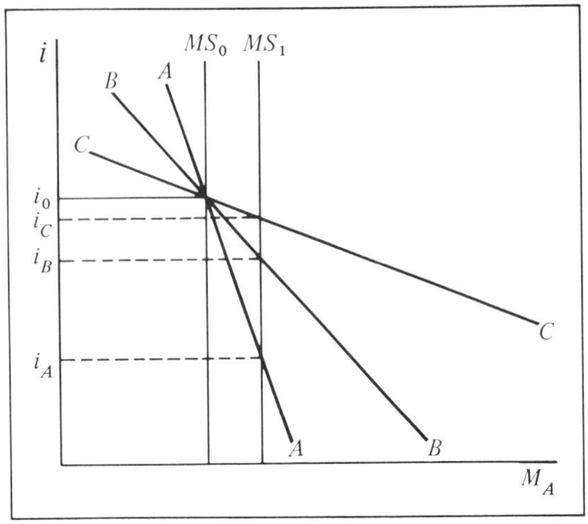

FIGURE 10:27
The interest elasticity of the asset demand for money

Now that we have described the theoretical properties of the asset demand for money that contributes to the success of monetary policy, what is the actual elasticity of the schedule in question? Its actual slope can be determined through econometric estimation and the evidence from numerous studies for the United States, which, while they are based on the total demand for money, suggest that the slope is fairly inelastic—approximately *AA*. The precise estimate depends upon whether short- or long-term interest rates are used, and on the measure of money (the *M*-1s or M_2).

Once the interest rate changes, the variable that responds most directly is the purchase of producer and consumer durable goods, which we call investment. How responsive investment is to a change in the interest rate is a measure of its elasticity. Monetary policy will be potent if, for a given change in the interest rate, investment spending responds significantly. In Figure 10:28 three possible investment demand schedules are plotted. If the actual schedule approximates *AA*, monetary policy will have a greater chance for success than if it approximates *CC*, for example.

The actual elasticity of the schedule can be estimated by econometric methods. Those estimations that have been made suggest that some classes of investment are not as sensitive to the interest rate as others, e.g., housing. As an approximation, schedule *BB* is more likely to be consistent with real-world conditions.

THE COUNTERCYCLICAL USE OF MONETARY POLICY

In the Keynesian interpretation of economic history an unstable investment demand schedule, due to waves of investor optimism and pessimism, is the cause of most business cycles. In this frame of reference the role of the

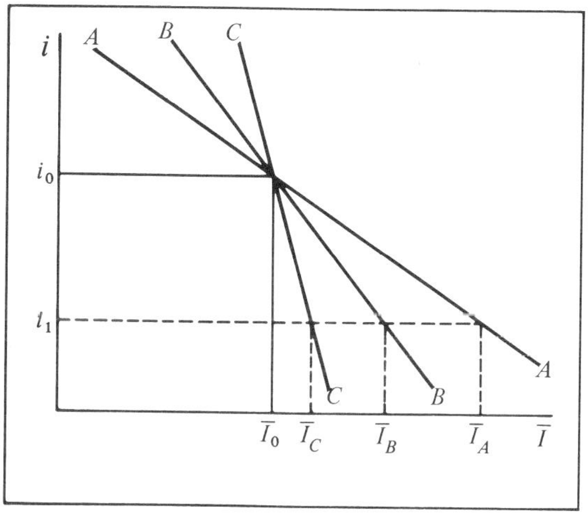

FIGURE 10:28
The interest elasticity of the investment demand schedule

money supply and the central bank is to provide compensatory changes in the market interest rate. That is, as businessmen and consumers become pessimistic about the future and the investment schedule shifts to the left, the money supply is supposed to be increased in order to drive down the rate of interest and thereby maintain a high employment level of investment. Conversely, when pessimism gives way to optimism and the investment schedule shifts to the right, the money supply is supposed to be reduced, forcing the interest rate to rise, again with the objective of maintaining high employment levels of investment.

To see compensatory monetary policy in action, assume that in

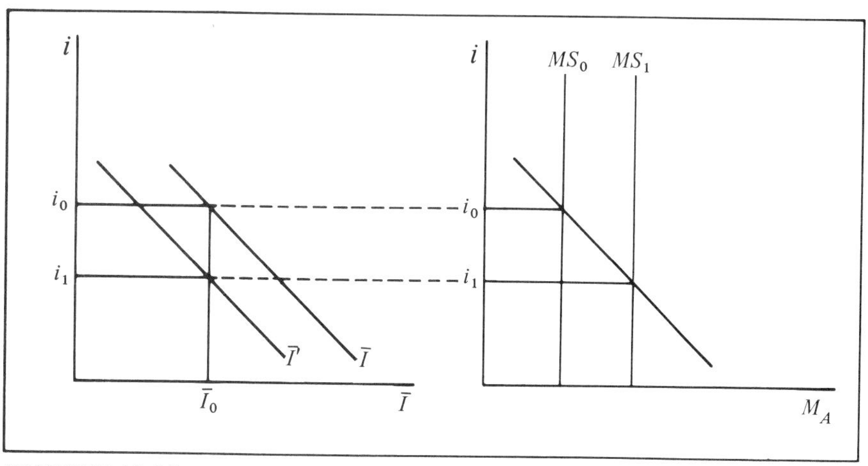

FIGURE 10:29
Compensatory monetary policy

Figure 10:29, investment level, $\bar{I}_0$, is consistent with high levels of employment. Then suppose that investment prospects appear bleak and the investment schedule shifts to the left, from $\bar{I}$ to $\bar{I}'$. In order to maintain investment at its high employment level, $\bar{I}_0$, the market rate of interest must be reduced from i_0 to i_1. This reduction will call forth an aggressive increase in the supply of money from MS_0 to MS_1. On the other hand, when investment prospects brighten and the investment schedule shifts back to the right, the interest rate must rise or else the desired level of investment will exceed I_0 and excess demand will prevail.

Thus, in the Keynesian framework countercyclical monetary policy calls for an expansion in the money supply (or its rate of growth) in the downswing of the cycle and a contraction (or slowing of its growth rate) in the upswing of the cycle. Both policies are designed to preserve the high employment rate of interest (and investment).

Factors complicating countercyclical policy

Several factors stand in the way of successful countercyclical monetary policy. They must be acknowledged and analyzed before a full appraisal of this policy's potential for stabilization can be made.

Elasticity of the asset demand for money

The success of countercyclical monetary policy depends upon the ability to manipulate the interest rate at will. If the asset demand schedule for money becomes highly elastic, it will set a floor below which the interest rate cannot be driven. If this rate is above that consistent with high employment, monetary policy will be insufficient to maintain high levels of employment. This is shown in Figure 10:30, where the market interest rate, i_{LT}, is above the high employment rate, i_{HE}.

In the *General Theory* Keynes speculated on this possibility, although he knew of no such case in the world. This situation has come to be called the special case of a *liquidity trap*. That is, the demand for liquidity (money) is so strong that at a certain interest rate wealth holders will willingly hold all increases in the money supply given in exchange for bonds.

Inelasticity of investment demand

A second qualification to the successful conduct of countercyclical monetary policy is to be found in the possible interest inelasticity of the investment demand schedule.

Suppose that in the downswing of the cycle the investment demand schedule is highly inelastic and lies close to the origin of the diagram. Then the possibility arises that even if the interest rate were driven to zero, the

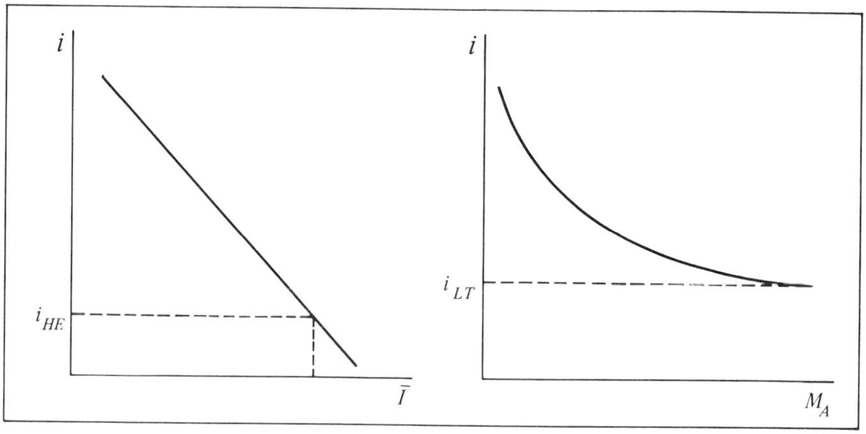

FIGURE 10:30
The liquidity trap

volume of investment would be insufficient to maintain a high level of employment. This situation is shown in Figure 10:31, where high levels of employment would require an $\bar{I}$ of the magnitude of $\bar{I}_{HE}$.

These two qualifications to the success of the countercyclical monetary policy justified, in the minds of many Keynesians, a primary reliance on countercyclical fiscal policy to stabilize employment at high levels. Thus, if the interest rate could not be forced low enough or if private investment was insufficient for high employment even at very low rates, government expenditures (or tax rates) could be used to accomplish the desired

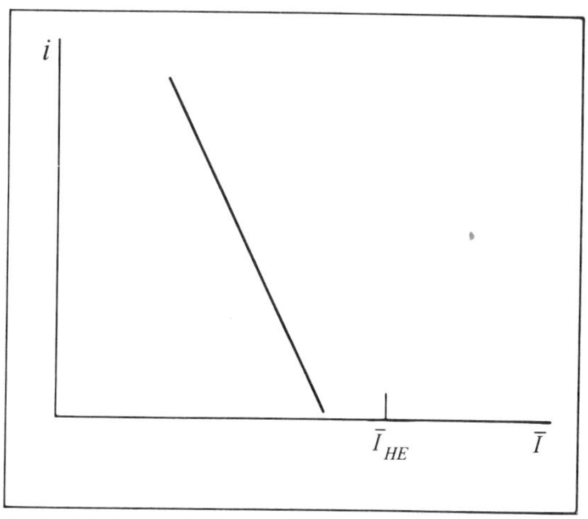

FIGURE 10:31
Inelasticity of investment demand

objectives regardless of what interest rates prevail. However, monetary policy might be able to make some contribution to employment policy, to the extent that it could keep interest rates low. Thus, Keynesian economists tended to argue for a permanent central bank policy of low interest rates. Fiscal policy, however, was to be the major stabilization tool, with monetary policy relegated to the subsidary role of maintaining low interest rates.

The problem of lags

A potentially far more serious qualification to the success of both countercyclical monetary and fiscal policy is the presence of lags in the operation of each. That is, the two policies do not operate in the instantaneous fashion described above. Because they do not, a number of economists, including some Keynesians, are increasingly reluctant to use them in a countercyclical fashion. In terms of time, Figure 10:32 sets forth the entire lag structure with which all discretionary policy must contend.

The first and basic lag consists of the passage of time from the point when action is needed until it is recognized that action is needed. Once it is recognized that some policy action is required, it takes additional time (the second lag) to formulate and execute a policy designed to deal with the problem. At this stage monetary policy is likely to have an advantage over fiscal policy, because the Open Market Committee of the Federal Reserve can frequently design a stabilization program more rapidly than the executive and legislative branches of the government. The first of these lags is appropriately called the *recognition lag,* while the second is called the *action lag*. These two together are called the *inside lag,* because they concern only authorities inside policymaking circles.

After the policy is formulated and executed—that is, after some change

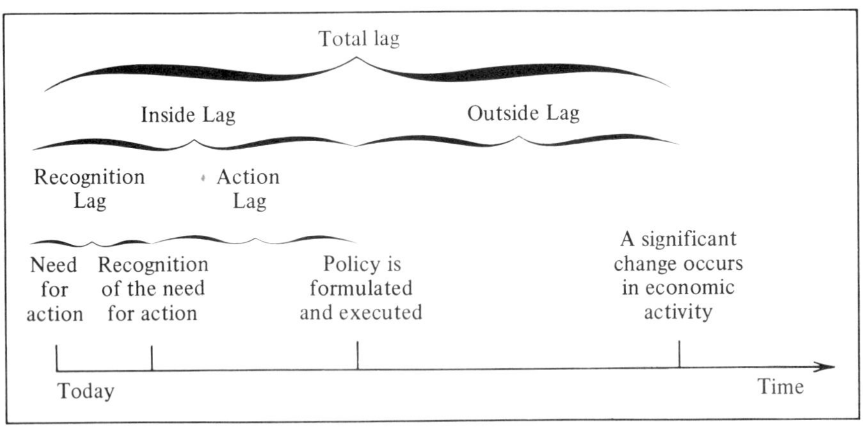

FIGURE 10:32
The lag structure for discretionary policy

in the money supply or fiscal variables takes place—the real sector of the economy must respond. The time it takes from the execution of policy until a significant change occurs in the real sector (in terms of real income and employment, or the price level) constitutes the *outside lag*. The extent of the outside lag is variable; sometimes it is short, at other times it is long. Its length may depend on such factors as the state of unemployment and the inflationary expectations held by labor and management or borrowers and lenders.

It is in the realm of the outside lag that fiscal policy is alleged to have an advantage over monetary policy, especially if fiscal policy involves some form of tax cut. This allegation rests on the fact that fiscal policy directly affects the spending stream—i.e., tax changes directly affect take-home pay, and government purchases directly affect aggregate demand—whereas monetary policy has its main impact on interest rates, to which business and consumers must then respond.

Regardless of the relative merits of fiscal and monetary policy, each operates with a lag that is long and variable, and these lags have implications for countercyclical policy. Suppose, for example, that a recession sets in and the money supply is increased in order to lower interest rates, and in this way maintain the high employment level of investment. Such a policy may actually become procyclical if, during the interval in which business and consumers are reacting to the lower rates, they suddenly become more optimistic about the future. In that case, an outward shifting investment demand schedule would confront lower interest rates and a policy with a countercyclical initial purpose would become procyclical—it would boom the boom. Conversely, a policy undertaken to curb a boom may have its impact, because of lags, in the downswing of the cycle. Thus, a recession could be forced into a deeper downturn or a depression.

Because of the existence of lags, countercyclical policy must be used with great care. To be successful, one must know the state of the economy not only today, when the policy is executed, but in the future, when the policy will have its major impact. If the economic situation cannot be predicted with some accuracy, countercyclical policy may become procyclical—rather than stabilize the economy, it may destabilize it.

The fact that lags exist has given rise to two different approaches to monetary policy. Those who believe that erratic movements in the investment schedule are the major cause of the business cycle, and that with econometric models one can foretell the future with some accuracy, generally advocate a discretionary countercyclical monetary policy involving variable changes in the money supply designed to produce high-employment interest rates. Those who hold similar beliefs about the cause of the cycle, but take the view that econometric models are often an unreliable guide to the future, frequently advocate a monetary policy that promotes a more or less stable growth rate for the money supply. Thus, even though they are Keynesians, they advocate a monetary policy that is consistent with that urged by economists who have a monetary interpretation of the business cycle. (This shows that is may be difficult to pinpoint who is and who is not a Keynesian.)

SUMMARY

In this chapter a relatively simple macroeconomic model was formulated, consisting of three markets, or sectors, in which supply and demand are the basic determinants of the interest rate, the level of real income, employment, and the level of commodity prices.

To understand the functioning of this model, an increase in the money supply was analyzed in a step-by-step fashion. Next, the use of countercyclical monetary policy was discussed, together with the problems that arise because that policy operates with a lag that can be long and of variable length. Because of the lag, countercyclical policy may inadvertently destabilize the economy. This potential gives rise to two different approaches to implementing countercyclical policy: one calling for a variable growth rate of the money supply, and designed to achieve an interest rate consistent with high levels of employment; the other calling for a stable growth rate for the money supply. Both policies have been advocated by economists who identify themselves as Keynesians.

STUDY QUESTIONS

1. Explain why aggregate saving can be regarded as equivalent to the aggregate supply of goods and services for nonconsumption purposes.
2. If an increase in investment in the Keynesian model always brings forth an equivalent increase in saving, why doesn't a rise in saving bring forth an equal increase in investment?
3. In the Keynesian framework, why is the interest elasticity of the investment schedule important?
4. How would the central bank be likely to respond to a leftward shift in the investment schedule (if monetary policy was correct before the shift)?
5. Suppose that income and expenditures could be perfectly synchronized. Would money balances be held in such a society?
6. Show how a rise in money wages relative to prices would look in the labor market.
7. What is the importance of the so-called Keynesian unemployment equilibrium?
8. Explain why a Keynesian economist might argue that changes in the money supply are equivalent to changes in the money wage rate.

9. How would a Keynesian economist likely explain the presence of large-scale unemployment?
10. Does the existence of lags complicate monetary policy? If so, how?

SELECTED REFERENCES AND READINGS

Hansen, Alvin. *A Guide to Keynes.* New York: McGraw-Hill, 1953.

Harris, Seymour. *The New Economics.* London: Dobson, 1960. An exceptional collection of early views on Keynes's *General Theory.*

Hicks, John. "Mr. Keynes and the Classics: A Suggested Interpretation." Reprinted in *Critical Essays in Monetary Theory.* London: Oxford University Press, 1967.

Johnson, Harry. "Monetary Theory and Policy." *American Economic Review,* Vol. 52, No. 2 (June 1962).

_____. "The General Theory after Twenty-Five Years." *American Economic Review,* Vol. 51, No. 2 (May 1961).

_____. "A Quantity Theorist's Monetary History of the United States." *Economic Journal,* Vol. 75, No. 2 (June 1965).

Keynes, John M. *The General Theory of Employment, Interest and Money.* London: Macmillan, 1936.

Klein, Lawrence. *The Keynesian Revolution.* 2nd ed. New York: Macmillan, 1966.

Laidler, David E. W. *The Demand for Money.* 2nd ed. New York: Dunn-Donnelley, 1977.

Leijonhufvud, Axel. *On Keynesian Economics and the Economics of Keynes.* New York: Oxford University Press, 1969.

Lekachman, Robert, ed. *Keynes' General Theory: Reports of Three Decades.* London: Macmillan, 1964.

Makinen, Gail E. *Money, the Price Level, and Interest Rates.* Englewood Cliffs, N.J.: Prentice-Hall, 1977. See especially Chapters 5, 7, and 8.

Patinkin, Don. *Money, Interest and Prices.* 2nd ed. New York: Harper and Row, 1965.

Smith, Warren. "A Graphical Exposition of the Complete Keynesian System." *Southern Economic Journal,* Vol. 23, No. 4 (Oct. 1956).

Thorn, Richard. "A Transaction Theory of the Demand for Money." *Weltwirtschaftliches Archiv,* Vol. 110, No. 3 (1974).

Tobin, James. "The Interest-Elasticity of Transactions Demand for Cash." *Review of Economics and Statistics,* Vol. 38, No. 3 (Aug. 1956).

_____. "Liquidity Preference as Behavior Towards Risk." *Review of Economic Studies,* Vol. 25, No. 1 (Feb. 1958).

Wright, A. L. "The Genesis of the Multiplier Theory." *Oxford Economic Papers* Vol. 8, No. 2 (June 1956).

APPENDIX A– THE DERIVATION OF THE KEYNESIAN SPECULATIVE DEMAND FOR MONEY

Chapter 10 presented, instead of the speculative demand for money, a simplified version called the asset demand for money. In this appendix the correct Keynesian derivation of the speculative demand schedule will be developed.

In the model derived from Keynes's *General Theory* the individual wealth owner is given the option of holding his assets in either of two forms: money or very long term bonds (consols). Since bonds yield interest, while money per se has no explicit yield, it would appear that for the rational individual the choice would be a simple one—only bonds would be held. However, the obvious choice is not always the right one. When one contemplates the purchase of a bond, one knows that movements in the market interest rate can affect the market price of the bond. If the market price changes, it may impose either a capital gain or loss upon the bond owner. This must be considered in calculating the profitability of the bond option.

Thus, in considering whether to purchase a bond, the wealth owner must compare the current market interest rate with that *expected* to prevail in the near future. The expected interest rate is called by Keynes the individual's *normal* rate. If the expected or normal rate is higher than the current market rate, holding bonds will impose a capital loss upon the individual, which will have to be offset against the interest paid by the bond in order to calculate the true yield from holding bonds.

To simplify the selection process for the wealth owner, we can derive a value for the current interest rate that will leave him indifferent as to whether he holds bonds or money. This is the value of the current interest rate that, given his expected or normal rate, will make the yield on the bond zero. Once this computation is completed, all that must be done is to compare the actual market interest rate with the calculated value of that rate which reduces the yield on the bonds to zero. If the actual market rate is greater than the calculated rate, the individual will become a bond holder because his yield will be positive; if it is lower, he will become a money holder because the yield on bonds will be negative.

To see this, let i_c stand for the current market interest rate, i_e for the expected or normal interest rate, and $g = (i_c/i_e) - 1$ be the capital gain or loss on the consol per dollar invested.[1] We now seek to calculate a value for i_c that makes the total yield on the consol, $g + i_c$, equal to zero, or

$$g + i_c = 0\,; \quad g = \frac{i_c}{i_e} - 1$$

which by substitution is

$$\frac{i_c}{i_e} - 1 + i_c = 0 \qquad (10A{:}1)$$

and

$$\frac{i_c}{i_e} + i_c = 1 \qquad (10A{:}2)$$

which can be expressed as

$$i_c\left(\frac{1}{i_e} + 1\right) = 1 \qquad (10A{:}3)$$

or

$$i_c\,\frac{1 + i_e}{i_e} = 1 \qquad (10A{:}4)$$

which, by manipulation, becomes

$$i_c = \frac{1}{\dfrac{1 + i_e}{i_e}} \qquad (10A{:}5)$$

and

$$i_c = \frac{i_e}{1 + i_e} \qquad (10A{:}6)$$

[1] To see that g represents the capital gain or loss per dollar held as bonds, assume that $i_c = i_e = .04$. In this case, the capital gain or loss is zero. If $i_c = .05$ and $i_e = .04$, the market price of the consol is expected to rise from \$1 to \$1.25, which, when subtracted from the investment of \$1, yields a capital gain per dollar of 25% or 25 cents.

Given the individual's normal or expected market interest rate, the value of the current market rate that will make him indifferent between holding bonds or money can be calculated. For example, assume that $i_e = .04$. By substituting this value into Equation (10A:6), the value of i_c making the individual indifferent is .0385. If the actual market interest rate is greater than .0385, the individual will hold bonds because their yield will be positive. To verify this, assume i_c is equal to .039 and substitute this value into Equation (10A:1) to compute the total yield from bonds, or

$$\frac{.039}{.04} - 1 + .039 = .014$$

Since the yield on the bond option is positive, *only* bonds will be held in the portfolio of this wealth owner.

Calculations such as these produce for the individual wealth owner a discontinuous demand schedule for speculative money balances. That is, at current market interest rates above .0385, only bonds are held, whereas for rates below that, all of the individual's wealth (measured as W_0) will be held in the form of money. This produces a demand schedule such as that shown in Figure 10A:1.

In order to derive the demand schedule for speculative balances by all individuals, their separate schedules must be aggregated. A downward-sloping demand schedule will be produced as long as we have diversity among individuals concerning expected or normal market interest rates. If everyone has the same expected rate, the aggregate schedule will resemble Figure 10A:1.

A diversity of normal rates will produce a diversity of corresponding

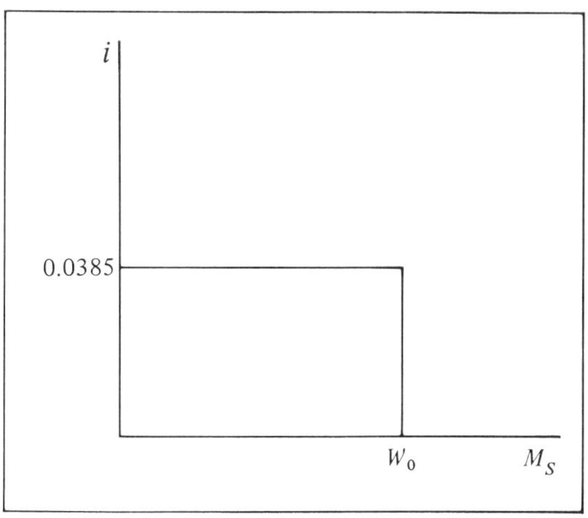

FIGURE 10A:1
The speculative demand for money by the individual

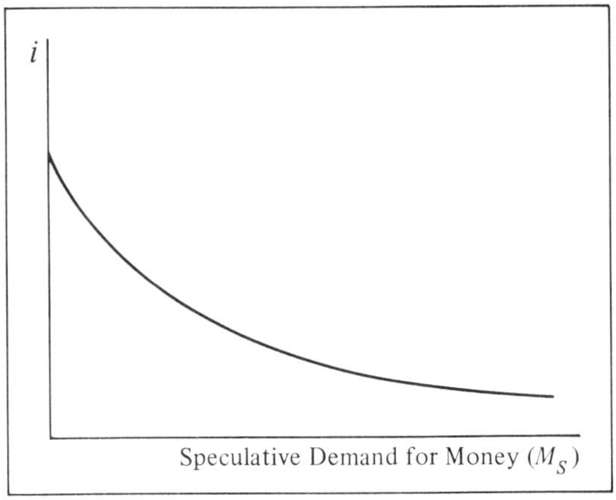

FIGURE 10A:2
The aggregate speculative-demand-for-money schedule

values of the current rate which will render the bond yield zero. As the actual value of the current market rate is lowered from some high level, we should expect to find more and more individuals who become money holders. Such considerations produce a continuous demand schedule such as Figure 10A:2.

It must be remembered that the aggregate demand schedule is drawn under the assumption that each wealth owner has in the back of his mind some expected or normal rate to which the market rate will move in the near future. If these expectations are not met, revisions should take place in the normal rate, which could cause the demand schedule for speculative balances to shift. In his *General Theory* Keynes expressed the view that it should be unstable—shifting from time to time in response to changing expectations or even in response to the announced policy of the central bank as to whether it desired higher or lower interest rates.

Subsequent research on the demand for money has failed to produce evidence in support of this view. The principal findings of these studies is that a very high proportion of the demand for money can be explained by income and an interest rate. If the demand for money were subject to random shifts over time, one would not expect those two variables to explain such a high proportion of the demand for money.

APPENDIX B– A CRITIQUE OF THE MONETARY THEORY OF KEYNES

The model developed in this chapter incorporates a monetary sector that corresponds basically to that derivable from Keynes's *General Theory*. Over the past four decades the Keynesian approach to money has been subject to a great deal of criticism, which has stimulated a number of studies designed to correct some of the problems. Several of these are discussed in Appendix 10C and these two appendices should be read as one.

Keynes's major innovation was the speculative demand for money. This contribution distinguished him from what are called the classical economists. Therefore, most of the criticism of his monetary theory centers around this motive for holding money.

The first major problem with the speculative demand for money is that the wealth of society is aggregated into only two assets—money and bonds. All other assets, such as equities, real capital, and inventories of durable goods, are made perfect substitutes for bonds. While the two-asset model vastly simplifies monetary analysis, it raises two basic problems. First, it implies an unrealistic type of portfolio behavior on the part of wealth owners—they hold either all money or all bonds, never both. In practice, a diversified portfolio is the norm, and the two-asset model cannot explain such behavior. Second, both bonds and money are equally affected by inflation, since both have fixed nominal values. Therefore, inflation does not directly affect asset selection or portfolio behavior. It may do so indirectly if it causes wealth holders to revise their expectations of the normal interest rate. If the portfolio had contained an asset with a market price that moved with the general price level, the effect of inflation on the demand for money could be analyzed much more precisely.

A second major problem arose from the manner in which Keynes presented what he called the "liquidity preference" theory of interest rates. He suggested that the market rate of interest was a purely monetary phenomenon—determined only by the supply of and demand for money. This was in sharp contrast to the view then prevailing that the interest rate was determined by nonmonetary forces—only saving and investment. This issue of the fundamental determinants of the interest rate prevails to this day. Mainstream opinion, which emerges from the model developed in this chapter, is that the rate of interest depends upon both monetary and real factors. As our example of an increase in the money supply showed, so long as unemployed resources are present, the interest rate will fall. However, an examination of the problems in Appendix 10D will demonstrate that an increase in saving will also serve to lower interest rates, while an increase in investment will raise them. Thus, nonmonetary factors can influence the rate of interest. Only in the special circumstances of the liquidity trap is the interest rate a purely monetary phenomenon.

A third major problem connected with the Keynesian model concerns the transmission mechanism by which a change in the money supply affects the commodity market. As we have seen, this mechanism is limited to a change in the interest rate that, by affecting the cost of capital, alters the rate of investment. Other possible routes for money to influence economic activity were eliminated or neglected. In subsequent work by Keynesian economists the routes of transmission have been expanded to include one that affects the flow of funds through financial intermediaries into the market for new housing, and one that affects consumption expenditures produced by a change in the nominal value of wealth held as bonds caused by a change in market interest rates.

Some non-Keynesian theorists have emphasized an additional wealth effect induced by exchanging money for bonds. This change in wealth influences aggregate spending on both durable and nondurable goods. It is produced when bonds are replaced by money. In this type of swap the former, which are both an asset and a liability, are replaced by the latter, which is only an asset. Such a swap has the effect of altering the nominal wealth of society. This alternative route by which money can directly influence the level of economic activity is sometimes called the "real balance effect."

Fourth and finally, it is claimed that the monetary theory of Keynes embodies two quite different approaches to money. On the one hand, the transactions demand for money represents an application of a sort of institutional approach to money, for it says that given the institutional arrangements of American society (payment practices), income and expenditures are not synchronized. Therefore, money balances will be held. Moreover, the implication is that the relationship between income and money holdings is a proportional one, i.e., as income doubles, so does the quantity of money demanded.

On the other hand, the speculative demand for money involves an exercise in capital theory, for it relates the holding of an asset to economic variables—the current market rate of interest in relation to the expected rate of interest. A unified approach should attempt to link both motives for holding money to economic variables.

APPENDIX C—REFINEMENTS TO THE MONETARY THEORY OF KEYNES

Beginning in the early 1950s, a number of efforts were made to amend several of the shortcomings in the original monetary theory of Lord Keynes. The first was designed to create a uniform approach to monetary theory by applying capital theory to the transactions demand for money. This work also questioned the linear relationship between income and the quantity of money held for transactions. It suggested that the relationship was not linear. Rather, as income grew, the quantity of money held for transactions could grow by much less (in a nonproportional manner).

In the original Keynesian formulation of the transactions demand only money is held to bridge the gap between income and expenditures. There is no reason why this should be so. Consider the case in which the individual receives his income on Monday and spends it all at one time on Friday. There is nothing to prevent him from buying an income-producing asset (a bond) on Monday, holding it for its income during the week, and exchanging it for money just before making his expenditures on Friday. This example served as the inspiration for some highly creative work done independently by Professors James Tobin and William Baumol.[1]

Taking their inspiration from a problem common to the asset management of business—that of determining the optimum inventory of raw materials—they were able to draw some interesting conclusions, one of which was that monetary policy had the potential to be much more powerful than many Keynesians were willing to concede.

Following the general outlines of the Baumol–Tobin approach, in applying capital theory to the transactions demand for money, money balances held to make expenditures are considered a sort of inventory and the goal of the individual is to minimize the costs associated with that inventory. When money is held to make expenditures, two costs are associated with its holding. The first involves the expenses necessary to convert other assets (in this case, bonds) to money. These expenses are both monetary—the fee necessary to sell bonds on an organized financial market—and nonmone-

[1] W. J. Baumol, "The Transactions Demand for Cash: An Inventory Theoretic Approach," *Quarterly Journal of Economics,* Vol. 66, No. 4 (Nov. 1952): 545–56. James Tobin, "The Interest-Elasticity of Transactions Demand for Cash," *Review of Economics and Statistics,* Vol. 38, No. 3 (Aug. 1956): 241–7.

tary—the physical exertion and inconvenience involved in making the conversion. Both expenses are called the *brokerage fee*. Second, each dollar held as money involves the loss of interest the individual could have earned by holding his wealth in a bond form. In deciding how much money to hold over any given period, the goal is to minimize the sum of these costs. It is assumed that in order to compute his optimum inventory of money, the individual has certain uniform expenditures to make over a given time period, symbolized by Y.

The individual can make one conversion of bonds for money equal to the total of his planned expenditures at the beginning of the period over which the expenditures are to be made, or he may make as many uniform conversions as he wishes over the expenditure period. Each conversion will involve a brokerage fee, as defined above, and the total brokerage fee will be equal to the number of conversions into money times the brokerage fee, or (Y/M) (b), where M denotes the amount of bonds converted to money and b is the brokerage fee per conversion.

Every time bonds are converted into money, the individual forgoes interest income. The total interest income forgone over the expenditure period is equal to the average money holding per *conversion* period or, $M/2$, multiplied by the interest rate applicable to the expenditure period, or i.[2]

The problem then posed to the individual is to minimize the sum of these two costs, symbolized by C, associated with his money holding over the expenditure period, or

$$\text{Minimize } C = \frac{Y(b)}{M} + \frac{M(i)}{2} \qquad (10C{:}1)$$

This can be done by differentiating C with respect to M, setting the result equal to zero and solving the equation, or

$$\frac{dC}{dM} = \frac{-Y(b)}{M^2} + \frac{i}{2} = 0 \qquad (10C{:}2)$$

$$\frac{Y(b)}{M^2} = \frac{i}{2} \qquad (10C{:}3)$$

$$\frac{1}{M^2} = \frac{i}{2Y(b)} \qquad (10C{:}4)$$

[2] For example, if the expenditure period is one year and bonds are converted into money at the beginning of the year, average money holding is $(M/2)$ and the interest forgone is $(M/2)(i)$, where i is the annual rate of interest. If bonds are converted into money twice per year, the semiannual cost consists of the average money balances held per half-year, $(M/2)$, multiplied by the semiannual interest rate, $(i/2)$—or $(M/2)(i/2)$. The annual cost is, therefore, $(M/2)(i/2) + (M/2)(i/2)$, or $(M/2)(i)$, or the average money holding per conversion period (half-year) multiplied by the annual rate of interest, or the rate prevailing over the expenditure period.

$$M^2 = \frac{2Y(b)}{i} \qquad (10C:5)$$

$$M = \sqrt{\frac{2Y(b)}{i}} \qquad (10C:6)$$

Since the average money holding of the individual per period is $M/2$, Equation 10C:6 becomes

$$\frac{M}{2} = \frac{1}{2}\sqrt{\frac{2Y(b)}{i}} = \sqrt{\frac{Y(b)}{2i}} \qquad (10C:7)$$

Therefore, the nominal money holdings for the cost-minimizing individual will vary directly with the square root of planned nominal expenditures and inversely with the square root of the market interest rate. The function can be made into one for real-money balances, M/P, by making expenditures and the brokerage fee real magnitudes, that is, by dividing each nominal magnitude by a suitable price index, P.

Before the implications of the Baumol–Tobin construct are explored, several factors qualifying the analysis ought to be understood. First, the brokerage fee has obvious importance. If its value were zero, no money would be held to make transactions and the wealth owner would merely synchronize bond sales with planned purchases. Second, the brokerage fee has been assumed to be constant regardless of the size of the conversion of bonds for money. This is unrealistic to a degree, but the principal cost involved in the brokerage fee is supposedly the time and inconvenience involved in converting bonds into money. It is not the commission charged by the intermediary to dispose of the issue on the financial market. When viewed this way, any lack of realism seems minimal.

Finally, any cost associated with the acquisition of the bonds has been omitted from the discussion. That is, at the beginning of the planned expenditure period, an individual could have received some portion of his income and used it to add to his stock of bond holdings. The acquisition of these bonds obviously involves costs, both monetary and nonmonetary. The occurrence of such costs is usually handled by saying that their explicit consideration does not alter the ultimate conclusions of the analysis, so long as they do not vary directly with the amount of bonds purchased and are relatively small. Thus, they enter the analysis much as do the disposition or conversion costs.

The implications of the Baumol–Tobin model are several. First, the demand for real cash balances, M/P, will rise by less than the rise in real income (or real expenditures), implying both that substantial scale economies exist in holding money balances and that, in the terminology of microeconomic theory, money is a necessity. One therefore ought to observe a secular rise in the velocity of money over time. Data produced by Friedman would tend to contradict this implication.[3] Second, in this model the demand for real balances is invariant with respect to changes in the price level; therefore inflation can only affect the demand for money by altering the rate of interest. Third, the power of monetary policy is greatly enhanced. Suppose, for example, that the supply of money is increased, creating a disparity between actual and desired balances. This model implies that for a given interest rate, nominal income must rise by the square of any increase in nominal balances before equilibrium can be restored. Fourth, no doubt should exist that the transactions demand has been formally recognized on a methodological level with the speculative demand, for now the individual, in deciding whether to hold wealth in a money or a bond form for transactions purposes, must consider (among other variables) the market rate of interest. This permits the total demand for real money balances to be written in one general functional form as

$$\frac{M}{P} = f\left(\frac{Y}{P}, i\right) \qquad (10C:8)$$

In the late 1950s the fertile mind of James Tobin formulated a model in which the simultaneous desire to avert risk and to maximize the utility from wealth would lead an individual to choose a diversified portfolio consisting of both money and bonds.[4] The presentation of the Tobin model here is based on simplifications introduced by David Laidler.[5]

As stated above, Tobin's demonstration of a diversified portfolio is based on the premise that an individual desires to maximize the utility from his wealth and seeks to avoid the risk associated with holding his wealth in various forms. Since the portfolio will consist only of bonds and money, the type of risk associated with bond holding involves alteration in their market value (capital gains or losses) resulting from uncertainty over the future rate of interest.[6] If the portfolio consists only of money, this risk is zero, for risk arises only if bonds are held. On the other hand, if the

[3] M. Friedman and A. J. Schwartz, *A Monetary History of the United States* (Princeton, N.J.: Princeton University Press, 1963), pp. 678–9.

[4] James Tobin, "Liquidity Preference as Behavior Towards Risk," *Review of Economic Studies*, Vol 25 (Feb. 1958): 65–86. The principles stated in this analysis can also be applied to an expanded portfolio. However, in a world that includes equities and commodity inventories, movements in commodity prices may be important because they affect the yield on money. In the two-asset world of money and bonds changes in the price level can be neglected, for they affect money and bonds in the same way. Thus, money can be assumed to have a zero explicit yield.

[5] David E. W. Laidler, *The Demand for Money* (Scranton, Pa.: Intext, 1969), pp. 67–76.

[6] Uncertainty over the future rate of interest is one feature distinguishing this model from Keynes's. In the derivation of the speculative demand schedule the assumption was made that each individual had a "normal" rate in mind where the current rate was expected to move to in the near future. In this model the individual is uncertain about the future rate and views it in terms of a probability distribution of possible rates.

portfolio consists only of bonds, the risk is maximized. Portfolios consisting of both bonds and money involve intermediate levels of risk depending on the extent to which they approach either extreme.

Despite the risk attached to bond holdings, such a portfolio has an advantage over a portfolio consisting solely of money—it yields an explicit income. This income is composed of two parts: an interest income that is known with certainty, and capital gains or losses that depend upon movements in the interest rate. To simplify the analysis, we will assume that the individual wealth owner assesses the probabilities of making capital gains and losses on bonds in such a way that the expected value of such gains and losses is zero. If this assumption is made, the expected yield from holding bonds will be equal to the market rate of interest.[7]

In order to determine the optimum combination of money and bonds for the individual, it will be necessary for him to express his subjective preferences between the utility from his expected wealth and his aversion to risk. In addition, it will be necessary to determine the tradeoff that exists in the marketplace between wealth and risk. Thus, the problem that must be solved is very similar to the constrained welfare maximization problem of consumer choice presented in microeconomic textbooks.

Figure 10C:1 represents the graphical construct in which the Tobin

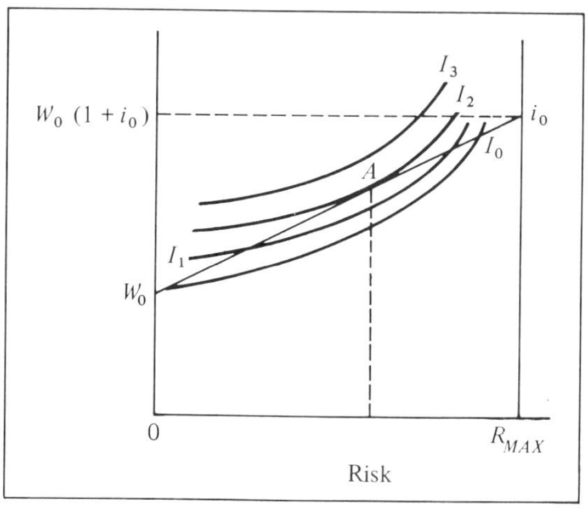

FIGURE 10C:1
Portfolio choice under uncertainty

[7] The assumption of a zero expected capital gain or loss is not critical. It could be positive or negative. However, if an alternative value is used, the growth path or budget constraint that transforms present wealth into future wealth would depend not only on the present rate of interest, but also on the adjustment for the expected rate of capital gain or loss. Such an adjustment complicates the analysis, for it makes it difficult to relate the speculative demand for money to the rate of interest unless it can be shown that the expected rate of capital gain or loss is related systematically to the rate of interest.

approach can be developed. Its horizontal axis measures the risk of capital gain or loss associated with uncertainty about the future rate of interest. As the portfolio becomes more heavily concentrated in bonds, the degree of risk increases until it reaches a maximum when all assets have been converted to bonds. That maximum is denoted as R_{MAX}. The vertical axis measures the expected value of the portfolio. For the end of any given period, it may not be the actual value, but rather the value the individual believes will prevail, given his expectations of future interest rates. If actual events correspond with those expected, the actual and expected values of the portfolio will be equal.

If the initial position of the portfolio is given by W_0, its expected value at the end of the period under consideration would be $W_0(1 + i_0)$ if the entire portfolio were invested in bonds. Thus, the growth of the value of assets would depend on the market interest rate, i_0, for it has been assumed that the expected value of capital gains or losses is zero. The growth path by which W_0 approaches $W_0(1 + i_0)$ is shown by the solid line designated (i_0). This growth path can be conceived of as the analog of the budget constraint in the theory of consumer behavior, for it gives all combinations of risk and expected wealth objectively open to the individual in the marketplace.

The subjective tradeoff of the individual is given by indifference curves, each of which measures alternative levels of expected wealth and risk that leave the individual equally well off. To induce the individual to bear more risk, the expected value of his wealth must be increased. Because the individual avers risk and increases in wealth yield diminishing utility, ever-larger increases in expected wealth are necessary to induce him to bear uniform additional increments of risk. Thus, the indifference curves slope upward and to the right. Additionally, higher-level indifference curves are preferred to those lying at lower levels, for they yield higher expected wealth for the same level of risk; for a given level of expected wealth, they represent lower levels of risk. These indifference curves are shown in Figure 10C:1 as I_0, I_1, I_2, and I_3.

The optimum, or utility-maximizing, portfolio for the individual will result when his subjective tradeoff is equal to the objective or market tradeoff. This situation is shown in Figure 10C:1 by the point *A*, which indicates a portfolio weighted more heavily toward bonds than money. The expected value of this portfolio at the end of the period can be obtained by moving directly over to the vertical axis.

In order to derive a demand schedule for idle or speculative balances, Figure 10C:1 must be amended to show alternative rates of interest. If the rate is not i_0, but a higher rate such as i_1, the growth path of expected wealth must be above that for i_0 so long as the evaluation of risk remains constant, for the slope of the path is given by

$$\frac{W_0(1 + i) - W_0}{R_{MAX}} \tag{10C:9}$$

or

$$\frac{iW_0}{R_{MAX}} \qquad (10C:10)$$

So long as W and R_{MAX} remain constant, the value of the slope of the expansion path will depend on i. Figure 10C:2 gives several points of equilibria for various values of the market rate of interest. These are designated as A, B, and C, and they indicate that as the market interest rate rises, the individual is willing to bear more risk by holding more bonds and less money.[8] When this inverse relationship is graphed, it will yield the usual continuous speculative demand schedule, shown as Figure 10C:3. It is important to note that this demand schedule is for the individual wealth owner.

Such a continuous schedule did not emerge in the formal Keynesian model developed in this chapter, for the individual had an either/or choice and acted as if he knew with certainty the future rate of interest. This knowledge permitted the computation of the critical current rate ($\bar{i}_c$), and whenever the actual current rate was above its critical value, the individual held only bonds; when it was below its critical value he held only money. Such reasoning would produce for the individual a discontinuous demand function such as shown in Figure 10C:4. The smooth, continuous down-

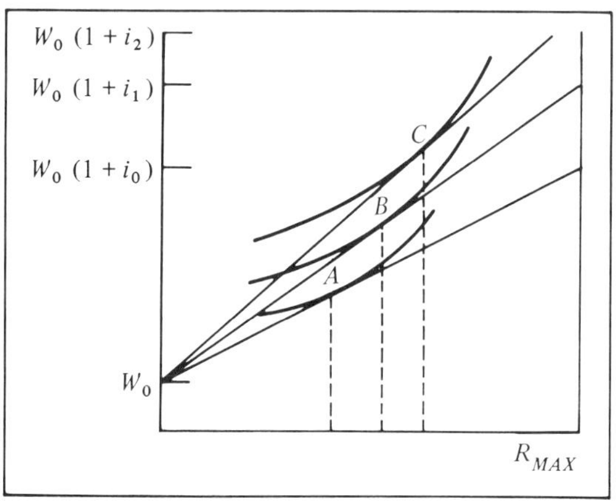

FIGURE 10C:2
Equilibrium with alternative interest rates

[8] It should be obvious that this conclusion results from the position of the indifference curves. Had the slopes of the schedules been constructed differently, it would have been possible to produce the opposite conclusion. Whether rising interest rates increase or decrease, the demand for money can only be resolved empirically. The available evidence using both short and long interest rates is that an inverse relationship is present.

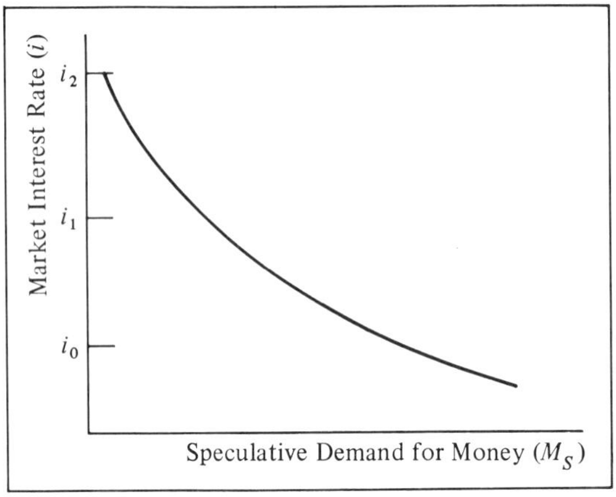

FIGURE 10C:3
Demand for money by a utility-maximizing individual

ward-sloping function was produced by summing these individual demand functions and assuming that the individuals had diverse normal rates and therefore diverse critical values of the current market rate.

Tobin's model can also be altered by allowing for changes in the level of risk attached to portfolios containing various combinations of bonds. While this refinement will not be presented here, its general conclusion should come as no surprise: If the level of risk rises for the same interest rate, i_0, fewer bonds and more money will be held in the individual's portfolio.

In summary, the work of Tobin permits the derivation of a demand

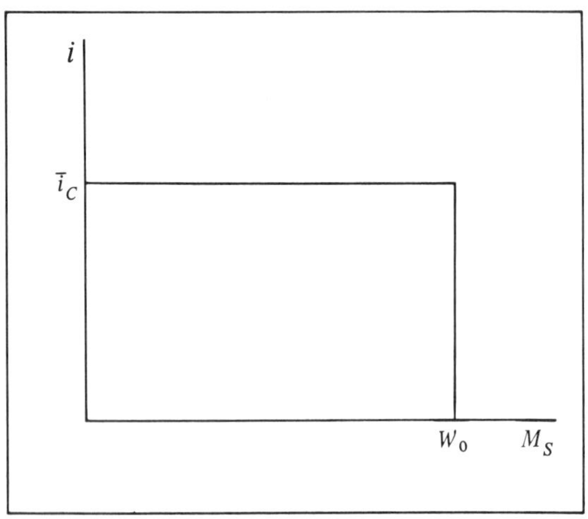

FIGURE 10C:4
Keynesian demand functions for speculative balances by the individual

schedule for speculative balances and explains a diversified portfolio that corresponds to those observed in the real world. His theorizing is based upon the wealth level of the individual, the current rate of interest (which actually serves as a proxy for the expected yield on bonds), and the risk of changes in the capital value of bonds. In many respects Tobin's formulation of the problem is markedly similar to the constrainted welfare-maximization problems of microeconomic theory.

APPENDIX D— OTHER PROBLEMS IN A MACROECONOMIC CONTEXT

In order to develop a greater appreciation for the functioning of the macroeconomic model developed in this chapter, several additional problems will be analyzed.

A RISE IN GOVERNMENT EXPENDITURES

Our first problem will be to trace through a rise in government spending that is not simultaneously covered by an equal rise in taxes. It should be noted that this problem is exactly similar to a rise in private investment spending.

In terms of the macroeconomic model, the rise in government expenditures is shown by a rightward shift in the $\bar{I}$ schedule from $\bar{I}$ to $\bar{I}'$, by the amount of the rise in the expenditures (see Figure 10D:1, Diagram A).

Businessmen now experience an influx of government orders for goods and services. They will expand production and fill these orders only if real profits rise. That is, the prices they charge must rise relative to the wages they pay. The rise in prices is due to the increase in per unit labor cost as output expands. Per unit labor cost rises because the marginal productivity of labor declines as output is increased (holding money wages constant).

Let us assume that businessmen believe labor is available to be hired at going money wages. Prices are now increased, which is translated into a rightward shift in the demand-for-labor schedule, leading to a rise in employment (see Figure 10D:1, Diagrams C and D). As employment rises, real income is increased, setting in motion the familiar multiplier process. This serves to increase the quantity of both private savings and taxes, or $\bar{S}$ (see Figure 10D:1, Diagram B).

As real income and the price level rise, nominal or money income also rises. Given the expenditure pattern of society, this will lead to a rise in the quantity of money held for transactions purposes (see Figure 10D:1, Diagram E). Since the money supply itself has not changed, the amount of money remaining to be held as an asset diminishes, and market interest

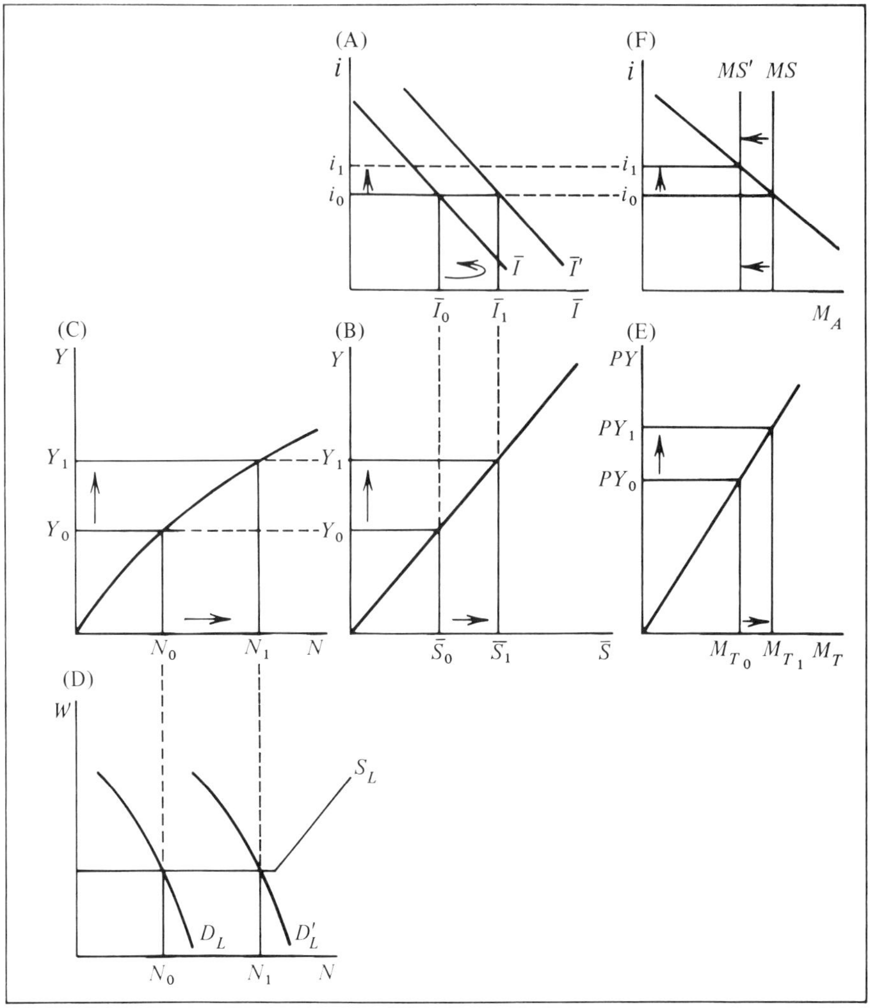

FIGURE 10D:1
The macroeconomic effect of a rise in government expenditures

rates rise (see Figure 10D:1, Diagram F). The rise in the interest rate will cause some private expenditures for producer and consumer durable goods to diminish, thereby undoing in part the overall effect of the rise in government expenditures. This rise in interest rates induced by government expenditures, which serves to displace in part private expenditures for capital goods, is called the crowding-out effect.

In order to measure the degree of "fiscal crowd-out," consider Figure 10D:2, which shows Diagrams F and A of Figure 10D:1 at the point where the rise in money income has forced the market rate of interest upward.

Since the difference between the two I schedules represents government

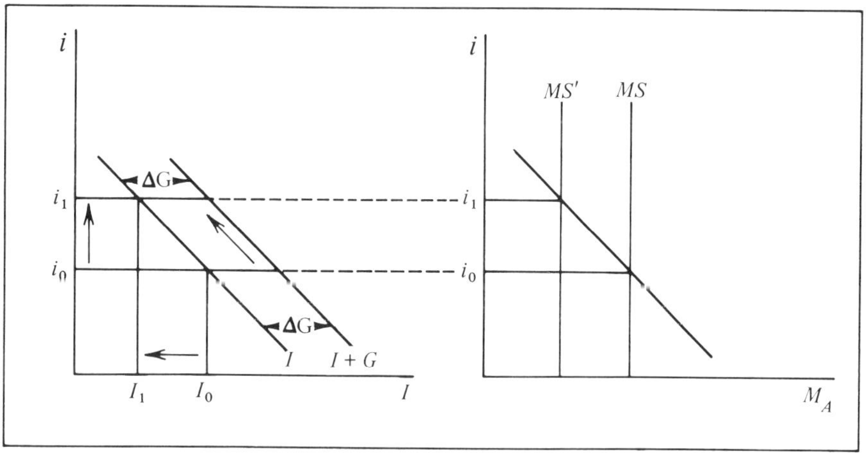

FIGURE 10D:2
The crowding-out effect of fiscal policy

expenditures, the crowd-out can be seen by reference to line I on the first $\bar{I}$ schedule. The rise in market interest rates from i_0 to i_1 will cause private capital expenditures to diminish from I_0 to I_1, or be crowded out by fiscal expenditures. Thus, the net impact of government expenditures will be less than its gross impact, i.e., it will not raise aggregate demand dollar for dollar.

The degree of the crowd-out is obviously related to the elasticity of private investment expenditures and the degree of unemployment. The more elastic this schedule is, the larger is the crowd-out. If the investment demand schedule were vertical (of zero elasticity) the crowd-out would be zero. However, under any circumstances, if full employment prevails, all government expenditures replace private expenditures dollar for dollar—i.e., crowd-out is complete.

AN INCREASE IN TAXES

As an anti-inflationary device, taxes are often increased. It is the purpose of this exercise to see why such action is undertaken.

In terms of Figure 10D:3, an increase in taxes will cause the $\bar{S}$ schedule to shift in a clockwise fashion (see Diagram B) from $\bar{S}$ to $\bar{S}'$.

As taxes rise, the disposable income of individuals (their income after taxes) declines. With less disposable income, consumption expenditures fall. Manufacturers receive fewer orders for replacement goods than previously. They cut back output, causing real income to decline (see Figure 10D:3, Diagrams C and D), thereby serving to raise the marginal physical productivity of labor. This reduces per unit labor cost and, consequently, the price level. This shifts the demand schedule for labor to the left, reducing the volume of employment.

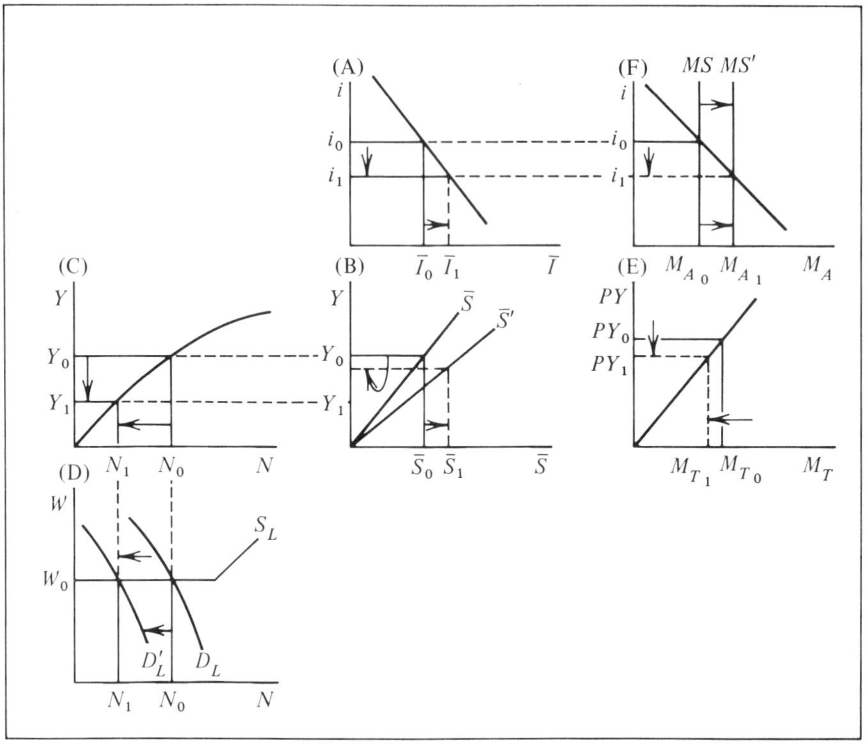

FIGURE 10D:3
The macroeconomic effects of a rise in taxes

As the price level and real income decline, nominal or money income also declines *(PY),* meaning that less money will be required for transactions (see Figure 10D:3, Diagram E).

Since the money supply has remained constant, more money will be available to be held as an asset, putting downward pressure on the interest rate (see Figure 10D:3, Diagram F). The decline in the interest rate then serves to stimulate private investment expenditures (see Diagram A). This serves to undo, in part, the initial rise in tax rates.

The end result should be lower real income and employment, a *higher* real wage, and *lower* market interest rates.

A CUT IN MONEY WAGES AS AN ANTIRECESSION TOOL

It has frequently been suggested that the problem of unemployment could be solved if only the unemployed or all workers in general would take a voluntary wage cut. This problem seeks to analyze the efficacy of such a solution.

The effect of a wage cut will appear simultaneously in two markets: the labor market and the money market. The first seems obvious, while the second does not. However, it must be remembered that when wages are cut, per unit labor costs fall and the price level declines. As the price level declines, the value of nominal income, PY, declines, and with it, the quantity of money needed for transactions.

Thus a reduction in wages from W_0 to W_1 will shift the labor supply schedule downward and appear to increase the volume of employment (see Figure 10D:4, Diagram D). However, since per unit labor costs have fallen, the price level will decline. This will shift the labor demand schedule to the left ($MPP_L \times P_1 < MPP_L \times P_0$) from D_L to D_L'.

If prices fall in proportion to the reduction in per unit labor costs, there will be no direct increase in employment. However, the fall in the price level will lead to a decrease in the quantity of money demanded. Since the supply of money will have remained constant, a larger quantity will be available to hold as an asset, serving to drive down the interest rate and stimulate investment. Thus, in the final analysis, the effectiveness of a wage

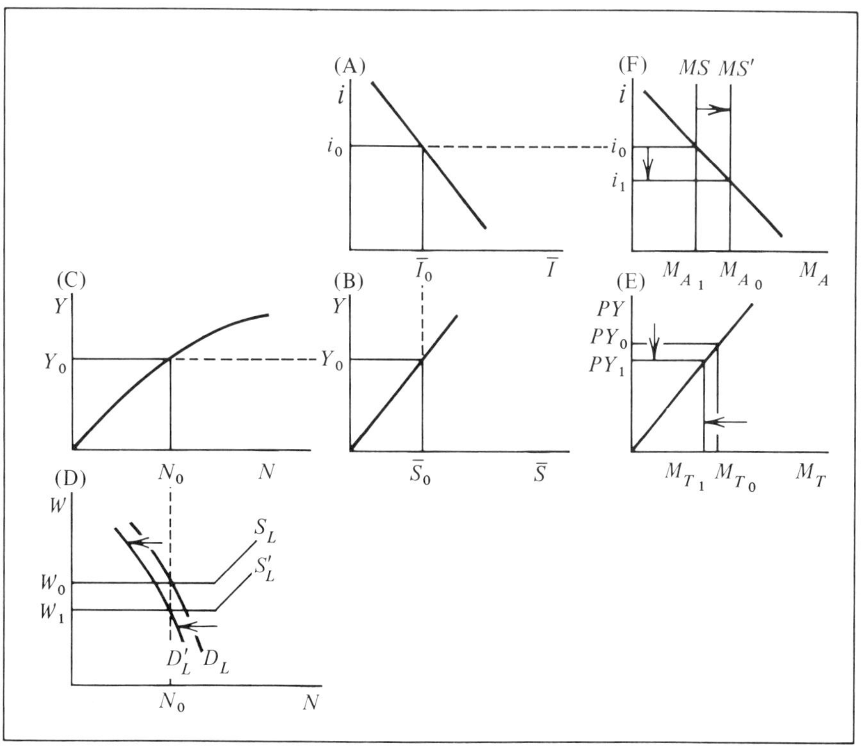

FIGURE 10D:4

The macroeconomic effects of a cut in money wages

cut to stimulate employment is exactly the same as an increase in the money supply keeping the price level constant.

What the wage cut succeeds in doing is increasing the real value of a given nominal money supply. Whether it will stimulate employment depends upon the same factors governing the effectiveness of an increase in the money supply to accomplish the same end.

APPENDIX E—THE *IS-LM* FRAMEWORK AS AN ALTERNATIVE MACROECONOMIC MODEL

A popular and alternative way to express the model developed in this chapter is to use the Hicks–Hansen *IS-LM* schedules. A principal shortcoming of this approach is that it includes only the commodity and money markets. Unless the labor market is introduced, it is excluded from discussion, making it easy to forget where the price level comes from and what is responsible for its change over time.

The *IS-LM* framework does, however, have an important advantage over the model developed and used in this chapter in that it permits the various points of equilibria to be seen both before and after a given policy change.

In this appendix this alternative framework is developed and an increase in the money supply is analyzed.

THE *IS* SCHEDULE

The *IS* schedule yields all combinations of the market interest rate and real income levels at which investment ($\bar{I}$) is equal to saving ($\bar{S}$)—hence the name is *IS* schedule. Thus, the *IS* schedule gives all combinations of real income and the market interest rate at which the demand for nonconsumption goods and services is equal to the supply. In other words, it gives all the points at which the commodity market is in equilibrium.

In terms of the model developed in this chapter, the *IS* schedule is derived by simply plotting all combinations of i and Y that yield $\bar{I} = \bar{S}$ or, in terms of Figure 10E:1, i_0, Y_0; i_1, Y_1; i_2, Y_2; etc.

THE *LM* SCHEDULE

The *LM* schedule yields all the combinations of the market interest rate and *money income* at which the supply of money (M) is equal to the demand for money (designated by Keynes as the L_1 or transactions demand and the L_2 or speculative demand—hence the name *LM* schedule).

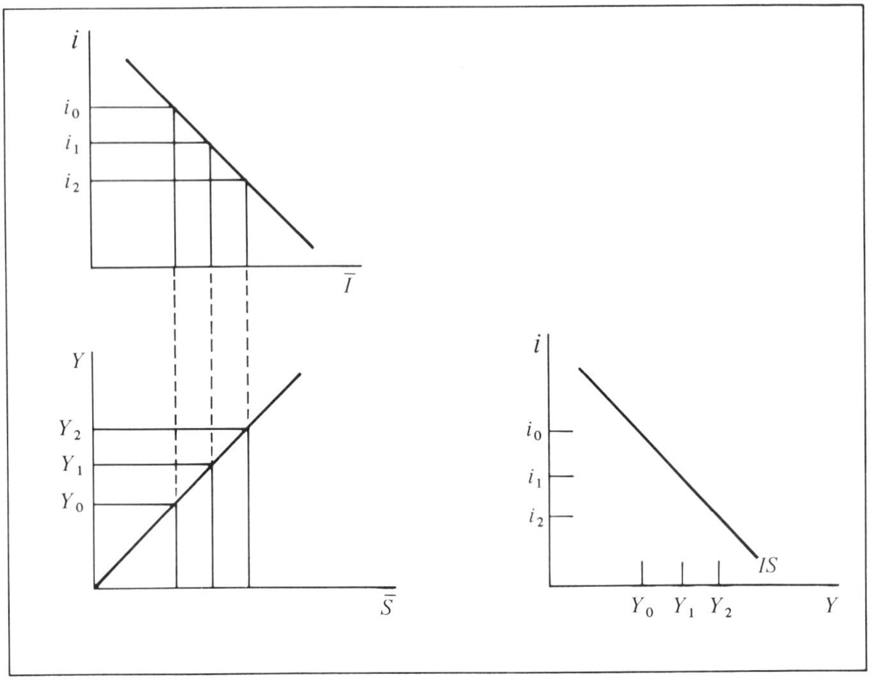

FIGURE 10E:1
The derivation of the IS *schedule*

Once the *LM* schedule is defined, an immediate problem is encountered, for one wishes to place the *LM* schedule in the same set of axes designated for the *IS* schedule. Yet the *LM* schedule is defined to depend on money income, whereas the *IS* schedule depends on real income. In order to derive an *LM* schedule compatible with the *IS* schedule, the demand for money will have to be made a demand for *real balances,* not *nominal balances*. To accomplish this, both the transactions and asset demand and the money supply will have to be divided by the price level—the nominal interest rate can still be used to measure the opportunity cost of holding money.

Once the money demand and supply schedules are divided by the price level, the *LM* schedule will be designated as *LM/P* to indicate that it is measured in real terms. Such a designation will not be required for the *IS* schedule, since it is already expressed in real terms. The *LM/P* schedule is derived in Figure 10E:2.

To start the derivation, Y_0 is assumed to be given, which fixes the quantity of money to be held for transactions, M_{T_0}/P. If this sum is subtracted from the real money supply, the interest rate must then be i_2 to

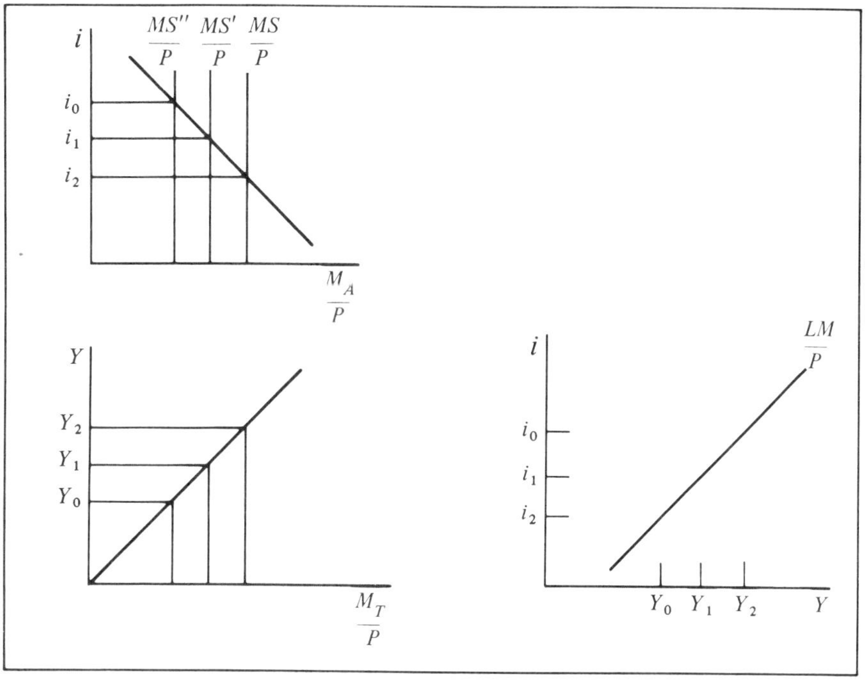

FIGURE 10E:2

The derivation of the $\frac{LM}{P}$ *schedule*

enable the residual supply, *MS/P*, to be held, thus ensuring equilibrium in the money market. If real income increases to Y_1, the residual supply will decline to *MS'/P* and the interest rate will then have to rise to i_1 to ensure money-market equilibrium. Similarly, if real income is Y_2, the interest rate will have to rise to i_0 to ensure continued equilibrium. If these points are plotted, the *LM* schedule will result. Throughout the derivation the price level, *P*, has been held constant. If the price level rises, the real money supply will decline, and for each level of real income—Y_0, Y_1, and Y_2—the market interest rate will have to be higher to ensure money-market equilibrium. In terms of the *LM* diagram, the schedule will be seen to shift upward.

MACROECONOMIC EQUILIBRIUM

When the *IS-LM* schedules are combined in the same diagram, their intersection yields the unique market interest rate and level of real income that ensures simultaneous equilibrium in both the money and commodity markets. Such a situation is shown in Figure 10E:3.

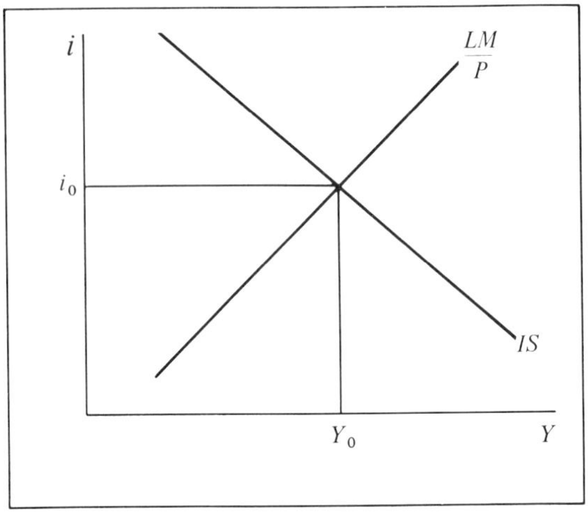

FIGURE 10E:3
Macro equilibrium using the IS-LM *framework*

AN INCREASE IN THE SUPPLY OF MONEY

To complete our discussion of the *IS-LM* macro model, an increase in the supply of money will be considered. Given the initial equilibrium shown in Figure 10E:4, the supply of real money will be assumed to increase. This action shifts the *LM* schedule in a rightward or downward direction from LM_0/P_0 to LM_1/P_0 (the reason for the shift is simply the reverse of the one

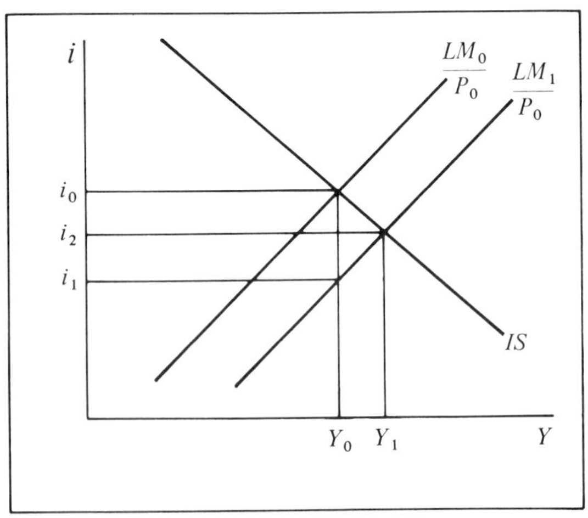

FIGURE 10E:4
An increase in the supply of money

above, with the difference that the price level is held constant while the nominal supply of money is increased). The initial drop in the interest rate from i_0 to i_1 corresponds to the so-called liquidity effect of an increase in the money supply discussed above.

The initial decline in the interest rate will lead to a desire to add to the stock of producer and consumer durables (i.e., investment increases) that, through the operation of the multiplier, will expand income and the demand for money. Upward pressure is put on the interest rate. If the price level remains constant, a new equilibrium interest rate and real income level will occur at i_2, Y_1. However, if, as noted above, labor experiences diminishes marginal productivity, per unit labor costs will rise, as will the price level. Since a rise in the price level reduces the real stock of money, the *LM* schedule will shift back in the direction from which it came—toward LM_0/P_0. So long as an unemployment equilibrium prevails initially, the new equilibrium will be to the right of i_0Y_0 but to the left of i_2Y_1 and will be characterized by lower interest rates and a higher level of real income and employment.

The student may judge whether this presentation of an increase in the money supply or that given in the more elaborate model in the body of the text is more conducive to understanding the process at work. Whatever decision is made, the problems presented in Appendix 10D should be redone in the *IS-LM* framework as an exercise to increase understanding of the functioning of alternative models.

11 THE IMPLEMENTATION OF MONETARY POLICY

The tools of general credit control discussed and evaluated in preceding chapters are used by the Federal Reserve with the objective of stabilizing economic activity. The formulation and execution of a program to achieve stability is commonly called *monetary policy*. To understand and evaluate monetary policy, the objectives to be achieved by it must first be set forth. They have been expressed from time to time by the Congress in such legislation as the Federal Reserve Act of 1913 and the Full-Employment Act of 1946. The much-debated and recently enacted Humphrey–Hawkins bill refines these objectives. The objectives that have emerged from this legislation, which are designed to improve the overall well-being of the country, are several. The most often repeated ones are the attainment of a high level of employment, the maintenance of a stable price level, the promotion of a high rate of real economic growth, and the sustentation over time of some semblance of balance in our international payments.

Ordinary experience has shown that these objectives may not be mutually compatible. Thus, the achievement of a low level of unemployment may cause the rate of change of the price level to accelerate, which will probably produce some imbalance in our international trade accounts.

Because of this incompatibility, the history of the United States is replete with instances wherein one objective has been held more important than others. In the nineteenth century equilibrium in the balance of payments was more highly regarded than, for example, the maintenance of full employment. The experience of the Great Depression pushed to the forefront the importance of minimizing unemployment regardless of the status of our international accounts. Our most recent experience suggests that curbing inflation is once again the uppermost objective of Federal Reserve policy.[1]

[1] From time to time the Federal Reserve has had different policy goals from those of Congress or of the executive branch, which is responsible for the execution of fiscal policy. The failure to harmonize fiscal and monetary policy because of different objectives is one source of conflict in our system, and is perhaps inevitable because no single group is responsible for the formulation and execution of the programs designed to achieve economic stabilization. It is the price asked of us to preserve the independence of our monetary authorities.

To be sure, the chairman of the Board of Governors is an active participant in the process of formulating and executing stabilization policies. However, when he has different objectives, it may be hard for him to be a full-time team player.

Regardless of the objective the Federal Reserve decides to promote through the use of monetary policy, its operations are handicapped in at least three ways. First, the Federal Reserve may not have any *direct* means of achieving a specific result. For example, open-market operations cannot directly change gross national product, employment, the price level, and so on. Rather, these variables respond indirectly to changes in the money supply and interest rates.

Second, the effect of a change in the tools of general credit control on the real sector of the economy is not immediate or absolutely predictable. Indeed, the response of the real sector to policy-induced stimulations is not very well understood by economists. Since the response that does occur involves such lengthy and uncertain time lags, it is totally impractical for the Federal Reserve to make continuous policy adjustments on the basis of observed changes in those variables selected as its goals. This second handicap is often briefly stated by saying that the effects of monetary changes on the real sector are subject to lags that are both long and of uncertain length. (The nature of these lags was explained extensively at the end of Chapter 10.)

Finally, the implementation and execution of monetary policy is handicapped in two respects by a lack of data. First, *current values* of the empirical estimators selected to measure the ultimate goals of monetary policy (e.g., the price index, the level of GNP, the unemployment rate) record primarily the effect of past central bank policies rather than the thrust of *current* policies. This is because monetary policy operates with a lag that is both long and variable. Second, the data making up the indices are collected, processed, and published at discrete intervals. Those for several price indices and the unemployment rate are gathered and published monthly, whereas data on GNP are only gathered quarterly and are subject to considerable error.[2] At least the second of these shortcomings in the data could be corrected to a large extent by investing more resources in data gathering so that we would have more frequent and complete sampling, especially for making GNP estimates.

Nevertheless, these limitations mean that data on current economic events are not available until sometime in the future. Because of this lag, it is not possible to base current policy on the current state of the economy.

Despite these handicaps, the central bank must function today. It must make decisions on the use of the tools of general credit control for stabilization purposes. How is it to know if the action it undertakes today will have the right impact, so that if continued, the ultimate objectives of

[2] For example, the preliminary third quarter 1979 growth rate for real GNP was announced in October 1979 as 2.4%. In November 1979 it was revised on the basis of more complete data to 3.5%. Finally, in December 1979 it was revised downward to 3.1%. (The error between the October and December figure is 29%.)

The unemployment rate and the change in the price indices are usually released one month after the data are gathered.

the policy will respond in the anticipated fashion? For example, suppose it desires a general reduction in the unemployment rate, so that two years hence it will have declined from 7% to 5 1/2%. What directive would it issue to the New York Federal Reserve, which conducts open-market operations for the system? Would it read: "Buy enough government securities to accomplish this goal in two years"? This is highly unlikely. The Open Market Committee would probably direct the so-called Trading Desk of the New York Federal Reserve to "ease monetary conditions." What, then, would the Trading Desk do, knowing that the results of its activities would not show up in the data on ultimate objectives for some time? Alternatively, suppose that on observing the trend in the data on ultimate objectives, the Federal Reserve believes monetary conditions to be "just right." It then directs the Trading Desk to "hold things as they are." How will the Trading Desk respond? To do nothing would not be in accord with the directive because the economy grows over time and to hold a monetary aggregate (the *M*-1s) or an interest rate constant will probably precipitate an economic downswing. The downswing would hardly be "keeping things as they are."

Thus, the formulators of monetary policy must have some way to measure the current state of monetary conditions and to judge whether policies undertaken today will have a greater, lesser, or neutral impact on their ultimate objectives relative to those previously pursued. As discussed above, this cannot be determined with any precision by looking at current movements in a price index or unemployment rate, because the impact of present policy is likely to have a major effect only in the future.

Thus, central bankers and economists have been interested in selecting what have come to be called *targets* and *indicators* of monetary policy. The purpose of these is to enable policymakers to judge whether monetary actions undertaken currently are moving economic activity in the right direction to achieve ultimate objectives.[3]

[3] The literature in this area is both confused and controversial, especially since targets and indicators are not consistently defined. As a result, the discussion here will rely on the distinction laid down by Brunner and Meltzer and used by Berger and Hamburger. See Karl Brunner and Allan Meltzer, "The Meaning of Monetary Indicators," in G. Horwich, editor, *Monetary Process and Policy* (Homewood, Ill.: Richard D. Irwin, 1967), pp. 187–217; Albert Berger, "The Implementation of Monetary Policy," *Monthly Review,* Federal Reserve Bank of St. Louis 53 (Mar. 1971): 20–30; and Michael Hamburger, "Indicators of Monetary Policy: The Arguments and the Evidence," in *Monetary Aggregates and Monetary Policy* (New York: Federal Reserve Bank of New York, 1974), pp. 20–27. Hence, much of the subsequent discussion should be taken as suggestive of practices by the central bank rather than as a statement of actual conditions.

For a good statement of the problem involved in implementation of monetary policy, see Thomas Saving, "Monetary-Policy Targets and Indicators," *Journal of Political Economy,* Supplement (Aug. 1967): 446–56. However, we will not use the distinction between targets and indicators that Saving makes, even though his presentation is excellent.

A recent paper questioning the need for the target–indicator approach that merits serious consideration is Benjamin Friedman, "Targets, Instruments, and Indicators of Monetary Policy," *Journal of Monetary Economics* 1 (1975): 443–73.

TARGETS AND INDICATORS OF MONETARY POLICY

The distinction between targets and indicators made in this text is based upon time. The *target* is an economic variable that the Federal Reserve Open Market Committee (FOMC) directs the Trading Desk to hold within specified ranges during the interval between its semimonthly meetings. Thus, the target may be viewed as a variable that the Trading Desk observes on a day-to-day basis to see whether its day-to-day operations in the financial markets are consistent with the directive from the FOMC.

On the other hand, the purpose of an *indicator* is to enable a policymaker to see whether in the near future the thrust of policy is in the right direction to accomplish the ultimate goals of the central bank. So nothing would prevent the same variable from serving as both a target and an indicator.

Thus, the operational target enables the policymaker to see whether in the very short run the effect of policy is in the right direction, while the indicator serves to give a more intermediate measure of the thrust of policy. Ultimately, in the longer run the measures selected as the objectives of policy will be used to judge whether the central bank was successful or not.

Table 11:1 is a schematic view of the implementation of monetary policy.

DESIRABLE CHARACTERISTICS OF TARGET AND INDICATOR

Since the purpose of targets and indicators is to provide the central bank with information on the day-to-day impact of its policies as well as to measure their thrust over the intermediate run of time, targets and indicators should possess certain desirable qualities.

First, each should be easily observable and reported in a timely and accurate manner. Especially in the case of the target, the information must be accurate in the very short run.

TABLE 11:1
The implementation of monetary policy

Policy Tools

1. Open-market operations
2. Reserve requirements
3. Discount rate

↓

Operational Targets

↓

Indicators

↓

Ultimate Objectives

1. High levels of employment
2. A stable price level
3. High rates of economic growth
4. Balance-of-payments equilibrium

that the Keynesians would be pleased with their assignment; in fact, given the theory of business cycles advanced by Lord Keynes, Keynesian economists might go so far as to suggest that the market interest rate would be a most unreliable target or indicator. For this reason, the Keynesians might be willing to share with the Monetarists a common set of target and indicator variables.[4]

Be that as it may, the Monetarists have claimed for themselves the monetary base as an operational target and the supply of money as an indicator. Despite some protests,[5] they have assigned to the Keynesians the level of free reserves[6] of the financial system as an operational target and market interest rates as an indicator of monetary policy.

In a format paralleling Table 11:1, Table 11:2 sets out the implementation framework favored by the Monetarists. They suggest it is compatible with some Keynesian theorizing (later, this suggestion will be the subject of a critical discussion).

If the Federal Reserve were to take the Keynesian route, it would set the indicator in terms of a desirable level of the relevant market interest rate

TABLE 11:2
Relative implementation routes for monetary policy

	Policy Tools 1. Open-market operations 2. Reserve requirements 3. Discount rate	
Keynesian ↓	↓	Monetarist ↓
Free Reserves ↓	Operational Targets ↓	Monetary Base ↓
Market Interest Rates ↘	Indicators ↓	Money Stock ↙
	Ultimate Objectives 1. High levels of employment 2. Stable price levels 3. High rates of economic growth 4. Balance-of-payments equilibrium	

[4] For a more detailed analysis of this issue, see Appendix 11A.

[5] William Poole, "Optimal Choice of Monetary Policy Instruments in a Simple Stochastic Macro Model," *Quarterly Journal of Economics,* Vol. 84, No. 2 (May 1970): 197–216, and "Rules-of-Thumb for Guiding Monetary Policy," in *Open Market Policies for Guiding Monetary Policy,* Board of Governors of the Federal Reserve System (July 1971); Richard G. Davis, "Implementing Open Market Policy with Monetary Aggregate Objectives," in *Monetary Aggregates and Monetary Policy* (New York: Federal Reserve Bank of New York, 1974); and M. J. Artis, "Monetary Policy in the 1970's in the Light of Recent Developments," in *Issues in Monetary Economics,* ed. Johnson and Nobay (London: Oxford University Press, 1974), pp. 517–47.

[6] The free reserves of the financial system are equal to the difference between excess reserves and those borrowed from the central bank.

over the next 6 or 12 months. It would then set the operational target in terms of a free reserve level it thinks consistent with the future level of the relevant interest rate. Finally, it would use its policy tools to achieve these results. Both a target and an indicator are used because the Federal Reserve's control over the level of free reserves is more comprehensive than its control over the relevant market interest rate.

Conversely, if it selected the Monetarist route, the Federal Reserve would set a desired range for money supply growth over the next 6 or 12 months, and then set the growth rate of the operational target (the monetary base) that it believes to be consistent with the growth rate of the money supply. In terms of the analysis of this text, the task for the Federal Reserve is to estimate both the movement in the money multiplier over this time period and the impact on the monetary base, which will be made by those over whom it has no control (e.g., the public, the commercial banks, the Treasury). It then uses its policy tools to make the relevant changes in the monetary base. As in the Keynesian case, both a target and an indicator are used because the Federal Reserve would have considerable difficulty in controlling the relevant measure of the money supply on a day-to-day or week-to-week basis.

An examination of Table 11:2 suggests that somehow changes in the supply of money in the Monetarist framework affect the ultimate objectives of policy in a different fashion than in the Keynesian approach. That is, the Monetarists believe that a change in the money supply works through different channels than those employed by the Keynesian model to alter economic activity. Nothing could be further from the truth.

Before an evaluation of the target–indicator set of each side is attempted, a brief discussion of the monetary transmission mechanism will be undertaken. While it may repeat some of what was already discussed in Chapter 10, it will provide deeper insights into most recent thinking on the way changes in the supply of money affect economic activity.

THE MONETARY TRANSMISSION MECHANISM

It was shown in Chapter 10 that changes in the supply of money affect the level of economic activity through the interest rate. Indeed, economists regard the interest rate channel to be very important in transmitting the influence of money to the real sector.

In terms of the analyses of Chapter 10, let the central bank buy government securities in the financial market in order to expand the reserves of depository institutions. This increase in reserves (the monetary base) through open-market operations will raise the actual excess reserve/demand deposit ratio above that desired by depository institutions. To restore equilibrium, they will lend out reserves by buying assets and creating deposits in the process. As they lend out these reserves, market interest rates will decline relative to the marginal yield on the existing capital stock. This will serve to stimulate new investment spending, which will expand total spending and employment, and perhaps drive up the price level as well.

The route from the change in the policy instruments to the ultimate objectives of policy is shown in Table 11:3.

In the Monetarist framework steps A, B, C, F, and G are emphasized, whereas the Keynesians lay stress on steps A, C, D, E, F, and G. However, in both frameworks an important channel transmitting money's influence to economic activity is the interest rate (or more correctly, the range of interest rates).

Within the general framework as outlined in Table 11:3, each side tends to emphasize different aspects of the montary transmission mechanism.

The Monetarists generally believe that open-market operations can directly alter the level of nominal wealth in the society, as well as affect the interest rate. When the Federal Reserve buys government interest-bearing securities, it does so with money. Every government interest-bearing security represents both an asset and a liability—an asset to the person who owns it, and a liability to the nation's taxpayers, who must provide the wherewithal to pay the interest on it and to retire it when it matures. Currency, on the other hand, is clearly an asset to the people who own it, but it represents a liability to no one, for it pays no interest, and since it never matures, it does not have to be repurchased. Thus, in the eyes of the Monetarists an open-market operation that swaps the non-interest-bearing

TABLE 11:3
The monetary transmission mechanism

A. Expansive open-market operations
↘ B. A rise in the monetary base
↘ C. An increase in the supply of money
↘ D. A decline in market interest rates
↘ E. A rise in the rate of of investment
↘ F. An increase in aggregate demand and employment
↘ G. A rise in the general level of prices

debt of the government (currency) for its interest-bearing debt (bonds) gives the society something that is only an asset and removes something that is both an asset and a liability. The result is a net addition to the wealth of society. As wealth rises, so does money spending. Thus, open-market operations can directly affect money spending on goods and services even if they have only a minimal effect on interest rates.

To most Keynesians this argument is farfetched, and if they concede such an effect is present, they regard its influence as minimal.

The Keynesians would argue that the scheme of affairs shown in Table 11:3 appears to limit the influence of the money supply to a single cost-of-capital route. The construction of Keynesian econometric models suggests that money's influence is transmitted in two other ways, which also involve interest rates.

The first of these channels involves the influence of market interest rates on the ability of financial intermediaries to transmit loanable funds to certain sensitive sectors of the economy, especially new housing. Whenever market interest rates rise above the ceilings permitted by Regulation Q, disintermediation tends to occur and the housing market is starved for mortgage money. This leads to a decline in new housing starts and a decrease in aggregate demand. Even without Regulation Q, disintermediation is likely to occur if the rates rise rapidly because financial intermediaries will be hit by a profit squeeze—their costs to keep and attract funds will rise relative to their earnings.

The second channel involves the influence of interest rates on the nominal wealth of society. Declining interest rates are thought to raise nominal wealth in two ways. The usual route involves the inverse relationship between the market prices of negotiable securities (bonds) and interest rates. The other results indirectly from the first. As the yield on bonds falls, individuals are led to purchase common stocks. This bids up their prices and raises the nominal wealth holding of all stock owners. The rise in wealth is, in turn, linked to increased spending largely on consumption-type goods.

Thus, in most of the large Keynesian-oriented econometric models the influence of changes in the money supply is transmitted to real output and employment through changes in the interest rate. The interest rate, in turn, alters the cost of capital and is the major influence on new housing starts and a determinant of consumption expenditures.

Thus, both the Keynesian and Monetarist views on the transmission mechanism can be subsumed within one general framework that highlights market interest rates, even though each may emphasize different aspects of the overall process.

This discussion raises, but leaves for the moment unanswered, this question: why is it that if money exerts an influence on economic activity through interest rates, the Monetarists prefer to use the money supply itself as the indicator of monetary policy?

AN EVALUATION OF EACH TARGET–INDICATOR SET

The evaluation of each target–indicator set consists of explaining how each is to work, and then judging if each can pass the tests specified as a desirable measure of the posture of monetary policy. These tests, it will be remembered, are three in number: (1) Is accurate information available on a timely basis? (2) Can the Federal Reserve control the variable? (3) Does a strong and predictable relationship exist between the indicator and the ultimate objectives of policy? In addition, when the target and indicator are different variables, a strong relationship must exist between them, since the target is essentially set to achieve a given change in the indicator.

Before we undertake this evaluation, we will discuss a problem of potentially great significance. This problem centers on specifying the precise empirical counterpart for each target and indicator set. For the Keynesians, this involves specifying the specific interest rate or rates that will serve as indicators. As the analysis to follow will suggest, the appropriate *rates* are both long term—the rates at which the business sector borrows its funds for capital investment—and short term—the comparative rates between short-term debt instruments, such as Treasury bills, and the rates paid depositors by financial intermediaries, especially those most committed to making loans for new housing.

As for the Monetarists, they must specify what measures of the money supply they want to use as an indicator—the M-1s, M_2, M_3, etc., or some combination of these. In addition, they must specify whether they wish to use the monetary base or some portion of it (e.g., the portion used to support private demand deposits) as their operational target.

The evaluation to follow will assume that each side has been able to specify the precise empirical counterpart to each variable used as a target and indicator.

The Keynesian set

Free reserves as an operational target

If the level of free reserves (the difference between the excess and borrowed reserves of the banking system) is taken to be the operational target, then large or growing amounts of free reserves are used as a measure of an *easing in monetary conditions*. Thus, if the FOMC issued the directive to ease monetary conditions, the Trading Desk might purchase government securities with an end to increasing the free reserves of the banking system. If the demand schedule for free reserves discussed in Chapter 4 remains constant, the increase in the supply of free reserves will probably be lent out, leading to a general easing of monetary conditions. However, if the demand schedule for free reserves is subject to shift, then the increase in the supply of free reserves may be willingly held with no easing of monetary conditions. During the various stages of the business cycle, it seems likely that the banks' demand schedule for free reserves will shift, rendering their level a poor guide to the ease or tightness of monetary conditions. This discussion implies that the Federal Reserve does not control the level of free reserves, which is generally true. Hence, using it as a target fails at least one of the tests. In addition, there is no evidence that their level or rate of change is in any way, much less directly and predictably, related to the objectives of monetary policy. Their level may be fairly highly correlated with market interest rates, however.

The popularity among central bankers of the level of free reserves as an unofficial target, and perhaps an indicator, of monetary policy appears to be connected to the availability of information regarding free reserves on a weekly basis (the level of free reserves does pass test number one). This popularity predates the formation of the Keynesian approach to macroeconomic theory by a considerable number of years.[7] Moreover, it is questionable whether Keynesians would endorse the level of free reserves as a target of monetary policy.

Interest rates as an indicator

A great deal of evidence suggests that for a considerable number of Keynesians, market interest rates are either a target or an indicator of monetary policy. In their view low or falling market rates mean monetary ease, whereas high or rising market rates generally typify tight monetary conditions.

This use of market interest rates as a target or indicator by the Keynesians is rather curious. According to Lord Keynes's view of the business cycle, interest rates are subject to substantial influences by forces not under the control of the central bank, and hence their movements in the short run are likely to be a poor guide for current central bank actions. Nevertheless, since money affects economic activity through interest rates, Keynesians use interest rates in the financial sections of their models, and rely on their movements to measure the current posture of monetary policy.

More recently, Monetarists have claimed that during inflationary periods caused by a too-rapid growth in the money supply, market interest rates *rise*, not *fall*. Thus, an increase in the rate of issuing money leads ultimately to *higher*, not *lower*, interest rates. For this reason, the Monetarists contend, market interest rates are particularly misleading indicators of monetary policy.

[7] In their monumental monetary history of the United States, Milton Friedman and Anna Schwartz demonstrate that this target or indicator was used frequently and mistakenly by officials of the Federal Reserve, especially during the onset of the Great Depression in 1929–1933. On several occasions during which the money supply was contracting by 29%–34% (depending on the M_1 or M_2 measure), Federal Reserve officials judged monetary policy to be easy because free reserves were rising. See *A Monetary History of the United States* (Princeton, N.J.: Princeton University Press, 1963), Chapter 7, "The Great Contraction, 1929–33."

Before these two shortcomings are considered in detail, it should be noted that a wide variety of market interest rates are available on a daily basis. Moreover, Keynesian-oriented econometric models show that market interest rates have a direct and predictable relationship to the ultimate objectives of monetary policy.

Interest rates and the business cycle The first criticism of the interest rate as a target or indicator can be considered in terms of Keynes's interpretation of the forces responsible for the cyclical flow of economic activity. According to his view, the business cycle is due basically to changes in the expectations of individuals as to the future profitability of capital investment. If they should become pessimistic about the future, they will decrease the rate of investment and aggregate demand will fall, which will put downward pressure on interest rates. Supposedly, the outlook of individuals is subject to rapid change—a recession can be set in motion quickly, as can a revival of economic activity.

Insofar as the conduct of monetary policy is concerned, the Keynesian interpretation of economic history implies that short-run movements in market interest rates may be due to causes that cannot be accurately estimated by the central bank. Because of this, the central bank either should not use market interest rates as a target or indicator, or it should use them only with great caution. For example, suppose the Federal Reserve uses an interest rate as a target and is satisfied with current economic conditions—they are just right. The Open Market Committee then issues a directive to the Account Manager to "keep things as they are." However, just as the directive is issued, assume than an economic downturn is set in motion because of business pessimism. The downturn, by decreasing the demand for money, should cause interest rates to decline—which, under the circumstances, is desirable. However, the Account Manager, mindful of the directive, now contracts the money supply or slows its growth rate (if free reserves are a target, their level or rate of growth would be used) in order to bring the interest rate back to its previous level. This is, of course, the wrong policy to pursue, for it will aggravate the downturn. The error on the part of the central bank arises because it does not have exclusive control over the interest rate and may find it difficult in the short run to understand what is causing the rate to change. Because information on economic activity often lags behind actual events, the central bank may persist in an incorrect policy for some time, with the result that a mild recession may be turned into a major downturn.

Inflation and market interest rates Perhaps a more serious criticism of the use of the interest rate either as a target or an indicator arises from the allegation that during an inflation, market interest rates provide a misleading measure of the effect of monetary policy.

This critique can be traced through using Table 11:3. Initially, a higher rate of increase in the supply of money will bring about a decrease in market interest rates (steps A through D). However, it will probably lead to a rise in the price level as well (step G), which, in turn, will cause the nominal interest rate to rise. The Monetarists contend that the Keynesians neglect this stage of development in their view of affairs. Moreover, the Keynesians are apt to judge the rise in market rates as an indication that monetary conditions are becoming tight and urge the central bank to engineer a further increase in the rate of money creation. This should only lead to a further increase in the rate of inflation and still higher market rates. Thus, reliance on interest rates as an indicator of monetary policy is likely to lead to serious errors.

According to the Monetarist critique, inflation-induced increases in market interest rates, that result from too rapid an increase in the money supply, give the appearance of tight monetary conditions when, in fact, conditions are easy. This misleading impression is derived from observing and incorrectly understanding two events. First, high market rates of interest need not be high *real* rates of interest. The real rates are the relevant variables for decisions on whether or not to add to the capital stock. That is, they are the correct measures of the cost of capital. Second, since inflation causes market interest rates to rise, it is responsible for the disintermediation and consequent decline in the flow of loanable funds into the housing mortgage market. Paradoxically, "easy money leads ultimately to tight credit." Similarly, inflation-induced rises in market rates, by reducing the capitalized or market value of nominal wealth, cause a decrease in consumption spending by households.

In order to see more closely how inflation is supposed to affect market interest rates, the work of the American economist Irving Fisher will be examined.

The Fisherian theory of interest rates Irving Fisher of Yale University was the first economist to study the effects of inflation on market interest rates systematically. Beginning in 1896 and culminating in 1930, Fisher devoted four books[8] and many articles to this subject, including some fascinating attempts (which must have been very laborious in a precomputer era) to verify his hypothesis empirically.

Fisher's basic supposition was that when individuals lend money, they realize that they are lending command over real resources. Hence, when they are repaid, they wish to receive back the same command over real resources, plus a premium (i.e., interest) equal to what they could have earned (again measured in real terms) in an alternative use of the money. How, then, does inflation, or the rise in the general level of commodity

[8] See his *Appreciation and Interest* (New York: Macmillan, 1896), *The Rate of Interest* (New York: Macmillan, 1907), *The Purchasing Power of Money* (New York: Macmillan, 1912), and *The Theory of Interest* (New York: Macmillan, 1930). A more detailed diagrammatic presentation of Fisher's theory of interest rates is reserved for Chapter 13.

prices, affect this relationship? Quite simply, the market interest rate will have to rise, for it is the means by which the real purchasing power of the principal sum lent and the interest payment received are preserved.

To see how this occurs, let us contrast two one-year loans. The first is made when no inflation is expected to take place, while the second is made with the certainty that prices at the end of the year will be 8% higher (i.e., the inflation rate is 8%).

Case I Under conditions of stable prices, an individual will lend (supply loanable funds which are the money counterpart of saving) $100 at an interest rate of 5%. One year hence, he will receive in return $105, which will purchase 5% more goods and services than it would purchase today. In this environment of stable prices 5% can be thought of as the real rate of interest.

Case II The saver/lender contemplates the same loan as in Case I, but knows with certainty that the price level will be 8% higher one year from now. To preserve the purchasing power of his capital and the interest payment he received in Case I, how much should he ask as a *market* interest rate?

To keep the purchasing power of his capital constant will require an additional $8, while to keep the purchasing power of his real interest payment of $5 constant will require the payment of $5.40. Therefore, he requests of the investor/borrower $13.40 in interest or a rate of 13.4%.

Will the investor/borrower, who in Case I was willing to pay 5%, now pay 13.4% for the same amount of dollars? Yes, so long as his expected rate of inflation coincides with that of the saver/lender, because in the situation envisioned in Case II his income from investing the borrowed funds should rise by 8% in addition to the rise resulting from the investment. If Fisher's reasoning is correct, the effect of expected inflation is to raise market interest rates. In the case at hand, they rise from 5% to 13.4%. This effect of inflation on the market interest rate is popularly called the Fisher Effect.

Conceptually, the market rate of interest, i, can be viewed as the sum of the real rate, r (which would prevail with no expected inflation), plus the sum of the expected rate of inflation, p^e, and the product of the real rate and the inflation rate, rp^e, or

$$i = r + p^e + rp^e$$

Thus, according to Fisher's theory, high market rates of interest during an inflation are compatible with low real rates of interest. In Case II, while the nominal rate was 13.4%, the real rate was 5%. Clearly, what the lender/saver and borrower/investor are concerned with is the real yield on the sum lent and borrowed. The inflation rate is linked by Fisher to the rate of growth of the money supply. The higher the growth rate relative to the growth rate of real output, the higher will be the rate of inflation, and thus the market rate of interest.

In order to evaluate the possibility that inflation-induced rises in the interest rate can mislead the monetary authorities into believing that monetary conditions are tight, the operation of the Fisher Effect must be placed in the context of the Keynesian model. In that context expected inflation will have an impact only on the investment schedule, since we assumed that saving depends only on real income. Thus, expected inflation will have an initial impact on the commodity market only.

Since expected inflation will raise the nominal profit per year expected from an investment project, it will raise the nominal interest rate required to equate expected profit with the current cost of the investment project. To see this, consider the simple case of an investment project that yields a net profit of \$1,000 per year forever and that costs \$5,000 to construct today. Using the formula for a consol (see Equation 6:1), the investment project yields a return of 20%, or

$$\$5{,}000 = \frac{\$1{,}000}{i}$$

$$5 = \frac{1}{i}$$

$$.20 = i$$

where 20% can be considered as the real rate of return on the project. Now, if both prices and production costs are expected to double, nominal profits will also double to \$2,000 per year. If current investment costs are held constant at \$5,000 per year, the nominal yield on the investment project (the interest rate that will equate future profits with current project costs) will rise from 20% to 40% (the real yield is still 20%).

In terms of Figure 10:20, the investment demand schedule in the commodity market will shift upward, thereby exerting upward pressure on the market interest rate.

It is this inflation-induced rise in the nominal yield on investment that will put upward pressure on interest rates and lead monetary authorities to misleading conclusions regarding the posture of monetary policy.

Easy money and tight credit The theory of market interest rates put forth by Fisher can also be used to explain how easy money leads to tight credit.

A more rapid rate of increase in the money supply will cause the rate of inflation to increase, which will, after the inflation becomes anticipated, cause interest rates (both short and long) to rise. As short-term rates rise, financial intermediaries will find it increasingly difficult to attract and retain their deposits because their earnings will not rise as fast as the costs of retaining their deposits.[9] Even if earnings did rise as fast, the Regulation Q ceilings on interest paid on deposits may prevent intermediaries from effectively competing for funds.

As the financial intermediaries lose deposits (in terms of our previous discussion, lending moves from an indirect to a direct route), they find it more difficult to make new loans or extend old ones. Credit is then said to be tight.

The Keynesian set–a summary While the Keynesian targets and indicators pass most of the tests set forth above, our analysis suggests that they fail one major test: they are not under the exclusive control of the Federal Reserve. Take the interest rate indicator. It is subject to two influences that will cause it to change and that lie beyond the control of the central bank. The first can be seen most clearly when the investment demand schedule shifts because of a change in the expectations of the future profitability of investment in a stable price environment. The second influence concerns the effect of expected changes in the price level (i.e., inflation). Fisher's theory tells us that if prices are expected to rise, the result will be a rise in interest rates.

Each of these two influences, originating in the commodity market or real sector of the model, has an effect on market interest rates independent of any actions by the Federal Reserve. These movements in the interest rate may cause the Federal Reserve to pursue actions that further destabilize the economy.

The Monetarist approach

As noted above, the Monetarists claim for themselves the monetary base as an operational target and the money supply as an indicator or measure of the thrust of monetary policy. How well do these two variables pass the tests posed earlier in this chapter?

The monetary base as an operational target

When the monetary base is used as a target, an increase in its growth rate relative to either the most recent past or some long-run average rate suggests that monetary conditions are easier. The possibility of relating the current growth rate to either of two past rates (which can be different) may lead to confusion if the comparison is not clarified. Thus, if the historic

[9] The lag of earnings behind costs arises from the fact that only a small portion of the assets of most intermediaries come due or are turned over in any one year. It is only the portion turned over that can be invested in new higher-yielding securities. In the meantime, to retain their deposits, the intermediaries will have to increase the interest they pay to all their creditors. Obviously, at some point, costs will outrun profits and disintermediation will occur.

average rate is 4%, the most recent past rate 12%, and the current rate 8%, monetary conditions would be taken to be easy compared with the long span of history, but restrictive with respect to the most recent past. Therefore, a high rate of growth of the monetary base must not always be taken to mean a turn toward monetary ease, for it can indicate a tightening of conditions.

The data-collection facilities of the Federal Reserve are good, and accurate data on the monetary base are published on a weekly basis. Its desirability, then, as an operational target depends ultimately on whether the central bank can control its movement over time. Two factors hinder this ability in the very short run: the borrowing of reserves by depository institutions with deficiencies through discounting and advances, and fluctuations in the amount of float outstanding. However, since weekly information on the value of each of these items is available, the Federal Reserve can undertake appropriate remedial action, if necessary, to keep the growth of the base within specified limits. The base, therefore, appears to have a number of desirable properties that enable it to pass most of the tests specified above.

The money supply as an indicator

As with the monetary base, the *relative* growth rate of the money supply is used to measure monetary conditions in the Monetarists' framework. The confusion about which past rate of increase to relate it to when speaking of the ease or tightness of current conditions is also present.

The use of the money supply as an indicator is complicated both by the unavailability of accurate data on this variable on a weekly or monthly basis, and by the fact that the Federal Reserve does not have direct control over it.

As to data on the money supply, the banks that belong to the Federal Reserve report their deposit liabilities to the central bank on a more frequent basis than depository institutions that are not members. The absence of more frequent data on the deposits of nonmember depository institutions would present no problem to the Federal Reserve if these liabilities grew at the same rate as those of member banks. Unfortunately, this is not generally true, so the monthly data on the money supply reported by the Federal Reserve is subject to errors. Its value depends on the relative growth rate of the deposit liabilities of member and nonmember depository institutions.

A more serious problem in using the money supply as an indicator arises from the fact that the Federal Reserve does not directly control this variable, but only the monetary base. Standing between the base and the supply of money, it will be remembered, is the money multiplier. The value of the multiplier depends on the portfolio decisions of the public (its currency/demand deposit and time/demand deposit ratios), and depository institutions (their excess reserve/demand deposit ratio), and on the decision by the Treasury as to the depository for its funds (i.e., the value of the Treasury deposit/demand deposit ratio).[10]

In order to control movements in the supply of money the Federal Reserve must be able to estimate the value of the money multiplier. Then, through suitable manipulations of the monetary base, it will be able to produce the desired results.

The existence of extensive historical data on the components of the money multiplier provides the means by which the Federal Reserve can estimate its future movements. While such data are of great value, there are various random and unpredictable influences on the variables making up the multiplier. If these influences are truly random, they should average out over the longer run and have no lasting influence on the money supply. However, in the shorter run they may be consistently negative or positive. If so, they will cause the actual value of the multiplier to differ consistently from its predicted value. If this is the case, the Federal Reserve may, over the short run, have to contend with a money supply that grows at either a faster or slower rate than is desired. This, of course, raises the possibility that the Federal Reserve cannot control the money supply over the intermediate run of time. In further support of this possibility, several Keynesian economists[11] have pointed to the second half of the 1930s as an example of a period during which the money supply slipped from control of the central bank. The large buildup of excess reserves from 1934 to the beginning of World War II suggests to them that the Federal Reserve had little control over the money supply. Large excess reserves supposedly gave commercial banks a great deal of room to maneuver and rendered them basically immune to open-market operations. In terms of the money multiplier, all increases in the monetary base could be offset by decreases in the multiplier (i.e., the excess reserve/demand deposit ratio could rise, resulting in a decrease in the multiplier). Needless to add, since this interpretation of history conflicts with that of the Monetarists, it is controversial.

The relationship of the money supply to economic activity

We have already explored in this chapter the transmission mechanism by which a change in the money supply exerts its effects on the real sector of the economy. However, standing between the money supply, M, and total

[10] This last ratio is relevant within the context of the more elaborate multiplier developed in Chapter 9.

[11] See Paul Samuelson, "Reflections on the Merits and Demerits of Monetarism," in *Issues in Fiscal and Monetary Policy: The Eclectic Economist Views the Controversy,* ed. James J. Diamond (Chicago: DePaul University, 1971); and James Tobin, "A Monetary Interpretation of History: A Review Article," *American Economic Review,* Vol. 55, No. 3 (June 1965): 464–85.

money spending on gross national product, PY, is the velocity or turnover rate of money, V; or $MV = PY$. If the velocity of money were highly erratic or subject to unpredictable changes, control by the Federal Reserve over the money supply would not yield control over money spending, PY. The possibility that velocity may be erratic has long been recognized by Monetarists as well as by other economists, and a good deal of research effort has gone into explaining the stability of the velocity of money. Stability here means that movements in velocity can be accounted for by prior movements in such variables as the market rate of interest, the expected rate of inflation, and real income. These studies, which are too numerous to mention, have generally found that the velocity of money is highly stable in the sense that almost all of its movements over time can be accounted for by prior movements in the "explanatory" variables noted above.[12] To the extent that the past is a good basis for predicting the future, the stability of velocity supports the view advanced by the Monetarists that economic activity is reliably related to the money supply.

It should be noted that the velocity, or turnover rate of money, is the reciprocal of the demand for money. If, for example, the demand for money is expressed as $M = kPY$, k then becomes the reciprocal of velocity. If interest rates rise, k should fall relative to PY, that is, individuals will desire to hold smaller money balances. Desiring to hold smaller balances, they spend the undesired portion of their actual balances and the turnover rate or velocity of the existing money stock rises.

Discussions then, about the stability of velocity, are also about the stability of the demand for money. If individuals believe velocity to be unstable, they also believe the demand for money to be unstable. Needless to add, stability of money demand is a basic tenet of Keynesian models.

In addition to the work on estimating the stability of velocity, other pioneering econometric work, largely by Milton Friedman and Anna Schwartz, was designed to show that on both a secular and a cyclical basis the recorded statistics on the money supply were highly related to money income. These studies also implied that velocity was stable and unlikely to be a problem in any attempt to control the course of money income over time by controlling the money supply.

The secular evidence The earliest effort (by Friedman) was to show that the supply of money per unit of output (where money is measured as M_2)[13] was highly correlated with the price level over a long period of time. Thus,

[12] For a sample of these studies, see David E. W. Laidler, *The Demand for Money: Theories and Evidence*, 2nd. edition (New York: Dun-Donnelley, 1977), Chapters 6, 7, and 8.

[13] M_2 must be used in these long-run studies because banks prior to 1913 never separated their deposits, since the same reserve requirements were applied to all deposits. Moreover, this measure of M_2 uses only commercial bank deposits.

what Friedman compares is M/Y and P. If velocity is fairly constant, then M/Y and P should be highly correlated with each other. Popularly termed the *secular evidence,* it is shown in Figure 11:1. The correlation is substantial over the longer run, even though over the shorter run it is not.[14]

However, as pointed out when this evidence was first presented, and as acknowledged by Friedman and his followers, correlation does not mean cause and effect. At most, it means that the two series are related—they have positive covariability. (Covariability of A and B is consistent with A causing B, B causing A, or both A and B responding positively to some cause, C.) Thus, this evidence does not necessarily substantiate the Monetarist position.

The cyclical evidence Of far greater importance was another piece of evidence—that related to the business cycle. Friedman and Schwartz[15] compared the rate of change of the money supply (M_2) with the peaks and

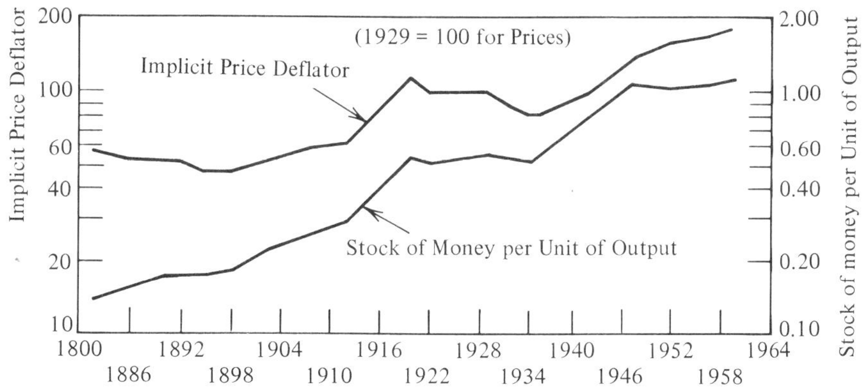

FIGURE 11:1
The secular evidence (Courtesy of Milton Friedman, "The Supply of Money and Changes in Prices and Output," in The Relationship of Prices to Economic Stability and Growth, *85th Congress, 2nd Session, Joint Economic Committee (Washington, D.C.: U.S. Government Printing Office, March 31, 1958), p. 247.)*

[14] The lack of a strong short-run correlation may be due to the fact that increases in the supply of money frequently bring forth temporary changes in real output, as well as temporary changes in the velocity or turnover rate of money. These changes ultimately vanish and the true longer-run relationship then prevails.

In place of the money stock one could have used the monetary base. Our previous analysis has indicated that the value of the money multiplier is fairly constant over time. If this is the case, the monetary base and the money supply will show a strong positive correlation. Thus, the monetary base might suffice both as a target and an indicator.

[15] See Milton Friedman and Anna J. Schwartz, "Money and Business Cycles," *The Review of Economics and Statistics,* Vol. 45, No. 1, Part 2 (Feb. 1963): 32–79.

troughs of 23 business cycles from 1867 to 1960.[16] The results were startling and are shown in Figure 11:2.

1. The rate of change of the money stock decreased before the peak of *each* cycle.
2. The rate of change of the money stock increased before the trough of *each* cycle.
3. The lag of economic activity behind the change in the rate of growth of the money supply is long and of variable length.
4. In the six cycles wherein the rate of change in the money stock became negative (i.e., the money stock declined absolutely), the depression in economic activity was deeper than in all of the other cycles. However, there appears to be no correlation between the magnitude of the contraction of the money stock and the contraction in the level of economic activity.

This evidence strongly indicates that the stock of money is the cause of the business cycle. However, as was pointed out by a British economist in the Keynesian–Radcliffe spirit, Nicholas Kaldor,[17] this evidence is consistent with reverse causation, i.e., with changes in economic activity causing the money stock to change. Suppose, for example, that in an economy experiencing a recession the government increases its expenditure rate. It thus places a larger volume of orders with firms. These orders are supported with checks drawn on newly created demand deposits. The business firms might first respond by drawing down inventories. As the inventories fall below normal levels, the firms would place orders for more goods, which would lead ultimately to expanded production and employment and a revival in economic activity. This sequence of events would show itself in the data as a rise in the rate of increase in the money supply followed by a rise in the level of gross national product. However, the money supply change clearly did not cause the change in the level of GNP. Thus, the cyclical evidence does not directly support only the Monetarist theory.

Recent Monetarist theorizing, which will be explored more completely in the chapters to follow, suggests that there should be a correlation between the rate of change of the money supply and the rate of change of any of several measures of economic activity (most notably GNP or national income). When these are compared, as shown in Figure 11:3, neither series consistently leads the others.

[16] It bears emphasizing that in this study the *rate of change* of M_2 is being compared with the *level* of GNP during various phases of the business cycle. The rate of change of GNP is not used. Again, this early study employs an older definition of M_2, one in which only commercial bank deposits are used.

[17] Nicholas Kaldor, "The New Monetarism," *Lloyds Bank Review* (July 1970): 1–17. See Appendix 11A for a discussion of how the procyclical growth rate of the money supply results when the interest rate is used as an indicator of monetary policy.

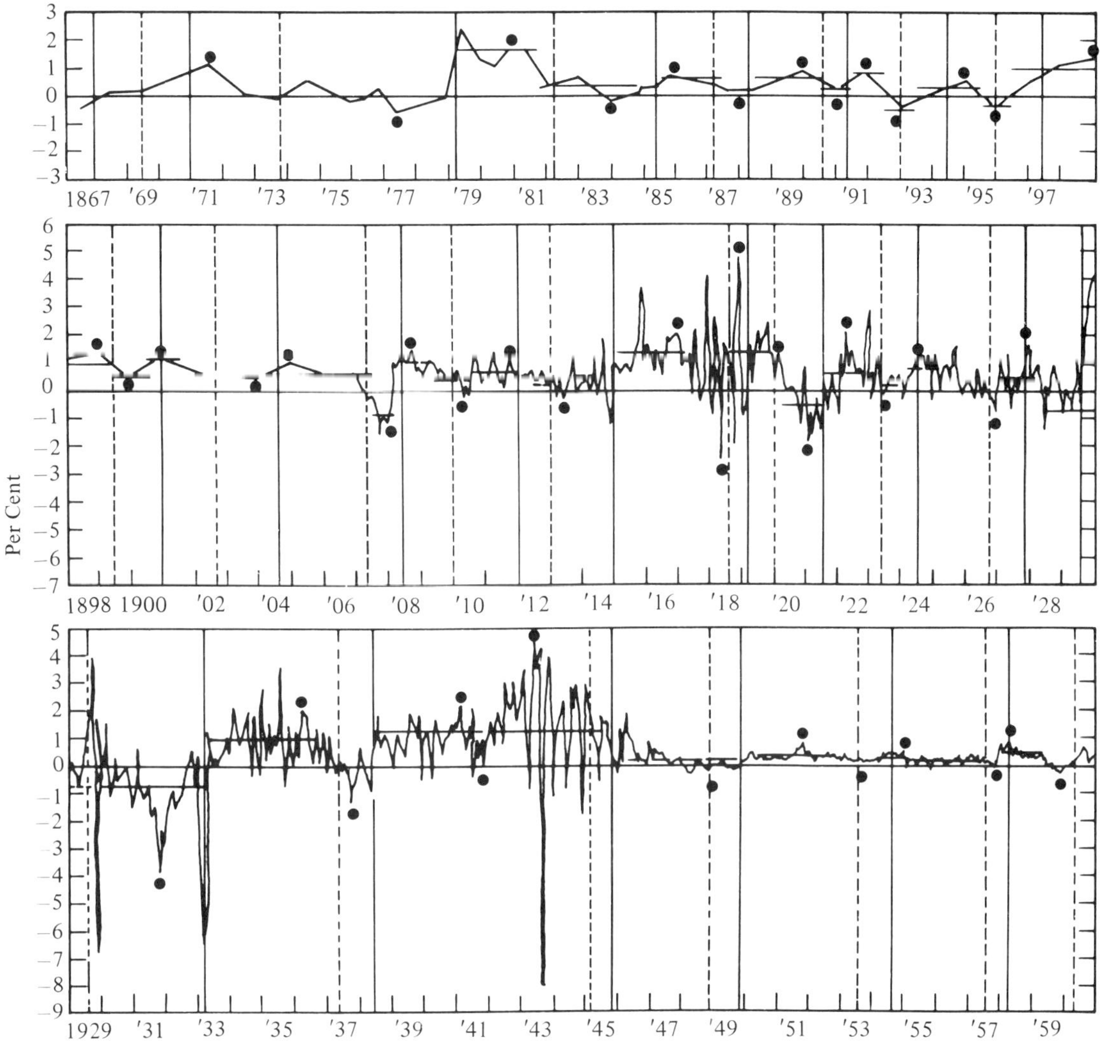

FIGURE 11:2

The cyclical evidence. Note: Solid vertical lines represent reference cycle troughs: broken lines, peaks. Dots represent peaks and troughs of specific cycles. The horizontal broken lines represent high and low steps in the rate of change. (In the annual or semiannual segment, 1867–1907, the change in natural logarithm from one date to the next in the data underlying the money supply was divided by the number of months intervening, and the quotient plotted at the middle of the month halfway between. In the monthly segment, 1907–1960, the month-to-month change in natural logarithm was plotted in the middle of the second month. Reference dates are courtesy of the National Bureau.)

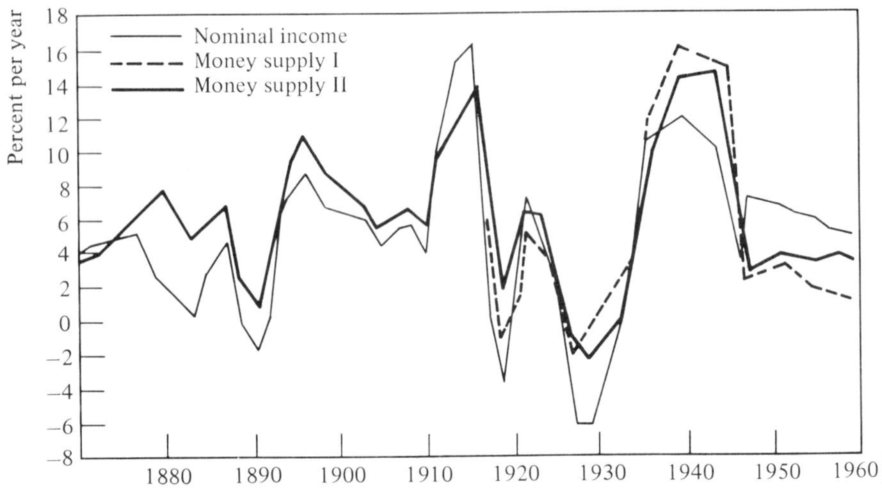

FIGURE 11:3
The relationship between the rate of change in nominal income and the money stock, 1870–1961, excluding intracyclical effects. (Courtesy of Milton Friedman, Dollars and Deficits: Inflation, Monetary Policy and the Balance of Payments, *© 1968, p. 128. Reprinted by permission of Prentice-Hall, Inc., Englewood Cliffs, New Jersey.) Note: Money Supply I consists of currency and the demand deposits of commercial banks. Money Supply II adds time deposits of commercial banks.*

Other evidence (to be evaluated) is also adduced in support of Monetarist claims that there is a strong and positive link between the supply of money and the ultimate objectives of monetary policy. This partial critique of the evidence that there is such a link is not meant to deny that it exists. It only questions the validity of the method used to substantiate the relationship.[18]

The Monetarist set—a summary Our analysis of the target and indicator set preferred by the Monetarists shows that it passes most of the tests for an ideal set put forth in this chapter. A potential source of trouble for the money supply as an indicator arises because it is alleged that velocity is unstable, and hence a strong and predictable relationship does not exist between the supply of money and any goal set forth for nominal gross national product. To the extent that velocity is unstable, the money supply will be an unreliable indicator of monetary policy.

[18] For a more sophisticated approach to the subject of causality, see Christopher Sims, "Money, Income, and Causality," *American Economic Review,* Vol. 62, No. 4 (Sept. 1972): 540–53.

Keynesianism versus Monetarism

Our analysis of the target–indicator set used by each side suggested that neither measured up to all the tests posed for an ideal target and indicator. In the Keynesian set instability in the real sector involving mainly the investment demand schedule could lead the Federal Reserve into incorrect policies. In the Monetarist set instability in the financial sector involving the velocity of money (or demand for money) could render Federal Reserve attempts to hit a goal set for nominal income (GNP) difficult, if not impossible, to accomplish.

Since both sets involve potential shortcomings, it might appear that the Federal Reserve is left without any measure of the posture of monetary policy. William Poole has proposed that one way out of this dilemma is for the Federal Reserve to use either the interest rate or the money supply as an indicator, depending on whether it believes the real sector or the monetary sector is more stable.[19]

To understand Poole's proposal, consider first a situation such as that depicted by Figure 10:21. The Federal Reserve regards income level Y_0 to be "just right." If the interest rate is used as the indicator, then i_0 is regarded as "just right." Similarly, if the money supply is used as an indicator, then the present quantity is "just right." Now, let us explore the case in which the Federal Reserve believes the real sector to be more unstable than the monetary sector. That is, for given interest rates, policymakers do not know the precise amounts of investment that are planned, while they do know the precise amounts of money that will be demanded. According to Poole, under these conditions the money supply is the superior indicator. This can be seen if we suppose that the investment incentives of individuals become pessimistic, so that the investment demand schedule in Figure 10:21 shifts to the left. This leftward shift will put downward pressure on the interest rate, which will offset, in part, the worsened prospects for investment—so long as the money supply is held constant. On the other hand, if the Federal Reserve had maintained the interest rate at i_0, it would have been led to contract the money supply to keep the rate from falling. This contraction would have caused a larger decrease in income and employment than would have occurred if the money supply had been held constant.

Thus, if the Federal Reserve wishes to minimize the deviations of income

[19] William Poole, "Optimal Choice of Monetary Policy Instruments in a Simple Stochastic Linear Model," *Quarterly Journal of Economics* 84 (May 1970): 197–216. See also the somewhat critical papers by John Kareken, "The Federal Reserve's Modus Operandi," in *Controlling Monetary Aggregates* (Boston: Federal Reserve Bank of Boston, 1969), pp. 57–63; and Warren Smith, "On the Conduct of Monetary Policy," in *Public Finance and Stabilization Policy, Essays in Honor of Richard Musgrave* (Amsterdam: North Holland, 1974), pp. 203–29. A rigorous treatment of this subject in terms of the *IS-LM* curves is found in Appendix 11B.

from its goal value, and if it believes the real sector to be more unstable, then a money supply indicator is superior to one using the interest rate.

Conversely, consider the case wherein the instability is in the financial or monetary sector. Poole would conclude that in this situation the interest rate is the superior indicator. To verify this conclusion, suppose that the velocity of money rises. Since this is equivalent to a fall in the demand for money, it can be shown in Figure 10:21 either by shifting the transactions demand in a counterclockwise direction or by shifting the asset demand schedule to the left. Either action will cause the interest rate to decline, and when this decline is followed through the model, it will be seen to be expansionary, i.e., income will rise above its best level, Y_0.

If the Federal Reserve uses an interest rate indicator, then as the rate falls below i_0, it will contract the money supply. Similarly, should the demand for money rise or velocity fall, the interest rate will rise above i_0 and the Federal Reserve will be forced to expand the money supply to restore the rate to its "just right" level. These contractions and expansions should keep income at Y_0, i.e., minimize the deviations of income from its "just right" value.

On the other hand, had the Federal Reserve used the money supply as an indicator, it would have held the supply constant and not offset any of the changes in velocity or money demand. Under these circumstances, the deviations in the level of income from Y_0 would have been much greater. Hence, if the financial sector is thought to be more unstable than the real sector, the interest rates are a superior indicator to the money supply.

Since Keynesians, as a rule, believe the source of cyclical instability lies in the real sector, Poole's analysis might lead them to prefer the money supply to the interest rate as an indicator of monetary policy. In this instance, they would have much in common with the Monetarists.

CURRENT FEDERAL RESERVE PRACTICES

The analysis above has been organized with reference to what competing macroeconomic theories might suggest as the best target–indicator set. It did not suggest what set the Open Market Committee uses in its pursuit of monetary policy. The records of the committee's meetings suggest that both an interest rate (that paid for federal funds) and three measures of the money supply (*M*1, *M*2, and *M*3 as measured prior to 1980) have been used.[20]

The reason for this hybrid policy is that the Open Market Committee

[20] For a discussion of the use of indicators and the operations of the Open Market Committee during 1979, see Appendix 11C. On October 6, 1979, the Board of Governors announced that monetary policy would be conducted with primary emphasis on the growth of monetary aggregates. It is too early to know to what degree they are implementing such a policy. This change is discussed in Appendix 11C.

wants to be able to gauge the immediate impact of its actions on the money market. Therefore, an interest rate is used.[21] The selection of the federal funds rate is due to a desire to have an interest rate that is free from inflationary expectations, and therefore reflects the underlying conditions of the supply and demand for loanable funds. Since the federal funds rate applies to loans made on a daily basis, it is not itself directly subject to the effect of expectations of inflation, as a longer-run rate would be.

In the execution of monetary policy the Open Market Committee sets both quarterly and longer-run goals for the growth rate of the several monetary aggregates. Open-market operations are then conducted to carry out these goals. However, it can be shown that this approach using the federal funds rate as a target of monetary policy may lead the Federal Reserve to commit serious errors because the same federal funds rate can be consistent with different rates of growth of the monetary aggregates, or policy indicator.

To demonstrate this possibility, the market for federal funds is graphed in Figure 11:4. The demand schedule has the traditional downward slope, for a larger quantity will be demanded by depository institutions at a lower federal funds rate, other things being equal—that is, so long as the discount rate and the marginal yield on bank assets (represented by a suitable market interest rate) remain constant. Should either the discount rate or the market interest rate rise, however, the demand schedule for federal funds would shift to the right. The reason is rather straightforward. A rise in the discount

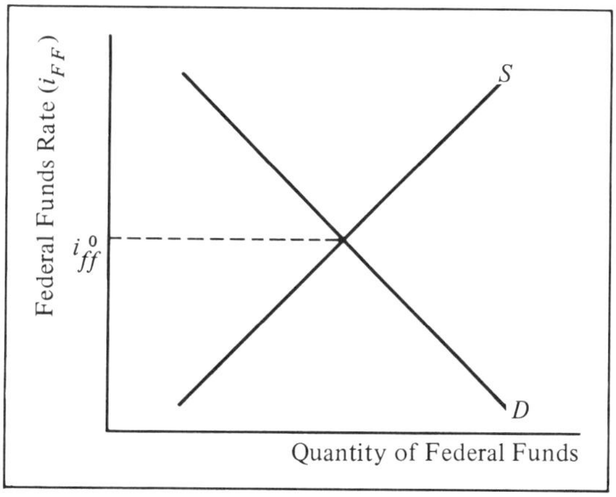

FIGURE 11:4
The federal funds market

[21] The Federal Reserve Act commits the Federal Reserve to maintain orderly conditions in the securities markets of the nation. Rapidly changing interest rates may lead to disorderly markets (e.g., panic selling). For this reason, the Open Market Committee may desire to be mindful of changes in interest rates.

rate will lead depository institutions that desired to borrow reserves to shift from the discount window of the Federal Reserve to the market for federal funds. Similarly, should an increase in credit demand by the public lead to a rise in market interest rates, depository institutions would be led to borrow more heavily in the federal funds market in order to increase their own lending capability.

The supply schedule drawn in Figure 11:4 should conform to one normally drawn for commodities, for lending depository institutions should desire to supply a larger quantity of their excess reserves to the federal funds market as the rate in that market rises. The supply schedule should shift mainly in response to open-market operations, for they alter the amount of excess reserves depository institutions can make available to the market.

Given this elementary description of the federal funds market, we can see the possibility for error when the federal funds rate is used as a target and monetary aggregates are used as indicators of monetary policy. Suppose that the current federal funds rate is i^0_{ff}, which is consistent with the Federal Reserve's chosen value for the target. In terms of our previous discussion, the Trading Desk is told to "keep things as they are." However, if there is an unanticipated rise in the demand for credit, market interest rates should be pushed up. This, in turn, will shift the demand schedule for federal funds to the right, putting upward pressure on the rate i_{ff}. Mindful of its directive, the Trading Desk would buy government securities in an effort to increase the supply of federal funds. As a consequence of the open-market operation, the monetary base is increased and the growth rate of the money supply rises. On the other hand, should there be an unanticipated weakening in credit demand so that market interest rates tend to decline, the demand schedule for federal funds would shift to the left, causing the rate to fall below i^0_{ff}. Again, mindful of its directive, the Trading Desk would sell government securities, decreasing the reserves of depository institutions and the supply of federal funds. The result is a reversal of the above, i.e., the growth rate of the money supply would decline.

This analysis demonstrates that the same federal funds rate, i^0_{ff}, can be compatible with different rates of growth of the money supply. Hence, no close and predictable relationship need prevail between the target and the indicator.

In using its current target–indicator combination, the Federal Reserve must be implicitly assuming that the demand schedule for federal funds is relatively stable. Thus, changes in the funds rate are governed by shifts in the supply schedule. If this is true, then to accelerate the growth rate of the money supply, the target rate for federal funds would have to be lowered through open-market operations; a converse operation would be used to achieve opposite results. When, however, the demand schedule is subject to frequent shifts, the Trading Desk is faced with a problem in interpreting movements in the federal funds rate. Is a falling rate due to a decrease in demand or to an increase in supply? Each situation is unlikely to dictate the same response by the Trading Desk.

SUMMARY

Because the impact of monetary actions on economic activity has a lag that is both long and variable, and because there is also a lag in collecting information on the current status of the economy, policymakers find it difficult to know whether monetary actions undertaken today are moving economic activity in the right direction for achieving the goals set forth for policy. For this reason, they have sought operational targets and indicators that will supply them with the required information.

Since economists differ on the best way to conceptualize the functioning of an economy, it should come as no surprise that they disagree on the best target–indicator set. As our analysis showed, however, economists of different schools may prefer to use the same set.

Our discussion came to several disconcerting conclusions. First, no target–indicator set examined meets all the tests set forth. To enable the Federal Reserve to use one or the other set, Poole suggested that the choice at a given time be based on the sector, the real or financial, that the Federal Reserve regarded as the more unstable. Second, some of the economic difficulties that have beset our country from time to time may have been caused by an incorrect use of targets and indicators by those individuals charged with the responsibility for stabilizing the economy. Finally, we still do not know precisely the different avenues through which the supply of money affects economic activity and the relative importance of each avenue.

STUDY QUESTIONS

1. Explain the meaning of the phrase "easy money leads ultimately to tight credit."
2. What are the basic problems that arise in the use of monetary policy?
3. What are the desired characteristics of a target and an indicator?
4. Under what circumstances might a Keynesian find the money supply a superior indicator of monetary policy?
5. What stands between the money stock and money spending? What are some of the implications of this variable for monetary policy?
6. How does uncertainty influence the selection of an indicator of monetary policy?
7. Explain how the maintenance of a given federal funds rate can be consistent with several alternative growth rates of the money supply.
8. Why have some argued that during the great contraction of 1929–1933, when the money supply declined by almost one-third, monetary policy was easy?
9. What is the nature of the controversy over the cyclical evidence on the relationship between money and economic activity?

SELECTED REFERENCES AND READINGS

Artis, M. J. "Monetary Policy in the 1970's in the Light of Recent Developments." *Issues in Monetary Economics,* edited by H. G. Johnson and A. R. Nobay. London: Oxford University Press, 1974.

Brunner, Karl, ed. *Targets and Indicators of Monetary Policy.* San Francisco: Chandler, 1969.

Burger, Albert E. "The Implementation Problem of Monetary Policy." *Monthly Review,* Federal Reserve Bank of St. Louis 53 (Mar. 1971).

Davis, Richard G. "Implementing Open Market Policy with Monetary Aggregate Objectives." In *Monetary Aggregates and Monetary Policy.* New York: Federal Reserve Bank of New York, 1974.

Friedman, Benjamin. "Targets, Instruments, and Indicators of Monetary Policy." *Journal of Monetary Economics,* Vol. 1, No. 4 (Oct. 1975).

Friedman, Milton, and Schwartz, Anna. *A Monetary History of the United States, 1867–1960.* Princeton, N.J.: Princeton University Press, 1963. Chapter 7.

______. "Money and Business Cycles." *The Review of Economics and Statistics,* Vol. 45, No. 1, Part 2 (Feb. 1963).

Hamburger, Michael J. "Indicators of Monetary Policy: The Arguments and the Evidence." *American Economic Review,* Vol. 60, No. 2 (May 1970).

Holms, Allan. "The Problem of the Open Market Manager." In *Controlling Monetary Aggregates II: The Implementation.* Boston: Federal Reserve Bank of Boston, Sept. 1972.

Kaldor, Nicholas. "The New Monetarism." *Lloyds Bank Review* 97 (July 1970).

______. "Reply to Friedman:" *Lloyds Bank Review* 98 (Oct. 1970).

Kaufman, George. "The Strange Journey of Monetary Indicators." *Journal of Financial and Quantitative Analysis,* Vol. 7, No. 2 (May 1972).

Meltzer, Allan, Horwich, George, and Hendershott, Patric. "The Appropriate Indicators of Monetary Policy." In *Savings and Residential Financing, 1969 Conference and Proceedings.* Chicago, 1969.

Poole, William. "Optimal Choice of Monetary Policy Instruments in a Simple Stochastic Macro Model." *Quarterly Journal of Economics,* Vol. 84, No. 2 (May 1970).

______. "Rules-of-Thumb for Guiding Monetary Policy." in *Open Market Policies for Guiding Monetary Policy.* Board of Governors of the Federal Reserve System, July 1971.

Saving, Thomas. "Monetary-Policy Targets and Indicators." *Journal of Political Economy,* Vol. 65, No. 4 (Aug. 1967).

11

APPENDIX A– INTEREST RATES AS AN INDICATOR OF FEDERAL RESERVE POLICY AND THE PROCYCLICAL GROWTH OF THE MONEY SUPPLY

11

Our examination of the numerous business cycles that have occurred since the formation of the Federal Reserve System shows a general procyclical growth rate of the money supply. This behavior can be rationalized quite easily if the interest rate is assumed to be an indicator of monetary policy, a position in accord with well-known practices of the Federal Reserve System.

We start our explanation for the procyclical growth rate of the money supply by assuming that we are in the initial phase of an economic expansion characterized by a high level of unemployment and a relatively stable price level.

The Federal Reserve desires to aid the recovery in an effort to reduce unemployment. It does this by holding interest rates at a low level. However, as the recovery gathers momentum, the increased demand for money and credit will undoubtedly put upward pressure on market interest rates. The Federal Reserve may interpret this development as a decrease in the supply of credit that, if allowed to continue, will bring the expansion to a halt. It therefore expands the monetary base and the supply of money. This serves to accelerate the rate of economic expansion. As the recovery progresses, the unemployment rate may fall to a lower level and the rate of inflation will start to rise.

It is at this juncture in the expansion phase of the business cycle that the response of the Federal Reserve to continued upward pressure on interest rates is important. If the monetary base is expanded further in an effort to hold down interest rates, the economic recovery may become inflationary. However, if the Federal Reserve becomes concerned about the inflation rate, it may raise its interest rate indicator. However, if the boom is well underway, the initial increase in the interest rate indicator may be insufficient to restrain it, and the Federal Reserve may be led to further expand the money supply. Further expansion may occur if actual market rates exceed the indicator rates. Under these circumstances, the account manager may further increase the growth rate of the monetary base in order to hold interest rates below their indicator levels.

Ultimately, as the inflation rate rises, the Federal Reserve will focus attention on promoting price level stability. To achieve this goal, the interest rate indicator will be raised and the growth rate of the money supply curtailed. As this lower growth rate takes hold, the economic expansion will come to an end and a contraction will be set in motion.

The contraction and concomitant decrease in demand for money and credit will put downward pressure on interest rates. If the Federal Reserve mistakenly believes this decrease in interest rates is due to an increase in the supply of credit, it may further tighten the monetary base in an effort to raise interest rates to their indicator levels. Because of lags in the collection of accurate data and the fact that the inflation rate does not decrease abruptly when the money supply is contracted, the Federal Reserve may persist in a contractionary policy long after such a policy is warranted.

The net result of using the interest rate as an indicator of monetary policy is that the money supply grows in a procyclical fashion. That is, its growth rate expands in the upswing of the cycle because the Federal Reserve desires to promote economic expansion by holding interest rates down. As the upswing continues, if the interest rate indicator is not adjusted appropriately, the Federal Reserve may turn the expansion into an inflationary boom. Then, in an effort to correct for past policies, the Federal Reserve may precipitate a major downturn in economic activity, which could be exacerbated if the interest rate indicator is set too high. During the downswing the growth rate of the money supply will be decreased.

11

APPENDIX B–THE IMPLEMENTATION OF MONETARY POLICY IN AN *IS-LM* CONTEXT

11

The purpose of this appendix is to put the implementation of monetary policy as presented by William Poole into an *IS-LM* framework.

Poole's conclusion is that the money supply is a superior indicator for monetary policy when the real sector is unstable, whereas the interest rate is superior when the monetary sector is unstable.

Figure 11B:1 is designed to show the first conclusion. The *LM* schedule is drawn for a money supply and money demand that are known with certainty by the Federal Reserve. Therefore, its position is assumed not to be subject to shift. The *IS* schedule, however, is subject to random shifts. Based upon fiscal variables (tax rates and government spending) and the projections of private spending for consumption and investment, $E(IS)$ represents the expected value of the *IS* schedule. Because this schedule is subject to random shifts, IS_1 and IS_2 represent the range of its possible values.

The objective of the Federal Reserve is to keep income as close to its ideal level, Y_0, as possible, i.e., to minimize the deviations of income about Y_0.

If the Federal Reserve selects the interest rate as the indicator of monetary policy, then rate i_0 will be the correct one, i.e., compatible with income level Y_0. When i_0 is selected as the indicator, the Federal Reserve will make any changes in the money supply that are required to keep i_0 constant. In essence, this means that the *LM* curve becomes horizontal at i_0. Since the *IS* schedule is subject to random fluctuations between IS_1 and IS_2, a horizontal *LM* schedule will cause the range of deviation of income to fall between Y_4 and Y_3.

On the other hand, should the Federal Reserve select the money supply as an indicator and keep its value constant, the range of deviation of income from its ideal value of Y_0 would be only Y_2–Y_1, which is less than Y_4–Y_3. How much less depends on the slope of the *LM* schedule. As a special case, consider a vertical *LM* schedule. Here the money supply would clearly be the superior indicator for then, if it were held constant, income

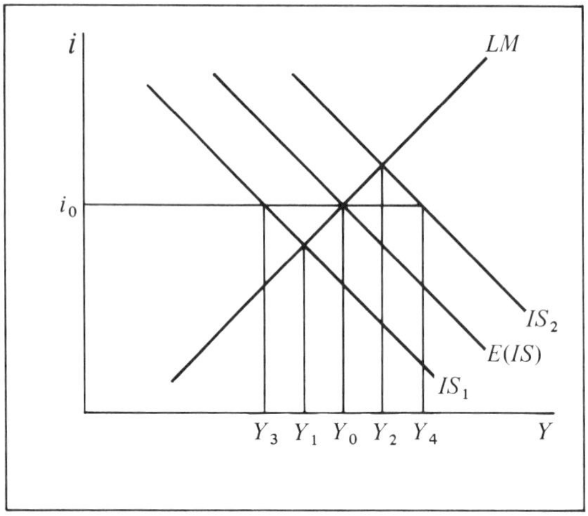

FIGURE 11B:1
An unstable real sector

would not deviate from $\mathbf{Y}_0$. (A vertical *LM* schedule will arise if both the money supply and money demand schedules are insensitive to the rate of interest.)

Should the monetary sector be unstable because of erratic shifts in velocity, then it will be the *LM* schedule that will shift, while the *IS* schedule will remain stationary. Under these circumstances, Poole concludes that the interest rate is preferable to the money supply as an indicator. This conclusion can be substantiated by examining Figure 11B:2. There $E(LM)$ represents the expected value of the *LM* schedule, while LM_1 and LM_2 represent the range of its random fluctuations.

If the Federal Reserve uses an interest rate indicator, it will adjust the money supply to offset any changes in velocity whenever the interest rate departs from i_0. Such a compensatory policy should contribute to maintaining income continuously at Y_0. If, however, it uses a money supply indicator, holding the money supply constant will produce a variation in income about Y_0 of $Y_2–Y_1$. Thus, if the monetary sector is thought to be more unstable than the real sector, the interest rate is superior to the money supply as an indicator.

Figure 11B:2 also shows that should the *IS* schedule approximate the vertical (which results when investment and saving are unrelated to the interest rate), the Federal Reserve could use either a money supply or interest rate indicator. In this case, it would make no difference because changes in the money supply would not change income. (This conclusion holds only if money operates through the interest rate channel.)

Suppose, however, that both sectors are unstable. In that case, which indicator is to be preferred? The choice is determined by two main factors:

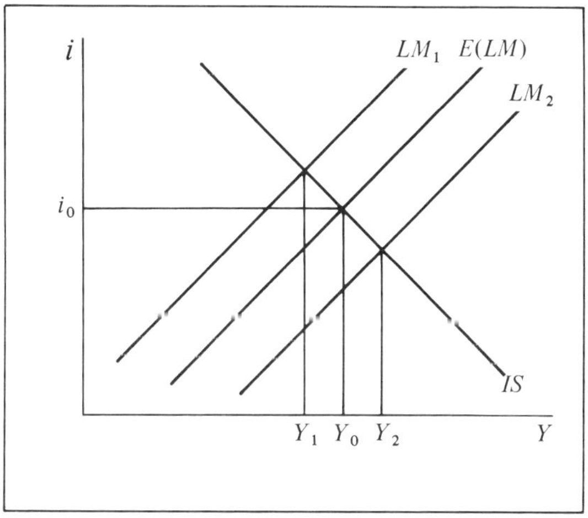

FIGURE 11B:2
An unstable monetary sector

which sector is the more stable, and the slopes (elasticities) of the two schedules. Consider first the situation where each schedule is unstable, but the *IS* schedule is more unstable than the *LM* schedule. This is shown in Figure 11B:3, where the horizontal shift of the *IS* schedule is greater than that of the *LM* schedule. In order to simplify the diagram, the *IS* schedule will be assumed to shift to the right, whereas the *LM* schedule shifts to the left. Thus, *E*(*IS*) and *E*(*LM*) represent the expected value of each schedule, while IS_p and LM_p represent the probable values of each schedule due to

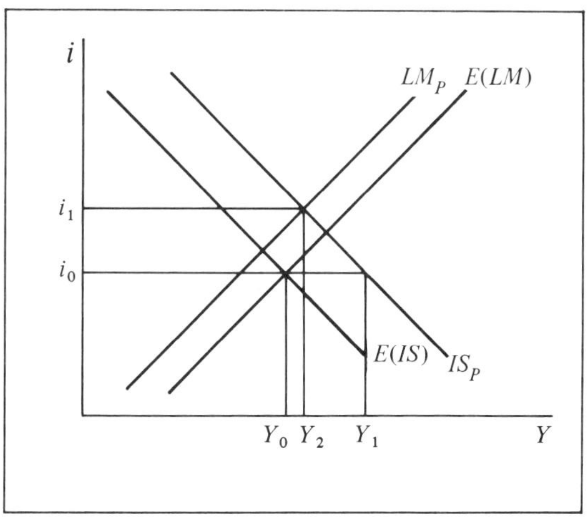

FIGURE 11B:3
Both sectors unstable

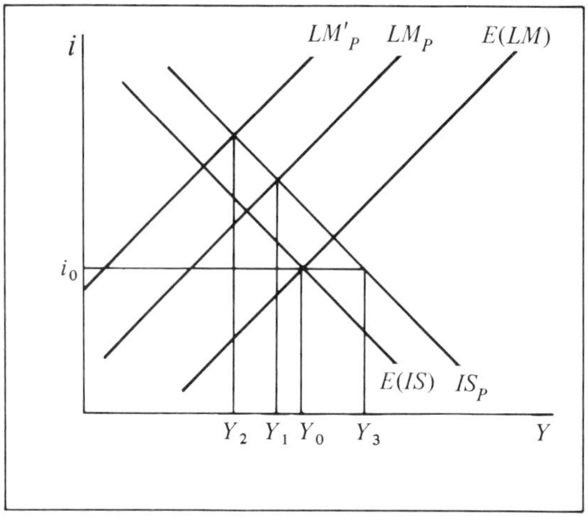

FIGURE 11B:4
LM *more unstable than* IS

random shifts. If the interest rate is stabilized at i_0, the divergence of income from its "just right" value will be $Y_0 - Y_1$; whereas if the money supply is held constant, the divergence of income will be $Y_2 - Y_0$. Thus, neglecting the slope or elasticity of each schedule, if the *IS* schedule is more unstable than the *LM* schedule, a money supply indicator is to be preferred. However, should the *LM* schedule be more unstable, the interest rate indicator is not necessarily superior. The choice depends not only on the extent to which the *LM* schedule is less stable, but on the elasticities of the two schedules as well.

First, in Figure 11B:4 we demonstrate the case where the *LM* schedule is more unstable than the *IS* schedule. Again, assume the *IS* schedule is subject to shifts to the right from *E*(*IS*) to IS_p, while the *LM* schedule is subject to two possible shifts, from *E*(*LM*) to LM_p to LM'_p. In both instances the expected shift in the *LM* schedule exceeds that of the *IS* schedule. However, in the case where the expected shift is only slightly larger (LM_p), it is still better to use a money supply indicator. When the money supply is held constant, the variation of income from its desired level is $Y_0 - Y_1$, whereas it is $Y_3 - Y_0$ when the interest rate is stablilized. However, should the probable shift of the *LM* schedule be to LM'_p, the income variation would be $Y_0 - Y_2$, which exceeds the other two variations.

However, the probable shifting in the two schedules is not the only consideration in judging which indicator the central bank should use in the conduct of monetary policy. The slopes or elasticities of the two schedules must be considered. To see this, let us examine the case shown in Figure 11B:5. If the *LM* schedule is very inelastic (i.e., the demand for and supply of money is highly insensitive to the interest rate), then an interest rate indicator should be preferred. In the extreme case of a vertical *LM* schedule,

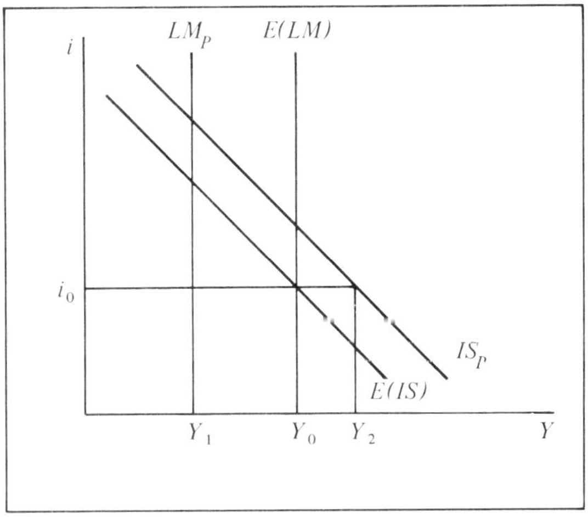

FIGURE 11B:5
An inelastic LM *schedule*

stabilization of the money supply will result in a divergence of income from its ideal value of $Y_0 - Y_1$, whereas stabilization of the interest rate will result in a divergence of only $Y_2 - Y_0$. The latter divergence will be smaller so long as the *LM* schedule is inelastic and its expected shift is greater than that of the *IS* schedule.

On the other hand, should the *LM* schedule become increasingly horizontal, only a stable money supply will work to minimize fluctuations about Y_0.

Figure 11B:6 is designed to show that should the *IS* schedule become

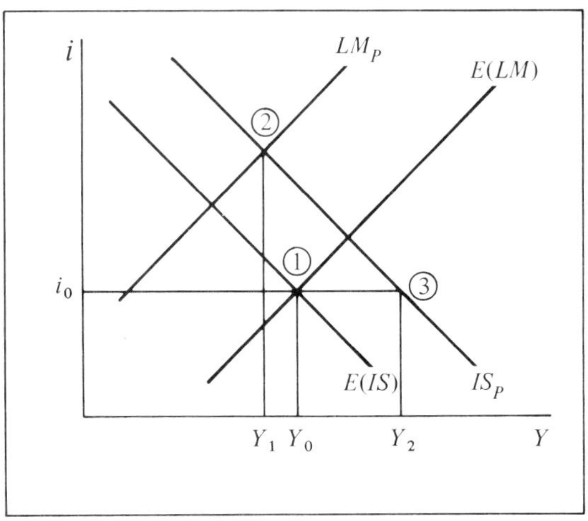

FIGURE 11B:6
An inelastic IS *schedule*

increasingly inelastic (i.e., investment becomes insensitive to the interest rate), the money supply would be a better indicator than the interest rate, even though the *LM* schedule is more unstable than the *IS*. To see this, note that should the money supply be used as indicator, the new equilibrium point is②, whereas if the interest rate indicator is used, point③becomes the relevant one. The deviation of income from the ideal is only $Y_0 - Y_1$, as opposed to $Y_2 - Y_0$. To see the relevance of the elasticity of the *IS* schedule, allow it to become increasingly inelastic. This can be done by rotating IS_p in a clockwise direction around point③. As it is rotated, point② will move out along LM_p, causing the deviations of income about Y_0 to become first smaller, then increasingly larger. However, until the *IS* schedule becomes vertical, the deviations of income from Y_0 will never be as large as they would be if the interest rate served as the indicator. Hence, it follows that the money supply is a superior policy guide when the *IS* schedule is inelastic.

11 11

APPENDIX C- DELIBERATIONS OF THE FEDERAL OPEN MARKET COMMITTEE IN 1979

For several years the Federal Reserve Bank of St. Louis, in the March issue of its *Monthly Review,* summarizes the activities of the Federal Open Market Committee (FOMC) for the preceding year. These summaries are prepared from the "Record of Policy Actions of the Federal Open Market Committee." The "Record" is released a few days after the relevant FOMC meeting. It is subsequently published in the *Federal Reserve Bulletin* and "Records" for the entire year are published in the *Annual Report of the Board of Governors*. The "Records", as well as the masterful summaries by Richard Lang in the St. Louis *Monthly Reviews,* contain a wealth of information on such topics as targets and indicators of monetary policy, how members of the FOMC voted on various resolutions, and the actual phrasing of the directives given to the Trading Desk or the Account Manager of the New York Federal Reserve Bank.

In this Appendix we will concentrate on what may be the most important change in monetary policy in this century. It occurred on October 6, 1979, when the Federal Reserve announced that in its conduct of monetary policy greater emphasis would be placed on control of the monetary aggregates rather than confining short-term fluctuations in the federal funds rate. Control of the aggregates was to be accomplished by using bank reserves as a target of policy rather than the federal funds rate. Many economists interpreted this change by the Federal Reserve to be its movement into the Monetarist camp.

Why did such a fundamental change in Federal Reserve policy occur? According to the Federal Reserve, it was designed to

assure better control over the expansion of money and bank credit, help curb speculative excesses in financial, foreign exchange, and commodity markets and thereby serve to dampen inflationary forces[1]

[1] "Announcements: Monetary Policy Actions," *Federal Reserve Bulletin* (October 1979): 830.

One might rephrase the above to read that by confining the federal funds rate to a narrow range, the Federal Reserve admits it has lost control over the monetary aggregates, and it was the aggregates which were important in explaining inflation and speculation.

Figures 11C:1 and 11C:2 below show that while the Federal Reserve was successful in keeping the federal funds rate within a narrow band, it was unsuccessful in keeping M_1 and M_2 within their tolerance ranges.

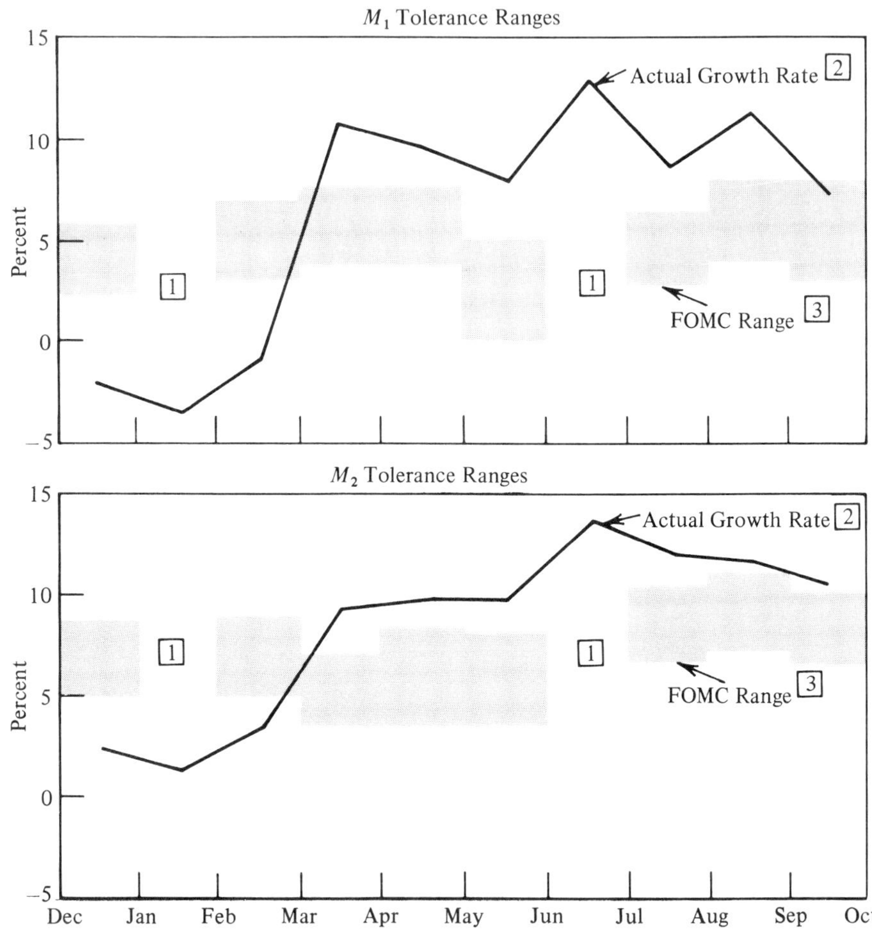

FIGURE 11C:1

FOMC short-run ranges for monetary aggregates. Note: After the October 6, 1979 FOMC meeting, the FOMC no longer specified tolerance ranges for M_1 *and* M_2 *in the same manner. (1) During the January–February and June–July periods, ranges for* M_1 *and* M_2 *were not specified by the FOMC. (2) Actual growth-rate data are revised as of January 10, 1980. (3) The shaded areas represent two-month ranges adopted by the Committee at each regularly scheduled meeting. (Courtesy of the Federal Reserve Bank of St. Louis.)*

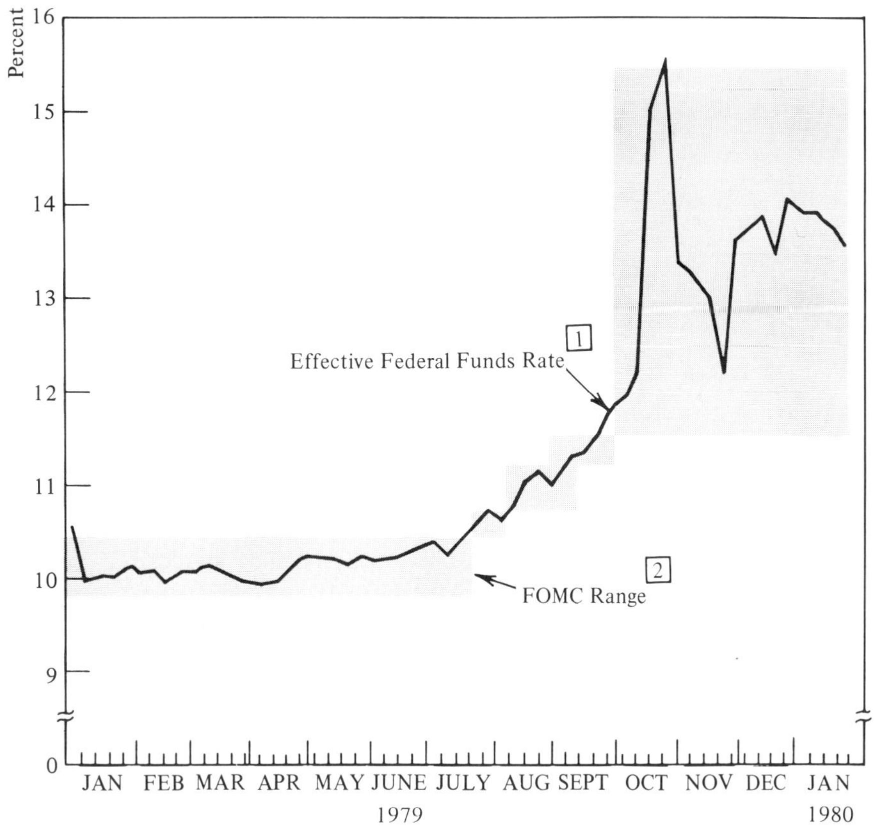

FIGURE 11C:2
FOMC ranges for the federal funds rate. (1) Weekly averages of effective daily rates. (2) At each meeting during 1979, the FOMC established a range for the federal funds rate. These ranges are indicated for the first full week during which they were in effect. (Courtesy of the Federal Reserve Bank of St. Louis.)

From the "Record" we learn that the FOMC was especially concerned with the expansion of both monetary aggregates and bank credit, which had been increasing at rapid rates after the first quarter of 1979. The issue of how to slow monetary growth to keep the aggregates within their 1979 ranges was the catalyst for the change in the FOMC's short-run operating procedures.

The FOMC recognized that the relationship between bank reserves, which they sought to control, and the growth of monetary aggregates was not precise and did not guarantee that the growth of the aggregates would diminish in the fourth quarter of 1979. The FOMC also recognized that this change in operating procedure could be accompanied initially by substantial increases in interest rates and that movements in the rates would be more uncertain.

In conjunction with the October 6 meeting it is instructive to read the actual directive issued by the FOMC to the manager of the open market account. The "Report" states:

> *. . . the Committee instructed the Manager to restrain expansion of bank reserves to a pace consistent with the growth from September to December at an annual rate on the order of 4.5% for M_1 and about 7.5% in M_2 and M_3, provided that in the period before the next regular meeting the federal funds rate remained generally within a range of 11.5%–15.5%.*

Subsequent directives have been similarly explicit about the growth rates of the aggregates. At the March 7, 1980 meeting, the FOMC widened the federal funds rate range to 11.5 to 18%.

Several aspects of the new operating procedures should be noted. First, the FOMC no longer targets on a specific level of the federal funds rate as its short-run operating objective. Second, the range of permissible variation of the federal funds rate has been increased from a one-half to three quarter percentage point range to one which is now some 6.5 percentage points. Third, while the directive specifies the desired growth rate of the monetary aggregates, the Account Manager must manipulate the reserves available to the banking system. The FOMC does not specify the desired reserve growth. It is left to the staffs of the Board of Governors and the New York Federal Reserve's Open Market Desk to establish guidelines for the growth of the reserve aggregate. Rather than controlling total bank reserves or the monetary base, the FOMC has selected unborrowed bank reserves as its target (i.e., total bank reserves less those reserves borrowed through discounts and advances). In the future, this may be changed to one or another of the reserve aggregates.

12 INFLATION AND UNEMPLOYMENT

The intense, long and intractable depression experienced by the major industrial countries during much of the period between the two world wars did much to make the causes and cures of unemployment the major focus of analysis for economists. Measured in terms of output lost forever when men and machines which might otherwise have remained employed remain idle, this era imposed upon the whole of society a tremendous cost, not to speak of the individual deprivations and psychological burdens that prolonged inability to find employment must ultimately bring.

This era of the Great Depression served also to impress upon economists in general that the analytical framework of orthodox macroeconomic theory was unable to provide either an explanation of or a cure for this major disaster. The popularity of the approach to macroeconomic theory expounded by Lord Keynes can be traced in large part to the fact that it provided both a timely framework of analysis and a distinct set of policies for dealing with unemployment.

For many economists who familiarized themselves with this paradigm and its policy implications, unemployment and recessions were to be a thing of the past and for a fairly long time after World War II, it looked as though this assessment may have been correct. Not only were the recessions of the period mild by historic standards, but from 1961 to 1969 the United States experienced the longest sustained upward period of economic expansion since the National Bureau of Economic Research started to date business cycles starting with the one of 1854. For over 100 months the real growth rate of the U.S. economy was positive. However, in the aftermath of the Vietnam War this came to an end and the United States experienced its highest unemployment rate since the Great Depression of the 1930s.

Throughout the post–World War II period of sustained economic progress, the rise in the general level of commodity prices, or inflation, had been a nagging problem. When the rate of increase reached double-digit proportions in the early 1970s, dire warnings were sounded that the American way of life was in deep trouble.

The joint occurrence of inflation and unemployment is puzzling to many economists, for economic theory suggests quite an opposite relationship. That is, that unemployment results from inadequate or deficient aggregate demand, whereas inflation results from demand in excess of the full-employment level of output. Thus, their joint occurrence clearly requires some special circumstances.

Nevertheless, for some time, at least since the pioneering statistical work of Irving Fisher in 1926,[1] independently rediscovered by A. W. Phillips in 1957,[2] economists have believed that there may, in fact, be a link between inflation and unemployment. The exact nature of this link and the degree to which it is permanent will be discussed in detail later in this chapter. For the time being, it should be noted that this link remains the subject of intense controversy among economists. Before we investigate this topic, we will analyze the subjects of inflation and unemployment separately.

INFLATION

Our discussion of inflation begins with a definition. Then the costs of inflation will be indicated. Finally, some theories of its causes and cures will be considered.[3]

A definition

Inflation is usually defined as a sustained rise in a broadly based index of commodity prices over a given period of time. The essential elements in the definition are several. First, inflation involves the movement in the general level of commodity prices, *not* changes in relative commodity prices, which measure the terms on which one good exchanges for another. Even when the price level is stable, it is not uncommon for the price or exchange value of one good or service to change in relation to another. Supply-and-demand conditions in individual markets are subject to frequent changes. When they do change, individual prices also change. In a dynamic society one should expect the structure of relative prices to change continuously. Therefore, inflation is a situation in which, on the average, *all* individual prices are rising in terms of whatever is called money.

Second, the movement in the price level must be somewhat substantial

[1] Irving Fisher, "A Statistical Relation between Unemployment and Price Changes," *International Labor Review* (June 1926): 785–92.

[2] A. W. Phillips, "The Relation between Unemployment and the Rate of Change of Money Wages in the United Kingdom, 1862–1957," *Economica*, Vol. 25, No. 100 (Dec. 1958): 283–99. Note that this work does not take the same view of unemployment as Fisher's. Fisher's article relates employment to the level of wages, whereas Phillips's relates it to the rate of change of wages.

[3] For the interested student, four rather extensive surveys of inflation exist. See Martin Bronfenbrenner and Franklyn Holzman, "Survey of Inflation Theory," *American Economic Review*, Vol. 53, No. 4 (Sept. 1963): 593–661; Harry Johnson, "A Survey of Theories of Inflation," in *Essays in Monetary Economics* (London: Unwin University Books, 1967), pp. 104–42; David Laidler and Michael Parkin, "Inflation: A Survey," *Economic Journal*, Vol. 85, No. 4 (Dec. 1975): 741–809; and Helmut Frisch, "Inflation Theory 1963–1975: A 'Second Generation' Survey," *Journal of Economic Literature*, Vol. 15, No. 4 (Dec. 1977): 1289–1317.

and sustained over a time period longer than a day, a week, or a month. Often, the time period is one of several years or more.[4]

In the United States the price level, and hence the rate of inflation, can be measured according to three separate price indices: the consumer price index (CPI), the producer price index (PPI), and the GNP deflator. As Table 12:1 shows, they do not always tell the same story as far as the rate of inflation is concerned. For that reason, a brief description of each is in order. The CPI results from a survey of the spending habits of a group of typical American families. Periodically, the Bureau of Labor Statistics carries out such a survey and from it compiles a so-called market basket, which represents these families' purchases of goods and services. In general, the importance of each item in the market basket is determined by the percentage of income devoted to its purchase. Then, every month in various cities across the United States this market basket is priced. If the prices of the goods and services composing the market basket increase by 1%, the CPI rises by 1%, and so on. An inherent problem with this index is that the longer it is used after an initial survey of the spending habits of typical individuals, the less representative of actual spending habits the makeup of the market basket may become. This is because as relative prices change and as income rises, individuals are likely to change the way they allocate or spend their income. Thus, the bureau updates its survey from time to time.

The producer price index is also calculated monthly, but unlike the consumer price index, it does not include the prices of any services. The PPI was formerly the wholesale price index. The new index was designed to avoid some of the double counting that was found in the old index. One advantage of the PPI is that it may catch early price level increases that only show up later in consumer prices. Thus, it may anticipate changes in the CPI.

The GNP deflator is only available on a quarterly basis. It represents the most broadly based measure of a change in the general level of prices. When the Department of Commerce calculates the gross national product in current prices, it also calculates it in terms of the prices prevailing in some base period (e.g., 1972). The difference between GNP valued in current prices and constant prices (1972 prices) is a measure of the change in the price level. For example, if GNP valued in terms of 1976 prices was \$1.8 trillion, whereas in terms of 1972 prices it was \$1.2 trillion, then between 1972 and 1976 the GNP deflator or price index would have

[4] To every definition some exception can always be found. The most intense inflation ever recorded occurred in Hungary after World War II. From July 1945 to August 1, 1946, the price level rose from 7964 to 24×10^{28}. In the last two months of this episode the rate of inflation was, respectively, $8.4 \times 10^{5}\%$ and $41.9 \times 10^{15}\%$.

TABLE 12:1
The rate of inflation: 1939–1979

Year	CPI 1967 = 100 Index	CPI % Change	PPI * 1967 = 100 Index	PPI % Change	GNP Deflator 1972 = 100 Index	GNP Deflator % Change
1939	41.6				28.5	
1940	42.0	.9			29.1	2.1
1941	44.1	2.4			31.3	9.8
1942	48.8	10.7			34.4	9.9
1943	51.8	6.1			36.2	5.2
1944	52.7	1.7			37.0	2.2
1945	53.9	2.2			37.9	2.4
1946	58.5	8.5			44.0	16.1
1947	66.9	14.4	74.0		49.7	13.0
1948	72.1	7.7	79.9	8.0	53.1	6.8
1949	71.4	−1.2	77.6	−3.0	52.6	−.1
1950	72.1	1.0	79.0	1.8	53.6	1.9
1951	77.8	7.9	86.5	9.5	57.3	6.9
1952	79.5	2.2	86.0	−0.6	58.0	1.2
1953	80.1	.8	85.1	−1.1	58.9	1.6
1954	80.5	.5	85.3	1.2	59.7	1.4
1955	80.2	−.4	85.5	.2	61.0	2.2
1956	81.4	1.1	87.9	2.8	62.9	3.1
1957	84.3	3.6	91.1	3.6	65.0	3.3
1958	86.6	2.7	93.2	2.3	66.1	1.7
1959	87.3	.8	93.0	−.2	67.5	2.1
1960	88.7	1.6	93.7	.8	68.7	1.8
1961	89.6	1.0	93.7	—	69.3	1.5
1962	90.6	1.1	94.0	.3	70.6	1.9
1963	91.7	1.2	93.7	−.3	71.6	1.4
1964	92.9	1.3	94.1	.4	72.7	1.5
1965	94.5	1.7	95.7	1.7	74.3	2.2
1966	97.2	2.9	98.8	3.2	76.8	3.4
1967	100.0	2.8	100.0	1.2	79.0	2.9
1968	104.2	4.2	102.9	2.9	82.6	4.6
1969	109.8	5.4	106.6	3.6	86.7	5.0
1970	116.3	5.9	110.3	3.5	91.4	5.4
1971	121.3	4.3	113.7	3.1	96.0	5.0
1972	125.3	3.3	117.2	3.1	100.0	4.2
1973	133.1	6.2	127.9	9.1	105.8	5.8
1974	147.7	11.0	147.5	15.3	116.0	9.6
1975	161.3	9.2	163.4	10.8	127.2	9.7
1976	170.5	5.7	170.3	4.2	133.8	5.2
1977	181.5	6.5	180.6	6.0	141.6	5.8
1978	195.4	7.6	194.6	7.8	152.0	7.3
1979	217.4	11.3	216.1	11.0	165.5	8.9

(Courtesy of *Survey of Current Business, Department of Commerce* (Washington, D.C.: United States Government Printing Office).)
*Producer price index is for total finished goods.

advanced 1.5 times—or the inflation rate would have been 50% over the four-year period.

Even though all price indices suffer from some sort of deficiency, they are about as good a measure of the rate of inflation as can be constructed.

Cost of inflation

Why has inflation been the cause of such concern throughout much of recorded history? In ancient Rome the rate of inflation became so serious that the Emperor Diocletian issued an edict imposing extensive wage and price controls in an effort to curb it. Four years later he was forced to abdicate. In 1971 Richard Nixon felt compelled to do the same thing. The fact that he was also forced from office is thought by most to be purely coincidental. The concern that led these two leaders to recommend similar policies nearly 17 centuries apart is related to what is perceived to be the costs of inflation. To this discussion we now turn.

For analytical purposes, a basic distinction is required when the costs of inflation are discussed. The cost to society as a whole must be distinguished from the cost to the individuals who compose the society. The distinction does not mean that the one cost is in some sense more important than the other. It is made because the burden to society, which is a net loss to everyone, must be distinguished from the loss to one individual, which (the analysis will show) is offset by a gain to another individual. From the perspective of the individual, the main effect of inflation is one of redistribution—the income and wealth of society are redistributed. While this may be viewed as a cost by the individual, it is not a cost to society, for nothing is lost to the group as a whole.

A second reason for distinguishing the cost of inflation is to compare it with the analogous cost to society of unemployment, so that if society is faced with a choice between less unemployment and more inflation, it will have some basis upon which to choose.

The social cost of inflation[5]

In Chapter 2 the social usefulness of money was shown to arise because money as a medium of exchange and unit of account reduces the costs of acquiring information and making transactions. Because of its usefulness in these two roles, individuals would probably come to hold some of it as an inventory, with the amount held determined by a balancing at the margin of its productivity and its holding cost. The principal holding cost of money, it was noted, is represented by the rate at which its purchasing power is

[5] The social cost of inflation will occur even if the rate of inflation is known with perfect certainty, whereas the cost to the individual arises primarily because inflation is unanticipated. If it were fully anticipated, most of the cost to the individual could be avoided, in theory.

diminished, i.e., the rate of inflation. The higher the rate of inflation, the greater becomes the marginal cost of holding money and, consequently, the less of it individuals will hold.

When individuals hold smaller money balances, they must alter the way they arrange their transactions chains, or the way an initial bundle of commodities or labor time is converted into an ultimate bundle of goods and services. Thus, because of the increased cost of holding money, individuals move from an optimal transactions arrangement to one less optimal and less efficient. Time and effort hitherto devoted to the production of goods or to leisure will now have to be devoted to exchange.

As a practical example, one way to avoid the effect of inflation is to hold less money, and hold a larger fraction of wealth in either commodities with prices that move with the general level of prices, or in financial assets with yields that adjust to the inflation. To the extent this is accomplished, the transaction chain is lengthened, for now it involves using money to buy a real or financial asset and then converting that asset back to money before purchasing the ultimate good or service.

For business units, the escape from the burden of inflation may involve going to the bank more frequently with deposits (i.e., of converting them from demand to time and back again before purchases are made): increasing the average inventory of goods: paying employees more frequently, offering less favorable credit terms to customers, and, in general, devoting more time and attention to holding smaller money balances per unit of transactions. For households, it may mean rushing more frequently to the market to exchange money for goods, financial assets, foreign currencies, or precious metals. It may also mean an increase in barter transactions, which are more time consuming than similar monetary transactions.

Thus, for both businesses and households, the lengthened transaction chain induced by inflation causes time and energy to be diverted from the production of goods and services, or from leisure, to making exchanges. In addition, inflation encourages the maintenance of excessive inventories of producer and consumer goods. Finally, since money balances are also held as a form of insurance against unexpected contingencies, smaller real money holdings tend to reduce peace of mind, and therefore the real income of households.[6]

Economic efficiency and a variable rate of inflation

A further cost imposed upon society results not from inflation per se, but from a variable rate of inflation. Most inflations are of this variety. The rate

[6] This final argument may need some clarification. Income can be regarded as the flow of total utility to the household. Utility that arises from the holding of money may be in the form of peace of mind and the ease in making transactions. If lower real balances are held, less utility, and thus income, accrues to the household. Obviously, "income" here includes something in addition to what is counted in GNP.

is not steady but moves first faster, then slower, and so on. The cause of this variable rate of movement will be discussed later. In part, it results from attempts by the government to "do something about inflation."

As noted in most principles textbooks, among the basic problems to be solved in any society are what to produce and how to produce it (or how to use one's own resources). In many countries, including our own, these problems are solved by the price system (or market system), which serves in a largely unseen fashion to coordinate economic activity. In the process the price system resolves these problems. The essential information to be gained from the resolution of these problems through the price system concerns the structure of relative prices. That is, the price of one good relative to another, of one factor relative to another, of product prices relative to factor prices, of prices today relative to prices tomorrow, and so forth. However, information about relative prices is often transmitted through the absolute price level. When the absolute price level is stable or growing at a constant rate, changes in relative prices are easy to isolate by seller or buyer. However, when the rate of inflation is variable, it becomes increasingly difficult for the buyer and seller to disentangle a change in relative prices from a change in the absolute price level.

To clarify this difference, consider the case of a producer who experiences a 10% increase in orders in a given year. Should he respond by increasing the rate of production? He will do so only if his real rate of profit increases. He has already calculated his profit-maximizing level of output and knows that real profit will not increase if, as he raises prices in the face of expanded output, his production costs rise proportionately. In this case, the relative positions of marginal revenue and marginal cost remain unchanged. If, however, marginal revenue rises relative to marginal cost, a profit incentive to expand output is created. The producer must decide what kind of a situation confronts him.

If the increase in orders occurred in a stable price level environment, the producer could be fairly certain that a shift in relative demand had taken place. That is, demand for other goods had declined while it had risen for his product. As a consequence, when he expands output, productive factors will be available at present prices (and marginal revenue will rise relative to marginal cost). However, in an inflationary environment, the producer may be uncertain whether the increase in orders represents a shift in relative demand or is merely part of the overall rise in money demand. Depending upon his interpretation, he may alter the flow of production, the price of the product, or the employment rate.

Regardless of the individual producer's decision, the variable rate of inflation creates greater uncertainty in the minds of all. The price system is not an efficient coordinator and allocator of economic activity, and a cost is imposed upon society because of the lessened ability of the economic system to efficiently transform resources into goods, services, and leisure.

How serious are these social costs from inflation, or its variable rate? A number of economists believe that for the United States, these costs are rather small. A leading spokesman for this view is Professor James Tobin of Yale University. In his presidential address before the American Economic Association, Tobin declared:

> *According to economic theory, the ultimate social cost of anticipated inflation is the wasteful use of resources to economize holdings of currency and other noninterest-bearing means of payment. I suspect that intelligent laymen would be utterly astounded if they realized that* this *is the great evil economists are talking about. They have imagined a much more devastating cataclysm, with Vesuvius vengefully punishing the sinners below. Extra trips between savings banks and commercial banks? What an anti-climax!*[7]

There is little doubt how Tobin would vote on a tradeoff between unemployment and inflation.

For the magnitude of the inflation historically experienced by the United States, Tobin's calculations appear quite realistic. Clearly, there must be some other aspect of inflation that causes governments to tremble and some to foresee doom. This aspect of inflation is related primarily to its effect on the distribution of income and wealth among the members of the private sector, and between the private sector and the government. The redistribution among members of the private sector arises primarily because inflation is unanticipated, whereas redistributions between the private sector and the government occur whether inflation is anticipated or not.

Let us consider first the redistribution from the private sector to the government.

Inflation and tax revenue

Inflation serves to increase the real tax revenue of the government by enabling it to extract a higher proportion of real income in the form of income taxes and to expropriate a portion of the wealth of society held in the form of money.

Inflation and the progressive income tax In the United States, as elsewhere, the federal income tax rate structure is generally progressive, i.e., the higher one's income, the greater is the fraction of that income paid to the government in taxes. Thus, when the amount of dollars earned by the

[7] James Tobin, "Inflation and Unemployment," *American Economic Review,* Vol. 62, No. 1 (Mar. 1972): 15. To calculate the social costs, Tobin continues:

> [W]ith the means of payment-currency plus demand deposits—equal currently to 20% of GNP, an extra percentage point of anticipated inflation embodied in nominal interest rates produces in principal a social cost of 2/10 of 1% of GNP per year. This is an outside estimate. An unknown, but substantial, share of the stock of money belongs to holders who are not trying to economize cash balances and are not near any margin where they would be induced to spend resources for this purpose.

typical individual rises, these additional dollars are taxed at higher percentage rates. Suppose that prices rise by 20% per year, as do the amount of dollars earned by the typical wage earner. The real wage of the individual would be preserved, but under a system of progressive taxes his or her real take-home pay would decline. To see this, take any two years and assume that in year 1 income is $10,000, while in year 2 it is $12,000, and that the tax rate is 20% of the first $10,000 of income and 40% for the next $2,000. In year 1 take-home pay is $8,000, while in year 2 it is $9,200 (or $10,000 × .8 plus $2,000 × .6). However, since prices have risen 20%, the $9,200 will only buy $7,667 in terms of the prices in year 1. The progressive income tax has therefore decreased the real income of the typical taxpayer. This burden is likely to become especially severe if the individual's income in year 1 is so low as to escape taxation altogether. In year 2 inflation serves to push it into the taxable range, and taxation operates to reduce his real income to a very impoverished level. This type of income redistribution can be minimized by imposing income taxes on real rather than nominal income.

Inflation as a tax on money wealth Inflation was defined at the beginning of this chapter as a sustained rise in the general level of prices. It could alternatively be defined as a sustained fall in the purchasing power of money. It is the wealth of society held in a money form that is usually diminished by inflation. This lost purchasing power is not a net loss to society, for it is transferred to those who issue money.

To simplify the explanation, assume initially that the government issues all the money to pay for its expenditures, and that the economy is operating at full employment. In this situation, if government expenditures rise, the money supply must also rise, and since the economy is at full employment, the price level will rise in proportion to the increase in money issue.

If initially the price level is stable, the public will hold, say, $1,000 in real-money balances. The government now issues $100 in new notes to pay for its increased expenditures. The money supply has now risen by 10% and the price level will rise by 10% from an initial level of 1.0 to 1.1. The new nominal money supply of $1,100 now has a real value of only $1,000 $\left(\frac{M}{P} = \frac{\$1{,}100}{1.1}\right)$. Thus, when the government issued $100 in new notes to pay for its expenditures, the rise in the price level served to decrease the purchasing power of the existing money supply of $1,000 by exactly $100. The inflationary issue of new money served to reduce by 10% the value of the previously existing wealth of society held in the form of money, thereby providing the government with resources equal to $100. The effect of this issue of new notes is identical to that of a situation where the government sends out tax collectors to seize 10% of the existing money supply.

Furthermore, the rise in the price level may well prompt the public to desire to hold smaller real-money balances. If this choice is made, the public will seek to get rid of its undesired dollars by spending them. Since real output cannot expand, the price level merely rises in proportion to the increased spending, and the same nominal dollars are now fewer real dollars.

Since the price level has risen, the government must now issue more nominal dollars if it desires to command the same amount of real resources that it previously obtained at a lower price level. Of course, this action pushes the price level still higher and takes away from the public a larger proportion of its money wealth. The public may respond by desiring to hold still fewer real dollars. Then spending rises, and the price level rises still higher, and so on as the process becomes repetitive. An important question is, will the monetary system ultimately break down? That is, will the public come ultimately to abandon the use of money and arrange their transactions chains by barter or resort to using foreign currencies? A breakdown may occur if the government attempts to use too many resources financed through the issue of money. What, then, determines the maximum amount of revenue that the government can raise through money issue? The answer to this question is analogous to the answer to the question concerning what price should be charged by a seller who is interested in maximizing his sales revenue.

When a seller has sales maximization as his goal, he will reduce the price of his product so long as the lowered price generates a positive increase in marginal revenue. He will cease reducing the price when the final increase in marginal revenue is zero. At this price, total revenue will be maximized. It will be recalled from microeconomic principles that the point on the demand schedule corresponding to zero marginal revenue occurs when the demand schedule is unit elastic. This is shown in Figure 12:1.

Suppose now that Figure 12:1 is regarded as a demand schedule for real-money balances. The price axis in this case will measure the cost of holding money (the anticipated rate of inflation). If the government wishes to maximize its command over real resources (revenue) from inflation, it should set its rate of money issue at that rate designed to produce the anticipated rate of inflation designated as $P_{REV.\ MAX.}$ in Figure 12:1. If its rate of money issue produces a higher rate of anticipated inflation, its revenue will be below the maximum possible rate, whereas if it produces a lower anticipated rate, it will forego revenue.

The usual conditions facing governments that resort to financing expenditures by money issue are precisely those that lead to hyperinflation. The discussion concerning revenue that accrues through inflationary issues of money can become more complicated when banks are allowed to issue money in addition to that issued by the government. The banks then share in the revenue arising from money creation. This situation can be seen when it is realized that banks create money by acquiring assets. The income that accrues to banks is then equal to the product of the interest rate and the amount of assets acquired. Since the assets acquired are equal to the

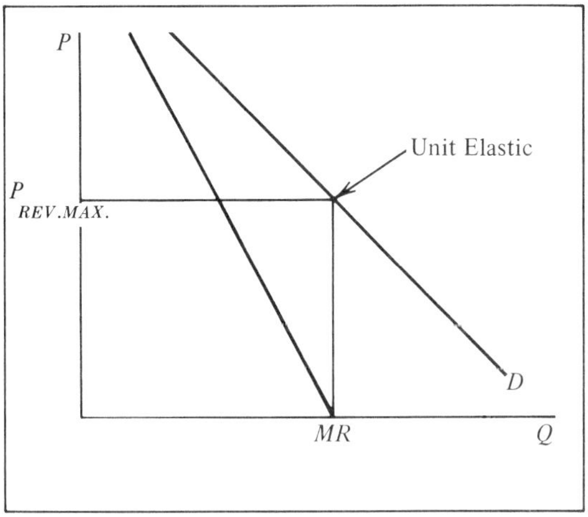

FIGURE 12:1
Price that maximizes total revenue

deposits created, the revenue accruing to banks per annum is equal to $i \times {}^{D}D$. If we take the case where banks renew the loans forever, the present value of it revenue is equal to $\frac{i \times \Delta D}{i}$, which is simply equal to the increase in its deposits or ΔD.

This analysis assumes that the rate of interest, i, fully adjusts to the inflation rate. If it does not, the banks then share their revenue with their customers by granting them loans at subsidized interest rates, i.e., at interest rates that do not reflect the inflation.

Redistributions among the private sector

The major reason for redistributions of income and wealth among individuals during an inflationary period is that the rate of inflation is incorrectly anticipated. However, redistribution can occur even if inflation becomes perfectly anticipated—if, at the time contracts were entered into, the inflation rate was not anticipated. The principal income redistribution is between wage earner and profit recipient; the wealth redistribution is between debtor and creditor.

Income redistribution The conventional wisdom among economists is that since wages are often fixed by contract while profits represent a residual claim on revenue, inflation, by catching workers unprepared, causes prices and profits to rise relative to wages. *Unanticipated* inflation thus serves to transfer income from wage earners to profit recipients.

There are not many data in support of the conventional wisdom. Early empirical work by Wesley C. Mitchell[8] on the Greenback era in post–Civil War United States, that of Earl Hamilton[9] on sixteenth- and seventeenth-century Europe, and that of Alvin Hansen[10] on the post–World War I inflation in the United States appeared to lend strong support to this hypothesis. Hamilton's work was even cited by Keynes in support of his view that "profit inflation" was a great stimulus to economic growth.

Work of a more recent vintage, however, has seriously undermined the wage-lag hypothesis. Studies by Alchian and Kessel,[11] Kessel and Alchian,[12] and Felix[13] have shown that this earlier work made insufficient allowances for the influence of factors other than inflation on the movement of wages over time. Some of these earlier conclusions were particularly sensitive to the time period concerned (for example, Alchian and Kessel show that the supposed 30% decline in real wages in Spain from 1520 to 1600 reported by Hamilton can be turned into a 4% *rise* if one uses as dates of reference 1522–1602). Later work using data from the post–World War II period in the United States by Bach and Ando,[14] Bach and Stephenson,[15] Conard,[16] and Phelps[17] has produced such mixed results that the only safe conclusion about the wage-lag hypothesis is that it may have occurred from time to time, but it certainly has not been universal.

Wealth redistribution The wealth redistribution that occurs during inflation is one from creditor to debtor or from lender to borrower. It occurs, theoretically, because interest rates do not adjust to compensate fully for inflation. This failure to adjust fully is usually ascribed to a failure to anticipate inflation correctly (i.e., underanticipation), or to the liquidity

[8] W.C. Mitchell, *A History of Greenbacks* (Chicago: University of Chicago Press, 1903).

[9] E. J. Hamilton, "American Treasure and the Rise of Capitalism (1500–1700)," *Economica* 9 (Nov. 1929): 338–57; *American Treasure and the Price Revolution in Spain, 1501–1650* (Cambridge, Mass.: Harvard University Press, 1934); *Money, Prices, and Wages in Valencia, Aragon, and Navarre, 1351–1500* (Cambridge, Mass.: Harvard University Press, 1936).

[10] Alvin Hansen, "Factors Affecting the Trend in Real Wages," *American Economic Review*, Vol. 15, No. 1 (1925): 27–42.

[11] A. A. Alchian and R. A. Kessell, "The Meaning and Validity of the Inflation-Induced Lag of Wages Behind Prices," *American Economic Review*, Vol. 50, No. 1 (Mar. 1960): 43–66.

[12] R. A. Kessell and A. A. Alchian, "Redistribution of Wealth through Inflation," *Science*, No. 130 (Sept. 1959): 535–9.

[13] D. Felix, "Profit Inflation and Industrial Growth: The Historic Record and Contemporary Analogies," *Quarterly Journal of Economics*, Vol. 70 (Aug. 1956): 441–63.

[14] G. L. Bach and A. Ando, "The Redistributional Effects of Inflation," *Review of Economics and Statistics*, Vol. 34, No. 1 (Feb. 1957): 1–13.

[15] G. L. Bach and J. B. Stephenson, "Inflation and the Redistribution of Wealth," *Review of Economics and Statistics*, Vol. 61, No. 1 (Feb. 1974): 1–13.

[16] J. W. Conard,"The Causes and Consequences of Inflation," in *Commission on Money and Credit* (Englewood Cliffs, New Jersey: Prentice-Hall, 1964).

[17] E. S. Phelps, "Inflation in a Theory of Public Finance," *Swedish Journal of Economics*, Vol. 75 (1973): 67–82.

effects of new-money creation by banks, which serves to depress interest rates.

It should also be noted that even if the inflation rate is correctly anticipated when loans are made, but then changes in subsequent years because of some random influence, the lender may still lose and the borrower gain.

Attempts have been made to trace the net transfer of wealth induced by inflation. Such efforts have generally been handicapped by the fact that the government is one of the main borrowers. The underadjustment of interest rates means that the government gains at the expense of those who lend to it. However, the government consists of the individuals who compose the society. So if inflation eases the government's debt burden, it eases the tax burden of those who must service that debt, i.e., they need work fewer hours to pay off the debt.

If the wealthy in society lend to the government, they lose; if they also pay the majority of the taxes, inflation eases their burden—and they gain. Whether on balance they gain or lose depends on the degree to which bond ownership corresponds with tax liabilities.

As with the question of the effects of inflation on wage earners and profit recipients, the empirical evidence as to the degree of the gain and loss through wealth redistributions is incomplete. It shows that interest rates do not fully adjust to reflect inflation, but exactly who gains and who loses is complicated by the fact that the government is a heavy borrower, and is both a debtor and creditor. In a world where definiteness is a virtue, these conclusions must surely be regarded as unsatisfactory.

Transfers of income and wealth are classified by economists as redistributions, and are not considered burdens or losses for society. Nevertheless, they should not be regarded as something desirable, for they contain the seeds of social conflict. Those who have gained naturally attribute it to their superior wisdom, insight, or virtue, whereas those who have lost attribute it to inflation and believe that something should be done to redress the balance. It is inflation's capacity to cause social divisiveness and to polarize society that makes it a concern of governments.

Inflation and economic efficiency

Unanticipated inflation can also lead to a misallocation of economic resources because it gives rise to mistaken estimates of changes in relative prices. For example, individuals may mistake a rise in money wages for a rise in the real wage and offer more labor time; sellers may fail to anticipate future price increases in their productive inputs and, as a result, contract to supply their output at too low a price. Such errors could, of course, be made even if the price level were stable, but they are more likely to occur when the general level of prices is also rising. These errors are also more costly to avoid when the price level is rising—for instance, new price lists or catalogs must be issued more frequently, or goods must be sold under more uncertain conditions (e.g., buyers must pay the price of the merchandise when it is delivered rather than when it is ordered). Thus, unanticipated inflation is likely to increase the possibility of resource misallocation.

Inflation and changes in relative prices

The social discontent associated with inflation is exacerbated by the fact that changes in relative prices, and thus the distribution of income, are often blamed on inflation when, in fact, other nonmonetary factors are responsible for them, e.g., shifts in supply-and-demand conditions.

An examination of the consumer price index for 1967–1975 shows that changes in relative prices occurred over this period. While food prices increased 75.4%, rents only rose 37.3%, transportation services 52.7%, and medical care 79.1%. The change in all items was 61.2%. What caused these changes in relative prices? Most probably changes in conditions of supply and demand, although one should not rule out the possibility that all these prices may ultimately rise proportionately, except that some may rise faster over a given period than others. Naturally, those sellers whose prices have lagged behind the general average are apt to blame their lack of good fortune on inflation.

Summary—costs of inflation

Thus far, our discussion has been concerned with the social loss from inflation, and its ability to redistribute income and wealth. The social cost was measured by the additional time and effort that must be devoted to arranging less efficient means of transactions, and by the loss of peace and security that comes from holding less wealth in a money form.

The income and wealth redistributions occur between the public and private sectors, and among the members of the private sector. While some of the redistributions are a consequence of unanticipated inflation, others can arise even if the rate of inflation is known with certainty (e.g., that from the private sector to the government). It is the redistributional aspects of inflation that are most likely to be of concern to the government and the public, largely because they are the source of social divisiveness.

The causes of inflation

It is natural to associate inflation with money, for inflation can only occur in a society that uses money. So long as a unit of account is absent, a society can only have relative prices. Good A can be expressed in terms of goods B, C, D, etc. Similarly, good B can be expressed in terms of A, C, D, etc., and so on for all the goods traded in the society. In a system of relative prices it is not possible for the price of all goods to advance simultaneously. A can rise relative to B, C, D, B can advance relative to D, but fall in terms of A and C. The price of all goods can advance only if some one thing is used as a unit of account. When A, B, C, D, etc. are expressed in terms of dollars, each of their respective prices can rise or, alternatively, the price of money (its purchasing power) can be said to fall. Thus, the possibility of inflation depends on the existence of money, and there are a number of economists who believe that it depends *only* on money. Other economists reject this position. They believe that since supply as well as demand determines prices, some inflations are cost induced. That is, production cost increases induced by monopolies, oil sheiks, trade unions, and other factors play a prominent role in explaining the inflationary cycle. These economists therefore prefer, for analytical purposes, to distinguish between *demand–pull* and *cost–push* inflations.

We shall first examine the proposition that inflation is strictly a monetary phenomenon. The proponents of this view are popularly known as Monetarists.

The monetarist view

One of the leading Monetarists, Professor Milton Friedman, has declared:

> *Inflation is always and everywhere a monetary phenomenon resulting from and accompanied by a rise in the quantity of money relative to output. This generalization is not an arithmetical proposition or a truism, and it does not require a rigid relation between the rate of rise in prices and in the quantity of money. The precise rate at which prices rise for a given rate of rise in the quantity of money depends on such factors as past price behavior, current changes in the structure of labor and product markets, and fiscal policy. The monetary character of inflation . . . is an empirical generalization backed by a wide range of evidence. . . . It follows that the only effective way to stop inflation is to restrain the rate of growth of the quantity of money.*[18]

This statement not only contains Professor Friedman's analysis of the cause of inflation, it also suggests its cure. Note especially his claim that monopoly (either of auto companies, public utilities, or trade unions) does not cause inflation and his failure to recommend wage and price controls as a method of cure.

To understand Friedman's conclusions fully requires some detailed knowledge of his analytical framework. In a somewhat simplified version Friedman uses what we called earlier the Equation of Exchange. This states the truism that total money spending (the product of the money supply, M, and its turnover rate or velocity, V), MV, is equal to the market price of all

[18] Milton Friedman, "What Price Guideposts," in *Guidelines: Formal Controls of the Marketplace,* ed. R. Z. Aliber and G. P. Schultz (Chicago: University of Chicago Press, 1966), p. 18.

goods and services sold (the product of a suitable price index, P, and real output, Y), PY. Thus, $MV = PY$.

Individuals such as Friedman believe that the value of real output, Y, and its growth over time depend upon the rate of accumulation of capital, the supply of labor, the degree to which the market structure of the economy is characterized by competition or monopoly, the degree of technological innovation, and so on.

This list of factors determining real output does not include the growth in the supply of money. However, as will be shown later, the growth rate of the money supply can induce temporary changes in both real output, Y, and the turnover rate or velocity of money, V. Because change in the growth rate of the money supply can accomplish these temporary changes, Friedman does not believe there is a rigid relationship between the money supply, M, and the price level, P. However, when one observes the longer span of time, these temporary changes in Y and V should have canceled out and the proportionate relationship between M and P should then be evident.

The Monetarists also deny that cost–push is the cause of inflation. That is, they dispute the commonly held view that large corporations, trade unions, public utilities, oil sheiks, and other powerful groups can cause inflation. The popularity of cost–push as a cause of inflation, they believe derives from the deceptiveness of appearance and the desire of governmental authorities to shift the blame for inflation to someone else.[19] They rightly claim that the view that monopolies, trade unions, and other powerful

[19] Monetarists often include in their discussions of the popular view of cost–push inflations an ingenious little example from an elementary textbook that shows that a demand-induced rise in prices comes to be viewed as cost–push in nature.

> Pretend that for some reason people's desire for meat increases. . . . Housewives reveal an increased demand by buying more meat than formerly at the current prices in the meat markets. . . . [T]he increased demand takes it toll of inventories. . . . [The] butcher will buy more meat than usual the next day in order to restore his inventory from its abnormally low level. . . . Just as butchers use inventories, so packers . . . also rely on inventories. . . . [A]ssume that the first day's change in demand was within that inventory limit and, therefore, was met without a price increase.
>
> Packers restore inventories by instructing their cattle buyers . . . to buy more cattle than usual. But with all the packers restoring their inventories in this manner, the number of cattle available for sale each day are inadequate to meet the increased total demand *at the old price*. . . .
>
> [T]he buyers will begin to raise their offers . . . until the price rises to the point where the packers will not want to buy more meat . . . than is available from the cattlemen. . . .
>
> [T]he packers experience *a rise in costs* . . . [so] the packers must charge a higher price to butchers if they are to continue as profitable meat packers. . . . The butchers, in turn, post higher prices to the housewives. When housewives complain about the higher price, the butcher in all innocence, honesty, and correctness says that it isn't his fault. The cost of meat has gone up. . . . And the packers can honestly say the same thing.

To almost all participants, therefore, a rise in price produced by excess demand appears to take the form of a rise in costs that enforces a higher price. See Armen A. Alchian and William R. Allen, *University Economics* (Belmont, Cal.: Wadsworth Publishing Co., 1964), pp. 106–7.

groups cause inflation results from an elementary confusion between *high* prices and *rising* prices and is inconsistent with the orthodox theory of monopoly behavior. According to orthodox theory, a monopolist sets a relative price for his product that maximizes profits in *real* terms. The monopolist then maintains that *real* price by adjusting *nominal* price to allow for inflation. Thus, given the degree of monopoly power possessed by the monopolist, inflation is no incentive for him to raise prices other than to keep pace or catch up with inflation. Since real prices are already established at profit-maximizing levels, any further upward adjustments would reduce profits. On the other hand, if prices are being raised by the monopolist to exploit a hitherto unexploited monopoly potential, the question arises as to why those gains were forgone in the past. In either case, rising real prices by a monopolist would be inconsistent with rational behavior. Thus, for those who believe in orthodox theory, the presence of monopoly is not the cause of inflation.

This conclusion should be qualified to allow for certain special circumstances. First, if over time the industrial structure becomes increasingly monopolized or oligopolized, it could lead to rising prices. Thus, Monetarists claim that much of the rise in prices during the 1930s was due to New Deal legislation (e.g., the Agriculture Adjustment Act, the National Industrial Recovery Act, the Fair Labor Standards Act, the Waggoner Act) that sanctioned and encouraged the growth of monopolistic elements in the U.S. economy.

Second, the growth of monopolistic elements may evoke a rise in the money supply. Consider, for example, a situation in which a competitive market structure becomes monopolized. Output will be reduced and prices will rise. The reduction of output will, however, lead to a corresponding reduction in the employment of labor, i.e., unemployment will rise. If the government does nothing, over time this unemployment will cause wages, costs, and prices to fall in other industries, as the unemployed workers become absorbed back into the working force. Once the transition period is over, unless V or Y has been affected, P must be the same as it was before the formation of the monopoly—only relative prices will have changed. If the government responds to the rise in unemployment caused by the formation of the monopoly by increasing aggregate money demand, MV, the price level increase would have to be permanent to reduce it.

Finally, the effect on the domestic price level of an action such as the huge price increases of the OPEC oil cartel is, in the Monetarist view, similar to that produced by the formation of a domestic monopoly. That is, the level of output will fall initially and the price level will rise. However, as relative factor prices adjust (real wages fall) over time, output will once again rise; and if money growth is held constant, the price level will fall to its long run trend. Ultimately, only relative prices will change—oil will then be relatively more expensive.

In conclusion, for the Monetarists, inflation is always a monetary phenomenon set in motion by a rise in the money stock or its growth rate relative to the growth rate of real output. Consequently, the cure for inflation is a reduction of the growth rate of the money stock. Attempts to control inflation with wage and price controls are regarded as positively harmful. This is because, in the Monetarist view, since the supply of money governs the rate of increase in the price level, the only effect of wage and price controls is to suppress inflation, not to cure it. The suppression leads ultimately to disequilibrium conditions (i.e., a divergence between supply and demand) in individual markets. Disequilibrium leads ultimately to some means of rationing such as by chance, favoritism, or bribery; it induces individuals to spend much time and effort avoiding the controls; it causes the government to increase the size of its bureaucracy and its invasion of individual freedom; and it works to destroy the social cohesiveness of society as individuals seeking their own interest are led to become violators of the law.

The Keynesian view

While few Keynesian economists would disagree with the proposition that *some* inflations can be attributed to a rapid growth of the supply of money relative to real output, the Keynesian analysis of inflation tends strongly to abstract from the role of money as the cause. The Keynesians have done much to popularize the distinction between demand-induced and cost-induced inflations, and to curb the latter, they have urged the adoption of wage and price guidelines or, as these have been called in more recent years, "incomes policy."

While a presentation of all the Keynesian models of inflation is a formidable task, several will be analyzed in an effort to convey the flavor of this school's approach to the problem.

Demand–pull inflation Shortly after the *General Theory* appeared, Keynes himself showed how its analytical apparatus could be applied to the problem of inflation.

In November 1939, just after Britain entered World War II, Keynes published three articles in the London *Times* under the title "How to Pay for the War." In general outlines the approach to inflation set forth in these articles is quite similar to the Monetarist approach. Keynes directs attention to the upward pull on prices exercised by aggregate demand as the cause of inflation. However, he differs notably from the Monetarists in directing attention not to the supply of money, but to the spending flow of total expenditures. Indeed, the only way the stock of money enters this analysis is through its influence on interest-sensitive expenditures, and perhaps through the influence of real-money balances on spending. In sum, the money supply is relegated to a very minor role as a cause of inflation.

Keynes's work drew attention to the so-called *inflationary gap,* which occurs when the sum of the investment demand by the private sector and the government for goods and services ($\bar{I}$) exceeds the supply made available through private saving and taxation ($\bar{S}$) at the existing level of commodity prices. The inflationary gap is shown in Figure 12:2.

The diagram has one intriguing feature. It implies that one and only one income level measures full employment. Before that level of income is reached, the price level is stable, whereas after that point, the price level will rise without limit.

Keynes realized that a mere rise in the price level would not close the inflationary gap, for excess demand in the commodity market is matched by excess demand in the labor market. Thus, both commodity prices and wages would rise in an effort to restore equilibrium and the gap would remain open so long as expenditures exceeded output at full employment. Ultimately, the rise in the price level would close the inflationary gap through various means. First, with a progressive tax structure, the real take-home pay of labor would diminish, decreasing consumption and perhaps investment. Second, the rise in the price level would decrease the real value of the money supply, forcing market interest rates to rise and interest-sensitive expenditures to fall. Finally, inflation could be redistributing income from individuals with a low marginal propensity to save (wage earners) to those with a higher marginal propensity to save (profit recipients), thus increasing total saving. How long and to what heights the price level would rise before equilibrium was restored remains unspecified.

Rather than wait for inflation to close the gap, fiscal policy could be used to increase taxes and reduce expenditures, and monetary policy could be directed toward decreasing the money supply or its growth rate. The Keynesian preference, revealed over time, was to rely on fiscal policy to accomplish the task, since it supposedly exerted a direct impact on expenditures, whereas monetary policy operated indirectly through interest rates.

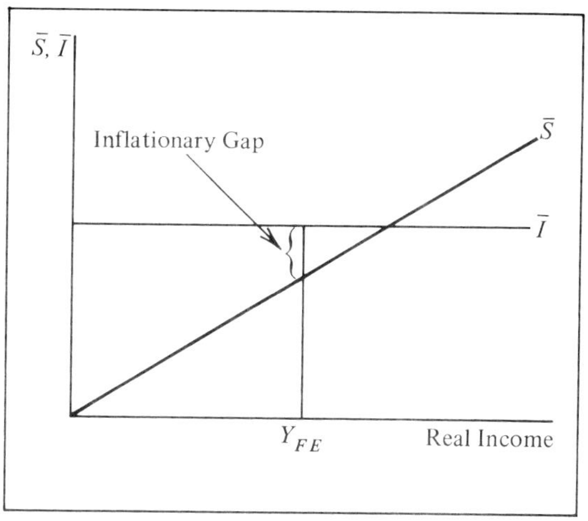

FIGURE 12:2
The inflationary gap

This concentration by Keynesians on the flow of desired expenditures as the cause of the pull of demand on the price level leads to the conclusion that a society can have nonmonetary inflations; their cause must obviously be too high a level of $C + I + G$. The only consequence of the behavior of the money supply is as a factor determining the interest rate. If C, I, or G is insensitive to interest rate changes, money would play no role in inflation. Yet, the history of inflations the world over stands as a testament to the opposite conclusion—they are inevitably *associated* with a growth rate of the money supply above its long-run trend.

Cost–push inflation In the United States Keynesian economists as a group have been the leading proponents of cost–push explanations of inflation. Perhaps this is because in the Keynesian model the price level depends upon per unit labor costs plus a markup for profit. Such a theory of price level determination draws immediate attention to the wage rate or the rate of profit as a price-determining factor.

Regardless of the origin of this view of inflation, Keynesians are fond of talking about vast sectors of the market in which "administered prices prevail." In the words of John Kenneth Galbraith, in vast sectors of the U.S. economy firms and trade unions have "power over prices—the plenary power to set them within a considerable range. . . ." Apparently, any price that is not set by a continuous bid-and-ask auction process is administered—which means most prices. That this means that business firms and trade unions have the power to set prices in complete neglect of supply-and-demand conditions is doubtful.

In the late 1950s Keynesian economists became convinced that cost–push was responsible for the rise in the price level that occurred in an environment they believed was not characterized by full employment. Since that time they have argued for wage and price guidelines.[20] Such guidelines were popular when Walter Heller was chairman of the Council of Economic Advisers (1961–1965).

In a similar vein the Keynesians have argued that U.S. inflation during the 1973–1980 period can be attributed to special circumstances arising from the OPEC oil cartel, the precariously low level reached by world food production,[21] and the effect of rising interest rates.

[20] In retrospect, the rise in the price level in the late 1950s seems insignificant. Measured by the consumer price index, the rate of change was 3.6% in 1957: 2.7% in 1958, .8% in 1959, and 1.6% in 1960. The respective unemployment rates were 4.3%, 6.8%, 5.5%, and 5.5%. Measured against a full-employment rate of unemployment of 4%, these rates of unemployment were thought to be conducive to falling or constant rather than rising prices.

[21] See, for example, D. E. Hathaway, "Food Prices and Inflation," *Brooking Papers on Economic Activity* 1 (1974): 63–109, and W. Nordhaus and J. Shoven, "Inflation 1973: The Year of Infamy," *Challenge* (May–June 1974): 14–23. Rising interest rates will, indeed, push up the consumer price index because they form the major component of housing costs. For the Monetarists this results in somewhat of a paradox—tight money which initially leads to rising interest rates increases the rate of inflation whereas easy money initially decreases the rate of inflation!

Demand–pull and cost–push distinguished Whether inflation results from excess demand pulling up the price level or rising costs of production pushing it up, the price level still rises. Quite clearly, one ought to know what is making the price level rise in order to prepare an appropriate stabilization program. Thus, Keynesian economists attempted early to devise tests to distinguish the two types of inflation. In the demand–pull type, rising prices and *falling* unemployment are supposed to go together, for the rise in the price level results from excess demand, which can lead to some decreases in unemployment through tighter labor markets. On the other hand, if rising prices go hand in hand with *rising* unemployment, cost–push inflation is at work. This conclusion follows from the theory as to the source of cost–push: trade unions force up wages, thereby leading to a decrease in the quantity of labor demanded (a rise in unemployment) and an increase in production costs. This is translated into a rise in the price level.

In actual fact it may be difficult to disentangle whether inflation is demand–pull or cost–push, for with either type of inflation money wages will be rising. If the pressure of aggregate demand varies over time in response to policy, it could produce a situation where prices rise because of a delayed wage increase from a past period of strong demand, while unemployment rises because current demand pressure is lessened as a result of the anti-inflationary policy. This sequence will produce a period of rising prices and rising unemployment characteristic of cost–push inflation. In addition, large firms and trade unions may consider periods of strong demand the best time to exercise what market power they may have to raise wages and prices, for such increases will be more difficult to spot and easier to rationalize when other prices are rising as well.

Such is the general Keynesian line of reasoning. It emphasizes two types of inflation and provides policies believed to be effective in dealing with each. For inflations diagnosed to be cost–push in nature, wage and price controls, anathema to the Monetarists, are called for.

The American experience with inflation

Figure 12:3 shows the U.S. experience with inflation over the past century.[22] A most striking conclusion from the figure is that the period subsequent to World War II looks quite different from the previous period—it is one of more or less continuous rise in prices. In fact, since 1950 the quarterly GNP deflator has *never* declined. This has prompted the observation that we now live in a new secular age of inflation.

[22] These data are subject to the general caveat that they are not all comparable. The price index, represented by the GNP deflator, is by no means homogeneous. The index for 1874–1909 is based upon estimates made by Robert Gallman; for 1910–1946, the data are estimated by Simon Kuznet, while for 1947–1979, the official Commerce Department figures are used. In addition, the composition of GNP has changed drastically over this period.

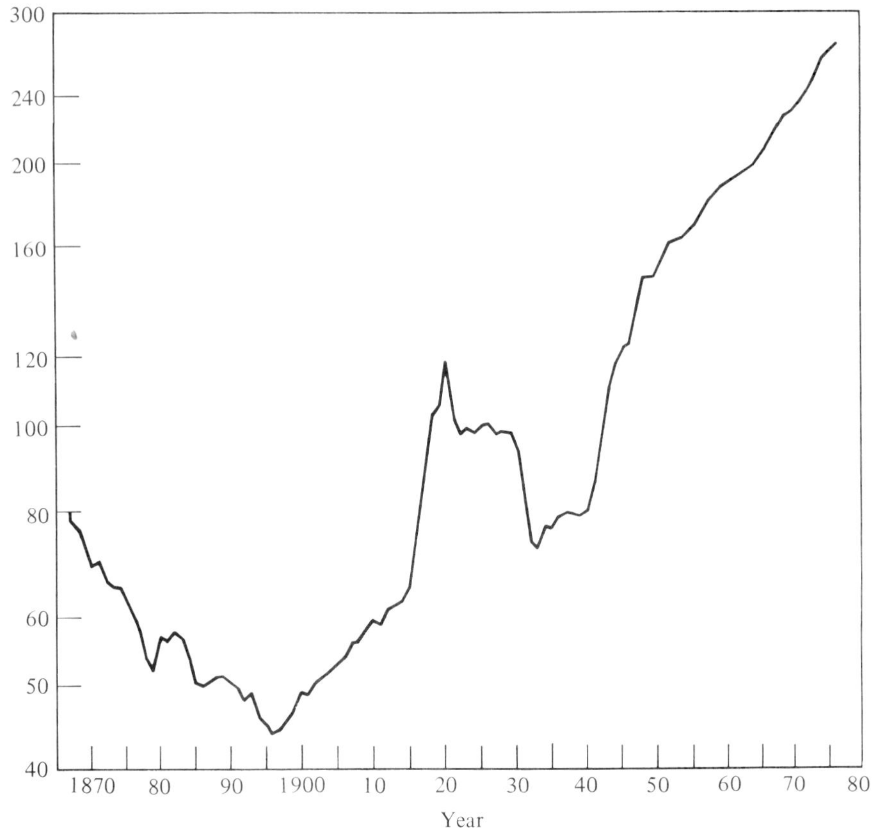

FIGURE 12:3
The price index, 1867–1979 (1929 = 100)

If the early period depicted by Figure 12:3 is examined, it is seen that for almost 30 years following the Civil War the price level declined. This caused great distress for American farmers, giving rise to the agitation for the free coinage of silver in an effort to raise prices. Beginning in 1895, the price level started what was to be a 25-year rise, culminating (at the end of World War I) in the highest level ever attained. Interestingly, on the eve of World War I the price level stood at approximately the same value it had attained at the end of the Civil War some 50 years earlier.

The decade of the 1920s was one of rough price stability. It was followed by a sharp decline as the United States slid into the Great Depression. In 1932 the price level was slightly below the value it had attained some 67 years earlier. However, from that time to the present the movement has been steadily upward. Are we now in a new era of inflation? Several factors point to a positive answer.

First, since the end of World War II the stability of the U.S. economy has improved dramatically. Not only have we had fewer recessions, but they have been less intense. If the price level is going to decline, it will most likely do so during recessions, when demand weakens and puts downward pressure on prices. If monetary and fiscal policy or some combination of fortuitous circumstances makes recessions fewer in number and less intense, there will be less opportunity for the price level to decline. Other things being constant, a more stable economy will impart an upward bias to the price level.

Second, an increasing share of GNP is accounted for by markets wherein oligopolies and monopolies are present. Without a continuous auction process for determining prices, firms in these industries will be slow to respond to demand declines with price reductions, both because they cannot predict the duration of a decline and, in the case of oligopolies, because price changes may precipitate price wars if they are interpreted by rivals as aggressive attempts to increase market share. Given such market structures, with infrequent and mild recessions, price reductions are likely to be infrequent or slow in coming.

Third, a number of legislative provisions, and also some arranged through private contract, have introduced several rigidities into the wage-and-price structure, which makes it increasingly difficult for wages and prices to fall promptly. Among these are minimum wage laws, the provision of ample unemployment benefits supplemented by private bargaining arrangements, commodity price supports, and the provisions of services by government. When these are coupled with fewer and more mild recessions, they impart a continuous inflationary bias to the economy.

Finally, for at least a decade or more starting in the early 1960s, policymakers believed that a tradeoff existed between the level of unemployment and the rate of inflation. Perhaps because of the legacy of the 1930s, they placed a higher priority on reducing unemployment than on reducing the rate of inflation. Monetary and fiscal policy was directed toward achieving their social preferences, i.e., to exploiting the tradeoff. The result was that while this view was in vogue, policy imparted an inflationary bias to the economy. Later, we will discuss the validity of the tradeoff, for few ideas have occupied such an important and controversial place in macroeconomic theory.

UNEMPLOYMENT

The social concern over involuntary unemployment is understandable. Workers and machines that could be used to augment our material well-being are allowed to stand idle. This lost output can never be recovered; it represents a net loss to society. Measured by this standard, the 25% unemployment rate reached in the depth of the Great Depression was a tragic loss to this country. The Depression also gave rise to a general Keynesian view of the unemployed as consisting of large numbers of relatively homogeneous workers who, given a sufficient increase in demand, would once again be employed.[23] Moreover, these unemployed workers could do little to increase aggregate employment by offering their services at reduced wages. The effectiveness of such actions would, as we showed earlier, depend upon the same conditions as would an increase in the nominal supply of money.

According to this popular Keynesian view, since the general cause of unemployment is deficient aggregate demand, its cure must rest on an increase in demand. This demand, it was assumed, could be brought about by an appropriate combination of monetary and fiscal policies.

The structuralist view

During the late 1950s and early 1960s a new explanation of the cause of unemployment appeared to challenge the prevailing-deficient-demand theory. This alternative explanation was inspired by our own experience with unemployment during these two decades. From the advent of the Korean War until 1958, unemployment in the United States was below 5% except for 1954. It rose to a recession high of 6.8% in 1958 and did not fall below 5% for the next seven years. Drawing upon this experience, the alternative view postulated that a continued high rate of unemployment was due to certain structural changes occurring in the U.S. economy. That is, it was caused by structural changes in the composition of labor skill availability relative to labor skill requirements. It was argued that this structural mismatch could arise in several ways, regardless of the level of aggregate demand. For example, technology can change (the automated elevator), the demand for certain products can diminish or disappear (cheap oil diminished the demand for coal), raw materials may be exhausted in a given geographic area (iron ore mining in northern Michigan and Minnesota), a factory or industry may change its location (textiles moving from New England to the South), or the proportion of different skill groups in the population may change over time. So long as the labor force can adapt to these changes, the changes should not aggravate the unemployment problem. However, people may be unwilling or reluctant to move from one geographic area to another, or their labor skills may limit their transferability to other jobs or be obsolete in general. To deal with this type of structural unemployment, it was argued, one should not attempt to manipulate aggregate demand. Such manipulations would merely lead to bottlenecks and increase the rate of inflation. Rather, correct policy should center on adapting the unem-

[23] In the United States the unemployment rate is not determined by counting the number of individuals who receive unemployment benefits. Rather, once per month 50,000 households selected according to accepted statistical sampling procedures are surveyed. The survey ascertains the number of individuals in the household who are working full or part-time, seeking employment, have been laid off or have quit their job, etc. From this monthly sample survey, a national unemployment rate is calculated.

ployed to available job openings through retraining or by paying moving allowances so that workers can go to areas where their skills are in demand.

The job-search view

More recently, several other competing theories of unemployment have emerged. One, concerned with job search, will be developed more comprehensively below as the Monetarist explanation of unemployment. In this view, unemployment is the result of voluntary choice by individuals who quit their jobs to search for another or who are entering the labor market for the first time. Because these persons lack information on the opportunities available to them in the labor market (e.g., on types of jobs, levels of wages, location of jobs, working conditions), they must search the market to acquire the necessary information on which to base their choices. In this view, high unemployment rates result not from a deficiency in demand, but from the inefficiency of the labor market in supplying the necessary information on which workers can act. To reduce the search time, and hence the average amount of time people are unemployed, will necessitate several policies. One would be an expansion of such agencies as the Federal–State Employment Service to improve the quality and speed of worker–job matches to reduce turnover rate; another would improve vocational counseling and expanded job opportunities for youths to reduce their high job turnover rates; others would provide training and job restructuring to relieve skill shortages in certain occupations and support geographic mobility to reduce pockets of high unemployment while good jobs remain unfilled elsewhere. Finally, laws could be devised to eliminate institutional barriers, such as union restrictions on entry and occupational licensing, which increase unemployment by reducing the efficiency of job searching.

A variant of the job-search explanation of unemployment attributes to social insurance and minimum wage legislation some of the high duration of unemployment. For individuals laid off from their jobs, the search for a new position in a given or new geographic area would be instituted more rapidly if the level of unemployment benefits and other related social insurance payments were not so high. Since these benefits are exempt from all taxation, they provide some individuals with an income that approaches their after-tax income from a full-time job. This high tax-free income is thought to prolong the search time for a new job, thereby prolonging the duration of individual unemployment and raising the unemployment rate. In addition, the high real level of the minimum wage is believed to contribute to the high teenage unemployment rate. It does this chiefly by discouraging employers from providing teenagers with meaningful jobs containing substantial on-the-job training content. Rather, employers are led to provide dead-end type jobs in which the employee's contribution to the income of the firm at least matches the wage paid. Because there are so many of these dead-end jobs available, teens quit frequently and remain unemployed longer than they would otherwise.[24] From the perspective of this variant of the job-search theory, public policy should seek to reduce the real minimum wage paid by the employer (either through subsidy or by maintaining its nominal level and reducing its real level through inflation) and offer some means of reducing the level of unemployment benefits and related social insurance payments (by, for example, subjecting them to taxation).

The dual labor market view

As a final interpretation of the cause of unemployment, we will consider what has been called the dual labor market hypothesis. Its interpretation of the cause of unemployment is somewhat similar to the variant of the job-search explanation explained above, except that it sees the cause of high labor turnover and unemployment in sociological and institutional practices rather than social insurance programs and minimum wage laws.

The dual labor market hypothesis views the economy as being composed, at least conceptually, of two labor markets: a primary and a secondary market. The primary sector is characterized by good jobs, high wages, satisfactory working conditions, employment stability, and prospects for advancement. In the secondary sector, on the other hand, jobs are bad, pay is low, working conditions are undesirable, layoffs are frequent, there are few chances for promotion, and job turnover is high.

Most unemployment in the primary sector is viewed by the proponents of the dual labor market hypothesis as Keynesian in nature—involuntary; and the individual so afflicted generally waits to regain his lost position, although temporary employment may be accepted elsewhere. Unemployment in the secondary sector is vastly different. It is the result of people quitting one low-paying job and going to another. This high quit rate exists because firms in the secondary sector provide jobs with little specific training content and only limited chances for advancement. Also, the wage rates for many of these jobs tend to be uniform.[25] As a result, workers find little incentive to perform adequately on the job and they adopt poor work habits—indifference or lack of interest in the job, reporting late for work or not at all, and quitting frequently. The development of poor work habits

[24] An excellent exposition of this alternative version of job search is to be found in Martin Feldstein, "The Economics of the New Unemployment," *The Public Interest,* No. 33 (Fall 1973): 3–42. As will be explained more completely below, this lack of relevant information on job opportunities, the social insurance program, and the minimum wage legislation are believed by those expounding this view both to increase over time and to maintain at a high level what they call the "natural rate of unemployment."

[25] The analysis of this group is rather silent on why the secondary sector provides only this type of job. It should also be noted in terms of our discussion to follow, that the dual labor market theory can be used as an explanation for the high level of the "natural unemployment rate." From that viewpoint, it has additional links to the job-search explanation of unemployment.

makes it increasingly difficult for the individual to move to the primary sector. Moreover, since these secondary-sector jobs provide little on-the-job training (because of the unstable work force, management has little incentive to provide such training—the benefits do not justify the training costs), even after holding many jobs, secondary-sector workers do not have the transferable skills that enhance employability in the primary sector.

One would be inclined to believe that if the wage disparity between the two sectors were very great, a substantial profit incentive would be provided to upgrade workers from the secondary sector. There are two reasons why, even with a substantial disparity, this upgrading does not occur. First, there are the so-called *restrictive practices,* which range from such legalized barriers to upgrading as licenses granted by authorities, to union practices designed to create an artificial scarcity of labor. Restrictive union practices range from regulations governing the number of apprentices to negotiated high real wages—and these cause employers to hire fewer workers than are willing to work at that high real wage rate.

The second reason for continued duality in the labor market is alleged to be discrimination. One variant, termed *statistical discrimination,* arises in an effort to simplify hiring procedures. Some employers simply assume that individuals with certain characteristics (related to age, sex, race, Vietnam war service, etc.) will have poor work habits. Thus, they reject applicants with these characteristics out of hand, which serves to increase the supply of labor to the secondary sector. This kind of discrimination is supported by both secondary-sector employers and primary-sector employees, for it lowers the wage the former must pay, and by reducing the supply of labor available to the primary sector, it raises the wages received by the latter. It also reduces the screening costs of primary-sector employers.

The other type of discrimination is the outright variety with which perhaps the majority of Americans identify the word. This variant is also based on age, sex, race, religion, and like characteristics, and produces the same economic effect as the statistical variety.

Advocates of the dual labor market thesis propose a multifold approach to its solution. An important part of this approach is the use of the legal power of the government to end discrimination. By this means, they hope that secondary-sector workers will be able to enter the primary sector, where they will acquire valuable on-the-job training and the "social acceptability" of the established group of primary-sector workers. Neither of these factors can be bought by sending someone to school. Both must be acquired on the job in the primary sector.

Second, they advocate federal programs ranging from attempts to transform secondary-sector jobs into primary-sector jobs (through such things as extending the minimum wage to cover more workers, encouraging unionization, and expanding coverage by social insurance legislation) and the promotion of a long-run, stable full-employment policy. A basic idea behind such proposals is that if one makes secondary-sector jobs costly enough for the employer, they will be transformed into primary-sector jobs. Moreover, a continued policy of full employment will encourage employers to incur the costs of training and providing career benefits to secondary-sector workers, thereby transforming them into primary-sector employees. So long as employers are convinced that the macroeconomic policies of the government are applied in a stop-and-go fashion, they will not make an effort to upgrade workers. Rather, they will tend to rely on temporary workers and subcontractors.

It should be obvious that the dual labor market hypothesis and the job-search hypothesis conflict sharply on their public policy approaches to the unemployment problem. In fact, the job-search recommendations are, in some ways, the exact opposite of those put forth by the dual labor market advocates. Still, it is not necessary to view these two theories of unemployment as competing. They may be taken, instead, as an important set of complementary perspectives on the nature of unemployment. However, to do this, public policy will have to be developed within a framework that allows policymakers to sift out the valid from the invalid assumptions and propositions of each theory.

THE INFLATION–UNEMPLOYMENT TRADEOFF

Now that we have completed our discussion of inflation and unemployment, we can investigate at some length one of the most interesting and controversial ideas in macroeconomic theory: the view that a tradeoff exists between the two such that more of one means less of the other.

The idea that there is a tradeoff between inflation and unemployment is not exactly new. As noted earlier, Irving Fisher established the relationship statistically in 1926. It appears to have been forgotten, though, and it certainly contradicts a view noted with regard to Figure 12:2: that there is one unique full-employment point, to the right of which inflation grows continuously, and to the left of which the price level is stable.

The rediscovery of the tradeoff was made in 1957 by the British economist and long-time professor at the London School of Economics, A. W. Phillips (1914–1975).

The Phillips curve

In 1958 Professor Phillips published the results of an investigation into the relationship between the rate of unemployment and the rate of change of *money* wages. Utilizing annual data for Great Britain from 1861 to 1913, Phillips's original work suggested that an apparently stable and permanent relationship existed between these two variables. The stability of the relationship was inferred from the fact that, with minor exceptions, the relationship that fits for the data for 1861–1913 also seems to fit about as well for the data covering 1913–1948 and 1948–1957.

A hypothetical Phillips relationship is shown in Figure 12:4, where each dot represents a paired relationship between the rate of change of money wages in a given year and the average unemployment rate of that year. Phillips rationalized his findings by suggesting that when labor markets are tight (unemployment low), demand pressures would lead to larger wage increases than when unemployment is high and demand slack. Thus, the rate of increase of money wages was made to depend on the level of unemployment.

The original Phillips curve was in later work transformed into a relationship between the rate of change of the price level and the rate of unemployment. This was done by assuming that prices would change whenever wages rose more rapidly than labor productivity. Thus, if the average rate of productivity growth per year were subtracted from the rate of change of wages, it should yield the rate of change of prices.

For example, if productivity rose on an average of 2% per year, a wage increase of 2% should be noninflationary, for it would leave per unit labor costs constant. Thus, the point on the original Phillips curve corresponding to a percentage wage change of 2% and, say, unemployment of 8% would be transformed into a new point corresponding to 0% inflation and 8% unemployment. Each point on the original Phillips curve could then be transformed into a point of the revised Phillips curve. Figure 12:5 represents such a transformation.

Seldom has such a piece of research so totally caught the attention and interest of economists. In a very short time Phillips's work became the centerpiece of macroeconomic theory and was used as a major policy

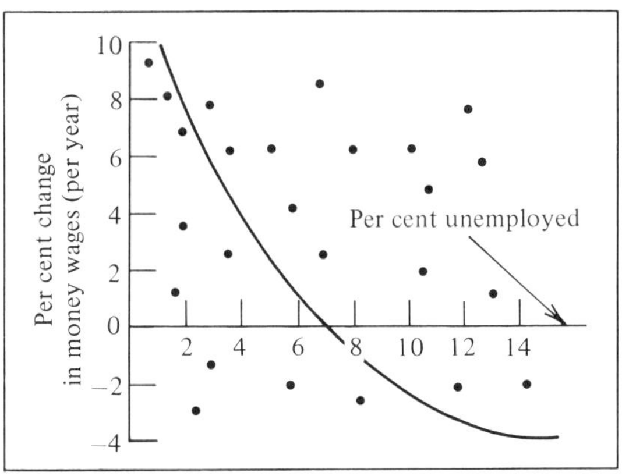

FIGURE 12:4
A hypothetical Phillips curve

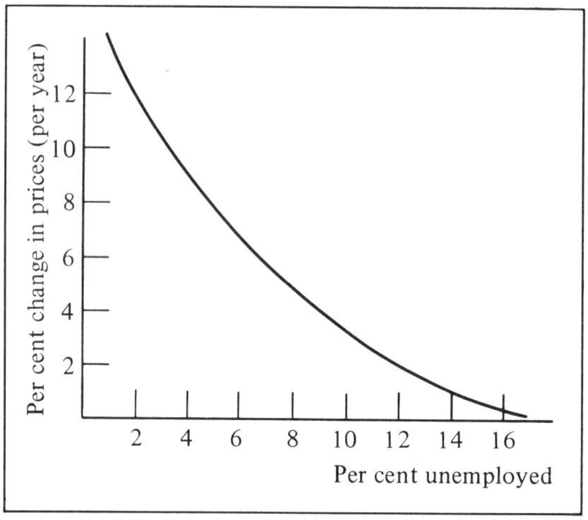

FIGURE 12:5
A transformed Phillips curve

device. It was almost a decade before any serious criticism of the theory was made. We will turn in a moment to a discussion of this criticism. However, let us see first why the Phillips curve was so readily accepted by economists.

Acceptance of the Phillips curve

The Phillips curve was generally accepted for a theoretical and a policy reason. On the theoretical level, the Keynesian model is usually thought to be one equation short, in the sense that while the price level depends on per unit labor costs and the latter depend on the wage rate, there is no equation to explain the wage rate. Rather, it is said to depend upon historical and institutional circumstances. From this viewpoint, a rigorous statement as to the cause of inflation becomes difficult and the door is open to all sorts of ad hocry. The Phillips curve was seized upon to remedy this shortcoming by providing the missing equation. Changes in prices now depended upon conditions in the labor market or, more precisely, the rate of unemployment. As demand presses upon labor markets, money wages rise, pushing up production costs and the price level.

From a policy viewpoint, the Phillips curve implied, at least for Britain, that a *permanent* decrease in unemployment could be purchased for a *permanent* increase in the rate of inflation. How long a time was meant by permanent is debatable. If not forever, at least for the foreseeable future. There is ample evidence that during the 1960s the U.S. Council of Economic Advisers also believed in this tradeoff and proposed to make use of it, even though the data suggested that the Phillips curve for this country was not

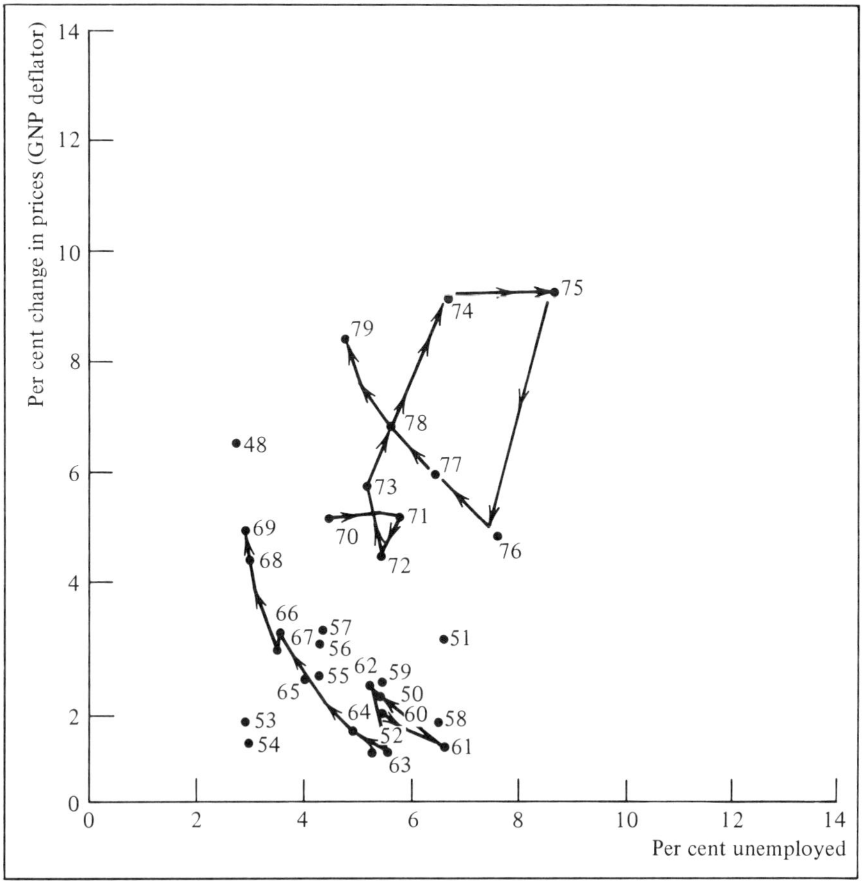

FIGURE 12:6
U.S. Phillips curve data for 1948–1979

as stable as that for Britain. Quite clearly, the data for the past decade shown in Figure 12:6 imply that the tradeoff is highly unstable.[26]

The attack on the Phillips curve

In the late 1960s a considerable theoretical attack was mounted on the Phillips relationship by the leading Monetarist Milton Friedman[27] and by an

[26] See, for example, James Tobin, *The New Economics One Decade Older* (Princeton, N.J.: Princeton University Press, 1972); Arthur Okun, *The Political Economy of Prosperity* (Washington D.C.: Brookings Institution, 1970); and the 1962 Annual Report of the *Council of Economic Advisors* (1962).

[27] Milton Friedman, "The Role of Monetary Policy," *American Economic Review*, Vol. 58, No. 1 (Mar. 1968): 1–17.

individual of Keynesian persuasion, Professor Edmund Phelps of Columbia University.[28] The crux of the problem of the Phillips curve is really part of a broader controversy that is summarized in the chapters to follow. This controversy involves the degree to which the real and monetary sectors of the economy are separate from each other. That is, can a change in the money supply cause a *permanent* change in such real variables as the level of employment? Reference to Chapter 10 shows that in orthodox Keynesian theory a change in the money supply can induce a permanent change in the level of employment. ("Permanent" in this context simply means a fairly long time period.) The Monetarists of today, as did their pre-Keynesian forebears, deny this. As the Phillips curve is plotted in its original form, it suggests a permanent relationship between a monetary variable (money wages) and a real variable (employment). Monetarists argue that this relationship is at best transitory and that no permanent relationship can exist—that is, that monetary variables cannot change real variables permanently. The correct variable influencing the long-run behavior of labor is not the *money wage* but the *real wage*.

Their view as to the transitory nature of the Phillips relationship depends on the fact that inflation accomplishes an amazing paradoxical feat—it simultaneously reduces the real wage paid by the employer and raises the real wage received by the employee! To see this, let us consider the theoretical foundations offered for the Phillips curve.

The Keynesian explanation of the Phillips curve

In order to provide a comparison for the Monetarist view of the Phillips curve, a brief review of the Keynesian approach is in order. Recall the discussion of the effect of an increase in the supply of money in Chapter 10. The increase in the money supply lowered the market rate of interest, which increased the quantity of desired investment. This increase, aided by the multiplier, led to an expansion of income, a decrease in the marginal productivity of labor, a rise in per unit labor costs, and an increase in the price level. In the labor market this sequence resulted in an outward shift in the labor demand schedule (measured as the product of the marginal physical product of labor and the price level). In terms of Figure 12:7, the labor demand schedule shifts from $D_L(P_0)$ to $D_L(P_1)$ and employment rises from N_0 to N_1. The increase in employment was accomplished by a

[28] E. S. Phelps, "Phillips Curve, Expectations of Inflation and Optimal Employment Over Time," *Economica* 34 (Aug. 1967): 254–81; and "Money Wage Dynamics and Labor Market Equilibrium," in *Micro-Economic Foundations of Employment and Inflation Theory* (New York: Norton 1970). See also the papers in this volume by A. A. Alchian, "Information, Costs, Pricing, and Resource Unemployment"; and C. Holt, "Job Search, Phillips' Wage Relation, and Union Influence: Theory and Evidence."

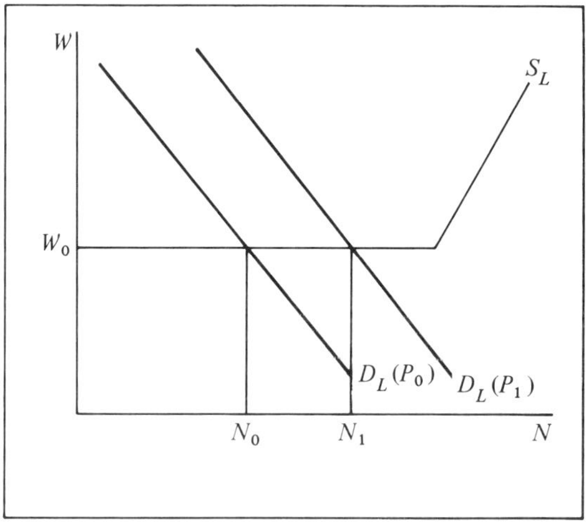

FIGURE 12:7
An increase in the demand for labor

reduction in the *real* wage. Money wages remained constant at W_0, while the price level rose from P_0 to P_1.

In terms of the Phillips curve shown as Figure 12:8, the economy moved from a point such as A to one such as B. To keep the economy's inflation rate and unemployment level at a combination such as B will, if we allow for a growth in the labor force and capital stock, necessitate a continual expansion in demand and a continuous rise in the price level such as given by point B.

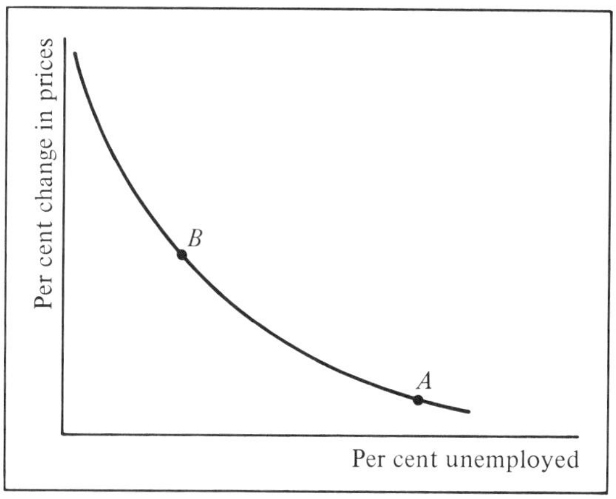

FIGURE 12:8
A movement along the Phillips curve

Note carefully, however, that labor suffers only a once-for-all decrease in its real wage in moving to B. Once at B, its real wage will increase as labor productivity rises. This follows from the method of deriving the revised Phillips curve, which says that the change in the price level plus the change in labor productivity equals the change in money wages. As long as productivity is positive, prices will rise by less than wages, and the real wage will rise over time.

The same conclusion will follow if the supply schedule of labor is allowed to be positively related to the money wage, as shown in Figure 12:9. In this case, it will simply take a larger change in the price level to produce the movement from A to B on the Phillips curve. It does not alter the conclusion that a once-for-all decrease in the real wage will be required to accomplish the movement along the Phillips curve.

The Monetarist critique The Monetarists argue that the Keynesian analysis is incomplete, and because it is, a Phillips relationship appears to emerge. The incompleteness is related to the implication that the suppliers of labor suffer from some form of *money illusion*. That is, they will supply the same quantity of labor for a lower real wage and will not react to the fall in its purchasing power.

To remedy this shortcoming and explain why a short-run Phillips curve can exist, the Monetarists draw the labor supply schedule as shown in Figure 12:9. However, the supply schedule is drawn with reference to the price level that wage earners *expect* to prevail over the term of their work contract. Thus, in Figure 12:9 we have a demand schedule for labor that responds to the *actual* price level and a supply schedule that responds to

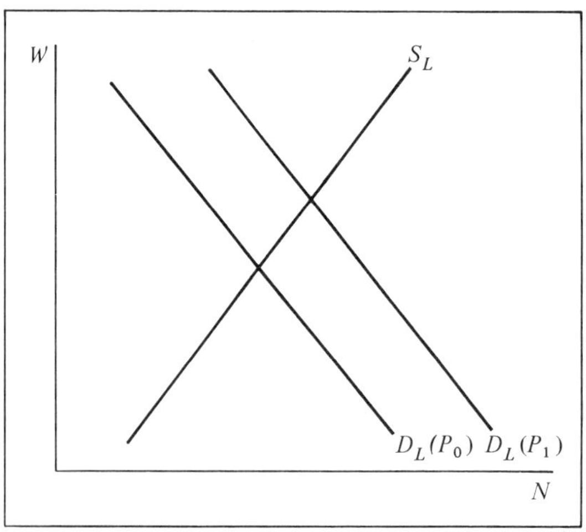

FIGURE 12:9
A positively sloped labor supply schedule

the *expected* price level. Both demand and supply depend on a real wage. The lower the real wage management must pay, the greater will be the quantity of labor demanded by management, while the larger the real wage, the greater will be the quantity of labor supplied by workers. The reason for the distinction in real wages paid by management and received by workers is the belief that the sellers of final products know better than workers the actual conditions of the market. This is not to suggest that labor is oblivious of changes in prices. As the analysis to follow will show, the sooner workers adjust to actual market conditions, the more transitory is the Phillips curve.

Before we discuss the Monetarists' position in depth we must first define their concept of labor market equilibrium, the short run, and the special characteristics of unemployment that prevail in that equilibrium. The Monetarist concept of equilibrium prevails in the labor market whenever the actual rate of inflation is equal to the rate of inflation expected by workers. Under these circumstances, there are no forces causing either the demand schedule or the supply schedule of labor to shift. The prevailing real wage for a given number of labor hours is that which management wants to pay and labor expects to receive. Hence, the labor market is in equilibrium. The short run, then, is the period of time during which the actual rate of inflation differs from the expected rate of inflation. It is therefore a period of disequilibrium in which the supply and demand schedules are likely to shift in the labor market so that the rate of unemployment changes.

Finally, when the labor market is in equilibrium, the unemployment rate that prevails is called the *natural rate* and is derived from the difference between those individuals who are working and the labor force. Whenever the natural unemployment rate prevails, it does not mean that no one ever quits his or her job. It only requires that the number of job quits be balanced by new hires so that the rate of unemployment remains constant.

To show the natural unemployment rate, Figure 12:9 must be amended to include the labor force. This is down in Figure 12:10. The demand schedule is drawn for the actual price level (P_0^A), whereas the supply schedule of labor depends on the expected price level (P_0^E). Both demand and supply depend, then, on the real wage, $\frac{W_0}{P^A}$ and $\frac{W_0}{P^E}$.

In a simplistic sense the labor force can be conceived of as the maximum amount of labor time available in the economy. As shown in Figure 12:10, it is a constant. In actuality, it is likely to depend on the real wage. It will do no harm to neglect the latter qualification. The difference, then, between the labor force, N_{LF}, and the number of people working, N_0, represents the natural level of unemployment.

The natural level of unemployment is not necessarily constant. It depends on the structural characteristics of the labor market. For example, it depends upon the age–sex mix of workers; the extent, availability, and

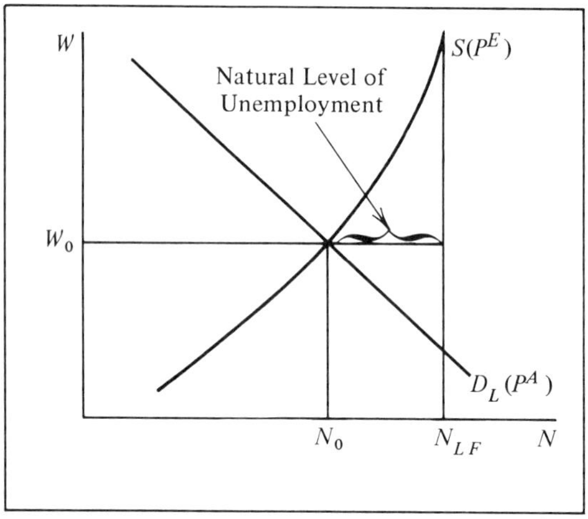

FIGURE 12:10
The natural level of unemployment

duration of unemployment benefits; the extent of monopoly or competition in the product market; and the barriers to working in various occupations such as apprenticeship rules and union cards. Since these factors are not constant, the natural unemployment level need not be constant over time.

The Monetarists would agree in general terms with the sequence of events whereby an increase in the supply of money leads ultimately to an increase in the demand for labor. In terms of Figure 12:11, the final step in

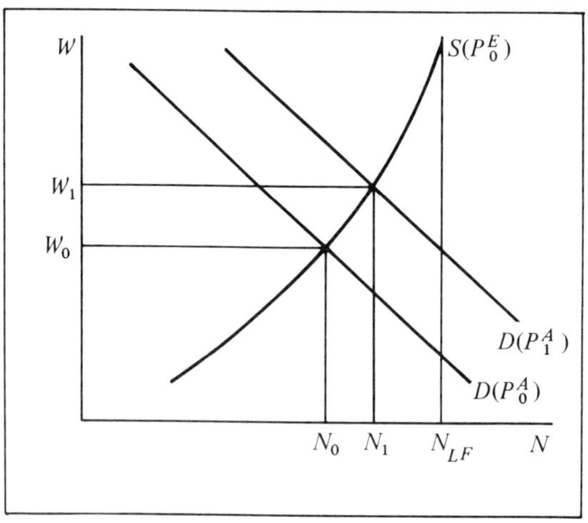

FIGURE 12:11
The effect of inflation in the labor market

the sequence appears as a shift in the demand schedule for labor from $D(P_0^A)$ to $D(P_1^A)$, where P^A is the actual level of prices while P^E is the expected price level.

Once the price level starts to rise, inflation works its magic—it lowers the real wage paid by management while it raises that received by labor. The rise in the price level from P_0^A to P_1^A increases the demand for labor (shown in Figure 12:11), which leads to a rise in money wages from W_0 to W_1. Since those who supply labor services expect prices to remain constant (P_0^E), they treat the rise in money wages from W_0 to W_1 as a rise in the real wage,

$$\frac{W_1}{P_0^E} > \frac{W_1}{P_0^E},$$

and offer more labor time. Employment rises from N_0 to N_1 and unemployment falls below its natural rate. In particular, as money wages rise, those who are unemployed and looking for a job at a wage above W_0 now take one because for them, the real wage has risen. In terms of the Phillips curve as shown in Figure 12:8, we move from A to B, just as the Keynesian approach would suggest.[29] However, this analysis is incomplete, for labor will one day discover that its price level expectations were wrong—that actual prices have risen. What, then, will its reaction be? First, it will probably revise upward its expected price level to P_1^E. When this occurs, the prevailing money wage, W_1, will be regarded as a lower real wage, W_1/P_1^E, and less labor time will be offered. The supply schedule of labor will shift to the left and the same amount of labor time will now be forthcoming only at a higher money wage. This can be seen in Figure 12:12. The amount of employment will fall from N_1 toward N_0, as money wages rise from W_1 toward W_2, and the unemployment rate will once again approach its natural level. What is the implication for the Phillips curve of this adjustment on the part of labor? In terms of the curve, the economy moves from B to a point such as C in Figure 12:13. That is, for the same actual inflation rate, unemployment is back again at its natural rate.

If the government now wishes to lower the unemployment rate, it must engineer a rise in the price level above that expected by labor. In Monetarist terminology, the government will have to *accelerate* the rate of inflation. So long as the actual rise in prices is above that expected, inflation will again work its magic by reducing the real wage paid by management while raising that which labor receives. If the government is successful, the economy will move along a new higher Phillips curve from C to D (each

[29] This analysis provides a sophisticated statement of why Friedman believes that a rise in the money supply need not produce an immediate and proportionate increase in the price level. This is because it can first produce a temporary change in real output. However, when output is again back to its original level, the rise in the money supply will produce a more or less proportionate change in the price level.

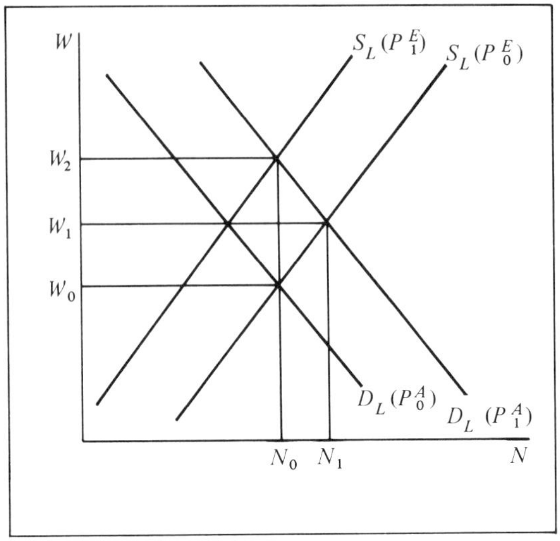

FIGURE 12:12
The supply of labor and a change in expected prices

higher Phillips curve is drawn for a given expected inflation rate). If labor catches on to the fact that its real wage has again fallen, it will demand higher money wages, which will move the unemployment rate toward E.

From analyses such as this, the Monetarists conclude: (1) the short-run Phillips curve tradeoff occurs as the Keynesians say it does; (2) there are, however, many short-run Phillips curves, each one depending on the rate of inflation expected by labor (the higher the expected rate, the higher the

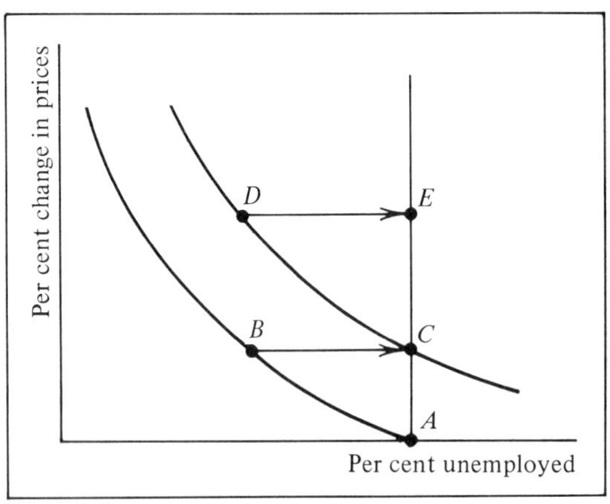

FIGURE 12:13
Changes in price expectations and the Phillips curve

Phillips curve); (3) the "true" or long-run Phillips curve is vertical, connecting such points as A, C, and E; (4) the true tradeoff given by the Phillips curve is less unemployment today versus an acceleration in the rate of inflation tomorrow; (5) an accelerating inflation rate leads ultimately to hyperinflation, the breakdown of the monetary system, and a reversion to barter methods of exchange. Finally, it should be noted that the Monetarists' explanation of the Phillips curve can be translated into their theory of the business cycle. According to their theory, an acceleration in the growth rate of the money supply leads to a rise in the price level, which, because it simultaneously causes the real wage paid by business to fall and that received by labor to rise, causes an expansion in output. The rise in real output is, however, essentially transitory, for it will fall when labor seeks an adjustment in its nominal wage to compensate for the unexpected rise in prices. The process of restoring the real wage received by labor may be protracted since each increase in wages leads to a further rise in the price level. This entire sequence is designed to show that changes in the money supply cannot permanently change real variables. It also provides an insight into the Monetarist view that demand–pull and cost–push inflation both occur as part of one integrated cycle. The initial increase in the money supply increases demand, which serves to pull up prices as well as increase output and employment (the classic symptoms of demand–pull inflation). However, when labor catches on to the rise in the price level, it asks for wage increases to compensate. These increases serve to raise production costs, which pushes up the price level and causes employment and output to fall (the classic symptoms of cost–push inflation). Currently, the simultaneous rise in both the unemployment rate and the rate of inflation (the worst of both worlds) is called *stagflation*. It is frequently alleged that a stagflation cannot be explained by economic theory, for rising unemployment implies a softening of markets, which should be a condition for falling, not rising, prices. Commentators who offer this opinion neglect the inflation-induced increase in labor costs that leads to both rising prices and rising unemployment. As explained by the Monetarists, these two phases of the business cycle are but separate parts of one integrated theory of the cycle. Clearly, in this interpretation, the cost–push phase is caused by an earlier demand–pull phase. It does not occur autonomously and does not depend upon trade unions in the labor market. It would occur even in a perfectly competitive labor market setting. It will be recalled that according to the Monetarists, trade unions may cause high prices: but not rising prices, the essence of inflation.

The analysis also suggests that the Monetarists believe that an increase in spending financed by new-money creation is the cause of inflation. Its cure is to reduce the growth rate of the money supply to parallel the growth in real output.

It should be noted that this analysis does not imply that Monetarists have no concern for unemployment. In fact, they believe that some of the unemployment that prevails when the labor market is in equilibrium is *socially desirable*. It consists of people who have quit their jobs to devote full time to seeking a new one that will pay a superior real wage.

Even though the Monetarists believe some unemployment is socially desirable, they say that efforts should be made to decrease its average duration. That is, individuals should be matched with a desirable job as quickly as possible, for otherwise socially useful output is forgone. How, then, is the natural rate of unemployment to be reduced? In a number of ways. First, information on job market opportunities should be made available to as wide an audience as possible at low cost. Such information would reduce search time and the average length of unemployment. Second, since liberal unemployment benefits tend to prolong search activity, they should be reduced. Third, the ability of trade unions to raise wages by excluding individuals from participating in certain lines of work should be curtailed. Fourth, minimum wage laws should be revised to exclude teenagers since Monetarists believe such laws are a major factor in the high unemployment rates in this group. Finally, a number of other federal laws pertaining to wages (e.g., the Davis–Bacon Act) keep them at artificially high levels and thereby contribute to unemployment. These should be eliminated.

Nowhere in this scheme does one find a role for fiscal and monetary stimulus as policies for curing unemployment. They are thought to have no permanent effect on the rate of unemployment.

Whether the Monetarists are right or wrong is, as in so many other instances, an empirical proposition. However, the estimation techniques presently available may not be able to capture adequately the adjustment of wages to expected changes in the price level. Using present techniques, the data for the United States show that wages do not adjust fully to incorporate the ongoing inflation. Since they adjust somewhat, the tradeoff between inflation and unemployment is much worse than a simple Phillips curve would suggest.[30]

The Keynesian counterclaim The Keynesian response to the Monetarist view is straightforward. It recognizes that inflationary expectations may affect the level of the wages that labor asks, and to the extent that they do, the simple Phillips curve is simplistic and unsatisfactory. The Keynesians now acknowledge that inflationary expectations may be a factor causing the Phillips curve to shift over time.

They do, however, disagree with a substantial part of the Monetarists'

[30] See, for example, the evidence in Otto Eckstein and Roger Brinner, *The Inflationary Process in the United States,* Joint Economic Committee, Congress of the United States (Washington, D.C.: U.S. Government Printing Office, 1972); R. M. Solow, *Price Expectations and the Behavior of the Price Level* (Manchester: Manchester University Press, 1969); and Alex Cukierman, "A Test of the 'No Tradeoff in the Long-Run' Hypothesis," *Econometrica,* Vol. 42, No. 6 (Nov. 1974): 1069–80.

theories on the behavior of the labor market. The implied behavior is simply not observed. First, according to Monetarist theory, the individuals who are unemployed during a state of equilibrium in the labor market (they are a part of the natural unemployment) are those who will not work at the prevailing real wage (W_0 / P_0^E). They have *quit* their jobs to devote all their time to searching out a new job that, given their expectations of future inflation, will yield them a higher real wage (one in excess of W_0 / P_0^E). A great deal of evidence on labor market behavior suggests that this is not how workers look for new jobs. Many seek a new position while remaining employed at their current position—especially academic economists. Second, a considerable amount of new job searching appears to be the consequence of dissatisfaction and frustration rather than some quest for financial improvement. Third, the Monetarist analysis suggests that the number of people quitting their jobs should move inversely with the cycle. That is, it implies that job quits should diminish when unemployment is low and wage rates are rising rapidly. Quite the opposite is true. The quit rate moves with the cycle. Nevertheless, Keynesians would acknowledge that the idea that some individuals voluntarily leave their jobs in order to seek others means that some unemployment is socially efficient.

The most telling criticism leveled at the Monetarists' view is that no one is ever laid off in their model *during an economic downturn*—everyone who becomes unemployed was induced first to quit his or job. To see this absence of layoffs, let us reverse the initial sequence. Rather than an increase in the supply of money, consider a decrease. The analysis is reversed, As output falls, the marginal physical product of labor *rises,* per unit labor costs and the price level *fall,* and the demand for labor in Figure 12:14 shifts to the left from $D(P_1^A)$ to $D(P_2^A)$. Money wages decline from W_0 to W_1. Workers now treat the fall in money wages as a fall in their real wage $\left(\frac{W_0}{P_1^E} > \frac{W_1}{P_1^E}\right)$ because each money wage is deflated by a constant expected price level, P_1^E. Rather than accept what they perceive to be a cut in their real wage, some workers withdraw their labor time from the market, i.e., they quit and search for better-paying positions, and employment falls by N_1N_2.[31]

After considering the Monetarist analysis, the Keynesian view appears to be that expectations of inflation on the part of labor reduce, but do not render invalid, the tradeoff suggested by the Phillips curve.

[31] This statement must be qualified initially in order to recognize that in any economy certain industries will be declining. They will lay off workers. In addition, new entrants will be joining the labor force, which, in periods of recession, will add to the overall unemployment. Nevertheless, how do Monetarists respond to this criticism of their model? They argue that layoffs do occur, but those laid off represent *voluntary* unemployment. They are voluntary because firms know that employees will refuse to work for lower wages and will quit. Hence, rather than use the market mechanism of cutting wages and letting workers quit, they simply lay them off. Either way, unemployment is voluntary.

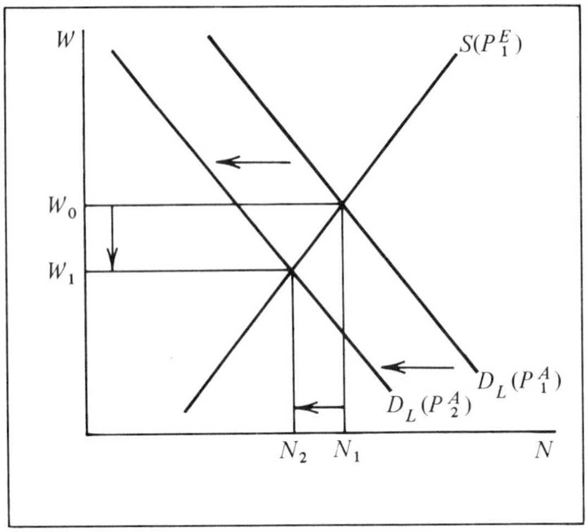

FIGURE 12:14
A fall in money wages and a rise in unemployment

Rational expectations and the Phillips curve

Recent theoretical contributions have questioned the correctness of the theory underlying both the Keynesian and earlier Monetarist rationalizations (the accelerationist view)[32] for the Phillips curve tradeoff. This critique also casts doubt on the correctness of the methods used to estimate the extent to which inflationary expectations are incorporated into wage rates. This new contribution is both simple and compelling. It is best explained by contrasting it with common features of the Keynesian and Monetarist views on the tradeoff.

In the Keynesian view, for there to be a tradeoff, workers must be fooled into working for a lower real wage. Thus, monetary and fiscal policy must be used to inflate the price level relative to money wages so that the real wage falls. In the Monetarist view, a tradeoff exists as long as the rate of inflation is accelerated and prices rise relative to money wages. Again, workers are fooled. At least in the short run they never quite catch on to what is occurring. In both views, the errors on the part of workers are said

[32] Robert Barro, "Rational Expectations and the Role of Monetary Policy," *Journal of Monetary Economics,* Vol. 2, No. 1 (Mar. 1976): 1–32; Robert E. Lucas, "Expectations and the Neutrality of Money," *Journal of Economic Theory,* Vol. 4, No. 2 (June 1972): 103–24; Thomas J. Sargent, "A Classical Macroeconomic Model for the United States," *Journal of Political Economy,* Vol. 84, No. 2 (Apr. 1976): 207–37; and Thomas J. Sargent and Neil Wallace, "Rational Expectations and the Theory of Economic Policy," *Journal of Monetary Economics,* Vol. 2, No. 2 (June 1976): 169–83. The rational expectations view is set forth in a rigorous fashion in Appendix 12A.

to be systematic, meaning that they will not average out to be zero over the longer run. Workers always lose.

In the accelerationist view, workers lose because in forecasting the future rate of inflation they use some weighted average of past rates of inflation. This method of forecasting will produce a continuous underestimate of inflation as long as the rate accelerates. Rational expectation exponents question whether expectations are formed in this fashion. They do so for several reasons. First, substantial financial gains could be made from eliminating these *systematic* errors. Second, individuals have available to them a great deal of information drawn from economic theory and supported by empirical evidence on how inflation is actually generated. Why shouldn't individuals use all of this information in forming their expectations? Rational expectations exponents believe they do and that they act accordingly. Thus, through one device or another, market participants, be they workers, lenders, sellers of goods and services, or whatever, attempt to protect their real wage, real interest rates, and real selling price by incorporating into their market behavior their expectations of the future inflationary consequences of government and central bank policies. In turn, their expectations depend on what theory teaches as the likely inflationary consequences of those policies.

The implications of the theory of rational expectations are very supportive of those who question the use of countercyclical monetary and fiscal policy. The theory implies that since individuals will fully incorporate into their wage, interest rate, and selling prices their expectations of the price level consequences of government and central bank actions, these actions will have little or no impact on such real variables as employment, investment, and output, for they will have been discounted and neutralized in advance.

The implications of rational expectations for the Phillips curve tradeoff are devastating. First, they deny completely that Keynesian-type policies will work, for, as we have seen, workers are required to suffer a decline in their real wage for an economy to move up the curve. The rational expectations view holds that individuals cannot be repeatedly fooled by government policies that attempt to exploit the tradeoff. Since workers take into account all available information before making decisions with regard to wage contracts, they will come to understand the policy actions of the government. In one way or another, workers will act to protect their real wage. When this is accomplished, the Phillips curve tradeoff no longer exists with respect to systematic policy actions of the monetary and fiscal authorities.

Second, the rational expectations view also denies the validity of the accelerationists' explanation for the short-run tradeoff. This, it will be remembered, requires the government to accelerate the growth rate of the price level in order to continuously fool labor, and hence exploit the tradeoff. Such an explanation also relies on irrational behavior on the part of workers. Since they would come to understand the inflation-generating process, they would undertake appropriate action to protect their real wage. Thus, all nominal magnitudes would adjust simultaneously with the increase in nominal money demand. No real variables would change. There can be no Phillips curve tradeoff except that caused by purely unanticipated surprises or shocks.

This so-called "rational expectations view" is increasingly being incorporated into Monetarist thinking on the effectiveness of discretionary monetary and fiscal policy to deal with problems of unemployment and inflation.

It should be noted that by "rational expectations" one does not mean that economic agents have perfect foresight or that their expectations are always accurate. Quite the contrary. "Rational expectations" means only that economic agents make use of all available information to forecast market developments. Sometime they will make errors in forecasting future inflation (because, for example, the data are influenced by such things as wildcat strikes, weather conditions, and political upheavals), but the average value of these errors will be zero. Economic agents will not be led to make systematic ovcr- or underestimates of the rate of inflation or deflation. A theory based on rational expectations appears intuitively more plausible than alternative theories, especially considering the profits that can be made from improved forecasts.

The public policy implications of "rational expectations" is straightforward. The only conceivable way that public policy can have even a short-run influence on employment or prices is for that policy to be completely unexpected. This implies that policymakers must either act in an unpredictable or random fashion, or that they must secretly change how they react to a given change in economic conditions. It should be added that once their secretly contrived policy becomes known, the public would learn to predict these changes, just as they predict the policy itself. From this it follows that monetary and fiscal policy should concentrate on maintaining a steady rate of inflation (zero is considered the best) rather than attempting to manipulate the rate of inflation.

Economists, mainly Keynesian, have reacted to rational expectations in different ways. On one level, they agree that there is ample evidence to suggest that such expectations play an important role in markets where a continuous auction process is present (e.g., the stock market). They disagree that other markets, primarily the ones for some goods and services and labor contracts, display evidence of rational expectations. Such phenomena as long-term labor contracts that do not contain safeguards against inflation suggest "irrationality."

While skeptics concede that there is an incentive to improve forecasts, they point out that the acquisition and utilization of relevant information is costly. Moreover, the quantity of information may be vast. They further point out that understanding the forces generating inflation is not simple, as a quick perusal of two or three economic journals will show. How individuals go about learning the actual process of inflation is unclear. Until we understand this, they argue, we cannot know whether they behave "rationally." Nevertheless, a good deal will be heard about rational expectations during the 1980s.

SUMMARY

The great social loss related to involuntary unemployment rightly gives a high place to the study of its causes and cures. The popularity of the Keynesian analytical framework is due in large measure to its ability to focus on the apparent causes of unemployment and to provide a program for dealing with this most urgent of problems.

However, economies both in times past and today have been beset with the nagging problem of inflation. Much effort has been devoted to understanding the causes of inflation and its consequences, which were seen to be largely distributional, but with the result that they can lead to the breakup of social cohesiveness. The social loss from inflation comes mainly from inducing smaller real-money holding, thereby decreasing the efficiency of monetary exchange. Extreme inflation can lead to a return to barter, which rejects all the benefits of monetary exchange.

Once the social losses due to unemployment and inflation are isolated, they invite a comparison as to which is worse, and if they can be traded off one against the other, they suggest appropriate public policies, For this reason, the Phillips curve became popular, for it showed the existence of an apparently permanent tradeoff between the two.

The Phillips curve brought forth a bitter counterattack by those who believed that changes in the supply of money cannot cause permanent changes in real variables. The critics have formulated an explanation for a temporary tradeoff of the type suggested by the Phillips curve that hinges on the ability of inflation to simultaneously lower the real wage paid by employers and raise the real wage received by employees. Because inflation can accomplish this in the short run, unemployment will dip below its "natural" rate and many will perceive that "good times" are at hand. To the extent that expectations are rational, the "good times" are believed to be of short duration.

STUDY QUESTIONS

1. Why might the simultaneous occurrence of inflation and unemployment be puzzling to some?
2. Each month the Bureau of Labor Statistics releases the Consumer Price Index. The monthly rise in the price level is then attributed to one or more components of the index, e.g., food, clothing, fuel, medical care. What do you see as the major problems connected with this approach?

3. Why can't inflation occur in a nonmonetary economy?
4. Would inflation entail any social cost if its rate were held to a constant but positive amount?
5. What should the government attempt to do if it wishes to maximize its revenue from inflationary increases in the money supply?
6. Suppose that significant segments of the labor and manufacturing sectors of the economy become monopolized. Should this cause inflation?
7. How did Keynes envision the closing of the inflationary gap? Explain in relation to Figure 12:2, which shows the gap.
8. Suppose the recorded statistics on unemployment rose. How might an adherent to the job-search view rationalize this and why would such a person be less concerned about it than one who views unemployment in rather simple Keynesian terms?
9. Explain in general how minimum wage legislation may be responsible for increases in the unemployment rate.
10. Does a Phillips curve exist?
11. Does the "natural rate of unemployment" mean an unchanging rate?
12. Why is it important to understand if individuals act rationally?
13. Does inflation lead ultimately to unemployment and recession?
14. If prices are rising, shouldn't output also be increasing?

SELECTED REFERENCES AND READINGS

Bach, George, and Ando, Albert. "The Redistribution Effects of Inflation." *Review of Economics and Statistics,* Vol. 34, No. 1 (Feb. 1957).

——— and Stephenson, James. "Inflation and the Redistribution of Wealth." *Review of Economics and Statistics,* Vol. 61, No. 1 (Feb. 1974).

Barro, Robert J. "Rational Expectations and the Role of Monetary Policy." *Journal of Monetary Economics,* Vol. 2, No. 1 (Mar. 1976).

Bronfenbrenner, Martin, and Holzman, Franklyn. "Survey of Inflation Theory." *American Economic Review,* Vol. 53, No. 4 (Sept. 1963).

Eckstein, Otto, and Brinner, Roger. *The Inflationary Process in the United States.* Joint Economic Committee. Washington, D.C.: U.S. Government Printing Office, 1972.

Feldstein, Martin. "The Economics of the New Unemployment." *The Public Interest,* No. 33 (Fall 1973).

Fisher, Irving. *Appreciation and Interest.* New York: Macmillan, 1896.

———. "A Statistical Relationship between Unemployment and Price Changes." *International Labor Review* (June 1926).

———. *The Rate of Interest.* New York: Macmillan, 1907.

———. *The Purchasing Power of Money.* New York: Macmillan, 1912.

———. *The Theory of Interest.* New York: Augustus Kelley, Reprints of Economic Classics, 1971.

Friedman, Milton. "Nobel Lecture: Inflation and Unemployment." *Journal of Political Economy,* Vol. 85, No. 3 (May/June 1977).

———. "The Role of Monetary Policy." *American Economic Review,* Vol. 58, No. 1 (Mar. 1968).

———. "What Price Guideposts?" In *Guidelines: Informal Controls and the Market Place,* edited by George Schultz and Robert Aliber. Chicago: University of Chicago Press, 1969.

———. *Unemployment Versus Inflation?* Occasional Paper 44. London: Institute of Economic Affairs, 1975.

Frisch, Helmut. "Inflation Theory, 1963–1975: A 'Second Generation' Survey." *Journal of Economic Literature,* Vol. 15, No. 4 (Dec. 1977).

Gordon, Robert J. "Recent Developments in the Theory of Inflation and Unemployment." *Journal of Monetary Economics,* Vol. 2, No. 2 (Apr. 1976).

———. "The Demand for and Supply of Inflation." *The Journal of Law and Economics,* Vol. 18, No. 3 (Dec. 1975).

Humphrey, Thomas. "Changing Views of the Phillips' Curve." *Economic Review,* Federal Reserve Bank of Richmond (July 1973).

———. "Some Recent Developments in Phillips' Curve Analysis." *Economic Review,* Federal Reserve Bank of Richmond (Jan./Feb. 1978).

Johnson, Harry. "A Survey of Theories of Inflation." In *Essays in Monetary Economics.* London: Unwin University Books, 1967.

Laidler, David, and Parkin, Michael. "Inflation: A Survey." *The Economic Journal,* Vol. 85, No. 340 (Dec. 1975).

Lipsey, Richard. "The Relation between Unemployment and the Rate of Change in Money Wages in the United Kingdom, 1862–1957: A Further Analysis." *Economica,* Vol. 27, No. 1 (Feb. 1960).

Machlup, Fritz. "Another View of Cost–Push and Demand–Pull Inflation." *Review of Economics and Statistics,* Vol. 42, No. 2 (May 1960).

McMillan, R. A. "A Re-examination of the 'Full Employment' Goal." *Economic Review,* Federal Reserve Bank of Cleveland (Mar./Apr. 1973).

Makinen, Gail. *Money, The Price Level, and Interest Rates.* Englewood Cliffs, N.J.: Prentice-Hall, 1977. Chapter 11.

Modigliani, Franco. "The Monetarist Controversy or, Should We Forsake Stabilization Policies?" *American Economic Review,* Vol. 67, No 1 (Mar. 1977).

Morley, Samuel. *The Economics of Inflation.* Hinsdale, Ill.: Dryden Press, 1971.

Okun, Arthur. *The Political Economy of Prosperity.* Washington, D.C.: Brookings Institution, 1970.

Phelps, Edmund. "Phillips' Curves, Expectations of Inflation and Optimal Unemployment Overtime." *Economica,* Vol. 34, No. 135 (Aug. 1967).

Phillips, A. W. "The Relationship between Unemployment and the Rate of Change of Money Wages in the United Kingdom, 1862–1957." *Economica,* Vol. 25, No. 100 (Dec. 1958).

Samuelson, Paul, and Solow, Robert. "Analytical Aspects of Anti-Inflation Policy." *American Economic Review,* Vol. 50, No. 2 (May 1960).

Schultze, Charles. "Recent Inflation in the United States." In *Employment, Growth and Price Levels.* Joint Economic Committee, 86th Congress: 1st Session, Washington, D.C.: U.S. Government Printing Office. 1959.

Solow, Robert, *Price Expectations and the Behavior of the Price Level.* Manchester; Manchester University Press: 1969.

———. "The Intelligent Citizen's Guide to Inflation." *The Public Interest:* No. 38 (Winter 1975).

Tobin, James. "Inflation and Unemployment." *American Economic Review,* Vol. 62, No. 1 (Mar. 1972).

APPENDIX A– A MATHEMATICAL DEVELOPMENT OF THE PHILLIPS CURVE THEORY

12

The discussion of the development of the Phillips curve in this chapter can be supplemented and made more rigorous by the application of a few elementary mathematical concepts.

As noted, the original Phillips curve expressed the notion that the percentage rate of change of money wages depended upon the percentage rate of unemployment. By assuming that the general level of prices results from a constant markup applied to per unit labor costs, the Phillips curve could be expressed as a relationship relating the percentage rate of inflation, P, to the rate of unemployment, U, or

$$P = a_0 + a_1 U \tag{12A:1}$$

where the numerical value of the coefficient a_1 indicates the tradeoff between inflation and unemployment. The coefficient should take on a negative value, indicating that as the unemployment rate increases, the rate of inflation decreases.

The simple relationship expressed by Equation (12A:1) implies that the tradeoff is fixed and permanent throughout time and gives to policymakers a range of choices whereby the rate of unemployment can be substituted for a faster or slower rate of change of commodity prices.

However, soon after the Phillips curve was presented in the late 1950s investigations of historical experience suggested that a stable, enduring tradeoff did not exist. They further suggested that the Phillips curve was subject to shifts over time. This finding led to several efforts to augment the Phillips equation with variables thought to explain the shifts, such as productivity changes, profits, trade union effects, the age–sex mix of the labor force, and the dispersion of unemployment. To incorporate these additional influences, Equation (12A:1) was modified to resemble Equation (12A:2), where X represents the totality of these other influences, or

$$P = a_0 + a_1 U + X \tag{12A:2}$$

The expectations of the public on the future rate of change of prices, or the rate of inflation, was absent from the discussion of the variables thought to shift the Phillips curve.

Increasingly, during the late 1960s and early 1970s expectations of price inflation were thought to be the important variable explaining the shift in or the worsening of the Phillips curve tradeoff. Such a belief led to the substitution of the expected rate of inflation, P^e, for the variables, summarized by X, in Equation (12A:2). This yielded

$$P = a_0 + a_1 U + a_2 P^e \tag{12A:3}$$

This modification of the Phillips curve was largely due to the efforts of the Monetarists. Their arguments implied that the value of the a_2 coefficient was unity, which meant that in the longer run the expected rate of inflation was fully incorporated into the wage rate, and hence the actual rate of price increases as well.

If it were true that $a_2 = 1$, then $P^e = P$, and the sellers of both labor services and final products would not suffer from money illusion. Changes in the money supply could not, therefore, permanently change real variables.

Moreover, as long as $P^e = P$, since $P - P^e = 0$, the unemployment rate or U would be equal to $-a_0/a_1$, which would then be defined as its natural rate, What that rate would be was thought to depend on a number of characteristics of the labor market.

As long as $P^e = P$, the natural rate of unemployment can prevail regardless of the rate of inflation, so long as it is fully anticipated. If, however, the rate of inflation is not fully anticipated ($P > P^e$), departures from the natural rate are possible. One such departure was seen to arise from an acceleration or deceleration in the money supply. This so-called *accelerationist view* can be more readily understood when the mechanism by which expectations were thought to be formed is explained.

As Equation (12A:3) stands, it contains one unobserved variable, the expected rate of inflation, P^e. In order to quantify this argument, assumptions were made concerning how the public forms its expectations. A common assumption stated that they were formed adaptively, or through an error-learning process. This can be expressed as

$$P^e_T - P^e_{T-1} = \beta(P_{T-1} - P^e_{T-1}) \tag{12A:4}$$

where the change in expected prices this period ($P^e_T - P^e_{T-1}$) is equal to some fraction ($0 < \beta < 1$) of the difference between the actual rate of inflation last period, P_{T-1}, and the expected rate of that same period, or P^e_{T-1}. If the adjustment factor, β, is equal to .6, and the actual inflation rate and the expected rate of last period were, respectively, 12% and 8%, Equation (12A:4) then says that the expected rate of inflation this period will be revised upward by 60% of the error, or 2.4%. Such revisions will continue until the error is eliminated.

Such an error-learning mechanism is mathematically equivalent to the proposition that the expected rate of inflation is equal to a geometrically weighted average of all past actual rates of inflation, with the weights summing to one, or

$$P_T^e = \Sigma\omega_i P_{T-i}, \Sigma\omega_i = 1 \tag{12A:5}$$

Thus, Equation (12A:5) says that the current expected rate of inflation is equal to a weighted average of past actual rates of inflation, where the weights decline geometrically—the farther back in history one goes, the smaller is the weight given that experience.

So long as β does not equal unity, expectations of inflation will always lag behind the actual rate of inflation, although the gap will continuously decrease as long as the actual rate remains constant. However, if the actual rate is accelerated, the gap will not decrease. This fact, then, became the basis for the Monetarists' claim that only by accelerating the inflation rate could the unemployment rate be held below its natural level, i.e., could a Phillips curve tradeoff be maintained in the longer run.

The empirical value of the coefficient a_2 in Equation (12A:3) therefore became very important, given that the expected price series was formed according to Equations (12A:4) and (12A:5). A variety of empirical tests covering a number of countries in the world during a number of historical epochs, as well as single countries during different epochs, all seemed to yield a coefficient of less than unity. This evidence suggests that a tradeoff of the type envisioned by the Phillips curve does exist. It should be noted, however, that in several countries it was discovered that as the inflation rate accelerated, the calculated value of the coefficient a_2 increased.

It was not long before several individuals raised objections to the assumption that expectations were formed adaptively. They pointed out that the assumption that expectations are based only on past price level increases overlooks all other pertinent evidence on how inflation is generated. Hence, the public is assumed to ignore the growth rate of the money supply, movements in the exchange rate, the announced policies of the central bank and the government, and other information. All this information could be used by the public to reduce the errors in their predictions of the actual movements in the price level. To neglect to take account of this relevant information would imply that the public is wrong about systematic movements in the price level. Such behavior was said to be irrational.

As noted in the main body of this chapter, the implications of "rational expectations" are that the authorities who make policy cannot engineer a tradeoff between inflation and unemployment except by surprising the public through completely unexpected or random actions. It should also be noted that the assumption of "rational expectations" implies that the tradeoff disappears completely for an acceleration of the money supply, for the public understands how inflation is generated, and an acceleration of the money supply cannot fool them.

To incorporate the "rational expectations" view into our mathematical presentation is a rather straightforward task. It merely requires several additional equations relating to various assumptions of behavior.

First, the inflation rate is assumed to depend on the growth rate of the money stock per unit of output, M, and on random shocks to the economic system (such as those arising from strikes, crop failures, political upheavals, etc., which are unrelated to money supply growth), z, or

$$P = M + z \tag{12A:6}$$

Since the average or expected value of z over the longer run is equal to zero, Equation (12A:6) states that the course of inflation depends upon the growth rate of the money supply per unit of output.

Next, we must specify a policy reaction function governing the rate at which the authorities increase the money supply. For simplicity, we assume that the central bank alters the growth rate depending on the degree of excess supply or demand in the commodity market during the previous time period, or Y_{T-1}.

However, since the central bank does not control the money supply directly, but only the monetary base, the growth rate of the money supply is also subject to other random influences summarized by Z, which causes the actual growth rate of the money supply to alter from its desired path over time, or

$$M = M(Y_{T-1}) + Z \tag{12A:7}$$

Note also that Z can represent monetary surprises engineered by the central bank. To the extent that Z is random, its average value over time should be zero.

Next, we must specify an equation that indicates how rational expectations of inflation are formed. With reference to Equation (12A:6), we see that the actual inflation rate depends on the actual growth rate of the nominal money supply per unit of output plus a random term whose average value over time is zero. Hence, the expected inflation rate, P^e, is equal to the expected growth rate of the nominal money supply per unit of output, M^e, or

$$P^e = M^e \tag{12A:8}$$

Finally, to complete our model, we must specify the determinants of the expected growth rate of the nominal money supply. The determinants depend on the nature of the policy reaction function. As set forth in Equation (12A:7), the nominal supply is related to excess supply or demand in the commodity market over past periods, plus a random variable. Because the average value of the random component, Z, is zero, the growth rate of M^e is related to the systematic or predictable component of the reaction function, Y_{T-1}, or

$$M^e = M(Y_{T-1}) \tag{12A:9}$$

Since rational economic agents are assumed to have the same information as policymakers, they too can predict Y_{T-1}, and therefore M^e and P^e, and act accordingly in their wage and price demands. It follows, then, that only the random or unpredictable changes given by z in Equation (12A:6) and Z in Equation (12A:7) can generate a Phillips-type tradeoff. This conclusion follows when Equation (12A:3) is subject to successive substitutions from Equations (12A:6), (12A:7), (12A:8), and (12A:9).

$$P - P^e = a_0 + a_1 U$$

which, after the substitutions yields,

$$z + Z = a_0 + a_1 U \tag{12A:10}$$

Since Z can include surprise changes in the money supply engineered by the monetary authorities, it follows that it is only through this route that policymakers can attempt to influence the unemployment rate.

13

THE GIBSON PARADOX AND THE TERM STRUCTURE OF INTEREST RATES

Because inflation is usually associated with extreme changes in an economic system, it has long stimulated the analytical curiosity of economists. One interesting problem is the behavior of market interest rates during a period of inflation. The evidence from a wide variety of countries with vastly different institutional structures during different historical periods is that inflation is generally—indeed, almost universally—associated with rising (and usually high) levels of market interest rates. The man on the street might find nothing unusual about this relationship. After all, inflation is a rise in the price level, and interest rates might be thought of as the price of money. Hence, as prices in general rise, so should the price of money. Yet this positive relationship between market interest rates and the price level has perplexed a good many economists. Being able to explain it has been thought crucial to understanding how an economic system functions. More concretely, it has been thought that a good understanding of the cause of this relationship would provide the means to answering the questions of the origin of the business cycle and whether changes in the supply of money can permanently change variables such as the *real* rate of interest.

THE RICARDO–TOOKE CONUNDRUM

The relationship between rising commodity prices and market interest rates played a central role in an early nineteenth century debate among British economists over the cause of the inflation in England during the Napoleonic

Wars (which they measured by the rise in the price of gold bullion in terms of the inconvertible paper pound note).[1]

The accepted monetary theory of the day viewed the interest rate as the principal linkage between the supply of money and economic activity. (Economic activity was measured by employment and the price level in a fashion quite similar to that of the Keynesian model presented in Chapter 10.) In this theory the banks that gain excess reserves use them to acquire debts in the process of creating deposit money or bank notes. The increased purchases of debts by the banks serve to raise their prices and reduce market interest rates. The fall in market interest rates increases the desired level of investment, which, in turn, serves to increase aggregate demand. The increase in aggregate demand would then cause a rise in commodity prices. The key relationship to keep in mind here is that the rise in the money supply leads to lower market interest rates, which leads to rising commodity prices (inflation). Once the money supply ceases to expand, the rise in commodity prices would come to a halt and interest rates would then return to their previous level. However, during the period of inflation or rising prices, interest rates should be at historically *low* levels and vice versa. Thus, economic theory implied a behavior for the interest rate at variance with most of recorded economic history.

David Ricardo, one of the founders of modern economics, strongly advocated the view that British inflation was linked to an overissue of paper pounds during the war to finance the activities of the government. One of the foremost antagonists of this view was Thomas Tooke, a pioneer in the statistical investigation of economic phenomena. Tooke's view was that the premium on bullion (British inflation) was due partly to the necessity to import much grain because of bad harvests, and partly to the need to make large advances of funds abroad to maintain an army on the continent of Europe. In his *History of Prices* Tooke showed that Ricardo and his followers could not possibly have the correct explanation for inflation. He did this by demonstrating that movements in the general level of commodity prices and market interest rates were positively correlated; that is, high price levels and high interest rates go together, as do low price levels and low interest rates. In addition, when first differences of successive years were taken, rising price levels and rising interest rates were seen to move together, as did falling price levels and falling interest rates.

Tooke used an interesting method to explain this relationship, which has

[1] At the advent of the first Napoleonic War in 1797, Great Britain suspended the convertibility of the pound sterling into gold. The paper or inconvertible pound then depreciated relative to gold and other convertible currencies. The premium on gold bullion was then used as evidence by David Ricardo and his followers that the pound had been overissued. Their logic was that an overissue of notes had driven up British prices relative to those abroad, causing British exports to fall and imports to rise. The depreciation of the pound was then necessary to restore equilibrium to the balance of payments. Thus, the depreciation or premium on gold was evidence of an overissue of currency. Had price indices been available, the issue might have been resolved more directly.

been employed by many others. As Tooke saw it, the price level was determined by aggregate demand and aggregate supply. Since interest rates were a cost of production, whenever they rose the price level would also rise. Therefore, let some autonomous force increase aggregate demand. This would lead to a rise in the demand for money, and consequently, a rise in interest rates. This, in turn, would lead to a rise in production costs, which would push up the price level—hence the positive correlation between the two.[2]

Because Tooke's view on the cause of the business cycle was at variance with the accepted monetary interpretation, his work, including his empirical findings, was ignored. Monetary theory continued to teach a mechanism linking the money supply to the price level that would generate expected data on prices and interest rates at variance with much of recorded history!

GIBSON'S PARADOX

The early work of Tooke showing a positive correlation between the level of commodity prices and market interest rates was dramatically confirmed by an empirical study conducted by an English banker, A. H. Gibson, first published in 1923 and updated in 1926.[3] The original Gibson findings are reproduced in Figure 13:1; they do, in fact, show "a sympathetic movement" between the yield on consols and the course of wholesale prices.[4] More recent work by Shiller and Siegel covering the period from 1729–1974 for Great Britain is shown in Figure 13:2.

The Gibson study came to the early attention of Lord Keynes (then merely J. M. Keynes), who was very impressed with its findings.

> *For the extraordinary thing is that the "Gibson Paradox"—as we may fairly call it—is one of the most completely established empirical facts within the whole field of quantitive economics, though theoretical economists have mostly ignored it.*[5]

[2] The error in this reasoning can be found using microeconomic theory. The interest rate represents the cost of capital and is thus a fixed cost, since it does not vary with output in the short run. As an element of fixed cost, it does not affect the marginal cost or short-run supply schedule. Hence, it does not determine prices.

In the United States the view that rising interest rates cause rising prices was long forcefully advocated by the former chairman of the Joint Economic Committee, the late Congressman Wright Patman of Texas. In a recent paper, using a full-cost model in which interest costs would affect prices, Steven Seelig was unable to uncover evidence to support the congressman's claim. See his "Rising Interest Rates and Cost Push Inflation," *Journal of Finance*, No. 4, Vol. 29 (Sept. 1974): 1049–61.

[3] A. H. Gibson, "The Future Course of High-Class Investment Values," *Bankers' Magazine*, Vol. 115, No. 946 (Jan. 1923): 15–34; and "The Road to Economic Recovery, Some Reflections," *Bankers' Magazine*, Vol. 122, No. 992 (Nov. 1926): 595–612.

[4] It should be noted that Gibson himself provided no intelligent explanation for this relationship. When the two curves moved in opposite directions in 1924–1926, Gibson speculated that it "may be due to the spreading of communist doctrines in this country unduly depressing Government credit. . . ."

[5] J. M. Keynes, *A Treatise on Money*, Vol. II, *The Applied Theory of Money* (London: Macmillan, 1930), p. 198.

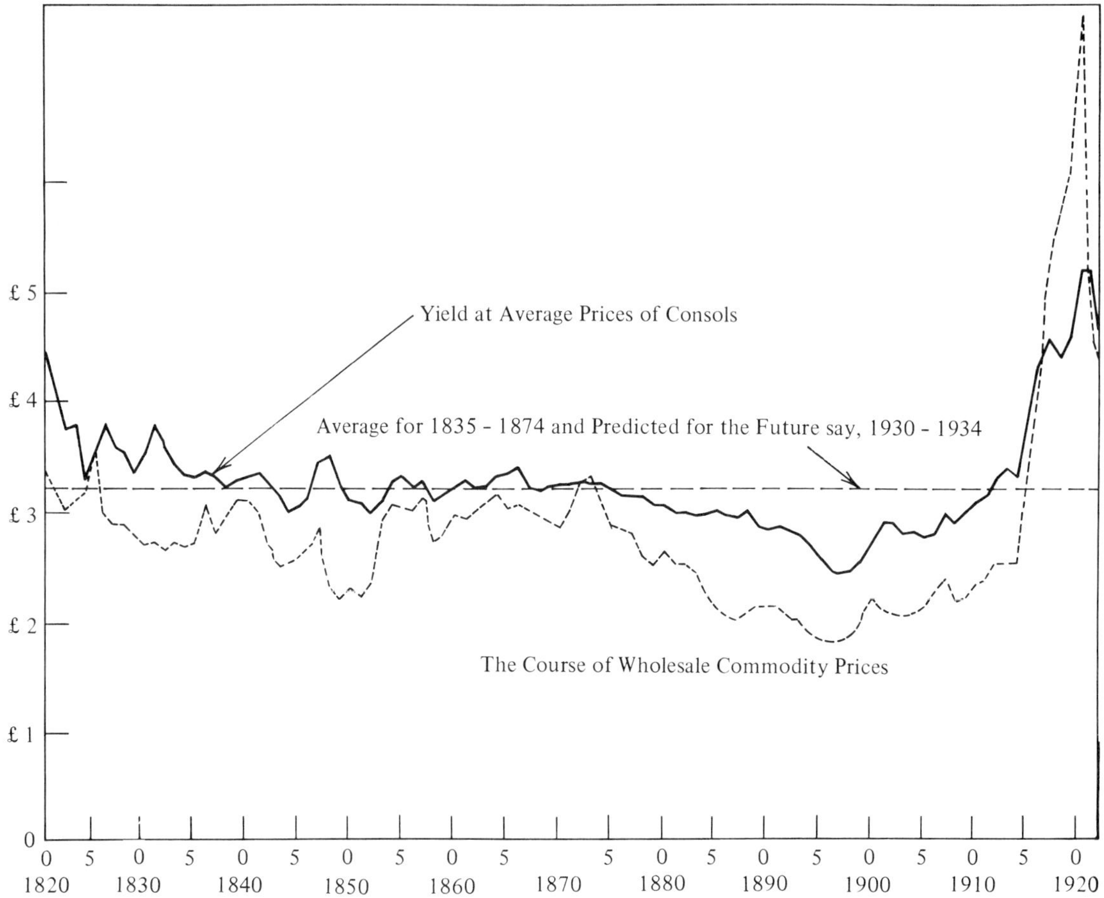

FIGURE 13:1
The original Gibson study. The curve representing wholesale commodity prices is based on index numbers compiled by Mr. Sauerbeck for 1820–1912, and by the Statist *(in continuation) for 1913–1922, and is plotted to a suitable scale for the purpose of close comparison with the curve representing the yield of Consols. For the year 1914 the curves are based on averages for the first seven months of the year. Lowest average yield for any year of Consols during last 100 years, £2. 8s. 11d. for 1897; highest, £5. 6s. 5d. for 1920. Average for the 40 years 1835–1874, £3. 4s. 6d. For full explanations of certain divergencies shown between the curves, see relative letterpress. No curve is shown representing the course of the* price *of consols, because such a curve would be misleading, on account of the reductions in the rate of interest in 1889 and 1903, provided for by the Conversion Scheme of 1888.*

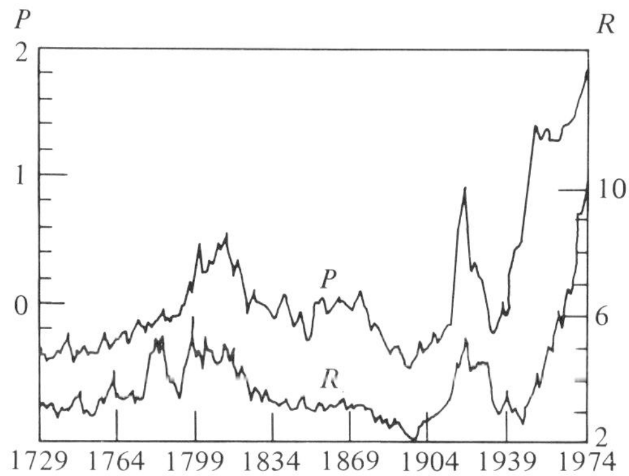

FIGURE 13:2
*The price level and long-term interest rate for Great Britain, 1729–1974. The log of the price index (*P*) and the long-term interest rate (*R*), British data. (Courtesy of Robert Shiller and Jeremy Siegel, "The Gibson Paradox and Historical Movements in Real Interest Rates,"* Journal of Political Economy, *Vol. 85, No. 5 (Oct./Nov. 1977).)*

Keynes set about to provide a theoretical explanation for this relationship. By a rather remarkable coincidence, the great Swedish economist Knut Wicksell, aware of the controversy between the Ricardians and Tooke, had provided an explanation virtually identical to Keynes's for the phenomenon some 30 years earlier (his work was not available in English until the late 1930s).

The Keynes–Wicksell resolution

In the Keynes–Wicksell framework a major technological innovation or other event occurs (e.g., the discovery of new territory or mineral resource or the advent of a war) that increases the expected profitability of capital investment. Investment then expands, which serves to put upward pressure on the market interest rate. As interest rates rise, the desired excess reserve holdings of banks become less than their actual holding of excess reserves. To restore equality between the two, the banks make loans, create deposits, or issue new notes, and expand the supply of money. The rise in the money supply serves to finance the rise in aggregate demand. In an economy tending always to full employment, the rise in money demand causes the price level to rise.

Once the desired and actual reserve holdings of the banks are again equal, no more money will be created and prices will stop rising. However, during the disequilibrium interval inflation and high interest rates will coexist. Once the inflation ceases, a high price level and high interest rates will continue until some other change occurs in the expected profit calculations of entrepreneurs.

Keynes and Wicksell were thus able to rationalize the findings of Tooke and Gibson.

The Fisher resolution

In 1895, at the request of the American Economic Association, Irving Fisher began what was to become a lengthy study of the effect of commodity price changes on the rate of interest. He devoted four books and numerous articles to this subject. From this research, he developed a monetary theory of the business cycle.

Earlier, in our discussion of the targets and indicators of money policy, the Fisherian theory of the effect of inflation on interest rates was presented. This analysis can be put in graphic terms to show the conditions under which the market interest rate will adjust to the rate of inflation.[6]

Figure 13:3 depicts the demand for and supply of loanable funds in the financial market. The demand for loanable funds (D_I) is the financial counterpart of the demand for real goods for investment, whereas the supply of loanable funds (S_S) is the financial counterpart of individual savings. The supply can be augmented by the flow of new money created by depository institutions (S_{CB}).[7] The equilibrium interest rate, r_O, can be called the real rate and represents the lending rate that would prevail in the absence of inflation.

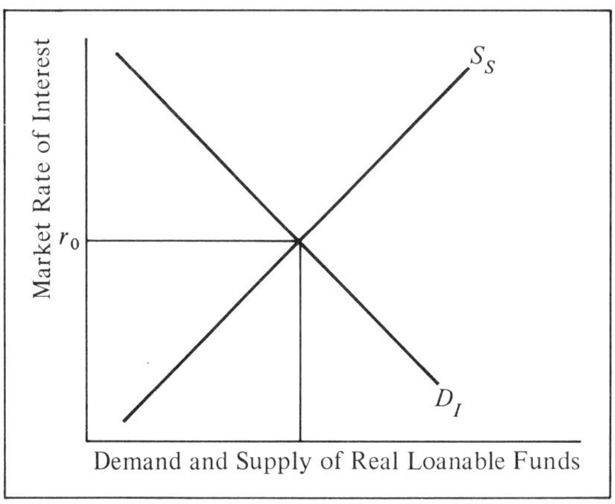

FIGURE 13:3
Demand for and supply of loanable funds

[6] For a more extensive graphical treatment, see W. A. Bomberger and G. E. Makinen, "The Fisher Effect: A Graphical Treatment and Some Econometric Implications," *Journal of Finance,* Vol. 32, No. 3 (June 1977): 719–33.

[7] The demand for loanable funds can also arise from a government budget deficit and a desire on the part of individuals to hoard money. Similarly, the supply of loanable funds can be augmented by a government budget surplus. These alternative sources of demand and supply will be neglected in the analysis to follow.

Now, says Fisher, suppose the money supply expands (either because someone discovers gold or the government prints up paper money). The expansion in money spending will drive up the level of commodity prices. The inventories acquired by businessmen can be expected to appreciate in value at the rate of inflation. Thus, businessmen are ready to pay more for the loanable funds they borrow. As a maximum, they will pay per year a sum or percentage equal to the appreciation in their inventory, i.e., the actual rate of inflation. This being the case, the demand schedule for loanable funds will shift up by the amount of the inflation (ΔP^A). This is shown in Figure 13:4.

So long as lenders do not react to the ongoing inflation, the real rate of interest ($r_1 - \Delta P^A$) paid by the borrower falls. This can be seen by subtracting from the new market rate, r_1, the amount of the inflation, ΔP^A. To accomplish this, move to the intersection of D_I' and S_S. Then move directly down to the zero inflation demand schedule, D_I, and then over to the vertical axis. The market rate, r_2, then represents the real rate paid by the borrower (and received by the lender). It is not surprising that if the real rate paid by borrowers declines, then a larger quantity of loanable funds will be borrowed. This is seen in Figure 13:4 ($LF_1 - LF_0$).

Once the savers react to the inflation, they will ask a premium to preserve the real purchasing power of the principal lent and the interest received. When this occurs, the supply schedule of loanable funds will shift up from S_S to S_S' by the amount of the expected inflation. Figure 13:5 shows such an adjustment. In this case, the new market rate, r_3, is greater than the real rate, r_0, by the amount of the inflation. Thus, high money rates of interest need not be high real rates of interest. Note also that if the change in the market rate reflects the inflation rate correctly, the amount of real loanable

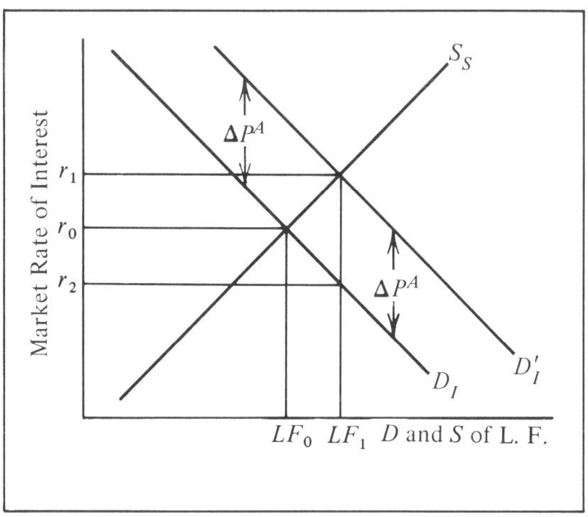

FIGURE 13:4
Inflation and the demand for loanable funds

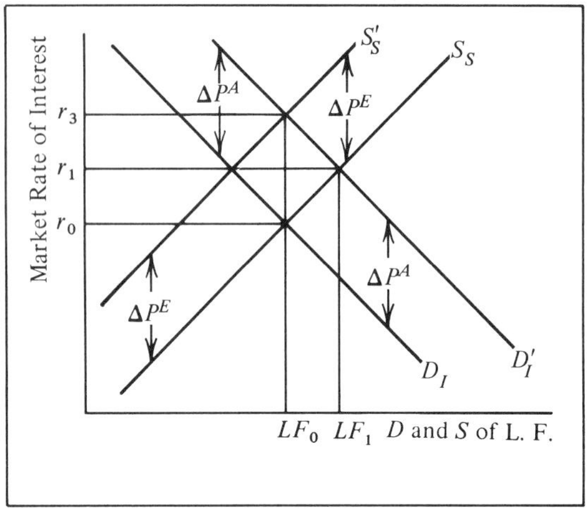

FIGURE 13:5
Inflation and the supply of loanable funds

funds lent and borrowed will be exactly the same, LF_0; it is as if there were no inflation.

Be that as it may, Fisher believed that for two reasons the market rate would not adjust quickly to the ongoing inflation, i.e., that the real rate of interest would decline.

> *First, . . . we are so accustomed in our business dealings to consider money as the one stable thing—to think of a "dollar as a dollar" regardless of the passage of time, that we reluctantly yield to this process of readjustment, thus rendering it very slow and imperfect. This inadequacy and tardiness of adjustment are fostered, moreover, by law and custom, which arbitrarily tend to keep down the* [*money*] *rate of interest.*[8]

Second, the inflation-induced rise in the demand for loanable funds that causes interest to rise also has an effect on the supply of money from banks (or, in general, from depository institutions), for, according to Fisher, bankers "are led to become more enterprising. Beguiled by the higher nominal rates into a belief that fairly high [real] interest is being realized, they extend their loans, deposit currency [demand deposits in contemporary language] . . . expands . . . ."[9]

The activities of depository institutions can be seen in diagrammatic terms in Figure 13:6. By creating demand deposits or notes, they increase the supply of loanable funds, shifting S_S to S_{S+CB}. The nominal or market rate of interest declines from r_1 to r_4. The decline in the market rate serves to reduce the real rate as well (in this case to r_5).

In terms of our money supply analysis of Chapter 4, the inflation-induced

[8] Irving Fisher, *The Purchasing Power of Money* (New York: Macmillan, 1912), pp. 57–8.
[9] Ibid.

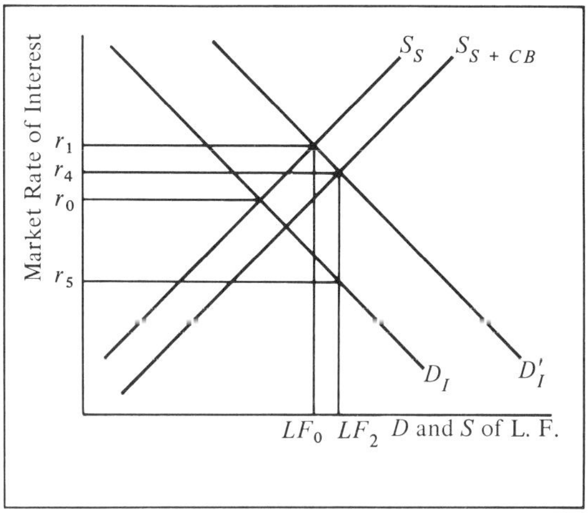

FIGURE 13:6
Money creation and the real rate of interest

rise in the market rate from r_0 to r_1 is taken by depository institutions to be a rise in the real rate, which causes the desired excess-reserve-to-demand-deposit ratio to be less than the actual ratio. In an effort to restore equilibrium between the two, depository institutions make loans and create deposits.

Once depository institutions recognize that the real rate of interest is not r_4 but r_5, they will realize that their real rate of return has fallen and that as a consequence, the ratio of excess reserve to demand deposits is now at an abnormally low level. To raise the ratio, they will refuse both to make new loans and to renew old loans. In some cases they may even call in outstanding loans. The net effect is to contract the supply of money. Since this action reverses the original procedure shown in Figure 13:6, the nominal interest rate rises, as does the real rate.

Full adjustment of the market interest rate to inflation

Whether the market interest rate adjusts fully to the inflation rate, and the length of time it takes for the adjustment to be completed, are two very important issues.

If the market interest rate does not fully adjust to the inflation rate, then the real rate of interest will have fallen and the amount of real loanable funds demanded and supplied will have risen. Since loanable funds are, in the main, the money counterpart of saving and investment, a fall in the real rate means that these two variables have also changed. Since inflation in Fisher's analysis was instituted by an increase in the supply of money, a lack of full adjustment of the real rate to inflation means that a monetary change caused a permanent change in real variables—the real interest rate, investment, and saving. The reader will recall that the Monetarists deny the possibility of such an occurrence.

Second, if the adjustment is complete but takes many years to occur, then variations in the supply of money can be used in a short-run stabilization context, for they can alter real variables.

Empirical evidence on both points is mixed, but, in general, shows underadjustment and a long period for the real rate to rise toward its original level (at least several decades).[10]

It should also be noted that because the real rate fails to adjust completely and rapidly, inflation does appear to redistribute wealth from creditors to debtors. Why underadjustment occurs is an area for further investigation.

Keynes–Wicksell and Fisher compared

The Keynes–Wicksell and Fisher resolutions of the Gibson paradox have much in common. In each, movements in the money multiplier (due to changes in the desired ratio of excess reserves to demand deposits) lead to an increase in the supply of money and money spending, which either directly or in a contributory fashion causes the price level to rise. Thus, each can be said to be a monetary theory of the business cycle in which the money multiplier plays an important (in Fisher's view) or a dominant role (Keynes–Wicksell). In Fisher's approach a change in the monetary base may initiate the cycle.

In the Keynes–Wicksell explanation of the cycle, however, the initiation factor is a change in investor expectations due to such occurrences as changes in technology, news of land or mineral discoveries, and impending military conflict. From this viewpoint, Keynes–Wicksell could be said to have a nonmonetary view of the cycle. However, unless the money supply changes in their model, the results reported by Gibson cannot be explained by Keynes–Wicksell.

The *General Theory* and the Gibson paradox

It is claimed by Monetarists that the response of the economic model that emerges from Keynes's *General Theory* to a change in the supply of money will generate evidence that is inconsistent with Gibson's findings. Hence,

[10] The empirical evidence on these points is extensive. The best of it can be found in Thomas Sargent, "Commodity Price Expectations and the Interest Rate," *Quarterly Journal of Economics*, Vol. 83, No. 330 (Feb. 1969): 127–40; William Gibson, "Price Expectations Effects on Interest Rates," *Journal of Finance*, Vol. 25, No. 1 (Mar. 1970): 19–34; "The Lag in the Effect of Monetary Policy on Income and Interest Rates," *Quarterly Journal of Economics*, Vol. 84, No. 335 (May 1970): 288–300; "Interest Rates and Monetary Policy," *Journal of Political Economy*, Vol. 78, No. 3 (May/June 1970): 431–54; and "Interest Rates and Inflationary Expectations: New Evidence," *American Economic Review*, Vol. 61, No. 5 (Dec. 1971): 854–65; and William Yohe and Dennis Karnosky, "Interest Rates and Price Level Changes, 1952–69," *Monthly Review*, Federal Reserve Bank of St. Louis, Vol. 51, No. 12 (Dec. 1969): 18–38.

they conclude the *General Theory* model is an invalid abstraction of the way in which an economy functions.

Quite clearly, the extensive problem worked out in Chapter 10 featuring an increase in the money supply is what the Monetarists have in mind. In that problem it was shown that an increase in the supply of money would *lower* interest rates (both market and real) and lead to some increases in the price level. These results are clearly inconsistent with Gibson's findings.

There is a reasonable way the *General Theory* model can be revised to generate expected results that are consistent with those Gibson recorded.[11] One need merely require that the origin of the change in behavior in the model be a rise in investment spending or government spending (a problem considered in Appendix 10D).

A rise in government expenditures or in the purchase of producer or consumer durables will expand aggregate demand, putting upward pressure on both the price level and market interest rates. As this occurs, nothing prevents depository institutions from supplying a larger quantity of money. Our earlier reasoning making the desired ratio of excess reserves to demand deposits sensitive to the market interest rate would imply some increase as depository institutions reduce their holdings of excess reserves. Moreover, a rise in government spending relative to taxes, if large, will certainly invite some Federal Reserve purchases of government bonds to support their prices and ease the government's borrowing burden. This action, of course, increases the monetary base and permits a more intense or prolonged expansion in demand to take place.

There is, therefore, no inherent limitation in the model from the *General Theory* that makes it unable to explain results such as those reported by Gibson. Unlike the Monetarist interpretation of history, the interpretation given by those who adhere to the *General Theory* attributes the cause of the business cycle to nonmonetary events—in the case at hand, to the expectations of those who purchase durable goods and to the government. Moreover, contrary to the earlier Keynesian explanation of the Gibson paradox, the resolution from the *General Theory* does not require any increase in the money supply to take place.[12]

[11] It would seem strange that the same person who applied the name "Gibson paradox" to the observed relationship between interest rates and the price level would produce a model that could only generate the opposite results!

[12] Recent econometric work of a sophisticated nature (spectral analysis) has been used by Shiller and Siegel to unravel the Gibson paradox. They *reject* the hypothesis of Irving Fisher that expectations of inflation cause the correlation observed by Gibson. They propose instead an explanation that centers in the financing used by governments during wartime and the distributional effects of unanticipated inflation. As such, their work is similar to that which emerges from the Keynesian *General Theory* model explained above. See their "The Gibson Paradox and Historical Movements in the Real Interest Rate," *Journal of Political Economy,* Vol. 85, No. 5 (Oct. 1977): 891–909.

Summary—the Gibson paradox

The Gibson paradox involves the observed positive correlation between market interest rates and the index of commodity prices. It was called a paradox by Keynes because accepted monetary theory implied that there should be a negative relationship between the two series.

The resolution of the paradox is of interest for several reasons, foremost among which is that it may provide the key to the cause of the business cycle. Second, the extent to which market interest rates adjust to inflation, and the length of time it takes to complete the adjustment, provide evidence on whether changes in the supply of money can permanently change real variables and whether monetary policy can be used as a stabilization tool.

The resolution of the paradox put forth by Keynes–Wicksell and Fisher implies a monetary theory of the business cycle, whereas the one that emerges from Keynes's later work, the *General Theory,* implies a nonmonetary theory of the cycle.

THE LEVEL OF INTEREST RATES

The preceding discussion of the Gibson paradox was designed, in part, to demonstrate the effect of inflation and expectations of inflation on the market interest rate. It was also intended to distinguish the real rate from the market rate. Elsewhere in this text we have discussed various aspects of market interest rates and some of the factors influencing them. In this chapter we present a systematic discussion of market interest rates.

At various places in previous discussions the words "the interest rate" have been used as though only one market interest rate existed. It should by now be obvious that this expression is a shorthand reference for a *structure* of market interest rates. A brief glance at the financial page of a daily newspaper will reveal a bewildering variety of market interest rates, even for the same borrower. For example, federal government securities will carry many different market rates. Moreover, the market rates on private securities are different from those on government issues, and the yield on the issues by different levels of government are by no means uniform. What factors account for these differences? Several have been thought to be of primary importance:

1. Marketability or liquidity;
2. Default risk;
3. Taxation;
4. Time to maturity.

It is undoubtedly the relationship between yield and time to maturity that has most intrigued economists, in part because the relationship is subject to change and the pattern is sometimes observed to be descending and at other times to be ascending. However, let us first examine the other three

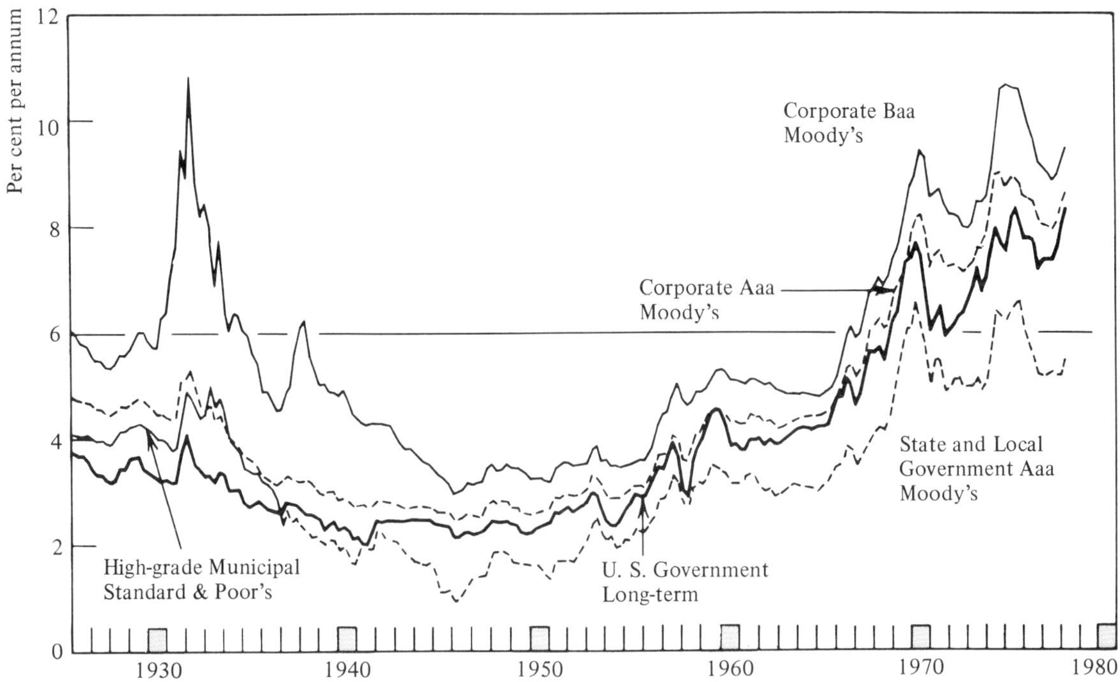

FIGURE 13:7
Long-term bond yields (Courtesy of the U.S. Treasury)

factors considered important in explaining the difference between market yields. The yields plotted in Figure 13:7 are thought to reflect in large measure these three influences.

Default risk

Note first that corporate bonds with a higher default risk (those labeled Baa by Moody's)[13] bear a higher yield than those with a lower default risk (Moody's Aaa). Both corporate issues bear a higher yield than comparable U.S. government securities, on which the risk of default is near zero. Hence, an important consideration in lending money is the risk that what is lent will not be returned as promised. To induce lenders to undertake such a risk, interest rates will have to be higher than on loans for which such a risk is less or nonexistent.

[13] There are two major credit rating services for financial securities: Moody's and Standard and Poor. Their rating systems are similar in structure to the grades given students—A's are better than B's, which are better than C's. Thus, Aaa-rated securities are more secure (less risky) than Baa-rated ones.

Note also that Figure 13:7 shows that the market's evaluation of the default risk is not constant over time. This can be seen by comparing the difference in market interest rates or yield differential between the different types of securities. The differential on private securities was very high in the 1930s when business failures were numerous. The yield differential between Aaa- and Baa-rated securities also widened. The default risk appears to have fallen during the prosperous years of World War II and during the long continuous cyclical upswing of the 1960s. During the more turbulent 1970s, the market's evaluation of the risk of default appears to have risen, for the differential between Aaa- and Baa-rated securities has tended to widen.

Tax treatment

It may come as something of a surprise that Figure 13:7 shows that state and municipal securities bear a lower market interest rate or yield than comparable issues of the federal government. This difference has little to do with the market's evaluation of the default risk; rather, it reflects the special tax treatment accorded the coupon interest on these securities: it is exempt from federal income taxation. The exemption means that lenders are willing to supply funds to this sector of the market at a lower interest rate.[14] How much lower depends on the lenders' marginal income tax bracket. Thus, the data plotted in Figure 13:7 show that the value of the tax exemption is sufficiently strong to overcome the higher default risk implicit in state and municipal securities.

Marketability or liquidity

The remaining influence determining the level of interest rates is the marketability or liquidity of the security in question.

Earlier, we defined a security to be highly liquid if it could be quickly disposed of at or about the price paid for it. Obviously, then, the degree of liquidity depends on how quickly the asset can be sold and the price or exchange value realized in relation to its cost.

Liquidity or marketability depends on many factors related to a security's time to maturity, how widely the issuer is known, the extent of a secondary market for the security, the volume of transactions in the market (whether heavy or thin), the time and effort required to learn about the security, and so on.

The most liquid of all assets is the non-interest-bearing debt of the Treasury (in low denominations) and its short-term interest-bearing debt

[14] This exemption is equivalent to a federal government subsidy to states and municipalities. This result is the same as if these levels of government borrowed at prevailing rates and then received a cash grant to offset their borrowing costs.

(e.g., Treasury bills). Since these assets have a short time in maturity, they are little affected by changes in market interest rates. Also they are issued by a well-known borrower and there is a highly organized, nationwide resale market for them.

As the liquidity or marketability of a security decreases, the market rate on the security should rise, providing the necessary incentive for lenders to buy it. To a degree, the yield differentials shown in Figure 13:7 reflect differing degrees of liquidity.

THE TERM STRUCTURE OF INTEREST RATES

While the yield differences between different types of securities have attracted the attention and intellectual curiosity of economists, such attention and effort are insignificant compared to the effort spent to explain the relationship between long- and short-term rates. In investigating this relationship, it is essential that all attributes of the securities be held constant except the length of time to maturity (when the security will be paid off by the borrower). Thus, one might, for example, examine only the yield pattern of federal government securities.

The relationship between long- and short-term securities is called the *term structure of interest rates* and is shown graphically by a yield curve. Such a curve is constructed in a diagram similar to Figure 13:8. On the horizontal axis, the scale shows the time to maturity, while the scale on the

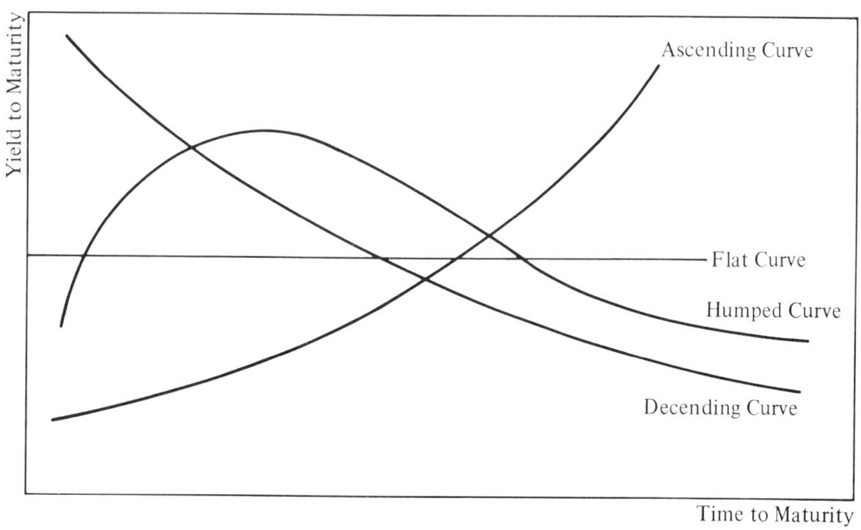

FIGURE 13:8
Alternative yield curves

vertical axis records yield to maturity, or the rate of return an individual would realize on his investment if the security were held to maturity.

In a diagram such as Figure 13:8, how would the typical yield curve look for government securities? On the basis of our discussion above, one might be tempted to say that the curve will be ascending. That is, as the time to maturity lengthens, the yield to maturity will rise. Indeed, such a curve is a logical possibility. However, at least three other general configurations have occurred, and all are shown in the diagram. Since each of these is a possible yield curve, any theory explaining the term structure of interest rates must be capable of explaining how each could emerge.

Reference to Figure 13:9 shows that several possible yield curves have characterized the market for government securities during the past several years. It also shows that the level of the yield curve has been subject to rather large shifts over time.

As with so many other phenomena in economics, no single explanation for the term structure has been universally accepted. We shall discuss three

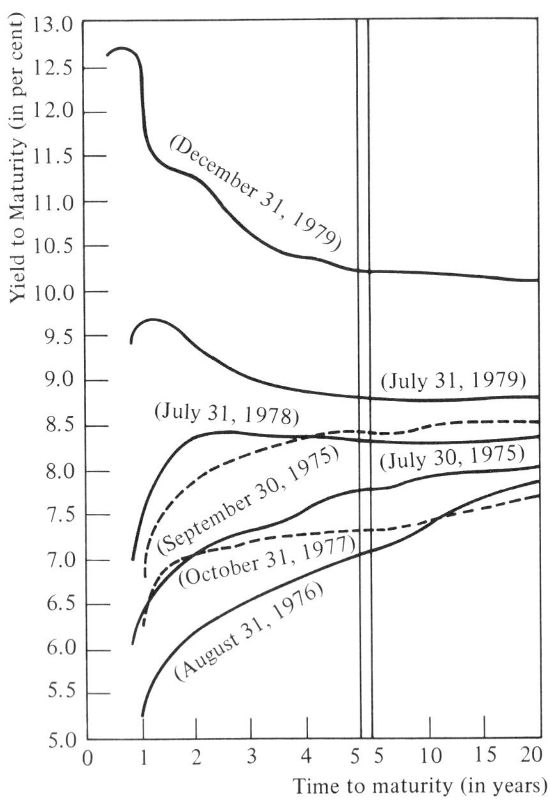

FIGURE 13:9
Government yield curves (Courtesy of the U.S. Treasury)

of these explanations, each of which is capable of explaining the four possible yield curves. These three theories are, however, interdependent to a degree.

The expectations hypothesis

The expectations hypothesis, which was given its first clear statement by Irving Fisher,[15] finds many adherents (in one form or another) among economists. It holds that the long-term interest rate is the average of the current short-term rate and the short-term rates expected to prevail over the time period in question. Thus, the market rate on a security maturing in five years is the average of the one-year rates prevailing and expected to prevail over the next five years.

A more rigorous statement of this theory requires several assumptions:

1. The securities in question have no default risk.
2. Investors have complete, certain, and accurate forecasts of all future short-term rates.
3. Investors desire to maximize profits.
4. Transactions costs in buying and selling securities are neglected.

These assumptions imply that investors are indifferent (have no preferences) between long- and short-dated securities. The securities, then, are perfect substitutes for each other in the lender's portfolio. They also tell us that investors will buy and sell in such a way as to maximize their profits.

Suppose, then, that an investor has available a quantity of funds that he wishes to commit for two years. Should he purchase a two-year security that currently yields 10% or a one-year security yielding 8%? His choice depends on his expectations about short-term rates in the second year, for he has the option of buying the one-year security today and investing the proceeds one year hence in another one-year security. Thus, the expected rate on one-year securities one year from now is crucial to the choice. If this were 10%, his average return over two years by investing sequentially would be approximately 9%, which is below what could be earned by investing in a two-year security. However, should the expected rate by 13%, his average yield by investing sequentially would be above 10%, the return on the two-year security. Thus, given expectations about short-term interest rates, the desire to maximize profits will drive the long-term rate to be the average of current and expected short-term rates.

This analysis can be used to explain why expectations of rising interest rates will produce an ascending yield curve. If lenders expect interest rates

[15] See "Appreciation and Interest," *Publications of the American Economic Association* (Aug. 1896): 23–9, 88-92. Perhaps it is best expressed by Friedrich A. Lutz, "The Structure of Interest Rates," *Quarterly Journal of Economics*, Vol. 55, No. 4 (Nov. 1940): 36–63.

to rise in the future, then they will consider present interest rates low. They will, therefore, lend at short term, depressing short-term interest rates. Borrowers, on the other hand, will want to borrow at long term to lock themselves into low long-term rates. They therefore increase the demand for funds in the long end of the market, forcing up the long-term rate. It follows, then, that expectations of rising interest rates will produce an ascending yield curve, in which the long-term rate is the average of the current and expected short-term rates.

A descending yield curve is seen as evidence that investors believe market interest rates will be lower in the future, i.e., that they are abnormally high. Reacting to their expectations, lenders will lend at long term to take advantage of the now high rates, and borrowers will borrow in the short sector to avoid being locked into today's high rates for a long period. As a consequence, the supply of funds in the long end of the market will increase, driving down long-term rates, while the demand for funds at the short end will rise, driving up short-term rates.

A flat or horizontal yield curve is seen as evidence that investors believe the present short rates will prevail over the relevant time horizon, i.e., they will neither rise nor fall. A humped curve implies that investors expect rates to rise in the near future, but fall in the long run.

The term structure as a measure of expected inflation

So far in our analysis we have not considered why investors expect future short-term interest rates to rise or fall. One reason why they would is related to their forecast of the future rate of inflation.

If investors are indifferent about investing either at short or long term (in market terminology, the market is said to be dominated by risk-neutral as opposed to risk-averse or risk-accepting individuals), then the real rate of interest should be the same for all maturities of the same type of security. Thus, if the yield curve plotted real yields rather than market yields, it would appear as a horizontal line. Then only inflationary expectations would cause market yields to differ from real yields. That being the case, the yield curve can be used as the market's forecast of the future rate of inflation. Thus, an ascending curve implies an expectation of a rising inflation rate, whereas a descending curve would imply a forecast of a declining rate of inflation.

We conclude this discussion about the expectations hypothesis by noting one of the criticisms raised against it. This concerns its basic premise: that the long-term rate is the average of the relevant short-term rates. In explaining this concept, one customarily compares a two-, three-, or five-year security with a comparable series of one-year securities (otherwise the mathematics would become too cumbersome). However, consider the case of a consol or perpetual security. Before purchasing a consol, the investor would be required to compare its yield with the present short-term yield and all short-term rates expected to prevail until the end of time! This is not to imply that expectations are unimportant in determining the yield curve, but rather that the specific formulation that has long characterized this approach is questionable.

The market segmentation hypothesis

A second theory of the term structure that occupies a prominent place is the so-called market segmentation hypothesis. It seems to be more popular among market analysts than among economists. It draws attention to a fact observed in our discussion of financial intermediaries in Chapter 3. That is, lending institutions have a strong tendency to match the maturity of their assets with that of their liabilities. Thus, insurance companies, which have long-term liabilities, also hold long-term assets; whereas money market mutual funds have short-term liabilities matched by short-term assets. Similar observations can be made about other intermediaries. There are several reasons for this observed behavior. First, in some instances the law limits the type of lending that can be done or the assets that these institutions can acquire. Second, a financial institution with a certain liability structure prefers a comparable asset structure to ensure a *certainty* of income, even if it does not ensure a maximum yield. For example, insurance companies and pension funds can calculate with reasonable accuracy the amount they must pay out in the future for accidents, disability, death, and retirements. Given their knowledge of future outflow, they can today invest premiums to ensure themselves either certainty of yield and profits or uncertainty of yield and possibly greater profits. That is, by investing in long-term securities with yields that are known today, they can guarantee themselves a certain income flow. On the other hand, they can invest in successive short-term securities and, in effect, bet on their future income and yield. So long as such investors are risk averse, they will confine their assets acquisitions to long-term securities. Note that this kind of risk aversion leads to a preference for long-dated securities, whereas in the liquidity premium theory (to be discussed below) aversion leads to a preference for short-dated securities.

Similar considerations lead money market mutual funds to prefer short-term assets. Commercial banks present a somewhat special case. Because their liabilities are largely demand in nature, they will invest heavily in short-term assets and require a premium to invest in longer maturities, as the liquidity premium theory predicts. The investment behavior of many financial intermediaries leads to what is known as market segmentation—investors who confine their activities to one segment of the market, who do not buy both long and short maturities.

The assumption of complete segmentation is a strong one, but more or less necessary for the theory. To see that this is the case, it must be understood that market segmentation implies that the yield curve can be explained by activities of individual segments of the market and that the long-term rate need not be the average of the current and expected short-term rates. For example, a rising yield curve can indicate a heavy demand for loanable funds by long-term borrowers and a sparse supply by lenders, together with reverse conditions in the short-term sector. There is no necessary relationship between long and short rates. This situation can happen only if markets are segmented. If they are not, and some lenders can operate in all different segments of the market, then profit opportunities will arise that tend to make the yield curve conform to that suggested by the expectations theory. This can be demonstrated if we suppose that some segmentation does occur and that some lenders have a decided preference for short-term loans. The long-term rate, then, will not be the average of the current and expected short-term rates, unless there are some lenders who are willing to operate in all sectors of the market. Should these lenders exist, they will exploit an obvious profit opportunity: in their eyes short-term rates are low relative to long-term rates. They will, therefore, increase the demand for short-term funds (raising interest rates in that sector) and increase the supply of funds to the long-term sector (depressing the rate there), until the long rate is the average of the current and expected short-term rates. This is why one must believe that markets are completely segmented in order to consider the segmentation theory a satisfactory explanation of the yield curve.

Those who adhere to this explanation of the yield curve often assign to commercial banks and general monetary conditions a crucial role in determining the ultimate shape of the yield curve. An increase in the rate of growth of the monetary base that produces monetary ease will lead commercial banks in particular to buy short-term Treasury securities. This will increase the flow of loanable funds to the short sector, depressing short-term market yields relative to long-term yields and produce an ascending yield curve. Just the reverse happens when monetary conditions are tightened. Then commercial banks become borrowers in the short sector to meet loan demands. They sell Treasury bills, depressing their price and raising short-term yields relative to long-term yields. The result is a declining yield curve. (Other depository institutions do not figure prominently in this explanation because laws circumscribe the types of assets they can purchase to a far greater extent than banks.)

The liquidity premium hypothesis

The liquidity premium hypothesis is a variation on both the expectations and market segmentation theories.[16] It shares with the latter a belief that markets are segmented. The segmentation arises because the market is

[16] The most articulate statement of this view is to be found in J. R. Hicks, *Value and Capital* (London: Oxford at the Clarendon Press, 1939, 2nd ed. 1946), pp. 144–9.

dominated by investors who are risk averse. That is, they wish to avoid risk and will accept it only if compensated by additional interest. Since a yield curve is plotted for securities with the same default risk, it is obvious that the risk involved must be of some other variety. Indeed, this is the case and refers to a type of risk we noted in Chapter 6: whenever market interest rates change by the same fraction, the market price will fluctuate more for long-term securities than for short-term securities. It is this type of risk that commands a premium. The amount of that premium will depend on the collective valuation of lenders.

Under this theory, the yield curve will normally slope upward because of the liquidity premium.[17] It will only slope downward or become flat if short-term rates are expected to fall in excess of, or so that they are equal to, the liquidity premium. Under most conditions, one would expect an ascending yield curve. It is the emphasis on expectations that causes some economists to classify this hypothesis as a variation on the expectations theory.

THE IMPORTANCE OF THEORIES OF THE TERM STRUCTURE

It might be tempting to dismiss this controversy among economists over the term structure as just so much arcane nonsense, of no importance to the world of decision making. If little else has been learned from the pages of this text, it is hoped the reader now knows that controversies arise over matters of substance. So it is here. Among the important practical issues involved, several should be noted and discussed. First, the expectations and market segmentation hypotheses imply very different things about the substitutability of various securities. The expectations theory implies that they are, in general, very good substitutes: investors are indifferent between long- and short-dated securities. The segmentation theory implies much the opposite: different-maturity securities are very poor substitutes.

Whether securities are good or poor substitutes can play an important role in the evaluation of targets and indicators. Among Keynesian economists, the short-term interest rate is often a preferred operational target, while the long-term rate is an indicator. For these two rates to function adequately, there must be a stable and predictable relationship between them. Changes in the short-term rate will be generalized to the long-term sector only if different-maturity securities are good substitutes for one another. If markets are segmented, short- and long-term interest rates would not be a useful set of targets and indicators for the conduct of monetary policy.

[17] Borrowers must not be as risk averse as lenders. If they are, they will prefer to borrow on a succession of short-term loans. Should this occur, short-term rates will be at a premium relative to long-term rates. Hence, borrowers must either be less risk averse than lenders or risk neutral.

Another consequence of deducing the correct explanation concerns the financing of business and government in a cost-minimizing way. The expectations hypothesis suggests that when an upward-sloping yield curve prevails, the time is at hand for borrowing long, even though current long rates are above short rates. Conversely, for a declining curve, it is better to borrow for "short term" even though short-term rates are above long-term rates.

Summary—market interest rates and the term structure

Two different objectives were attempted in this second portion of the chapter. First, material presented elsewhere was gathered together to explain systematically the differences in market interest rates, for although economists are fond of speaking of "the" interest rate, in fact a number of different rates are found in the market. Second, we considered the term structure, or relationship between short- and long-term rates. Three different hypotheses were examined and some of the implications for the correct view were drawn. While the available data are in accord with all explanations, economists tend to stress the important role of expectations as an explanatory variable.

CONCLUSION

This chapter discussed interest rates in terms of the loanable funds theory. The demand for these funds was seen largely to come from those desiring to make capital investments. To this could be added the demand by government to finance a budget deficit and the desire by individuals to hoard money. The supply of these funds comes from saving, new-money creation, government budget surpluses, and the dishoarding of money. The interplay of demand and supply determines the market rate of interest. In the absence of inflation and expectations of inflation, the market rate was also the real rate of interest.

We then allowed inflation to affect the market and real rate of interest, and examined the Gibson paradox and the various attempts to resolve it. The importance of the resolution was seen to be the insight that it provides into the cause of business cycles and the adjustment of the economy to cyclical disturbances.

Finally, the last part of the chapter was devoted to explaining the relationship of interest rates on securities of similar maturities and on securities of different maturities, or the term structure of interest rates.

STUDY QUESTIONS

1. If individuals expect the rate of inflation to decline dramatically, what do you think would happen to market interest rates? Explain.

2. How might one argue that both Keynes and Wicksell have a monetary theory of the business cycle?
3. From any previous discussion in the text, does it appear plausible that a change in the money multiplier would lead to or cause inflation? From this answer, what is your feeling about the plausibility of the Keynes–Wicksell explanation of the Gibson paradox?
4. Explain why yield curves can slope upward.
5. Why might borrowers prefer to borrow at long term today even though long-term rates exceed short-term rates?
6. Explain under what conditions a descending yield curve indicates that the market expects the rate of inflation to decline.
7. Why is complete market segmentation crucial to the segmentation explanation of the term structure?
8. Explain why complete segmentation of markets would eliminate the usefulness of interest rates as targets and indicators of monetary policy.

SELECTED REFERENCES AND READINGS

Bomberger, William, and Makinen, Gail. "The Fisher Effect: Graphical Treatment and Some Econometric Implications." *Journal of Finance,* Vol. 32, No. 3 (June 1977).

Fisher, Irving. *The Purchasing Power of Money.* New York: Macmillan, 1912.

Gibson, A. H. "The Future Course of High-Class Investment Values." *Banker's Magazine,* Vol. 115, No. 946 (Jan. 1923).

———. "The Road to Economic Recovery, Some Reflections." *Banker's Magazine,* Vol. 122, No. 992 (Nov. 1926).

Keynes, John M. *A Treatise on Money.* Vol. II. *The Applied Theory of Money.* London: Macmillan, 1930.

Macaulay, Frederick R. *The Movement of Interest Rates, Bond Yields, and Stock Prices in the United States Since 1856.* New York: National Bureau of Economic Research, 1938. Chapter 6, "Interest Rates and Commodity Prices."

Makinen, Gail. *Money, the Price Level, and Interest Rates.* Englewood Cliffs, N.J.: Prentice-Hall, 1977. Chapter 3.

Malkiel, Burton. *The Term Structure of Interest Rates.* Princeton, N.J.: Princeton University Press, 1966.

Michaelson, Jacob B. *The Term Structure of Interest Rates.* New York: Intext Educational Publishers, 1973.

Shiller, Robert, and Siegel, Jeremy. "The Gibson Paradox and Historical Movements in Real Interest Rates." *Journal of Political Economy,* Vol. 85, No. 5 (Oct./Nov. 1977).

14

THE GREAT DEBATE OVER THE IMPORTANCE OF MONEY

Basic differences of opinion might seem to suggest that economics is without a consistent methodology, or that economists as a group are unable to come to any firm conclusions. However, basic disagreements are inevitable in a profession where no one ideology prevails; where some individuals prefer to focus attention on the short run, while others take a longer-run perspective; and where some are more concerned with efficiency, while others hold considerations of equity in higher regard.[1] Among the famous debates of economics, none has been more acrimonious or more long-lasting than that over the importance of money.

Before the general acceptance of the Keynesian approach to macroeconomics, few economists doubted the importance of money as a determinant of nominal values such as money wages, money interest rates, and money income. Indeed, for the pre-Keynesian economic orthodoxy, money was of supreme importance as a determinant of nominal values. On the other hand, real values such as the real wage, real interest rate, real income, and employment were determined by forces that, over the longer run, had little if anything to do with the supply of money. Thus, somewhat paradoxically, while money was important as a determinant of nominal values, it was unimportant as a determinant of real economic values, especially employment. In the words of these pre-Keynesian economists, money was neutral in its effect on the real sector of the economy. The prevailing belief was that variations in the supply of money (or its growth rate) could exert no systematic or lasting influence on the real wage, employment, real income, or the real interest rate.[2]

[1] The participants in this debate are the economists recognized by their professional colleagues. In contrast to the medical or legal profession, anyone can call him or herself an economist. Without legal recourse to prevent such an appellation, one often finds oneself identified with a group containing all sorts of cranks and knaves.

[2] This is not to suggest that a barter economy was seen by the pre-Keynesians as no different from a monetary economy. To the extent that improvements in the monetary system (e.g., the introduction of checks, which increased the efficiency of exchange) reduced the time, effort, and material resources devoted to exchange, money was non-neutral. However, this is not the type of non-neutrality under consideration here.

This idea of the neutrality of money is clearly opposed to the conclusion drawn in Chapter 10, which was based upon the Keynesian approach to macroeconomic theory. There it was seen that changes in the money supply could cause systematic changes in real variables, e.g., they could lower the real wage and the real rate of interest while raising the level of employment and real income. This ability of money to change real variables permanently is, of course, a primary message of the Phillips curve relationship.

It is no wonder that the *General Theory* generated heated debate after its publication in 1936. Once the Keynesian approach to macroeconomics became orthodox, the older doctrines, in which the neutrality of money occupied such a prominent position, were shunted aside. However, in the United States these doctrines were by no means cast into oblivion. They occupied a place of some importance in the courses in economics given at various academic institutions, most notably the University of Chicago after Milton Friedman assumed a position there in 1946.

Another early "keeper of the flame" was Professor Karl Brunner, an immigrant from Switzerland in the early 1950s. Friedman and Brunner, together with Professors Phillip Cagan, Anna Schwartz, Allan Meltzer, David Meiselman, David Fand, and several economists at the Federal Reserve Bank of St. Louis, became the vanguard in the revival of the pre-Keynesian view of money, under the name *Monetarism*. The ideas, theories, and empirical investigations of this group, which questioned the assumptions, relevance, and predictive capability of the ruling Keynesian model, met with limited success until the mid-1960s and the onset of inflation in the United States associated with the financing of the war in Vietnam.

The Monetarists had a ready analysis to explain the cause of the inflation and to provide a theoretically sure-fire cure, both of which initially eluded the prevailing Keynesian-oriented policymakers. The latter consistently underestimated the strength of the inflationary surge in the U.S. economy.

Thus, during the late 1960s and throughout the 1970s a loud and growing debate was waged between the Monetarists and the Keynesians that continues to this day. Its central feature is the importance of the supply of money as a determinant of real economic variables and the price level. While the various components of this debate are interesting in themselves, they are also of concern because they imply the pursuit of markedly different monetary and fiscal policies for purposes of economic stabilization.

To set out the nature of this debate and issues involved is by no means an easy task. For one thing, economists do not agree on the essential elements of the debate. For another, consistent views are not held by all members of both camps. That is, some economists identified as Keynesian may be sympathetic to a Monetarist position on one or more issues, and vice versa. A reading of the vast literature on this controversy reveals dissention over philosophy, methodology, interpretations of economic history, whether public policy should seek to fine-tune the economy, whether the short or long run is the proper perspective for policy, the empirical values of certain crucial elasticities, etc.

Thus, it would appear difficult if not impossible to distill a list of issues that all or even a majority of economists would agree constitutes the core of the debate over the importance of money. Notwithstanding this, the following scheme of reference will be used to set out the nature of the controversy and to organize the subsequent discussion. It is your author's view that these are the essential elements of the debate.[3]

1. The neutrality of money
2. The proportionality of the money stock and the level of prices
3. The monetary theory of the price level
4. The causality of money
   a. The monetary transmission mechanism
   b. The role of money in cyclical disturbances
   c. The role of fiscal policy
   d. Empirical verification of the causality of money
5. The exogeneity of money

As will be demonstrated, a great deal of the controversy over these propositions could be resolved by suitable empirical tests (if they could be contrived), for in Friedman's words, "the basic differences among economists are empirical not theoretical. . . .[4]

Because the issues between the Monetarists and the Keynesians are basically empirical, and individuals may not all place the same value on empirical tests, consistent views are not held by all members of both camps. Thus, some Keynesians may agree with the Monetarist view on some of the five propositions given above, and the Monetarists may similarly agree with the Keynesian analysis on some points. For that reason, when a view is described as Keynesian (or Monetarist) it must not be interpreted as meaning that all Keynesians (or all Monetarists) subscribe to it as an article of faith. To be sure, the view of each group on a specific issue may not even be homogeneous.

As we explore the components of the debate, we will see that they are interrelated. Moreover, our discussion of the five propositions will enable us to draw together a great deal of the analysis that has been made thus far in previous chapters.

[3] For alternative taxonomies (which are consistent with the five propositions set out here), see Milton Friedman, "The Counter-Revolution in Monetary Theory," *First Wincott Memorial Lecture* (London: The Institute of Economic Affairs, 1970); Karl Brunner, "A Survey of Selected Issues in Monetary Theory," *Schweizerische Zeitschrift Für Volkswirtschaft Und Statistik* 107 (Winter 1971); and Thomas Mayer, "The Structure of Monetarism," *Kredit und Kapital* 8 (1975): 191–217 and 293–315; and the related discussion by Karl Brunner, Harry G. Johnson, Phillip Cagan, David Laidler, Benjamin Friedman, and Martin Bronfenbrenner.

[4] Milton Friedman, National Bureau of Economic Research *Occasional Paper* 112 (1971): 61.

THE NEUTRALITY OF MONEY

A central proposition of the debate concerns the neutrality of money. That is, what do changes in the supply of money accomplish? Do they cause changes to take place in real variables such as real wages, employment, real income, and the real interest rate? If so, are these changes permanent or merely transitory? And if transitory, how long is the time period of change—decades or merely days?

The Keynesian view

There is little doubt that, in the Keynesian monetary theory as presented in this text, money is not neutral. So long as an unemployment equilibrium prevails, an increase in the supply of money will produce permanent changes in real variables—interest rates, income, wages, and employment. This conclusion is reinforced by the Keynesian use of and belief in the permanency of the tradeoff shown by the Phillips curve. The original curve depicts a relationship between a money variable (the change in money wages) and a real variable (the percentage of unemployment). This is the quintessence of the non-neutrality of money.

While the Phillips curve shows that the tradeoff is permanent, does permanent mean forever (in the absence of any unexpected shock to the system)? Here the Keynesian may hedge a bit, for the focus of his analysis is the rather ill-defined "short run" and Keynes himself expressed the opinion that in the long run we are all dead. Thus, a permanent tradeoff is likely to be envisioned as permanent within the relevant time period for public policy, however that is defined.[5]

Thus, under circumstances other than those associated with Keynesian full employment, money is non-neutral in the Keynesian world.

The Monetarist view

The Monetarist view on the abilities of changes in the money supply to change real variables was set forth in detail in previous chapters. With regard to both the level of employment and the real rate of interest, changes in the supply of money were seen to exert transitory non-neutral effects. Thus, if the rate of increase of the money supply is accelerated, it will produce some initial rise in the level of commodity prices. This rise in the price level has been seen to perform the paradoxical feat of raising the perceived real interest rate and wage rate received by the lender/saver and

[5] So as not to understate the Keynesians' case, we noted earlier that they distinguish between the simple or very-short-run Phillips curve tradeoff and a longer-run or expectations-augmented Phillips curve in which the expectations of workers regarding inflation enters as a variable worsening, but not eliminating, the tradeoff, i.e., their long-run Phillips curve is not vertical.

worker, while lowering these same real variables for the borrower/investor and the employer. So long as the actual inflation rate is incorrectly anticipated by the lender/saver and the worker, the real interest rate will be below its natural level and the volume of employment will be above its natural level (i.e., the unemployment rate will be below its natural rate). These non-neutral effects of an increase in the money supply will, however, be only transitory. How long, then, is a transitory time period? Here Monetarists can give no discrete time estimate applicable to all situations. The time interval depends on the speed with which the participants in the financial and labor markets adapt their anticipations to the actual course of events. If this is fast, the time interval will be short; if not, it will be longer. Prevailing opinion is that the speed of adaptation depends in large part on the nature of policies being pursued by the monetary and fiscal authorities. If they are a complete surprise, the adaptation will take longer than if they are a continuation of well-established policies. When the latter prevail, market participants rationally include them in their expectations of the future course of events—especially their likely effect on the rate of inflation.

Milton Friedman has suggested that for the United States "in the short-run, which may be as much as five or ten years, monetary charges affect primarily output; over decades, on the other hand, the rate of monetary growth affects primarily prices."[6]

In his early work on the effects of inflation on U.S. interest rates, Irving Fisher saw the transition period as lasting a decade or more.[7] Subsequent empirical estimates using more recent U.S. data are supportive of Fisher's conclusion.[8]

Thus, in the main, the Monetarist analysis envisions an economy as resting at a natural rate of unemployment and a natural real interest rate, with temporary departures from this state of affairs being produced by accelerations or decelerations in the growth rate of the money supply. These changes in money produce unanticipated changes in the price level, and this leads to short-run or transitory changes in real variables. From this, it follows that Monetarists can believe in the short-run tradeoff as given by the Phillips curve. However, in the longer run, when the actual course of movements in the price level is fully anticipated, the Phillips curve is vertical at the natural rate of unemployment and money is neutral.

Qualifying this general conclusion on the Monetarist view on the neutrality of money are a number of suggestions, by both Monetarists and others, why one should believe in the long-run non-neutrality of money. For rates of inflation similar to those experienced by the United States, these considerations are of minor significance. Foremost among them is the

[6] Milton Friedman, "The Counter-Revolution in Monetary Theory," pp. 23–4.

[7] Irving Fisher, *The Theory of Interest* (New York: Macmillan, 1930).

[8] For a listing of these studies, see footnote 10 in Chapter 13.

belief that if the rate of inflation (caused by a higher rate of growth of the money supply) should increase, individuals and business will be led to hold smaller money balances. Since money yields utility to its holder by easing the process of exchange and providing peace of mind against an uncertain future, smaller money holdings reduce the flow of utility to the individual. Since the flow of utility is a part of the real income of the individual, a smaller flow means a reduced real income. Hence, an increase in the supply of money reduces a real variable—income—and is, therefore, non-neutral.[9]

The importance of neutrality

The importance of the neutrality of money derives from its implications for the conduct of monetary policy. If the Monetarists are correct, then discretionary changes in the supply of money should have no lasting effect on real interest rates, real output, and employment. Instead, their lasting effect will be on the general level of prices. Under these circumstances, the rate of increase of the money supply should be geared to producing whatever long-run rate of inflation (including zero) society desires. It should come as no surprise, then, that a central tenet of Monetarist monetary policy is the desirability of a more or less constant growth rate for the supply of money.[10]

If, however, the Keynesian view is correct (meaning that the transition period is very long), then a case can be made for a variable growth rate of the money supply as a part of a program to stabilize income and employment.[11]

It should now be apparent that the issue of neutrality is empirical, in the sense that it cannot be settled by theoretical argument.

[9] See Milton Friedman, "The Optimum Quantity of Money," in *The Optimum Quantity of Money and Other Essays* (Chicago: Aldine, 1970), pp. 14–5; Phillip Cagan, "The Non-Neutrality of Money in the Long-Run," *Journal of Money, Credit and Banking,* Vol. 1, No. 2 (May 1969): 207–27; and James Tobin, "Friedman's Theoretical Framework," *Journal of Political Economy,* Vol. 80, No. 5 (Sept.–Oct. 1972): 852–63.

For other developments, see Benjamin Klein, "Income Velocity, Interest Rates, and the Money Supply Multiplier," *Journal of Money, Credit and Banking,* Vol. 5, No. 2 (May 1973): 656–68. This paper also contains an argument for expecting the long-run nonneutrality of money.

[10] Monetarists differ on the conduct of monetary policy. Some of their new adherents, associated with the Federal Reserve Bank of St. Louis, call for discretionary changes in the rate of growth of the money supply, in the belief that they can cause the growth rate of income to remain on its long-run path. These conclusions are derived from their econometric studies. The old guard among the Monetarists, led by Friedman, opposes discretionary changes, for they believe that income responds to these changes with a lag that is both long and uncertain.

[11] Since some Keynesians find Friedman's argument that monetary policy works with a long and uncertain lag compelling, they might accept his policy recommendation centering on a constant growth rate for the money supply, however measured.

THE PROPORTIONALITY OF THE MONEY STOCK AND THE GENERAL LEVEL OF PRICES

One of the great empirical regularities discovered when data covering long periods of time are plotted (such as in Figures 1:1 or 11:1) is that the stock of money per unit of real output (in terms of the Equation of Exchange, $MV = PY$, this is expressed as M/Y) is roughly proportional to the general level of prices, P. This long-run proportionality has been adduced as evidence in support of the Monetarist position. Before we examine the validity of this claim, let us look at the Keynesian approach.

The Keynesian view

The Keynesian analysis is primarily concerned with the short run, and generally assumes the presence of an unemployment equilibrium. In this context, an increase in the money supply will lead both to a permanent expansion in real output, Y, and to a lower interest rate. The latter will increase the quantity of money demanded (or, equivalently, lead to a fall in velocity, V). Because Y rises and V falls, an increase in the money supply, M, should not be expected to produce a proportional change in the price level, P. This conclusion follows, of course, from the tradeoff given by the Phillips curve. This lack of proportionality between M and P in the short run is also consistent with the data, as can be seen when a segment of time is isolated (take, for example, the period 1933–1937, using the price index in Figure 1:1). The Keynesian analysis is largely silent on the longer-run relationship between M and P. However, to the extent that the tradeoff given by the Phillips curve can be exploited, one should expect Keynesians to argue that proportionality need not characterize the longer run.

The Monetarist view

The Monetarists' view is for all purposes identical to the Keynesians' for the short run, or period of transition, for their analysis supports the short-run non-neutrality of money (for different reasons, to be sure). Thus, increases in the growth rate of the money supply lead initially to some rise in the price level, and a large rise in real output. Since such increases also lead, initially, to a reduction in the market rate of interest, the velocity of money should fall in the short run. Since V falls and Y rises, a change in M will not produce a proportional change in the level of prices, P.

However, these changes in velocity and real output are mainly transitory. To the extent that money is neutral, real output will ultimately fall back to its original level (or long-run growth path) and the price level will then rise faster than the growth in the money supply (the price level, so to speak, will catch up with the previous growth in the money supply). As inflationary expectations cause market interest rates to rise (as explained by Fisher), the velocity of money will start to rise and will probably exceed its former level (this is the counterpart of the long-run non-neutrality argument given above). To the extent that velocity remains permanently higher, the price level will be proportionately greater than the mere growth rate of the money stock itself would imply.

The Monetarist view on the relationship between the money supply and the price level is conveniently summarized by Milton Friedman:

1. *There is a consistent though not precise relation between the rate of growth of the quantity of money and the rate of growth of nominal income.*
2. *This relationship is not obvious to the naked eye largely because it takes time for changes in monetary growth to affect income and how long it takes is itself variable.*
3. *On the average, a change in the rate of monetary growth produces a change in the rate of growth of nominal income about six to nine months later. This is an average and does not hold in every individual case.*
4. *The changed rate of growth of nominal income typically shows up first in output and hardly at all in prices.*
5. *On the average, the effect on prices comes about six to nine months after the effect on income and output, so the total delay between a change in monetary growth and a change in the rate of inflation averages something like 12–18 months.*
6. *Even after allowance for the delay in the effect of monetary growth, the relation is far from perfect. There's many a slip "twixt the monetary change and the income change."*
7. *In the short-run, which may be as much as five or ten years, monetary changes affect primarily output; over decades, on the other hand, the rate of monetary growth affects primarily prices.*[12]

Over the longer run, the Monetarist view is that M and P need not be strictly proportional, for various institutional developments (among others) can affect the long-run trend of velocity—checking accounts and the transfer of money by wire, for example. These developments increase the speed with which money is transferred from one party to another. Since velocity is subject to some long-run trend, M and P lose their close proportionality.

A MONETARY THEORY OF THE PRICE LEVEL

An important aspect of the great debate concerns the factors responsible for determining the level of prices, which, for policy purposes, translates into what determines the rate of inflation. This aspect of the debate may appear redundant, given the discussion above on neutrality and proportion-

[12] Milton Friedman, "The Counter-Revolution in Monetary Theory," pp. 22–5.

ality. However, those two propositions do not preclude nonmonetary factors from influencing the price level, and one aspect of the great debate is centered on such a possibility.

The Keynesian view

The Keynesian view of the determinants of the price level, and hence the rate of inflation, is heterogeneous. While it does not exclude the supply of money from an important role, it does not accord it an exclusive or even a prominent place among explanations.

In the Keynesian model set forth in Chapter 10 the price level depended upon per unit labor costs and a markup for the elements in "profit." Such an approach draws attention to the supply (or cost) side as a determinant of the price level, and away from the supply of money or aggregate demand as a causal factor.[13] Thus, anything capable of raising per unit labor costs or profit markups becomes a possible explanation for inflation. The behavior of wages over time is prominent among such cost–push explanations, both among American and British Keynesians. In these theories the rate of wage increase is viewed as largely independent of the level of unemployment (which leads one to wonder what has become of the Phillips curve); it depends on personal concepts of equity or on what is occurring in foreign countries. These theories seem to rely more on sociology than on economics for their frame of reference, and to be increasingly popular as the inflationary period continues.[14]

[13] Among Keynesians, Paul Samuelson summarizes this view very concisely in the following three propositions, which he regards as both Keynesian and incompatible with Monetarism:

1. *Even when the money supply is held constant, any significant changes in thriftiness and the propensity to consume can be expected to have systematic independent effects on the money value of current output, affecting average prices or aggregate production or both.*
2. *Even when the money supply is held constant, an exogenous burst of investment opportunities or animal spirits on the part of business can be expected to have systematic effects on total GNP.*
3. *Even when the money supply is held constant, increases in public expenditures or reductions in tax rates—and even increases in public expenditures balanced by increases in taxation—can be expected to have systematic effects upon aggregate GNP.*

See his "Reflections on the Merits and Demerits of Monetarism," in *Issues in Fiscal and Monetary Policy: The Eclectic Economist Views the Controversy,* James J. Diamond, ed. (Chicago, Ill.: DePaul University, 1971), p. 7.

For an excellent discussion of the nonmonetary theories of inflation put forth by Keynesians, see David Fand, "Some Issues in Monetary Economics," *Monthly Review,* Federal Reserve Bank of St. Louis 52 (Jan. 1970): 20–3.

[14] For the view of an American Keynesian, see Arthur Okun, "The Great Stagflation Swamp," address to the Economics Club of Chicago (Oct. 6, 1977); for the British view, see R. F. Kahn, "Thoughts on the Behavior of Wages and Monetarism," *Lloyds Bank Review* (Jan. 1976): 1–11; and J. R. Hicks, "What Is Wrong with Monetarism," *Lloyds Bank Review* (Oct. 1976): 1–13.

The Keynesians do not always have recourse to trade union power to explain inflation, however. For those who adhere to the tradeoff given by the Phillips curve, merely running the economy at a high level of activity (a low-unemployment rate), which produces a tight labor market (one characterized by high demand), will generate wage increases in excess of productivity increases, which will raise per unit labor costs, and hence the price level. How much per unit labor costs will rise depends on the particular structure of the labor market, which includes its mix of ages, sexes, and skills.

Finally, as an additional cost–push element, one finds in Keynesian explanations of inflation reference to the rise in the price of a crucial commodity. In recent times oil and certain agricultural crops have been prime candidates, while in times past it was the price of steel products. This approach to explaining the cause of inflation arises from a method of constructing a price level common to many Keynesians. The level is made to depend upon a suitable weighted sum of individual prices. Hence, in investigating the cause of the rise in the average of all prices, one is led naturally to an investigation of the price behavior of individual commodities or industries. Such an approach runs the risk of confusing a change in relative prices with a change in the level of all prices, and leads to the neglect of aggregate demand as the major cause of inflation.[15]

In summary, the Keynesian view concentrates heavily on explaining inflation by reference to nonmonetary phenomena ranging from the behavior of trade unions to the prices of certain "critical" commodities.

The Monetarist view

The Monetarists typically view the price level in terms of the Equation of Exchange, in which it emerges as the balancing factor between aggregate demand, MV, and the level of real output, Y. Holding this view, they echo Friedman's claim that the price level is a monetary phenomenon and "inflation is always and everywhere a monetary phenomenon in the sense that it can be produced only by a more rapid increase in the quantity of money than in output."

In their explanation of the inflationary cycle, rising money wages play an important role in pushing up the price level. However, these increases in cost are not the cause of inflation, but are the result of prior price level increases produced by an expansion of aggregate demand, and are designed to preserve the purchasing power of money wages (i.e., to keep the real wage constant). If these increases in money wages did not occur, the real wage would be depressed and real output would be permanently larger.

[15] This is not to suggest that the price behavior of such commodities as oil may not lead to a rise in the overall price index. However, its lasting effect upon prices in general is more likely to be the consequence of its ability to decrease the level of output.

The Monetarist view on the neutrality of money precludes this. Thus, an integral part of any inflationary cycle will include a rise in money wages that is designed to preserve real wages. Because the rise in money wages is apt to lag behind the initial rise in aggregate demand that ignites the inflation, Monetarists believe that individuals come to confuse cause and effect.[16] Such views are often encouraged by the government, which seeks to shift the blame for its own actions to others.

We have also noted that Monetarists do not hold labor unions, corporations, or public utilities responsible for inflation. This, they believe, confuses high prices with rising prices.

Finally, the Monetarist view of the key-commodity theory of inflation is usually considered along two lines. The first dismisses it as an elementary confusion between a change in relative prices and a change in the price level. The second is to explain that its effect upon the price level will be temporary. That is, the price of a key commodity such as oil is increased by reducing output. This restriction serves to reduce aggregate real output as well. Given such a decline in Y, the price level, P, will rise to maintain equality between demand and supply. However, the decline in Y may result in some unemployment. In addition, over the longer run, the increase in the supply of labor will have less oil input to work with. This will lead to a fall in the wage rate. As wages decline relative to other input prices, production costs and prices will decline. Thus, over the longer run the net result will be a change in relative prices—goods containing oil will cost relatively more than goods which use labor intensively.

A summary

The importance of an explanation of the determination of the price level is to be found in the area of public policy. As long as one views the price level as always and everywhere a monetary phenomenon, then inflation can be controlled and price level stability achieved only through monetary means. Wage and price controls as anti-inflationary weapons are not only useless, but positively harmful in the sense that they postpone the inevitable, lead to less efficient ways to obtain wage and price increases, and encourage individuals to violate the law, which weakens the social cohesiveness of society. On the other hand, a Keynesian perspective on inflation, especially that viewed as cost–push in nature, argues that controls, or what is now called an incomes policy, are an essential anti-inflationary weapon.

The key-commodity interpretation of inflation, which focuses attention on the supply or cost side, has an implication for policy that appears to be

[16] Recently, among Monetarists, Karl Brunner has proposed that the distinction between demand–pull and cost–push inflations be dropped. Rather, he believes it more analytically meaningful to distinguish between a price-theoretical and a "sociological" view of price–wage movements.

neglected by the Monetarists. It leads to the view that means other than monetary may be an effective way to combat inflation.

The rise in world oil prices during 1973–1974 requires all oil-importing countries to transfer to the oil-producing countries a larger proportion of their real gross national product. Thus, real per capita GNP must decline, which serves to impoverish the existing population of the importing country. This impoverishment is accomplished because the price level must rise relative to the money wage rate, i.e., the real wage must fall. Such a decrease in the real wage may be met by worker resistance. The workers will demand compensatory money wage adjustments, which could set off a cost–push inflation independent of any prior demand–pull phase. To deal with this problem, the government has several options. One is to allow the unemployment rate to rise, hoping that this will decrease the ability of labor to push money wages higher. The longer these unemployed workers remain unemployed, the greater is the likelihood that they will seek employment by offering their services at reduced real wages. Alternatively, the government may seek to persuade labor that it must moderate its wage demand in the face of rising prices—no easy task. This appears to be the essence of the social contract approach of the British government in dealing with the problem of oil price increases.

As far as the United States is concerned, Monetarists such as Milton Friedman seem to discount the permanent addition to the price level attributable to the oil price hike of 1973–1974:

> *I have no doubt that the oil crisis of late 1973 and early 1974, by making the country poorer, raised the price level. I have variously estimated that as having been about 1 1/2 percent. Spread that over the three years, and you have about 1/2 percentage point, per year.*[17]

THE CAUSALITY OF MONEY

A theme repeated throughout this text concerns the cause of business cycles. Is the cycle attributable primarily to monetary conditions, or is it due mainly to the instability of various components of the real sector of the economy (the demand for producer and consumer durable goods)?

The cause of the business cycle remains one of the major points of contention in the great debate. Several other points of disagreement are involved in this discussion of the causality of money, and they must be distinguished to clarify the discussion. These other points are: (1) the mechanism whereby the influence of a change in the money supply is transmitted to the markets for goods, services, and labor; (2) the role of fiscal policy; and (3) empirical verifications of respective positions.

[17] "The Monetarist Controversy," remarks by Franco Modigliani and Milton Friedman, *Economic Review* (Supplement), Federal Reserve Bank of San Francisco (1977): 17.

The transmission mechanism

We have already discussed the nature of the transmission mechanism whereby a change in the supply of money exerts its influence on the real sector. The discussion here will repeat some of that presentation, as well as introduce material on the evolution of the Keynesian view on the importance of money.

The Keynesian view

The Keynesian view, which emerged shortly after the publication of the *General Theory,* concentrated on the market interest rate (presumably a group of long-term interest rates) as the crucial variable in the transmission process, much as noted in our discussion in Chapter 10. Next, the responsiveness (or elasticity) of investment spending to a change in the interest rate was perceived to be important. Thus, the effectiveness of monetary policy was seen to depend on the interest elasticity of both the demand for money and the demand for producer and consumer durable goods.

Naturally, attempts were made to ascertain the values of these elasticities. The earliest attempts were made by circulating questionnaires to business, and by the case study method. Paul Samuelson provides a graphic description of the results of these early and primitive efforts:

> *In 1939 Oxford questionnaires were sent to businessmen and investors asking whether interest rates were of any importance to them. To a man they all answered: No, no importance whatsoever! So, this is coffin nail No. 1 on the importance of money. At the Harvard Business School, the late Professor Ebersole did case studies on finance, and what do you think they all showed, every one of them? They showed that money and finance were of no importance. If that doesn't convince you, let's turn to econometrics. Professor Tinbergen of Rotterdam did the first econometric studies—giant computer models for an economy. He tried regression coefficients, and no matter how he regressed investment on the interest rate, he always got a zero coefficient.*
>
> *Finally, if more is necessary, economic theory came to the rescue of this view and people like Sir John Hicks said that as far as short-term investment is concerned, interest is of no consequence as a cost, and as far as long-term investment is concerned, uncertainty is so great that it completely swamps interest which leaves you with only a minuscule of intermediate investment that is interest elastic. Well, that was the 1939 view. Unfortunately, some people get frozen into what they learned in their youth, and those views still prevail in some circles. Still these fellows are dying out in this country.*[18]

[18] Paul Samuelson, "Money, Interest Rates, and Economic Activity," in *Proceedings of A Symposium on Money, Interest Rates and Economic Activity* (New York: American Bankers Association, 1967), p. 22.

Elsewhere Samuelson adds that experience during the 1930s contributed to the view that money doesn't matter. This involved the inflow into the United States of billions of dollars because of distrust of Hitler's Europe, producing, in the eyes of at least Alvin Hansen, a controlled experiment in which the reserves of the banking system were vastly expanded and yet no commensurate expansion in business activity or even in the total money supply was achieved. See his "Reflections on the Merits and Demerits of Monetarism," pp. 11–2.

This early attempt by Keynesians to verify the importance of money was later, during the Monetarist revival, translated into the rallying cry that for the Keynesian, "money doesn't matter." However, rallying cries do not settle the question. A more sophisticated statement of the Keynesians' position can be gleaned from an examination of the monetary sector of their computerized models of the U.S. economy.

As these Keynesian models are presently constructed, the influence of money is transmitted through three different routes. We have identified these as cost-of-capital, wealth, and credit-availability channels. The first of these routes is sometimes called the substitution effect (or the portfolio adjustment effect), for it leads individuals to substitute higher-yielding assets for lower-yielding ones, following a change in yields induced by a change in the money supply. The late Professor Warren Smith, a Keynesian, provides a very good description of the workings of the substitution effect following the purchase by the Federal Reserve of Treasury bills:

A purchase of, say, Treasury bills by the Federal Reserve will directly lower the yield on bills and, by a process of arbitrage involving a chain of portfolio substitutions, will exert downward pressure on interest rates of financial assets generally. Moreover—and more important—the expansion of bank reserves will enable the banking system to expand its assets. . . . But the bulk of the addition to reserves will ordinarily be used to make loan accommodation available on more favorable terms, and to buy securities, thereby exerting a further downward effect on security yields.

With the expected yield on a unit of real capital initially unchanged, the decline in the yield on financial assets, and the more favorable terms on which new debt can be issued, the balance sheet of households and businesses will be thrown out of equilibrium. The adjustment toward a new equilibrium will take the form of a sale of existing financial assets and the issuance of new debt to acquire real capital and claims thereto. This will raise the price of existing units of real capital—or equity claims against these units—relative to the (initially unchanged) cost of producing new units, thereby opening up a gap between desired and actual stocks, a gap that will be closed by production of new capital goods. This stock adjustment approach is readily applicable, with some variations to suit the circumstances, to the demands for a wide variety of both business and consumer capital—including plant and equipment, inventories, residential construction, and consumer durable goods.[19]

As far as the Keynesians are concerned, the swap of Treasury bills for money will not directly create wealth, for they believe the public does not include tax liabilities for bond debt service in their personal balance sheets.

[19] Warren L. Smith, "A Neo-Keynesian View of Monetary Policy," *Controlling Aggregates* (Boston: Federal Reserve Bank of Boston, 1969), pp. 106–10. See Samuelson, "Reflections on the Merits and Demerits of Monetarism," pp. 8–10.

Thus, since both bonds and money are regarded by the public only as assets, open-market operations do not alter the nominal wealth of society.[20]

However, an open-market operation does cause market interest rates to change, and this change produces a wealth effect in the Keynesian framework. This wealth effect results from the fact that at a lower interest rate, the present or capitalized value of the expected income stream, represented either by government bonds or by real capital assets (or by their equity claim equivalents), ought to rise.[21] Believing themselves to be wealthier, individuals are led to buy more of all goods and services, as well as assets.

Finally, Keynesians generally believe that capital markets do not function smoothly in the sense that the interest rate alone determines the allocation of credit to prospective borrowers. Other nonprice means are thought to be of importance in the rationing process. This belief in nonprice methods of credit rationing leads to a Keynesian view that if an excess supply of loanable funds emerges in one sector of the capital market, it will not

[20] As to the general Keynesian position, we are told by Samuelson that "all men are mortal. Most men do not concern themselves with the well-being of their remote posterity. Hence, government bonds as an asset are not completely offset in their minds by the recognition of the liability of paying taxes in perpetuity to carry the interest of those bonds. Only if people live forever, foreseeing correctly the tax payments they (or the posterity as dear to them in the most remote future as in their own lifetime well-being) must make on account of the perpetual future interest payments on government bonds—only then would it be true to say that retirement of public debt would have no substantive effects upon the reckoning of wealth, the level of spending, and the level of prices generally." See his "Reflections on the Merits and Demerits of Monetarism," p. 9.

Another prominent neo-Keynesian, James Tobin, admits that over the years he has vacillated on the wealth potential of government bonds. In 1952 he asked: "How is it possible that society merely by the device of incurring a debt to itself can deceive itself into believing that it is wealthier? Do not the additional taxes, which are necessary to carry the interest charges, reduce the value of other components of private wealth? There certainly must be effects in this direction." See "Asset Holdings and Spending Decisions," *American Economic Review, Papers and Proceedings* 42 (May 1952): 109–23. Reprinted in *Essays in Economics,* Vol. 1, *Macro Economics,* p. 91. In 1963, in demonstrating that the issuance of long-term government securities can be expansionary, Tobin assumes they increase, dollar for dollar, net private wealth. See his "An Essay on the Principles of Debt Management," p. 378–98. In 1971 he believes that government bond issues do, to a degree, increase private wealth because future tax liabilities are probably discounted at a higher rate than future interest claims against the government.

[21] To see how this wealth effect operates, consider the simple case of debt security known as a consol. Its present value is equal to its coupon rate of interest divided by the market rate, or

$$PV = \frac{\text{coupon interest or payment per \$100}}{\text{market interest rate}}$$

If the coupon is \$4 (or 4%) and the market rate is 4%, the consol will fetch \$100 in the market. Should the market rate fall to 2%, the present value or price of the consol will rise to \$200. So long as the liabilities on the taxpayers to service the consol are disregarded, the nominal wealth of society rises when market interest rates fall.

automatically flow to other sectors characterized by excess demand. Monetary policy is thus seen to work in a discriminatory fashion against certain sectors, especially housing.

Again, we quote from Warren Smith in order to describe the operation of the credit availability channel:

The portfolio and wealth effects appear to constitute the basic channels through which monetary policy has its initial impact on economic activity. In addition, however, the institutional arrangements for providing financing to certain sectors of the economy may be such as to give monetary policy a special leverage over the availability of credit to these sectors, thereby affecting their ability to spend.[22]

The portfolio, wealth, and credit-availability effects can be labeled *initial*. They are followed by *secondary* effects:

Working through portfolio effects, wealth effects, and credit availability effects, the initial impacts of monetary policy will generate additional income, and this will further increase the demand for consumer nondurable goods and services. It will also expand the demand for services of durable goods, thereby giving a further boost to the desired stocks of these goods. Thus, the familiar magnification of demand through multiplier and accelerator effects comes into play.[23]

The Monetarist view

The Monetarists have made a considerable effort to differentiate their view on the transmission mechanism from what they describe as the Keynesian view. They have taken two different approaches. Under the first, they have called their general frame of reference the *relative price or price-theoretic approach* to money, to distinguish it from the Keynesian interest rate approach. However, this distinction is at best superficial, for the relative prices of various financial and real assets depend upon their respective yields or interest rates. Thus, whether changes in the money supply affect interest rates or the prices of various assets is immaterial, since both are merely two ways of expressing the same point of view.

Second, Monetarists claim that the Keynesian discussion of the effectiveness of money concentrates on a narrow range of interest rates (mainly those on financial assets), whereas in their view one must concentrate on the whole range of interest rates—those on both real and financial assets. This approach is best expressed by Milton Friedman:

The Keynesians regard a change in the quantity of money as affecting, in the first instance, "the" interest rate, interpreted as a market rate on a fairly narrow class of financial liabilities. They regard spending as affected only "indirectly" as the

[22] "A Neo-Keynesian View of Monetary Policy," pp. 107–9.

[23] Ibid.

> *changed interest rate alters the profitability of investment spending, again interpreted fairly narrowly, and investment spending, through the multiplier affects total spending.*[24]

If the statement by Professor Warren Smith quoted above is taken to be the Keynesian view, this statement by Friedman of the Monetarist position is quite misleading.

To facilitate comparison with the Keynesian view, the following quotation from the work of Friedman and Meiselman is reproduced at length. It involves the purchase by the Federal Reserve of Treasury bills. Because the initial situation is identical to that posited by Smith in stating the Keynesian view, the student may judge if the respective positions are different.

> *In order to persuade holders of Government bills to sell them, the monetary authorities had to make it attractive for them to do so. This means that the initial effect of the open-market operation is twofold: it made prices of bills higher (i.e., yields on them lower) than they otherwise would have been; it changed the structure of assets held by the community—excluding of course the monetary authorities. The community now holds a larger nominal amount of Government bills yielding less on the market than prior to the open-market operation.*
>
> *If money and bills (or perfect substitutes for bills) were the only form in which the community held assets . . . this would be the end of effects on existing balance sheets. For any further effects we would have to look for the effect of the changed bill yield on expenditures financed by borrowing in the form of bills or of the changed income from bills on expenditures.*
>
> *Given other assets, this is far from the end of the matter. Since the community voluntarily exchanged bills for money under the inducement of a higher price, there is a sense in which its new balance sheet is a "desired" or "equilibrium" balance sheet. But the sense is a highly restricted one. The balance sheet is in momentary but not longer-run equilibrium. The major function of money and the basic source of its social utility is to enable individuals to avoid barter by separating the purchase of particular goods from the sale of particular goods. Money is a temporary abode of purchasing power to which the proceeds from attractive selling opportunities can be added pending decisions what to buy and from which attractive buying opportunities can be financed pending the finding of attractive selling opportunities. Money performs this function no less in the market for assets than in the market for current services. In our example, individuals parted with bills for money because they saw an attractive selling opportunity. But this does not mean that they want to hold the new amount of money indefinitely or even for any very long period. The shift to money is more likely to be a temporary shift which is simply an intermediate step in the rearrangement of the balance sheet in light of the altered circumstances.*
>
> *The initial change in the structure of assets therefore introduces a deviation*

[24] *NBER Occasional Paper* No. 112, p. 28. This attempt by Monetarists to draw a distinction between their work and that of the Keynesians may stem from their desire to draw attention away from the early Keynesian view that the effectiveness of monetary policy rests on the interest elasticity of money demand and investment. Monetarists believe that the influence of money on economic activity is far more pervasive than these two elasticities might lead people to believe.

> *between the structure of assets desired under the new circumstances and the actual structure; the community holds more money and fewer assets other than bills that it desires. It will seek to correct this discrepancy by converting money into other assets. Let us suppose that the community first turns to marketable securities. In the process of trying to acquire more of them, it will of course bid up their prices (i.e., lower the yield on them), since the amount available at any point of time is fixed. But this will again introduce a disequilibrium in the balance sheet and induce the community to continue the process further, say, by trying to shift to nonmarketable securities and to real assets. In this way, the process of readjusting the portfolio leads to a bidding up of the prices not only of fixed money claims but also of equities and such real assets as houses, land, and the like. The rises in the prices of such assets raises "the" price level and so contributes to reducing the apparent "excess" money stock by reducing its real value, thereby moderating the changes in interest rates needed to achieve equilibrium.*
>
> *The rise in the nominal price of real assets (i.e., the fall in rates of interest) has further effects. On the supply side, it makes it more profitable to produce such assets and hence leads to an increase in the demand for resources employed in their production, and perhaps a bidding up of the prices of such resources. On the demand side, the rise in prices will temper the rise in amount demanded because it means a rise in the prices of assets relative to the current prices of services. It now becomes cheaper, for example, to acquire housing services by renting a house instead of buying one, to acquire the services of automobiles by renting the use of an automobile rather than buying one, and so on down the line. The readjustment of the portfolio, whose first impact we have assumed to be directed towards the acquisition of additional assets, therefore produces a partly offsetting shift toward direct acquisition of services, in the process widening the range of goods for which the money demand increases. This is equivalent to saying that lower interest rates lead to an increase in what is generally termed consumption expenditures relative to what is generally termed saving or investment.*
>
> *Of course, we describe the process in this particular order only for expositional purposes. The first impact may be on goods rather than securities. And more generally, the readjustment will take place simultaneously in all areas, though perhaps at a faster rate in some than in others. An initial increase in the stock of money will tend, via its impact on the demand for other assets, to produce an increase in money expenditures on all varieties of them and hence on both what is termed investment and what is termed consumption; it will tend, via its impact on the relative prices of assets and flows of services, to produce an increase in money expenditures for consumer services and hence a further increase in what are termed consumption expenditures. Whether the reaction is manifested sooner in investment expenditures or in consumption expenditures, whether the major quantitative effect is on the one or the other, whether the effect is mostly in prices or quantities, what the initial and subsequent impacts are on interest rates—these are all matters that depend on the speed with which the economic participants react, on the technical problems involved in readjusting various categories of expenditures, on the state of supply conditions and employment at the time in question, and the like.*[25]

This quotation indicates that both sides use a general portfolio approach in which the substitution effect working through relative interest rates (or

[25] Milton Friedman and David Meiselman, "The Relative Stability of Monetary Velocity," pp. 219–21.

relative asset prices) is the major route or channel through which monetary influences are transmitted to the markets for goods, services, and labor.

Nevertheless, the Monetarist view of the transmission mechanism differs in three respects from the Keynesian. First, the Monetarists' wealth effect is produced by the exchange of money for government bonds, for the latter represent both an asset and a liability, while the former is only an asset. Second, for the Monetarists, an increase in the supply of money may lead to the direct purchase of nondurable goods and services, whereas in the Keynesian approach such purchases result, in the main, from the working of the multiplier principle. Whether the Monetarists are correct is again an empirical question. It would seem plausible that such purchases may be explained by their view of the wealth effect.

Third, Monetarists minimize the importance of credit rationing. Their rationale is that the housing industry does not form a focal locus of monetary policy. Rather, capital markets are more flexible and fluid than the Keynesian view acknowledges. Loanable funds that do not flow through intermediaries into housing (historically because of factors such as Regulation Q) manage to find their ways into other sectors of the market.

Despite the obvious similarities in the attitudes taken by both sides to the question of the influence of money on economic activity, each has adopted markedly different research strategies to measure that influence.

The Keynesian approach has centered on constructing elaborate economic models comprising hundreds of equations, many of which are designed to capture the influence of money. This approach is dictated in part by the Keynesian belief that economic disturbances are likely to arise in particular sectors of the economy. Hence, great allocative detail is necessary to enable the policymaker to isolate and deal with the disturbance. (Note the relevance of this type of model to the Keynesian view of the cause of inflation.)

On the other hand, the Monetarists contend that little information is gained from such elaborate models for several reasons. First, the influence of money on economic activity works through so many channels, it is impossible to capture all of them. Second, what is important for economic activity is aggregate money demand, and to alter this variable, one does not need an extensive model. Because capital markets are believed to be fairly fluid, a given increase in the money supply will produce an almost identical effect on aggregate demand, regardless of where it is introduced in the model (although the relative income of the various sectors may not be immune to how money is introduced into the economy). Finally, since economic disturbances are unlikely to originate in the real sector, an elaborate breakdown of the markets for goods and services to isolate such disturbances seems uncalled for.[26] For these reasons, most Monetarist

[26] On the other hand, if one wished to explain the structure of interest rates or the behavior of *relative* interest rates and the *allocation pattern* of credit flows, a more elaborate model would be consistent with the Monetarist approach. Monetarists believe that credit policies (Regulation Q) have allocative consequences, with negligible spillover into aggregative effects.

macroeconomic models are relatively simple, with few equations (ten or less).

Whether the simple Monetarist models or the more elaborate Keynesian models have a better forecasting record is highly debatable and depends on the tests used.

The cause of cyclical disturbances

By this time the various positions on the basic cause of the business cycle should be well known. One of the foremost monetary theorists of this century, the late Professor Harry G. Johnson, puts the issue succinctly:

> *This . . . is . . . the crux of the issue prevailing between Keynesians and Monetarists: the Keynesian position is that the real economy is highly unstable and that monetary management has both little relevance to it and little control over it; the Monetarist position, on the contrary, is that the real economy is inherently fairly stable, but can be destabilized by monetary developments, which therefore, need to be controlled as far as possible by intelligent monetary policy. The monetarist position . . . seems to me the only alternative consistent with the facts . . . of historical experience.*[27]

The use of the word *unstable* to characterize the Keynesian view of the real sector is unfortunate and ambiguous. In commenting on a similar Monetarist assertion, Professor Lawrence Klein objected to the use of this word as a characteristic of the Keynesian position:

> *I don't think it is correct to say that Post-Keynesians contend that the economy is inherently unstable. They may contend that it is oscillatory or subject to fluctuations and it has a tendency to move about a position of underemployment equilibrium, but this is far different from saying that the economy is unstable.*[28]

Klein apparently interprets *unstable* to mean that if an economy is pushed from a point of equilibrium by some shock, its oscillations diverge in larger and larger swings rather than converging toward a new equilibrium. However, the usual Keynesian meaning of *unstable* is that the investment demand schedule is subject to more random shifts than, for example, the money demand schedule, and that small changes in investment, through the multiplier process, produce comparatively large changes in output. The volatility of the investment demand schedule thus yields an explanation of

[27] Harry G. Johnson, *Inflation and the Monetarist Controversy* (Amsterdam: North-Holland, 1972), pp. 6–7.

[28] Lawrence Klein, "The State of the Monetarist Debate," *Monthly Review,* Federal Reserve Bank of St. Louis (Sept. 1973): 11.

the business cycle (and, incidentally, a rationalization for the use of compensatory fiscal policy).

The Keynesian view

Professor Franco Modigliani perhaps best summarizes the Keynesian view when he says:

> *Non-Monetarists accept what I regard to be the fundamental practical message of* The General Theory: *that a private enterprise economy using an intangible money* needs *to be stabilized,* can *be stabilized, and therefore* should *be stabilized by appropriate monetary and fiscal policies. Monetarists, by contrast, take the view that there is no serious need to stabilize the economy; that even if there were a need, it could not be done, for stabilization policies would be more likely to increase than to decrease instability. . . .* [29]

The Monetarist view

One of the central propositions of Monetarism is that changes in the supply of money are the dominant determinant in explaining movements of money income over time. Monetarism starts from the proposition that the demand schedule for (or velocity of) money is highly stable. This (stability) does not mean that velocity is rigid or constant over time, but rather that its movements over time can be explained by certain variables, e.g., interest rates and the rate of inflation. Given a stable value for velocity, V, the movement in money income, PY, can be explained mainly by variations in the movement of the supply of money, M.[30] Additionally, Monetarism asserts that the movement in the money supply itself is dominated by movements in the monetary base rather than by movements in the money multiplier. The reason for the latter condition is that changes in the money multiplier are due mainly to movements in economic conditions (e.g., the

[29] Franco Modigliani, "The Monetarist Controversy or, Should We Forsake Stabilization Policies?," *American Economic Review,* Vol. 67, No. 2 (Mar. 1977): 1 [italics in the original].

[30] In an early statement of the Monetarist position Milton Friedman specified that its followers believe that the velocity of money function is not only highly stable, but more stable than functions such as the consumption function, which plays a prominent role in Keynesian analysis. This point is very important, because the consumption function is the source of the Keynesian multiplier that stands between changes in such variables as investment and government spending and subsequent changes in national income. If the consumption function is unstable, the multiplier will be subject to unexplained changes in value, which will make the relationship between changes in expenditures and subsequent changes in income uncertain.

This belief in the superior stability of the velocity function explains why Monetarists prefer to calibrate change in income in terms of a stable V and the supply of money, M. See Milton Friedman, "The Quantity Theory of Money: A Restatement," in M. Friedman, ed., *Studies in the Quantity Theory of Money* (Chicago: University of Chicago Press, 1956).

currency/demand deposit ratio) or to expectations concerning future economic events (e.g., the desired excess reserve/demand deposit ratio). If the multiplier were to dominate movements in the money supply, it could be argued that nonmonetary forces are the basic cause of the business cycle.[31]

From this interpretation of the source of movements in money income over time, the Monetarists conclude that the central bank (the Federal Reserve) is responsible for the majority of business cycles experienced in this country (at least since its inception). The central bank either forces or permits the monetary base to grow too rapidly or too slowly, with a consequent impact on the money supply and the course of economic activity. This view is appropriately summarized by Allan Meltzer:

> *Large changes in the growth rate of money become a main source of instability . . . the Federal Reserve permits or forces the stock of money to grow at too high or too low a rate for too long a time. Excessive expansions and contractions of money become the main cause of the fluctuations in output and of inflations or deflations. Inappropriate public policies, not changes in private expenditures, become the main cause of instability.*[32]

Nevertheless, despite Monetarist rhetoric, investment expenditures are observed to undergo substantial changes from time to time. In explaining this, Monetarists argue that major *instabilities* and *uncertainties* in such private sector expenditures do not cause the business cycle. Rather, they represent the response of the private sector to the behavior of the government. In particular, the Monetarists believe that major *uncertainties* arise from tax and expenditure policies that are, or are proposed to be, pursued by the government, and from the actions of its regulatory agencies, whereas the stop-and-go nature of money, credit, and fiscal policies leads to *instability* in private expenditures. Friedman and Schwartz note with particular approval the analysis of Kenneth Roose, which attributes to

[31] Interestingly, a Monetarist might agree with the Keynesians that the real sector is inherently unstable, but nevertheless continue to adhere to a belief that as long as the supply of money is prevented from growing erratically, money income will grow in a stable fashion over time.

This position is possible if the Monetarist believes that the velocity of money is highly inelastic with regard to the interest rate, for then changes in investment expenditures or saving will affect the interest rate, but will not affect (or will affect only negligibly) the velocity of money. Since V will be virtually constant, even with an unstable real sector, the course of money income, PY, over time, will be governed by movements in the supply of money, M.

For those who have mastered the *IS-LM* framework, this case is analogous to a vertical *LM* curve. An unstable *IS* curve will be seen to produce interest rate changes, but no change in income. Moreover, changes in income can only be provided by changes in the supply of money that shift the *LM* schedule.

[32] Allan Meltzer, "The Role of Money: Comment," *Controlling Monetary Aggregates*, p. 29.

government policy the very low level of private investment during the period 1933–1941.[33]

The stability of the velocity of money

Aside from this discussion of respective interpretations of economic history by Keynesians and Monetarists, the broader issue of the causality of money has raised the question about the importance of the stability of the velocity of money. Obviously, this stability is of great importance to the Monetarists, but is it inconsistent with the Keynesian approach to macroeconomic theory? Most assuredly not. The Keynesian model does not assume that the demand for money is unstable. A host of empirical papers on the demand for money prepared by Keynesian economists attest to their belief in the stability of the demand for or velocity of money. Nevertheless, the Keynesians still prefer to explain changes in income in terms of changes in expenditures and a multiplier derived from the consumption function.

The role of fiscal policy

It is in the use of fiscal policy that we find the greatest difference between the Monetarists and the Keynesians. However, the Monetarist view on the effectiveness of fiscal policy is somewhat obscure. Part of the obscurity arises from a failure to distinguish between countercyclical and allocative fiscal policy.

The Keynesian view

For the Keynesians, countercyclical fiscal policy is the chief means available to policymakers to stabilize economic activity and maintain high employment levels. Their preference for fiscal over monetary policy rests on two basic reasons. First, if consumer and business spending is insensitive to interest rate changes, or the demand for money is highly interest elastic, monetary policy would be largely ineffective in their theoretical approach

[33] *A Monetary History of the United States, 1867–1960.* Among government programs reducing the incentive to invest, Roose mentions the NIRA, National Labor Relations Act, minimum wage laws, social security taxes, federal provision for unemployment compensation, the Undistributed Profits Tax Law, the Securities Act of 1933 and the Securities Exchange Act of 1934, restrictions on public utility holding companies, the TVA, the Home Owners Loan Corporation, the Federal Farm Mortgage Corporation, the nationalization of gold, unbalanced budgets, Roosevelt's attacks on monopoly and "economic royalists," the attempt to reorganize the Supreme Court, the rise of the CIO-AFL, and tolerance of the sit-down strike. The effect of all these policies was to (1) reduce the profitability of business, (2) weaken business confidence, (3) expand government into areas traditionally reserved for business, and (4) threaten the sanctity of private contracts and property.

as a countercyclical tool. Second, fiscal policy, by directly and immediately altering the disposable income of consumers and the profitability of capital projects, is thought to have a faster and more direct impact on economic activity than monetary policy, which acts through the indirect interest rate route.[34]

Professor Warren Smith's brief description of the Keynesian view of countercyclical fiscal policy is worth repeating here, because it brings out what many in the Keynesian school regard as the principal point at issue between them and the Monetarists: the interest elasticity of the demand for money (or the slope of the *LM* curve).

> *An increase in government purchases of goods and services, with tax rates constant, would affect the economy by three different routes. First, there would be a direct expansionary income effect resulting from the purchase of output by the government. Second, there would be an expansionary* wealth effect *as the private sector, experiencing an increment to its wealth entirely in the form of net claims against the government, increased its demand for real capital in an effort to diversify its portfolios. These income and wealth effects would set off a multiplier–accelerator process of economic expansion. The expansion, in turn, would activate a partially offsetting monetary effect as the rise in income increased the demand for money. If the dial settings of the monetary instruments remained unchanged, this would drive up interest rates. The rise in interest rates would cause some reductions in those types of expenditures that were sensitive to interest rates through portfolio, wealth, and availability effects.*
>
> *The wealth effect of fiscal policy may be quite powerful, particularly because it is cumulative—that is, it continues to operate until the budget has been brought back into balance, thereby shutting off the increase in net claims against the government. . . .*
>
> *If we neglect the wealth effect . . . we are left with the income effect and the offsetting monetary effect. The monetary effect will be greater (a) the greater the proportion of expenditures in GNP that are affected by interest rates, (b) the greater (in absolute value) is the average interest elasticity of these expenditures, (c) the greater is the income elasticity of demand for money, (d) the smaller (in absolute value) is the interest elasticity of demand for money and (e) the smaller is the interest elasticity of the supply of money.*
>
> *Only if the interest elasticity of both the demand for and supply of money are zero will the monetary effect completely cancel out the income effect. . . . Since the empirical evidence is overwhelming that both money demand and money supply possess some degree of interest elasticity, it seems clear that fiscal policy is capable of exerting an independent effect on income.*[35]

[34] This brief statement neglects the question of lags. Both monetary and fiscal policy involve lags. In fiscal policy the so-called administrative lag is important and involves the time it takes Congress to change expenditures or taxes to deal with a problem.

[35] "A Neo-Keynesian View of Monetary Policy," pp. 111–2. Professor Smith neglects the effectiveness of tax changes as a countercyclical fiscal policy tool. Recent Keynesian theorizing now concedes that the effectiveness of tax cuts depends upon whether the public regards them as permanent or temporary. To the extent that such changes are regarded as temporary, they will be largely offset by counterchanges in saving, e.g., temporary tax cuts will generate higher saving rates.

The importance of the interest elasticity of the demand for money to the success of fiscal policy in the Keynesian model should be obvious in view of the monetary theory developed in Chapter 10. In that context, an outward shift in the $\bar{I}$ schedule caused the interest rate to rise so long as the money supply was held constant. The degree to which the interest rate rose depended upon the interest elasticity of the demand for money. The lower the value of the elasticity (i.e., the more inelastic the demand schedule), the higher would be the rise in the interest rate. Finally, the higher the rise in the interest rate, the larger would be the amount of *fiscal crowd-out*—the displacement of private sector expenditures by those of the public sector. In the extremes, if the interest elasticity of money demand were zero, the rise in the interest rate would be sufficient to ensure total crowd-out—thus, it would follow that countercyclical fiscal policy is ineffective.[36] For this reason, the interest elasticity of the demand for money was long thought to be of vital importance in the debate between the Monetarists and the Keynesians. Milton Friedman now denies that zero interest elasticity is essential to the Monetarist position. He is willing to accept some positive elasticity so long as it is not infinite.[37]

The Monetarist view

The Monetarist position on countercyclical fiscal policy has been evolving over the past several years. If we neglect the fact that Monetarists believe that the activities of the government are responsible, in large measure, for the observed instability of private expenditures, an early quotation from Milton Friedman will reveal their initial position:

> *I believe that the state of the government budget matters; matters a great deal—for some things. The state of the government budget determines what fraction of the nation's income is spent through the government and what fraction is spent by individuals privately. The state of the government budget determines what the level of our taxes is, how much of our income we turn over to the government. The state of the government budget has a considerable effect on interest rates. If the Federal Government runs a large deficit, this means the government has to borrow in the markets, which raises the demand for loanable funds and so tends to raise interest rates. . . . But—and I come to my main point—in my opinion, the*

[36] Even though ineffective as a countercyclical tool, fiscal policy, under these circumstances, would still have a role to play in allocating resources between their use in the private and public sectors.

[37] See, for example, his "Comments on the Critics," *Journal of Political Economy,* Vol. 80, No. 5 (Sept.–Oct. 1972): 917. Interestingly enough, in his earlier empirical work Friedman alone among a vast number of economists who were devoted to the subject was able to demonstrate that the demand for money was so inelastic with regard to the interest rate that it could be approximated by zero. One wonders why such effort was devoted to such a mundane subject unless it was once regarded as important.

state of the budget itself has no significant effect on the course of nominal income, on inflation, on deflation, or on cyclical fluctuations.[38]

Several years later Friedman provided a more complete statement of his view on the effectiveness of countercyclical fiscal policy. He now believes that its effect "is certain to be temporary and likely to be minor,"[39] with any sustained effect (on nominal income) depending upon how the government operations are financed. His analysis, from which these conclusions are drawn, has a bearing on his present belief that the interest elasticity of money demand is not a distinguishing characteristic of Monetarism.

Suppose, says Friedman, that the government raises taxes to decrease demand. In terms of Figure 10:21, the $\bar{S}$ schedule would shift out and income would fall, causing unemployment to rise and the market interest rate to decline. This decrease in income and employment would be minor, according to Friedman, because the fall in interest rates would stimulate a vast amount of new spending, which would tend to offset the initial decline in income. Hence, the ultimate effect of the tax hike is "likely to be minor." Its effect would also be "temporary" because it is a once-and-for-all shift in the $\bar{S}$ schedule, and its effect on income will be superseded by a monetary effect in the longer run. The monetary effect occurs because the tax hike, to the extent that it produces a budget surplus, produces one that will recur year after year. If the Treasury disposes of this continuing surplus by buying back government bonds owned by the central bank, the monetary base will decline and the money supply will contract. The continuous contraction of the money supply will become the dominant force explaining the subsequent movement of nominal income.

A still more recent statement by Brunner[40] incorporates into the Monetarists' view of countercyclical fiscal policy their concept of the natural rate of unemployment. An expansionary increase in government expenditures will increase output in the short run only if it catches labor unprepared for the initial rise in prices. Unemployment then falls below its natural level and output rises above normal. When labor ultimately realizes that its real wage has fallen and seeks a compensatory adjustment, unemployment will then rise back toward its natural rate and output will decrease to its normal level. It is during this return to normal levels of output that government expenditures exert their principal crowding-out effect on private expenditures.

Over the longer run other aspects of fiscal policy may have a greater effect on the level of output and employment. These involve the impact of government expenditures on the real capital stock of the country, and the

[38] Milton Friedman, *Monetary vs. Fiscal Policy* (New York: Norton, 1969), pp. 50–1.
[39] "Comments on the Critics," p. 915.
[40] Karl Brunner, "Issues of Post-Keynesian Monetary Analysis," *Kredit und Kapital*, Vol. 9, Heft 1 (1976): 24–55.

extent to which these expenditures involve the provision of extensive social services. If government expenditures decrease the growth of the nation's capital stock and increase the real amount of social services available to labor, they serve to raise the natural rate of unemployment and lower the normal level of output. Moreover, Brunner expresses the fear that government behavior involves the systematic attrition of property rights, which serves to further reduce the growth rate of private capital and raise the natural rate of unemployment.[41]

Finally, the Monetarists have a view on the allocative role of fiscal policy (which may be unacceptable to Keynesians). This position is effectively stated by Professor David Fand:

> *If we move away from short-run stabilization problems and focus on the longer-run allocative effects of alternative policies, there appears to be a reversal of positions. Thus, suppose it was necessary for the Government to select a policy to effect a permanent change in the rate of capital formation. Monetarists would have to find some fiscal policy while (some) Fiscalists would seek to achieve this result with monetary policy. Although Monetarists believe that control of the money stock is the appropriate and preferred instrument for dealing with stabilization problems, they also believe that monetary actions have their permanent effects on prices. As a consequence, it follows that fiscal policy may be the only instrument to bring about permanent changes in interest rates, capital formation (and possibly the long-term rate of growth) as well as permanently changing the resource flow from the private to the public sector. . . .*
>
> *. . . Since Monetarists postulate that in the long-run money is essentially a veil (having its permanent effects primarily on prices), they would of necessity have to rely on some kind of fiscal action if public policy required some changes in interest rates and rates of return.*[42]

Since they have fundamentally different theories of the cause of business cycles, it should come as no surprise that Keynesians and Monetarists have very different views on the effectiveness of countercyclical fiscal policy.

Empirical verification

Empirical verification of the causality of money has occupied a prominent place in the debate between the Monetarists and the Keynesians, and is likely to continue to do so as long as both are of the opinion that the issues

[41] A superficial distinction between Monetarism and Keynesianism is supposedly in their respective views on the desirability of government intervention in the economy. Monetarists, as a group, appear more disposed to depend on the operation of market forces, whereas Keynesians generally are more disposed to altering those market outcomes, including the distribution of income, they find objectionable on personal grounds. This distinction would suggest that the major differences between the two schools are ideological, or based on value judgments. A fair reading of the literature would suggest that the issues involved here are of more substance than the desirability of government intervention in the economic process.

[42] David Fand, "Monetarism and Fiscalism," *Banca Nazionale del Lavoro Quarterly Review,* No. 94 (Sept. 1970): 23–4.

between them are empirical rather than theoretical. Some of the empirical evidence has been discussed in Chapters 11 and 12. Little purpose would be served in reviewing it again. Suffice it to say that the evidence thus far adduced is inconclusive, being consistent both with the Monetarist position and with its denial. That is to say, the evidence does not unambiguously support the Monetarist hypothesis; it is consistent with a properly understood Keynesian view as well.

It is over the origin of the Great Depression of 1929–1933 that a great deal of the controversy has been generated. Surprisingly, for such a major event in economic history, very little rigorous work has been done until very recently to explain its origins. Economists have been too willing to accept the impressions of those living at the time as to the origin of this event.

It was Milton Friedman who, in his presidential address to the American Economic Association, set out the issue clearly, claiming that the Depression was monetary in origin, and a testimony to the potency of monetary policy:

> *The revival of belief in the potency of monetary policy was fostered also by a re-evaluation of the role money played from 1929 to 1933. Keynes and most other economists of the time believed that the Great Contraction in the United States occurred despite aggressive expansionary policies by the monetary authorities—they did their best, but their best was not good enough. Recent studies have demonstrated that the facts are precisely the reverse; the U.S. monetary authorities followed highly deflationary policies. The quantity of money in the United States fell by one-third in the course of the contraction. And it fell, not because there were no willing borrowers—not because the horse would not drink. It fell because the Federal Reserve System forced or permitted a sharp reduction in the monetary base, because it failed to exercise the responsibilities assigned to it in the Federal Reserve Act to provide liquidity to the banking system. The Great Contraction is tragic testimony to the power of monetary policy—not, as Keynes and so many of his contemporaries believed, evidence of its impotence.*[43]

In this assessment of monetary policy Friedman fails to note the dramatic role played by the money multiplier in explaining the course of events in this era. In particular, there was a sharp rise in both the currency/demand deposit and total reserve/demand deposit ratios during the 1929–1933 period.[44] Friedman and Schwartz attribute the rise in the former to a lack of confidence in the banking system because of widespread failures. The rise in the latter, they believe, reflects the buildup of precautionary reserves

[43] Milton Friedman, "The Role of Monetary Policy," *American Economic Review,* Vol. 58, No. 1 (Mar. 1968): 3.

[44] In *A Monetary History of the United States* these two ratios are expressed in a slightly different manner as the currency/money supply and reserve/deposit ratios, because Friedman gives a different development of the multiplier. A reformulation of these ratios in terms of those used in this text does not alter any of the following conclusions.

against bank runs, because the Federal Reserve failed to assist banks during the period when currency drains were especially heavy.

For a full appreciation of the Keynesian critique of this position, it should be noted that while the currency/demand deposit ratio rose a bit in late 1933 and 1934, in July 1960 it was at almost the same level as in July 1932. The reserve/demand deposit ratio continued to rise throughout the decade of the 1930s. In 1940 almost one-half of all commercial bank reserves were in excess of legal requirements. Moreover, the Treasury bill rate was driven down in the late 1930s to almost zero (from 1938 to 1940 it was about .014 percent—the Treasury was borrowing at short term virtually for free!).

Friedman attributes this buildup of excess reserves to the continued precautionary demand by banks to guard against bank runs, and to their desire to be able to offset any changes in their legal reserve requirements that might arise from the exercise by the Federal Reserve of its newly acquired power to alter reserve requirements. The low yield on Treasury bills, according to Friedman, had no influence on the holding of bank reserves, for they are regarded by him as insensitive to interest rates.

The Keynesian interpretation of the cause of the Great Depression is quite the opposite. It was caused by the collapse of the investment demand schedule, which was due, in part, to the increased uncertainty following the stock market collapse and widespread bank failures.[45] The contraction of investment spending caused, via the multiplier, a massive decrease in income, which in turn led to a decrease in the demand for money. Given a positively sloped money supply schedule, the leftward shift of the demand for money would be recorded as a fall in the stock of money.

The Keynesian denial of Friedman's interpretation is based upon several pieces of evidence. First, contrary to Friedman's assertion in his presidential address, his own data reveal that the monetary base did *not* decline, but rose throughout the period 1929–1933—in July 1932, for example, it was more than 10% higher than in July 1929.[46] Thus, the large contraction in the money stock was produced by a decline in the money multiplier (produced by a rise in the two ratios).

[45] Professor Peter Temin's recent book on the origins of the Great Depression questions both the Keynesian and the Monetarist interpretations. His finding is that a large unexplained decrease in consumption (a downward shift in the consumption function) set in motion the Depression. The decline in the stock of money and the wave of bank failures are interpreted as the consequence of the Depression, not its cause.

This view has been attacked by Arthur E. Gandolfi and James R. Lathian and by Thomas Mayer. In order, the works of these individuals are: *Did Monetary Forces Cause the Great Depression?* (New York: Norton, 1976); "Did Monetary Forces Cause the Great Depression? A Review Essay," *Journal of Money, Credit and Banking,* Vol. 9, No. 4 (Nov. 1977): 679–91; "Consumption in the Great Depression," *Journal of Political Economy,* Vol. 86, No. 1 (Feb. 1978): 139–46. For other recent works supporting the Keynesian view, see C. P. Kindleberger, *The World in Depression, 1929 to 1939* (London: Allen Lane, 1973); and C. L. Barber, "On the Origins of the Great Depression," *Southern Economic Journal,* Vol. 44, No. 3 (Jan. 1978): 432–56.

[46] How Friedman could have made such an error remains an unanswered question.

If the currency/demand deposit ratio rose because of widespread fears of the solvency of the banking system, why, the Keynesians ask of the Monetarists, was it still at the same level in July 1960 as in July 1932 (its lowest point in the twentieth century)? Surely 30 years of experience and the advent of deposit insurance should have convinced the public that banks were safe.[47] As to the rise in the reserve/demand deposit ratio and the decline in the Treasury bill rate, Keynesians interpret these as reflecting mainly a lack of borrowers. Thus, banks invested their surplus funds in Treasury bills to such a degree that they drove their yields to practically zero. Any further additions to those reserves through open-market operations would have resulted in currency holdings by the banks. In this situation the banks' demand for excess reserves was in a virtual liquidity trap—money did not matter and monetary policy was impotent.[48]

As with the empirical evidence offered to support other Monetarist and Keynesian positions, the origin of the Great Depression is still an open subject of controversy. It remains to be seen what would constitute convincing evidence.

A summary of the causality of money

Our discussion of the causality of money has ranged over several topics, for this aspect of the debate is complex. The major importance of this discussion is in the area of public policy.

It is basic to the Monetarist position that changes in the supply of money are the dominant factor in explaining the longer-run movements in nominal income. A high degree of stability in the growth of money income can, therefore, be accomplished by inducing a stable growth rate in the money

[47] Among neo-Keynesians, Nicholas Kaldor believes the rise to be due to changes in the relative magnitude of expenditures paid for in paper currency (goods and services) relative to those paid for by check (financial or income expenditures). Among Monetarists, Phillip Cagan has provided an explanation for the rise in the ratio and its subsequent failure to decline. The initial rise during the first half of the 1930s he attributes to bank failures and panic. During the second half of the 1930s, after the failure and panic subsided, the ratio remained high because of the introduction by banks of service charges on checking accounts, which led individuals to economize on the use of demand deposits, and because of a general decline in the rate of interest paid on savings deposits. During World War II the high ratio was sustained because currency transactions were used as a means of tax evasion, as was currency holding. After the war, Cagan believes, the rise in check service charges is the principal reason the ratio has failed to decline. See Phillip Cagan, *Determinants and Effects of Changes in the Stock of Money, 1875–1960* (New York: NBER, 1965), pp. 132–4. It should be noted that Cagan's conjectures are not supported by any empirical work.

[48] For an extensive discussion of this point, see James Tobin, "A Monetary Interpretation of History: A Review Article," *American Economic Review,* Vol. 55, No. 3 (June 1965): 470–2. Among contemporary observers of the period, Lauchlin Currie, generally regarded as an early follower of Keynes, wrote in 1935 that the buildup of excess reserves in the period 1932–1934 could not be attributed to an alleged lack of loans suitable as bank assets, for a large quantity of government securities, among other possible outlets, were available for the surplus reserves of banks. See Lauchlin Currie, *The Supply and Control of Money in the United States* (Cambridge, Mass.: Harvard University Press, 1934), pp. 121–3.

supply. The money supply, then, becomes the principal indicator of monetary policy, while the monetary base, the variable under direct control of the Federal Reserve, becomes the target of policy.

The actual growth rate of the money supply could be any number the policymakers desire. However, certain considerations (principally the efficiency of monetary exchange) suggest that the growth rate should provide a stable price level over the longer run.

In the Monetarist framework fiscal policy performs only an allocative role. That is, government expenditure and tax policies decide the fraction of total resources available for public use and the fraction available for private use. Since the long-run growth of money income is determined by the supply of money, countercyclical fiscal policy has no role to play. Indeed, the use of fiscal policy in either role is viewed with misgivings by Monetarists, for it creates uncertainties that lead to instabilities in private spending. In addition, fiscal policy can alter the amount of the capital stock available to the private sector, and this, together with its provision of social services (e.g., unemployment compensation, food stamps, housing allowances), may raise the natural rate of unemployment.

Keynesians, on the other hand, while they do not deny that variations in the supply of money may cause some business cycles, believe that the majority of cycles are caused by instabilities in private sector spending, especially for durable goods. In order to maintain the level of growth rate of aggregate demand, fiscal policy (supported by monetary policy) must supplement private spending, rising when the latter falls and declining when the latter rises.

In addition, since the principal channel by which money affects economic activity is through its effects on interest rates, Keynesians are apt to rely on these in deciding the proper growth rate for the money supply.

This discussion of the respective public policies emerging from Monetarist and Keynesian assessments of the importance of the supply of money suggests that Monetarists may be more concerned with control of inflation, while Keynesians are more concerned with the minimization of unemployment. Such a conclusion is unwarranted. The Monetarists are as concerned with the social waste resulting from unemployment as are the Keynesians. However, their policies to reduce unemployment are markedly different. Manipulating aggregate demand through fiscal policy along Keynesian lines, they argue, will only work temporarily so long as labor does not accurately adjust to a change in the price level. Once it does, the fiscally induced change in demand is undone. It is better, the Monetarists believe, to reduce the natural rate of unemployment along *microeconomic* rather than macroeconomic lines, using such policies as reform of the minimum wage and unemployment insurance, reductions in barriers to entry into professions or skilled trades that have been erected merely to reduce the available supply, provision of low-cost information on job opportunities, and allowances to increase the mobility of labor. These policy changes, the Monetarists claim, can permanently lower the long-run level of unemployment.

THE EXOGENEITY OF MONEY[49]

A significant part of the debate between the Monetarists and the Keynesians has involved empirical testing of alternative hypotheses that sometimes pits rival propositions against one another. In any such empirical tests the movement in one variable over time, called the dependent or *endogenous* variable, is explained by movements in other variables, called the independent or *exogenous* variables. To minimize the bias in the estimate of the effects of the exogenous variables on the endogenous variable, the former must be truly independent of movements in the latter, i.e., movements in the endogenous variable must not cause movements in the exogenous variables. If they do, the estimates will be biased and the independent variables will not be truly exogenous. Since this aspect of estimation is an integral part of modern statistics, it is not subject to debate.

Where the controversy erupts is over the nature of empirical tests that apparently violate these rules of estimation. Monetarists employ tests in which the movement in money income (the endogenous variable) is explained by movements in the nominal money supply (the exogenous variable) among other variables.[50] Keynesians object on the grounds that this type of test violates established rules of statistics. They point out that the money supply is not a truly exogenous variable for at least two reasons. First, historic movements in income have often caused the Federal Reserve to change the money supply so as to moderate the course of business cycles. Second, movements in the money multiplier, a basic determinant of the money supply, often respond to movements in income, either directly through the currency/demand deposit ratio, or indirectly through the effect of income on interest rates that then cause changes in the excess reserve/demand deposit ratio. For these two reasons, the money supply must be regarded, in part, as an endogenous variable.

In an effort to get around these Keynesian criticisms Monetarists now supplement such tests with a detailed analysis of changes in the money stock. This is designed to show that the feedback from income to the money supply is minimal.

Another tendency in Monetarist literature is to call any variable that the authorities can control an exogenous variable, and then to carry out empirical tests as though the variable were exogenous in a statistical sense as well. Thus, since the money supply and the monetary base can be controlled by the Federal Reserve, they are regarded as exogenous, even

[49] This section is somewhat technical and requires some knowledge of statistics for complete comprehension.

[50] In discussing the exogeneity of money we have reference to the nominal supply of money, for the Federal Reserve cannot control the real stock of money. It is the public, through its spending habits and their impact on the price level, that governs the real stock of money.

In Chapter 11, pp. 322–4, the discussion of the cyclical evidence adduced by Monetarists in support of their claims is really a discussion of the exogeneity of money. The counter explanation of this evidence given by Nicholas Kaldor is also a claim that money is not exogenous but endogenous.

though history is replete with instances when the Federal Reserve chose not to exercise control (e.g., in the financing of various wars the Federal Reserve has permitted the money supply to accommodate the financing needs of the Treasury). Such a careless use of statistical procedures calls forth Keynesian condemnation.

Finally, we may ask how essential an exogenous money supply is to the Monetarist position on the causality of money. Suppose that the money supply could not be controlled by the Federal Reserve, but expanded automatically according to the demand for it. Would this cancel its effectiveness as the major force explaining subsequent movements in money income? The answer quite clearly is no. It is quite possible for the money supply to be both endogenous and powerful in explaining movements in money income. For example, suppose that the supply of money did automatically respond to a change in desired expenditures on the part of the public. What would happen if, for whatever reason, the money supply were prevented from making such an automatic response? It is quite possible that nominal income would not increase at all, but rather newly desired expenditures would simply displace already existing expenditures, i.e., complete crowd-out would occur. This would be the case in the Keynesian model if the demand for money were insensitive to the interest rate and the supply of money were held constant.

It would, therefore, be possible for one to argue that, even with an endogenous money supply, changes in money income are caused by changes in the money supply. Thus, causality and exogeneity are not tied together.

SUMMARY

This chapter undertook a rather ambitious task: to summarize as clearly, comprehensively, and succinctly as possible a major debate among economists over the effectiveness of the supply of money. As a result of reading it, one should have a fairly good idea of what it means to be a Monetarist and what it means to be a Keynesian.

Both sides view the supply of money as a very important variable for economic stabilization purposes. However, a variety of views, ranging from technical to philosophical, separate the two schools. Among the technical differences, we noted their respective positions on the role of monetary and nonmonetary factors as causes of the business cycle, the nature of the transmission mechanism, the effectiveness of fiscal policy for economic stabilization, the degree to which the money supply is exogenous, and whether changes in the money supply exert any lasting influence on real economic variables or whether their influence is only on the price level.

From a philosophical perspective, each side has different views as to whether a market-oriented economy will stabilize at a high level of employment in the absence of government-instituted monetary and fiscal policies. Each side, therefore, has quite different views on the desirability of government intervention in the economy. However, because of the presence of long and variable lags in the effect of monetary and fiscal policy on economic activity, the difference between the two schools on this issue is less than clear-cut.

Since the current debate has historic origins that reach long into the past and will undoubtedly continue long into the future as new empirical and theoretical work alters individual views, the conclusions stated in this chapter should be regarded as tentative.

While some may be inclined to dismiss this discussion as arcane academic nonsense, your author believes in the wisdom of an old Jewish proverb that says, "When scholars disagree, the public and the truth will both benefit."

STUDY QUESTIONS

1. Why is the issue of the neutrality of money important?
2. Would your views on the use of countercyclical monetary policy be affected if you thought money was neutral only in the very long run?
3. Evaluate the statement that a Monetarist is a person who believes that money matters.
4. Will the rise in the price of oil or any other commodity produce a permanently higher price level?
5. Are government bonds wealth? What are the issues involved and why are they important?
6. Why is the stability of the velocity of money important to the Monetarist view?
7. Is fiscal policy important to Monetarists?
8. Could the Federal Reserve prevent Christmas buying by refusing to issue currency? Could it produce Christmas in July by issuing a great deal of currency? Does this say anything about the importance of money?
9. How important is crowding out to the Monetarist position?
10. What are the major differences between the Keynesian and Monetarist views of the transmission mechanism whereby a change in the money supply leads to changes in the real sector (i.e., real income and employment)?

SELECTED REFERENCES AND READINGS

Blinder, Alan, and Solow, Robert. "Does Fiscal Policy Matter?" *Journal of Public Economics,* Vol. 2, No. 4 (Nov. 1973).

Bronfenbrenner, Martin. "Thomas Mayer on Monetarism." *Kredit und Kapital,* Vol. 8, Heft. 1 (1975).

Brunner, Karl. "Issues of Post-Keynesian Monetary Analysis." *Kredit und Kapital,* Vol. 9, Heft. 1 (1976).

———. "The Role of Money and Monetary Policy." *Monthly Review,* Federal Reserve Bank of St. Louis (July 1968).

———. "The 'Monetatist Revolution' in Monetary Theory." *Weltwirtschaftliches Archiv,* Vol. 106, No. 1 (1970).

———. "A Survey of Selected Issues in Monetary Theory." *Schweizerische Zeitschrift Für Volkswirtschaft und Statistik* 107 (Winter 1971).

. "The State of the Monetarist Debate." *Monthly Review,* Federal Reserve Bank of St. Louis (Sept. 1973).

———. and Meltzer, Allan. "Money, Debt, and Economic Activity." *Journal of Political Economy,* Vol. 80, No. 5 (Sept.–Oct. 1972).

Cagan, Phillip, "Monetarism in Historical Perspective." *Kredit und Kapital,* Vol. 9, Heft. 2 (1976).

David, Richard G. "The Role of the Money Supply in Business Cycles." In *Essays in Domestic and International Finance.* New York: Federal Reserve Bank of New York, 1969.

Fand, David. "Keynesian Monetary Theories, Stabilization Policy, and Recent Inflation." *Journal of Money, Credit and Banking,* Vol. 1, No. 3 (Aug. 1969).

———. "Some Issues in Monetary Economics." *Monthly Review,* Federal Reserve Bank of St. Louis (Jan. 1970).

———. "Monetarism and Fiscalism." *Banca Nazionale del Lavoro Quarterly Review,* No. 94 (Sept. 1970).

Friedman, Benjamin. "The Theoretical Nondebate about Monetarism." *Kredit und Kapital,* Vol. 8, Heft. 2 (1975).

Friedman, Milton. *The Counter-Revolution in Monetary Theory, First Wincott Memorial Lecture.* London: Institute of Economic Affairs, 1970.

———. "The Monetary Studies of the National Bureau." In *Monetary Economics, Readings on Current Issues,* edited by William Gibson and George Kaufman. New York: McGraw-Hill, 1971.

———. "A Monetary Theory of National Income." *Journal of Political Economy,* Vol. 79, No. 2 (Mar.–Apr. 1971).

———. "A Theoretical Framework for Monetary Analysis." *Journal of Political Economy,* Vol. 78, No. 2 (Mar.–Apr. 1970).

———, and Schwartz, Anna. "Money and Business Cycles." *The Review of Economics and Statistics,* Vol. 45, No. 1, Part 2 (Feb. 1963).

Hicks, John R. "What Is Wrong with Monetarism." *Lloyds Bank Review,* No. 118 (Oct. 1975).

Johnson, Harry. "The Keynesian Revolution and the Monetarist Counter-Revolution." *American Economic Review,* Vol. 61, No. 2 (May 1971).

———. *Inflation and the Monetarist Controversy.* Amsterdam: North–Holland, 1972.

———. "Comments on Mayer on Monetarism." *Kredit und Kapital,* Vol. 9, Heft. 2 (1976).

———. "What Is Right with Monetarism." *Lloyds Bank Review,* No. 120 (Apr. 1976).

———, and Nobay, A. Robert. "Monetarism: A Historic–Theoretic Perspective." *Journal of Economic Literature,* Vol. 15, No. 2 (June 1977).

Kahn, Richard. "Thoughts on the Behavior of Wages and Monetarism." *Lloyds Bank Review,* No. 119 (Jan. 1976).

Kaldor, Nicholas. "The New Monetarism." *Lloyds Bank Review,* No. 97 (July 1970); and "Reply to Friedman" (Oct. 1970).

Klein, Lawrence. "The State of the Monetarist Debate." *Monthly Review,* Federal Reserve Bank of St. Louis (Sept. 1973).

Laidler, David E. W. "Mayer on Monetarism: Comments from a British Point of View." *Kredit und Kapital,* Vol. 9, Heft. 1 (1976).

Mayer, Thomas. "The Structure of Monetarism." *Kredit und Kapital,* Vol. 8, Heft. 2 (1975).

Park, Yung Chul. "Some Current Issues on the Transmission Process of Monetary Policy." *International Monetary Fund Papers,* Vol. 19, No. 1 (1972).

Parkin, Michael. "Where Is Britain's Inflation Going?" *Lloyds Bank Review,* No. 117 (July 1975).

Samuelson, Paul. "Money, Interest Rates and Economic Activity." In *Proceedings of a Symposium on Money, Interest Rates and Economic Activity.* New York: American Bankers Association, 1967.

———. "Reflections on the Merits and Demerits of Monetarism." In *Issues in Fiscal and Monetary Policy: The Eclectic Economist Views the Controversy,* edited by J. Diamond. Chicago: DePaul University, 1971.

Spencer, Roger. "Channels of Monetary Influence, A Survey." *Monthly Review,* Federal Reserve Bank of St. Louis (Nov. 1974).

———, and Yohe, William. "The 'Crowding-Out' of Private Expenditures by Fiscal Policy Actions." *Monthly Review,* Federal Reserve Bank of St. Louis (Oct. 1970).

Tobin, James. "A Monetary Interpretation of History: A Review Article." *American Economic Review,* Vol. 55, No. 3 (June 1965).

———. "Friedman's Theoretical Framework." *Journal of Political Economy,* Vol. 80, No. 5 (Sept.–Oct. 1972).

15 ELECTRONIC FUNDS TRANSFERS

The process of exchange has evolved in response to the introduction of means through which it can be made more efficient, in the sense of reducing the time and cost involved when an initial bundle of goods and services is converted by its owner into a more desirable bundle.

Because monetary exchange is a more efficient means of making transactions, it largely replaced barter. Monetary exchange, though, itself evolved over time as paper instruments came to replace metal coins. This evolution can also be explained in terms of the reduction of the time and cost of making transactions. Paper currency or bank notes came into widespread use because they had distinct advantages over metal coins, largely in terms of superior transportability (especially when large sums were involved). Checks came to replace both currency and coins in many transactions because they have various cost-saving advantages: for example, ease of transportation in any amount and between individuals; they also involve much less loss due to theft and provide a convenient form of receipt. Nevertheless, exchanges involving checks are not instantaneous and costless. They take time and involve the use of capital and labor when money balances must be transferred from payer to payee. If the sums involved are large, the time required to transfer balances becomes increasingly important.

With the advent of high-speed computers, electronic impulses that travel at the speed of light substantially reduced the time and costs involved in making exchanges. These computerized approaches to transferring funds are several in number and are popularly termed Electronic Funds Transfer Systems (EFT for short). They speed the transfer of funds by communicating information relating to payments by electronic means rather than by the use of paper instruments. From the perspective of time and cost of transactions, EFT can be viewed as a means for further increasing the efficiency of monetary exchange. It should be of interest to explore how it would alter the conclusions reached in this text on the appropriate definition of money, the determinants of the supply of and the demand for money, the use and effectiveness of the instruments of general credit control, the appropriateness of the set of targets and indicators of monetary policy, and the transmission mechanism whereby changes in the supply of money influence economic activity.

Because EFT is yet in the initial stage of implementation, few definitive statements about its ultimate effects can be made. Some of what is said in this chapter must therefore be conjectural in nature. Moreover, our conclusions will be subject to the outcome of certain legal cases and proposed changes to regulations governing financial institutions.

The basic legal questions that must be resolved involve both commercial banks and the other financial intermediaries, which we identified in Chapter 5 as thrifts. When commercial banks commenced to deploy some of the EFT equipment, such as machines that dispense money automatically (remote teller machines) and perform other routine bank services, legal questions arose as to whether these machines were branch banks, especially when they were installed in locations other than at the banks' established branches. Since these machines permit the interstate transfer of funds, there is a question about the legality of interstate branch banking. Thus far the majority of court cases have held that these remote teller machines are branch banks within the meaning of the law and are subject to the rules and regulations governing the establishment of branches. Since U.S. law forbids interstate branch banking, the use of remote teller machines is further restricted. As a holdover from the time when thrifts could not transfer deposits by check, many state laws are silent on their right to establish branches. Hence, they are given an advantage in the installation of remote teller and other EFT equipment. This advantage, of course, will alter the structure of financial institutions in the United States. Partly as a result of this regulatory inequity, legislation that would exempt the teller machines of commercial banks from the limitations of branch banking has been enacted in some states and is pending in others.

To give some order to the discussion, the impact of EFT-induced changes will be organized in terms of its implications for:

1. A definition of money
2. The market structure of financial institutions
3. The portfolio selections by depository institutions
4. The theory of the supply of money
5. The theory of the demand for money (or velocity)
6. The effectiveness of the instruments of monetary policy
7. The selection of the appropriate set of targets and indicators
8. The transmission mechanism

Before these issues are examined, we will first explore the nature of EFT systems and the nomenclature that has evolved to describe them.

DESCRIPTION OF SOME EFT SYSTEMS[1]

For the sake of clarity and simplicity, EFT systems can be grouped into three categories: teller machines, point-of-sale systems, and automated clearing houses. These systems differ in types of payments handled and in means of processing.

[1] Reproduced in total from William C. Niblack, "Development of Electronic Funds Transfer Systems," *Monthly Review,* Federal Reserve Bank of St. Louis, Vol. 58, No. 9 (Sept. 1976): 11–2.

Teller machines

Machines through which an individual may conduct various routine banking services can be grouped under the heading of teller machines. Much of the recent EFTS development has involved these machines, which are called customer-bank communication terminals (CBCTs) by the Comptroller of the Currency and remote service units (RSUs) by the Federal Home Loan Bank Board. In principle, these machines can be located either on a bank's premises or elsewhere, conceivably at great distances from the bank. They may be manned or automatic and vary greatly in complexity, ranging from simple communications terminals to more complicated automated teller machines (ATMs). Services which ATMs can typically perform include receiving deposits, dispensing funds from checking or savings accounts, transferring funds between accounts, making credit card advances, and receiving payments. The less complicated manned terminals handle the communications between the customer and his bank while the receipt or disbursing of funds is physically accomplished by the clerk who operates the terminal.

Teller machines are usually accessed by a combination of magnetic stripe card (on which account information is encoded) and a personal identification number which, for security reasons, is known only to the customer. If the device is connected "on-line" to the bank's computer, the customer's account is updated immediately; otherwise, a record maintained in the machine is periodically delivered to the bank for processing.

Point-of-sale systems

On-line Systems which allow customers to transfer funds to merchants in order to make purchases are usually called point-of-sale (POS) systems. Systems of this type may be used for check authorizations and credit card transactions in which funds are immediately transferred from the purchaser's account to the merchant's account. Conceivably, they could also be used for instantaneously transferring funds between businesses and/or individuals, using terminals or push-button telephones.

Large-scale POS systems generally operate in the following manner. On-line terminals are located at check-out counters or other points of sale. When making a purchase, a customer's card is inserted into a terminal which "reads" the data encoded on it. Other data concerning the transaction are entered manually by the clerk or through an electronic cash register or products code reader. If the customer's bank is different from the store's bank, a switching and processing center (SPC) connects the computers of the two banks. The computer at the customer's bank verifies that the card and identification code are valid and that the customer's account has sufficient funds. The customer's account is debited for the amount of the purchase while the store's account is credited for the same amount. Both parties to the transaction receive a printed statement at the time of the transaction, and the customer's regular bank statement contains a descriptive listing, much like those which many credit cards presently use. Since some 30 percent of personal checks are written to grocery or other retail stores, this type of system would allow automation of a substantial portion of check payments as well as many payments presently made by cash or credit card.

Automated clearing houses

Another type of EFT system, which is conceptually different from the two systems described above, is the automated clearing house (ACH). As the name suggests, an ACH is analogous to a traditional clearing house, in that it represents a system for the interbank clearing of debits and credits. The main difference between automated and conventional clearing houses is that the debit and credit items in an ACH exist in the form of electronic signals, whereas they are paper items in a conventional clearing-house operation. An ACH is thus not *a system for automating the handling and clearing of paper checks. The payment items must enter the system in the form of electronic data, usually computer-generated magnetic tape.*

To illustrate how an ACH works, consider how a payroll payment could be made directly to an employee's checking or savings account through an ACH. The employee authorizes his employer to make such direct payments, eliminating the need for a check to pass through the employee's hands, be endorsed, cashed or deposited, and sent through the check clearing process to the employer's bank. The employer prepares the payroll data on computer tape and sends it to the company's bank. The bank directly credits the employee's account if he is a customer and combines the data for the remaining payees with those from other employers on a magnetic tape. This consolidated tape is delivered or transmitted to the ACH, where a computer processes all the data for a day in a single run, sorting out all payees for each participating bank. Each bank then receives a computer tape (or paper advice if it is not equipped to handle tape) which lists the payees and the amount to be credited to each account. The employer's accounts are debited by the originating banks. Net settlement among the banks is accomplished in the same manner as with paper checks.

ACHs are especially suited for handling recurring payments, such as payroll, social security, or pension payments, or recurring payments made by individuals. Payors would authorize their banks to pay a specified amount to a payee (mortgage lender, insurance company, etc.) on a specified date. Parties to these types of payments would receive a descriptive statement documenting the payment.

Many types of payments—those where the payee and amount vary—are not amenable to this type of preauthorization. The case of regularly recurring bills of varying amounts, such as utility bills, represents a middle ground between the extremes of identical recurring payments and more or less random payments. The customer could, for example, authorize his bank to pay the amount billed by a specified creditor. Since many people are reluctant to give such broad power to their banks, a system called Bill Check has been developed. This type of payment allows the customer to control the amount and timing of payments to creditors but still achieves some of the benefits of ACHs.

An ACH thus differs considerably from teller machines and POS systems. The ACH is essentially a "batch" processing system used for the interbank settlement of recurring credits and debits, whereas many of the other systems allow instantaneous transfers of funds between the customer and his bank or from the customer to third parties.

A DEFINITION OF MONEY

Money has been defined in this text as those assets used as dominant transactions media, and included currency and the deposits of financial institutions against which checks can be drawn. The simple advent of EFT technology would have done little to change this definition of the money supply, for in the main it serves merely to eliminate the writing of paper instructions to depository institutions to transfer ownership of a demand deposit. Rather an electronic signal now accomplishes the transfer. Demand deposit accounts do not vanish. Only the means for transferring ownership changes—paper gives way to electronic signals. Nevertheless, EFT brings with it several other changes that commend to policymakers a broader definition of money.

First, EFT should greatly reduce the costs of making transfers from one asset to another. This should make it easier to shift balances from short-term government securities, mutual funds, insurance reserves, and commercial paper to demand deposits. As such transfers become easier, households may come to regard these nonmonetary assets as fully equivalent to those assets included in the narrow measure of money. However, since depository institutions will soon be allowed to pay explicit interest on demand deposits at competitive rates, such transfers may continue to be as uncommon for households as they are today.

Second, since the use of EFT technology will permit the prearranged deposit of wage and salary income and the payment of various recurring obligations, it may create uncertainty as to the prevailing balance in the account of any individual at a depository institution. To avoid the inconvenience of overdrawn accounts, depository institutions will be under pressure to make available more generous lines of credit and overdraft facilities to household customers. The sums of these permissible overdrafts may also have to be included as a part of the money supply. Granting overdrafts will be facilitated by computer technology, which reduces the cost of accumulating, storing, and retrieving large amounts of information on the credit worthiness of potential borrowers.

The problem that the increased ease of transferring funds and overdraft facilities poses for monetary policy is that through EFT these can come to exert an increasingly dominant influence on money spending. If they are excluded from the definition of money, their effect on spending will show up in velocity. To the extent that they make the movements of velocity over time less predictable (or more unstable), they make it more difficult for monetary policy to guide the subsequent movements in economic activity, regardless of whether the money supply or the structure of interest rates is used as an indicator. The issue here is analogous to one faced in the mid-nineteenth century when demand deposits became increasingly important, and ultimately the dominant, means of making transactions.

Of course, EFT will not be introduced overnight. During the period of its gradual implementation, however, the use of the M-1s or M_2 as the correct measure of the money supply may become increasingly unrealistic for policy purposes.

THE MARKET STRUCTURE OF FINANCIAL INSTITUTIONS

Financial institutions operate in a market setting that is quite similar to that known to ordinary business firms. Indeed, much of the early discussion in this text viewed the financial institution as a firm whose product was money.

As such, financial firms have much in common with other firms. They have cost and revenue schedules (both average and marginal), they are assumed to be profit oriented, their pricing decisions depend on whether they face competitors or have monopoly power, and so on. However, financial institutions are unlike many business firms in that their entry into the financial market is regulated. That is, not everyone can form a depository institution and enter the market. Regulations govern conditions of entry, giving due regard to competitive pressure, public convenience, financial soundness of existing institutions, and similar considerations. As a result, the market is filled with different-size firms that have different cost structures. Thus, regulation, by raising barriers to entry, has had the effect of permitting inefficient firms to survive. It does this by sheltering many firms from competitive pressure.

The effect of EFT on market structure is somewhat uncertain. At first glance it might seem reasonable to conclude that large firms could, through the use of teller machines and point-of-sale systems, invade markets held by smaller inefficient firms, in the process driving them from the market. However, this conclusion is not so convincing. Remote teller machines are not inordinately expensive and they may make it possible for small depository institutions to place "branches" in territory presently served by their larger competitors.

Point-of-sale systems, on the other hand, involve high fixed outlays to be put in place, even though the marginal cost to process a single transaction may be rather small. The high fixed costs to set up a POS system will likely work to the competitive disadvantage of smaller firms.

Automated clearing houses, whether operated by the Federal Reserve or by private organizations, are unlikely to give the large firm an advantage. It is a long-standing principle of antitrust law that all competing firms should be granted access to a unique resource such as a clearing house, even though it may have been developed by others. As long as this principle prevails, small depository institutions should be able, upon payment of a reasonable fee, to gain access to the facility.

Whether and to what extent EFT systems will be employed depends ultimately on the cost per transaction relative to the cost of conventional checks. Our limited cost information thus far suggests that a fairly substantial volume of transactions must be made before average cost per transaction falls below comparable costs for conventional methods.

Nevertheless, over the longer run the implementation of EFT should serve to increase the degree of competition among financial institutions. Therefore, the interest rates payable to depositors should rise and the rates charged borrowers should fall. Since the difference between the two rates helps to determine profits, one should expect EFT to squeeze profit margins. Indeed, this is what one anticipates generally from increased competition.

THE PORTFOLIO SELECTIONS OF DEPOSITORY INSTITUTIONS

EFT has the potential to increase both the frequency and the rapidity with which the portfolios of wealth holders can be adjusted. That is, individuals can with greater frequency and at lower costs alter the types of assets they own. This implies that depository institutions as a group and individually should expect greater variability in the day-to-day total of their liabilities. Whether this occurs will depend in part on the ability of these institutions to set competitive rates of interest on their deposits. If they can rapidly adjust to changes in the market, increased variability of deposit totals should be minimized. However, should financial institutions be unable to meet rapid changes in market conditions, they will likely find it prudent to hold more liquid portfolios, i.e., hold more cash and short-term highly marketable securities such as Treasury bills.

Deposit variability may pose special problems for some of the depository institutions, for example, savings and loan associations. Laws currently limit the types of assets they can acquire, and thus constrain their flexibility to meet sudden and large deposit withdrawals. As a consequence, one should expect EFT to increase pressure to change the law in the direction of granting financial institutions greater freedom to manage and diversity their portfolios. The Depository Institutions Deregulation and Monetary Control Act of 1980 did grant greater freedom to savings and loans associations to diversify their portfolios. Up to 20% of their assets can now be invested in consumer loans, commercial paper, and corporate debt securities.

THE THEORY OF THE SUPPLY OF MONEY

As developed in this text, the supply of money was the product of the monetary base and a multiplier whose complexity depended upon the definition of money, the type of financial intermediaries included in the system and the degree to which other than individuals were allowed to hold deposits (i.e., are Treasury holdings of deposits included?) The development and implementation of EFT will affect both the base and the multiplier, which may, on balance, make the money supply less predictable (more unstable).

Concerning first the base, EFT should reduce substantially the amount and variability of float, whose short-run movements are a major source of unpredictable gyrations in the base. It will be remembered that float arises because of the time needed to clear paper instruments. By reducing the volume of paper that requires clearing, EFT should cause float to decline considerably. Of course, computerized operations are also subject to mechanical failure, so float may from time to time become a serious matter.

Nevertheless, the overall reduction in float and the decrease in its variation will contribute substantially to the degree of control the Federal Reserve exercises over the monetary base.

The expected changes in the money multiplier are quite another thing. These are likely to be highly unpredictable until the EFT system is fully implemented.

EFT will have an effect on both currency and demand deposits, affecting thereby the currency/demand deposit ratio in the multiplier. How the ratio will be affected, and in which direction, is uncertain and will depend upon whether EFT is a better substitute for transactions made with currency than for those made by check. It is expected that average currency balances held by households will decline, both because transactions currently made by currency can be made by EFT and because the availability of automated teller machines will enable individuals to make more frequent withdrawals of currency. The effect of EFT on demand deposits will depend, in part, on monetary authorities granting the institutions the right to pay interest on their accounts at competitive rates. To the extent that they do, the incentive to hold demand deposits will not be diminished. Additionally, if EFT leads to the expected reduction in the costs of operating depository institutions, it may increase the proportion of households that maintain checking accounts. Such a development could change further the currency/demand deposit ratio. Any factor changing the amount of demand deposits will alter the value of the ratios in which these deposits appear, and hence the value of the multiplier.

Finally, since all depository institutions will soon face uniform reserve requirements imposed by the Federal Reserve, the multiplier will become more stable. Forecasting the net impact of these expected changes on the money multiplier may not be easy, since there is no prior historic experience upon which to draw. So long as EFT is introduced gradually, its effect on the multiplier will be distributed over time, giving the Federal Reserve an opportunity to adjust its operations to meet the uncertainty. Once the EFT system is in place, the movement of the money supply multiplier should stabilize and be more predictably related to changes in economic variables, much as the multiplier related to the current system behaves.

THE THEORY OF THE DEMAND FOR MONEY

As viewed in this text, the demand for money was a demand for currency and checking account balances, whose sum was the empirical counterpart of M-1B. The demand for money was also reconciled with the concept of the velocity or turnover rate of the money stock. The two were seen to be reciprocals; thus, any factor causing the demand for money to rise caused its velocity or turnover rate to fall.

Two factors explaining a great deal of the movement in the demand for money over time were real income, and the market interest rate, which serves as a proxy for the opportunity cost of holding money. It is in the area of the demand for *M*-1*B* that EFT is expected to have its greatest impact. The net effect cannot be accurately predicted, for the final outcome will depend on the relative strength of a number of competing factors.

First, from a purely accounting viewpoint, the recorded statistics on the money stock will decline as a result of the reduction in "mail float." This type of float arises because the individual who draws a check deducts the amount from his deposit balance before it is added to the balance of the check's recipient. Since the sum involved will still be recorded on the books of depository institutions, the result will be a larger total of demand deposits on the books of depository institutions than on the books of its depositors. Since EFT will provide instantaneous clearing, it should reduce the amount of "mail float."[2]

It has been held that mail float tends to hide some of the random fluctuations in the demand for money. With its elimination, these random fluctuations should then show up more clearly as unexplained movements in velocity.

Second, since the turnover rates of currency and demand deposits are not equal, any change brought by EFT in their relative contribution to the total money stock should alter its velocity. In addition, since EFT will lower the cost of maintaining a checking account, it should increase the proportion of households owning such balances. This increase in ownership should serve further to reduce velocity because household holding of demand deposits is not as sensitive to interest rate changes as are corporate holdings.

Third, since EFT should lower considerably the cost of moving funds into and out of demand deposit accounts, it should lower the demand for *M*-1*B* or raise its velocity. This should come about since both households and business will have an incentive to minimize the resources they hold in balances that do not yield a competitive rate of return. To the extent that depository institutions are able to offer a competitive interest rate on their demand deposit accounts, it should blunt the incentive to transfer balances back and forth between various assets. In fact, competitive interest payments on demand deposits should serve to increase the demand for them, which will cause velocity to decline.

[2] Interestingly, "mail float" gives rise to conflicting incentives for the introduction of EFT. Those who receive checks will welcome the ability of EFT to enable them to secure more rapid additions to their account balances. However, those who draw checks may count on "mail float" to enable them to write more checks than their balances will cover at any moment. These individuals should resist the introduction of EFT.

If EFT does lessen "floating" checks, it may also result in a substantial increase in the demand by consumers for overdraft accounts.

Fourth, if extensive overdraft facilities are made available to households, together with preauthorized payment of bills, the demand for *M*-1*B* should decline and its related velocity should rise.

Fifth, depository institutions, particularly commercial banks, provide a number of services to their business customers (maintain their checking accounts, do their payroll, pay their dividends, provide lock-box services, etc.). As payment for these services, they generally require business to maintain demand deposit balances that are not available for business use, and these deposits can be viewed as an interest-free loan to depository institutions. Since EFT has the potential to reduce the cost of operating depository institutions through reducing the need for conventional branches and for the clearing and processing of checks, they should require of business smaller "compensating balances." It might even serve to end the practice altogether. Nevertheless, any reduction in these balances held by business will reduce the demand for *M*-1*B* and cause its velocity to rise.

Finally, it is speculated that since EFT will reduce some business expenses, especially those related to paying employees (a computer tape containing all employee pay information can be transmitted to depository institutions, thereby eliminating the need to pay by check), employees will be paid more frequently, which will reduce their demand for money or raise velocity.[3]

In summary, the introduction of EFT will exert a number of conflicting influences on the demand for or velocity of the *M*-1*B* measure of money. While overall it is expected that the demand for *M*-1*B* balances will decline or its velocity rise, the magnitude of this change will depend, in part, on whether depository institutions are financially able to pay a competitive rate of interest on their demand deposit accounts. Unfortunately for monetary management, the introduction of EFT will cause great uncertainty in the precise movement of velocity because past historical experience will not serve as a guide for prediction purposes.

It should be noted that the broader the measure of money used, the less impact EFT will have on its related velocity.

REGULATION Q

We noted in Chapter 3 the disruptive effects of Regulation Q on the financial system, especially its role in the so-called credit crunches. We also noted that the Monetary Control Act of 1980 provided for the phasing out of this regulation over the next six years. During the transition period, Regulation Q can still cause problems for an EFT based system. This arises because EFT can reduce the costs of shifting from one asset to another. As a result,

[3] This conclusion follows from the simple demand-for-money model developed in the body of this text. It does not follow from the money demand specification postulated by Baumol and Tobin and presented in Appendix 10C.

it will be easier for households and business to shift the composition of their wealth from the accounts of depository institutions to other assets. Hence, EFT contains the potential to create or make more serious the "credit crunches" or waves of disintermediation which have beset the U. S. financial system since the mid-1960's.

Once Regulation Q is phased out, one can envision depository institutions offering a spectrum of depository accounts ranging from those payable on demand to those with a time-maturity structure bearing interest rates that are competitive with the market yields on other securities with similar maturity and risk characteristics. Under such circumstances, the incentive to shift funds from depository institutions to other assets would be greatly reduced, imparting greater stability to the *M*-1*B* velocity of money.

THE EFFECTIVENESS OF THE INSTRUMENTS OF MONETARY POLICY

One of the prerequisites for effective monetary policy is the timely flow of accurate information. Since EFT should enable the Federal Reserve to gather financial data of greater variety and accuracy than hitherto, the central bankers should be able to reduce the recognition lag, thereby improving their conduct of monetary policy.

Much of the analysis in the preceding chapters on the instruments of general credit control indicated the superiority of open-market operations as the principal tool of central banking. The development of EFT should not alter this situation, for the monetary base will remain the principal determinant of the money supply regardless of how it is measured. Open-market operations will remain the best way to alter the value of the base. Changes in the institutional arrangement of financial markets should not alter the qualitative superiority of open-market operations as a tool of monetary management. In fact, EFT may enhance their superiority because it should cause bank float, a persistent cause of unanticipated changes in the monetary base, to fall substantially. This will enable central bankers to concentrate their open-market operations on achieving dynamic objectives unencumbered by the need to iron out unwanted changes in the base due to float.

It was with respect to reserve requirements that EFT was expected to raise special problems for the Federal Reserve. It has long been recognized that every dollar held as reserves earns zero income for depository institutions, particularly commercial banks. It is as though the income that could have been earned by these impounded funds is taxed at a rate of 100%. This "tax" would not be of great concern were it not for the fact that the reserve requirements vary according to the types of deposits and depository institutions. These differences gave special advantages to those depository institutions that did not belong to the Federal Reserve. Under the circumstances, the Federal Reserve was threatened with a massive loss of members. Fortunately, Congress redressed this problem in the Monetary Control Act of 1980. As noted above, the provisions of this act will subject all depository institutions to uniform reserve requirements after an initial phase-in period. Because of this timely change, EFT should pose no threat to this instrument of monetary policy.

The use of the discount rate, never highly regarded as a credit control device, should not be altered by the introduction of EFT. It will still be used in an attempt to ration the reserves depository institutions desire to borrow from the Federal Reserve to augment their lending power. In addition, the discount rate will also retain whatever ability it has to signal major changes in monetary policy.

In summary, the tools of general credit control should, in a fully implemented EFT system, function much as they do today.

THE SELECTION OF THE APPROPRIATE SET OF TARGETS AND INDICATORS

Our discussion has identified several reasons to suspect that the introduction of EFT will increase the instability and uncertainty of both the money multiplier—and hence the relationship of the monetary base to the money supply—and the velocity of or demand for money. We have questioned as well the appropriate definition of money for purposes of monetary control.

The discussion in Chapter 11 of the criteria for selecting the appropriate set of targets and indicators for monetary policy indicated that the choice depended upon the relative stability of the monetary versus the real sector of the economy.

The introduction of EFT should bias the selection of the best set in favor of the Keynesian approach, which centers on interest rates, at least during the introduction phase. This is because it is believed that EFT will cause great instability in both the supply and demand functions for money, and increased instability in the monetary sector enhances the use of the interest rate for stabilization purposes. On the other hand, to reduce the expected instability of the velocity function, a more comprehensive measure of the money supply could be used. Unfortunately, finding the precise empirical counterpart may not be easy during a transition phase in which overdrafts and lines of credit will take on increasing importance, and the interest rates depository institutions are permitted to pay will be in the process of deregulation.

THE TRANSMISSION MECHANISM

The route by which the influence of changes in the money supply are transmitted to the real sector has been explored extensively. For the Keynesians, the influence is divided into changes in the cost of capital, the influence of interest rate changes on nominal wealth, and the flow of funds through financial intermediaries into certain crucial sectors such as housing. In the Keynesian approach, therefore, EFT should alter somewhat the relative importance of the flow of funds through intermediaries.

To the extent that EFT increases the variability of deposit balances at depository institutions, pressures will arise to make their asset structures increasingly diversified and more liquid. Hence, they will tend to be less specialized and, as the Regulation Q ceilings are removed, better able to withstand the waves of disintermediation and intermediation that beset the financial system. Since they will be less specialized, the flow of funds to certain sectors may decrease. Offsetting this advantage, to a degree, would be a less cautious lending policy.

As credit markets become more competitive and flexible under EFT, less reliance should have to be placed on any noninterest channels that have been used to ration the available supply of loanable funds. Thus, the Federal Reserve will have to rely more on interest rates as an allocator of funds than hitherto. However, the expected greater availability to households of overdraft facilities and lines of credit may diminish the contractionary influence of monetary policy unless the Federal Reserve adapts to this situation.

For the Monetarists, the introduction of EFT should not alter their view of the transmission mechanism, which centers on the play of interest rates, and on the alterations to the wealth of society that result when noninterest-bearing currency and interest-bearing government securities are swapped.

For both sides, EFT, by decreasing the costs and time involved in effecting transactions, should reduce the spread between the interest rate at which savers lend and investors borrow and the economic resources used in the whole exchange process. Reducing the spread should put downward pressure on the interest rate, while decreasing resources used in exchange should exert a downward pressure on the level of prices.

SUMMARY

The evolution of the process of exchange has been one of gradual increases in the efficiency with which an initial bundle of goods and services is converted by its owner into a more preferred bundle. Thus, barter gave way to monetary exchange, and within monetary exchange the use of metal gave way to paper instruments. These now appear about to yield to electronic impulses.

The discussion of electronic funds transfers was placed toward the end of the book for strategic reasons. After having discussed the concept of money, its creation, the instruments of central banking, the targets and indicators of monetary policy, and the route through which money affects economic activity, the framework was in place for evaluating the probable impact of this major technological innovation in the exchange process. The special problems posed by the introduction of EFT could, therefore, be distinguished from those that would remain after a full-fledged EFT system is in place.

STUDY QUESTIONS

1. Explain the incentive that exists to reduce the time involved in making transactions or exchanges.
2. What is the implication of EFT for the definition of money?
3. Suppose we continue to define money as $M1-B$. What would be the expected effect of EFT on the velocity of money?
4. What does EFT imply for the ability of the Federal Reserve to control the supply of money?
5. Evaluate the proposition that the problems posed by EFT are only likely to occur during its introductory phase.

SELECTED REFERENCES AND READINGS

Arthur D. Little, Inc. *The Consequences of Electronic Funds Transfer.* National Science Foundation, 1975.

Atkinson, Thomas R., and Ritter, Lawrence S. "Monetary Theory and Policy in the Payments System of the Future." *Journal of Money, Credit, and Banking,* Vol. 2, No. 4 (Nov. 1970).

Bender, Mark. *EFTS: Electronic Funds Transfer Systems—Elements and Impact.* Port Washington, N.Y.: Kennikat Press, 1975.

EFT in the United States: Policy Recommendations and the Public Interest. The Final Report of the National Commission on Electronic Fund Transfers. Washington, D.C., 1977.

Federal Reserve Bank of Boston. *The Economics of a National Electronic Funds Transfer System.* Conference Series No. 13 (Oct. 1974).

Flannery, Mark J., and Jafee, Dwight M. *The Economic Implications of an Electronic Monetary Transfer System.* Lexington, Mass.: Lexington Books, 1973.

Gambs, Carl M. *The Economics of an Automated Payments System.* Ph.D. dissertation, Yale University, 1972.

Hester, Donald D. "Monetary Policy in the 'Checkless' Economy." *Journal of Finance,* Vol. 27, No. 2 (May 1972).

Hosemann, Michael J. "Measuring the Impact of Electronic Funds Transfer Systems on Float." *Journal of Bank Research* (Autumn 1972).

Kane, Edward J. "Institutional Implications of the Changing Regulatory and Technological Framework of S and L Competition." Second Annual Conference of the Federal Home Loan Bank of San Francisco, December 9–10, 1976.

Mandell, Lewis. "EFTS and Competition in National Banks." *Proceeding of a Conference on Bank Structure and Competition.* Chicago: Federal Reserve Bank, 1976.

Moroney, John R., and Wilbratte, Barry J. "Money and Money Substitutes: A Time-Series Analysis of Household Portfolios." *Journal of Money, Credit, and Banking,* Vol. 8, No. 2 (May 1976).

Niblack, William C. "Development of Electronic Funds Transfer Systems." *Monthly Review,* Federal Reserve Bank of St. Louis (Sept. 1976).

Phillips, Almarin. "Competitive Policy for Depository Institutions." In *Promoting Competition in Regulated Markets,* edited by Almarin Phillips. Washington D.C.: Brookings Institution, 1975.

Richardson, Davis W. "The Emerging ERA of Electronic Money: Some Implications for Monetary Policy." *Journal of Bank Research* (Winter 1973).

Silber, William, ed. *Financial Innovation.* Lexington, Mass.: Lexington Books, 1975. See especially article by A. J. Meigs, "Recent Innovations: Do They Require a New Framework for Monetary Analysis?"

White, Kenneth J. "The Effect of Bank Credit Cards on the Household Transactions Demand for Money." *Journal of Money, Credit and Banking,* Vol. 8, No. 1 (Feb. 1976).

16

MONEY IN AN OPEN ECONOMY

16

Our discussion of money has proceeded largely in the context of a closed economy that has no commercial relations with other economies. This is admittedly an unrealistic abstraction. The United States does not exist in isolation from other nations, but is part of a worldwide network of trade, commerce, and finance. From time to time, events related to international economic affairs intrude into the daily lives of Americans. The prices of oil and coffee make us aware that our way of life depends on decisions made and circumstances occurring beyond our borders. Newspapers feature headlines on the foreign exchange value of the dollar and Walter Cronkite solemnly reports the monthly statistics on the international balance of trade. Frequently, he also reports what initiatives the government plans to undertake to deal with the problems presented by a persistent adverse trade balance. The close observer will often note that the intended reponse is likely to have implications for employment, economic growth, the rate of inflation, and other domestic areas. Thus, the international sector of the U.S. economy is linked to domestic economic activity. Yet, it often comes as a surprise to learn that the United States economy is largely self-sufficient. Foreign trade in goods and services is but a small percentage of our gross national product. Using either exports or imports, the percentage is less than 6%. Other countries, our leading trading partners, have far more open economies. For Japan, the relevant percentage is approximately 12%, for Great Britain 24%, Canada 20%, Germany 20%, Belgium 37%, Norway 43%, and the Netherlands 48%.

THE ROLE OF MONEY IN AN OPEN ECONOMY

In its broad functions the role of money in an open economy is not very different from its role in a closed economy, such as that discussed in Chapter 2. There, monetary exchange was seen to have considerable advantages for a typical Robinson Crusoe. These advantages hold as well in an open economy. The only difference is that since the world does not have a common unit of account, any given transactions chain by which an initial endowment of goods and services is converted into an ultimately more desirable combination may have as one of its links the conversion of domestic currency into foreign currency. Thus, a part of the following discussion of the role of money in an open economy will necessarily involve an explanation of the determination of foreign exchange rates and their implications for domestic economic activity.

Before we proceed to a consideration of some of the basic tools and concepts of the theory of international trade and commerce, let us note carefully why international exchange is desirable. Once we have examined the benefits that accrue from open international commerce, or free trade, an evaluation of which of the several international financial systems is most supportive of that end will be more meaningful.

THE CASE FOR FREE TRADE

In Chapter 2, to explain the advantages of monetary exchange over barter, a hypothetical Robinson Crusoe figure was used. It was seen that by exchange, Crusoe was able to convert the goods and services he produced most efficiently for those he could not produce, or that were differentiated in some way from those he produced, or that were identical to those he could produce, but only less efficiently. The advantages from trade that accrued to Crusoe were also available to those with whom he traded (his trading partners), for they would find in his goods and services the same advantages he found in theirs. As a result of the exchange, all parties should find themselves in a better position (i.e., enjoying a higher level of satisfaction) than before trade. This example demonstrates how free or unencumbered internal trade serves to make all consumers better off (or at least no worse off), in the sense that it increases the range of goods and services available to satisfy individual needs and desires. This argument applies to international trade as well. The United States imports a considerable range of raw materials and finished goods that cannot be produced domestically, or that are differentiated from domestic substitutes, or that are identical to those that would be produced, but are lower in price.

Free trade has one additional benefit: production is concentrated in those areas of the world where it is accomplished most efficiently. Thus, given the resources available to the world, free trade will ensure that world output will be maximized.[1] Because free trade is generally recognized as preferable to any other alternative, the ideal organization of the means of international finance should be supportive of this goal. In terms of our Robinson Crusoe analogy, if the transactions chain has as one of its links

[1] Note carefully what is left unsaid. The case for free trade does not guarantee that every nation of the world will be able to produce every commodity it wishes; it does not guarantee that every employee will have a lifetime job in a chosen occupation; and it does not guarantee that every investor will recover a normal profit on this invested capital. In fact, the more dynamic the world economy, the greater is the likelihood that some individuals will lose their jobs and have to be retrained for others, and that some fixed capital will become redundant and relatively worthless. Thus, in a world of free trade producer and consumer interests might clash.

the conversion of dollars for foreign currency, the international monetary system should make this possible, so long as Crusoe is willing to pay the price.

To facilitate an understanding of the nature of alternative international monetary systems, some of the terminology used, such as "balance of payments," must be explained and the functioning of foreign exchange markets examined. Then, a foreign trade sector will be added to the macro model developed in Chapter 10.

THE BALANCE OF INTERNATIONAL PAYMENTS

The balance of international payments is an accounting record that records all the transactions between the citizens of the United States (both individuals and corporate) and the citizens of the rest of the world. It includes all transactions involving merchandise (goods), services, and the flow of financial capital.

It is customary to divide the balance-of-payments account into two portions. The upper, called the *current account,* records the transactions involving goods and services undertaken by both private citizens and the government. The lower portion, called the *capital account,* records transactions involving the flow of money funds for the purchase of stocks, bonds, and real estate, and for deposit in financial institutions. The current account is frequently subdivided to separate merchandise transactions from all others. The difference between goods sold and purchased is called the *balance of trade.*

Before examining the balance of payments of the United States, answers should be provided to two questions. First, why do nations keep such records? Historically, the practice can be traced to the British, who began to use them to support an economic policy whose basic tenet was that it was desirable to export as great a sum as possible relative to imports.[2] Even after this policy was discarded, it was still considered desirable to maintain such records, for international transactions can affect the domestic money supply, aggregate demand, interest rates, employment, the price level, and other economic variables. Without such records, it might well be impossible to isolate what is causing these variables to change. Depending

[2] This view of trade policy was called *mercantilism* by Adam Smith. It was practiced in England for some 250 years, from 1500 to 1750, when it gave way to the doctrines of free trade. Several reasons have been advanced to explain the mercantilist policies. Among them is one that suggests that the mercantilists viewed the economy as one of low growth with a fixed number of jobs. In this context imports would cause a loss of jobs, while exports would stimulate employment. Thus, their policy of promoting the latter and retarding the former. Quite clearly, mercantilism was a producer- rather than a consumer-oriented doctrine. Adam Smith, together with a fellow Scot, David Hume, did much to show that mercantilism could not be successful, in the long run and that free trade was perferable in terms of efficient resource use and consumer well-being.

upon the cause of change, public policy might be different. For example, monetary policy might be different if it were known that reductions in the monetary base were due to a gold outflow induced by a balance-of-trade deficit as opposed to a transfer of Treasury balances from commercial banks to the Federal Reserve. Because such information is useful for internal policy purposes, nations still find it to their advantages to maintain such records.

The second question asks whether the balance of payments always balances. The answer is yes, it always balances. However, one should not identify balance with equilibrium. Thus, while the balance-of-payments account always balances, it is not always in equilibrium. To separate these two concepts, we must first explain why the balance of payments always balances. This occurs because in compiling the transactions, double-entry bookkeeping is used. In terms of the familiar *T*-account, every entry on one side of the account is balanced by an entry of equal magnitude on the other side, or by one of equal magnitude but opposite sign on the same side.

If the balance of payments always balances, how, then, can we have a balance-of-payments deficit or surplus? What is the meaning of such phrases? When people speak of surpluses or deficits they are talking about a disequilibrium, which they attempt to measure by using a portion of the transactions that enter the payments accounts. In particular, an attempt is made to separate two types of entries—those that occur for their own sake, because they help to maximize either consumer well-being or the profits of investors, and those that occur in response to the first category. The former are called *autonomous* entries or transactions, while the latter are called appropriately *induced* or financing entries. In calculating a deficit or surplus, only the autonomous transactions should be used. However, as the discussion to follow will show, it is difficult in certain instances to separate the autonomous from the induced. Hence, the surplus or deficit is, at best, only an approximation to the ideal. It will also be shown that a balance-of-payments disequilibrium is only applicable to a world in which the exchange rate of one currency for another is fixed. Where perfectly flexible rates of exchange prevail, the balance of payments must always be in equilibrium.

Table 16:1 represents a typical balance-of-payments account. It contains transactions related to merchandise, services, unilateral transfers, and financial flows for the purchase of stocks, bonds, and real estate and for deposits in financial institutions.

Current account

The current account functions for the nation much as the income statement does for a business. It records as credits the current sales to foreigners by the nation of goods and services and the gifts it receives from abroad, and

TABLE 16:1
Balance of international payments

Current Account	
Items Generating Payments (Debits)	Items Generating Receipts (Credits)
Imports of merchandise	Exports of merchandise a. Private b. Government
Balance of Trade	
(Debits > Credits = Deficit)	(Credits > Debits = Surplus)
Plus	
Purchases of travel, transportation, and other services	Sales of travel, transportation, and other services
Remittances, pensions, and other unilateral transfers	Remittances, pensions, and other unilateral transfers
Dividends and interest remitted	Dividends and interest received
Balance on Current Account	
(Debits > Credits = Deficit)	(Credits > Debits = Surplus)
Capital Account	
Items Increasing Assets or Decreasing Liabilities (Debit)	Items Increasing Liabilities or Decreasing Assets (Credits)
Long-term capital payments	Long-term capital receipts
Short-term capital payments	Short-term capital receipts
(Debits > Credits = Deficit)	(Credits > Debits = Surplus)

treats as current expenses (i.e., records as debits) the purchases by the nation of goods and services from foreigners and the gifts it makes abroad. Most of the transactions are self-explanatory, but a few may require special explication. Why, for example, are dividends and interest received from foreign investment or paid to foreigners recorded in the current account? The reason is that such receipts or payments are regarded as arising from the current services of capital. That is, capital provides current services in producing current output. Dividends, then, are regarded as the payment made for those services.

The item "pensions" records the receipts by foreigners from the U.S. pension system (either private or public—social security) and the receipt by U.S. citizens of pensions from foreign sources. It should also be noted that the current account records expenditures abroad by American tourists and of foreign tourists visiting the United States. (If U.S. tourists fly abroad on a U.S. carrier, the transaction is treated as a domestic one and does not enter the balance of payments.)

A subsection of the current account or the current account itself is said to be in surplus whenever the total credits exceed total debits. Whenever debits exceed credits, the subsection is said to be in deficit.[3]

Capital account

The capital account functions for the nation as the balance sheet functions for a business. It records increases in U.S.-owned assets abroad or decreases in U.S. liabilities to foreigners as debits, and decreases in U.S.-owned assets abroad or increases in U.S. liabilities to foreigners as credits.

Under the heading "long-term capital" is recorded the purchase by U.S. citizens of foreign bonds, equities (stock), and real estate, certain deposits in financial institutions, as well as the retention of earnings by U.S.-owned subsidiary companies abroad (e.g., Ford Motor of Germany is treated as a German firm). These transactions are recorded as debits in the capital account, while similar transactions in which foreigners are the initiating parties are recorded as credits (increases in U.S. liabilities abroad).

Under the heading "short-term capital" is recorded the purchase of securities whose time to maturity is one year or less or which are of a demand nature. Hence, short-term capital includes bank deposits, Treasury bills, and any debt security, regardless of its time to maturity when issued, that is within one year of redemption at time of purchase.

The capital account records all liabilities to foreigners, both private individuals and official institutions, e.g., foreign central banks.

Whenever total debits exceed total credits, the United States is said to have a net outflow of capital, or to be a net capital exporter, or to have a deficit on capital account. The opposite occurs when total credits in the capital accounts exceed debits. We are then a capital importer.

Some illustrative entries

To understand how double-entry bookkeeping works and to distinguish autonomous from induced entries, consider the following rather typical transactions.

First, assume that an American decides to purchase a Japanese automobile. The purchase is an autonomous transaction and is recorded as merchandise imported. Suppose the automobile is paid for with a check drawn on an American bank. The Japanese exporter deposits the check in his bank, which then acquires a claim on the U.S. financial system. This rise in U.S. liabilities to foreigners is the induced transaction and appears as a credit to short-term capital borrowing. (The American financial system is in essence borrowing from Japan).

[3] When the balance of trade is in surplus, some call this a favorable balance of trade. What is favorable about this state is uncertain, for it implies that the U.S. has fewer goods and services than it would have had had a deficit prevailed. The term *favorable* is a holdover from mercantilism.

Next, assume that a U.S. subsidiary company located in France pays a dividend to its U.S. parent firm. This dividend is an autonomous entry and will appear as a credit to "dividends and interest" in the current account. When the U.S. parent deposits the dividend check in its bank, the U.S. financial system will acquire a claim on the French banking system. The induced entry will appear in the capital account as a debit under short-term capital lending.

Suppose now that the U.S. government ships surplus military equipment to a foreign ally. The cost value of the equipment would appear as military exports (credit) (an autonomous transaction). The induced entry would not appear in the capital account, as the equipment is a gift and no money is received. Instead, the offsetting induced entry would appear as a unilateral transfer (a transfer for which no *quid pro quo* is expected). In this instance both transactions are confined to the current account.

Consider now the case where an American firm purchases equity shares in a German firm. The autonomous entry will be recorded as long-term capital lending, while the induced entry that arises when the Germans deposit the check in their bank, will represent an increase in German claims on the American financial system, i.e., as short-term capital borrowing by American depository institutions.

Thus far the short-term capital account has been used to record the offsetting transactions that serve to finance the autonomous entries. That is, the short-term capital account has been used to record induced transactions. This need not be the case in all instances. Several autonomous transactions can involve short-term capital flows. An American bank, for example, may invest funds in Canadian Treasury bills because their yields exceed comparable yields on U.S. securities. This flow of "interest-sensitive" or "hot" money to Canada would be recorded as short-term capital lending (debit), while the offsetting credit would appear as short-term capital borrowing (the claims of the Canadian banking system on the U.S. financial system would rise following the deposit of the check purchasing the bills). Moreover, speculative flows of funds to take advantage of expected changes in exchange rates would also appear as both autonomous and induced entries in the short-term capital account. Since the short-term capital account contains both types of entries, and it is impossible to separate them, it is consequently possible to calculate only an approximate measure of the balance-of-payments surplus or deficit.

Some relationships among the balance-of-payments entries

From the transactions examined above it is plain that a number of relations exist among the balance-of-payments accounts. The most common tie current account items to those in the capital account.

However, if a longer time span is considered, other relationships become evident. For example, capital outflow, especially long term, which expands foreign productive capacity, can serve to reduce U.S. exports and to increase U.S. imports. It also serves to produce a flow of dividends and interest to the United States.

Similarly, capital inflow to the United States, to the extent that it expands productive capacity, may reduce U.S. imports and expand U.S. exports to foreign markets. Recent investments by Sony and Volkswagen are clear examples of the former. To the extent that foreign investment in the United States is profitable, dividend and interest outflows from the United States will rise.

Moreover, foreign investment can raise the standard of living of recipient nations. A rising standard may lead to the purchase of foreign goods. Thus, U.S. exports and imports may rise as an indirect consequence of foreign investment.

Other relationships are also possible, but those involving foreign investment are undoubtedly the most complex and difficult to disentangle.[4]

THE BALANCE OF PAYMENTS OF THE UNITED STATES

Now that the general format of the balance of payments has been discussed and a range of typical transactions examined, we shall consider the balance of payments of the United States in some detail. Table 16:2 presents the U.S. balance of payments for 1977.[5] Technically, the U.S. Department of Commerce has not calculated a net balance-of-payments deficit or surplus since 1975. This is to recognize the use by the United States of flexible exchange rates. As will be explained after the discussion of the foreign exchange market, the sum of autonomous transactions is zero and a net balance cannot be computed. However, it is possible to reconstruct a net position from the recorded statistics. The 1977 number results from that reconstruction. Surely the curious will think this a serious inconsistency. How can a net position be constructed when it must theoretically sum to zero? No sleight of hand is involved. Basically, a net position can be computed for two reasons. First, it is not possible to separate data into autonomous and induced transactions. Any attempt will only be partially successful. Thus, a net balance may result. Second, and relevant to the case at hand, the balance of payments shown in Table 16:2 attempts to

[4] For two attempts, see H. Peter Gray and Gail Makinen, "The Balance of Payments Contributions of Multinational Firms," *Journal of Business* (July 1967):339–43; and Gail Makinen, "The Pay-off Period of Direct Foreign Investment of the U.S. Automotive Industry," *Journal of Business* (Oct. 1970):395–409.

[5] The format of this table is different from that of Table 16:1, the reason being that the available data are designed to calculate a specific net balance. Nevertheless, the balance of trade and that on current account are calculated, as well as a balance of some long-term capital transactions.

TABLE 16:2
The balance of payments of the United States for 1977 (billions of dollars)

Current Account	Debit	Credit	Net
Merchandise exports		$120.6	–
Merchandise imports	$151.6		–
Balance of trade	–	–	–$31.0
Travel and transportation	17.6	14.5	–3.1
Other services	4.2	8.9	4.7
Remittances, pensions, and other unilateral transfers (including government)	19.3	32.1	12.8
U.S. military	5.7	7.1	1.4
Balance on current account			–$15.2
U.S. government capital flows, net (excluding reserve transactions)	–	–	–3.7
U.S. direct investment abroad*	–	–	–12.2
Foreign direct investment in U.S.	–	–	3.3
U.S. purchases of foreign securities, net	–	–	–5.4
Foreign purchases of U.S. securities (excluding Treasury issues), net	–	–	2.9
Net change in long term claims on foreigners	–	–	–.7
Net change in long-term liabilities to foreigners	–	–	–.2
Balance on current account and long-term capital (basic balance)			–$31.2
Net change in short-term claims	–	–	–3.0
Statistical discrepancy	–	–	–1.0
Official reserve transactions balance			–$35.2

Courtesy *Survey of Current Business* (June 1978).
*For balance-of-payments accounting, direct investment is distinguished from portfolio investment. It includes the purchase of equity securities in foreign firms more than 10% owned by a U.S. parent firm. It also includes establishing a U.S. subsidiary abroad. Portfolio investment includes the purchase of equities in firms less than 10% owned by a U.S. parent firm and the purchase of debt securities (e.g., bonds).

measure the net magnitude of foreign transactions that could contribute to dollar holdings by foreign central banks. These holdings, under fixed exchange rates, could be used to exert pressure on the U.S. stock of gold and other official reserves. This net balance, therefore, omits a number of autonomous transactions that were thought unlikely to put dollars in the hands of foreign central banks.

According to Table 16:2, the United States had a balance-of-trade deficit of $31 billion, a current account deficit of $15.2 billion, a deficit on basic balance of $31.2 billion, and an overall deficit of $35.2 billion.

We have already discussed the meaning of the balances of trade and the current account. The concept of the "basic balance" has yet to be discussed. Its purpose is to measure the long-run balance-of-payments position of the United States. Therefore, all short-term capital is excluded. Except for military transactions and government grants, the components of the basic balance respond primarily to market forces consisting of price differentials and investment opportunities among trading economies. If one is primarily concerned with international flows of resources, with the benefits received from international commerce, with the impact of international trade on domestic income and production, or with estimates of long-run movements in exports and imports, the "basic balance" would be a good yardstick and tool of analysis.

Since private short-term capital movements are primarily in response to transitory phenomena (e.g., interest rate differentials, expectations of changes in the value of currencies, fear of political upheaval), they are excluded from the basic balance. Because they respond to factors regarded as transitory, short-term capital movements are readily reversible. As such, they create enough volatility to make them incompatible with longer-run or basic concepts.

Statistical discrepancies arise because the various components that enter the balance of payments are often obtained from samples or may escape counting altogether. Some think that a large part of the discrepancy consists of unrecorded short-term capital movements.

Finally, the "official reserve transactions balance" is designed to record the net change in the assets counted as U.S. monetary reserves and net changes in U.S. liabilities to foreign official agencies (principally central banks). During the era when the United States maintained fixed exchange rates, this balance indicated the direct pressure that might be exerted by official agencies on the U.S. stock of gold and official reserves.

To conclude this discussion of the balance of payments, Table 16:3 presents in a highly aggregated form the U.S. balance-of-payments experience since the end of World War II.[6]

THE FOREIGN EXCHANGE MARKET

In its economic characteristics the foreign exchange market closely resembles the markets for financial securities and raw material commodities, and conforms closely to the competitive ideal found in microeconomic text-

[6] In examining Department of Commerce literature, one notices that from 1960 through 1975 the United States also used a so-called net liquidity balance as a measure of the overall balance-of-payments deficit or surplus. It differed from the official reserve transactions balance in its treatment of short-term capital. One has the feeling that there was a little sleight-of-hand going into the makeup of these definitions. That is to say, these measures were designed in part to mask the true nature of the deficit in the U.S. balance of payments and to confuse foreign dollar holders as to the seriousness of the protracted buildup of dollar liabilities abroad. This experience is discussed in Chapter 17.

TABLE 16:3
The U.S. balance of payments since World War II

Year	Balance of Trade	Balance of Current Account	Basic Balance	Official Reserve Transactions Balance
1946	6.7	4.9	—	—
1947	10.1	9.0	—	—
1948	5.7	2.4	—	—
1949	5.3	.9	—	—
1950	1.1	-1.8	—	—
1951	3.1	.9	—	—
1952	2.6	.6	—	—
1953	1.4	-1.3	—	—
1954	2.6	.2	—	—
1955	2.9	.4	—	—
1956	4.8	2.7	—	—
1957	6.3	4.8	—	—
1958	3.5	.8	—	—
1959	1.1	-1.3	—	—
1960	4.9	2.8	−1.2	−3.4
1961	5.6	3.8	0.0	−1.3
1962	4.5	3.4	−1.0	−2.7
1963	5.2	4.4	−1.4	−1.9
1964	6.8	6.8	−.1	−1.5
1965	5.0	5.4	−1.8	−1.3
1966	3.8	3.0	−2.6	.2
1967	3.8	2.6	−4.0	−3.4
1968	.6	.6	−2.3	1.6
1969	.6	.4	−3.9	2.7
1970	2.6	2.4	−3.8	−9.8
1971	−2.3	−1.4	−10.6	−29.8
1972	−6.4	−6.0	−11.1	−10.4
1973	1.0	6.9	−1.0	−5.3
1974	−5.3	1.7	−10.9	−8.8
1975	9.0	18.4	3.9	−4.7
1976	−9.4	4.3	−14.5	−10.6
1977	−31.1	−15.2	−31.2	−35.2
1978	—	—	—	—

Courtesy of the *Survey of Current Business* (June 1978).

books. A standard or homogeneous product (i.e., currency in the case at hand) is bought and sold and the market has so many buyers and sellers that no one of them has the power to make or set the exchange rate. Rather, price is said to be determined by the market. This is subject to the qualification that from time to time central banks may intervene to alter the price. Through the use of telex machines and telephones, the foreign exchange market is highly integrated and worldwide in scope.

This market serves to determine the price of one country's currency in terms of all others. Its functioning can be explained by using simple supply-and-demand schedules. Table 16:4 shows selected foreign exchange rates. These rates are explained in two different ways: foreign currency expressed in terms of the dollar, and the dollar expressed in terms of foreign currency. Thus, .4627 British pound is equal to one dollar or 2.16 dollars are equal to one British pound.

In order to simplify our explanation of the foreign exchange rate, the rest of the world will be assumed to use a common unit of account, the pound sterling (£). Thus, the exchange rate to be explained is the dollar/pound rate ($/£). In Figure 16:1 the vertical axis measures the $/£ rate, that is, the price of the pound in dollars. The horizontal axis measures the quantity of pounds demanded and supplied.

To understand why the demand schedule has the usual downward slope, consider a product that sells for £1,000. Will individuals in the United States demand a larger quantity of this product if they must give $1 per pound than if they must give $4 per pound? That is, will they demand a larger quantity if the U.S. price is $1,000 rather than $4,000? Generally, the answer will be yes. The lower the price, the larger will be the quantity demanded. Thus, the fewer dollars an American must give per pound, the larger will be the quantity of pounds demanded. From this it follows that the demand schedule should have the normal downward slope. This discussion also indicates that the demand for pounds is closely related to the demand for imported goods and services, and to the demand for foreign financial assets and real estate as well.

On the other hand, the citizens of the pound country supply their currency to the American market in order to purchase American goods, services, financial assets, and real estate. Thus, the supply of pounds

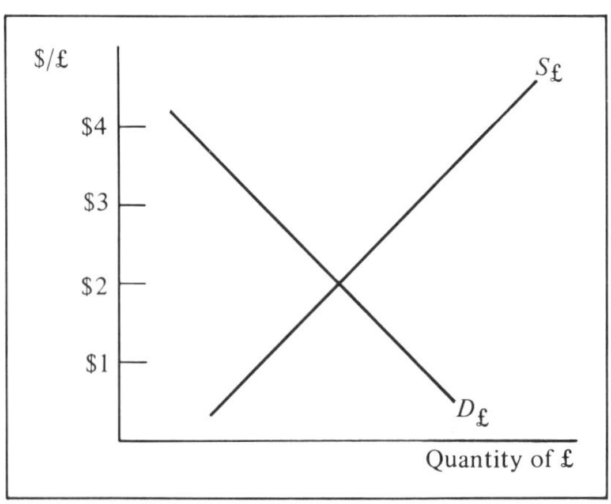

FIGURE 16:1
The foreign exchange market

TABLE 16:4

Selected Foreign Exchange Rates (September 24, 1979)

NEW YORK (AP) Foreign Exchange, New York prices

	Fgn. currency in dollars		Dollar in fgn. currency	
	Mon.	Fri.	Mon.	Fri.
Argentina	.0007	.0007	1421.0	1421.0
Australia	1.1280	1.1280	.8865	.8865
Austria	.0787	.0785	12.70	12.73
Belgium	.0353	.0352	28.36	28.42
Bolivia	.0495	.0495	20.20	20.20
Brazil	.0343	.0343	29.14	29.14
Britain	2.1613	2.1625	.4627	.4624
30 day fut	2.1597	2.1596	.4630	.4630
60 day fut	2.1558	2.1571	.4639	.4636
90 day fut	2.1531	2.1541	.4644	.4642
Canada	.8560	.8563	1.1682	1.1678
30 day fut	.8576	.8569	1.1660	1.1671
60 day fut	.8577	.8573	1.1659	1.1665
90 day fut	.8580	.8577	1.1655	1.1659
Chile	.0256	.0256	39.00	39.00
Colombia	.0233	.0233	42.88	42.88
Denmark	.1947	.1964	5.1370	5.0916
yEgypt	1.45	1.42	.6915	.6915
Ecuador	.0356	.0356	28.10	28.10
Finland	.2666	.2670	3.7515	3.7445
France	.2407	.2407	4.1540	4.1540
Greece	.0273	.0273	36.60	36.60
Holland	.5123	.5115	1.9518	1.9550
Hong Kong	.1987	.1987	5.0320	5.0320
yIndia	.1256	.1256	7.9600	7.9600
Indonesia	.0016	.0016	625.00	625.00
Iran	.01320	.01320	71.50	71.50
Ireland	2.1270	2.1205	.4701	.4716
Israel	.0369	.0369	27.10	27.10
Italy	.001239	.001243	806.75	804.50
Japan	.004500	.004500	222.20	222.22
30 day fut	.004510	.004514	221.70	221.55
60 day fut	.004530	.004534	220.75	220.55
90 day fut	.004551	.004555	5219.75	219.75
Jordan	3.3501	3.3355	.29850	.29980
Kuwait	3.6160	3.6223	.2765	.2761
Lebanon	.3056	.3058	3.2725	3.2700
Mexico	.0439	.0439	22.76	22.77
New Zealand	1.0007	1.0030	.9993	.9970
Norway	.2017	.2005	4.9585	4.9875
yPeru	.004300	.004300	233.58	233.58
Phillippines	.1360	.1360	7.3500	7.3500
Portugal	.0203	.0203	49.20	49.12
Saudi Arabia	.2978	.2989	3.3580	3.3450
Singapore	.4664	.4664	2.1440	2.1440
xSo. Africa	1.2043	1.2042	.8303	.8304
Spain	.0151	.0151	66.03	66.03
Sweden	.2401	.2397	4.1640	4.1719
Switzerlnd	.6349	.6377	1.5750	1.5680
30 day fut	.6415	.6435	1.5588	1.5540
60 day fut	.6473	.6500	1.5448	1.5385
90 day fut	.6537	.6562	1.5298	1.5240
Turkey	.0212	.0212	47.10	47.10
Uruguay	.1226	.1226	8.1550	8.1550
Venzuela	.2329	.2329	4.2937	4.2937
W. Germany	.5655	.5670	1.7682	1.7635
30 day fut	.5680	.5694	1.7606	1.7561
60 day fut	.5701	.5723	1.7541	1.7474
90 day fut	.5731	.5751	1.7449	1.7385

Midday prices at New York & San Francisco banks, gathered by Bank of America, New York.

x—Floating. y—Official rate.

represents a demand for things exported from the United States. The more dollars that individuals in the United States are willing to give per pound, the larger should be the quantity that foreigners are willing to supply. It follows, then, that the supply schedule should have the usual upward slope. The intersection of the supply and demand schedules yields the equilibrium price of pounds in terms of dollars or the foreign exchange rate.

The role of arbitrage

In actual foreign exchange markets more than one exchange rate is determined. From Table 16:4 it can be seen that a dollar rate is determined for the currency of each of the leading trading countries of the world. What ensures that the dollar/pound, dollar/franc rate will be translated into the corrected pound/franc rate? For example, suppose the dollar/pound rate is $2 and the dollar/franc rate is 50 cents. Will 4 francs exchange for 1 pound? So long as individuals are free to maximize private profit, the market will ensure the 4 francs exchange for one pound (sometimes called the cross rate of exchange). To see why, suppose that while the dollar/pound rate is $2 and the dollar/franc rate is 50 cents, 3 francs exchange for 1 pound. In such a situation profit possibilities arise. A trader could sell dollars for francs, realizing two per dollar sold. Then 3 francs (worth $1.50) could be sold per pound, and then converted into $2. The gross profit per pound would be 50 cents. This simultaneous buying and selling (or arbitrage) cannot continue forever. The relative supplies and demands for the three currencies will be altered so that the cross rates of exchange will be consistent. Individuals called arbitragers will also be responsible for seeing that a uniform dollar/pound rate prevails throughout the worldwide market, i.e., that the rate is not $2.00 in New York and $1.75 in London.

The forward exchange market

An examination of the exchange quotations in Table 16:4 will show for several currencies both a current quotation (called the spot rate, for it represents the price paid "on the spot" for currency) and a future quotation (called the forward rate, for it represents the price paid today for the future delivery of currency). The forward rate is necessary because some commercial transactions require payment to be made in the future or income to be received from foreign sources in the future. Individuals making such payments or receiving such income might wish to know with certainty today the dollar values involved rather than wait and make conversions in the future in the spot market. For example, an American exporter might sell an automobile for £4,000, to be paid for 60 days in the future. How much will the exporter realize in dollars? One way for the exporter to avoid uncertainty would be to offer today to exchange £4,000 for a given number of dollars in 60 days. In essence, the contract the exporter signs commits him to sell his pounds for dollars in 60 days, but at an exchange rate determined at the time the contract is signed and not at the (uncertain) exchange rate that will actually exist in 60 days. Thus, the exporter knows at the time he signs the contract exactly how many dollars he will receive even though he will not get them for 60 days.

The forward exchange market enables the exporter to do this.[7] Similarly, an American bank could buy a 90-day Canadian Treasury bill with a market rate of interest of 12%. However, should the exchange rate move in favor of the U.S. dollar, the U.S. bank could suffer a net loss on the purchase. To avoid this and at the same time calculate the actual yield on the bill, the American bank can offer to sell Canadian dollars for U.S. dollars in 90 days when the Treasury bill matures, at an exchange rate determined now.

Having seen how the forward market functions, it should come as no surprise that this market is an important part of the infrastructure of international trade and commerce.

The elasticity and shiftability of the demand and supply schedules

No investigation of the mechanism determining a market price would be complete without a discussion of the factors explaining both the elasticity of the relevant schedules and what causes them to shift over time.

Elasticity

When one focuses on the market for any good, the elasticity of the demand schedule is thought to depend upon the availability of substitutes. The more substitutes and the closer they are to the good in question, the more elastic the demand schedule in question. This is also true for foreign exchange markets. Since the demand for foreign currency mainly represents the demand for foreign goods, services, and so forth, the schedule should be increasingly more elastic the greater the availability and range of domestic substitutes. Where many substitutes are available, slight changes in the exchange rate will lead to large shifts in demand between domestic and foreign goods. Consequently, the quantity demanded of foreign currency will be sensitive to small changes in the exchange rate, i.e., it will be relatively elastic.

For a commodity such as wheat, the supply schedule is the marginal cost schedule. This is not true for foreign exchanges. Here, the supply schedule depends upon the demand by foreigners for American goods, services,

[7] One might legitimately ask why the American exporter did not price the goods in dollars to avoid the difficulty. Indeed, this could be done. Note, however, that this merely shifts the uncertainty to the importer, who will not know the pound cost attached to the automobile unless he can have recourse to the forward exchange market.

financial assets, and so on. Thus, its elasticity will depend upon the range of foreign-produced substitutes. The more foreign substitutes there are, the more will small changes in the exchange rate lead to large shifts between U.S. and foreign goods, i.e., the more elastic the supply schedule of foreign currency will be.

Shiftability

When deriving the demand schedule for an individual commodity, it is customary to hold constant such factors as tastes and preferences, real income, the prices of substitutes and complements, and various expectational elements. Similarly, when deriving the demand and supply schedules for foreign exchange, a comparable range of variables must be held constant. These include tastes and preferences, real income and price levels in both the United States and the rest of the world, and a host of expectational elements concerning the future course of economic events and the balance of payments. Several examples are constructed below to demonstrate the possible influence of changes in each of these factors on the foreign exchange rate.

Consider first a rise in real income in the United States relative to the rest of the world. U.S. citizens will then be able to purchase more of all goods including imports. As shown in Figure 16:2, the demand for pounds rises from D to D', and the exchange rate rises or depreciates, i.e., it would take more dollars to purchase a pound.[8]

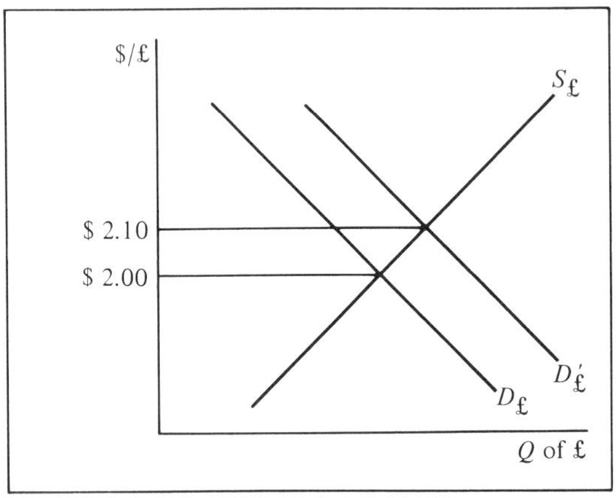

FIGURE 16:2
A rise in real income in the United States

[8] It is correct to say that the exchange rate *rises* or depreciates only if the foreign currency is quoted in terms of the dollar. Should the dollar be quoted in terms of foreign currency, a depreciation will cause the rate to fall, for this rate is the reciprocal of the first rate mentioned.

Conversely, should the real income of the leading trading partners of the United States rise at a faster rate, the supply schedule of foreign exchange would shift to the right and the exchange rate would appreciate or fall.[9]

A rise in the price level in the United States relative to the rest of the world presents a somewhat more complicated situation. The first effect of such a rise would be to increase the demand for foreign exchange in Figure 16:3 from *D* to *D'*, since foreign substitutes are now cheaper. Second, since foreign substitutes are now relatively cheaper, some foreign buyers will switch from American goods to their own domestic goods. This causes the supply schedule of pounds to shift to the left from *S* to *S'*. The net result is a dollar depreciation.

Suppose now that economic prospects look bright for the United States in that a high rate of real economic growth is expected. Foreigners might become convinced that business profits will be high, which will lead to a rise in equity prices. As a result, their demand for U.S. securities will rise and the supply of foreign currency will shift to the right. Without drawing the diagram to show this case, a rightward shift in supply will cause the exchange rate to fall and the dollar to appreciate.

Finally, suppose that the prospects for the United States balance of payments do not look good because, for example, a deficit has persisted, the inflation rate is high and expected to remain so, or the economic growth rate is low and there is little prospect it will rise. Under these circumstances

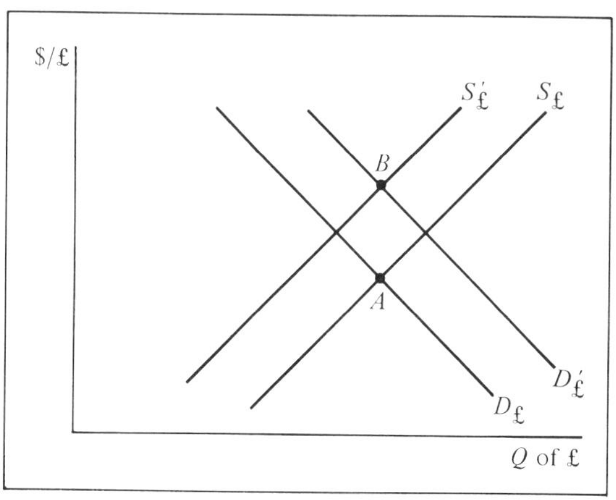

FIGURE 16:3
U.S. prices rise relative to those abroad

[9] For the dollar to appreciate, it is not only necessary for real income in foreign countries to grow faster than ours, but their tastes and preferences must be somewhat comparable to ours. Thus, a faster rise in real income will ensure a growth in their imports from us relative to our imports from them. It is possible for the reverse to take place if foreign tastes and preferences are not strongly in favor of U.S. goods.

individuals might believe that the dollar will continue to depreciate. This may lead to speculation, i.e., individuals may sell dollars today and buy them back later after the depreciation they expect has taken place. While such a game is dangerous, it always attracts players. Speculation against the dollar can be shown by a rightward shift of the demand schedule for foreign currency and, possibly as a leftward shift of the supply schedule. Either or both actions will lead to a depreciation of the dollar.

Other cases could be contrived and their implications for the exchange rate examined. However, those given should suffice for a reasonable understanding of the functioning of the foreign exchange markets.

FOREIGN EXCHANGES AND THE BALANCE OF PAYMENTS

When demand and supply schedules are drawn, they refer to things that would happen under the hypothesized circumstances. For example, the demand schedule refers to quantities of a good or service individuals would be *willing* to purchase at a corresponding series of prices, holding constant such variables as were discussed above. This is also true for the demand for foreign currencies. This demand represents what individuals would like to do in order to maximize their well-being or their profit. Seen from such a perspective, the foreign exchange rate is determined by the *autonomous* items making up a hypothetical balance of payments. That is, only the autonomous items that would be entered on the balance of payments would go to determine such demand and supply schedules as those depicted in Figures 16:1 through 16:3. The induced transactions only occur after the fact. They help to determine past rates of exchange but not the rate expected to prevail in the future. Only the autonomous transactions are relevant.

Given this situation, it is possible both to define a theoretical balance-of-payments deficit or surplus and to see why neither can arise if the exchange rate is truly flexible. In terms of Figure 16:4, the demand for foreign currency arises from those transactions that enter the balance of payments as debits. On the other hand, the supply of foreign currency reflects the transactions that enter as credits. At P_E, the autonomous debits are equal in value to the autonomous credits and the balance of payments is in equilibrium.[10] So long as a flexible exchange rate system is in force and the flexibility of the rate is not impeded by government intervention, the balance of payments will always be in equilibrium and there can be no deficit or surplus. From this it follows that a surplus or deficit is characteristic of disequilibrium and arises from the fact that the exchange rate is

[10] Thus, while the value of the credits on the balance of payments will always *equal* the value of the debits (because of double-entry bookkeeping), this equality does not mean that the balance of payments is in *equilibrium*.

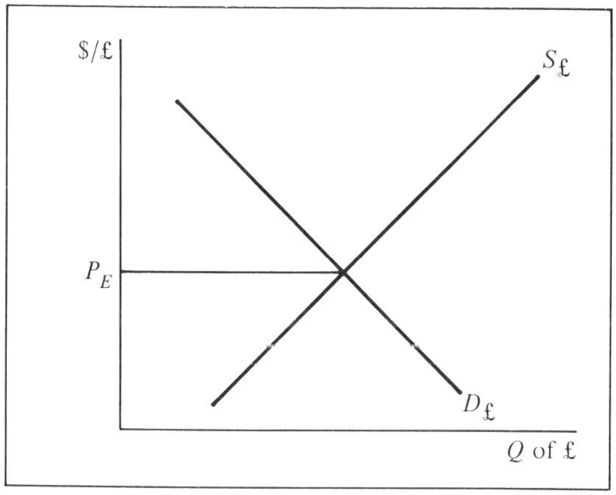

FIGURE 16:4
The balance of payments in equilibrium

fixed and not permitted to change. In Figure 16:5 both a surplus and deficit are shown. The latter would arise if, for example, the exchange rate were held at P_D, which is below the equilibrium or market clearing price, P_E. As a result, the autonomous demand for foreign exchange would exceed the supply arising from autonomous transactions. It is customary in such a situation to say that the dollar is overvalued, i.e., it takes too many units of foreign currency to buy a dollar.

Just the opposite holds for a surplus. The exchange rate is held above the equilibrium rate. In this case, the dollar would be said to be undervalued, or too cheap in terms of the pound. By how much the exchange rate must

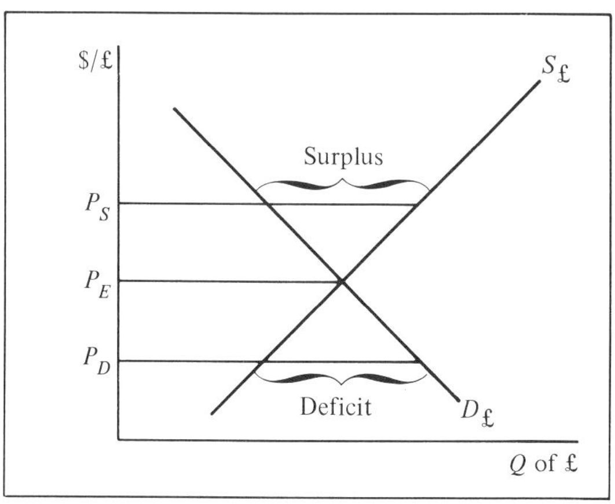

FIGURE 16:5
Balance of payments disequilibrium

change in each situation to establish equilibrium depends, of course, on the elasticities of the supply and demand schedules. The more elastic each schedule, the smaller will be the required change.

Having examined how the balance of payments appears in the foreign exchange market, it is now convenient to analyze how deficits and surplus may be corrected.

FIXED VERSUS FLEXIBLE EXCHANGE RATES

Fixed rates

Before discussing how balance-of-payments disequilibria are corrected under fixed exchange rates, it is necessary to explain reasons for, and consequences of, fixed exchange rates.

The origin of fixed rates

Historically, fixed exchange rates resulted from the practice by nations of defining their unit of account in terms of gold (or silver). Should the dollar be defined as 20 grains of fine gold and the pound as 40 grains, the exchange rate would be $2 to the pound. On the other hand, each nation could announce a purchase price of gold. Should the U.S. price be $30 per ounce and the British price be £15, the exchange rate would also be $2 to the pound. Fixed exchange rates emerged, then, when nations started to use precious metals as means of exchange. Fixed rates are a natural part of the international monetary system known as the gold standard.[11]

Adjustment under fixed rates

To see the potential difficulties when exchange rates are fixed, ask yourself what would happen if the government decided to fix the price of wheat at $4 per bushel, and hold it there for the forseeable future. So long as the equilibrium market clearing price was also $4, no difficulties would arise. Should new land come into production, or a new hybrid seed be discovered, so that supply was increased, the government would be required to purchase and hold in storage all the excess supply at the fixed price. On the other

[11] This is not to say that the exchange rates are rigid under a fixed exchange rate regime. Since costs are involved in transporting gold from country to country, the exchange rate can vary around *parity* (or $2 per £ 1), depending on the range of costs. Suppose that it costs 4 cents per pound to ship and insure gold from the United States to Britain. The dollar/pound rate could rise in New York to $2.04 before Americans would ship gold to London rather than send a pound check. Similarly, the rate could fall as low as $1.96 before the British would be willing to ship gold to New York rather than send a dollar check. The upper rate of $2.04 was called the *gold export point,* while the lower rate, $1.96, was called the *gold import point.* Within this band, $1.96–$2.04, market forces were free to set the prevailing exchange rate.

hand, should the demand schedule shift to the right and exceed supply at the $4 price, the government would then have to supply the deficiency from its inventories. If none exist, it would be forced to adopt some rationing method or allow the price to rise. Obviously, neither disequilibrium could persist in the long run without large government expenditures (and taxes) in the case of a surplus, or extensive government restrictions on consumers' behavior in the case of a shortage.

When a government fixes an exchange rate, it invites the same kind of difficulties that arise when it fixes the price of wheat—demand may exceed supply, or supply may exceed demand. To deal with the two situations, it has many of the same options. In the short run it can sell gold or foreign currencies from its inventories, or add to them should supply exceed demand. It can also contemplate changing the exchange rate. That is to say, it can raise the purchase price of gold (or *devalue* its currency), or lower the purchase price (and *revalue* its currency).

To maintain a fixed rate over the longer run, the country must adopt policies to ensure that the demand and supply schedules intersect reasonably close to price P_E in Figure 16:5. What policies should be pursued and how can the government get the schedules to shift? To answer these questions, recall the explanation of the factors that cause the schedules to shift. Two of these factors are relevant here: price level changes and income changes.[12]

Suppose U.S. prices are rising at a faster rate than those of other trading partner nations. Americans will increasingly shift to the purchase of foreign substitutes and foreigners will purchase their own domestic substitutes. The net result is a balance-of-payments deficit. To remove the deficit, the government could alter the parity exchange rate, i.e., devalue. However, an examination of history will show that other steps are likely to be taken. First, the payments imbalance will set in motion its own corrective mechanism. The nation with the deficit will find itself transferring gold to the surplus nation. It will be recalled from Chapter 8 that the gold transfer alters the monetary base and the money supply of each nation (unless offset or sterilized by defensive open-market operations). The change in relative money supplies should operate on interest rates and aggregate demand in each country. In the deficit country real income and the rate of inflation should fall, whereas in the surplus country they should rise. These changes, in turn, should operate on the demand and supply of foreign currencies, serving to push the exchange rate back toward equilibrium. These so-called natural forces of adjustment can be augmented or hastened if the respective governments in each country undertake policies that reinforce the direction of movement of the monetary base. Thus, the central bank of the deficit

[12] It should come as no surprise that the solution to balance-of-payments problems is subject to controversy. The pre-Keynesians argued that price level changes would be the means for correction, whereas the Keynesians emphasized changes in real income.

country must sell government securities and raise reserve requirements, while the central bank in the surplus country must do the opposite.

These monetary changes can be reinforced by fiscal policy. In the deficit country taxes should be raised and expenditures reduced, whereas in the surplus country the opposite policies should be followed.

Several aspects of this adjustment process should be noted, for they are likely to bear on its acceptability. First, both monetary and fiscal policy operate with a lag that is both long and variable. Hence, the time required to restore equilibrium to the balance of payments may be protracted. Second, the pressure to restore equilibrium is asymmetrical. The deficit country is under pressure to end the outflow of gold, whereas the surplus country always has the option of offsetting the inflow. The pressure on the deficit country arises because gold, being the international means of payment, is the available asset through which it participates in international commerce. Should its gold losses be substantial, it may no longer be able to engage in foreign trade. Third, the adjustment process calls for deflation in the deficit country and expansion and inflation in the surplus country. Quite understandably, countries have often expressed opposition to the purposeful creation of inflation. Hence, the burden of adjustment may be borne mainly by the deficit country. Finally, when fixed exchange rates are used, a country must harmonize the goals of high employment and price level stability (internal stability) with balance-of-payments equilibrium (external stability).

Often, countries with prolonged balance-of-payments difficulties have chosen an alternative solution to the adjustment mechanism just outlined. It is analogous to the rationing scheme in the wheat example, because the country does not wish to officially devalue its currency. Since the demand for foreign exchange exceeds the supply at the existing rate, this alternative concentrates on a number of devices designed to reduce demand. These devices include the imposition of a tax on foreign goods and services (a tariff), the specification of quotas that limit the amount of imports, the auctioning off of the available foreign exchange to the highest bidder, and the use of official multiple exchange rates. All are designed to *suppress* the deficit rather than to deal with its underlying causes.

Flexible rates

As the name implies, flexible rates are free to adjust, so that neither excess demand nor excess supply persists. The value of payments made to foreigners is always equal to the value of receipts from foreigners. Thus, under a system of flexible exchange rates, the balance of payments can have no domestic impact via a change in the monetary base or money supply. To see this more clearly, consider the case posed above under a fixed exchange rate regime: the price level in the United States is rising at a faster rate than that of our trading partners. As in the fixed rate situation, the demand for foreign currency would rise and the supply would fall. However, with flexible exchange rates, this will result in an immediate depreciation in the exchange rate.[13] The depreciation of the currency serves to raise the domestic price of foreign goods and services, i.e., depreciation restores the relative prices of domestic and foreign goods and services. Since relative prices remain unchanged, the volume of trade and commerce remains constant, but its money value may rise. Moreover, since the exchange rate adjusts to eliminate any excess demand or supply in the exchange market, the monetary base in *each country* remains unaffected by the balance of payments. Since it does, the money supply, interest rates, employment, the rate of inflation, and so forth are effectively isolated in all countries from external developments.[14]

If flexible exchange rates work to insulate any country from developments abroad and to ensure that it can use monetary and fiscal policy to advance its own internal goals of employment and price stability, why hasn't the world used them throughout much of recorded history? Is there a fly in the ointment?

One reason for not using them is historic; another is their alleged deficiencies. Historically, the use of precious metals as money gave rise to fixed exchange rates. The longer they were used, the more familiar the world became with their functioning and the larger or more extensive became the vested interests in seeing that they were maintained. To rationalize the fixed exchange rate system, arguments were made alleging deficiencies in the flexible rate system. We now turn to an examination of these allegations. However, it would be a disservice not to evaluate fixed rates at the same time. Hence, a contrast-and-comparison approach will be used.

The relative merits of each system

In the beginning of this chapter it was stated that the desirable attributes of any international monetary system are that it contribute to the maximum freedom in the exchange of goods and services, and that it facilitate the international flow of capital. Certain desirable consequences were expected:

[13] Often the words *depreciation* and *devaluation* are used interchangeably. They should not be. The devaluation of the currency requires an act by the monetary authority, whereas the market automatically depreciates an overvalued currency. Men devalue, while markets depreciate.

[14] This may not be true for the real volume of goods exported. If tastes should change in one country so that it preferred the goods of another, the exchange rate would depreciate as its citizens sought to purchase more foreign goods and services. The depreciation of the foreign exchange rate serves to turn the *terms of trade* against the country. That is, the country must now export more goods to obtain one unit of imports than it did before the change in tastes. Hence, overall the country has fewer goods and services per capita. This is not to imply that its real income has fallen. Even though the volume of goods per capita declines, the total utility from them will have risen or else the trade would not have been undertaken.

world output of goods and services and the well-being of consumers would be maximized. We should be especially concerned with which exchange rate regime allows the closest approach to the ideal situation.

Promotion of international trade and commerce

Fixed exchange rates are alleged to be superior in the promotion of international trade and commerce because they minimize the uncertainty about the price at which purchases and sales will be made. Both sellers and buyers know the exchange rate, and hence the price involved in the transaction, even if payment is to be made in the future. This is not true with flexible exchange rates. Since they introduce greater uncertainty, traders will prefer domestic to international commerce and the volume of trade will fall.

This alleged advantage of fixed rates is deficient on several grounds. First, despite their name, the rates are in fact not fixed. Historical experience suggests that they are adjustable, i.e., subject to devaluation and revaluation. Such discrete change in rates may, however, be less uncertain than day-to-day or continuous fluctuations. Second, and more important, the existence of a forward exchange market does much to lessen the degree of uncertainty.[15] However, since forward contracts can usually be made only for a limited future period (30, 60, 90, or 180 days), uncertainty does remain for long-term capital projects (it does in the adjustable rate system as well). Moreover, history shows that fixed rates may engender trade restrictions (tariffs, quotas, etc.) as nations attempt to defend overvalued currencies. On balance, it does not appear that fixed exchange rates have any inherent superiority over flexible rates in promoting trade and commerce. Possibly, the contrary is true.

Promotion of internal economic stability

It is agreed by all that when flexible exchange rates are used, monetary and fiscal policy can be employed to deal with domestic problems without having to worry about balance-of-payments consequences. However, it is argued by some that once these tools are freed from a balance-of-payments constraint, they will be used excessively regardless of their inflationary consequences. Hence, flexible rates could impart an inflationary bias to the world economy. The argument is of dubious validity. Governments in fixed exchange rate regimes have shown little compunction in devaluing currencies when their domestic policies result in an overvalued exchange rate and balance-of-payments deficits. There is little evidence to suggest that the presence of fixed exchange rates makes governments more cautious in the

[15] Using the forward exchange market to reduce uncertainty may increase slightly the transactions costs of buying and selling.

use of fiscal and monetary policy. A depreciating exchange rate is as good a signal of domestic inflation as is a rise in the price index.

A variant of the argument that flexible exchange rates impart an inflationary bias is that they raise the average inflation rate experienced by a country. The argument usually starts with an ongoing inflation and a depreciating exchange rate. As a consequence, the domestic price of imports rises and the overall inflation rate is higher. This added inflation would not happen if the exchange rate were constant or fixed. As far as it goes, this argument is valid. Indeed, in the presence of domestic inflation, the exchange rate will depreciate in order to preserve the relative price of domestic goods and foreign substitutes. However, could a domestic inflation continue indefinitely in a fixed exchange rate regime? Of course not, for the country in question would ultimately run out of reserves and then the monetary authorities would be confronted with a choice involving a change in the exchange rate. The real issue involved in this variant is not whether flexible rates raise the average inflation rate, but what forces generate inflation.

The need for international reserves

Reserves of gold, silver, and suitable foreign currencies (those convertible into gold and silver) are required to provide short-term financing for balance-of-payments deficits whenever fixed exchange rates are used. Obviously, if the exchange rate cannot adjust, reserves must be used to finance any gap between export earnings and import expenditures. These reserves function somewhat analogously to the money balances held by individuals for transactions and precautionary purposes. The need for reserves is much reduced under a system of flexible exchange rates. Their major use in such a regime is to provide for an orderly transition from one equilibrium rate to another. That is, if the long-run prognosis is for the exchange rate to depreciate, it is desirable that the rate make the transition in an orderly fashion rather than gyrate in a way that would encourage destabilizing speculation. By using reserves, nations can ensure an orderly transition.

The advantage of smaller reserve holdings is that fewer resources are required to operate the international monetary system. When gold and silver are used for reserves, scarce resources are used to dig the metal from the ground, refine and process it, and then store it in vaults. Moreover, the metal itself is put to no useful purpose. Such a system is costly to put in place and to maintain. A flexible exchange rate regime reduces this cost.

Speculation

Speculation in the foreign exchange market arises because individuals believe that the present exchange rate is not an equilibrium one and that changes will take place in the near future. Speculators are especially likely to be active if, in a fixed exchange rate world, a country has a persistent balance-of-payments surplus or deficit, primarily the latter; and in a flexible rate world if the trade or current account is in surplus or deficit and shows little prospect for change.

Both types of regimes have been subject to massive speculative movements of short-term capital. Support of currencies by the monetary authorities is not costless by any means. Should the currency purchased in support of the effort depreciate or be devalued, the monetary authorities (and citizens of the country) will experience a loss of wealth. It will be transferred to the speculators. At this time, it is difficult to say which system is more or less immune from speculation.

Resource misallocation

Changes in the exchange rate serve to alter the relative price and hence the attractiveness of imports, exports, and import substitutes. When a currency depreciates, the result is a reduction in the price of exports to foreigners and an increase in the price of imports to domestic residents. Consequently, industries producing exports and import substitutes experience an increase in demand for their goods and services. Incentives are thus created to attract additional resources (labor and capital) into these industries and out of others. Should the depreciation prove to be transitory and unjustified by longer-run factors (e.g., income growth, price level changes, capital movements), any resources committed to the expansion of plant, equipment, capacity, and the specialized training of labor would be redundant and misallocated. Critics of flexible exchange rates imply that such misallocations would be frequent and extensive. However, this is unlikely. So long as the monetary and fiscal authorities provide a stable internal economy, few reasons exist for unjustified transitory changes in the exchange rate. Moreover, because capital and labor cannot be reallocated rapidly, prudent management would no doubt wait and see if the exchange rate changes were permanent before making significant changes to its fixed capital or labor force.

Periods of stress

Finally, it should be noted that fixed exchange rate regimes have frequently been suspended during periods of major stress in the international economy. Thus, periods of war and international financial crisis have seen fixed exchange rate regimes set aside for flexible systems or by some form of bilateral trade balancing. In Chapter 17 the historical experience will be considered in greater detail.

Summary The case for fixed exchange rates rests upon slender reeds. Almost all the alleged advantages for fixed rates really do not exist when a more comprehensive view is taken. In the end one must ask whether it is any more rational to fix the price of foreign exchange in the long run than it is to fix the price of wheat or sugar or any other good or service.

MONETARY AND FISCAL POLICY IN AN OPEN ECONOMY

In Chapter 10 a macroeconomic model was developed in order to analyze the role money plays as a determinant of economic activity. Several problems were examined in the context of this model to illustrate its functioning. However, the model developed in Chapter 10 did not include a foreign sector—it was a closed-economy model. We are now prepared to drop this restrictive assumption and develop an open-economy model. In such a model the relative roles of monetary and fiscal policy will be compared. Both a fixed and a flexible exchange rate regime will be considered.

Before monetary and fiscal policy can be analyzed, some preliminary work must be done in the nature of modifying the macroeconomic model to add a foreign trade sector. In addition, changes will have to be made to the commodity and money markets.

The commodity market in an open economy

In a closed economy GNP was measured as the sum of consumption (C), investment (I), and government spending for goods and services (G) or $C + I + G$, which represented a demand for purely domestic goods and services. In an open economy, we must add in the demand by foreigners for domestic goods (U.S. exports), X, and realize that now U.S. citizens can also purchase foreign goods. Thus, C, I, G, and X must be purged of any imports or foreign goods and services, Z. Hence, GNP in an open economy is equal to $C + I + G + X - Z$.

The money market

From Table 16:3 it can be seen that the value of transactions giving rise to balance-of-payments debits is seldom equal to those giving rise to credits. The settlement of the imbalance in a *fixed exchange rate regime* serves to change the monetary base and the domestic money supply. How this is accomplished is demonstrated in Chapter 8 but bears repeating here.

Suppose that the United States sells more goods abroad than it purchases, or receives a net inflow of capital. As a result, a greater value of checks will be deposited in the American financial system than will be drawn on it. In terms of Table 16:5 this is shown as a rise in demand deposits, DD, offset by an asset "due from foreign banks." When American depository institutions decide to repatriate their deposits in foreign banks, the Federal Reserve will be paid in gold or foreign exchange by the central bank of the

TABLE 16:5
A balance-of-payments surplus

Depository Institutions	
Due from foreign banks +	*DD* +

countries losing deposits. The rise in the gold stock is a rise in a source of the monetary base, and an increase in a source item increases high-powered money and the domestic money supply.

From the preceding discussion it can be seen that changes in the balance of payments can exert a direct effect both on the commodity and the money markets. It bears emphasis that the effect on the money market occurs only if fixed exchange rates are being used.

An open macroeconomic model

In order to convert the closed model to an open one, a diagram is needed to relate imports and exports to those variables thought to influence their behavior. Generally, it is believed that U.S. imports are positively related to domestic real income and negatively related to a rise in foreign prices relative to domestic prices. Similarly, U.S. exports are thought to respond positively to foreign real income and negatively to a rise in U.S. prices relative to foreign prices. If relative prices are held constant, imports and exports can be graphed as in Figure 16:6.

The diagram shows that imports vary positively with real income in the United States. However, since exports depend upon foreign real income, the export schedule is drawn to parallel (or be unresponsive to) U.S. real

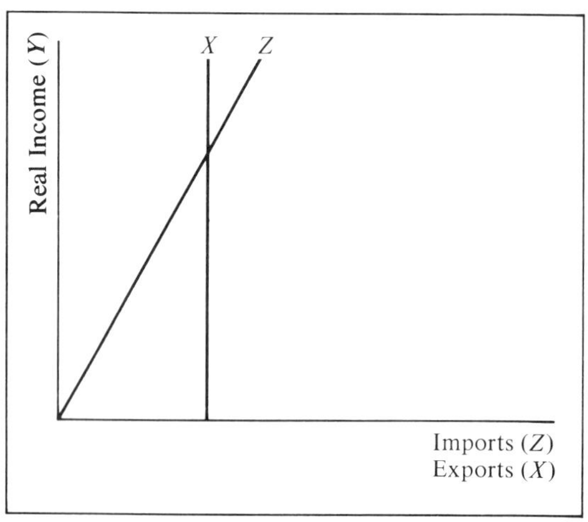

FIGURE 16:6
The foreign trade sector

income. Its position to the right of the origin of Figure 16:6 depends upon foreign real income. Should it grow, the *X* schedule will shift to the right.

If relative prices (foreign and domestic) change, the slope of the *Z* schedule and the position of the *X* schedule will change. To see this, let the price of domestic goods fall relative to the price of imports, i.e., they become cheaper. Given tastes and preferences, U.S. citizens should now consume more U.S. goods and fewer foreign goods at each level of real income. Thus, the *Z* schedule moves counterclockwise. On the other hand, since U.S. prices fall relative to the price of foreign goods, foreigners will purchase more U.S. exports and the *X* schedule will shift outward.

In Figure 16:7, Figure 16:6 is added to the macroeconomic model and an

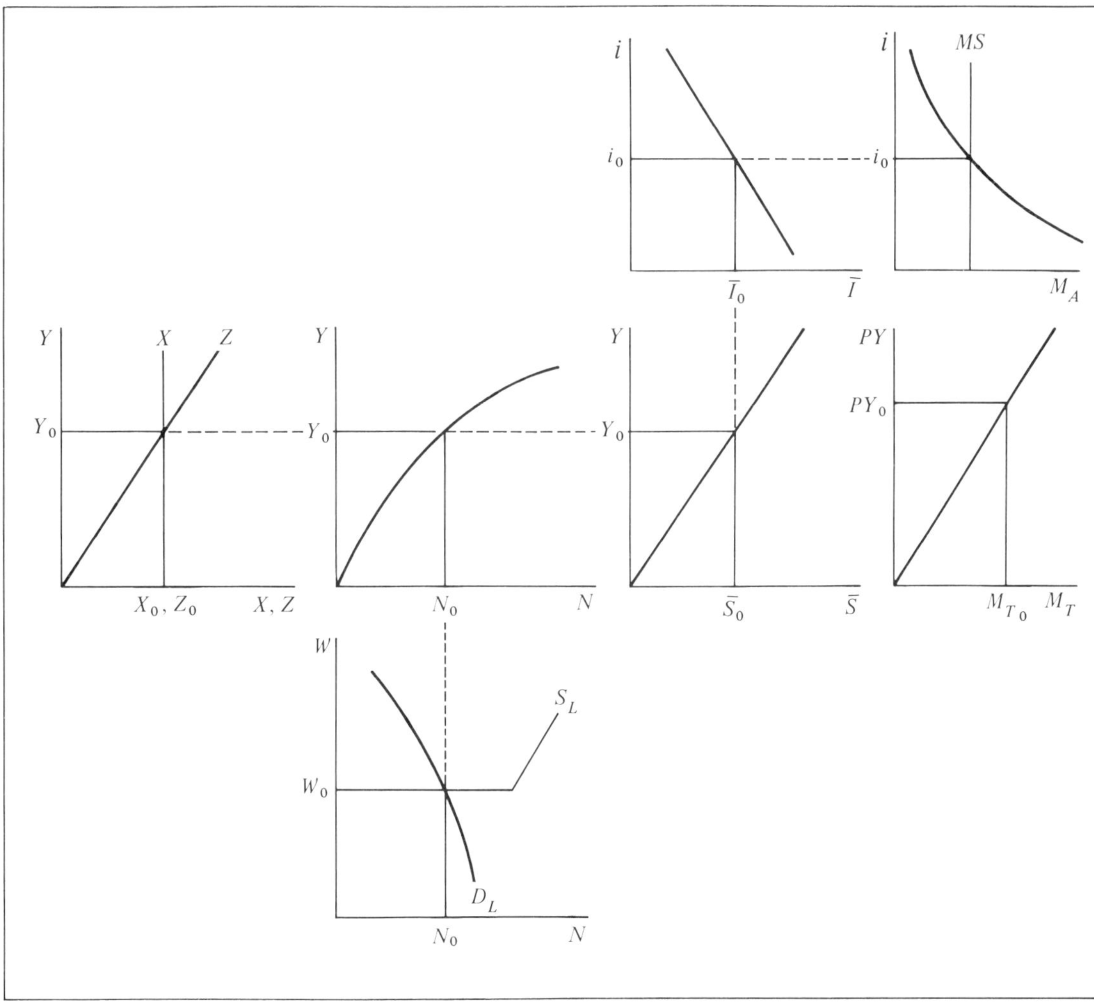

FIGURE 16:7
An open macroeconomic model

open economy is shown. In this model all markets are in equilibrium and the export of goods and services is equal to the value imported. Our interest in the open model is, among other things, to investigate the relative potency of monetary and fiscal policy in alternative exchange rate regimes.

The multiplier in an open economy

In investigating the intricacies of the model developed in Chapter 10 for a closed economy, it was noted that the commodity market contained a modified Keynesian multiplier—the modification being due to the addition of the ratio of tax revenue to income changes to the marginal propensity to save.

In an open economy the strength of the multiplier is in general reduced because imports exert an effect on domestic income and employment analogous to saving. This arises because imports represent a use of income for purposes other than the consumption of domestic goods and services. In an open economy income recipients can use their income for domestic consumption, to pay taxes, or for domestic saving, or they may use it to purchase foreign goods and services. To the extent that foreign goods and services are purchased, the domestic economy receives a smaller stimulus from any given change in demand. As a consequence, the multiplier for such an open economy should be smaller in value. To see this, in Figure 16:8, imports, Z, are added to the supply of domestic goods and services

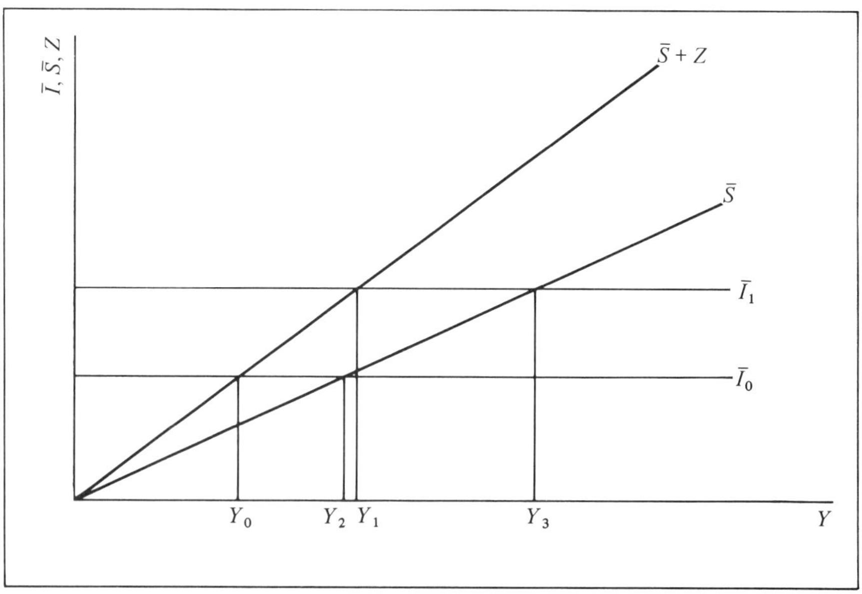

FIGURE 16:8
The effect of imports on the Keynesian multiplier

available for nonconsumption purposes, measured in Chapter 10 by $\bar{S}$. The new schedule $\bar{S} + Z$ then measures the total available supply of goods and services for nonconsumption purposes. A given increase in demand due to a rise in investment or government spending shifting, for example, $\bar{I}_0$ to $\bar{I}_1$ will result in a smaller increase in real income (from Y_0 to Y_1, as opposed to Y_2 to Y_3), the reason being that a part of the increase in demand is spent abroad, which expands the demand for foreign goods rather than for U.S. goods.

The larger the change in Z relative to a change in income (i.e., the higher the $\Delta Z/\Delta Y$ ratio, or marginal propensity to import), or the steeper the Z schedule, the smaller will be the change in income for a given change in aggregate demand.[16]

Monetary and fiscal policy in a fixed exchange rate regime[17]

Consider the case where the unemployment associated with income level Y_0 in Figure 16:9 is regarded as too high and an expansionary monetary policy is selected to reduce it. Consequently, the central bank engineers an increase in the money supply, shifting *MS* to the right. Interest rates fall, the quantity of desired investment increases, the multiplier operates, income and employment rise. However, as income rises, the value of imports in Diagram E begins to exceed the value of exports and a balance-of-payments deficit occurs. In the foreign exchange market, shown in Figure 16:10, the rise in real income shifts the demand for foreign currency to the right and at the fixed exchange rate, P_0, demand now exceeds supply, which measures the deficit. In addition, should financial funds be interest sensitive, the lower U.S. interest rates will cause a short-term capital outflow, further increasing the demand for foreign currency and exacerbating the balance-of-payments deficit.[18]

[16] This reduction in the strength of the multiplier can be shown mathematically. It will be recalled that the simple Keynesian multiplier for a closed economy is $1/1 - MPC$, which is the reciprocal of the slope of the saving schedule or $1/MPS$. However, in an open economy consumption includes imported goods. Thus, the marginal propensity to import (or MPZ) must be netted out. The multiplier then becomes $1/1 - MPC - MPZ$. Since $1 - MPC - MPZ = MPS$, the multiplier can be expressed as $1/MPS + MPZ$, which is the value of the reciprocal of the slope of the saving + import schedules in Figure 16:8. Adding the MPZ to the denominator reduces the multiplier.

[17] This analysis is fairly Keynesian in nature. Monetarists would probably disagree with its conclusions. For their approach, see Chapter 17.

[18] Since the deficit must be financed, the U.S. gold stock would start to diminish, reducing the monetary base. To prevent a decrease in the money supply, the Federal Reserve would have to engage in defensive open-market operations. Obviously, this cannot continue in the long run. Note carefully the implications of this example—it raises the fundamental question whether in a fixed exchange rate world the central bank can control the long-run supply of money. This analysis says that it cannot. Hence, the money supply is not subject to central bank control in a fixed exchange rate regime. In terms of the discussion in Chapter 14, the money supply is exogenous.

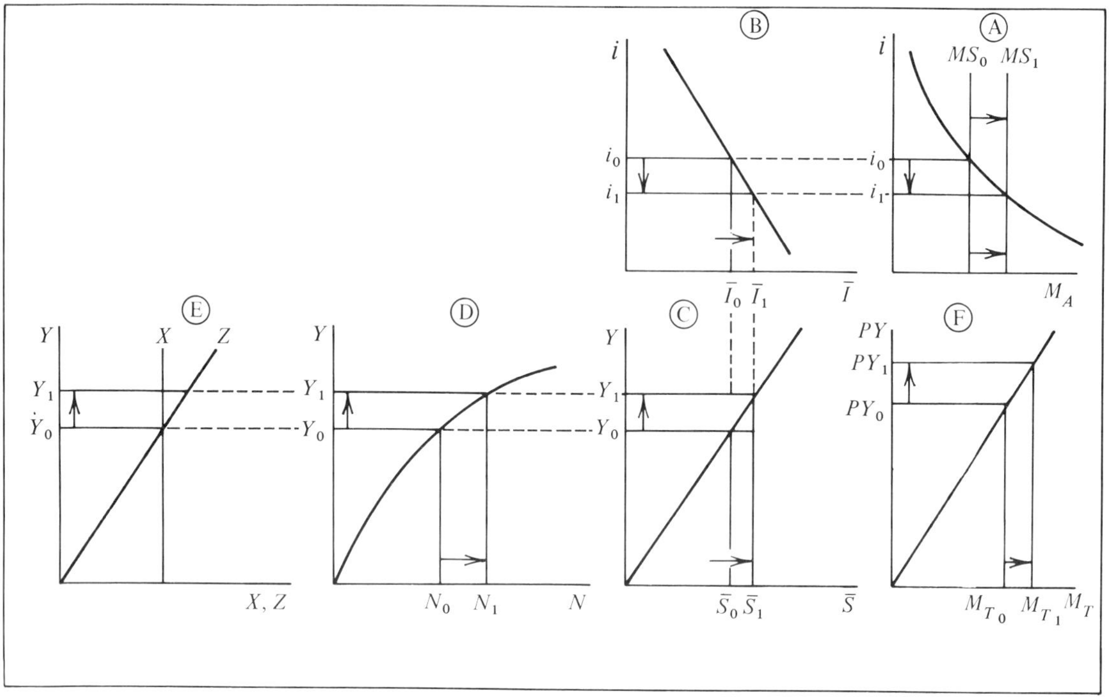

FIGURE 16:9
Monetary expansion in an open economy with fixed exchange rates

Thus, monetary policy cannot by itself be used to achieve both internal balance (a higher level of employment) and external balance (a balance-of-payments equilibrium). This shortcoming of monetary policy can be remedied if it is used in tandem with fiscal policy. To see this, return to the original situation of unemployment and balance-of-payments equilibrium shown by income level Y_0 in Figure 16:9. Government spending could be increased relative to tax revenue, shifting the $\bar{I}$ schedule to the right. The resulting rise in income would increase imports relative to exports and, simultaneously, increase the demand for foreign exchange, as in the case above where only monetary policy was used. However, in this case, the fiscally induced rise in income also serves to divert money balances into transactions use, exerting upward pressure on market interest rates. This rise in interest rates serves to attract short-term funds from abroad. In terms of Figure 16:10, the supply schedule of foreign exchange shifts to the right by the amount of the capital inflow. If the resultant rise in interest rates is insufficient to induce the amount of capital inflow necessary to maintain the exchange rate at P_0, monetary policy can now be tightened (i.e., the money supply or its growth rate reduced), which will raise the interest rate even higher—sufficiently high to attract the needed short-term capital to finance the deficit.

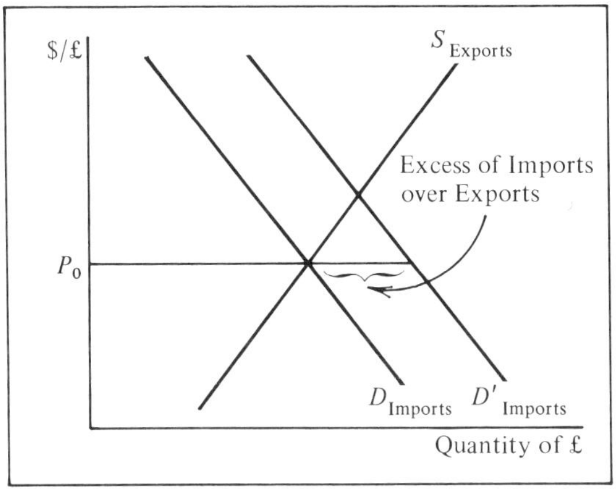

FIGURE 16:10
The foreign exchange market responding to an expansion in the supply of money

Thus, in the pursuit of two objectives—internal stability and external stability—both fiscal and monetary policy are needed. In the case under analysis, an expansionary fiscal policy is combined with a tight monetary policy. It should, of course, be noted, that if capital funds are insensitive to interest rate differentials so that monetary policy is ineffective, then fiscal policy cannot be used by itself—for two objectives, two policies must be used in a fixed exchange rate regime.

Monetary and fiscal policy in a variable exchange rate regime

Suppose that in the problem just presented the exchange rate regime were flexible. Would monetary policy by itself be ineffective? To answer the question, we must analyze the behavior of the exchange rate as the expansion in income causes imports to exceed exports. As in that original case, the expansion of income will shift the demand schedule for foreign exchange in Figure 16:11 from D to D'. However, because the rate is not fixed at P_0, it rises to P_1, or the dollar depreciates. As it depreciates, U.S. exports become less expensive abroad and imports become more expensive in the United States. The change in relative prices alters the desirability of exports and imports. If, because of lower interest rates, short-term capital flows out of the United States, the demand for foreign exchange will rise, causing a further depreciation of the exchange rate to P_2. As a result, the value of exports will exceed the value of imports, but foreign exchange receipts will still equal foreign exchange expenditures. This is shown in Figure 16:11. The U.S. monetary base remains constant and the money supply does not contract. Thus, using a flexible exchange rate regime

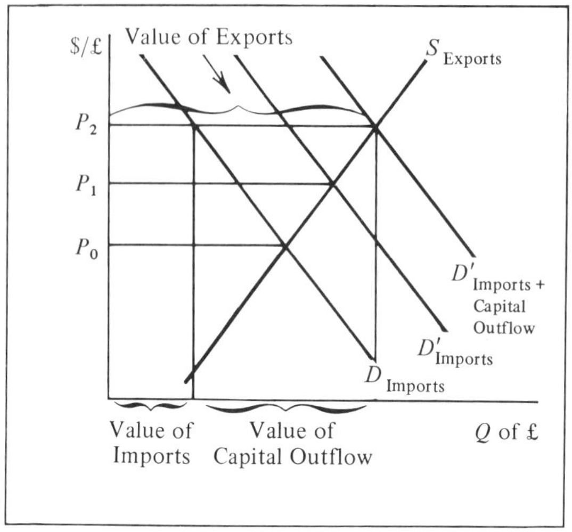

FIGURE 16:11
The response of the foreign exchange rate to monetary expansion

enhances the power of monetary policy. This occurs because in a flexible system external balance is always ensured. Therefore, only one policy tool is needed to accomplish one objective—internal balance.

This analysis also holds for fiscal policy. That is, it can be used for internal purposes without the necessity of considering its effect on the balance of payments. To see this, let us retrace the example used above. The rise in government expenditures would in Figure 16:9 be shown by a shift of the $\bar{I}$ schedule to the right. This would expand income and lead to a rise in market interest rates as money balances were increasingly used for transactions purposes. The expansion of income would also cause imports to exceed exports—a trade deficit would emerge. If the rise in interest rates fails to attract sufficient foreign capital to the United States so that a net deficit in the balance of payments still prevails, the exchange rate will deprepreciate sufficiently to ensure that foreign exchange receipts are equal to foreign exchange payments. That is, the depreciation will reduce the desire to import while it raises exports. This is shown in Figure 16:12. As import prices rise, U.S. citizens demand fewer of them and the Z schedule moves counterclockwise to Z'. Since U.S. exports are now cheaper, foreigners purchase more of them and the X schedule moves to the right to X'. The new equilibrium or intersection point is at a higher income level, a level induced by the monetary expansion.

In a flexible exchange rate regime, since one need not worry about the balance of payments or external balance, both monetary and fiscal policy can be used exclusively for domestic problems. Their relative effectiveness depends, of course, on the factors identified in a previous chapter, e.g., the

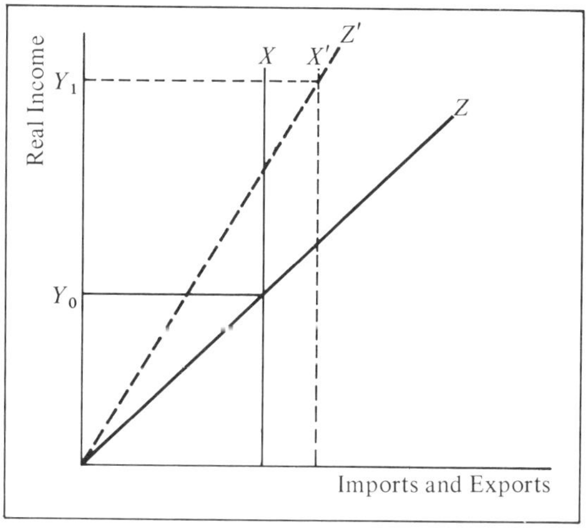

FIGURE 16:12
The response of the foreign trade sector to a depreciation of the dollar

interest elasticity of money demand and the interest sensitivity of expenditures (especially private investment).[19]

In an effort to understand more fully the functioning of an open economy, the student may wish to analyze such changes as: (1) a shift in foreign taste toward U.S. goods and the reverse; (2) a shift in U.S. taste toward foreign goods and the reverse; (3) an increase in domestic saving; (4) an autonomous decline in foreign real income; and (5) an increase in the demand for money.

CONCLUSION

No modern economy is self-sufficient. All are involved in international trade and commerce, which means external events influence such domestic variables as real income, employment, the price level, the money supply, and the standard of living. The degree of influence and its method of manifestation depend on whether a fixed or flexible exchange rate regime is used. The exchange rate regime also was seen to exercise a constraint on the effectiveness of monetary and fiscal policy, used individually or together.

To see that these conclusions were correct required the development of an open-economy macroeconomic model, an explanation of the functioning of foreign exchange markets, and an understanding of the balance of payments.

[19] See Appendix 16A for a discussion of monetary and fiscal policy in an open economy *IS-LM* model.

STUDY QUESTIONS

1. It has been said that the U.S. balance-of-trade deficit is due largely to the import of products produced by cheap foreign labor. To ensure high employment and high real wages in the United States, these products should be kept out. Evaluate this argument.
2. Why should the United States have been concerned about the cause of its balance-of-payments problem during the fixed exchange rate era?
3. How would you evaluate the statement that flexible exchange rates are inherently inflationary since they remove a constraint (balance-of-payments equilibrium) on the use of monetary and fiscal policy?
4. In a fixed exchange rate world, can the central bank of a small country control its own money supply?
5. Explain intuitively why the income multiplier should be smaller for an open economy than for a closed economy.
6. In a fixed exchange rate regime, suppose fiscal policy is used to expand income and employment. Suppose also that international capital flows are highly insensitive to relative interest rates. Will the expansive fiscal policy be successful?
7. Suppose that a balance-of-payments deficit occurs in a fixed exchange rate regime with large-scale unemployment. How should these two problems be solved, i.e., how can the balance of payments be pushed toward equilibrium at the same time that the unemployment rate is reduced?
8. Suppose a balance-of-payments surplus occurs in a fixed exchange rate regime under conditions of high employment—so high that inflation is present. How would you solve the combined problems?
9. Suppose fixed exchange rates exist and that a country has large-scale unemployment. Explain how the unemployment can be "exported" through devaluation. What might prevent a country from attempting such a policy?

SELECTED REFERENCES AND READINGS

Bator, Francis M. "The Simple Analytics of Welfare Maximization." *American Economic Review,* Vol. 47, No. 1 (Mar. 1957).

Gray, H. Peter. *International Trade, Investment, and Payments.* Boston: Houghton Mifflin Co., 1979.

_____. *The Economics of Business Investment Abroad.* London: Macmillan; New York: Crane Russak, 1972.

Gruber, William, Mehta, Dileep, and Vernon, Raymond. "The R & D Factor in International Trade and International Investment of United States Industries." *Journal of Political Economy,* Vol. 75, No 1 (Jan.–Feb. 1967).

Hufbauer, Gary C. and Adler, F. Michael. *Overseas Manufacturing Investment and the Balance of Payments*. Washington, D.C.: U.S. Treasury Department, 1968.

Kindleberger, Charles P. *American Business Abroad*. New Haven, Conn.: Yale University Press, 1969.

Levin, Jay H. "*IS, LM,* and External Equilibrium: Some Extensions." *Economia Internazionale,* Vol. 27, No. 2 (Mar. 1974).

Mundell, Robert A. "The Appropriate Use of Monetary and Fiscal Policy for Internal and External Stability." *International Monetary Fund Staff Papers* (Mar. 1962).

Reddaway, W. B., Perkins, J. O. N., Potter, S. J., and Taylor, C. T. *Effects of U.K. Direct Investment Overseas: An Interim Report and Final Report*. Cambridge: Cambridge University Press, 1967 and 1968.

Vernon, Raymond. "International Investment and International Trade in the Product Cycle." *Quarterly Journal of Economics,* Vol. 80, No. 2 (May 1966).

Wrightsman, Dwayne. "*IS, LM,* and External Equilibrium: A Graphical Analysis." *American Economic Review,* Vol. 60, No. 1 (Mar. 1970).

16

APPENDIX A– THE *IS-LM* MODEL IN AN OPEN ECONOMY

16

The *IS-LM* model developed in an earlier chapter to explain the functioning of a closed economy can be extended to accommodate an open economy. All that is required is the construction of a schedule depicting equilibrium positions in the balance of payments for various combinations of the interest rate and real income. This schedule will be designated the *EE* (external equilibrium) schedule.

Before the *EE* schedule is developed, the *IS* schedule will have to be modified for an open economy. Previously, the *IS* schedule depicted all combinations of the interest rate and real income levels at which investment was equal to saving. In an open economy an additional nonconsumption demand comes from exports, while an additional source of supply comes from imports. Hence, in an open economy the *IS* schedule traces all combinations of the interest rate and real income levels at which $I + X = S + Z$ (investment + exports = savings + imports). It follows that changes in imports and exports can lead to shifts in the *IS* schedule. A rise in exports or a fall in imports will shift *IS* to the right, whereas the reverse will shift it to the left. To derive the *EE* schedule, relative prices of foreign and domestic goods will be assumed to be constant.

Moving counterclockwise, Diagram A in Figure 16A:1 depicts net foreign investment, which is assumed to be sensitive to the rate of interest. That is, if domestic interest rates are low relative to foreign rates, Americans will tend to invest abroad, which will make net foreign investment positive. On the other hand, should the relative interest rate be high, foreigners will be more likely to invest in the United States, and U.S. net foreign investment will be negative.

Diagram C shows net exports of goods and services. Since exports are assumed to depend on foreign income, while imports depend on U.S.

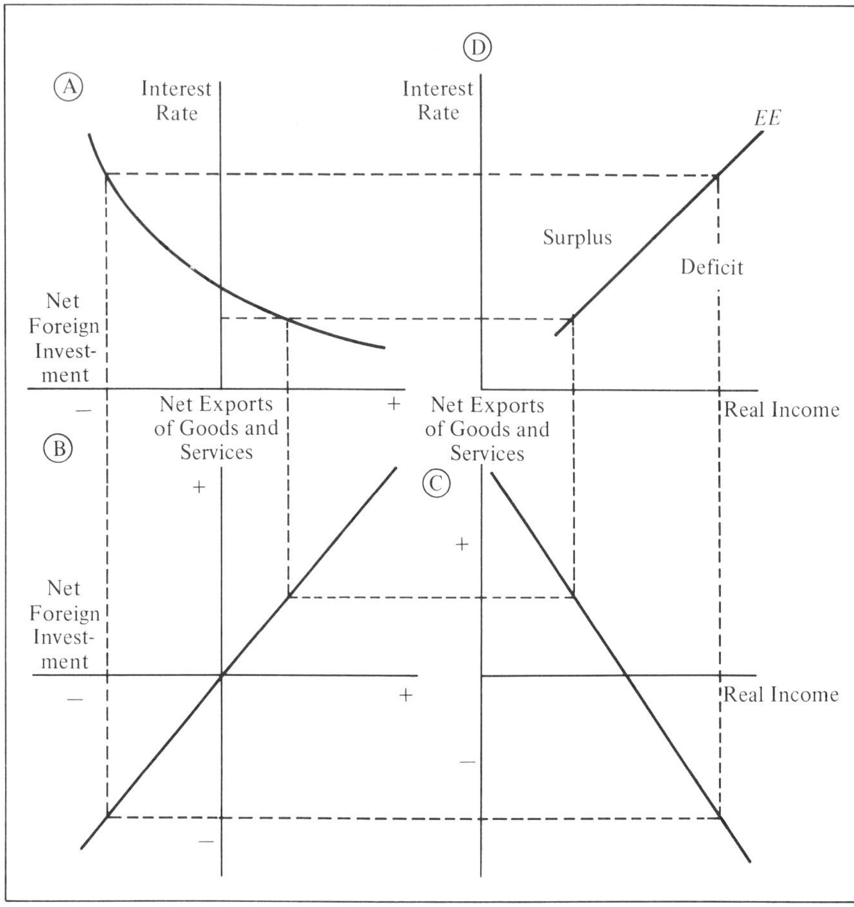

FIGURE 16A:1
The derivation of the external equilibrium schedule

income, as the latter rises, net exports will decline, ultimately becoming zero and then negative (i.e., exports will be less than imports). Diagram B shows the conditions for balance of payments equilibrium. A negative net foreign investment (i.e., foreigners investing [net] in the United States) will require a negative balance in goods and services to balance out total foreign receipts and payments. Similarly, a positive net foreign investment (i.e., U.S. funds flowing out [net] to the rest of the world) will require a positive balance on goods and services to make total foreign receipts and payments balance. Thus, the line is at 45 degrees.

Starting from Diagram A, straight lines can be drawn to trace out the *EE* schedule, showing all combinations of real income and interest rates at which the balance of payments is in equilibrium. As drawn, the *EE* schedule has an upward slope that depends on: (1) the interest sensitivity of net foreign investment, and (2) the income sensitivity of imports. Its shiftability depends upon the sensitivity of imports and exports to changes in relative prices. Since its shiftability has yet to be demonstrated, suppose that domestic prices fall relative to foreign prices, and the fall is produced by a change in absolute prices or by a depreciation of the exchange rate. In either case, exports should be stimulated and imports retarded. The net effect will be to shift the schedule in Diagram C to the right, i.e., at each income level, net exports of goods and services should be greater. As a result, the *EE* schedule will shift to the right; the converse will occur for a rise in export prices relative to import prices. Finally, the area to the left of the *EE* schedule measures balance-of-payments surpluses, whereas the area to the right measures deficits.

In Figure 16A:2 the *EE* schedule is combined with the *IS* and *LM* schedules to depict an open economy in equilibrium. As drawn, the *EE* schedule is assumed to be steeper than the *LM* schedule. This need not be the case, and depends on whether capital funds are more sensitive to the interest rate than in the demand for money. The line Y_{FE} denotes full-employment income. As shown, the economy is in an unemployment equilibrium.

Given a fixed exchange rate regime, can monetary policy itself be used to restore full employment? A sufficient expansion of the monetary base will shift the *LM* schedule to *LM'*. While this shift will result in both commodity and money-market equilibrium at point *A*, the balance of payments will be in deficit. The interest rate is too low and the resultant capital outflow is greater than any surplus on current account. The deficit

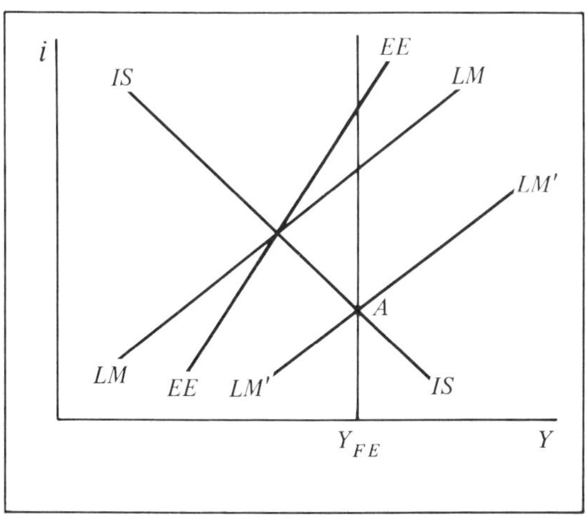

FIGURE 16A:2
An expansion in the monetary base

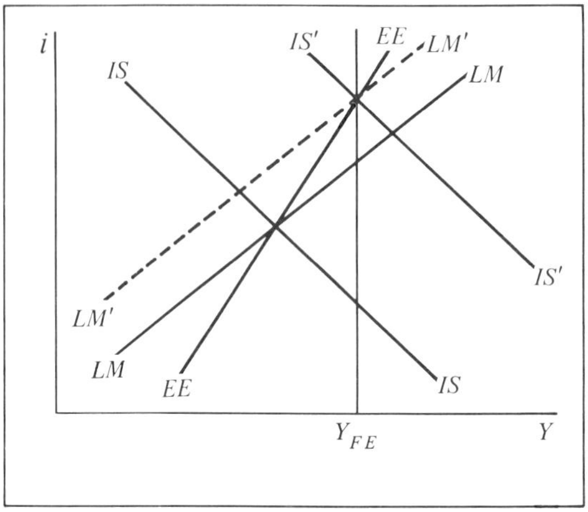

FIGURE 16A:3
Expansionary fiscal and contractionary monetary policies

will serve to contract the monetary base and shift the *LM* schedule back to the left. Obviously, position *A* is untenable. The country in question cannot rely on monetary policy alone. However, both monetary and fiscal policy can be used to accomplish the task. To see this, Figure 16A:3 is drawn showing the effect of an expansionary fiscal policy, which shifts the *IS* schedule to the right to *IS'*. To offset the resultant balance-of-payments deficit, monetary policy is tightened to raise the interest rate sufficiently to draw in enough foreign funds to offset the deficit on current account (the *LM* schedule is shifted to the left to *LM'*).[1]

This example demonstrates the point made in the text that when one wishes to achieve both internal stability (high employment) and external stability (balance-of-payments equilibrium), one needs two policies—monetary and fiscal. It must be recalled that this necessity holds when fixed exchange rates are assumed to prevail.

Consider now the same problem in a flexible exchange rate regime. Again, an unemployment equilibrium is assumed to prevail, and is shown as point *A* in Figure 16A:4. Again, the money supply growth rate is accelerated, shifting the *LM* schedule to the right to *LM'*. The resulting deficit in the balance of payments causes the dollar to depreciate, which serves to change relative prices—exports are now cheaper, while imports are more expensive. The resultant expansion of the former and contraction of the latter will accomplish two things: (1) the *IS* schedule will shift to the

[1] Should the *EE* schedule be less steep than the *LM* schedule, monetary policy would have to be expansionary and the *LM* schedule would be shifted to the right to lower interest rates. Left by itself, the balance-of-payments surplus, by expanding the monetary base, would ultimately shift the *LM* schedule to the right.

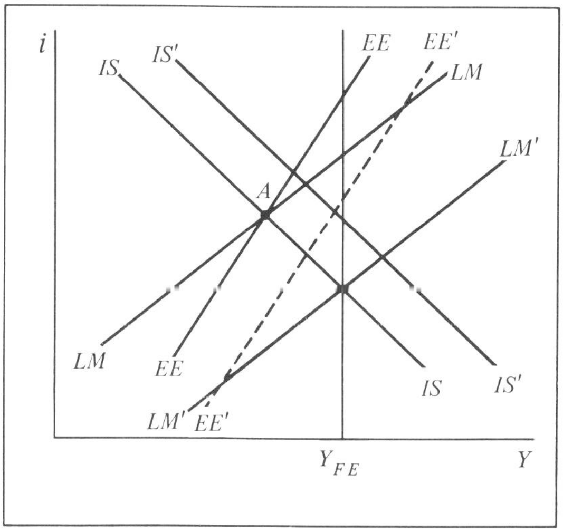

FIGURE 16A:4
Expansionary monetary policy in a flexible exchange rate regime

right in the direction of IS'; (2) since the balance of trade will improve at each income level, the EE schedule should shift downward or to the right in the direction of EE'. Ultimately, given the appropriate change in the money supply, joint internal and external equilibrium should prevail at Y_{FE}.

Suppose that fiscal policy alone had been used to accomplish the full-employment objective. A suitable cut in taxes or rise in government expenditures should shift the IS schedule to the right, as in Figure 16A:5,

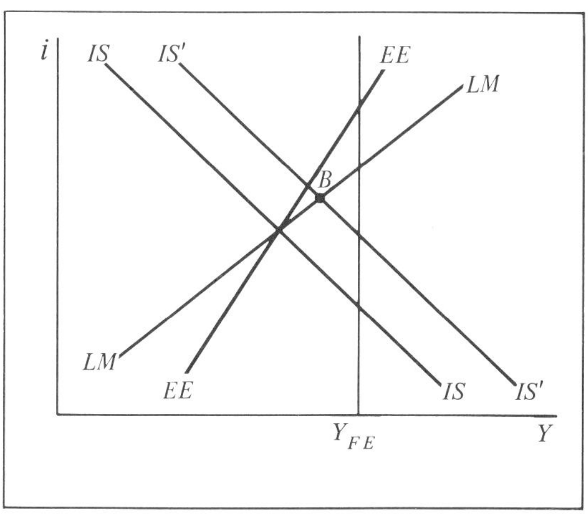

FIGURE 16A:5
Expansionary fiscal policy in a flexible exchange rate regime

to IS'. At point B, the balance of payments is in deficit. As a result, the exchange rate will depreciate, making exports cheaper and imports more expensive. Consequently, the net trade balance at each level of income should rise, shifting the IS schedule further to the right and the EE schedule downward or to the right also. Sufficient changes in the fiscal variables will ensure that IS, LM, and EE intersect at Y_{FE}.

This example demonstrates that the use of flexible exchange rates essentially prevents the balance of payments from exercising a constraint on fiscal policy—and, as shown above, on monetary policy as well. These policies can then be used exclusively for domestic purposes.

To further appreciate the operation of an open economy, consider the situation in which both fixed and floating rates are used and the IS, LM, and EE schedules intersect to the right of Y_{FE}—this is the situation of full employment and inflation. Then, consider the case in which the IS and LM schedules intersect to the right of Y_{FE}, but lie in the surplus area of the balance of payments. Finally, construct the same case, but assume they lie in the deficit area.

17 THE EVOLUTION OF THE INTERNATIONAL MONETARY SYSTEM

THE GOLD STANDARD

Throughout most of the nineteenth century international trade and commerce were carried on by the leading trading nations within a regime of fixed exchange rates that resulted from the use of an international gold standard. The center of this system was the great financial and commercial city of London, whose banks provided both the credit that made world trade and finance possible and the oversight that allowed the system to function. However, from time to time the system was disrupted by periods of extreme economic stress often associated with wars. The United States, for example, suspended the gold convertibility of the dollar at the onset of the Civil War in 1861. For the next eighteen years the dollar was allowed to float in the foreign exchange markets and its exchange value was determined by the forces of supply and demand. In 1879 the United States returned to the gold standard at the exchange parity that had prevailed in 1861.

Although the international monetary system of the nineteenth century is often regarded with nostalgia by those who yearn for a return to a simpler, more romantic past, its so-called golden age was comparatively brief. While precise dating is difficult, it appears to have functioned very well in the last two decades of the nineteenth century and the first thirteen years of the twentieth century, until the advent of World War I in August 1914. This 34-year period was filled with events that could have led to balance-of-payments difficulties for many nations: world trade grew tremendously, there were large international flows of capital, an enormous number of people left Europe for the New World, and inflation rates were not uniform in the various trading nations. Despite the potential for serious problems, however, few developed. The achievement of high levels of economic growth and employment (or internal stability) in the major trading nations coincided with reasonable overall balance in their international accounts (or external stability).

Whether this harmonious state would have continued had it not been for World War I is impossible to know. The major belligerent powers suspended the gold convertibility of their currencies in August 1914 and placed rigid controls on exports, imports, and the movement of capital. The great international city of London was closed and its efforts were concentrated on financing Allied war needs. Since the United States was officially a neutral nation until April 1917, the nations of the world increasingly turned to New York City to finance trade, capital requirements, and the necessities of war. Thus New York City grew to rival London as a financial center. At the end of the war the United States for the first time in its history was an international creditor nation. That is, the value of U.S. loans and capital invested abroad exceeded similar foreign claims on the United States.

The rise of New York City as a major rival to London and the international creditor status of the United States served to complicate the new world monetary system, which was reconstructed during the 1920s.

THE GOLD EXCHANGE STANDARD

The reconstruction of the international monetary system proceeded slowly following the Armistice of November 1918 and the peace treaties worked out in 1919. The new system was fully implemented when Britain returned to the gold standard in 1925. The new system was somewhat different from the old in that an expedient was found to economize on gold. A gold exchange standard was contrived whereby nations began to count as part of their gold reserves the currencies of other nations (e.g., drafts, bills of exchange, Treasury bills) that were convertible into gold. For example, France or Austria would hold U.S. Treasury bills or commercial bills of exchange as a part of their international reserves, for these were convertible into gold. The same was true for the British pound. Eventually, both the United States and Britain had foreign liabilities in excess of their gold reserves. Such a situation could continue only so long as all did not want gold at the same time. If an international run developed, the system could break down or have severe difficulties. Thus, the gold exchange standard was a fragile one, whose smooth functioning depended especially on confidence in the stability of the United States and Britain. It might have been strengthened by the emergence of some lender of last resort, or by extensive cooperation among the central banks of the world. Such cooperation did develop to a limited degree.[1]

As a legacy of the war, two conditions added instability to the new world order. The first concerned the restoration of the gold convertibility of currencies. The proper parity or exchange rate became an issue, since all

[1] For a discussion of this cooperation among central bankers, see Lester V. Chandler, *Benjamin Strong, Central Banker* (Washington, D.C.: The Brookings Institution, 1958); and Stephen V. O. Clarke, *Central Bank Cooperation, 1924–31* (New York: The Federal Reserve Bank of New York, 1967).

the nations of the world had not experienced the same rate of inflation. If they were all to return to the gold standard at the prewar parity, some currencies would be overvalued while others would be undervalued. Many countries did readjust their parities. Great Britain did not. Despite full knowledge of the economic consequences of an overvalued currency, the British restored the prewar exchange rate to the pound—$4.86. Given relative price levels, Britain's currency was overvalued. Recall from Chapter 16 that if an economy's currency is overvalued, exports will be less than imports. Under a gold standard, this results in a loss of gold, which cannot continue indefinitely. Eventually, the economy must lower its prices relative to the prices of other countries in order to stimulate exports and retard imports. Deflationary policies, though, have the unfortunate side effect of raising unemployment, at least temporarily. In order to maintain its overvalued exchange rate, Britain was forced to follow deflationary policies for the better part of the 1920s and early 1930s. Britain's precarious position was exacerbated by the growth of New York as a financial center. For two great financial centers to function smoothly, it is necessary that their interest rate structures be similar. Should New York, for example, have higher short-term rates than London, funds would flow out from Britain, resulting in an excess supply of pounds and putting additional downward pressure on an overvalued exchange rate. The time might come when the British government would feel that the further deflation and unemployment required to save the pound were not politically possible. In this case, the international monetary system would break down.

Second, during the postwar period many nations were encumbered with war-related debts and indemnities. The Allied nations owed the United States for the funds they had borrowed to finance the war, and Germany (and her allies) owned an indemnity to the Allies as the price of her acknowledged guilt in causing the war. The payment of all these debts according to schedule came to depend on rather fragile conditions. Since the Allies would not accept payment in kind, the German government borrowed funds in New York to pay the indemnity. The recipient Allied nations then used these funds to repay their war debts. All went well so long as the chain of lending remained intact. It was to come undone in the late 1920s.

Thus, after World War I the new international monetary system, featuring the gold exchange standard, was one with two financial centers whose interest rate policies had to be coordinated, in which the United States was a creditor nation, in which some currencies were overvalued (especially that of a major trading nation, Great Britain), and in which a cycle of lending was necessary to facilitate the scheduled payment of debts and indemnities.

The fragility of the system was dramatically exposed in the summer of 1931, some 18 months after the onset of the world Depression. In July of that year one of the Rothschild banks in Vienna, the Kredit Anstalt, experienced difficulties in paying its depositors. Individuals and banks of other countries then withdrew funds from Austria in such a volume that she suspended convertibility of her currency. An international run then began on the German mark and, finally, on the British pound. In September 1931 Britain suspended gold convertibility, and the pound promptly lost about one-third of its value in relation to the dollar. Other nations followed suit, and the international monetary system collapsed.

The 1930s

The system did not recover until after the Second World War. International trade was increasingly forced into bilateral lines and away from free exchange, the world split into currency blocs, restrictions were placed on capital flows, tariffs and quotas were imposed, discriminatory preferences were granted to some countries and not to others, and so on. Some of these developments were inevitable, given the rise of fascism and Nazism on the continent of Europe. Nevertheless, the United States did much to bring about the disintegration of the world order. In 1931 the Congress passed the highest tariff in U.S. history in an effort, in part, to maintain the United States both as a creditor nation and one that had a trade surplus.[2] Naturally, U.S. policy invited foreign retaliation. Moreover, in the first year of the New Deal the government began a fruitless and ill-advised experiment involving increases in the dollar price of gold that were thought capable of raising domestic prices (in an effort to aid debtors).[3] The only effect of this experiment was to devalue the dollar and encourage foreigners to engage in offsetting devaluations of their own. In the meantime valuable time was lost in which an early recovery might have been set in motion.

One can only speculate on the possible evolution of the international monetary system had the decade of the 1930s not drawn to a close with the beginning of the most destructive war ever known. Some progress was made during the decade toward liberalizing world trade and payments,

[2] If a country is a net creditor, it must have an excess of imports over exports to provide the wherewithal to repatriate dividends and interest from its foreign investment, unless it is prepared to lend. Such a policy cannot be followed in the long run, however, as ultimately the debt service will require an import surplus.

[3] Perhaps the totality of the collapse during the Great Depression and the desire for a quick solution made all sorts of ill-conceived ideas appear respectable. One such idea was advanced by Professor George Warren, an agricultural economist from Cornell University, and his long-time colleague, the noted statistician Frank Pearson. With a series of statistical computations, they tried to show that for some 100 years there had been a close relationship between the price level, production, and an increase in the value of the world's gold stock. Their "quick-fix" solution proposed that all that had to be done was to raise the domestic price of gold and the United States would be lifted out of the Depression. This argument was taken up by President Roosevelt and the purchase price of gold was raised in successive stages from $20.67 to $35.00 per ounce. When the hoped-for miracle did not occur, Warren and Pearson went back to Cornell. This was not the first time that a positive correlation was mistaken for cause and effect, and doubtless will not be the last.

especially after Congress passed the Reciprocal Trade Act of 1934. Moreover, in 1936 France was allowed to devalue the franc without the fear of retaliation by the United States and Britain. These three countries then stabilized the exchange value of their currencies and commenced a period of informal cooperation on international monetary matters.

The world financial community seems to have learned two main lessons from the tragic series of events in the 1930s, which were then used to reconstruct the international monetary system in the post–World War II period. The first lesson was that a system of free and unencumbered trade, commerce, and finance is preferable to its alternatives. To achieve this, the nations of the world community were called upon to give up competitive devaluations, quotas, tariffs, exchange controls, discriminations of all kinds, and other dubious attempts to achieve an advantage. Second, something analogous to a central bank had to be created to (1) provide nations facing temporary balance-of-payments problems with additional sources of financing so that they would not have to resort to the devices listed above, and (2) provide an adequate growth of international reserves to finance the long-run growth of trade and commerce. It should be noted that these lessons took for granted the desirability of fixed exchange rates.

BRETTON WOODS—1944

To formulate a new monetary system for the postwar world, delegates from the Allied Nations met at Bretton Woods, New Hampshire, in 1944. Both the United States and Great Britain brought plans for a new system. While they had much in common, the delegates adopted the American Plan (drawn up by Assistant Secretary of the Treasury Harry D. White) over the British proposal (put forth by Lord Keynes).

Under the White Plan, the Allied Nations founded the International Monetary Fund (IMF), which was not a central bank, although it subsequently came to exercise some of the powers of such an institution. By the terms of the IMF Agreement, each nation pledged itself to fixed exchange rates and promised to alter the rate only as a last recourse to deal with a "fundamental disequilibrium" in its balance of payments and only after prior consultation with the Fund (if the change in parity was to be greater than 10%). To give the exchange rate some flexibility, it would be allowed to fluctuate ±1% of its parity. Thus, while the new system was not the gold standard reestablished, it bore several superficial resemblences: fixed exchange rates and a band resembling the old gold import and export points. Since resort to changes in parity or pegged rates has been frequent, the new system is often called the adjustable peg system.

To make it possible for countries to deal with temporary or short-run balance-of-payments problems, the Fund acquired lending reserves consisting of gold and national currencies. These assets were acquired by imposing upon members a "quota," which each paid partly in gold and partly in its own national currency. Subject to certain restrictions, a nation could draw on these resources to finance short-term balance-of-payment difficulties. These drawings subsequently had to be repaid, with interest, to the Fund. As the Fund's lending practices evolved, it came to impose certain reforms on the borrowing countries as a condition to using Fund resources, e.g., reform of the tax system, balanced budgets, reductions in monetary growth.

As originally constituted, the Fund's Articles of Agreement did not provide for any systematic means for increasing the supply of reserves to finance the long-run growth in trade and commerce. Supposedly, this was to be accomplished by periodic increases in quotas and the normal growth in the world's gold supply. However, the long-run growth in international reserves that did take place was increasingly regarded as inadequate. In 1969 the Fund started to act like a world central bank when it began to create international reserves in the form of "paper gold" or Special Drawing Rights (SDR's). Before these later developments are discussed in detail, the early history of the IMF must be recounted, for it is related to the rebuilding of the world economy and the special position of the United States. It starts in 1945, with a prostrate Europe and a very powerful American dollar. It ends with the decade of the 1970s, in which Europe emerged as a powerful economic entity, the dollar was dethroned, and flexible exchange rates became the centerpiece of the new system. This evolution has been called the march down the road from dollar shortage to dollar glut.

1945–1958

In the immediate postwar period the major trading nations of the world, with the exception of the United States, maintained their tight wartime exchange controls and regulations on imports, exports, and capital movements. In this early period only the United States had a currency convertible into gold. Other nations did not, and required restrictions to conserve what resources of gold and convertible currencies they possessed, in order to rebuild their devastated economies.

The imposition of controls was accompanied by trade forced into bilateral lines, somewhat similar to the situation of the 1930s. A common practice was a trade treaty between two nations under which "X" dollars of trade could take place, subject to a certain percentage overrun of either imports or exports. That is, the treaty would permit trade to exceed the agreed upon amount by up to a certain percent. The latter was then settled in gold or a convertible currency—the dollar. This early role of the dollar gave the United States a strategic place in the international monetary system. The dollar became a so-called key currency, a special status shared to a far lesser degree by the British pound. This special status had both benefits and costs to the United States, as well as to the international monetary system.

For the United States, the principal benefits, as shown by history, was that for much of the postwar period we did not have to worry about or pay close attention to the state of our balance of payments, even though government officials did express concern at the persistence of deficits. Thus, the United States could engage in the rebuilding of the world economy and conduct a very extensive, expensive, and expansive foreign policy, called by some the era of the Pax Americana. This foreign policy was increasingly financed by the willingness of foreigners to hold dollars. This, of course, imparted instability to the system as dollar liabilities grew larger than U.S. gold reserves.

The main burden or cost to the United States of having a "key" currency was that devaluation was "out of the question" or "politically unacceptable" as a means of solving a balance-of-payments problem. The United States could not seek relief from balance-of-payments deficits as other nations had.

Perhaps the major benefit of the dollar system occurred early in this period. The U.S. deficit provided the principal means by which international reserves and liquidity grew. This growth was regarded as desirable, for by providing foreigners with needed reserves, it hastened the day when trade restrictions could be abolished and the world returned to multilateral payments. However, as the U.S. deficit proved to be intractable, foreign central bankers began to question whether the increased supply of dollars bore any resemblance to the growth in the world demand for reserves. This doubt subjected the world monetary system to periodic crises of confidence. In the early 1970s the virtual avalanche of dollars inundating foreign central banks precipitated an international run and the United States was forced to suspend the dollar's gold convertibility. This does, however, get us a little ahead of the story. We shall return to it later.

As the decade following the end of World War II drew to a close, trade and commerce began to take on an increasing multilateral character. This was made possible by the growth in international reserves due in large part to the U.S. deficit; the Marshall Plan, which helped to rebuild Europe; a substantial devaluation of the major European currencies in 1949, which served to undervalue each relative to the dollar; the creation of the European Payments Union, which made multilateral balance-of-payments settlements possible,[4] and the general revival of economic growth and progress in general.

In December 1958 the major trading nations of Europe announced that henceforth their currencies would be convertible both in the sense that one could sell or convert Dutch guilders for French francs and that the

[4] The formation of a payments union makes it possible for a given volume of trade to be conducted on a smaller reserve base. The payments union functions as a clearing house, in that each country's debt to another becomes a debt to the payments union, which then offsets the debts, requiring reserves to be used only to settle net debts. In this way trade can be conducted with a smaller volume of international reserves.

respective governments would officially convert their currencies into the key currency, the dollar, at a fixed rate ±1%. (The dollar, in turn, was officially convertible into gold.) This return to convertibility was accomplished by dismantling a host of foreign trade restrictions.

1959–1968

In this decade the international monetary system conceived at Bretton Woods came into full bloom. However, unanticipated developments revealed weaknesses in the original grand design and the IMF found it increasingly difficult to respond to them. Of prime importance was the growth of massive amounts of destabilizing speculative capital. Its movement from country to country in anticipation of parity changes put a severe strain on the system. Of lesser importance was the development of the Eurodollar and London gold markets.

Many factors were undoubtedly responsible for the growth of speculation. In particular, countries appeared to be more concerned with high levels of employment than with balance-of-payments equilibrium. When attainment of the former overvalued the exchange rate, it was often devalued. According to the IMF's Articles of Agreement, the par value or parity of a currency was to be changed only if the country's balance of payments was in "fundamental disequilibrium" (either deficit or surplus). However, no criteria were set forth to determine when such a state prevailed. Persistent deficits or surpluses ultimately became the test relied upon by the market, even though they may have been unrelated to any underlying structural changes in the economy. Moreover, in a fixed exchange rate regime speculation is almost costless and the possible gain for a short-term commitment of funds is very large.

While speculation occurs because individuals believe exchange rates to be either over- or undervalued, one might ask why central banks try to prevent the adjustment of exchange rates, what means they have available to maintain existing rates, and why they are not always successful. There are several reasons for attempting to maintain exchange rates that are obviously in disequilibrium. First, some countries base their economic growth around an export sector. Exports flourish when exchange rates are undervalued (i.e., they are cheap in foreign countries); in effect, an undervalued exchange rate acts as a subsidy to exports. The postwar revival and growth of West Germany and Japan, for instance, can be linked to undervalued currencies. Second, devaluation is often a tangible admission of the failure of government policy, perhaps that designed to curb inflation. Since some governments are reluctant to admit failure, they are willing to limp along with an overvalued exchange rate. Other reasons could also be put forth.

In theory, a central bank has unlimited resources to maintain an undervalued exchange rate. It can always supply an unlimited amount of its own currency for foreign currency. However, in the process it runs the risk of losing control over its own money supply and monetary base. Each unit of its own currency supplied to the market expands its domestic monetary base just as would open-market operations. To prevent its money supply from rising, the central bank must then sell securities in the open market and/or raise reserve requirements. In the process of defending its exchange rate, the central bank then accumulates large quantities of foreign currency. Domestic money or goods are traded for foreign money and the central bank accumulates additional inventories of foreign currency. Such a policy does not seem viable in the long run as it becomes increasingly probable that the central bank will not be able to sell the foreign currency at the price paid for it, i.e., they are likely to sustain large losses.

Should the speculation become massive, involving billions of dollars in one or a few days, the dimension of compensatory open-market sales could prove to be very disruptive to domestic financial markets. In such a circumstance the central bank may be forced to yield to market pressure and allow the exchange rate to adjust. This happened many times during the era of fixed exchange rates.

In the early part of the decade 1959–1968, the pound sterling was subjected to frequent and massive speculative pressure as the British balance of payments was in frequent and persistent deficit. The pound sterling was devalued to $2.80 in 1949 and to $2.40 in November 1967.

The IMF was helpful in counteracting the effects of speculation, but its resources proved to be insufficient in the short run, even though quotas were increased on several occasions. In part to compensate for this inadequacy, the central bankers of the leading industrial and trading countries began to cooperate on an informal basis. Out of this cooperation came so-called currency swaps, which are really short-term loans. For example, to deal with massive speculation against the British pound, the Bank of England would arrange with the Federal Reserve to borrow American dollars for a short period of time, subject to an exchange rate guarantee. The British would then draw on these dollars to buy pounds in an effort to ease the speculation against the pound. Later, when the speculative pressure was spent, usually after the British government instituted short-run measures to improve the balance of payments, it would buy back the dollars and repay the Federal Reserve.

These informal contacts among central bankers were made more permanent when, toward the end of 1961, the bankers began to hold regular meetings to discuss many important issues concerning the international monetary system. This arrangement came to be called the Group of Ten.[5]

[5] The members of this group were the United States, the United Kingdom, Germany, Italy, the Netherlands, Belgium, France, Canada, Japan, and Sweden.

Unfortunately, this group weakened the IMF since it unsurped some of its functions and purposes, even though it arose because of a shortcoming in the system.

The London gold market

Called by some a barbarous relic, gold is revered by others as the ultimate standard of value. Until 1954 no official market for gold existed in the postwar world. In that year an active private market for gold was reopened in London. Initially, the market price for gold was closely in line with the official price of $35 per ounce set by the U.S. Treasury. This free market served both to maintain a role for gold in the international monetary system, since central banks participated in it, and as an index of confidence in the dollar. Whenever the market price rose above the $35 official price, the market was de facto devaluing the dollar.

Since the London gold market presented a focal point for an international run on the dollar, the central banks of the United States, Belgium, France, Germany, the Netherlands, Switzerland, and the United Kingdom attempted to stabilize the market through the formation of a gold pool in October 1960. The pool lasted until 1968, when the respective countries announced that they would no longer support the market price. They then established a two-tier price system—private transactions could take place at the market price, whereas central banks would deal with one another at the official price of $35. They also promised not to deal in the private market, and hence to forgo potential profits. The two-tier system ended in August 1971 when the United States suspended the gold convertibility of the dollar. This action reduced substantially the role of gold in the international monetary system. However, while the London gold market functioned from 1954 to 1968, it provided a continual source of pressure on the international monetary system by providing a means whereby private foreign holders of dollars could obtain gold from the U.S. Treasury. Thus, it provided a means by which all foreign-held dollar liabilities were potentially subject to gold redemption.

The Eurodollar market

The Eurodollar market developed as the dollar became the means for conducting world trade. During the mid to late 1960s this market grew very rapidly. It is of interest because it represents a vast pool of what is essentially "stateless" money. That is, it consists of deposits (largely of a savings nature) denominated in dollars that are included in the narrow definition of the money supply of no country. These deposits could influence purchases in many countries, yet were under the control of no country. In part, the development of Eurodollars was symptomatic of the growing financial integration of the Western world.

Briefly, the functioning of the Eurodollar market allows a degree of intermediation that parallels the historic relationship of those depository institutions called thrifts in Chapter 5 to commercial banks in the United States. This relationship can raise the velocity or turnover rate of the narrow definition of the money supply. The same holds true for Eurodollars. They represent deposits that give rise to credit that can be used to buy American or foreign goods and services, yet are controllable by no nation. The Eurodollar market is discussed in detail in Appendix 17A. In that discussion it will be seen how the Federal Reserve deals with Eurodollars. It should also be noted that the existence of this market does not imply that the money supply of the United States is beyond the control of the Federal Reserve. Nevertheless, the Eurodollar market complicates domestic monetary management by central banks, and increases the pool of speculative capital funds that are a source of constant concern to the IMF.

The growth of international reserves

Of increasing concern in the 1959–1968 decade was the source of the long-run growth of international reserves, or liquidity. This growth had been provided by the deficit in the U.S. balance of payments and by gold sales from the Republic of South Africa and the Soviet Union. The former method of increasing reserves was regarded as transitory, and perhaps dangerous, especially as official dollar holdings came to exceed U.S. reserves of gold. The latter method was thought to be both inadequate and precarious. Thus, pressure built to provide a systematic assured means for the stable long-run growth of reserves.[6] A number of proposals were put forth, and several conferences were held for the purpose of discussing the nature of the new reserve growth mechanism. However, little came from these early discussions. It was not until the United States ran a balance-of-payments surplus (measured on an official settlements basis) in both 1968 and 1969 that a sense of urgency began to pervade official circles. Finally, in late 1969 the IMF members agreed to the creation of a first round of so-called paper gold, or Special Drawing Rights (SDR's). Initially, each SDR was defined to be equal to 1/35 ounce of gold or equal to one U.S. dollar. Later, the exchange value of the SDR was made to depend upon the exchange value of a pool of 14 currencies. In September 1980, this pool was reduced to only five currencies: dollar, mark, franc, yen, and pound. This initial issue of SDR's was very ill-timed, for the U.S. balance-of-payments surplus was in fact transitory. It was suddenly and dramatically

[6] It was by no means universally accepted that reserve growth had been inadequate. Those who felt that it had been pointed to the recurrent speculation to which the system was subjected as evidence in support of their view. Others argued that the recurrent and prolonged balance-of-payments problems of the deficit countries were caused by expansive monetary and fiscal policies. These, in turn, drove up prices in the deficit countries, caused the balance-of-payments problems, and, mistakenly, led to the conclusion that reserve growth was insufficient. Quite the contrary, said the critics. The system suffered from too much liquidity, not too little.

to become a deficit, which was to cause a dollar hemorrhage in the international monetary system, from which the system did not recover. Rather, its form changed dramatically.

Summary

In the decade 1959–1968 the system developed at Bretton Woods began to function in a world relatively free from encumbrances on international trade, finance, and payments. As the system began to function, it proved unable to deal with massive movements of speculative funds. This failure gave rise to a supplementary body known as the Group of Ten. Even their resources could not halt some of the speculative flows. In large part the inability of some countries, mainly the United States and the United Kingdom, to maintain reasonable equilibrium in their balance of payments was responsible for the speculation. The small cost in relation to the large potential gain served only to encourage speculation once it started. This was undoubtedly a major unanticipated shortcoming of the international financial system constructed by the Bretton Woods Conference.

1969–1971

The cornerstone of the postwar international monetary system was the dollar. It can be argued that the United States did not seek this role, that the events of history forced it upon her. Regardless of the truth of this assertion, the dollar did occupy this role. The acute dollar shortage of the postwar era gave way, at first slowly, to a dollar glut, which, in turn, led to a fundamental change in the international payments system. This glut reached a peak in 1971, which caused an international run on the dollar and resulted in a suspension of its convertibility into gold. The growing dollar glut is tied to the U.S. balance-of-payments position. We now turn to a discussion of developments in the U.S. balance of payments in the postwar period, for they are a critical part of the history of change of the international monetary system.

The period immediately prior to the return to convertibility by the major European countries in 1958 may in retrospect mark the highpoint of the dollar in the postwar era. The gold reserves of the United States stood in excess of $22 billion, which were thought more than sufficient to silence any alarmist concern over the ultimate convertibility of the dollar.[7]

The return to convertibility in 1958 was marked by a U.S. gold loss of $2.3 billion. Losses continued, with the exception of 1969, over the next 14 years (see Table 17:1). Not only did U.S. gold reserves dwindle, but

[7] The immense size of the gold reserves is misleading. At least one-half served as a gold reserve requirement for Federal Reserve notes and member bank deposits at the Federal Reserve. As the gold stock diminished, this reserve requirement was removed in stages.

TABLE 17:1
Balance-of-payments deficits and related gold losses (billions of dollars)

Year	Deficit (−) Measured by Reserve Asset Transactions	Changes in Gold Reserves
1956		+ 0.3
1957		+ 0.8
1958		− 2.3
1959		− 1.1
1960	− 3.4	− 1.7
1961	− 1.3	− 0.9
1962	− 2.7	− 0.9
1963	− 1.9	− 0.5
1964	− 1.5	− 0.1
1965	− 1.3	− 1.7
1966	− 0.2	− 0.6
1967	− 3.4	− 1.2
1968	+ 1.6	− 1.2
1969	+ 2.7	+ 1.0
1970	− 9.8	− 0.8
1971	− 29.8	− 0.9
1972	− 10.4	− 0.5
1973	− 5.3	—

liabilities to foreign central banks also rose dramatically. Some observers saw this as a favorable development, for it was a means of redistributing reserves more evenly and hence promoted a return to multinational trade. To others, this development portended an increase in speculation and the ultimate end of the fixed exchange rate regime.

Official anxiety about the depletion of U.S. gold reserves became manifest early in the 1960s in a series of remedial actions. The mere need for such action was symptomatic of an overvalued dollar. The policies devised amounted to exchange controls on capital exports. The first of these was the interest equalization tax. It represented a tax on securities purchased by Americans from foreigners (exemptions were granted—notably to Canadians). The purpose of the legislation was to reduce the issuance of foreign securities in New York by increasing financing costs to foreigners by approximately 1% per annum. Next came, in 1965 and 1968, respectively, the Voluntary Foreign Credit Restraint Program and tbe Foreign Direct Investment Program. Both programs were designed to reduce the outflow of liquid capital funds by limiting lending overseas to some fractional increase over lending in a base period. All three constraints on lending arose because U.S. officials were convinced that the source of the nation's balance-of-payments difficulties was too large an outflow of capital, given the surplus on current account. Support for the official interpretation took the form of studies suggesting that the formation of the European Common Market was a major magnet drawing U.S. funds abroad. These studies also suggested that a faster U.S. growth rate would serve to improve rather than deteriorate the balance of payments, i.e., that the decrease in capital outflow would be greater than the rise in imports.

As further steps to support the dollar, the U.S. Treasury began to issue U.S. bonds denominated in foreign currencies. These were sold to foreign central banks and served to reduce gold losses for two reasons. Since they were interest bearing, they provided a preferable alternative to gold, which bore no interest. Second, they guaranteed the foreign central bank against any losses due to an exchange rate adjustment in the value of the dollar.

To other observers it seemed the exodus of U.S. capital was due to an overvalued dollar. American manufacturers came to believe that to produce domestically and export would place them at a substantial disadvantage in major foreign markets. The disadvantage was seen to arise from an overvalued dollar, which made their products less competitive.

Other than capital outflow, a major reason for the deterioration of the balance-of-payments situation was believed to be the foreign policy objectives of the United States. The maintenance of large armies in Europe, Japan, and Korea was seen as causing a large foreign exchange drain on the United States. This drain was made unacceptable as the war in Vietnam developed.

It should be noted that during the 1960s the dollar problem was not unmanageable. It was only with the onset of the war in Vietnam that the balance-of-payments situation began to deteriorate sharply. Not only was the overall balance in large deficit in 1970, 1971, and 1972, but the balances of trade and current account were also deteriorating, moving into deficits for the first time in this century.

As the official statistics in 1971 recorded the flood of dollars pouring into the international exchange market, speculative pressures against the dollar began to build. These were massive and in the main represented a movement out of the dollar and into the German mark. On May 3–4 the German central bank purchased \$1 billion, and in the first 40 minutes of trading on May 5 it bought an additional \$1 billion. At this point, the mark was allowed to float. That same morning the central banks of the Netherlands, Switzerland, Belgium, and Austria ended their official support of the dollar. The resulting depreciation of the dollar then became a sort of barometer of world confidence in the United States. This depreciation did not lead to a quick improvement in the U.S. balance of payments. On Sunday, August 15, President Nixon suspended the gold convertibility of the dollar and ushered in the most significant change in the international monetary system in two centuries—the era of flexible exchange rates was about to dawn.

From August until December 1971 exchange rates were on a sort of managed float. Central banks would intervene in the exchange markets to even out changes that were judged to be too rapid. The period was also one of a proliferation of exchange controls (especially on short-term capital), as well as other devices to impede trade (such as the 10% U.S. surcharge on imports).

December 1971–March 1973

In the autumn of 1971 the Group of Ten met in Washington in an effort to restore fixed exchange rates. It was the first meeting ever conducted for the purpose of adjusting exchange rates on a multilateral basis. It resulted in the so-called Smithsonian Agreement, which provided that the major currencies of the world would be revalued upward ranging from 17% for the yen to zero for the floating Canadian dollar. Moreover, the permissible band of fluctuation was increased from ±1% of parity to ±2 1/4%. Finally the official dollar price of gold was increased from $35 to $38 per ounce. This was a somewhat deceptive ploy to make it appear as though the gold value of the dollar had been changed rather than that the dollar value of other currencies had been altered. The agreement was hailed by President Nixon and Treasury Secretary John Connally as the greatest monetary reform in the history of mankind. Such exaggeration in the use of words has seldom been equaled, for scarcely was the ink dry on the agreement when it became obvious that the new exchange rates still left the dollar substantially overvalued.

In June 1972 Britain's deteriorating balance of payments forced her to float the pound. Moreover, it was apparent that the U.S. balance of payments was not responding quickly to the devaluation worked out in December. The dollar hemorrhage still flowed, although at a diminished rate. Speculation against the dollar continued, and in February 1973 a new series of exchange rates was announced. These rates were achieved by an official devaluation of the dollar, as the price of gold was raised from $38.00 to $42.20 per ounce. However, in the first quarter of 1973 the United States announced a balance-of-payments deficit of $10 billion and world confidence gave way. In March the world embarked on a flexible exchange regime. Originally, this experiment was thought to be necessary only for a short period of time. It has now lasted seven years, largely because of the policy of benign neglect adopted by the United States. U.S. policy seems to be based on the conviction that flexible exchange rates are the best means of preventing the future emergence of an overvalued dollar.

Beyond 1973

As the flexible rate system has evolved in practice, it has not been the case that (1) purely market forces determine the exchange rate and (2) every country allows its exchange rate to float against those of every other country. Rather, the float has been "dirty" in the sense that central banks enter the markets from time to time to maintain exchange rates they think are desirable. However, we have not seen competitive depreciations engineered by countries in the hope of achieving some short-run gains in employment. It has been the stated policy of the United States to enter the market only to smooth out wide fluctuations in the rate or to prevent what are called "disorderly markets" or adjustments. This means that the Federal Reserve will allow the exchange rate to move along whatever trend is dictated by the market, but will seek to avoid large disruptive or potentially destabilizing changes in rates, such as might be instigated by speculators. In late 1978 U.S. resolve was put to the test. As the U.S. balances on trade and current accounts deteriorated in 1977 and 1978, it appeared as though the dollar/mark and dollar/yen rates were headed for further depreciation. Speculators then moved against the dollar, despite the fact that the trade balance showed some improvement and U.S. interest rates were above those of its leading trading partners. This led U.S. officials to believe that the speculation-induced depreciation far exceeded any decline related to fundamental factors. To support the dollar, in an effort to prevent disorderly markets, the United States drew resources from the IMF, increased gold sales, arranged swaps with the Japanese, German, and Swiss central banks, and announced plans to sell $10 billion in foreign-denominated securities in the Japanese, German, and Swiss capital markets. In addition, it markedly reduced the growth rate of the monetary aggregates. These actions were successful both in halting the depreciation and then in reversing it, i.e., the dollar began to appreciate. It is of interest that actions such as these were quite characteristic of the old fixed exchange rate system. This should not come as a surprise, for in both systems speculation can occur.

It should also be noted that not all exchange rates in the current system are flexible. Some countries in the so-called dollar bloc peg their exchange rate rigidly to the U.S. dollar. For such a country, the exchange rate vis-à-vis nondollar currencies depends on movements in the dollar. Similarly, the countries of the European Economic Community, in an effort to evolve a monetary union, are establishing rigid links between their own currencies with no permissible range of fluctuations. Someday the exchange rate between the German mark and the French franc will be as rigid as that between the dollar in Ohio and the dollar in Georgia.

OPEC and the international monetary system

In late 1973 and early 1974 the most successful cartel ever organized, the Organization of Petroleum Exporting Countries, effected a quadrupling of oil prices. This extortive rise in the price of a crucial commodity would have caused great strain regardless of the nature of the international monetary system. As the situation developed, however, the international monetary system appeared to play a minor role in adjusting balance-of-payments deficits and surpluses among the importing and exporting nations. This was primarily because OPEC oil is quoted in terms of the dollar. For the United States, this means that the exchange rate cannot adjust to restore the trade imbalance between itself and the OPEC nations. What occurs is that dollars are paid to an OPEC country, which then *recycles* or lends those "petrodollars" not used to purchase goods and services back to the financial system of the leading industrial countries. Since the absorptive capacity of most OPEC countries for imports is limited, many dollars are recycled back to the United States. Others are recycled into the Eurodollar market.

The recycling causes problems because the recycled dollars do not offset precisely the deficits of the respective countries. That is, the OPEC countries do not return or match as loans the oil deficits of the consuming countries. In this instance the international monetary system has a role to play. Those nations with uncovered oil deficits should, other things being equal, experience a depreciation of their currencies relative to those consuming countries where the amount of recycled petrodollars is greater than the oil deficit. The depreciation–appreciation then serves to restore overall balance of payments. Whether this is occurring or not is difficult to discern from the respective movements in exchange rates. It appears that two types of methods are used by those nations that do not get sufficient recycled OPEC profits to finance the oil deficits. First, contrary to all past experience, the central banks of these countries commenced to borrow funds in private markets—from Eurodollar banks and U.S. banks, in particular. Thus, the private market appears, at least initially, to be recycling the petrodollars. Second, as private credit began to dry up, the deficit countries have looked increasingly to more traditional methods of finance, e.g., to the IMF, to the expanded Group of 10, and to other support facilities provided by central banks.

A second problem posed by the OPEC petrodollars stems from their *shiftability*. That is, the OPEC countries can shift their deposits from one financial center to another. Such massive shifts of short-term funds can create disorderly exchange markets, increase the need for central bank cooperation, and increase the need for IMF involvement as a lender of last resort.

Ultimately, the OPEC oil imports will have to be paid for in goods and services. Such real transfers have not yet occurred to any significant degree. Thus far the oil has been paid for by pieces of paper, or entries in bank books called money.

THE CAUSE OF THE U.S. BALANCE-OF-PAYMENTS PROBLEM

When data on the U.S. balance of trade, current account, capital account, and the overall balance of payments in the post-World War II period are examined, they show great variation over time. The balance of trade slowly deteriorates until in 1971 the U.S. faced its first trade deficit in this century.

The balance on current account, dominated by the trade balance, also shows deterioration. The amount of long-term capital lent abroad varies markedly. Finally, the overall balance shows a steady deficit with a magnitude that varies from time to time. What forces supposedly account for these assorted movements? It should come as no surprise that economists do not agree in their interpretations of these events. While it might be convenient to divide interpretations along Keynesian–Monetarist lines, it may not be correct to do so. For several hundred years, before the world heard of Keynesianism and Monetarism, analytical assessments of movements in balance of payments have differed. However, old and new views have much in common. For one group of economists or observers, movements in the demand for, or supply of, money dominate all other causes in explaining surpluses or deficits in international accounts, whereas for others, changes in real variables exercise the dominant influence. That is, even if the money variables were held constant, changes in the real variables would still produce variations in the balance of international transactions.[8] Today, Monetarists and Keynesians tend to divide along the same grounds. The Monetarist view can be expressed quite simply. In a fixed exchange rate regime changes in the growth rate of the money supply produce variations (surpluses or deficits) in the balance of payments, whereas in a flexible rate regime they produce variations in the exchange rate. Moreover, for changes in real variables to affect either the balance of payments or the exchange rate, they must affect either the supply of or demand for money. Keynesians, on the other hand, are likely to assert that variations in the balance of payments or the exchange rate are due to nonmonetary changes in the different components of the balance of payments, and that such changes would occur even if the monetary variables were held neutral.

These alternative assessments of the source of balance-of-payments problems would be of little importance if they did not imply markedly different policy prescriptions to effect a cure. The nature of these policies is exactly the same as those we examined for dealing with domestic business cycles.

The monetary or Monetarist explanation[9]

The Monetarist interpretation of historical movements in the balance of payments is based on a model that is similar to the model used to explain

[8] These alternative interpretations emerged very early in economics. For the view from Sweden in the mid-eighteenth century, see Robert V. Eagly, *The Swedish Bullionist Controversy* (Philadelphia: American Philosophical Society, 1971); for England, see Denis P. O'Brien, *The Classical Economists* (London: Oxford University Press, 1975).

[9] The monetary view is summarized in Jacob A. Frenkel, "A Monetary Approach to the Exchange Rate: Doctrinal Aspects and Empirical Evidence," *Scandinavian Journal of Economics,* Vol. 78, No. 2 (1976): 200–24; Harry G. Johnson, "The Monetary Approach to Balance-of-Payments Theory," *Economic Notes* 1 (1972): 20–39; and Thomas M. Humphrey, "A Monetarist Model of Exchange Rate Determination," *Economic Review,* Federal Reserve Bank of Richmond, Vol. 63, No. 1 (Jan.–Feb. 1977): 3–9.

the movement of economic activity in a closed economy. The Monetarist open-economy model is based on the following four assumptions:

1. National price levels are determined by the growth rate of the supply of money.[10]
2. The demand for money depends primarily on real income and market interest rates. (This is equivalent to the view that the velocity of money is stable.)
3. The equilibrium exchange rate between two currencies depends only on relative national price levels.
4. Expectational elements concerning the future course of inflation can influence the equilibrium exchange rate.

Monetarists would explain the balance of payments during a fixed exchange rate regime by reference to a growth rate of U.S. money supply relative to the money supply of its leading trading partners. Various real changes would be analyzed only in terms of their effects on either money supply or money demand.[11] Suppose, for example, the Federal Reserve accelerated the growth rate of the money supply. Given real income and the interest rate, the real stock of money would now exceed the demand for it. That is, an excess supply of money would exist. These balances would then be spent on domestic goods, services, and financial assets. Prices of these assets would tend to rise in the short run relative to the prices of comparable assets abroad. Buyers in the United States would then switch their demands from domestic to foreign substitutes, while domestic suppliers of these assets would seek to sell more in the United States and less abroad. At the same time, foreign suppliers of these assets would seek to sell more in the United States and less in their home countries. The combination of these factors works to increase U.S. imports and decrease exports. As a result, the balance of payments, if we suppose it was initially in balance, now moves into deficit. It is as though extra money unleashed in the United States spills over into the economies of its leading trading partners. It is not possible to specify beforehand which components of the balance of payments will be most likely to deteriorate, or at what rate, for this will depend on conditions of supply and demand in particular markets at particular times.

As the balance of payments deteriorates, central banks will come into possession of dollars, the counterpart of their surpluses, and present them for conversion into gold. The decrease in the U.S. gold stock, the international component of its monetary base, will lead to a contraction in the

[10] It will be remembered that this is a long-run proposition. In the short run changes in the growth rate of the money supply can bring forth temporary changes in real income and velocity.

[11] By real changes, references is made to crop failures, income losses due to strikes or acts of God, foreign wars, the formation of trading blocs such as the European Economic Community, OPEC oil prices increases, the closing of the Suez Canal, the world food shortage in 1973–1974, etc.

growth rate of the money supply. Those U.S. trading partners with surpluses will, of course, be experiencing the opposite condition.

This analysis ignores the fact that, to some extent, the U.S. dollar is still an international reserve or key currency, as it was during much of the postwar era. Since it is, foreign central banks accumulate dollars and treat them as gold. Thus, the deficit country, the United States, does not suffer a reserve loss, whereas the surplus countries enjoy a rise in their reserves. The monetary base of the world rises, as does the world money supply and the world rate of inflation.

A central conclusion of this discussion is that in the longer run the monetary authorities of each country can only control the domestic part of their respective monetary bases (i.e., that part supplied in the main by open-market operations). They do not control their domestic money supplies. It might be argued that this is not so, for cannot surplus countries always offset the increases in the international portion of the monetary base by appropriate open-market operations designed to decrease the domestic portion? Monetarists would argue that they cannot do so in the longer run. Consider the consequences of such a policy. The surplus country acquires gold or foreign currencies, but loses investment and consumption goods. The accumulation of reserves is matched by a transfer of wealth from domestic to foreign consumers. Can any government pursue such a policy in the long run? The Monetarists think not.

The above analysis does not apply when flexible exchange rates are used. As in the fixed exchange case, an acceleration in the growth rate of the money stock will create an excess supply. As it is spent, the domestic price level will rise. In contrast to the fixed exchange case, though, the exchange rate will depreciate in order to restore the relative price between domestic and foreign goods. By how much will the exchange rate depreciate? This will depend upon the rate of U.S. inflation relative to that abroad. The exchange rate will adjust so that the price of foreign substitutes (in dollars) is equal to the price of domestic assets (neglecting transportation charges). Suppose, however, that the exchange rate is not flexible. For example, suppose that U.S. prices are twice as high as foreign prices, but one U.S. dollar exchanges for each unit of foreign currency. The dollar is overvalued relative to its "purchasing power parity."[12] In such a circumstance incentives are immediately created for both foreigners and U.S. citizens to buy foreign goods. U.S. exports would fall and imports rise until the exchange rate is pushed in the direction dictated by relative price levels. Thus, according to Monetarists, the exchange rate can only deviate from that indicated by relative prices for a short period of time.

When the analytical frame of reference shifts to a dynamic context, expectational elements become an important part of the Monetarist model. For example, using the flexible system above, if buyers in the United States

[12] Where purchasing power parity is measured by relative price levels. The phrase was coined by the Swedish economist Gustav Cassals, in explaining the exchange rate expected to prevail between countries using flexible exchange rates.

expect prices to rise faster domestically than in foreign countries, they will also expect the exchange rate to depreciate. In such a situation there are profit incentives to sell currency now and buy it back after it has depreciated. Thus, movements in the exchange rate may be governed by the expected price level rather than by the actual price level.

To understand the Monetarist view more fully, we shall consider a "real" change in the international system. Suppose that foreign oil producers form a cartel whose purpose is to raise prices by restricting supply. In a fixed exchange rate system oil prices rise directly, as does the domestic price level. The real stock of money declines and is less than the desired demand for money (which depends on real income and the interest rate). That is, excess money demand now exists in the market. In order to build up money balances money holders now refrain from spending. Aggregate demand declines as individuals buy fewer goods, services, and financial assets. As a result, the prices of these assets fall and will continue to fall until the real money stock is equal to the demand for it.[13] The end result will be an absolute decline in the prices of some goods relative to oil, which is also a change in relative prices. From this example it can be seen that the monetary approach to the balance of payments can handle changes in real variables. It does so by analyzing how these changes affect either the supply or demand for money.

To return to an explanation for the historical course of the U.S. balance of payments, the Monetarists would argue that its deterioration was due to a faster growth rate in the U.S. money supply relative to the growth rates for its leading trading partners. However, an increase in the supply of—or, alternatively, in demand for—money is only a *proximate* cause, for many factors affect supply and demand. A good understanding of the Monetarist view requires the investigation of various historical periods to explain the growth of the money supply. Undoubtedly, Monetarists would explain the sharp deterioration in the U.S. balance of trade and payments in the early 1970s to the financing of the war in Vietnam by the printing of money rather than by the sale of bonds to the public. The depreciation of the dollar in the late 1970s would likewise be attributed to the continued financing of the budget deficit by the printing of money and the expectation that this method of financing will continue, with its consequence for domestic inflation.

The Keynesian explanation

We give only a brief discussion of the Keynesian explanation, for much of Chapter 16 was devoted to the theories of that school, and discussed the relative effectiveness of monetary and fiscal policy in an open economy. The essential point missing from that explanation was a discussion of the causes of balance-of-payments problems (either deficit or surplus). In the Keynesian view the initating factor is likely to be real in nature, rather than

[13] The central bank could always increase the nominal money supply to offset the rise in oil prices and the price level.

a faster or slower growth rate in the money supply. This change is, moreover, likely to show up as a change or shift in the items that constitute the balance of payments, e.g., exports decline, dividends and remittances rise, unilateral transfers rise, capital export declines. In fact, Keynesian economists can explain most of the movements in the balance of payments by reference to such real variables. Thus, during the late 1950s and early 1960s the U.S. balance-of-payments problem was due to too large an outflow of capital relative to the surplus on current account. The outflow, in turn, was linked to the growth of multinational corporations, which found Europe a particularly attractive outlet for investment. This was supposedly because of the formation of the European Common Market. Moreover, this investment was seen to be both export decreasing and import increasing, and hence worked to reduce the overall U.S. current account surplus. Further, such investment transferred U.S. technology abroad, which served to weaken our trade balance. This diagnosis resulted in a mixed bag of policies. First, domestic growth was stimulated to make the U.S. a more attractive setting for investment.[14] Second, exchange controls were placed on capital movements, in the guise of various taxes and of both voluntary and compulsory lending restraints. In the late 1960s and early 1970s the continued deterioration in the trade balance and overall balance was attributed to the war in Vietnam. The war necessitated the direct cost of maintaining a large army in Asia, and the indirect cost of using imported raw materials to produce munitions. Finally, the depreciation of the dollar after 1975 is attributed to the OPEC oil cartel, and a faster growth rate in the United States relative to the growth rates of its principal trading partners. Heard throughout the entire period was the oft-repeated opinion that U.S. export industries perform poorly because of low productivity, lack of concern with foreign markets, too many government regulations, unfair taxation, a host of discriminatory practices by foreigners against U.S. goods and services, and so forth. Finally, many point to the revival of industries in Europe and Asia and allege that relative production efficiences are changing, which works a hardship on U.S. firms.

Essentially, insofar as the non-Monetarist school is concerned, there has been a series of shocks that have had a cumulative negative effect on the U.S. balance of payments and exchange rate over the past three decades. Each of these shocks has generally necessitated a separate policy to deal with it—sometimes fiscal, sometimes monetary, sometimes commercial.

CONCLUSION

This chapter explained the historical evolution of the international monetary system in the twentieth century. For most of the period the world used fixed (or adjustable) exchange rates with a gold standard, a gold exchange

[14] Note that, according to the monetary view of the balance of payments, this policy is likely to lead to a larger, not smaller, deficit.

standard, and a dollar standard supplemented by the IMF. Since the mid-1970s the world has moved increasingly toward a flexible exchange rate standard, largely because of the influence of the United States.

Throughout most of the post–World War II period the course of the international monetary system was tied to developments in the United States and its balance-of-payments position. It was the seeming uncontrollability of the U.S. balance-of-payments deficit that brought an end to the international monetary system forged at Bretton Woods in 1944. The future seems to be with flexible rates and relatively freely functioning exchange markets.

Finally, we discussed in some detail the Monetarist view as to the cause of balance-of-payments difficulties and the efficacy of various cures. The proximate cause of difficulties was seen to be in money supply or demand, and for cures to be effective, these variables must be changed. On the other hand, the Keynesian view tends to downplay money and to elevate nonmonetary or real factors as the cause of the difficulties, even if the monetary variables are held neutral.

STUDY QUESTIONS

1. It has been said that a virtue of the gold standard was that international exchange rates were fixed, which permitted the world to function as if a uniform single-currency system prevailed. Evaluate this contention.
2. In what sense was the fragility of the gold exchange standard similar to the fragility of the domestic monetary system of a given country before central banking?
3. Explain why the presence of over- and undervalued exchange rates creates problems for an international monetary system.
4. Explain the costs and benefits to the United States from having a "key currency." Do you think that the United States could have effectively devalued the dollar in the late 1950s or early 1960s?
5. Explain how the early London gold market presented a focal point for an international run on the dollar.
6. Can an individual who owns a Eurodollar deposit write a check on that deposit?
7. Present arguments both for and against the proposition that the long-run growth of international reserves in the period before 1970 was inadequate.
8. Distinguish the *recycling* of "petrodollars" from their *shiftability.* What problems are presented by each?
9. What does it mean to say that a currency is overvalued relative to its "purchasing power parity"? If this were true, what incentives would be created to restore parity?

SELECTED REFERENCES AND READINGS

Bloomfield, Arthur I. *Monetary Policy under the International Gold Standard.* New York: Federal Reserve Bank of New York, 1959.

Clarke, Stephen V. O. *Central Bank Cooperation: 1924–31.* New York: Federal Reserve Bank of New York, 1967.

———. *The Reconstruction of the International Monetary System: The Attempts of 1922 and 1933.* Princeton, N.J. Princeton Studies in International Finance, No. 33, 1973.

———. *Exchange-Rate Stabilization in the Mid-1930's: Negotiating the Tripartite Agreement.* Princeton, N.J. Princeton Studies in International Finance, No. 41, 1977.

Coombs, Charles A. "Treasury and Federal Reserve Foreign Exchange Operations." *Monthly Review,* Federal Reserve Bank of New York (Oct. 1971).

Frenkel, Jacob A. "A Monetary Approach to the Exchange Rate: Doctrinal Aspects and Empirical Evidence." In *The Economics of Exchange Rates,* edited by Jacob A. Frenkel and Harry Gordon Johnson. Reading, Mass.: Addison-Wesley Publishing Co., 1978.

Friedman, Milton. "The Euro-dollar Market: Some First Principles." *Monthly Review,* Federal Reserve Bank of St. Louis (July 1971).

Galbraith, John Kenneth. *Money, Whence It Came, Where It Went.* Boston: Houghton Mifflin Co., 1975.

Gray, H. Peter. *International Trade, Investment, and Payments.* Boston: Houghton Mifflin Co., 1979.

Greene, Margaret L. "Special Drawing Rights: A Major Step in the Evolution of the World's Monetary System." *Monthly Review,* Federal Reserve Bank of New York (Jan. 1968).

Hetzel, Robert L., and Lawler, Thomas A. "The Cause of the Dollar Depreciation." *Economic Review,* Federal Reserve Bank of Richmond (May–June 1978).

Humphrey, Thomas M. "A Monetarist Model of World Inflation and the Balance of Payments." *Economic Review,* Federal Reserve Bank of Richmond (Nov.–Dec. 1976).

Johnson, Harry Gordon. "The Monetary Approach to Balance-of-Payments Theory." In *The Monetary Approach to the Balance of Payments,* edited by Jacob A. Frenkel and Harry Gordon Johnson. Toronto, Canada: University of Toronto Press, 1976.

Klopstock, Fred H. "The International Status of the Dollar." *Essays in International Finance,* No. 28, Princeton University (May 1957).

———. "Eurodollars in the Liquidity and Reserve Management of U.S. Banks." *Monthly Review,* Federal Reserve Bank of New York (July 1968).

McCloskey, D. N., and Zecher, J. R. "How the Gold Standard Worked, 1880–1913." In *The Monetary Approach to the Balance of Payments,* edited by Jacob A. Frenkel and Harry Gordon Johnson. Toronto, Canada: University of Toronto Press, 1976.

Moggridge, Donald E. *British Monetary Policy 1924–1931: The Norman Conquest of $4.86*. New York: Cambridge University Press, 1972.

Tew, Brian. *The Evolution of the International Monetary System 1945–77*. New York: John Wiley & Sons, 1977.

Yeager, Leland B. *International Monetary Relations*. New York: Harper & Row, 1966.

17

APPENDIX A–THE EURODOLLAR MARKET

17

As the decade of the 1960s drew to a close, a phenomenon known as the Eurodollar market came to command much attention in the financial press, appeared to be understood by few, and implied to many a murky dominance of the U.S. financial system and money supply by forces other than the Federal Reserve. Subsequent developments have, on the whole, put this market into a more balanced perspective. Our task will be to define this market, explain its origin and growth, and explore its implications for domestic monetary policy.

Eurodollars are the deposit liabilities of European banks located outside the United States that are denominated in dollars. They are not bundles of American currency sitting around Europe, but deposits expressed in terms of dollars in banks outside the United States. These banks can be foreign owned or the foreign branches of U.S. banks. The only requirement is that the bank be located outside the United States. Initially "Eurodollars" meant that these banks must be located in Europe, but increasingly the term came to imply dollar deposits in any foreign bank. These deposits can be owned by foreigners or by American citizens.

The origin of the Eurodollar market lies mainly in the actions of the Soviet Union, which wanted to hold dollar balances outside the control of the United States.[1] The growth of the market, especially in the late 1960s, is attributable to the combined effects of Regulation Q, the several controls placed upon the outflow of capital from the United States,[2] and the marginally higher reserve requirements imposed by the Federal Reserve relative to the voluntary cash reserves held by foreign banks.

The ability of the Eurodollar banks to create dollar deposits has been the subject of a great deal of controversy. Some have said that they have no such ability, while others have claimed it to be unlimited. The truth lies at neither extreme. To see this, we must see how Eurodollar banks create deposits, and the relationship of these deposits to the American money supply. Both the creation and relationship can be most easily understood if Eurobanks are viewed as having the same relationship to U.S. commercial

[1] Soviet accounts in the United States were impounded during and after World War II.

[2] It will be remembered from Chapter 17 that these controls consisted of the interest equalization tax, the Voluntary Foreign Credit Restraint Program, and the Foreign Direct Investment Program.

TABLE 17A:1

U.S. Depository Institutions		U.K. Eurobank	
	Domestic deposits − $100	Deposits in U.S. bank + $100	Eurodollar deposits + $100
	Eurobank deposits + $100		

banks as do other depository institutions identified as thrifts in Chapter 5. It will be recalled that for thrifts to create credit, they must as a group receive a primary deposit. The amount of credit created depends upon the redeposit feature, that is, on the amount of credit that is redeposited in these nonbank institutions after the credit-creation process starts. Similarly, a Eurodollar bank must receive a primary deposit, which consists of "native" dollars from the U.S. financial system. That is, someone holding a deposit in an American depository institution (historically this was true only for commercial banks) must transfer the deposit to a Eurobank. How many Eurodollars can be created depends on the redeposit of these dollars in the Eurobanking system. From this perspective, Eurobanks can be seen as merely a higher level of intermediation. The extent of the intermediation depends, as with thrift institutions, on the spread between the borrowing and lending rates.

To demonstrate this analysis, consider a transfer of a deposit by an American from a U.S. bank to a British-owned bank that receives dollar deposits. The transaction shown in Table 17A:1 does not decrease the total deposits in U.S. depository institutions, their reserves, or the money supply.[3] However, it does give to the Eurobank additional lending power in the form of a claim on U.S. banks, against which the Eurobank can draw checks. Suppose the Eurobank, from prior experience, keeps a 10% reserve against its Eurodollar deposits. This being the case, $90 of its "deposit in U.S. banks" can be lent. Suppose the $90 is lent to a British firm importing from the United States. The British firm receives a check from the Eurobank drawn on its U.S. deposit. Upon making the loan, the Eurobank balance sheet appears as:

U.K. Eurobank			
Deposits in U.S. banks	$10	Eurodollar deposit	$100
Loans	$90		

What, then, does the American exporter do with the check? If it is deposited in the U.S. financial system, the balance of depository institutions would appear as:

[3] We have reference here to either the M-1A or M-1B measure of the money supply. Certain Eurodollar deposits are included in the M_2 and other M measures. It should be noted that Eurodollar deposits are mainly savings deposits. That is, an individual cannot draw a check against a Eurodollar deposit. The Eurodollar bank, in paying off the deposit, will give the depositor a check draw most likely on a U.S. commercial bank.

U.S. Depository Institutions

	Domestic deposits + \$90
	Eurobank deposits − \$90

If the American exporter deposits it in a Eurobank, the Eurobanking balance sheet would become:

Eurobanks

Deposits in U.S. banks	\$100	Eurodollar deposits	\$190
Loans	90		

This latter transaction does not change the liabilities or assets of U.S. depository institutions. Should the proceeds of each loan be redeposited in the Eurobanking system with no drains back into the U.S. financial system via deposits or into currency in circulation, total Eurodollar deposits would rise by the reciprocal of the voluntary cash reserve ratio used by Eurobanks multiplied by the amount of primary deposits (designated as "Deposit in U.S. banks"). This is, of course, analogous to the simple Case I of deposit creation explained in Chapter 4.

In the example above, the origin of the primary deposit was a transfer by an American of a dollar deposit from a U.S. depository institution to a British Eurobank. It could have also been the transfer by foreign central banks of their dollar-denominated foreign exchange reserves from the United States to the Eurodollar system. Indeed, there is ample evidence that in the late 1960s and early 1970s, when Eurodollar interest rates were high, foreign central banks were suppliers of primary deposits or reserves to the Eurodollar system. Thus, some portion of the credit created by the Eurodollar system was due to the recycling of reserves by foreign central banks.

This brings us to a very important part of the analysis of Eurodollar deposit creation, which concerns how national monetary authorities should account for Eurodollar deposits. These deposits are currently excluded from the narrow definitions of most of the money supplies of all nations. They are basically "stateless money." Nevertheless, these deposits and the credit they represent serve to finance and expand world spending. How should central banks deal with these deposits? Two options appear open. One is to neglect them, just as historically the deposits of nonbank intermediaries or thrifts were excluded from the narrow measure of U.S. money supply. These deposits and the credit they represent then become forces raising the velocity or turnover rate of this narrowly defined money. To account for them, the market interest rate influencing the demand for money should perhaps be the Eurodollar rate, or that rate should be added to relevant domestic interest rates. Alternatively, one could add to the domestic money supply those Eurodollars likely to be spent in the United

States (owned by both Americans and foreigners). This is basically how they are recorded in the M_2 measure of the U.S. money stock.

Now that the creation of Eurodollars has been explained, it is possible to see some of the consequences for domestic economic activity, in particular the credit crunches of 1966, 1968–1970, and 1973. During these periods of tight credit U.S. banks borrowed Eurodollars to expand their domestic lending power and, in the process, avoided to some extent the Federal Reserve's tight money policy. To see how this is done, suppose that in Table 17A:1 the Eurodollar bank with $100 due from an American bank (i.e., with a $100 deposit in an American bank) now lends $90 back to the American bank rather than to a British importer.

On the books of the American bank the deposit owed to the Eurobank is replaced by a nondeposit liability called, as an example, "due to foreign banks," or:

U.S. Depository Institutions

	Eurobank deposit	− $90
	Due to foreign banks	+ $90

Prior to September 4, 1969, the Federal Reserve did not impose legal reserve requirements on borrowings from foreign banks (including branches of U.S. banks). By borrowing from foreign banks, U.S. banks reduced their total deposits subject to legal reserve requirements. They were, as a consequence, able to come up with additional free reserves in order to increase their lending and, at least until the Federal Reserve caught on, circumvent some of the restrictive effects of monetary policy.

To explain the phenominal growth of the Eurodollar system in the late 1960s, assume, as was true then, that the United States is experiencing a period in which the Regulation Q ceilings are effective (i.e., that market interest rates are above those that depository institutions can pay on their deposits, so that they are faced with disintermediation). To reduce the disintermediation and increase their lending power, depository institutions must persuade large domestic customers to transfer their deposits to their European branches. The incentive to transfer comes from the promise of higher interest rates on deposits, because European branches are not bound by Regulation Q. After the transfer the loans of American depository institutions appear as:

U.S. Depository Institutions

	Domestic deposits	−
	Due to foreign branches	+

The books of the foreign branch would appear as:

Foreign branch	
Due from head office +	Eurodollar deposits +

This transfer simultaneously accomplishes three things: (1) it reduces disintermediation; (2) it allows the head office of the U.S. depository institution to reduce its average reserve requirements, thus enhancing its overall lending capacity; and (3) it gives the foreign branch lending capacity in the form of a primary deposit. In September 1969 legal reserves were imposed on sums due foreign branches, reducing the significance of the second effect.

With the removal of Regulation Q ceilings on large negotiable certificates of deposit, and the removal of controls on lending abroad by U.S. corporations and financial institutions, the growth of the Eurodollar market slowed and declined to some extent. This was due both to a decrease in the supply of primary deposits from U.S. sources and to a decrease in demand for Eurodollar funds, as borrowers once again could turn to New York for funds.

INDEX

D